LOGIC, SCIENCE AND DIALECTIC

Logic, Science, and Dialectic

Collected Papers in Greek Philosophy

G. E. L. Owen

edited by Martha Nussbaum

Cornell University Press

Ithaca, New York

First published in 1986 by Cornell University Press.

Library of Congress Cataloging in Publication Data

Printed in Great Britain

Owen, G. E. L. (Guilym Ellis Lane), 1922 –
Logic, science, and dialectic.

Includes bibliographical references and index.
1. Philosophy, Ancient—Addresses, essays, lectures.
I. Nussbaum, Martha Craven, 1947–
II. Title.
B171.087 1985 180 85-17479
ISBN 0-8014-1726-0

Contents

Preface

This was in every way Gwil Owen's project. He closely oversaw every aspect of the planning. Shortly before his sudden and tragic death in July 1982, we had an extended conference during which I learned his view on every matter of importance and got his agreement to every proposed alteration. I have done nothing on my own, beyond entirely trivial matters of editorial form. I feel fortunate indeed that this is so. It was his express wish, vigorously affirmed, that there be only the briefest and most mundane of prefaces to the book. Especially after the publication of a volume of essays in honour of his sixtieth birthday, which included an introductory account of his work and its importance,[1] he felt that any prefatory discussion of the contribution made by these essays would be inappropriate. I shall therefore confine myself to describing the scope of the volume, indicating the reasons for all departures from the originally published texts, and mentioning several further alterations that Owen would have made if he had lived to see the volume through to its completion.

The volume contains no material that was not completed for publication by Owen during his lifetime. It does include two posthumous publications. 'Philosophical Invective', which he had agreed to publish in the first number of the new journal *Oxford Studies in Ancient Philosophy*, appeared there a little more than a year after his death. At his death several footnotes were left blank; I supplied these references with the generous assistance of Albert Henrichs. The text indicates which notes we composed. 'Aristotelian Mechanics' was promised to a festschrift volume in honour of David Balme and was completed before Owen's death. The volume, edited by Allan Gotthelf, will appear in 1986. Owen did not leave behind any other finished work; there will be no further publications from his estate. (Through the kindness of his widow, Sally Owen, many of his manuscripts can be consulted at Cambridge University; several among these are eventually to be donated to Harvard University.) In addition to these two papers, this volume includes all the philosophical papers Owen published during his career. The only pieces of published writing which are, by his decision, omitted are: six book reviews, a brief commentary on papers by van der Waerden and Sambursky, a memorial notice of Gilbert Ryle, and an essay circulated in the *Notes* on *Metaphysics* Z reproduced by the Sub-Faculty of Philosophy at Oxford,

[1] *Language and Logos*, ed. M. Schofield and M.C. Nussbaum (Cambridge 1982).

which overlaps with 'Particular and General' and was thought by Owen to have been superseded by that article. (References to these other items may be found in the complete Bibliography of his work that is included in the festschrift volume *Language and Logos*.) Two of the published papers, 'Eleatic Questions' and 'Zeno and the Mathematicians', had appeared in a slightly revised version after their original publication, in the collection *Studies in Presocratic Philosophy*, edited by David Furley and R.E. Allen. Owen decided to include the revised version in both cases; and the pagination given in the margins here is the pagination of the revised versions. Many of his other published papers have also been reprinted in anthologies; but none of these was altered in any significant way.

The order of the papers is that chosen by Owen. In the first two sections the arrangement is chronological – though this is not, of course, meant to beg the question as far as the *Timaeus* is concerned. The Aristotle section opens with the general introduction to Aristotle written for the *Dictionary of Scientific Biography*. It continues with a group of papers about the criticism of Plato, turns to central issues of method and metaphysics, and finishes with several more specialized pieces.

The major change from the original texts is in the treatment of Greek. Owen's later articles used very little Greek that was not both transliterated in each occurrence in the text and translated somewhere in the text or notes. Once he saw how much interest his work was generating among philosophers not trained in the classical languages, he attempted, for the most part, to write in such a way as to make his work available to this wider audience – without, of course, in any way modifying his commitment to rigorous classical scholarship and to close philological argument where the issues called for it. Several of his earlier papers, by contrast, had a good deal of untranslated and untransliterated Greek, frequently even where no linguistic point was at issue. For this volume, Owen decided that he wanted to make all of the papers as available as possible to a non-specialist philosophical and student audience. He therefore decided that each occurrence of Greek in the text should be transliterated (with occasional exceptions in the case of lengthy citations), and that each occurrence of Greek should be translated somewhere (with minor exceptions in the case of particles and conjunctions mentioned in the course of stylistic discussion). Fortunately I was able to go over this with him case by case and to ascertain his preferred translations. (I should like here to acknowledge the help of Jonathan Barnes, Malcolm Schofield, and Richard Sorabji, who did this same thing earlier for those papers that appeared in their series of *Articles on Aristotle*, namely, 'Logic and Metaphysics in Some Earlier Works of Aristotle', 'The Platonism of Aristotle', ' "*Tithenai ta phainomena*" ', 'Aristotle on Time', and 'Aristotelian Pleasures'. As for the footnotes, we tried to pursue a similar policy, since Owen's notes are a tightly woven part of his arguments, and we wanted the reader to have access to the many important points made there. In only two cases, 'Eleatic Questions' and 'Plato on the Undepictable', were the notes so highly philological in character that we had made no clear decision about policy at the time of Owen's death. I have decided to retain the Greek characters in those two cases. Our policy in transliterating should be self-evident; it is the same one used by Barnes, Schofield and Sorabji. We use long marks (circumflexes) only to distinguish *êta* from *epsilon*, *ômega* from *omicron*; long and short *alpha*, *upsilon*, and *iota* are not distinguished. We include accents only where an important point turns on their presence or absence.

Other less important alterations include several added cross-references; the rewriting of some dedicatory material; and dozens of mechanical alterations, such as the supplying of fuller bibliographical references and the standardization of abbreviation and footnote form. In several cases these changes required the renumbering of footnotes. I have tried to help the reader of the original versions to locate references in this volume by placing in the margins the pagination of the original printed version (with the two exceptions noted above). In most cases page breaks are marked with a solidus.

Owen planned to make several further changes which, while relatively small, are too substantial for me to venture to make on his behalf. In '*Timaeus*' he planned to add a long footnote discussing recent stylometric work, in particular a thesis by Leonard Brandwood,[2] which, he believed, exposed some serious errors in Cherniss's use of the statistical evidence and supported his position against that of Cherniss. I hope that the student of this debate will be moved by this reference to pursue the issue further. In the same paper Owen planned to add, in a footnote, a discussion of the relationship between the two regress arguments in the *Parmenides*. In 'Inherence', he planned to add a postscript discussing the criteria for something's being a universal rather than a particular, since he felt that some of the discussion generated by this article could be sharpened by an explicit statement on this issue.

Owen wanted the Preface to say no more than this. I believe he would not have thought it inappropriate, however, for me to speak very briefly of the joy it has been to work closely through these extraordinary papers once again and to see the philosophical focus and power they exhibit when gathered together; of the equal and related joy of working with him on the project, to which, as to every enterprise, he brought his incomparable incisiveness and energy; and of the profound sense of loss that accompanies the knowledge that this will constitute his complete collected papers, rather than, as we thought, their first volume.

M.C.N.

[2] L. Brandwood, *The Dating of Plato's Works by the Stylistic Method: A Historical and Critical Survey*, Ph.D. Thesis, University of London, 1958, available from University Microfilms.

Acknowledgments

The papers in this book have been previously published as follows. The editor is grateful for permission to reprint them.

Chapter 1. 'Eleatic Questions', *Classical Quarterly* NS 10 (1960), 84-102. Reprinted in *Studies in Presocratic Philosophy*, ed. D.J. Furley and R.E. Allen, vol. 2 (London: Routledge and Kegan Paul, 1975), 48-81.
Chapter 2. 'Plato and Parmenides on the Timeless Present', *The Monist* 50 (1966), 317-40. Reprinted in *The Pre-Socratics*, ed. A.P.D. Mourelatos (Garden City, N.Y.: Doubleday, 1974), 271-92.
Chapter 3. 'Zeno and the Mathematicians', *Proceedings of the Aristotelian Society* 58 (1957-8), 199-222. Reprinted in *Zeno's Paradoxes*, ed. Wesley C. Salmon (Indianapolis: Bobbs-Merrill, 1970), 139-63; and in *Studies in Presocratic Philosophy*, vol. 2, 143-65.
Chapter 4. 'The Place of the *Timaeus* in Plato's Dialogues', *Classical Quarterly* NS 3 (1953), 79-95. Reprinted in *Studies in Plato's Metaphysics*, ed. R.E. Allen (London: Routledge and Kegan Paul, 1965), 313-38.
Chapter 5. 'Notes on Ryle's Plato', in *Ryle*, ed. O.P. Wood and G. Pitcher (Garden City, N.Y.: Doubleday, 1970), 341-72.
Chapter 6. 'Plato on Not-Being', in *Plato I: Metaphysics and Epistemology*, ed. G. Vlastos (Garden City, N.Y.: Doubleday, 1970, repr. University of Notre Dame Press, 1978), 223-67.
Chapter 7. 'Plato on the Undepictable', in *Exegesis and Argument*, ed. E.N. Lee *et al.*, *Phronesis* suppl. vol. 1 (Assen: Van Gorcum, 1973), 349-61.
Chapter 8. 'Aristotle: Method, Physics, and Cosmology', in *Dictionary of Scientific Biography*, ed. C.C. Gillespie, vol. 1 (New York: Charles Scribner's Sons, 1970), 250-8.
Chapter 9. 'A Proof in the *Peri Ideôn*', *Journal of Hellenic Studies* 77 (1957), 103-11. Reprinted in *Studies in Plato's Metaphysics*, 293-312.
Chapter 10. 'Logic and Metaphysics in some Earlier Works of Aristotle', in *Aristotle and Plato in the Mid-Fourth Century*, ed. I. Düring and G.E.L. Owen, Papers of the Symposium Aristotelicum held at Oxford in August, 1957 (Göteborg: Elanders Boktryckeri Aktiebolag, 1960), 163-90. Reprinted in German translation in *Metaphysik und Theologie des Aristoteles*, ed. F.-P. Hager (Darmstadt: Wissenschaftliche Buchgesellschaft, 1969), 399-435; and in English in *Articles on Aristotle*, ed. J. Barnes, M. Schofield, and R. Sorabji, vol. 3 (London: Duckworth, 1979), 13-32.

Chapter 11. 'The Platonism of Aristotle', *Proceedings of the British Academy* 51 (1966), 125-50. Reprinted in *Studies in the Philosophy of Thought and Action*, ed. P.F. Strawson (Oxford: Oxford University Press, 1968), 147-74; and in *Articles on Aristotle*, vol. 1 (1975), 14-34.

Chapter 12. 'Dialectic and Eristic in the Treatment of the Forms', in *Aristotle on Dialectic: the Topics*, ed. G.E.L. Owen, Papers of the Third Symposium Aristotelicum (Oxford: Oxford University Press, 1968), 103-25.

Chapter 13. '*Tithenai ta phainomena*', in *Aristote et les problèmes de méthode*, ed. S. Mansion, Papers of the Second Symposium Aristotelicum (Louvain: Publications Universitaires de Louvain, 1961), 83-103. Reprinted in *Aristotle*, ed. J.M.E. Moravcsik (Garden City, N.Y.: Doubleday, 1957), 167-90; and in *Articles on Aristotle*, vol. 1, 113-25.

Chapter 14. 'Inherence', *Phronesis* 10 (1965), 97-105. Reprinted in German translation in *Logik und Erkenntnislehre des Aristoteles*, ed. F.-P. Hager (Darmstadt: Wissenschaftliche Buchgesellschaft, 1972), 296-307.

Chapter 15. 'Aristotle on the Snares of Ontology', in *New Essays on Plato and Aristotle*, ed. R. Bambrough (London: Routledge and Kegan Paul, 1965), 69-75.

Chapter 16. 'Particular and General', *Proceedings of the Aristotelian Society* 79 (1978-9), 1-21.

Chapter 17. 'Aristotle on Time', in *Motion and Time, Space and Matter*, ed. P. Machamer and R. Turnbull (Columbus: Ohio State University Press, 1976), 3-27. Reprinted in *Articles on Aristotle*, vol. 3, 140-58.

Chapter 18. 'Aristotelian Mechanics', in *Aristotle on Nature and Living Things: Philosophical and Historical Studies*, ed. A. Gotthelf (Pittsburgh: Mathesis Publications, 1986).

Chapter 19. 'Aristotelian Pleasures', *Proceedings of the Aristotelian Society* 72 (1971-2), 135-52. Reprinted in *Articles on Aristotle*, vol. 2 (1977), 92-103.

Chapter 20. 'Philosophical Invective', *Oxford Studies in Ancient Philosophy* 1 (1983), 1-25.

Abbreviations

Plato

Cra.	*Cratylus*
Crit.	*Critias*
Ep.	*Epistulae*
Euthd.	*Euthydemus*
Gorg.	*Gorgias*
Parm.	*Parmenides*
Phd.	*Phaedo*
Phdr.	*Phaedrus*
Phil.	*Philebus*
Plt.	*Politicus* (*Statesman*)
Prot.	*Protagoras*
Rep.	*Republic*
Soph.	*Sophist*
Symp.	*Symposium*
Tht.	*Theaetetus*
Tim.	*Timaeus*

Aristotle

A.Pr.	*Analytica Priora*
A.Pst.	*Analytica Posteriora*
Cael.	*De Caelo*
De An.	*De Anima*
Div.	*De Divinatione per Somnum*
EE	*Ethica Eudemia*
EN	*Ethica Nicomachea*
GA	*De Generatione Animalium*
GC	*De Generatione et Corruptione*
HA	*Historia Animalium*
IA	*De Incessu Animalium*
Int.	*De Interpretatione*
Long.	*De Longitudine et Brevitate Vitae*
MA	*De Motu Animalium*
Mech.	*Mechanica*

Mem.	*De Memoria et Reminiscentia*
Meta.	*Metaphysica*
Meteor.	*Meteorologica*
MM	*Magna Moralia*
PA	*De Partibus Animalium*
Phys.	*Physica*
Pol.	*Politica*
Probl.	*Problemata*
Rhet.	*Rhetorica*
SE	*De Sophisticis Elenchis*
Sens.	*De Sensu*
Som.	*De Somno et Vigilia*
Top.	*Topica*

Other

AGP	*Archiv für Geschichte der Philosophie*
AJP	*American Journal of Philology*
Alex.	Alexander of Aphrodisias
in Metaph.	*In Aristotelis Metaphysica commentaria*, ed. M. Hayduck (Berlin 1891).
in Mete.	*In Aristotelis Meteorologicorum libros commentaria*, ed. M. Hayduck (Berlin 1899).
in SE	*In Aristotelis Sophisticos Elenchos commentarium*, ed. M. Wallies (Berlin 1898).
in Top.	*In Aristotelis Topicorum libros octo commentaria*, ed. M. Wallies (Berlin 1891).
Clem. *Strom.*	Clement of Alexandria, *Stromateis*
CP	*Classical Philology*
CQ	*Classical Quarterly*
CR	*Classical Review*
D.-K.	*Fragmente der Vorsokratiker*, ed. H. Diels and W. Kranz (14th edition, Dublin/Zürich 1969).
Hippolytus, *RH*	*Refutatio Omnium Haeresium*, ed. P. Wendland (Leipzig 1916).
HSCP	*Harvard Studies in Classical Philology*
JHP	*Journal of the History of Philosophy*
JHS	*Journal of Hellenic Studies*
J. Philol.	*Journal of Philology*
J. Philos.	*Journal of Philosophy*
K.-G.	R. Kühner and B. Gerth, *Ausführliche Grammatik der griechischen Sprache* (4th ed., Leverkusen 1955).
LSJ	*Greek-English Lexicon*, H.G. Liddell and R. Scott, new edition by H.S. Jones (Oxford 1925-40)
PAS	*Proceedings of the Aristotelian Society.*

PASS	*Proceedings of the Aristotelian Society*, Supplementary Vol.
Phil. Rev.	*Philosophical Review*
SVF	*Stoicorum Veterum Fragmenta*, ed. J. von Arnim (Vienna 1903).
TAPA	*Transactions of the American Philological Association*

I

THE PRESOCRATICS

1

Eleatic Questions

The following suggestions for the interpretation of Parmenides and Melissus **48**
can be grouped for convenience about one problem. This is the problem whether, as Aristotle thought and as most commentators still assume, Parmenides wrote his poem in the broad tradition of Ionian and Italian cosmology. The details of Aristotle's interpretation have been challenged over and again, but those who agree with his general assumptions take comfort from some or all of the following major arguments. First, the cosmogony which formed the last part of Parmenides' poem is expressly claimed by the goddess who expounds it to have some measure of truth or reliability in its own right, and indeed the very greatest measure possible for such an attempt. Second, the earlier arguments of the goddess prepare the ground for such a cosmogony in two ways. For in the first place these arguments themselves start from assumptions derived from earlier cosmologists, and are concerned merely to work out the implications of this traditional material. And, in the second place, they end by establishing the existence of a spherical universe: the framework of the physical world can be secured by logic even if the subsequent introduction of sensible qualities or 'powers' into this world marks some decline in logical rigour.

These views seem to me demonstrably false. As long as they are allowed to stand they obscure the structure and the originality of Parmenides' argument./

49

What measure of truth or reliability is claimed for the cosmogony?

Here our chief problem is the reinterpretation of a couplet which was already for Diels in 1897 the most controversial text in Parmenides. It occurs, according to Simplicius' quotation, at the end of the goddess's opening remarks.

* [Postscript 1971: I have made small corrections to the text as printed in 1960, and marked later comments by square brackets in the notes.]

χρεὼ δέ σε πάντα πυθέσθαι
ἠμὲν Ἀληθείης εὐκυκλέος ἀτρεμὲς ἦτορ
ἠδὲ βροτῶν δόξας, ταῖς οὐκ ἔνι πίστις ἀληθής.
ἀλλ' ἔμπης καὶ ταῦτα μαθήσεαι, ὡς τὰ δοκοῦντα
χρῆν δοκίμως εἶναι διὰ παντὸς πάντα περῶντα.[1]

(B 1. 28-32. In the first instance I shall quote fragments from the text of Diels-Kranz.)

Thus the final couplet follows a sharp denunciation of *brotôn doxai* (opinions of mortals), and subsequently this denunciation is driven home. When the goddess comes to the promised account of mortal ideas she calls it by the phrase which Empedocles took as a challenge – *kosmon emôn epeôn apatêlon* (the deceptive ordering [*or*: world] of my words) (B 8.52, cf. Emped. B 17.26). And it is certainly this same way of inquiry that she bars to her hearer in B 6.4-9, and B 7.1-5:[2] the way of mortals who know nothing, who wander deaf, blind and bemused, compelled by habit[3] to trust their aimless eye and sounding ear and tongue. Despite all this, Parmenides' readers have nursed the

[1] I.e., as I shall argue:

You must learn everything,
both the unshaken heart of rounded truth
and the opinions of mortals, which have in them no true belief.
Still, you shall learn these things too, namely how the things that seem
had to have genuine existence and to pervade everything without exception.

Or, with the reading περ ὄντα: had to have genuine existence: being indeed the whole of things.

[2] *Contra* those who follow Bernays in identifying this, the second of the false paths denounced by the goddess, with the theories of Heraclitus, and so have to distinguish it from the unheraclitean cosmology expounded in the last part of the poem. This thesis led Burnet to identify the cosmology with the *first* false path (*Early Greek Philosophy*[4] (London 1930), 183-4), though this path is the 'wholly unintelligible' line of sheer negation (B 2. 5): a preposterous equation that he did not try to make plausible. The second false path is the error not of Heraclitus but of all men: see the second section of this paper and W.J. Verdenius, *Parmenides* (Groningen 1942), app. J; W. Jaeger, *Theology of the Early Greek Philosophers* (Oxford 1947), 101; G. Kirk, *Heraclitus: the Cosmic Fragments* (Cambridge 1962), 211. To take this path is to suppose that *to be and not to be are the same and not the same* (B 6. 8-9: for the negative in τὸ οὐκ εἶναι cf. B 8. 40, where it cannot be explained as *oratio obliqua*). Gregory Vlastos, to whom I am indebted for making me reinforce and reconsider my argument at some salient points, argues: 'Those who deny any allusion to Heraclitus in Parmenides ... have yet to explain why in these lines Parmenides should (*a*) impute to *anyone* the belief in the identity of being and not-being (rather than merely the belief in not-being, which is bad enough ...) and (*b*) after saying οἷς τὸ πέλειν τε καὶ οὐκ εἶναι ταὐτὸν νενόμισται here, which would be quite sufficient to make his point, should add maliciously κοὐ ταὐτόν, producing the expression ταὐτὸν κοὐ ταὐτόν, which so strikingly parallels ὅλα καὶ οὐχ ὅλα in Heraclitus' (*AJP* 76 (1955), 341 n. 11). The explanation is given below, pp. 11ff. and n. 36. Both the points queried by V. are essential to Parmenides' criticism: ordinary men do not only want to keep both εἶναι and οὐκ εἶναι; in trying to distinguish them they confuse them. That is why *both* expressions in their ordinary use are empty names (B 8. 38-41). [On B 8. 38 L.E. Woodbury (*HSCP* 63 (1958), 145-60) argued for the reading τῷ πάντ' ὀνόμασται as against the Simplicius variant assumed here, τῷ πάντ' ὄνομ(α) ἔσται. The argument of the note does not turn on it; but there remains much disagreement on the sense and construction of the first text, and there is no known parallel for such a use of ὀνομάζειν without ἐπί governing the nominee-dative.]

[3] ἔθος πολύπειρον, B 7. 3, for which G. Calogero suggests 'l'esperienza della molteplicità delle cose' (*Studi sull'Eleatismo* (Rome 1932), 32 n. I); but if the adjective is πολύπειρος it is better taken with the accompanying σε. Perhaps from πολυπείρων, 'widespread'.

conviction that he meant to claim an independent validity for his cosmology, a reality of some kind or degree for the phenomena described in it. So there must be a saving clause in the denunciation. But where?

Wilamowitz found one in the goddess's promise to expound a *diakosmon eoikota panta* (B 8.60).[4] *Eoikota* he interpreted in a sense similar to that which it carries in the *Timaeus* 29b-d. Verdenius replied that without some such supplement as *tois etumoisi* (cf. Xenophanes B 35) the word can hardly have had this meaning for Parmenides;[5] and the same rejoinder rules out Reinhardt's 'Folgerichtigkeit und augenscheinlichkeit' and Kranz's 'wahrscheinlich-einleuchtend'. Verdenius himself cited Homer in support of the translation 'fitting' or 'proper',[6] and this sense is the more convincing in that the purpose for which the cosmology is fitting is announced in the next line of the poem: it is given simply *hôs ou mê pote tis se brotôn gnômê parelassêi* (so that no idea of mortals can outstrip you) (B 8.61),/ though these are still the same **50**
witless mortals, men at the mercy of the words they use (B 6.4-7; B 8.38-41, 53; B 9). So, on this construing of the lines, no ontological claims have been made and the cosmology need be no more than a dialectical device.

Nor, again, can any reality be conjured into the world of appearance from the ambiguous couplet B 8.53-4. 'Mortals decided to name two forms, of which it is not right to name one – and there they went astray': whether or not these words are meant to show that, as Aristotle supposed, one of the forms which dominate the cosmogony *is* logically respectable, what is certain and agreed is that the question cannot be settled from the obscure text. The interpretation of that text itself depends on the answer we give to our general problem.[7] So the saving qualification is still to seek.

Hence the importance of the couplet which ends the passage quoted above (B 1.31-2); for since Wilamowitz many interpreters have thought that on its most natural interpretation it expressly promises some sort of degree of reality to the contents of the cosmology.

The sole authority for the couplet is Simplicius, and he quotes it together with the three preceding lines (*De Caelo* 557. 25-558. 2 Heiberg). Of the four manuscripts used in Heiberg's text two, which share one archetype (A, F), give explicable and worthless variants for *mathêseai*. Of these two manuscripts one, which is particularly given to literal and accentual errors and improvements,[8] reads *perônta* in the last line as against *per onta* in the other three manuscripts. Despite these poor credentials *perônta* has been generally received.[9] Diels, as we shall see, had a special motive for adopting it, and those who did not follow Diels's interpretation seem to have accepted the reading on the ground that its better-attested rival would make the goddess claim, by a flat self-contradiction, that nothing existed but the *dokounta*. Whether she would be much happier to claim that all things are permeated by

[4] *Hermes* 34 (1899), 204-5. [5] Verdenius, op. cit., 50-1.

[6] ibid., citing *Odyssey* 3. 124-5 and 4. 239 (cf. 266).

[7] Cf. Kirk and Raven, *Presocratic Philosophers*[4] (Cambridge 1962), 281 n. 1, and by contrast Vlastos, *TAPA* 76 (1946), 74.

[8] Heiberg's A, which makes two other such slips in the five lines quoted.

[9] The sole recent exception is Zafiropoulo, *L'École éléate* (Paris 1950), 297.

those *dokounta* is an open question; but this is one dilemma that can be left to yield in due course to a general solvent.

All the manuscripts have *dokimôs* (and I have no doubt they are right). Wilamowitz explained the word in accordance with his Platonic reading of the *diakosmon eoikota*. He credited Parmenides with the theory that 'Neben die Wahrheit die in sich geschlossene konsequente Hypothese tritt. In diesem
51 Falle *ta/ dokounta dokimôs esti toiauta*, oder besser in der Rede des Eleaten *dokimôs esti*, die Hypothesen haben in einer probehaltigen Weise Realität'.[10] That is to say: provided our account of the phenomenal world can be got to conform to certain canons of internal consistency – even if as a whole it is vitiated by its premisses – then the phenomena can be allowed a modest but 'warranted' reality of their own. Kranz translated accordingly: 'Doch wirst du trotzdem auch dieses kennen lernen und zwar so, wie das (*ihnen*) Scheinende auf eine probehafte, wahrscheinliche Weise *sein* müßte, indem es alles ganz und gar durchdringt.' Grant the translation, and the saving clause has been found.

Diels replied that this interpretation will not square with Parmenides' ontology, and he was right.[11] There can be no degrees of reality: what exists must *pampan pelenai* (be entirely), on pain of being nothing at all.[12] But all such general issues apart, Wilamowitz's sense cannot be got from the Greek. Where *dokimôs* is attested elsewhere (Aeschylus, *Persae* 547, Xenophon, *Cyr.* 1. 6. 7) the lexica and the editors rightly translate it 'really, genuinely', and the earlier editors of Parmenides had no doubt that this was its sense in the present context.[13] The *dokimos* is the reliable man, not one who measures up to some standards but fails the main test.[14] So *dokimôs einai* is *assuredly to exist*; and this is what the phenomenal world can never do for Parmenides' goddess. The same fact defeats any attempt to read *dokimôs* as 'in a manner appropriate to *dokounta*'.[15] Avoiding these pitfalls, Verdenius followed

[10] Wilamowitz, l.c.; cf. K. Reinhardt, *Parmenides* (Bonn 1916), 9, Calogero, *Studi*, 31 n. 1.

[11] *Poetarum Philosophorum Fragmenta* (Berlin 1901), 60.

[12] B 8. 11, 15-18, 32-33. In line 33 most editors excise μή with Bergk and, with qualms, understand ἐόν as copulative = ἐὸν ἐπιδευές. But see H. Fraenkel, 'Parmenidesstudien' in *Wege und Formen frühgriechischen Denkens* (Munich 1960²), 192-3. The same sense can be got from Gomperz's ἔστι γὰρ οὐκ ἐπιδεές· μὴ ἐὸν δ' ἂν παντὸς ἐδεῖτο: *any* admixture of μὴ ὄν (any statement of the form οὐκ ἔστι) is as ruinous as taking the first wrong path at once. See below, pp. 10ff., 18-19.

[13] '*Plane*' Brandis (1813), '*clare*' Karsten (1835): both accordingly felt compelled to discard εἶναι for Peyron's ἰέναι.

[14] Arbenz, *Die Adjektiv auf* -ιμος (Zurich-Tübingen 1933), 38-41; Hermann Fraenkel, *Hermes* 60 (1925), 190. See, e.g., Aesch. *Persae* 87 (δόκιμος with inf. = 'able'), Democritus B 67, B 68. In Herodotus the sense 'renowned' becomes common, but never with the implication that the renown is not wholly deserved. The exception that may seem to tell for Wilamowitz is Heraclitus B 28, δοκέοντα γὰρ ὁ δοκιμώτατος γινώσκει, φυλάσσει. But if we give δοκιμώτατος here the weak sense of 'having the greatest (but finally undeserved) reputation' we spoil the aphorism, which is a paradox comparable with B 5 (καθαίρονται δ' ἄλλῳ αἵματι μιαινόμενοι), B 56 (ἐξηπάτηνται παραπλησίως 'Ομήρῳ, ὃς ἐγένετο τῶν 'Ελλήνων σοφώτερος πάντων), B 68 (describing the mysteries as ἄκεα). Such paradoxes trade on giving their full sense to certain expressions while putting them, as it were, in inverted commas: your 'sage' Homer was a fool, your 'purifications' are defilings, your 'δοκιμώτατος' is only an expert on δοκέοντα.

[15] Prompted perhaps by B 19, οὕτω τοι κατὰ δόξαν ἔφυ τάδε. This sense again might seem warranted by Heraclitus B 28 (see last note); but of course Heraclitus' characteristic word-play depends on there *not* being any such overt connection in sense between the words.

Hermann Fraenkel in translating the word 'acceptably'[16]; but he recognized that the reality of the appearances could not be acceptable to the goddess and therefore took this to mean 'acceptable *to mortals*'. He glossed the lines: 'How mortals starting from a certain principle were able to explain reality in detail in a manner satisfactory *to them.*'[17] The saving dative is far to seek (it is scarcely enough to argue that since it must be supplied with *dokounta* it can be imported elsewhere in the clause). But the weightier objection comes from an independent survey of the use of *dokimos*. Writing after Fraenkel, Arbenz showed by his discussion of the evidence that 'acceptable', however plausible at first sight, is still too weak a translation for this strong adjective. He was induced by that evidence to claim an original sense for the word that is not passive but active, 'receiving the enemy in battle' and hence 'steadfast, sure'.[18]/

Such difficulties with *dokimôs* seem to recommend Diels's emendation: *hôs* **52**
ta dokounta chrên dokimôs(ai) einai dia pantos panta perônta. Here, as in the older edition of Karsten, *perônta* takes on an excellent sense, describing not the appearances but the inquirer. But old snags give way to new. The elision is harsh, and harder to parallel than Diels supposed.[19] *Dokimôsai* he took for the equivalent of *dokimasai*, and on this assumption two interpretations of the clause *hôs ... einai* seem to be possible, depending on whether *einai* is taken with *dokounta* or with *dokimôsai*. The first is 'how one should examine the things that seem to exist' (the alternative taken most recently by Messrs. Kirk and Raven); the second is 'how one should test the appearances with regard to their reality' (Diels's original rendering[20]). The first requires a close coupling of *dokounta* and *einai* that the order of the text makes very improbable. The second ignores the fact that *dokimasai* with the infinitive would naturally mean '*approve* or *admit* their reality',[21] and this is certainly too hospitable for Parmenides' goddess. In his later editions Diels saw an escape-route: he reduced *einai* to a copulative role and took it closely with *hôs* ('wie man ... annehmen müsste, dass sich jenes Scheinwesen verhalte').[22] Such a reading is if anything strengthened by Reinhardt's objection that *dokimômi* must be equated not with *dokimazô* but with *dokeô* (= *oiomai*).[23] But the proverbial opposition of *dokein* and *einai* is enough to make any such weakening of *einai* implausible in this context, where the antithesis is inescapable. And

[16] Fraenkel (see n. 12 above) had suggested 'annehmbar, sich Anerkennung verschaffend.'

[17] *Parmenides*, 49-51.

[18] op. cit. (n. 14 above), comparing δόκιμος = ἐς δοκὴν ἀγαθός with ἄλκιμος = ἐς ἀλκὴν ἀγαθός: cf. D. Page, *Sappho and Alcaeus* (Oxford 1955), 184 (ad. loc. A 6).

[19] The elision in Xenophanes B 3. 5 was exorcized by Wilamowitz. Kirk and Raven (*Presocratic Philosophers*, 268) say 'the elision is otherwise unknown in hexameters', but editors have cited *Iliad* 11. 272, 13. 777, 17. 89.

[20] 'Wie man alles durchforschend das Scheinsein auf seine Echtheit prüfen musst', *Parmenides Lehrgedicht* (Berlin 1897), 59.

[21] LSJ. s.v. II: e.g. δεδοκιμασμένος ἱππεύειν.

[22] *Poet. Phil. Frag.* (1901), 60.

[23] Reinhardt, *Parmenides*, 6. The sense required by Diels is found only in the letter of 'Pherecydes', Diog. Laert. 1. 122. Hesychius gives δοκίμωμι· δοκέω, οἴομαι. Cf. Gow on Theocritus 30. 25 (apparently mis-read by LSJ. s.v.).

Reinhardt found other objections, arguing for instance that at this date *chrên* cannot be read as *chrê*: unless it is genuinely historic in tense it can express only what is contrary to fact, and as such it cannot introduce the general rule of procedure which Diels found in it.[24]

So much for a notorious deadlock. Between these lines of interpretation the choice is disheartening; but fortunately it seems also to be unnecessary. The competing answers are answers to a mistaken question.

The assumption on which the debate depends is put clearly by Verdenius. To settle the status of the cosmology, he observes, 'we should first examine the general character which the goddess attributes to her statements regarding human opinions. This is contained in the following lines' – namely, in the couplet we are discussing.[25] Thus the problem becomes: just what
53 comment on/ human opinions does the goddess volunteer in these lines? And this is the mistaken question.

The first step is to see, as Kranz and others have seen, that when the goddess promises *all' empês kai tauta mathêseai* her *tauta* is naturally taken to refer to the previous line. It means just 'the contents of mortal opinions'.[26] There is no true belief found among such opinions, nevertheless Parmenides shall be told these things too. And then without a connective the sentence continues: *hôs to dokounta chrên dokimôs einai dia pantos panta perônta*. Now according to the received view this is the goddess's own comment: her promise to say how the appearances can have a sort of reality, or how they can be tested, or whatever. But this gives the sentence an intolerable twist. It must now be supposed to mean: Still, you shall learn the contents of men's opinions *from me at second-hand – and at the same time learn from me at first-hand* how the appearances are to be allowed a sort of existence (or how to test them, etc.). But the connection that I have italicized is not in the text. The relative clause from *hôs* to *per onta* (or *perônta*) can only be epexegetic, elaborating the *tauta*: and *tauta*, on the natural reading, are the contents of human opinions. So the sense is: 'Still, you shall learn (at second-hand from me) these things too (*sc.* the content of mortal opinions), *namely* (still at second-hand and giving the general content of those opinions) how the things-that-seem had to have genuine existence (*dokimôs einai* in the only possible sense), being indeed the whole of things'[27] – or, if we read *perônta*, '... and to pervade everything without exception'.

To be sure, the twist of sense on which I have laid stress might also have been avoided by denying that *tauta* looks back to the preceding line. We might have held, as Diels and others have done, that the whole couplet is concerned with the goddess's own comment on mortal opinions. But if we say this all the old puzzles are restored. The only people who can say of the *dokounta* that and how they *dokimôs* exist are the mortals who believe in them (B 8.38), not the goddess.

[24] Reinhardt, op. cit., 7-9.
[25] Verdenius, *Parmenides*, 49.
[26] ταῦτα after δόξας is of course no obstacle: cf. e.g. *Od.* 3. 124-5.
[27] περ as *vel*, cf. J.D.D. Denniston, *Greek Particles*² (Oxford 1934), 482, 484.

If this is correct, the choice between *per onta* and *perônta* depends on a last minor point of interpretation. Suppose we take the couplet as anticipating some such general description of *dokounta* as that given in B 8. 38-40. In those lines mortals posit certain illusions, believing them real: in our couplet they claim/ that they assuredly exist. The illusions in question include coming to exist 54
and coming to an end, being and not being, shifting place and changing colour: in fact they are presumably all the ordinary manifestations of change and plurality. Then if these are the *dokounta* of our couplet we had better read *per onta*, for if the list comprises all the phenomena these must exhaust and not merely pervade the totality of things for those who believe in them. And in that case the tense of *chrên* must be taken to show that this is how things inevitably were from the start. But the past tense comes more firmly into its own on a slightly different interpretation. For suppose that by *dokounta* here the goddess means primarily just those two forms from which the cosmogony begins (B 8.53-54). The tense of the verb is wholly apt to the first stage of the cosmogony; and now *perônta* is just as attractive, for the forms are expressly said to permeate the universe (B 9.3). However, it is not clear that this pervasion of things by Light and Night could form part of the ordinary man's description of his world: it seems to be the goddess's independent commentary on the disastrous results of naming the two forms (B 8.53, B 9). So on balance I am inclined to keep *panta per onta* both as more appropriate to the content of mortals' beliefs and as the better-attested reading.[28] But no major point of interpretation now hangs on it.

If this general solution of an old puzzle is acceptable, it is worth seeing how much or how little it establishes. The goddess, we can now say, is not inconsistent in her denunciation of the mortal opinions she surveys; there is, after all, no saving clause. Her account of those opinions is not introduced as a contribution to early science. But to say this is not of course to deny that it was the most complete and plausible system its author knew how to produce. If the building of such a system was never his end, it could certainly be a means to his end; and for my part I take its purpose to be wholly dialectical. Parmenides set himself to give the correct or the most plausible analysis of those presuppositions on which ordinary men, and not just theorists, seem to build their picture of the physical world. (These are in fact presuppositions reached by analysis, but Parmenides presents them as conscious past decisions.[29]) Whittled down to their simplest and most economical they can be seen still to require the existence of at least two irreducibly different things in a constant process of/ interaction; and both the plurality and the process 55
have now, on Parmenides' view, been proven absurd.

But needless to say the points for which I have so far argued do not depend

[28] [But it must be noticed, as Mr. A.A. Long reminds me, that the form 'ὄν' is not found elsewhere in Parmenides apart from the highly reconstructed B 8. 57, where Diels-Kranz think it 'nur hier sicher'.]

[29] On this see Verdenius, *Parmenides*, 53 and app. E. With Parmenides, if not before, appears the ambiguity in νόμος and νομίζεσθαι which runs through fifth-century thought: 'unchallenged custom' (B 7. 3), 'arbitrary decision' (B 8. 53); the second an historical mirage thrown by the first, as the Social Contract was by current forms of society.

on the truth of these larger claims.

Do the arguments of the Alêtheia depend on assumptions derived from earlier cosmology?

Here I can best begin by illustrating the type of interpretation that I want to reject. Cornford maintained that Parmenides' whole argument depends on a premiss which 'states in a more abstract form the first assumption common to all his predecessors, Milesian or Pythagorean; ultimately there exists a One Being ... He considers what further attributes can, or cannot, logically belong to a being that is one.'[30] Following the same line of interpretation Raven held that Parmenides is really talking about the Pythagorean One: 'Unity,' he wrote, is 'postulated as an ultimate principle.'[31] Such theories are in fact answers to a familiar problem for which we must try a different solution. The problem is this: when the goddess begins her argument by distinguishing the right way of inquiry – *hê men hopôs éstin te kai hôs ouk ésti mê einai* – from a wrong way – *hê d'hôs ouk éstin te kai hôs chreôn esti mê einai* (B 2. 3-6) – what is the unexpressed subject of the verbs *éstin* and *ouk éstin*? Cornford and others import a subject from earlier cosmology, and by looking too far afield they overlook a remarkable argument.

(*a*) *The subject is not 'What is'.* Diels understood *to eon* as the subject. Cornford even proposed to introduce this into the text at B 2. 3 (*hê men hopôs eon ésti kai hôs ouk ésti mê einai*).[32] But there is a conclusive reason why this subject will not do. The reason is that it turns the *éstin* into a mere tautology and the *ouk éstin* correspondingly into a flat contradiction, whereas Parmenides thinks it necessary to *argue* for *éstin* and against *ouk éstin*. We shall come to the detail of his argument directly, but first this general point must be guarded against misunderstanding. No one will deny that, as the argument goes, *to eon* is a correct description of the subject. The point is that Parmenides purports to *prove* that it is a correct description, and that (as we shall see) his proof is not a disingenuous *petitio principii*, and therefore he
56 cannot be assuming it from the start. Cornford indeed seems to/ suppose that *to eon éstin* would not be a tautology for Parmenides, for he holds that it has to be incorporated in a group of special premisses on which, in his view, the whole argument depends.[33] But even if this paradox could be made out – if,

[30] F.M. Cornford, *Plato and Parmenides* (London 1939), 29. How far Cornford's picture of Parmenides' predecessors as sharing this assumption is acceptable is another question and one which lies outside this paper.

[31] J.E. Raven, *Pythagoreans and Eleatics* (Cambridge 1948), 176 and ch. iii *passim*. It is to be noticed that Mr Raven takes a different and, I believe, more plausible view in the later *Presocratic Philosophers* (see n. 44 below).

[32] *Plato and Parmenides*, 30 n. 2. As a parallel he cites B 6. 1, ἐὸν ἔμμεναι, yet within a few lines he destroys this parallel by taking the ἐόν with the immediately preceding infinitives (so Simplicius and Burnet, rightly; Cornford, op cit., 31 n. 2; see below, p. 15). in B 8. 3, as other editors have seen, ἐόν is part of the predicate (cf. *Laws* 904 a).

[33] *Plato and Parmenides*, 33. Of the other 'premisses' detected by Cornford one ('that which is is one and cannot be many') will be considered in part (*b*) of this section of the paper and the other ('that which is can be thought or known, and uttered or truly named; that which is not, cannot'), or an emended version of this, in part (*c*). None is in fact a 'premiss'.

that is to say, *eon* could be divorced from *einai* in such a way as to make the proposition non-tautologous (and of course Cornford does not profess to do this) – it would not affect the point. For, quite apart from the consideration that no such premiss is either recognized or required by the argument, the very fact that Parmenides argues for the existence of his subject proves that for him the assertion of its existence was no more a bare assumption than it was a bare tautology.

Yet a theory such as Cornford's does imply, wittingly or unwittingly, that Parmenides did not try to prove his *éstin*, and in face of this we need only remind ourselves of Parmenides' arguments on this head. The purpose of those arguments is well known: it is to rule out two wrong roads which, together with the remaining right road, make up an exhaustive set of possible answers to the question *éstin ê ouk éstin*? 'Does it exist or not?' The right path is an unqualified yes. The first wrong path is an equally unqualified no,[34] and this is rebutted at the start by the argument that what does not exist could not be thought or spoken of, *oute gar an gnoiês to ge mê eon (ou gar anuston) oute phrasais* (B 2. 7-8). (Later I shall suggest that this reply is itself reinforced by a further argument at the beginning of B 6.) There is no suggestion that anyone takes the first wrong road, which simply comes to saying that there is nothing whatever in existence. It is the second, the blind alley described in the latter part of B 6, that is followed by 'mortals' – i.e. by everyone in his daily business.[35] To take this well-trodden path (*patos anthrôpôn*, B 1. 27) is to say, very naturally, that the question *éstin ê ouk éstin*? can be answered either yes or no, depending on what one is talking about, and when, and where. Ordinary men want to keep *both einai* and *ouk einai* in use: horses exist, mermaids do not; there is sandy soil here but not there; there are dodos at one time, not at another. It is this qualified answer that Parmenides denounces as looking both ways (*dikranoi*, B 6. 5), moving in opposite directions (*palintropos keleuthos*, B 6. 9); and his first and fundamental argument against it is that it treats existence and non-existence as different and yet identical: *hois to pelein te kai ouk einai tauton nenomistai kou tauton* (B 6. 8-9). This clause, which has been con-/strued out of context by those who **57**
read it as a reference to Heraclitus,[36] has an exact sense in Parmenides'

[34] The two paths are 'It exists and *must* exist', 'It does not exist and *cannot*' (B 2. 3 and 5). The force of the 'must' and 'cannot' is shown by the remaining path, which says accordingly that the subject *can* but need not exist (ἔστι γὰρ εἶναι, cf. p. 15 below), and means by this that the question 'Does it exist?' has to be answered sometimes yes and sometimes no (see the text). In ruling out 'can' in favour of either 'must' or 'cannot' the other paths are ruling out this qualified answer. This warns us against saving that the third path is a conflation of the other two.

[35] *Pace* A.H. Coxon, who holds that Parmenides consistently distinguishes between ἄνθρωποι = *mankind as a whole* and βροτοί = *philosophers* (*CQ* 28 (1934), 134). I am obliged to him for a copy of his paper vigorously annotated with its author's second thoughts.

[36] Because they have to break it into two supposedly Heraclitean conjunctions: being and not-being, and same and not same (cf. Vlastos n. 2 above). Quite apart from the implausibility of the attempt to read these as actual echoes of Heraclitus (see the 'parallels' adduced by Kranz in his apparatus, *Vors.*[7] i. 233), this fragmentation destroys the sense and the grammar. The point is not that men simply identify being with not-being, or the same with the different, but that they cannot distinguish εἶναι and οὐκ εἶναι on their own terms without identifying them. Cornford, who does not claim a reference to Heraclitus here, commits the same fault of fragmentation

argument. Ordinary men and cosmologists alike try to distinguish existence from non-existence by saying, for instance, that lions do exist and mermaids do not; yet in distinguishing them they identify them, for (by the argument already brought against the first wrong road in B 2) if non-existent mermaids could be talked about they would be existent. Subsequently Parmenides essays to refute those who say that *éstin* is true at one time but not another (the elimination of *genesis* (coming to be) and *olethros* (ceasing to be) in B 8. 6-21), or true for one thing but not another (the proof that the subject is unitary and indivisible first introduced at B 8. 22-5), or true at one place but not another (the proof of spatial uniformity in B 8. 42-9: we shall return to these latter arguments). He is anxious to show that the second wrong road has no advantage over the first, and so to reduce the choice of answers to *pampan pelenai ê ouchi* (B 8. 11 and 15); to qualify the positive answer at all is to go wholly astray (B 8. 32-3[37]). And thus by elimination he tries to establish the conclusion he wants: *éstin.*

I confess that in face of this I do not see how it is possible to interpret Parmenides either as preoccupied merely with the truism that what exists exists, or as smuggling in the existence of his subject as a premiss in the argument.

(*b*) *Nor is the subject 'The One' or 'The One Being'.* Another premiss that Cornford detects behind Parmenides' argument is the proposition that what exists is single: 'That which is, is one and cannot be many.' This, he claims, must be a premiss, for Parmenides gives no proof of it.[38] Thus he is able from the start to pack unity as well as existence into the unexpressed subject of the argument; and then it is a short step to the claim that what Parmenides is discussing, albeit in this uncandid way, is just the One Being of Pythagorean cosmology. But this move to fill out the subject is one degree less plausible than the last. For not only does Parmenides prove the unity of his subject instead of (as Cornford believes) assuming it; he proves it at the second remove, from a theorem that he has previously provided about its existence. However, it is not hard to detect a reason why this was overlooked and indeed why Parmenides might seem to be offering no proof of unity at all. The reason seems to lie in a misreading of the first line of his proof./

58 The proof that the subject of the argument is single is of course just the proof that it is 'indivisible' and 'continuous', which is given in B 8. 22-5 and promised in the *hen* (one), *suneches* (continuous) of B 8. 6. The first line of the argument is always given in the form: *oude diaireton estin* (nor is it divided), *epei pan estin homoion*, where *pan estin homoion* is predicative and the premiss of the proof is that its subject is 'all alike'. But at once we run into difficulties. The passage is embedded in a long self-contained train of argument quoted as a

(*Plato and Parmenides*, 33): in a changing world, he says, men hold that things (*a*) are (at one time) and are not (at another), and (*b*) pass from being one thing (the same) to being another (not the same).

[37] See n. 12 above.

[38] *Plato and Parmenides*, 35.

whole by Simplicius,[39] and there is no previous point in the argument in which it has been concluded that the subject is homogeneous. Indeed it seems that the sense in which this is meant can only be gathered from the following lines: presumably the subject is *homoion* just in the sense that it is *suneches*, and then the supposed argument collapses into a mere *petitio principii* or, as Cornford might say, into the enunciation of an unsupported premiss. In any case it is unconnected with the arguments that precede it, and the deductive form in which it is cast is misleading.

But the picture is quite changed once it is seen that *homoion* here must have not predicative but adverbial force and that the *estin* before it must accordingly be read as *éstin*.[40] For several reasons this seems certain. First, *homoion* is parallel to the *têi mallon/cheiroteron* of the next two lines (B 8. 23-4), where the verb to be supplied from the first line can only be *éstin*: the subject exists uniformly, not somewhat the more in one part or somewhat the less. Next, it is this premiss that was proved in the preceding lines (B 8.6-21). For in those lines it is argued that, since there cannot be any change from non-existence to existence or vice versa, *houtôs ê pampan pelenai chreôn estin ê ouchi* (B 8. 11); and then the second alternative is ruled out as unintelligible (B 8. 15-18). So the proof has allegedly been given that the subject exists *pampan* or *homoion*, unqualifiedly, without intermission; and this is exactly the premiss required to prove that it is indivisible and single. Moreover, the form and placing of the *epei* clause in B 8. 22 shows that it takes up a conclusion previously established. For Parmenides' train of argument in B 8 breaks into four main stages which are clearly distinguished and correctly ordered in the programme given at the start,[41] and each succeeding movement is introduced by an *epei*-clause which, in the other cases at least, shows how the new argument depends on a proposition already proved. (Thus in the third movement B 8. 27 looks back/ to B 8. 6-21 and especially to line 21; and in 59
the fourth B 8. 42 looks back to B 8. 26-33 and especially to lines 26 and 30-1[42]) As we might expect, then, the second stage of the argument – the proof of unity and continuity in lines 22-5 – is no more an isolated and unargued pronouncement than the other stages. The unity of the subject is proved, not assumed *ab initio*.

It is worth noticing that all but the first of these reasons for reading *éstin homoion* could be satisfied by an alternative explanation of the lines which

[39] Simplicius, *Phys.* 145.1-146.25 Diels. Some have suggested that the passage is not continuous and that some lines have dropped out after B 8. 25 (cf. Zeller-Nestle i^7, 692). But it is not the case that Proclus quotes B 5 as though it directly followed B 8. 25: he turns to it with the words καὶ πάλιν (*in Parm.* 708. 14 Cousin).

[40] ὁμοιον and ὁμοια are used as standard adverbs with the dative: for the absolute use as here cf. Aeschylus, *Eum.* 240, ὁμοῖα χέρσον καὶ θάλασσαν ἐκπερῶν (Homer's γαῖαν ὁμοῦ καὶ πόντον), where as all editors have seen ὁμοῖα has adverbial force whether or not it is read as technically qualifying the nouns: so Parmenides in B 8. 22 (and perhaps the formula σε γῆρας τείρει ὁμοΐον, *Il.* 4. 315, which scholl. rightly use ὁμοίως to explain). The form ὁμοίως which appears in the fifth century is not found in Homer, Hesiod, or Parmenides, though ὁμῶς occurs in them all: notice that τοῖος kept its adverb τοῖον, as οἷος did οἷον and τοιοῦτος τοιαῦτα.

[41] See Additional Note A, p. 23 below.

[42] On this see pp. 17-21 below.

would leave *homoion* predicative. (But the first seems to me inescapable.) Up to this point the argument has been concerned only with variation in time: the sense in which it has been shown that the subject *pampan pelenai* is just that it has no temporal boundaries, no *genesis* or *olethros*. Now this is just the sense that Melissus later gave to *pan homoion*,[43] and the words can be construed in the same way in B 8. 22 without at all affecting the proposed interpretation. The fact that, on either version, the argument for continuity in lines 22-5 depends on the prior elimination of *temporal* starts and stops in lines 6-21 is of the first importance for understanding that argument, and we shall come back to it in another context. For the present we have sufficient grounds for dismissing these attempts to saddle Parmenides' argument with a subject from earlier cosmology.

(*c*) *But there is a subject.* Some interpreters gave up the quest for a subject. Hermann Fraenkel suggested that 'the *estin* is primarily used by Parmenides as a so-called impersonal, somewhat like "it rains" = "raining takes place" '.[44] But this move, soundly antiseptic as it is, is unconvincing because Parmenides goes on to prove various characteristics of the subject of his *éstin*. To supply that subject we have to repeat our question: What must it be *from the start* if it is to satisfy the demands of the argument? If it is not assumed to be existent and indivisible, what is it assumed to be? And the answer is clear and, I think, of great interest. The goddess maintains that to the question 'Does it exist?' only a positive answer can be given; the negative is ruled out by the plea that what does not exist cannot be distinguished in thought or speech (B 2. 7-8), and this plea is basic to the following arguments and recalled more than once in them (B 8. 8-9, 17-18, probably 34-6). This alone would give us the answer to our problem; but before drawing the moral we may take one more step to clarify the argument. The goddess's premiss in
60 this/ opening game is that what does not exist cannot be thought or spoken of or, what comes to the same, that what can be thought or spoken of exists. But this, after all, is far from self-evident. The plain men whose daily uses of language make up the second wrong path hold that plenty of things can be talked about which do not exist: they need not wait for Gorgias to tell them that they can think of Scylla and Chimaera.[45] So how are they to be

[43] Melissus B 7 = Simplicius, *Phys.* III. 22-3 Diels (cf. 112. 3-4): εἰ γὰρ ἑτεροιοῦται, ἀνάγκη τὸ ἐὸν μὴ ὁμοῖον εἶναι, ἀλλὰ ἀπόλλυσθαι τὸ πρόσθεν ἐόν, τὸ δὲ οὐκ ἐὸν γίνεσθαι.

[44] *CP* 41 (1946), 169, criticizing Verdenius's suggestion that the subject is 'All that exists, the total of things.' Cf. Calogero, *Studi*, 18; Kirk and Raven, *Presocratic Philosophers*, 269.

[45] Commentators are still seduced by Aristotle's loaded comment in *Meta* I 3. 984a29-b1 into diagnosing Parmenides' basic fallacy as a confusion between the existential and the predicative senses of εἶναι: as though he was (*a*) right to say that we cannot talk about a non-existent X but (*b*) wrong to suppose on this score that we cannot say 'X is not white'. Both (*a*) and (*b*) are groundless. Parmenides, though he certainly could not have drawn the necessary logical distinctions, might nevertheless fairly assume that, if one part of the world is white but not another, this can be formulated existentially as 'there is white, or a white thing, here but not there': the point may be confused but is not annulled by the use of τὸ λευκόν to mean both the colour and what has it. The move from ἀγένητον to ἀτρεμές is valid enough: what is mistaken is his claim that we cannot talk of the non-existent. We can, of course: mermaids, for instance. How we can is another matter, and Aristotle was not the first or last philosopher to fail to see his way through it; his failure that underlies his treatment of the Eleatics and their predecessors in A 3.

convinced that what can be talked or thought about must exist? It is this prior point that Parmenides seems anxious to establish in the opening couplet of B 6; and he argues it from something that plain men can be expected to concede, namely that what can be thought or spoken of *could* exist (even if they want to add that in fact, in particular cases, it does not). The couplet in question is *chrê to legein te noein t'eon emmenai·ésti gar einai, mêden d'ouk éstin.* I adopt the familiar version of Burnet: 'What can be spoken and thought of must exist; for it *can* exist, whereas nothing cannot.'[46] Hence, of course, it is *not* nothing; and hence it exists. That this celebrated fallacy[47] is the point of the lines seems certain on several scores. This seems to be the sole way of construing them that saves them from platitude.[48] And the presence of an important argument in the couplet is shown by the goddess's injunction to 'think that out' (*ta s'egô phrazesthai anôga*, B 6. 2), just as the fact that the argument is important to the reasoning in B 2 is proved by her immediate reference to the first wrong path (B 6. 3).[49] Moreover, this reading provides a context for B 3, which on a similar interpretation embodies the essential admission that Parmenides needs: what can be thought is identical with what *can* (not *must*) exist.

Either with or without this reinforcing argument, however, the subject of the reasoning is clear. What is declared to exist in B 2 is simply what can be talked or thought about; for the proof of its existence is that, if it did not exist, it could not be talked or thought about. (On our version of B 6. 1-2 the subject comes into the open there: *to legein te noein t'eon.*)[50] And it needs no

[46] [This translation, which I share with most English commentators since Burnet, may be followed with a certain pleasure through L. Taran's *Parmenides* (Princeton 1965). On p. 36 he declares it 'grammatically impossible', giving no reason but referring to a later discussion. In that discussion (p. 55) it has become 'possible'. Actuality is not far away: in his renderings of B 2. 2 and B 3 Taran himself adopts the proposed construction, giving the conventional explanation that the infinitives after the verb 'to be' have 'the value of datives'.]

[47] A, which can exist, is distinguished from B, which (poor thing) cannot: invalid, for to say 'nothing cannot exist' is not to ascribe compulsory non-existence to anything but to say that it is necessarily (truistically) true that what doesn't exist doesn't exist, and this unexciting reformulation disables the argument. The fallacy is the so-called *de re* interpretation of model statements.

[48] Kranz tries to save matters with an unwarranted 'nur': 'Nötig ist zu sagen und zu denken, das *nur* das Seiende ist; denn Sein ist, ein Nichts dagegen ist nicht.' The translation 'One must say and think that *what is, is*' is ruled out by pp. 10-12 above.

[49] Notice that Parmenides is refuting the first wrong path for the benefit of the plain men who take the second; for he refutes it from their premiss, that what can be thought of *can* exist. A convinced follower of the first wrong path would deny this by saying not only οὐκ ἔστιν but χρεών ἐστι μὴ εἶναι (B 2. 5), and with this Parmenides admits he could do nothing: it is παναπευθές (B 2. 6). But since no one takes this line it is enough to rule out οὐκ ἔστι from the plain man's assumptions.

[50] [Lest this mislead, it must be emphasized that the problem has never been to supply a *grammatical* subject for the ἔστιν and οὐκ ἔστιν of B 2 (save for emendators such as Cornford and Loenon), for there is sufficient evidence that, at the start of the argument at least, Parmenides is prepared to dispense with one. The problem is to decide what must be supposed true, from the start, of whatever it is that Parmenides exhibits in the course of his argument as existing without beginning or end or change or plurality. I argue that this subject must simply be what can be spoken and thought of (told forth, picked out in speech – φράζειν, λέγειν, φατίζειν, cf. the contrasted ἀνώνυμον, B 8. 17; distinguished and grasped in thought – γιγνώσκειν, νοεῖν). For one reviewer

proving that the subject of the argument can be talked and thought about, for we are talking and thinking about it. Hence indeed the temptation to say that the *éstin* has no subject; for Parmenides' argument need assume nothing save that we are thinking and talking of something, and this seems to be guaranteed by our framing or following the argument at all. The subject is
61 quite/ formal, until it is filled in with the attributes (beginning with existence) that are deduced for it; and because this seems to reduce to the vacuous discovery that the subject is just the subject, it is as tempting as it is certainly illogical and misleading to say that there is no subject at all.

Is this too small a mouse from the mountain? Philosophically it seems more like the giant that Parmenides' successors thought it. The comparison with Descartes' *cogito* is inescapable: both arguments cut free of inherited premisses, both start from an assumption whose denial is peculiarly self-refuting. This seems sufficient to establish that Parmenides does not, in the sense described, rest his argument on assumptions derived from earlier cosmologists.[51] To me it seems sufficient to establish him as the most radical and conscious pioneer known to us among the Presocratics.

But those who wish to set his poem inside an orthodox cosmological tradition have one prop left to rest on: the spherical universe, whose appearance is the outcome of the whole argument.

Does Parmenides argue for the existence of a spherical universe?

There is no novelty in denying, as I shall, that Parmenides' arguments set up a spherical world. But the reasons sometimes given for the denial seem to carry little weight.

One reason suggested is that Parmenides does not say that reality is a sphere, only that it is like one: *eukuklou sphairês enaligkion ogkôi* (like the mass of a well-rounded sphere) (B 8. 43).[52] But no doubt *sphaira* has its usual Homeric sense of 'ball', and a spherical world can certainly be compared to a ball.[53] Another reason is that Parmenides does not deal in spatial concepts at all: for him, nothing exists but thought.[54] But I do not for my part think that

---

this still left the subject too 'definite' (Kerferd, *CR* 1961, 26), and one can only ask what it would be to have a more indefinite subject than one which can merely be thought and spoken of: which of these attributes would it lack, and what nonsense would result? Another scholar, by contrast, found such an account of the subject 'rarefied and abstract' (A.P.D. Mourelatos, *The Route of Parmenides* (New Haven 1970), xiv) but himself proposed to translate the ἔστιν and οὐκ ἔστιν as '– is –' and '– is not –', 'with blanks in both the subject and the predicate place' (ibid. 55).]

[51] 'In the sense described': I am not of course denying that some of the ideas employed in the course of the argument may have been inherited from earlier theorists. This must be true of some of the cosmogony, and probably of at least the idea of πεῖρας in the Ἀλήθεια (see the third section of the paper).

[52] e.g. by Coxon, *CQ* 28 (1934), 140.

[53] A point most recently taken by Jameson, *Phronesis* 3 (1958), 15; but it does not go home, as he thinks, against Fraenkel (*Wege und Formen*, 196).

[54] Argued by Vlastos (*TAPA* 77 (1946), 66-77, *Gnomon* 25 (1953), 168) following von Fritz (*CP* 40 (1945), 236-42).

this is the necessary translation of B 3 (*to gar auto noein éstin te kai einai*) or that there is room in Parmenides' argument for such a thesis.[55] Again, Hermann Fraenkel rejected a spherical world in his analysis of the *sphaira*-passage: he set the lines in a wider context (B 8. 26-33 and 44-9) which he construed as a critique of Anaximander.[56] But the plausibility of this interpretation need not concern us now, for his wider context unhappily stops just short of the lines which/ settle the problem. These lines are the proof of continuity that is given **62**
in B 8. 22-5, and the importance of the proof is that it is precisely the same pattern of argument that is later given to show that what exists is like the mass of a rounded ball (B 8. 44-8; 44-5 are introductory). Since the repetition is beyond question deliberate, and since the argument is used at its first occurrence to prove that there is no part of reality that borders on nothing, it cannot be used at its second occurrence to prove that reality does border on nothing in all directions at an equal distance from a centre.[57]

This contention is correct, but to be conclusive it needs reinforcing at several points. The exact correspondence between the two occurrences of the argument scarcely needs proving. The proposition that the subject cannot be broken up by gaps of nothingness (*oude diaireton estin, epei pan éstin homoion*, B 8. 22 = *oute gar ouk eon ésti, to ken pauoi min hikneisthai eis homon*, B 8. 46) is followed by the complementary proposition that it cannot exist to a different degree at different points (*oude ti têi mallon ... oude ti cheiroteron*, B 8. 23-4 = *out' eon éstin hopôs eiê ken eontos têi mallon têi d'hêsson*, B 8. 47-8). The explanatory *epei pan estin asulon* of B 8. 48 answers to the *pan d'empleon estin eontos* of B 8. 24 which is itself in effect a restatement of the premiss *epei pan éstin homoion*. The *to ken pauoi min hikneisthai eis homon* of B 8. 46-7 matches the *to ken eirgoi min sunechesthai* of B 8. 23 (the sole difference being that in the later version of the argument the phrase attaches to the first proposition, and in the earlier to the second). If it had been noticed that the *hikneisthai eis homon* is no more than the earlier *sunechesthai* we might have been spared such eccentric renderings as Burnet's

[55] Vlastos argues that 'the thought which knows being could hardly be denied existence ... and since being is "all alike" (B 8. 22) [but see pp. 12-13 above on this reading], if thought is any part of being, all being must be thought' (*Gnomon* (1953), 168). This takes for granted that Parmenides must have faced squarely the question 'Is thinking of being a part of being?' Plato implies that he had not; for Parmenides constantly couples thinking and naming (B 2. 7-8; B 8. 17; B 8. 35-6), and in *Soph.* 244 c-d Plato argues that Parmenides does not face a dilemma in the relation of τὸ ὂν to its name: are there after all two things in existence or is the name a name of nothing? This is in effect the same problem as whether the νόημα is distinct from or identical with τὸ ἐόν, and (for what this is worth) Plato implies that it had not been faced. He implies the same at *Soph.* 248d-249a in making the Eleatic Stranger say that if reality contains life and soul and understanding it cannot be ἀκίνητον ἑστός.

[56] *Wege und Formen*, 186-97.

[57] [This argument met with one curious objection. W.K.C. Guthrie (*A History of Greek Philosophy*, vol. 2 (Cambridge 1965), 46) held that it would have seemed 'strange nonsense' to Parmenides since it anachronistically assumes a 'Euclidean' conception of space as continuing indefinitely in all directions instead of a primitive view of it as 'more like the curved and Einsteinian space'. No doubt if there is nonsense here it can be located. For his claim Guthrie quotes no evidence other than F.M. Cornford's paper 'On the Invention of Space' (*Essays in Honour of Gilbert Murray* (London 1936), 215-35; the thesis was briefly resumed in *Principium Sapientiae* (Cambridge 1952), 176-7). That paper is reviewed in Additional Note B on pp. 24 ff. below.]

'reaching out equally'; as Empedocles well knew,[58] the phrase means 'reaching to its like', *eon eonti pelazein*. For my part I can see no such difference between the two passages as Calogero detects.[59] He takes the vocabulary of the first to be 'static' and that of the second to be 'dynamic'. But *to ken pauoi min hikneisthai eis homon* is neither more nor less dynamic than the earlier *to ken eirgoi min sunechesthai* ... *eon gar eonti pelazei*: the primary sense of *pelazein*, like that of *hikneisthai*, is one of movement, but the reason why either verb is preferred to a more static counterpart must, here as elsewhere in the argument, be one of style and not of content.[60] The same holds good of the
63 later conclusion, *homôs en peirasi kurei* (B 8. 49), even if we/ read this as though it were *egkurei peirasi* ('gleichmäβig begegnet es seinen Grenzen', Kranz); but probably *kurei* has its weaker, copulative sense. Yet this very phrase engenders doubts about the parallel I have tried to draw between the arguments. How can the reasoning in B 8. 44-8 be the old argument for unbroken continuity, when it issues now in the assertion that its subject is contained equally within certain *boundaries*, *peirata*? Or when it is prefaced by the claim that the subject has a *peiras pumaton* (ultimate limit) and is *tetelesmenon pantothen* (complete on all sides), *eukuklou sphairês enaligkion ogkôi* (B 8. 42-3)? Moreover, if it is the same argument, what can be the point of repeating it in detail? These difficulties can be met by settling the course of the argument and the use that is made in it of one or two cardinal expressions.

Having argued that his subject has neither beginning nor end in time (B 8. 6-21), Parmenides goes on, in accordance with the programme he has laid down,[61] to prove its unity and continuity (B 8. 22-5). It is often assumed that at this point Parmenides is turning from existence in time to existence in space, from a refutation of *genesis* and *olethros* to a rejection of spatial division and variation. The impression is probably strengthened by the fact that when he repeats the argument for continuity it is in a context of spatial concepts (*sphaira*, *mesothen*, etc.). But the impression is surely false. For in the first place, as I have argued, the premiss of the continuity-argument at its first occurrence is taken from the refutation of *genesis* and *olethros* that precedes it, and consequently must carry a temporal sense. Secondly, this application of the preceding conclusion is clearly called for. For when it has been argued that the subject has neither beginning nor end in time it still remains to draw the corollaries, that there can be neither a succession of separate entities nor internal change in any one entity; and these corollaries are drawn in B 8. 22 and 23-24 respectively. Thirdly, the temporal import of the argument at its first occurrence is proved, not only by its being embedded in a context of temporal argument that reaches to B 8. 33, but by the fact that when Parmenides comes to resume the conclusions reached at B 8. 34-41 he mentions only ideas of temporal change (lines 40-1, where the only exception is *einai te kai ouchi*, and these are present because their misuse is taken to be

[58] Empedocles B 62. 6.

[59] *Studi*, 27 and n. 1.

[60] The 'Αλήθεια is full of metaphors of movement and arrested movement: motion on a path comes often (including the puzzling B 5), and arrested motion in B 6. 3; B 7. 3; B 8. 13-15 and 37. Cf. L. Woodbury, *HSCP* 63 (1958), 154.

[61] See Additional Note A, pp. 23ff. below.

basic to the other errors). Moreover, that *suneches* can have a temporal sense needs no arguing,[62] and that it must have it here/ is shown again by the **64**
couplet which introduced the refutation of *genesis*: *oude pot'ên oud' estai, epei nun éstin homou pan, hen, suneches*: *tina gar gennan dizêseai autou*? (Nor was it ever nor will it be, since it is now, all together, one, continuous: for what birth of it will you look for? B 8. 5-6). Thus one of our difficulties is resolved: Parmenides' reason for repeating the continuity-argument is that it is applied first in a temporal sense and then in a spatial.[63]

The next section of the argument (B 8. 26-33) remains within this temporal framework. It begins *autar akinêton megalôn en peirasi desmôn éstin anarchon apauston* (but it *is*, unchanged in the limits of great bonds, having neither beginning nor end), and thereby shows that in its turn it is applying the conclusions already reached. For just as the last two attributes have already been proved, and Parmenides at once refers to the proof (B 8. 27-8), so the possibility of any change whatever has been excluded by the argument for temporal continuity, and it is to this argument that Parmenides refers in order to establish that *tauton t' en tautôi te menon kath' heauto te keitai choutôs empedon authi menei* (remaining the same and in the same, it stays in its own right, and thus again it stands firm, B 8. 29-30). For, he says, 'mastering necessity holds it in the bonds of a limit that wards it about, since it is not permitted that what exists should be incomplete' (*ateleutêton*). For it is not lacking in anything; if it were, it would lack everything[64] (B 8. 30-3). Here the premiss that the subject is *ouk epideues* (not in need) or *ouk ateleutêton*, on which the proof of general immutability is made to depend,[65] is just a

[62] And if συνεχές then also in this context its opposite, διαιρετόν. (Thus Aristotle, maintaining against Parmenides that continuity does not preclude but always entails divisibility, can say that time and any process in time is συνεχής and therefore διαιρετός, *Phys.* VI 2. 232b23-26 *et al*). In this setting of temporal continuity it is natural to explain that τῇ in line 23, which is commonly read as implying an answering τῇ in 24, must have not its spatial sense but its wider meaning, 'in this respect' (Empedocles B 26. 10); but I doubt if Parmenides wants wholly to lose the spatial metaphor in τῇ, for not only this passage but the whole treatment of temporal variation is couched in spatial metaphor (the impossibility of any different *state of affairs* is pictured as being chained to one *place*, B 8. 14-15, 26-7, 30-1, 37-8); and Parmenides wants to keep open the possibility of a spatial application of the same arguments. (Karsten, pointing to the singularity of τῇ, here without an answering adverb and observing that the necessary contrast is carried by τι ... τι ..., emended so as to excise it; Stein proposed πῃ, plausibly in view of the source of contamination in B 8. 45 and 48.)

[63] [The surprise occasioned by this suggestion seems to stem from the correct but irrelevant feeling that the τῇ (with its implicit answering τῇ) in B 8. 23-4 cannot have a temporal *sense*. Very true: I take its sense, both here and in the later echoes in 45 and 48, to be 'in one respect ... (in another ...)'. But any suggestion that it could not be read as marking a temporal distinction is refuted by Aristotle's well-known reading of Empedocles B 26. 8-12 (*Phys.* 250b26-51a5): it is common ground to different interpreters that Aristotle understands the ἧ ... ἧ with their answering τῇ ... ταύτῇ as marking a temporal distinction, and whatever his error in doing so it would be preposterous to diagnose it as a mistake about Greek usage.]

[64] See n. 11 above.

[65] οὕνεκεν in B 8. 32 means 'because' (as generally in Homer: so Fraenkel in D. Furley and R.E. Allen (eds), *Studies in Presocratic Philosophy*, vol. 2 (London 1975), 30-1), not 'therefore' (as von Fritz argues in *CP* 41 (1946), 237-8). Von Fritz urges that to deduce immobility from finiteness would reverse the 'natural logical order' and depart from Parmenides' procedure of putting the 'more essential qualities of τὸ ἐόν' before the less, but he has not seen that the οὐκ ἀτελεύτητον is in fact the conclusion of the opening argument and the premiss of the next.

restatement of the *pan d'empleon estin eontos* in the continuity-proof; and the argument now given for this premiss, that to lack anything is to lack everything, is a reminder of the way in which the same proposition in the continuity-proof had been reached: namely by the opening argument that *pampan pelenai chreôn estin* because a yes-and-no answer to the question 'Does it exist?' is no better than a flat negative.

Now what is the sense within this argument of the statement that the subject has a *peiras* or *peirata* (B 8. 26 and 31)? Not, certainly, that it has *boundaries* in time, a beginning or an end: this is exactly what Parmenides denies from the start. The sense of 'consummation' or even 'perfection' that the word occasionally carries in Homer[66] is nearer to what we need, but (supposing we shelve the problem of reconciling this interpretation with the use of *apeiron* by other early thinkers and with Aristotle's generalization on the matter)[67] the sense is inappropriate in line 26, where as yet we know only that the subject is invariant in time and this fixity is the sole point made and
65 reitera-/ted in the context (B 8. 26-31). *Peiras* in fact is the mark of *invariancy*: this is certified by Parmenides' language (in both 26 and 31 the subject is chained and imprisoned by the *peiras*), and the same sense seems to be found in Pythagorean theory, for Aristotle's report of that theory may be taken to show that square numbers from one onwards exhibit *peras* because their sides are in *constant* ratio while oblong numbers exhibit *to apeiron* because with them the ratio varies.[68]

Similarly, to say that the subject of the argument is *ouk ateleutêton* (B 8. 32) is not to say that it has frontiers, as opposed to stretching *ad infinitum*. The sense of it is just that, since we cannot talk of what does not exist, we cannot say that there is still something lacking which could be supplied by any change. But this formulation, like Parmenides' own, is ambiguous, and the ambiguity gives him his transition to the final spatial conclusions in B 8. 42-9. If we do consider the possibility of change in *general*, there is an obvious temporal sense to be given to Parmenides' formula: the subject lacks nothing, in the sense that there is no state of affairs left for it to realize in the future. But movement has just been distinguished from other forms of change (B 8. 29-30, cf. the résumé at B 8. 41); and if we consider this form of change in particular there is an equally obvious *spatial* sense to be given to the formula: the subject is not *ateleutêton* or *epideues* in the sense that there is no empty or relatively empty space for anything to move into. In its first sense the formula insists that there cannot be an existential statement that is false at one time and true later; in its second it says that there cannot be an existential statement that is true of one place but not another. But Parmenides has no right yet to take the words in this second sense, for, as we have seen, at this point they are merely a restatement of the *pampan pelenai* and *pan empleon eontos* of the earlier arguments; and those expressions were to be understood in the temporal sense. Since Parmenides is a wholly honest and explicit reasoner he

[66] *Iliad* 18. 501; *Odyssey* 5. 289.

[67] Aristotle, *Phys.* III 4.203b4-15.

[68] See Ross's note on *Phys.* III 4.203a10-15; Raven, *Pythagoreans and Eleatics*, 188-94. [That this was Aristotle's sense is established by *Cat.* 15a28-32.]

sums up his interim conclusions in lines 34-41 and then, finally, turns to prove that his formula is equally true in its spatial interpretation.

He begins this last stage of the argument with the words *autar epei peiras pumaton, tetelesmenon esti pantothen* (B 8. 42-3). The *epei* shows that this proof in its turn depends on the conclusions already established; but even without the connective it should have seemed absurd to interpret *peiras* here as 'boundary', a/sense flatly incompatible with the whole train of argument in 66
which the word was first introduced. The epithet *pumaton*, so far from compelling that translation, itself recalls *peiratos ... to min amphis eergei*, a phrase used in a context where any suggestion of literal boundaries was out of the question (B 8. 31). So the sense is not in doubt: the opening words mean, in effect, 'Moreover, since it is utterly unchanging'. And the conclusion is drawn that, since there cannot be movement, there cannot be room for movement. *Tetelesmenon pantothen* is the exact spatial counterpart of the temporal *ouk ateleutêton* in B 8. 32; and in case this correspondence should escape any reader Parmenides reinforces his conclusion and shows its sense by transferring to this spatial context the very argument for continuity which was earlier, in its temporal application, associated with the *ouk ateleutêton* (B 8. 44-8). But before giving this argument Parmenides introduces his simile: the subject is *eukuklou sphairês enaligkion ogkôi, mesothen isopales pantêi* (uniform in every way from the centre), precisely because there is nothing true of it at one point or in one direction that is not true elsewhere. Its uniformity is like the perfect balance of a ball about its centre. (It is not of course a uniformity of *radius*: that is not the sense of *isopales*.) And the whole argument concludes: *hoi gar pantothen ison homôs en peirasi kurei* (B 8. 49). Here again is the metaphorical notion of being contained in *peirata*; here again is the equality which is *to isopales*, spatial indifference. And *homôs* does not of course mean 'at an equal distance from the centre': its meaning is given by the *hikneisthai eis homon* of lines 46-7. So the phrase has an exact sense: to the *peirata* of temporal invariance Parmenides has added the *homôs* of invariance in space.

So Parmenides' treatment of space exactly matches his treatment of time; there is no place in it for boundaries or a spherical universe. And if that is so there is a rider that deserves to be added. It is sometimes said that Melissus differed from Parmenides 'in holding that reality was spatially as well as temporally infinite'.[69] Both, we are told, agreed that 'reality is eternal'; but it was Melissus who saw the inconsistency of saying in the same breath that it had spatial frontiers. Thus it becomes an engaging puzzle why Melissus directs the brunt of his opening argument to proving that his subject is temporally infinite, whereas its spatial infinity – supposedly the major point of departure from Parmenides – is introduced by the almost perfunctory *all' hôsper estin/aei, houtô kai to megethos apeiron aei chrê einai* (for just as it is always, 67
so must it also be boundless in extent) (30 B 3).[70] To this puzzle we have a

[69] Burnet, *Early Greek Philosophy*⁴, 325.

[70] Vlastos (*Gnomon* 25 (1953), 34-5) thinks this fragment (= Simplicius, *Phys.* 109.31-2 Diels) to be concerned only with temporal infinity. His motive for trying to discount its natural meaning (and that of the following fragment, B 4) is that he does not see how to reconcile a spatial conclusion with B 9, which denies that τὸ ἐόν can be a *solid* (see this section of the paper).

clear answer. When Melissus indicates in these words that his argument for temporal infinity can be carried over, *mutatis mutandis*, to prove the corresponding point about space, he is not correcting Parmenides but following him without reservation. On the other hand, the point on which his opening argument is brought to bear is precisely the issue on which he does seem to differ from Parmenides: namely, on the form of those general conclusions which can be given both a temporal and a spatial application. For Parmenides had argued that, since there is no change, there can be no way of distinguishing the past and the future from the present: *oude pot' ên oud' estai, epei nun estin homou pan* (B 5.5).[71] In order to make the distinction there would have to be something true at one time that was not true at another. And, just as there is no purchase for temporal distinctions, so there is none for spatial: what exists exists *homou*, the mind makes no distinction between far and near (B 4).[72] Yet this conclusion raises in an acute form the difficulty besetting Parmenides' argument. The very proof which rules out all variation in time and space has to use language which implies temporal and spatial distinctions. It has to say that what exists is continuous, *eon gar eonti pelazei* (for what is is neighbour to what is); and that it remains the same; and that it is uniform in all directions. Just as Parmenides can only prove the unintelligibility of *ouk estin* by himself denying the existence of certain states of affairs, so he can only show the vacuousness of temporal and spatial distinctions by a proof which employs them. His argument, to adopt an analogy from Sextus and Wittgenstein, is a ladder which must be thrown away when one has climbed it. Melissus saw this hazard, and tried to evade it by reimporting the distinctions discarded by Parmenides: *aei ên ho ti ên kai aei estai* (it always was what it was and always will be) (30 B 1), *aei te ên kai aei estai* (it always was and always will be) (30 B 2). To him it seems clearly significant to say that reality always was and will be exactly the same, even though no description can be given to pick out one time from another; and thus his position is comparable to that of later philosophers who deny the 'identity of indiscernibles'[73] But he is at pains to explain that the distinctions he reimports do not entail divisibility in the obnoxious sense in which it had been rejected by Parmenides. To this end he argues that, since what exists is single, it cannot have a body; for otherwise it would have solidity (*pachos*)
68 and, consequently, distinguishable parts (*moria*),/ and then it would be no longer single (30 B 9). Here the word *morion* must evidently be understood in the light of the Eleatic attack on divisibility: the argument assumes that, on

[71] Fraenkel now challenges this reading of the lines (*Studies in Presocratic Philosophy*, vol. 2 (London 1975), 86, n. 46), arguing that otherwise Parmenides faces the dilemma I describe in the text; but the dilemma is genuine and Melissus' language shows that he recognized it. [See 'Plato and Parmenides on the Timeless Present', this volume, Chapter 2.]

[72] Clement, who quotes this fragment, interprets it in terms of temporal not spatial distance (*Strom.* v. 15), but shows that he found no warrant for this in the text by his words Παρμενίδης περὶ τῆς ἐλπίδος αἰνισσόμενος. The verbs σκίδνασθαι and συνίστασθαι call for a spatial interpretation.

[73] See for instance Max Black's description of a world containing a number of things having all their properties in common (*Mind* 61 (1952), 153-64) and on Parmenides' side cf. Russell's objection that there could be no way of establishing the existence of a plurality of such objects (*Inquiry into Meaning and Truth* (London 1951), 102).

the ordinary view of the world, a physical solid is divisible in the sense that parts can be identified and distinguished in it, either by finding or making gaps between them or by characterizing them as having more or less of something (hardness, say, or heat) than their neighbour; and it is this divisibility into parts against which Parmenides' argument in B 8. 44-8 is directed. So Melissus is anxious to point out that his subject is not such a solid: mere extension in time and space does not involve divisibility or prevent the subject from being *hen*, *suneches*. That Plato at any rate took this to be Melissus' point appears from his defence of Parmenides in *Timaeus* 37e-38a: what is unchanging, he says, can only be described in the present tense, for *ên* and *estai are* parts of time: they imply change and they break up the unity of the immutable. In reimporting such distinctions Melissus may of course have supposed himself to be not correcting but clarifying Parmenides' results. But one thing strongly suggests that he saw himself as a dissenter. For with those distinctions he couples an expression that Parmenides could never have used in any sense to describe his world: *apeiron*.

In sum: Parmenides' goddess does not claim that her cosmogony has any measure of truth or reliability in its own right; her subject-matter and her assumptions are not inherited from earlier cosmology; and she does not argue for a world that is spherical and everlasting. Parmenides did not write as a cosmologist. He wrote as a philosophical pioneer of the first water, and any attempt to put him back into the tradition that he aimed to demolish is a surrender to the diadoche-writers, a failure to take him at his word and 'judge by reasoning that much-contested proof'.

Additional note A 76

B 8. 2-4, The programme of the argument
(see p. 13, n. 41, and p. 18, n. 61 above)

In B 8. 2-4 the goddess gives a list of the 'signs' which mark the right road. This list is in fact a programme of the succeeding argument.

Simplicius twice quotes the lines in a longer context, which ensures that he is not trusting to memory (*Phys*. 78. 12-13, 145. 3-4 Diels), and then writes them:

Hôs agenêton eon kai anôlethron estin,
oulon mounogenes te kai atremes êd' ateleston.

That it is something that is without birth or death,
whole, unique, immovable, and ? endless?

But elsewhere, quoting the second line by itself and presumably from memory, he writes *êd' agenêton* for *êd' ateleston*, and so, in the same circumstances, do Plutarch and Proclus and the ps.-Plutarch *Stromateis*. Though Clement keeps this reading in quoting the whole couplet, it involves an impossible repetition when the line is coupled with its predecessor. This leaves small hope that Plutarch and Proclus are safe sources for the rest of the line, yet Kranz abandons the *oulon mounogenes* of Simplicius, Clement, and Philoponus for *esti gar oulomeles*, 'for it is whole of limb', which he takes from the isolated citations of the second line by Plutarch and Proclus. That reading must be rejected because (*a*) the *esti gar* occurs only in Plutarch and may well not be intended as part of the quotation (cf. a similar doubt over Plutarch's quotation of Heraclitus B 92), (*b*) the *gar* is inappropriate since *adiaireton* is to be proved from *agenêton anôlethron* and not vice versa, (*c*) the unreliability of Plutarch and Proclus in short quotations is notorious (see for instance Plutarch's quotation of Empedocles B 27, and on Proclus E.R. Dodds, *Gnomon* 27 (1955), 167 and now Jameson, *Phronesis* 3 (1958), 21). In face of this the apparent incongruity between *mounogenes* and *agenêton* can be discounted (Plato writes *heis hode monogenês ouranos gegonôs*, *Tim.* 31 b, and this would be a pleonasm if the epithet had the force suggested). But there is another correction to be made.

The lines give the programme of the argument. *Agenêton kai anôlethron* is proved in B 8. 6-21; *oulon mounogenes* (the exact equivalent is *hen, suneches* in line 6) is proved next in lines 22-5; *atremes* is
77 proved next in lines 26-33. Then, after resuming his/ interim conclusions in lines 34-41, Parmenides goes on finally to prove in lines 42-9 that his subject is *tetelesmenon pantothen*; and here the programme inexplicably ends with *êd' ateleston*. Diels, following Simplicius' mistaken attempt to find Melissus' *apeiron* in Parmenides (*Phys.* 29. 26-30. 5 Diels), explained *ateleston* as 'endlos' or 'ohne Ziel in der Zeit', but this will not do. For one thing, the word would be a mere repetition of *anôlethron* and the one redundancy in a very economical couplet; for another, the word is not to be found in Diels's sense. Homer couples it with *halion, autôs, maps*, and it connotes failure or unfulfilment (this is its sense in both the passages cited by Diels himself: *Iliad* 4. 26, *Odyssey* 16. 111). As such it is the equivalent of *ateleutêton* which Parmenides explains by *epideues* and which he expressly denies to characterize his subject (B 8. 33-4). And it is his assertion that the subject is *not ateleutêton* that is carried over and given a spatial application in the final argument that it is *tetelesmenon pantothen* (see the final section of this paper). So *êd' ateleston* cannot be right: what we want is just its opposite.

Brandis in 1813 proposed *oud' ateleston* (*Comm. Eleat.* i. 109-10, 138-40). But the reading is ungraceful and the authority of Karsten and Diels killed the attempt at emendation. I prefer *êde teleion*: a copyist was seduced by the reiteration of negative prefixes (*agenêton* ... *anôlethron* ... *atremes*) into writing *êd' ateleion* and this was corrected to the orthodox Homeric clausula *êd' ateleston* (*Il.* 4. 26). With this emendation the programme is complete. [Mourelatos, who prints this emendation (*Route*, 281), rightly notices the epic variant *telêen* as a possibility. An alternative *teleston* (Covotti) is palaeographically simpler but the adjective is not securely attested in Greek (and its existence is not of course guaranteed by that of the privative): if the Phaleron inscription *IG* ii^2 (*CIG* ii-iii ed. min. 4548) is read as providing for sacrifices *epi telestôn agathôn* (itself a debated reading), the phrase may mean 'in the presence of overseers who are men of worth'. Preller's *êd' atalanton* (cf. Emped. B 17. 19) is attractive, but for this item in the programme one would expect a forward reference to the *tetelesmenon* rather than the *isopales* of B 8. 42-4.]/

78

Additional note B

The shape of space

(see p. 17, n. 56 above)

In an essay 'On the Invention of Space' (*Essays in Honour of Gilbert Murray* (London 1936), 215-35) and a brief resumption of the same thesis in *Principium Sapientiae* (1962), 176-7, F.M. Cornford suggested that Greek conceptions of space changed radically about the middle of the fifth century B.C. His suggestion, ignored or courteously set aside by other scholars (e.g. Kirk-Raven, *PP* 110 n. 1), was adopted without more argument by Guthrie as a basis for his interpretation of Parmenides, B 8. 42-9 (*HGP* ii 46; he had been more tentative, ibid. i. 86). It may be worth recalling why Cornford's thesis did not command more assent.

The heads of his discussion were these. (1) He suggested that, since the characteristics of infinite 'Euclidean' space (among which he picked out that of having neither centre nor circumference) are not 'empirically observable', they were unlikely to be recognized by 'pre-Euclidean common sense'. He, by contrast, proposed to find an anticipation of 'Einsteinian', 'curved' space in the earlier Presocratics. On this supposed return to the unsophisticated I make no comment.

(2) More particularly, he suggested that 'Euclidean' space was invented by Greek mathematicians 'about the middle of the fifth century' and imported into physical theory as the 'void' of the atomists. The mathematicians, he supposed, recognized that their proofs implied the existence of such space when they came to axiomatize the proofs, i.e. undertook 'the examination

of first premisses'. (3) He further professed to find evidence that before this date space had been thought of as 'spherical', this evidence consisting chiefly in the point that the '*apeiron*' of Anaximander and the early Pythagoreans would bear such an interpretation. (4) Finally he claimed that thereafter into the next century this view 'persisted in the mind of most philosophers' and prompted opposition to the 'infinite void'.

Under (2), Cornford observed that the axiomatizing of mathematics is the project of which Plato in the *Republic* 'complains that it has been neglected', and that 'it was left for (Plato's) own school to *undertake* the task [my italics] and to carry it, as they supposed, to completion' – in the *fourth* century. Cornford did/ not offer to reconcile this with his date in the mid-fifth century or to **79**
adduce evidence for the earlier date. In fact the first mathematician credited with producing 'elements', i.e. with some attempt at axiomatization, is Hippocrates of Chios (Proclus *in Eucl.* 61), for whom Guthrie follows others in accepting a *floruit* of c. 430 (*HGP* i 219 n. 2). That is more than a decade after the Apollodoran *floruit* of Melissus (whom Guthrie himself dates 'in the middle of the fifth century', ibid. i 337), yet in Guthrie's view Melissus already had the conception of space that Parmenides, deprived of the new mathematics, supposedly lacked (ibid. ii 46). And then what of Zeno, writing probably twenty years earlier still? He had argued that the members of a plurality would have to be *megala hôste apeira einai*, 'so great as to be boundless' (Simpl. *in Phys.* 141. 8; *apeira to megethos*, 'boundless in extent', 139. 8-9). He assuredly did not mean that they would be so large as to be spherical. His argument patently makes use of a common view of space as allowing indefinite extension in any direction. When there is already evidence for that assumption in Parmenides' immediate circle, and none for the later mathematical contribution conjectured by Cornford, it is uncommon scholarship to neglect the first for the second.

To (3) and (4) Cornford gave less space than they seemed to call for (though certainly that space had its circularities). Under (3), apart from assuming that interpretation of Parmenides B 8. 42-9 which I have rejected, he was chiefly concerned to show that '*apeiron*' need not signify what is infinitely or indefinitely large and *could* be applied to what is finite but circular or spherical, and with drawing the inference that in some 'earliest cosmologies' it was so used of the universe about our world. For this use of the word his evidence came mainly from Porphyry's scholium on *Iliad* 14. 200 (iv 49-52 Dindorf = 189-93 Schrader) in which Porphyry, anxious to show that Homer does not contradict himself in speaking both of *peirata gaiês*, 'bounds of earth', and of *apeirona gaian*, 'boundless earth', insists that by the second phrase Homer means to allude to the spherical shape of the earth (52. 13-16 D = 192. 25-28 S). To support this anachronism (which becomes one more manifesto for Homer's infallibility in Heraclitus, *Hom. Probl.* 68-71 Oelm.), he argues that, while '*apeiron*' may be understood *kata megethos*, 'with reference to extent', or *kata plêthos*, 'with reference to number' (his examples, it may be noted, are *ei apeiros ho kosmos*, 'world', and *ei apeiroi hoi kosmoi*, 'worlds'), it can also among other uses be applied to the circumference of a circle or the surface of a sphere./ Thus (discounting his other instance from **80**
Homer) the word is used by the Attic dramatists of circles of people, rings without a bezel, seamless garments. And he tries, followed by Cornford, to read this sense into the only near-cosmological fragment he quotes (Euripides fr. 941: *horas ton hupsou tond' apeiron aithera/kai gên perix echonth' hugrais en agkalais*, 'you see this boundless heaven above you, which also holds earth round in its moist embrace'), although this neither says nor implies, what both interpreters claim, that the *aithêr* is called limitless *because* it encircles the earth (and hence must be circular in its total shape!); the apter parallels are Aristophanes, *Nubes* 393, and for the downward counterpart to the *hupsou apeiron aithera*, 'boundless heaven above', Xenophanes B 28 and Empedocles B 39. The sense of the word in Empedocles B 28 is no doubt fixed by its conjunction with '*sphairos*'; but this striking use will not serve Cornford's turn, since B 39 can be taken to show that Empedocles is contrasting it as his own use with the more common and objectionable applications of the word in cosmology (J. Bollack, *Empédocle* (Paris 1965-9), vol. i, 239-40, cf. Aristot. *De Caelo* 294a24-28). Nor could its application to a sphere be read back to explain Anaximander, for while no doubt the latter's *apeiron* now surrounds the world that came from it, equally certainly it preceded that world.

Indeed one may wonder how this theory of the *apeiron* was supposed to be confirmed by Parmenides, who so conspicuously rejected the 'limitless'; or why an interest in the character of a sphere's surface should be read into an argument designed to prove the continuity and balance of reality '*from the centre*'.

Under (4) Cornford added that, for some time after the mid-fifth century, the supposedly earlier view of space 'persisted in the minds of most philosophers'; but he cited only Plato and Aristotle. Plato cannot be discussed here; the issue presumably turns on the question whether the creation of the sphere in the *Timaeus* was proposed as (not an historical, but at least) an historically possible event. If it was, Plato did not assume an initial sphericality in the space available for his cosmogony. As for Aristotle, Guthrie observes that he 'mentions five considerations as leading to the belief that something is *apeiron* (sc. *Phys.* 203b15-30). We may take it that they include all the traditional aspects of the word up to and including his time' (*HGP* i 83). If that is so, it is enough to say that none of these considerations introduces the notion of finite sphericality. Nor does Aristotle anywhere represent himself as returning to a primitive view of space./

81 Positively, then, Zeno's arguments already give evidence of the only assumption about spatial continuity that is required for my interpretation of Parmenides, B 8. 42-9. Negatively, there is no evidence for any earlier assumption of a 'curved' or 'Einsteinian' space (whatever that might mean in the sixth century), and none for any mathematical revolution in this regard. Of course Greek views of space were steadily developed and clarified, from Hesiod's *chaos* on. But the development seems to have consisted in thinking harder about such natural assumptions as that one can always make another move in the line of the last one.

2

Plato and Parmenides on the Timeless Present

I

Some statements couched in the present tense have no reference to time. They 317
are, if you like, grammatically tensed but logically tenseless. Mathematical statements such as 'twice two is four' or 'there is a prime number between 125 and 128' are of this sort. So is the statement I have just made. To ask in good faith whether there is still the prime number there used to be between 125 and 128 would be to show that one did not understand the use of such statements, and so would any attempt to answer the question. It is tempting to take another step and talk of such timeless statements as statements about timeless entities. If the number 4 neither continues nor ceases to be twice two this is, surely, because the number 4 has no history of any kind, not even the being a day older today than yesterday. Other timeless statements might shake our confidence in this inference: 'clocks are devices for measuring time' is a timeless statement, but it is not about a class of timeless clocks. But, given a preoccupation with a favoured set of examples and a stage of thought at which men did not distinguish the properties of statements from the properties of the things they are about, we can expect timeless entities to appear as the natural proxies of timeless statements.

Now the fact that a grammatical tense can be detached from its tense-affiliations and put to a tenseless use is something that must be discovered at some time by somebody or some set of people. So far as I know it was discovered by the Greeks. It is commonly credited to one Greek in
particular, a pioneer from whose argu-/ments most subsequent Greek 318
troubles over time were to flow: Parmenides the Eleatic. Sometimes it is suggested that Parmenides took a hint from his alleged mentors, the Pythagoreans. 'We may assume' says one writer 'that he knew of the timeless present in mathematical statements.'[1] But what Aristotle tells us of Pythagorean mathematics is enough to undermine this assumption. According to him (esp. *Meta*. 1091a12-22) they confused the construction of

* This is a shortened version of a lecture given to the Philosophy Colloquium at Princeton University in January, 1964. The substance of another lecture delivered on that occasion can be found in 'Aristotle on Time', below, Chapter 17.

[1] W. Kneale, 'Time and Eternity in Theology', *PAS* 61 (1960-1), 90.

the series of natural numbers with the generation of the world. So Parmenides is our earliest candidate. His claim too has been disputed, and I shall try to clear up this dispute as I go, but not before I have done what I can to sharpen it and widen the issues at stake.

Parmenides seems to argue in the following way.[2] He begins, perplexingly enough, without specifying what the discussion is about, what the subject of his argument is. But the argument makes it clear that he does not want a specific subject on his hands: he wants to reason about whatever it is that can be a subject, whatever it is that can be talked and thought about. And he contends that if we have such a subject it must exist, since if it did not exist we should not have anything to talk about. (I think myself that he goes on to reinforce this argument with another and more interesting fallacy, but that is another story.) Then, having professedly proved the existence of his subject, he goes on to extract some other conclusions and occasionally to bolster them with independent arguments. He sets out his programme with the meticulous accuracy that characterizes his whole procedure: 'It exists without birth or death; whole, unique; and immovable; and perfect' (8. 3-4). And he goes on: 'Nor was it ever nor will it be; for it is now, all together, single, continuous.' The argument that he gives to support this – and we have no record of any other argument that he brought to bear on this point – is that the subject cannot have either a beginning or an end in time or indeed any temporal variation at all.

So the argument seems to be this. Let X be Parmenides' subject, viz., whatever we can talk or think about and so, derivatively, whatever there is.
319 Then (i) X is unchanging: it does not begin or/ cease to exist and nothing happens to it. Consequently (ii) nothing can be said of it in the past or future tense, not even that it has gone on and will go on being the same thing. So stated, the argument is plainly incomplete: we need some further assumption to get us from (i) to (ii). And it seems clear what the simplest assumption would be for this purpose. It is that, if X is to have a past distinct from its present, something must be true of that past which is not true of the present; and similarly with the future. Otherwise they could not be distinguished. And *ex hypothesi* this condition cannot be satisfied if nothing changes at all. We might put this, in a later idiom: times of which exactly the same things are true (at which the same states of affairs obtain, and which are not distinguished by their antecedents or sequels) are the same time. It is the identity of indiscernibles, with times and not objects for its arguments. But of course Parmenides could not say this. His assumption remains unstated. As such it need not come to anything more than the familiar readiness of the Greeks to picture the lapse of time as the parent and regulator and assessor of change.[3] When Aristotle came to argue that lapse of time is impossible

[2] For this interpretation and the textual readings on which it is based see 'Eleatic Questions', above, Chapter 1.

[3] See, e.g. C. Kahn, *Anaximander and the Origins of Greek Cosmology* (New York 1960), 170-1. If the variant *oud' ei* (better, with Coxon, *oude*) *chronos* at 8. 36 (Simplic. *in Phys*. 146.9) could be made plausible it would entail a clarity on Parmenides' part about the issue discussed in this paper which I have thought better not to assume.

without change he was the beneficiary of a century of discussion in which Parmenides' assumption had been pulled out and challenged.

So, on this interpretation of Parmenides, the force of the present tense in 'X exists' does not depend on its family connexion with other tenses of the verb. Those tenses have been scrapped, casualties of the argument. Just as Parmenides explodes the idea of non-existence on the way to propounding an existential statement, so he discards the distinctions imported by other tenses and then produces a statement in the present tense. The sense of his existential claim does not seem to him to require any complementary and contrasting use to be found for denials of existence, and his use of the present tense does not depend on leaving any complementary and contrasting use to the other tenses. On one view of it, he has managed to detense the verb, and the way is open for Plato's more sophisticated use of the same device./

On one view of it. As I shall show you, there can be other views. And to be **320**
fair I must advertise one of these views now, for it contradicts the conventional translation I have given of the essential lines in Parmenides. Hermann Fraenkel, in a footnote added to the reprint of his *Parmenidesstudien*,[4] argues that the words ordinarily rendered 'Nor was it ever now will it be' call for a different rendering, and in particular that the word translated 'ever', means rather 'at one time but not another' or, in this context, 'at some time in the past or future but not now.' The whole clause then means 'Nor is it the case that X existed at some time (*but not now*), or will exist at some time (*but not now*).' And thus Parmenides is arguing not for the timelessness but only for the temporal continuity of his subject. His denial comes merely to the claim that X not only existed at some past time but *also* exists now, and not only will exist at some future time but *also* exists now.

Now Fraenkel's reasons for this suggestion are weak. Later it will be worthwhile trying to reinforce them. Two are linguistic, one is philosophical, and I shall not dwell on the linguistic reasons. So far as the Greek goes, it just is not the case that the phrase *ou* (or *oude*) *pote*, which I translated '*not* (or *nor*) *ever*', would ordinarily have the sense that Fraenkel reads into it here.[5] It would *not* ordinarily mean 'not *at some particular time by contrast with others*' (Fraenkel gives no parallels for his sense): it would mean 'not *at any time*'. It is a joke to think that any Greek could claim *oupote ên kleptês oud' esomai* if by this he meant that he had not yet stopped being a thief and did not mean to give up the trade. (Given t as a time-variable, *pote* is $(\exists t)$ ... and *ou pote* is accordingly $-(\exists t)$ ...) And Fraenkel's second linguistic reason is no stronger. It is that he wants to emend the text elsewhere by importing a verb in the future tense; but even if all his assumptions about that other context were correct he would do better to bracket the doubtful verb as a gloss than tinker with the tense of
it.[6] In any event,/ as we shall see, the occasional appearance of different **321**

[4] *Wege und Formen frühgrieschichen Denkens*[3] (Munich 1968), 191, n. 1.

[5] Cf. W.K.C. Guthrie, *A History of Greek Philosophy*, vol.2 (Cambridge 1965), 30, n. 1. Of course Fraenkel knows this, but feels compelled to evade it by the arguments I go on to consider.

[6] If Proclus' *mimnei* is to be read in 8.29, the *menei* of 8.30 is better read as an intrusive gloss which had displaced some other verb, e.g. *pelei*.

tenses in Parmenides' argument is not ruled out by the interpretation that Fraenkel would like to undermine. But I want to turn from these points of scholarship and consider the substantial philosophical issue that is raised by Fraenkel's final and only serious argument.

This argument is that Parmenides cannot have intended to deny himself the use of different tenses in framing his conclusion, for in his case it would be flatly self-refuting, logical suicide, to do so. For Parmenides expressly concludes, from his polemic against the possibility of change, that his subject *remains* the same (8. 29-30). And to say this is to say that it still is what it was, and will continue to be what it is. So if Parmenides had used this as a premise for rejecting all tense-distinctions his conclusion would have disabled the premise on which it rested.

Now there are, on the face of it, other inconsistencies in what Parmenides says. He is ready, for instance, to use the language of motion in describing his immovable subject.[7] But this inconsistency is quite superficial: the jarring idioms can be neutralized without harming the argument. Fraenkel seems to have his finger on a far more radical incoherence. The only surprising thing is that he assumes that this type of incoherence is foreign to Parmenides' argument, when other evidence makes it overwhelmingly clear that it lies at the heart of the reasoning. Let me explain this. Parmenides argues, you remember, that any denial of existence is nonsense: the nonexistent cannot be thought or spoken of (2. 7-8), denials of existence are 'not sayable or thinkable' (8. 8-9). (More exactly, they are either self-refuting if they have a genuine subject or senseless if they have not.) Yet Parmenides sometimes puts this point by saying that there is no such thing as what is not (8. 46), that there is nothing except what there is (8. 36-7). He is driven to denying the existence of some kinds of thing – change and plurality *imprimis* – in order to maintain his thesis that nonexistence makes no sense. Nor would it help him to follow the more sophisticated path that seems to open at some moments in the argument (8. 38-41, 52-3, 9.1, 19.3) and recast these denials in the formal mode. He would still have to deny that there is anything for which such a/
322 word as 'change' stands. Yet just this is what his own conclusion should disable him from doing.

So, to repeat that memorable image from Wittgenstein, Parmenides' argument is a ladder to be climbed up and thrown away. Such arguments are not, put it picturesquely, horizontal deductions; if they parade as deductions they are patently self-defeating. They are not even of the form of a reductio ad absurdum, for there is no more benefit in negating their premisses than in asserting them. Gilbert Ryle has said something of such patterns of reasoning,[8] but I shall not generalize about them. They do not seem to form a genuine class, and I am sure that some of them are too substantial to be met by a call of contradiction. In particular I suspect Parmenides saw the oddity of his own argument. For instead of representing the denial of birth and death

[7] See 'Eleatic Questions', above, p. 18, n. 60.

[8] 'Philosophical Arguments', Inaugural Lecture (Oxford 1945), reprinted in *Logical Positivism*, ed. A.J. Ayer (Glencoe, Ill. 1959).

and change as final conclusions, corollaries to be drawn from the thesis that X exists, he is careful to call these *signs on the way* to that conclusion (8.2-3). Destinations do not contain the signs that lead to them, and travellers at their destination have no use for the signs.

In sum, then: it is characteristic of Parmenides that he should argue from the impossibility of change to the untenability of time-distinctions and yet, on the way, represent his argument as implying the permanent immutability of his subject. For this is the twin of that reasoning which moves from rejecting the concept of non-existence to simply asserting the existence of its subject, yet on the way represents the argument as denying the existence of change. Surely, we are inclined to say, if nonexistence is ruled out then there *is no such thing as* change? and then, equally surely, what there is must stay the same? Just these are the signposts, the intermediate rungs on Parmenides' ladder.

II

You will no doubt feel some unallayed qualms at this account. I promise to go looking for trouble directly. But first I want to strengthen my hand by noticing how such an interpretation throws light on some important moves made by Parmenides' near successors./

Anaxagoras is a notable example. He began his book with a sentence that **323**
is plainly framed as a flat contradiction of Parmenides on some major issues. Postulating a beginning of the physical world, he wrote: 'All things were together, limitless both in number and in smallness.' Parmenides had written 'Nor was it ever nor will it be, since it is now, all of it together, single, continuous.' 'All of it together, single' is discarded for 'All things together, limitless in number'. 'Continuous', which Parmenides understands (to Aristotle's indignation) as excluding divisibility into parts, is replaced by 'limitless in smallness' which is shortly afterwards explained by the continuous divisibility of things. Even 'together' takes on another sense; for part of Parmenides' argument was to deny not only temporal but spatial distinctions in the last analysis – to the mind, he says, distant things are present (B 4); whereas Anaxagoras' collection of seeds takes up limitless space. And now all that is left in Anaxagoras' sentence is the verb in the past tense, 'was'; and all that is left to be contradicted in the counterpart sentence in Parmenides is the phrase 'nor was it ever nor will it be'. Anaxagoras, I submit, must have read this phrase as disallowing the use of tenses other than the present.[9]

Thereafter he knocks home his point with a tattoo of tenses: 'all such things as were yet to be, all such things as were but are no more, all that now are, all

[9] It might be thought that Anaxagoras just meant to introduce a past tense in a sense other than that in which, on Fraenkel's view, Parmenides thought himself still entitled to it; i.e. A. might be saying 'This is how things were but are no longer.' But this would be a mistake: A. is at pains to insist that, so far as the state of affairs described in his opening sentence is concerned, matters are exactly the same now: 'Just as in the beginning, so now, all things must be together' (B 6).

such as will be ...' (B 12). Similarly, it is just when Empedocles is insisting on the progress of time (even though a circular progress) that he goes out of his way to snub Parmenides (B 17.26-9).

But the man whose position comes out in the sharpest relief is the later Eleatic, Melissus. That Melissus is given to improving on Parmenides where he thinks fit is common knowledge. Notice then how he introduces his thesis:

> It always was what it was and always will be. For if it had come into existence
> 324 there would necessarily be nothing before it did so./ Now if there had been nothing, there could not possibly have come anything out of nothing ... So since it did not come into existence it is and always was and always will be (DK B 1, 2).

With the word 'always' Melissus introduces others that found no place in Parmenides' verses: 'limitless' (in connexion with both time and space), 'eternal', 'the whole of time'. So Melissus is quite clear on what has been proved if one shows that what there is has neither beginning nor end nor any kind of change. What has been proved is that it did exist, does exist and will exist without change at all times in the past, present and future. What else? Whatever is true of any of these times is true of them all. So Melissus is in effect denying, what we took Parmenides to be in effect maintaining, the identity of indiscernibles in its application to times.

If this is so, Melissus' deductions must be horizontal deductions. That is, the premisses and intermediate steps must seem to him as solid and inalienable as the conclusions based on them. If the rejection of change shows that nothing new happened in the past or will happen in the future, then that *is* what it shows. And that this is Melissus' approach to the argument is clinched by his most remarkable departure from Parmenides' method. Namely, he wholly discards those arguments of Parmenides which hinge on the claim that some important expression has no sense, that what it purports to stand for cannot be 'spoken or thought'. The importance of this departure can hardly be overstressed (I cannot find that so far it has been stressed at all). For it was just that cry of 'unthinkable, unsayable' that compelled Parmenides to treat his own arguments as stages to be passed and then dismissed, since those arguments were compelled to use the very expressions branded unusable. Melissus can make nothing of this. He consistently treats the denial of existence and the description of change and plurality as significant; demonstrably false, but never unthinkable. Just how this shapes his argument against any beginning of existence, and finally commits him to a plurality of indiscernible times, I shall try to show you shortly. But first I must point to the trouble which I warned you still lay in wait for our interpretation. There seems to be a reason for doubting whether we are entitled to this sharp contrast between Parmenides and his follower. On the main issue/
325 Parmenides may be less single-minded than I have depicted him, and it is time to call his consistency in question.

III

The trouble is uncovered by an argument that occurs a few lines later in Parmenides' poem. He goes on to maintain that what there is cannot have come into existence either from nothing or from something.[10] And he gives two reasons for saying that it cannot have come into existence from nothing. First, the antecedent state of affairs would be indescribable, for to describe it would be to deny the existence of anything at that time; and this denial is nonsense. Secondly, he says: 'If it started from nothing, what (*ti chreos*) could have made it spring up later rather than earlier?' This is the argument to which Aristotle refers when he says that the Eleatics ruled out all change because they were unable to answer the question, what started the change (*Meta.* 984a29-984b1). Let us look harder at it.

It is, as you will have seen, the argument that Kant repeats in the antithesis to his First Antinomy and Moore discusses in his published lectures. 'Assume the world had a beginning. Then that beginning must come after a time in which the thing did not exist, i.e. an empty time. But nothing can begin to exist in an empty time, for no part of such a time can be picked out from the rest as furnishing a condition of existence.' Leibniz knew of the reasoning and discussed it in his third letter to Clarke. It is a very Greek pattern of argument. If the world starts from nothing, there can be no reason for it to start on Saturday rather than Thursday; and since it cannot start on both days there is no reason to suppose it started at all. Anaximander, asked why the earth stayed still in the middle of his universe, is credited with the reply that since the earth was symmetrically related to all the extremities of the universe there was no reason for it to move in any direction (*Cael.* 295b10-16). He probably used the same reasoning in deciding that the regular circles of the heavenly bodies are not interrupted when they go below the horizon. Aristotle retailored the argument/ to rebut the possibility of motion in a **326**
vacuum; the Academy adapted it to show that, since no physical sample of equality has more right to serve as a standard sample than any other, the standard sample cannot be physical. And Leibniz found an excellent example in Archimedes' mechanics and of course cited it as an illustration of his Principle of Sufficient Reason.

But there may be more to it than the Principle of Sufficient Reason. We can give Parmenides' argument more or less of an edge according to our interpretation of the phrase *husteron ê prosthen.* It may mean just 'later *or* earlier', and then the argument is: what reason is there for the world, if it comes from nothing, to start whenever it did (whether later or earlier)? But equally the phrase may mean 'later *rather than* earlier', and then the argument is: what reason is there for the world to start at a given time t rather than some earlier time $t-n$? And, since the same question can be raised in turn for $t-n$? and for any earlier time whatever, we have a regress on our hands; and

[10] I accept Reinhardt's emendation at 8.12 (cf. now Guthrie, op. cit., 28-9). But nothing in my present argument hangs on this.

Parmenides will have furnished Zeno not only with a simple pattern of *reductio ad absurdum* but with a destructive sample of the infinite regress, his two chief weapons.

Elsewhere in his third letter to Clarke, Leibniz recognizes this regress version of the argument. Discussing the supposition that 'God might have created the world several million years sooner', he says: 'since God does nothing without reason, and since there is no reason assignable why He did not create the world sooner, it will follow either that He created nothing at all, or that He produced the world before any assignable time – which is to say that the world is eternal.' In either version Leibniz would have none of the argument, for a reason which will have occurred to you already. The reason is that in all its versions the argument seems to assume the existence of absolute time, i.e. the existence of different times having all their properties, other than that of bare temporal order, in common. Yet surely this is just what Parmenides was supposed to be denying in his comment on 'was' and 'will be'? He seems now to be maintaining that if the world began at t it might equally have begun at $t - n$, and if at $t - n$ then at $t - nn$. But unless we borrow time from Newton and Melissus what are we to make of this glib distinction between t and $t - n$ and $t - nn$? It is not just that, as Kant puts it, no part of an empty time can be picked out from others as providing a sufficient
327 condition for the world to start. It/is that, on the view we took ourselves to have found in Parmenides, no part of an empty time (and generally no part of a time without events) can be picked out from others *at all*. It would be absurd to say that the beginning of things was to be brought forward by two days, or postponed sine die; and correspondingly absurd to ask why it should not be.

The suspicion that Parmenides is at least showing the cloven hoof here is reinforced by another consideration. As I said, he gives two arguments to show that what exists cannot come from nothing. Now it is this second argument that Melissus adapts to his own use. The first, which simply traded on the senselessness of all denials of existence, Melissus prudently and characteristically drops. It is the other, ready as it is to allow a use to the word 'nothing' and hospitable as it is to absolute time-distinctions, that is father to Melissus' own reasoning: 'If what comes first is nothing, there is no way in which that nothing can give rise to something'.

Let us pick the bones of the argument a little cleaner. Of the assumptions that it brings into play one is a principle (P) which for our purposes can be formulated quite broadly, to the effect that if anything is the case there must be some sufficient reason why it should be so and not otherwise. This is neither challenged nor expressly adduced by proponents of the argument. The mischief starts when it is put to work with two other assumptions, namely

(I) For any time t there is some time $t - n$ which is earlier than t, which taken together with P yields the corollary (c) that if any event occurs uniquely at t there is a sufficient reason for its not occurring at $t - n$; and

(II) There is an event, viz. the first event, which occurs uniquely at some time t but which *ex hypothesi* fails to satisfy the condition stated in (c).

Given a certain principle of explanation, then, propositions (I) and (II) cannot be jointly true. (Not that they are formally incompatible – this will be important later.) Leibniz accepts (II) and uses this as a lever to dislodge (I), and, with it, Newton's absolute time. Parmenides, on the other hand, is out to demolish (II). So, unless he is simply confused about the point of such arguments, he must surely accept (I). For the argument is a *reductio ad ab-/surdum*, and where a *reductio* depends on a number of independent **328**
premisses it can be used to destroy one of these only on the assumption that the others are true.

(I make no apology for picking at Parmenides' assumptions in this way. It is what his successors had to do in deciding what they must accept from him and what they could afford to reject. And Parmenides set the model for his successors in the care with which he uncovered the premisses on which his own arguments hinged, and the care with which he marked those theorems which had been proved and which were now to serve as the basis of a further proof. To talk of confusion in his case is to judge him by the standards that he and Zeno invented.)

Certainly Parmenides may be confused. One thing, though, he cannot be confused over. He cannot have thought that he was entitled to Assumption (I) merely on the strength of that troublesome step in the argument which depicts the subject as going on without change, 'standing fast, the same in the same place' (8. 29-30). For that step is inferred from the thesis that what exists can have no starts or stops: and this thesis in turn is established by means of the assumption we are discussing. In other words, Assumption (I) seems to be brought into play from the start of the reasoning. It is an independent premiss, and as such it may naturally be supposed to represent Parmenides' own conviction. And if that is so Parmenides is not a single-minded, and perhaps not any sort of, antagonist of temporal distinctions.

But we have gone too fast. We assumed that (I) and (II) must be logically independent assumptions. After all, Melissus was able to maintain (I) without (II); and Leibniz was able to maintain (II) without (I). So it did not occur to us that Parmenides could have assumed (I) merely because he took it to be naturally implied by the objectionable thesis (II). But this was a mistake.

It is far more likely that he did import Assumption (I) on just this ground – or even, if you prefer, that its connexion with (II) would have seemed so obvious that the question of importing and justifying it did not arise. For, if we set aside Leibniz's special pleading, it does seem obvious that if the world started from nothing there must have been some time before it started. It does seem obvious that, if there is a time when X begins to exist, this can only be distinguished from other times when X exists by the fact/ that X exists at **329**
that time but not at any earlier time. And if there are puzzles in this – there are indeed, and they will catch up with us later – at any rate they are not Parmenides' present concern. He is refuting the suggestion that what exists started from nothing. He has just attacked it on the supposition that to say that nothing existed before that time makes no sense. Now, in the lines we are discussing, he attacks it on the more natural and charitable assumption that

this does make sense. That is, he lets proposition (II) carry its conventional corollary (I). But this does not for a moment imply that he saw more sense in the corollary than in the hypothesis that seemed conventionally to entail it.

So the propositions that come into conflict in his *reductio ad absurdum* are just proposition (II) and that general principle of sufficient reason which lies unadvertised behind the argument. And it does not occur to him to jettison the latter. Perhaps it might have. When one recent writer pictures the first event as the 'spontaneous decay of an elementary particle in a static universe' (G.J. Whitrow, *The Natural Philosophy of Time* (London 1961), 32-3) he shows himself ready to abandon the principle, and this is not a recent liberty. Anaxagoras saw no need to satisfy Parmenides on this point when he described the beginning of this world from a static, characterless amalgam. In fact Parmenides' successors were generally content if they could meet his demand that there should never be a time at which there was simply nothing in existence. If they went on to picture a first event in a static (or otherwise timeless) world, they took no care to meet the query why it should have happened when it did. And in this their instinct, or their logic, may after all have been right.

Whether it was right is a question that I shall come back to. It does not lie on our way now. We were looking for signs of a cloven hoof, signs that Parmenides was ready to admit time-distinctions even in a world without events. And we have not found those signs. Parmenides' traditional claim to have been the first to attack temporal distinctions stands firm. It is Parmenides that Plato is echoing when he says in the *Timaeus* (37e-38a):

> Days, nights, months, years ... are all parts of time, and 'was' and 'will be' have come about as forms of time. We are wrong to apply them unthinkingly to what
> 330 is eternal. Of this we say that it was and/ is and will be, but strictly only 'is'
> belongs to it. 'Was' and 'will be' should be spoken of the process that goes on in time, for they are changes.

Indeed as soon as we attend to this echo we have another answer to an old objection. The difficulty was how to suppose that Parmenides meant to eliminate all talk of past and future, when he described his subject as remaining unchanged. The reply is that Plato knows of this conjunction and has no objection to it at all. He is as ready here as in his other dialogues, and as ready as his mentor Parmenides, to describe his own eternal entities the Forms as staying firm (29b) and as continuing always in the same state (28a, 29a, 37d, 38a). Indeed it is this very description of them that he uses when he goes on to prohibit any use of the past or future tense in talking of them (38a). And Aristotle repeats the point with enthusiasm:

> Things that exist always are not, as such, in time; for they are not contained by time (sc. there is no time before and after they exist), and their existence is not measured by time. A proof of this is that none of them is affected by time; for none of them is in it (*Phys.* 221b3-7).

How Plato came to terms with the anomaly is something we have yet to discuss. Meantime there can be no question that when he came to recognize the essential tenselessness of those propositions that most interested him – the analyses of ethical and nonethical concepts, the theorems of mathematics, and many more – it was Parmenides' dictum that gave him his model of explanation.

It was, as we shall see, an unfortunate model.

IV

Look back for a moment. Even without the benefit of Zeno's contribution, the Eleatics had set their successors some rich problems about time. We have isolated two in chief: one is the question whether and on what terms to discard time-or-tense-distinctions, with its attendant debate on the possibility of indiscernible times. The other is the question how to talk of a first event in time. The first question was aired by the disagreement between Parmenides and Melissus. The second was still better canvassed, but the prob-/lem to **331**
which it leads – whether for every time there must be some earlier time – may not have come into the open before Plato. However, Democritus seems to have noticed it: he argued that not everything came into existence, and his counter-example was time (*Phys.* 251b15-17). And there is other evidence that the logic of time continued to exercise the men of that century. Antiphon is even credited with saying that time is not a substance but a concept or a measure (*Doxographi Graeci* (Berlin 1879), 318.22), but in this insight his name is linked with that of a Peripatetic philosopher of much later date who no doubt supplied the formula. Let us shift from this thin ice and watch Plato coming to grips with the Eleatic issues.

With Plato's attempt to describe a beginning of time I shall deal on a later occasion. It has had the lion's share of recent discussion and its twin-issue, the discarding of tenses, demands a hearing. Moreover Plato made the first issue pretty much his own; just now I want to discuss him in the context of an older debate.

When Plato says that the past and future tenses have no place in our talk about unchanging things he is taking his stand with Parmenides and against Melissus. When he prefaces this with the comment that 'days, nights, years, are parts of time' he is calling attention to an oddity in Melissus' argument. Melissus had argued that something which is single and indivisible, as any Eleatic subject must be, could not have a body; for anything with a body has density (*pachos*), and consequently can be divided into parts; and anything with parts is no longer single and indivisible (B 9). Therein he took himself to be complying with Parmenides' requirement that what exists must be indivisible – the requirement that all Zeno's arguments are ultimately designed to protect. But in admitting past and present and future into time or in letting similar distinctions into infinite space he felt secure: divisibility into parts comes only with density, for dense things can be broken or scattered, and then one meets with the gaps that vexed Parmenides or the infinitely elusive smallest parts that delighted Zeno. Differences in time and space, he thinks, are quite another thing. Plato corrects him: time has parts just as certainly as a block of wood, so his evasion is unsuccessful. And his correction of Melissus is deliberate, for in his own dialogue *Parmenides* he is prepared to show how Zeno's puzzles over divisibility arise in connexion with time. This is another topic to be deferred for the present./

332 Now the use to which Plato puts Parmenides' device in the *Timaeus* is pretty widely agreed. When he says that 'was' and 'will be' are appropriate to our talk of the changing physical world, but that only 'is' and 'are' should be used in speaking of the timeless Forms, he is taken to have grasped the fact that such a statement as 'justice is a virtue' is temporally neutral or timeless, whereas such a statement as 'the moon is a satellite of the earth' is not timeless but, at best, temporally general. He has seen that, while the second statement properly collects such questions as whether the moon will continue to satisfy the description tomorrow, and how long it has done so, and even how old it is, it is a false analogy to coin such questions about justice. Faced with Parmenides' admirable discovery of the tenseless proposition he applies this discovery to elucidate the logic of those propositions which preoccupy him as a philosopher.

Is this the right story? I am going to sow some doubts.

Look again at the device that he has taken over from Parmenides. Does Parmenides manage to isolate a use of the verb which is wholly independent of tense-affiliations? Certainly (let us take this now for granted) he wants to discard the past and future tenses – just as surely as he wants to discard denials of existence. But there are considerations which leave his move ambiguous. It is not just his use of those expressions for permanence and durability which Plato was ready to echo. It is that, while denying that his subject can be said to have existed ever in the past or to be going to exist in the future, Parmenides insists that it exists now. His treatment of time is too like his treatment of existence. He wants to maintain the existence of his subject and yet at the same time to allow no sense to denying its existence; and similarly he wants to maintain its existence in the present while admitting no use for the statement that it existed in the past or will do so in the future.

In a recent paper Professor Kneale suggested a connexion between Parmenides' treatment of time and that puzzling piece of theological equipment, the eternal present that is enjoyed by God.[11] Augustine speaks easily of God's 'everpresent eternity'; he tells his Maker 'Your years neither go nor come, they stand all at once ... For you the present does not give place
333 to tomorrow or follow/ after yesterday; your present day is eternity' (*Conf.* xi 13). Nor is this odd move proprietary to theology. Philosophy has thriven on attempts to leave some expression its familiar use while cutting it off from its family connexions in the language. Think of the argument that any statement in the past tense must really be about the present or the future, because present or future evidence must constitute the whole ground for thinking it

[11] See p. 27 n. 1 above.

true or false. The manoeuvre fails, because to understand that some evidence is now available is to understand, inter alia, that it is false that that evidence was available but is so no longer. We reimport the past to mark out the sense of the present: without it we should have no right to the expression 'still', 'now', 'no longer'.

Parmenides' isolation of one tense from its fellows suggests a view of language which underlies some puzzles in the *Theaetetus* and *Cratylus* and which Plato very effectively dismantles in the *Sophist*. It is not a device which promises to throw much light on those propositions about the concept of justice or the cardinal number five which interest Plato. Let us see what Plato made of it.

In the *Timaeus* Plato seems to be under its spell. He is apparently ready to drop the word 'now' from timeless propositions, but he imports 'always' in its place (38a). And there are other clues, almost too familiar to list. He is ready to use the same adjectives in describing both the timelessness of the Forms and the temporal progress of the physical world. He calls them both 'everlasting', *aïdion* (e.g. 29a, 40b). And he uses the noble word 'eternal', *aiônion*, first of the existence of the Forms and then, in the same breath, of time itself, viz. the regular motions of the astronomical clock (37d) – to the despair of Cornford, who insisted that eternity (*aiôn*) was the prerogative of the Forms and wanted to emend the text in face of all the MSS and the ancient tradition.[12] But Cornford missed the argument. What Plato says is that the physical world cannot be *wholly or unqualifiedly* eternal (37d3-4: subsequently in 38b3 he coins the word 'di*aiônios*' for this notion). And the idiom is the familiar language of the Theory of Forms. Plato means to recall those canonical arguments in the *Phaedo* and *Republic* which show that while
things in this world can be beautiful or/ equal, large or single, they cannot be **334**
wholly or unqualifiedly so: in some other respect or relation they, unlike their respective Forms, will prove unequal or unbeautiful. Similarly with the eternity of the physical world. The movements of the planets, those movements which 'define and preserve the numbers of time' (38c), are both stable and unstable: the pattern is stable, but it is a pattern of change. The Forms, on the other hand, are simply stable. But then why are we not allowed to credit them with a stable past and future? Melissus is obviously fretting to be back in the conversation. How does Plato keep him out?

By a very compressed argument. He says:

> That which is always unchangingly in the same state cannot be growing older or younger by the lapse of time. It cannot ever become so, it cannot have become so at present, it will not be so hereafter. And in general nothing can belong to it of all the things that the process of becoming attaches to the shifting things we perceive (38a).

So the argument seems to be this. To go on in time, and thus to collect a past

[12] *Plato's Cosmology*, p. 98, n. 1; 'seems very plausible', H. Cherniss, *Aristotle's Criticism of Plato and The Academy* (Baltimore 1944), 419 n. 350.

and a future, is to grow older; but to grow older is to change; so what stays always the same cannot be staying so in time. Hence what stays always the same cannot collect a past or a future. Here, as you see, everything depends on what Plato means by 'growing older'.[13]

One thing that he does not mean is a change in the character of the subject, such as increasing decrepitude. For the description is meant equally to apply to the permanent furniture of the world, the stars and atoms. One thing that he may mean is the mere increase in age. This is suggested, both by his distinction between this and other characteristics of changing things, and by his claim that even to say of something that it 'was and is and will be' is to report it as changing. Now if this is his meaning we can expect paradoxes. Certainly we, like the Greeks, talk of becoming (or growing) older as readily as of becoming hotter or happier. But we do not, and neither did they, ordinarily talk of mere progress in time as a kind of *change* (*kinêsis, genesis*). We
335 expect to ask of/ any process of change how long it takes or how quickly it comes about, but the questions have no literal sense for our progress between different dates or ages. That progress is presupposed by, and not the subject of, our reports of change. Once reckon it among the familiar kinds of change, and the idea of complete stability finds itself curiously dispossessed. It cannot now, logically cannot, characterize anything that continues in time, yet the continuing in time is as essential to its logic as to that of change. What is left of it is a kind of logical torso supported, as in the *Timaeus*, by a present tense without past or future connexions.

And things are no different if Plato means something more than this by 'growing older'. For then he presumably means that to grow older is to have a history, in the sense that something is true of the subject at one time (something other than mere age) which is not true of it at another. But in Plato's view this is the case with all physical things. So again the idea of complete stability is dislodged from its hold on any temporal propositions save those couched in that degenerate tense, the eternal present. Later in the *Timaeus* Plato speaks of transient physical things as clinging precariously to existence, by contrast with the security of the Ideas. He is wrong. It is his stable forms which cling precariously to their stability, by virtue of their tenuous and disreputable hold on time.

In sum, it is part of the originality of Plato to have grasped, or half-grasped, an important fact about certain kinds of statement, namely that they are tenseless whereas others are tensed. But he tries to bring this contrast under his familiar distinction between the changeless and the changing. So he saddles the familiar distinction with a piece of conceptual apparatus taken from Parmenides, a tense-form which retains enough of a present sense to be coupled with expressions for permanence and stability, yet which has severed its links with the future and the past. Armed with this device Plato is able to turn the distinction between tensed and tenseless statements into a more congenial distinction between timebound and timeless, changing and

[13] 'Growing older *or younger*' (cf. *Parm.* 141a-d, 152a-e) called for separate discussion in a later lecture.

immutable, objects.

But at a price. The concept of stability has been stretched so that stability is no longer a function of time. And the interesting propositions, so far from staying tenseless, are restated in an artificial and degenerate tense-form. The theory for which we are asked to tolerate these anomalies will need to hold firm against/ scrutiny. But on scrutiny there seems to be something wrong at **336**
its roots.

V

What is wrong, I think, can be put very shortly. It is that to be tensed or tenseless is a property of statements and not of things, and that paradoxes come from confusing this distinction; just as they come from trying to manufacture necessary beings out of the logical necessity that attaches to certain statements. But how is the distinction to be recognized? One way, a good way, is to notice that tenseless statements are not proprietary to one sort of subject and tensed statements to another. And there seems to be evidence in another work of Plato that he did notice this, and brought the point home by a valid argument. I want to end by discussing that evidence. It occurs in the *Sophist*, in the criticism that the chief speaker brings against the so-called Friends of the Forms.[14]

The argument hinges on some special concepts of action and change which are brought into play a little earlier in the dialogue. An Eleatic stranger sets out to examine the theories of other philosophers with a view to extracting answers to a certain question. He wants to know, namely, what kinds of thing they count as real, or what general criteria they use in deciding that some kinds of thing exist and others do not. (Existence, reality: the Greek does not distinguish them here, and we need not.) After exposing the confusions of some earlier theorists he turns to two other parties: the Giants, who say that the sole criterion of reality is to be, or to have, a tangible physical body; and the Gods, who are 'friends of the Forms' and who say that the joint criteria of reality are to be knowable and to be free from change. And he professes to involve both of them in contradictions. The Giants are trapped by the admission that there are souls (good material souls, of course), and that souls can become wise and just. They are at once told that to become just is to come into some relation with justice – it is for justice to be possessed by, or to become present to, the soul/(247a5-6). So justice too must figure in the **337**
Giants' ontology, and no one would say that justice had a physical body. On the strength of this move the Eleatic proposes a more hospitable criterion of reality, to take care of justice as well. It is that real things are things which are able *to do something to another thing, or to have something done to them*, however little and however seldom (247d-e). This is the ambiguous formula on which

[14] My account of this argument lies close to that given by J.M.E. Moravcsik, in 'Being and Meaning in the *Sophist*', *Acta Philosophia Fennica* 14 (1962), 35-40, which should be consulted for its criticism of alternative views.

the later argument turns.

What does Plato mean by 'doing something or having something done to one'? The sole illustration he proffers is that justice can be possessed by, or can become present to and again depart from, a soul (247a5-9). Of course there is no suggestion that this activity makes any difference to the nature of justice – it would be nonsense to suggest that the concept of justice is revised when that virtue enters, or comes to be exhibited by, Tom Jones. In fact the requirement to be met if X is to be said to do something to Y, or to have something done to it by Y, seems to come to no more than this: that there should be statements in which the name of X stands as subject to some active or passive verb, and the name of Y stands accordingly as object or in the instrumental case; and that these statements should be at some time (but not timelessly) true. The class of verbs is undefined but wide. In particular it contains various expressions for the varying relations between justice and the just Mr. Jones.

Now turn to the Gods, the 'friends of the Forms'. Never mind whether they are Plato himself or, as some other friends of the Forms would like us to believe, a misguided minority in the Academy. They propose two criteria of reality, criteria that are severally necessary and jointly sufficient. What 'really exists', they say, is (a) always unchanging and (b) accessible to, or known by, the mind alone (248a). The characteristics are familiar enough from Plato's other accounts of the Forms. And the Eleatic sets himself to show that these criteria are mutually incompatible. His argument falls into two stages, and the question to be decided is whether the first stage is the back-bone of the case or merely something to be discarded when he gets to the second.

(A) He fastens first on the second criterion and the relationship that it postulates between the mind and reality. Surely, to know the Forms is either
338 to do something to them or to have something done/ to oneself by them (248b2-8)? But suppose knowing is doing something; then for a Form to be known is for something to be done to it: and if something is done to it, it is changed. But if it is changed by being known, the criteria conflict (248d10-e4).

The argument sounds preposterous. It is absurd to suggest that if Tom Jones got his head clear on the nature of justice this morning, he was performing some occult operation on that virtue. And between the steps of the argument (248c1-d9) the Eleatic stranger allows that his opponents may well jib at this; they will probably refuse to say that knowing is any kind of *doing*. In face of this he moves on to a second stage in his attack.

(B) He turns his attention now to the first criterion, that of immutability. This is the criterion which had to be saved by saying that coming to know Y is not doing anything to Y. But the Eleatic argues that the cost of maintaining it is higher than its friends have realised. They will have to deny any reality to intelligence. For intelligence entails life, and life and intelligence are found in the soul; and it would be absurd to say that something with a living and intelligent soul is something that does not change. So, again, the criteria are in conflict (248e6-249b6).

Most readers of Plato, I suspect, feel some relief when they come to this second argument. They are very ready to believe that in producing (B) the Eleatic has quietly dropped (A). He is content now to point out that even for the Friends of the Forms there must be one sort of changing thing in existence, viz. an intelligence going about its business; but he is not any longer pressing that deplorable point that in some sense the exercise of the intelligence must entail a change in its object. And there are two reasons for thinking that we have seen the last of (A). One is the sheer prima facie absurdity of saying that coming to know anything changes it. The second is that in the next few lines the Eleatic insists all over again that the objects of intelligence must be unchanging (249b8-c8).

But on a closer inspection these reasons lose their force. Bear in mind that the sort of change in question here is that which is implied by the vague notion of doing something or having something done to one. This, as we saw, covered the case in which justice came to be possessed by, or came to be present in, some soul. We had to explain it quite generally in terms of the active and passive uses of a very wide range of verbs. Now in this sense it seems beyond/ question that to say that Jones came to understand justice on 339
his tenth birthday is to describe a case of doing something to something. But it does not in the least imply that the question 'What is justice?' acquires a different answer once Jones has the Idea in view, nor that all the other generalizations by which I communicate my understanding of justice suddenly become reports of a transient state of affairs. Nor does it imply that my knowledge of justice is deficient if I do not know that it captured Jones's attention at lunch yesterday. In this respect the old requirement is absolute: justice must be immutable if there is to be any thinking about it. This is the point of the Eleatic's warning.

Still you may cavil at the suggestion that in having something done to it in this mild sense justice undergoes some change. But you have the answer by you. For if Plato can claim, as he does in the *Timaeus*, that even to have a history is to change, then to say that justice captured the attention of Jones yesterday is to report a change in the Form. For on such an account it is a sufficient condition of change that something should become true of the subject at some time that was not true before – even, for example, that some virtue came to be possessed, or understood, or manifested, or whatever.

If this is so, two points seem to follow. One is a point of detail: namely that, for all the objectors can show to the contrary, the argument (B) can be, as a first reading of the text would suggest, simply a reinforcing argument to (A). It is designed to cut away the chief reason for rejecting the conclusions of (A), namely the wish to cling to the first criterion and represent reality as unchanging.[15] The second point is more important for our purpose. It is that Plato will have recognized an important qualification to the claim that any statement about justice or a prime number is a tenseless statement, and

[15] This is certified, against some traditional misreadings of the passage, by the general conclusion in *Sophist* 249d: 'reality is all things that are unchanged and changed' *not* 'all things that are unchanged and some, viz. souls, that change'.

recognized this as a corollary of his own theory. It does seem reasonable to say that, if 'the number 3 is a prime number' is a tenseless statement about a number, 'the number of congressmen now in gaol is 3' is a tensed statement
340 about that number. Both statements might appear in the records of/a Pythagorean trying to establish the power and importance of 3. So I think that, so far as it goes, the claim is true. And I do not relish the thought of leaving Plato at this point wholly under the spell of Parmenides.

3

Zeno and the Mathematicians

At some time in the first half of the fifth century BC, Zeno invented the set of paradoxes on which his successors have sharpened their wits. The puzzles have come down to us in various versions, more or less incomplete and more or less reflecting the special interests of later writers. What we have left of Zeno's best-known work comes, on the most hopeful view, to less than two hundred words. Still, this has not stopped Zeno's admirers from trying, with all due caution, to reconstruct the programme of all or some of his arguments. I want to make one such programme plausible and to show how, if I am right, this makes some solutions to the puzzles beside the point. **143**

My second interest in the paper is this. Zeno, it is commonly said, was and wished to be the benefactor of Greek mathematics. By his day the Pythagoreans had brought mathematics to a high level of sophistication. But the foundations of their system were a nest of confusions, and Zeno was out to expose these confusions. One beneficial result of his arguments (on this familiar account) was to compel mathematicians to distinguish arithmetic from geometry.

This picture seems to me mistaken. Zeno neither had nor tried to have this effect on mathematics (though in other ways, no doubt, he did influence contemporary work in the science). But his arguments had a great effect on a later stage of mathematics, and the effect was not beneficial./

Zeno's programme **144**

Zeno certainly held, as a philosophical theory inherited from Parmenides, that there is only one thing in existence. This is an embarrassment to those who want to portray him as trying to set up a consistent logic for analysing the structure of space and time. For it means that he thought there was no such structure: any way of dividing things in time or space must carry absurdities. If this was his theory we should expect him to work out an exhaustive list of possible ways of dividing things and to set about refuting all the possibilities separately; and this, as I shall try to show, is what he does.

(Let me say at once that this talk of dividing is deliberately ambiguous. It is not always clear, for instance, whether Zeno is discussing the possibility of

* [Postscript 1971: I have made small corrections to the text as printed in 1958, and marked later comments by square brackets in the notes.]

producing a plurality by actually carving a thing up or by enumerating the fractions it must logically contain; but for most of the way we shall find the distinction irrelevant.[1] What matters is that whichever operation Zeno has in mind he is canvassing its logical and not its physical possibility.)

Some hold that Zeno was not committed to any philosophical tenet whatever. For he is credited with saying 'Show me what the *one* is and then I can tell you what things (in the plural) are';[2] and this is sometimes taken to show that he did not profess to understand even the one thing that Parmenides had left in existence. But the point of his words is just that, if you want to say that there are a number of things in existence, you have to specify what sort of thing counts as a unit in the plurality.[3] If there can be no such individuals as you claim there can be no such plurality either. And in particular if your individuals have to be marked off by spatial and temporal distinctions you have to be sure that your way of making such distinctions is not logically absurd.

Plato makes it clear that Zeno's major work was divided into separate arguments, each depending on some hypothesis and reducing the hypothesis to absurdity. We do not know the content of these hypotheses, but Plato is emphatic that every argument was designed to refute the proposition that there are a number of things in existence.[4] We certainly have reports of some of the arguments which began 'Suppose many things exist.' But we also have
145 a report of one which starts 'Suppose place exists.'[5]/ And Aristotle treats the familiar puzzles of *Achilles*, the *Arrow*, the *Stadium* and the *Dichotomy* as though these were designed in the first instance to refute the possibility of movement, not of plurality. It might be, of course, that these latter arguments came from another work of Zeno's.[6] But I shall try to show that they play an essential part in the attack on plurality.

[1] It is not clear even that Zeno used the word *diairein* and its cognates; but Parmenides had, and Zeno certainly used equivalent language in discussing Parmenides' topic (see A(1) below).

[2] Eudemus apud Simpl. *in Phys.* 97. 12-13, 138. 32-3.

[3] Cf. Alexander apud Simpl. *in Phys.* 99. 12-16.

[4] *Parmenides* 128e-128a, a version which became standard with later commentators (e.g. Simplicius *in Phys.* 139. 5-7.

[5] [Or so Diels-Kranz (i 498. 8-10) infer from Aristotle, *Phys.* 210b23, and its repetition by Simplicius (562. 4). But it seems likely from Aristotle's first statement of the puzzle at 209a24-5 and Simplicius' note there (534. 9-11), as well as from Eudemus (apud Simpl. 563. 18-20; cf. Philop. 510. 2-4, 599. 1-3 *et al.*), that the hypothesis was 'If each existing thing is somewhere' (or perhaps 'in (*a*) place' or 'in something', but cf. Simpl. 534. 10, 563. 20-4). And then the connection with plurality is evident. On the ordinary assumptions of physical divisibility that we shall see Zeno exploiting, plurality calls for spatial distinctions. So the force of Zeno's puzzle may have been: if each thing must be marked off by being somewhere, in some place, then that place in turn is a thing to be marked off, *ex hypothesi*, by being in some place; and so *ad inf.* (That the argument was a regress is clear from Aristotle, 11. cc.) There is no basis from which to start in locating things that are spatially distinct, for locations are themselves such things.]

[6] Not that the evidence that he wrote other works is strong: Plato seems not to know of them, yet he certainly knew of the arguments on motion (cf. *Phaedrus* 261d and the application of the *Arrow* in *Parmenides* 152b-e). [Of the four titles credited to Zeno by the Suda (29 A 2 *DK*) three are readily assigned, as librarians' variants, to the book known to Plato. The fourth, 'Exegesis of Empedocles' Verses' (Diels' evidence that the title could signify a polemic dissolves on scrutiny),

Zeno's major question then is: if you say there are many things in existence how do you distinguish your individuals? The answer in which he is chiefly interested is that the world and any part of it can be broken down into its individual parts by spatial and temporal divisions. And the paradoxes that I am anxious to discuss are those designed to meet this answer, namely those which are jointly planned to show that no method of dividing anything into spatial or temporal parts can be described without absurdity.

For suppose we ask whether such a division could be (theoretically, at least) continued indefinitely: whether any division can be followed by a sub-division, and so on, through an infinite number of steps. Let us say, to begin with, (A) that it does have an infinite number of steps. Then could such a division nevertheless ever be (or ever have been) completed? (A 1) One of Zeno's arguments is designed to show that it could not.

The paradox had two arms. The first began by arguing that the units in a collection can have no size at all: else they would have parts and be not units but collections of units.[7] The second began by arguing that, on the contrary, there cannot be anything that has no size at all; for there cannot be a thing which if it were added to or subtracted from something else would not affect the size of that thing.[8] So the first arm of the argument assumes that the units it describes are theoretically indivisible; and the point of this requirement comes out in the sequel, when Zeno shows that he is discussing the class of individuals produced by an *exhaustive* division of something, a division whose end-products cannot themselves be further divided. The second arm of the argument assumes, on the other hand, that its units must be capable of being added and subtracted in a sense in which these operations cannot apply to things without magnitude; and the point of this requirement comes out in the same sequel, for if a thing can be divided into parts (exhaustively or not) those parts/ must be capable of being added to make the thing, and in that **146**
case they must have some size, however small.

Next, to bring these requirements into one focus, Zeno went on to specify the collection of parts in which he was interested, namely the collection produced by completing a division in which every step has a successor. 'Each thing', he said, 'must have some size and thickness, and one part of it must be

---

was quite probably transferred to Zeno of Elea from Zeno of Citium, perhaps through the tendency of the Stoics to call their founder 'the first Zeno' (Clem. *Strom.* v 9; there was a later Stoic Zeno, Diog. Laert, vii 35). Heraclitus and Empedocles were of almost equal importance for the Stoics: between Heraclides' four books on Heraclitus and Cleanthes' four on the same subject it is unlikely that the Stoic Zeno took no hand in the exegesis (cf. Diels, *Doxographi Graeci* (Berlin 1879), 469-70); and as for Empedocles, Chrysippus introduces some major arguments by an exegesis of his verses (Galen in *SVF* ii 237.22-5). The theory of the four elements was acknowledged to him (*Dox. Gr.* 92 b-93 b), and by Stoic *oikeiôsis* he was credited with a cosmology based on final conflagration (Hippolytus, *RH* i 3) and his sphere-god became a *noeron pur* comparable to the *phronimon pur* of Heraclitus (ibid. ix 10).]

[7] Simplicius, op. cit., 139. 18-19: this argument at the start of the paradox is still overlooked by English editors, although its text and sense were settled by Hermann Fraenkel in *AJP*, 1942, 14-17 (= *Wege und Formen frühgriechischen Denkens*[3] Munich 1968), 211-14.

[8] Simplicius, op. cit., 139. 9-15.

separate [or perhaps just 'distinct'] from another. And the same holds good of the part which is in the lead – that too will have some size, and of it too some part will be in the lead. In fact to say this once is as good as saying it for ever, for no such part of the thing will be the last or unrelated to a further part.'[9] These words define a division so that there can be no last move in the sequence: for any fraction that is taken, a similar fraction can be taken of the remainder (the 'part in the lead'). In this, certainly, there is no clear implication that such a division can have been completed. But Zeno does make that assumption in drawing his conclusions. For he points out that, on one line of argument (that of the first arm), the parts produced by this division can have no size at all: they are end-products whose further division is logically impossible. And he also points out that, on the other line of argument (that of the second arm), since all the parts of such a collection must have some size the whole collection (and by the same token any part of it) must be infinite in size. And both conclusions are absurd. They were presented as an antinomy; but as a dilemma they are equally lethal. Either the parts have no size, and then there can be no such parts; or they have some size, and then the thing you set out to divide becomes infinitely big.[10]

Notice that Zeno is not first setting up a division which cannot have a last move and then asking, improperly, what the last move would be.[11] He is asking, legitimately, what the total outcome of the division would be; and for there to be such an outcome there must be a smallest part or parts.

The effect of the argument is to show an absurdity in the alternative for which we opted first, namely that if anything is infinitely divisible such a division can be carried right through. So now (A 2) we shall say that anything is infinitely divisible but that such divisions can never be completed. Then, supposing that the puzzle about Achilles and the tortoise[12] is a puzzle
147 about infinite divisibility, it is designed to block this escape-route. In/ order to overtake the tortoise Achilles must first reach the tortoise's starting-point; but by then the tortoise will have reached some further point. So then Achilles

[9] Simplicius, op. cit., 141. 1-6. A commoner but linguistically less easy version of the words runs 'Each thing must have some size and thickness and there must be another thing separate from it. And the same holds good of the thing in front: it too will have some size and there will be something in front of it ...' Taken in this way the words do not define the steps in the division but merely characterize its products by saying that the series has no last member. And there is no mention of parts (more exactly, none of the Greek genitives is understood as partitive) before the last line. Otherwise, for our purposes both versions come to the same.

[10] [That Zeno is here assuming, *per impossible*, that the division is *completed* is common doctrine to the Greek commentators: cf. Porphyry apud Simpl. *in Phys.* 139. 26-40. 6 (Simplicius rightly corrects Porphyry's slip and follows Alexander in assigning the argument to Zeno, 140. 21-6). Porphyry's account of the argument, and particularly the explanation in 140. 1-5, notoriously echoes Aristotle's discussion in *GC* 316a14-34 (see D.J. Furley, *Two Studies in the Greek Atomists* (Princeton 1967), 84-5), and in particular his *diêirêsthô pantêi* (140. 2) recalls Aristotle, 316a23-4; but without begging the question this cannot be argued to show that the gist of the argument was the invention of Aristotle and not, as the commentators claim (and as I have tried to argue from the texts they report), of the Eleatics. It is not relevant to criticize Zeno's arguments without noticing this assumption.]

[11] Cf. J.F. Thomson, 'Tasks and Super-tasks', *Analysis* 15 (1954-5), 6-7.

[12] Aristotle, *Physics* 239b14-29.

must reach this point, by which time the tortoise will have got on to another, and so forth: the series comes to no end. The moves which Achilles is required to make correspond to divisions of the intervening country, and the divisions are infinite, determined by the same general formula as in A 1. But on our present assumption Achilles cannot complete any such sequence of moves; so he cannot overtake the tortoise, whatever their relative speeds and however short the lead.

Now if I am right about the coupling of Zeno's arguments[13] it is beside the point to maintain, as a general solution of this puzzle, that an infinite division can be completed. For if we say this Zeno will take us back to A 1 and ask us about the character of the ultimate parts produced by the division. To make this clear, consider Aristotle's first solution to the puzzle – a solution which he later admits to be unsatisfactory but which he nevertheless thinks to be adequate *ad hominem*.[14] He replies that, provided we recognize that the time of the run can be divided in just the same way as the ground, Achilles can overtake the tortoise in a finite time; for the smaller his moves become the less time he needs to accomplish them, and these component times can diminish without limit. Then suppose we tell Achilles to mark in some way the end of each stage of the course in which he arrives at a point reached by the tortoise in the previous stage. Suppose also we satisfy Aristotle's requirement and allow these successive markings to follow each other at a speed which increases indefinitely, in inverse ratio to the ground covered at each stage; and suppose the marks become proportionately thinner and thinner. Then Zeno, as I understand him, argues that if Achilles claims to have finished his task we can ask about the positions of these marks, and in particular of the last two. If they are in the same place there is no stage determined by them, and if there is any distance between them, however small, this distance is the smallest stage in an infinite set of diminishing stages and therefore the course is infinitely long and not just infinitely divisible.

Two things, I take it, we must give Zeno: first, that of the series of movements that Achilles is supposed to make there can be no last member, just as of the stages of the division described/ in A 1 there can be no last **148**
stage; and second, that if either series can be completed it must be possible to describe the resulting state of affairs without absurdity. From these admissions Zeno infers that Achilles can never finish the run that brings him level with the tortoise. Any hope of salvation lies in looking at this inference.

Consider that other series of moves to which Professor Black once likened Achilles' run.[15] Hercules is required to cut off the Hydra's heads, but every time he cuts off a head another grows in its place. When can he finish the assignment? Never, if the task was correctly specified. For if some heads are left on Hercules has more work to do, and if all are off it was not the case that

[13] Notice the *proechein* which may have been common to both puzzles: Simplicius op. cit., 141. 4; Aristotle, op. cit., 239b17.

[14] op. cit., 233a21-31, 263a15-18: the solution is applied first to the *Dichotomy*, discussed below, but Aristotle took this to be the same puzzle as the *Achilles*.

[15] M. Black, 'Achilles and the Tortoise', *Analysis* 11(1950-51), 98 (= *Problems of Analysis* (Ithaca 1954), 105).

for every head cut off another head grows. But these are exhaustive alternatives, so there is *no* subsequent state of affairs of which it is logically possible to say truly: Hercules has finished his task. Now (as Mr Watling has already argued)[16] this is not the case with Achilles. There are plenty of states of affairs compatible with Achilles' having achieved his task of overtaking the tortoise: plenty of positions beside or beyond the tortoise that Achilles can have reached. It is just the case here that Achilles' movements have been so described that they have no last term, but not so that no subsequent state of affairs is compatible with his having completed the series. But to require anyone to finish an infinite division, as in A 1, is to start them on a Hydra-operation: there can be no state of affairs, no collection of bits, of which it is possible to say: Now the job is done. For either the bits do or they do not have some size, and that exhausts the subsequent possibilities. On this Zeno was right. His error was to construe his A 2 example on the model of A 1.

In a later paper[17] Black admits this difference in the sense in which Hercules and Achilles can be said to have taken on an infinite set of tasks. But he still holds that in either case 'talk of an infinite series of acts performed in a finite time is illegitimate'. For he now says that the description of Achilles' movements belongs to 'common-sense language' which, in contrast to the mathematical representation of space and time, 'does not permit talk of the indefinitely small' – that is, does not have a use for describing Achilles' movements as becoming as short as you like. But a guillotine is not an argument. If someone says, 'In making any movement you make an infinite
149 series of decreasing/ movements', we have no reason yet to reject this as an offence to common usage. It already looks like a recognizable application of mathematical language to the description of familiar events (we recall the graphic problems in school arithmetic): what it needs at once is clarification. We can ask 'What do you mean here by "infinite series"? Do you say that in walking from *a* to *d* I make a set of smaller walks of which the first takes me beyond *a* and the last brings me level with *d*? For then I cannot see how you define this sequence so as to let me draw on my knowledge of other uses of "infinite".' Suppose then he gives us a formula, as in A 1 or A 2, for defining the class of movements so that there can be no last move in the sequence bringing me level with *d*. Then we know how he is using the redescription of our movements that he has introduced. He has not uncovered an unsuspected set of events in our daily histories and he has not burdened us or Achilles with a new and crippling set of duties: the connection between our usual descriptions of Achilles' run and this sort of restatement is not in either of these ways a factual connection. What we have been given is a translation of those usual descriptions; where the second can be known, directly, to apply, the first can be known, derivatively, to apply. So no consequential question can arise about the applicability of the second. If we are told that the equation shows why Achilles never can catch the tortoise, we can only complain that

[16] J. Watling, 'The Sum of an Infinite Series', *Analysis* 13(1952-3), 41-2
[17] 'Is Achilles still running?' *Problems of Analysis*, 109-26.

the proffered rules of translation have broken down and go back to our request for clarification. Any attempt at this stage to reconstrue the expression 'series of moves with no last members' as specifying a Hydra-operation, an infinite parcelling of the ground such that no state of affairs is compatible with its completion, cancels the equation with our description of Achilles' run. And in this way 'common-sense language' is safeguarded; for it is the oscillation between bringing in the infinite series as a logically innocuous translation of ordinary statements and trying to reconstrue it on the model of the task in A 1 that breeds the puzzle.[18]

A closely associated paradox is the *Dichotomy*.[19] Before reaching your destination you must reach halfway, but before reaching that you must reach halfway to it; and so back. So in this series there is no first move, and you cannot get started. (It can of course also be made to show that there is no last move; Aristotle seems to take it so. But this was taken care of by the
Achilles.)/ Here again if you insist that there is a first move you are taken back 150
to A 1: either this move is no move, or it covers some distance, however small. The solution here is the same as for the *Achilles*. But Aristotle says that in face of this puzzle some theorists (certainly Xenocrates and apparently at one time Plato) postulated atomic distances, 'indivisible lines'.[20] That is, they challenged Zeno's disjunction 'Either no size at all; or some size, and then divisible' by adding 'Or some size, but *not* divisible.' Then the first or last move towards one's destination would be to cover such an atomic distance; for one could not logically be required to cover any fraction of it first. It is not certain whether the proponents of this theory thought that any measurable distance contained a finite or an infinite number of such distances. An argument for thinking that they meant the former is that this is assumed in the fourth-century polemic *On Indivisible Lines*. An argument for thinking the contrary is that the theory was held at a time when the difficulties of incommensurable lines were fully realized. It was a commonplace that the side and diagonal of a square cannot both be *finite* multiples of any unit of length whatever. If the latter account is true, those who introduced this theory were suggesting that an infinite division can have a last term: the products of such a division are not completely without magnitude, yet they

[18] ['Redescription', 'restatement', 'translation' and 'equation' are in fact all terms stronger than my argument needed. All that is required is that 'moving from A to B' should be represented as innocuously *entailing* 'moving to the halfway point between A and B, and the halfway point of the remainder, and thereafter every such halfway point in this infinite series' (or, in the case of the *Achilles*, a more sophisticated variant of this in which the position of the points is determined by the tortoise's initial lead and speed). The converse entailment is not needed for my purposes; and Benacerraf challenged it effectively ('Tasks, super-tasks and the modern Eleatics', *Journal of Philosophy* 59(1962), 765 ff.) by inventing a genie who set out to go from A to B but was afflicted with Proportional Dwindling. Only a half of the genie was left when he reached halfway, only a quarter when he was a quarter-way from home, and so on. There would be some of him to reach *every* halfway point in the infinite series yet none to arrive at B. Perhaps, in Professor Wiggins' words, 'if it takes a magical example to prove a conclusion this is significant in itself'; but it need not be pursued here.]

[19] Aristotle, *Physics* VI 239b11-14 (cf. 233a21-3).

[20] *Physics* I 187a1-3.

have no finite magnitude such that fractions of it can be specified. They would be, in fact, to all present intents and purposes, infinitesimals, vanishingly small quantities; and movement over such a distance is what writers on mechanics such as Heinrich Hertz have called *infinitely small* or *minimum displacements*. But whichever interpretation of the theory we give, it was an attempt to evade Zeno's dilemma in A 1.

Now it looks as though this attempt is met in advance by another of Zeno's arguments, that known as the *Stadium*.[21] On the prevalent interpretation of the argument this is certainly so; and I wish I could be sure of the truth of the interpretation. But it is fair to warn you that, if the moral of the argument is anything like that now found in it, the Greeks seem to have missed the point by a wide margin. Plato, who converted many of Zeno's arguments to his own use, made no use of this one and apparently saw no objection to postulating infinitesimals. Aristotle rejected infinitesimals, but he missed the sense of an argument that Plato had missed before him./

151 The puzzle sets up three parallel rows of bodies. All the bodies are equal in size; each row contains an equal number of them; and (a stipulation omitted in Aristotle's report) the bodies in each row are directly adjacent. One row (the *A*s) is stationary. The other two (*B*s and *C*s) meet at the mid-point of the *A*s and move on past each other at equal speeds, so that when the first *B* clears the last *A* in one direction the first *C*, moving in the opposite direction, clears the last *A* at the other end. Thus in the time that the first *B* passes half the *A*s, from mid-point to end, it passes all the *C*s. Let this time be t. But then if the first *B* takes t to pass n bodies (to wit, half the *A*s) it must take not t but $2t$ to pass $2n$ bodies (*viz.* all the *C*s). So the move which takes t also takes $2t$; this is the alleged puzzle, and plainly it depends on disregarding the relative motions of the bodies. The *C*s are moving, the *A*s are not. That is Aristotle's sole comment on the argument, and it is generally felt that if it is refuted by such a comment it was not worth the considerable space he gave it.

Suppose now that Zeno asks how we can specify the relative motions of the bodies. If we say that the first *B* can pass twice as many *C*s as *A*s in a given time, what we say entails that if in a given time it passes one *C* it also passes half an *A*. But suppose now that any *A* (and therefore any *B* or *C*) is an *infinitesimal* quantity. Then the *B* cannot pass half an *A*: it must pass all or nothing. And since *ex hypothesi* it *is* moving past the *A*s it must pass a whole *A* in the time that it passes one *C*. Yet, as we set up the problem, it would pass twice as many *C*s as *A*s in a given time. So when it passes one *C* it also passes two *C*s, and this gives Zeno his contradiction. It seems the simplest hypothesis that gives the problem any weight whatever.[22]

There is a familiar argument to show that, if lengths are made up of

[21] Aristotle, *Physics* VI 239b33-240a18.

[22] But it is possible that Zeno was out to explode the distinction between *moving* and *static*. Given that the distinction is relative, any one of the rows of bodies could be taken as providing the units of distance for assessing the speeds of the others. Trading on the fact that no row had prime right to this status, Zeno gave it to two of the rows in the same argument. [D.J. Furley propounds a very acceptable version of the paradox (*Two Studies*, 75); it seems to me however to yield a moral about indivisibility of a kind that he would like to avoid.]

infinitesimal lengths, everything that moves must move at the same speed.[23] Zeno goes one better than this. He argues (on the present interpretation at least) that, if bodies are made up of infinitesimal lengths, then even if bodies do move at the same speed they cannot move in opposite directions.

This argument, then, seems designed to destroy the last hope that the sort of division described in A 1 could theoretically by terminated, in the sense of producing any specifiable end-products. And the *Achilles* and the *Dichotomy* were devised to eliminate the alternative, that the world or any part of it was open to an in-/finite division that did not terminate in any end-product. The **152**
next question is whether Zeno faced the alternative (B) that any division terminates in some finite number of steps beyond which no further step is even logically possible.

Against one arm of this option he did not, as far as we know, think it worth arguing, namely the joint assertion that (*a*) anything is divisible for only a finite number of steps and (*b*) the products of such a division will have some finite size. For this could only be a thesis about physical possibilities: Zeno assumes without argument in A 1 that the conjunction of size with theoretical indivisibility would be a contradiction. Suppose, on the other hand, that the products of such a division are said to have no size: then the argument of A 1 that all parts must have some magnitude goes home against this thesis too. And suppose it is said that the products are vanishingly small, then the *Stadium* argument is equally effective here. For neither of these arguments requires that the end-products with which it deals should be produced by an infinite rather than a finite number of divisions.

However, I think that another of Zeno's arguments may be levelled directly against option B.[24] This is the argument that a collection containing a finite number of parts must also contain an infinite number of them. It must contain just the number that it does, whatever that number is; but between any two members there must be another member, so that the collection is infinitely numerous. The writer who reports this argument takes it to be concerned once again with the results of an infinite division.[25] But it can be understood more generally, as a foretaste of Bradley's paradox. Any two members of a collection must be separated by something if they are to be two things and not one; but by the same argument what separates them must itself be separated from each by something else; and so forth. I suspect that this is the correct interpretation because the argument then becomes complementary to one of Parmenides'. Parmenides had urged that if two things are separated it must be a gap, nothing; but this is to mistreat nothing as a substantial part of the world.[26] Zeno reinforces this by extracting a different embarrassment from the plea that things are separated not by nothing but by other intervening things, substantial parts of the world. And his argument begins from the consideration of a finite collection; so it may

[23] Cf. Russell, *Principles of Mathematics*[2] (New York 1943), 322.

[24] Simplicius, op. cit., 140. 28-33.

[25] ibid. 140. 34-5: Simplicius on his own authority?

[26] Diels-Kranz, *Vorsokratiker*[6] 28 B 8: 22, 46.

153 well/ be aimed at any who thought that there must be some finite number *n* such that the world could be divided into *n* things but not – logically not – into any number higher than *n*.

Certainly, this argument seems patently fallacious. For surely things may be separated by their common boundaries – by their edges, and nothing else. And it is absurd to ask what separates them from their edges, absurd for the reason that Plato and Aristotle drove home, that the edge of a thing is not another thing of the same type as what it borders, not a part that can be cut off its possessor. The moment that begins a stretch of time or the point that bounds a line is not any stretch, however small, of time or space. Otherwise it in turn has a beginning, and then Zeno's regress is afoot. And Zeno is accused of ignoring this distinction.

If that is so we can turn to the argument through which, if through any, Zeno exercised a major influence on the mathematics of science. For it is in this argument above all that he is accused of confusing edges with the things they border, or more precisely of confusing instants, which are the limits of time-stretches, with time-stretches. But it seems equally likely that he is now characteristically trying to seal off an escape-route from the last argument by showing how absurdities came from the attempt to *distinguish* moments from periods of time. This remaining puzzle is that known as the *Flying Arrow*. But before discussing it let me bring the mathematicians into the picture.

The mathematicians

Most handbooks written since the time of Paul Tannery will tell you the purpose of the arguments we have examined so far. By Zeno's day Greek mathematics, in the hands of the Pythagoreans, had come to exhibit the familiar picture of a sophisticated superstructure built on badly confused foundations. In his arguments on divisibility Zeno was out to expose these radical confusions, and he succeeded.

Following some other writers I am inclined to think this explanation a myth, and an obstructive myth. For first, the picture of Pythagorean mathematics, to the extent that it is intelligible, rests on quite inadequate evidence. And secondly (and for the present paper more relevantly), if there
154 were such a stage in the/ history of mathematics, Zeno's arguments would not be directed primarily at it.

Briefly, the theory ascribed to Zeno's contemporaries is this. It is mainly the work of Paul Tannery, but later writers have added to it. Cornford, one of the most important of these, credits the Pythagoreans with failing to distinguish physical bodies from geometrical solids, and with holding about these solids *both* that they are infinitely divisible *and* that they are divisible into atomic bits, which bits *both* have magnitude *and* have the properties of points without magnitude.[27] Indeed they seem to have held every possible

[27] P. Tannery, *Pour l'histoire de la science hellène* (Paris 1877), ch. 10; F.M. Cornford, *Plato and Parmenides* (London, 1939), 58-9, and papers in *CQ*, 1922-3.

opinion about the divisibility of bodies save the opinion that bodies are not divisible. Certainly, Zeno was anxious to find confusions in the claim that bodies are divisible at all. But to ensure that he was writing with a special target in view the target has been enlarged to the point where a shot in any direction will hit it.

This is not the place to hold an autopsy on the evidence for this theory. Much of the work has been done in print,[28] and what needs to be added can be deferred. What is to our purpose is that Zeno's arguments cannot have been directed against such a theory unless his whole programme was misconceived. For in order to provide his arguments with a target a theory had to be produced which houses every or nearly every incompatible view on the divisibility of bodies. But the direct refutation of such a theory would be to show the absurdity of holding any two or more of these views concurrently. What Zeno does is to distinguish each view and refute it in isolation. Thus he deals separately with absurdities arising from the addition of magnitudes (in A 1), although for Tannery the basic confusion in Pythagoreanism was the confusion between numbers and magnitudes. And he wrings separate embarrassments from the option that the ultimate parts of things have no magnitude and the alternative option that they have some magnitude, and again from the possibilities that a continuous dichotomy can and cannot be completed. In brief, his arguments seem designed to close not some but all avenues of escape to anyone holding the unremarkable belief that there is more than one thing in existence. To suppose that he is merely attacking the possibility of taking more than one of these avenues at once is to wreck the structure of his/ arguments and to neglect such evidence, internal and **155**
external, as we have of their motivation.

Now let me reset the scene by reminding you of some real teething-troubles that had overtaken mathematics by the time of Plato and Aristotle. The early Pythagoreans had certainly worked on the assumption that any two lengths can be represented as related to each other by a ratio of whole numbers. Any geometrical theorem could be applied in terms of the theory of numerical proportion that they had developed on this basis. But before Plato's day this assumption had run up against the discovery that lines could be constructed which bore no such proportion to each other. No matter what positive integer is assigned to the side of a square, no corresponding integer can be found to represent its diagonal.[29]

Some text-books would let you suppose that this discovery compelled mathematicians to jettison the old theory of proportion. But several reactions to it were possible. One was to retain the theory but restrict its scope: and this is just what Euclid does with it in the seventh Book of his *Elements*. One was to retain it *and* apply it to the sides and diagonals of squares by an accommodation that could be made as small as you please.[30] And one was

[28] In particular by Calogero and Heidel, van der Waerden, Fraenkel and Vlastos.

[29] Cf. Euclid, *Elements* X app. xxvii (Heiberg).

[30] An ingenious but infertile device. A rule was devised for constructing a series of fractions approaching as close as you please to the ratio between side and diagonal: the lines were

the reaction of Eudoxus: to remodel the theory radically by allowing the concepts of *addition* and *greater* and *less* to range over rationals and irrationals alike.

This is enough to certify that the discovery of incommensurables was a real crisis in mathematics, and to introduce another type of reaction to it. Some mathematicians gave up the model of a line as a multiple of unit parts, a model which made sense only on the old theory of proportion. They said instead, as Newton said later,[31] that a line should be considered as generated not by the summation of parts but by the fluxion or motion of a point: the extended line is the path of a moving thing without extension. This is said to be a relatively late reaction,[32] but it is already under attack in Plato's *Parmenides* and Aristotle's *Physics*; and this attack ushered in the period of Zeno's most powerful influence on mathematics. So far, it is plain, Zeno has made no appearance in the crisis. Some writers, hoping to find for him a directly influential role in the mathematics of his day, have suggested that the new picture of a line as the path of a moving point was a response not to the
156 discovery of incommensurable/ lines but to the arguments of Zeno; but this seems incredible. No one who had been vexed by those paradoxes can have hoped to evade them by introducing the idea of motion. In fact it is by an adaptation of some of Zeno's arguments that Plato rejects the new picture of a line; but Zeno himself had probably not talked of points and lines, and the later and precise concept of a point as something with location but without magnitude seems to have been produced to meet a difficulty that had little or nothing to do with his work.

When Plato turns to attack this account of a point in the *Parmenides*, he argues that a thing without parts cannot have a location.[33] For to have a location is to have surroundings, and this is to be in contact with something on various sides at various points: but a thing without parts cannot have different sides or points. This equation of location with surroundings is standard with the Greeks: Zeno had built one paradox on it,[34] and Aristotle was to give his own sophisticated version of it in the fourth Book of the *Physics*. Until it was replaced by the method of fixing location by co-ordinates, the formal objection to allowing a point location went unanswered. Aristotle inherited it,[35] as he inherited the corollary argument that a point cannot be said to move.[36] Moreover when Plato goes on to define the conditions under

---

described by a series of paired numbers such that always the square on the diagonal equalled twice the square on the side plus or minus one, and the approximate sides and diagonals defined by this construction were called the 'rational' sides and diagonals (Theon of Smyrna, 42. 10-44. 17 (Hiller), cf. Plato, *Rep.* 546c and Proclus' Commentary, ii. 27 (Kroll)).

[31] *Quadr. Curv.* (1704), intro. § 27.

[32] Sextus Empiricus, *adv. math.* X 281-2. The concept of a line that was superseded by the fluxion-model is probably not the innocuous one compared with it by Sextus (279-80) and Proclus (in Eucl. i 97-8).

[33] *Parm.* 138 a: part of the attack described by Aristotle in *Metaphysics* 992a 20-2.

[34] Diels-Kranz, op. cit., 229 B 5.

[35] *Physics* 212b24-5.

[36] *Parm.* 138c-d; *Phys.* 240b8-241a6.

which anything *can* be in contact with different things and, in particular, can be a member of a linear series of such things, he provides both the pattern and the terminology for Aristotle's own treatment of points and lines in the *Physics*.[37] Aristotle's insistence that a line can be composed only of smaller, indefinitely divisible lines and not of points without magnitude rests on Plato's treatment of the point as a thing that cannot have sides or neighbours; and it is more than likely that Plato's argument derives from Zeno's warning that the parts of anything must have some magnitude, however small.

Now it is this same distinction between lines and points that Aristotle turns against Zeno's remaining puzzle, the *Flying Arrow*; and his mishandling of both the distinction and the puzzle is the last topic I want to discuss./

The arrow **157**

Zeno's last paradox concerning motion is given by Aristotle in a form which, despite the depravity of the text, can be articulated as follows: Anything which occupies a space just as its own size is stationary. But in each moment of its flight an arrow can only occupy a space just its own size. Hence at each moment of its flight the arrow is not moving but stationary. But what is true of the arrow at each moment of a period is true of it throughout the period. Hence during the whole time of its flight the arrow is not moving but stationary.[38]

Aristotle says that the fallacy lies in assuming that any stretch of time is a collection of moments, a mistake parallel to thinking that any line is a collection of points. Now in a sense his diagnosis is right; but not in the sense that he gave to it. Before we come to this, however, one small point needs to be made. Aristotle is often represented as accusing Zeno of thinking that any time-stretch consists of a *finite* collection of moments. But we shall see that Zeno does not need this premiss (nor its denial, either). And as for Aristotle, he was equally anxious to deny that a period could be composed either of a finite or of an infinite number of moments. Define moments as having no magnitude, and Aristotle has learnt from Zeno to argue that no magnitude can be in either of these ways a sum of such parts.

Let us clear some issues by an imaginary conversation.

Aristotle: You claim that (*a*) in each moment of its flight the arrow must be stationary, since evidently it has no time to move; but (*b*) what is true of it at

[37] Terminology: *contact* (*haptesthai*), *in succession* (*ephexês*), *neighbouring* (*echesthai*), *Parm.* 148e and *Phys.* 226b18 ff. Plato defines the first by means of the other two, Aristotle defines the last by the first two.

[38] Aristotle, *Physics* 239b5-9; 30-31: on the text cf. H.D.P. Lee, *Zeno of Elea* (Cambridge 1936), 78-81. [The use of the term 'now' to mark the durationless instant, a term on which Aristotle's discussion of the *Arrow* so much relies, may not have been Zeno's. Perhaps the word is being groomed for this role in Plato's *Parmenides* 152b 2-e3; perhaps on the other hand Parmenides B 8. 5 suggested its exploitation to Zeno. But even if Zeno cast his premisses in terms of *hopotan* and *aei*, Aristotle can hardly be wrong in treating the puzzle as resolving a period of time into constituents which (so to speak) leave no room for movement.]

each *moment* is true of it throughout the whole *period*. Hence your conclusion. But you agree that moments have no magnitude (that, of course, is why the arrow cannot move in one). Consequently they cannot be added together to make a period of time, which does have a magnitude.

Zeno: You seem to be attacking my premiss (*b*). I grant what you say: indeed my argument depends on stressing this characteristic of points and moments. (You remember that I was accused of overlooking it last time). But the argument does not require that the moments should be added together. I merely assumed that if something was true at any and every moment of a period it was true throughout a period. It is ordinary sense and not bad logic
158 to say that if at any moment this afternoon I was asleep –/ at 4:30 as well as 2, and at any such precise time you care to take – then I was asleep throughout the afternoon.

Aristotle: But you cannot describe periods *exhaustively* in this way, in terms of moments. However many moments you can mention you are still only specifying the limits of the periods that separate them, and at any stage of the division you like it is these periods that make up the overall period. You can never have two neighbouring moments. So if it is correct to infer from the fact that at any time this afternoon I was asleep, to the fact that I was asleep all afternoon this can only be because 'at any time' means 'at all periods, however small'. And 'at 4:30' can only mean, in this context, 'at some period however small round 4:30'. Don't misunderstand me: I am not suggesting that such time-references as '4:30' are really specifications of periods of time: if they were, we should have to invent a new set of time-references to say when such periods began and ended; and it is absurd to ask how long 4:30 lasts. I am only suggesting that *here* what parades as a time-reference must be a shorthand specification for some small period of time.

Zeno: In as far as this argument differs from your first, it is trifling. To specify moments is surely enough to specify the limits of periods. But to say that therefore any formula phrased in terms of moments is indirectly about periods of time merely invites the converse reply: for to identify a period is to describe the moments that define it.

Aristotle: Nevertheless you do talk about moments in a way that is only appropriate to periods. You say, for instance, that the arrow is stationary at every moment of its flight. But in the section of my *Peri Kinêseôs* which introduces an attack on your paradoxes[39] I show that if there is no time in a moment for the arrow to move there is no time for it to be stationary either. Movement involves having different positions at different moments, and accordingly rest involves having the same position at different moments. But we are considering only one moment, so neither of these ideas applies. In making either of them apply you treat the single moment as a period of time itself containing different moments.

Zeno: Now, in effect, you are turning your attack to my premiss (*a*). But if it is true that at any moment of its flight the arrow is neither moving nor at rest

[39] *Physics* VI 239a23-239b4.

then, by my second premiss, the/ arrow is throughout its flight neither moving nor at rest. And as a paradox that will do – unless you can find some independent argument against my second premiss. Of course, if that premiss also depended on treating moments as small periods, the argument would collapse. But you have not shown this so far. **159**

Aristotle: It might be shown like this. Consider a spatial analogy to your argument about time. If a surface is uniformly red all over it is red in every part of it, however small the part. But it is not red or any other colour at every point, if by 'point' you mean something without extension. In the ordinary sense of 'red' we have no use for calling something without extension red. If we had such a use it must be because 'red' was used here in an unfamiliar sense. Likewise, even if it were legitimate to infer from 'The arrow was moving (or at rest, or neither) throughout the period', this could only show that the expression 'moving' (or the expression 'at rest', or both) was being used ambiguously between the two cases. Your second premiss, if it is true, rests on a pun; but if it rests on a pun the conclusion you want will not follow.

Zeno (by now a prey to sharp anachronism): This is surely wrong. For suppose a body is constantly increasing its speed: this state of affairs is naturally explained by saying that *at any moment* it moves at a speed greater than at any previous moment since its motion began. And here notice that the verb 'to move' is associated with the common expressions for velocity and that it can be paraphrased by the common equivalents, 'to change position' and so forth. So it is false that, if 'motion at an instant' had any use, 'motion' would have a different sense here from that which it usually carries.

Arbiter: You are both right and both wrong. Consider again the expressions 'X was moving at some moment *t*', 'X was moving throughout the period *p*'. Aristotle denied that the expression 'X was moving' had the same sense in both contexts. And in face of Zeno's reply we can add that any expansion of the expression, such as 'X was moving at velocity V', could not have the same sense in both. For consider how the methods of confirmation differ. Velocity is distance measured against time. The simple question, With what velocity did X traverse *d* in the period *p*? gets the simple answer, *d*/*p*. But the question, With what/ velocity was X moving at a time *t* inside the period? is complex. It **160**
calls for the concept of a limit – the possibility of measuring an indefinitely long series of distances against a corresponding series of times. It can be answered, for instance, by constructing a graph whose curve is indefinitely corrigible by further pairs of measurements. To be sure, once we have this graph we can replace our simple questions about speed over a period with a more sophisticated one. For whereas our first question merely demanded the overall speed (not the *average* speed: this is again complex), we can ask now whether X's speed over the period was constant. And this involves a different use of the graph. To say that X moved with a constant speed during the period is to say something doubly general, when to ascribe it that speed at one moment is to say something singly general: for now we ascribe it a speed at each moment in the period. But the possibility of operating on either of these levels of generality depends on being able to answer questions of our first, simple form, and the converse is not true. And thus Zeno's rejoinder fails. For

since in this way the possibility of talking about motion at a moment rests on the possibility of talking of motion over a period, the two uses of 'motion' are not the same. Likewise we could if we wished give a use to the expression 'colour at a point' by building on our ways of describing a colour over a space, but we could not begin the other way round without a radical change in the use of colour-words. But in another way Zeno was right. For to say that these are not the same use is not at all to say that Zeno's second premiss depends on a pun. The premiss is valid, and it is valid precisely because it is the sort of rule whereby we do give a use to such an expression as 'moving at a moment'. We rule that, when and only when it is correct to say 'X was moving throughout the period *p*', it is also correct to say 'X was moving at any moment *t* in *p*'. Aristotle's fallacy lay in supposing that to infer from the second formula to the first, one must regard the second as specifying a conjunction of moments exactly as long as the period specified in the first. He was in fact applying a simple model of induction, that model which set a premium on the exhaustive enumeration of cases and which Aristotle took to require strict synonymy between different occurrences of the predicate ('X-moving', for instance, in the inference from 'Each moment in *p* is a case of X-moving' to '*p* is a case of
161 X-moving'). And thus he failed to grasp that the two/ senses of 'moving' are not identical but yet systematically connected; and his failure to see this connection between the common uses of a common word led him to rule out one use entirely in favour of the other. His reply to Zeno rejects all uses of 'movement' other than that which can be described in terms of periods of time, just as the colour-model we considered exhibited all uses of 'red' as applicable to colour-stretches. And this is an unjustified departure from usage: it deprives us of a convenient method of characterizing motion which is common idiom for us and for the Greeks.

Now (and here we can drop the pretence of dialogue) if this is so Zeno's fallacy cannot lie in his second premiss. Therefore it lies in premiss (*a*), and in particular in the proposition 'There is no time to move in a moment' (with or without Aristotle's rider: 'and no time to rest either'). The picture we are given is of the arrow bottled up in a piece of time that fits it too closely to allow any movement. The moment is too short to fly in. But such talk of movement is appropriate only when we have in mind periods of time within which movements could be achieved. It is not false that movements can be achieved *within* moments: it is absurd either to say or to deny this, for moments are not pieces of time such that within them any process can either take place or lack the time to take place. But this certainly does not show that the arrow is not moving *at* any moment. It is, of course: we have seen the sense in which it is. Whether it is, is a question of fact and not of logic.

So, despite his contrast between moments and periods of time, Zeno was treating moments as stiflingly small periods. To that extent Aristotle was right in his diagnosis. But he did not apply the diagnosis where it was needed. His denial that there can be any talk of motion except in direct connection with periods of time is a surrender to Zeno; and his failure to come to grips with premiss (*a*) compels him to struggle against the wholly respectable premiss (*b*).

This surrender to Zeno had notable results in the history of dynamics. Notoriously, Aristotelian dynamics failed to deal adequately with acceleration; and it might be thought from what has been said that the failure lay in insisting that acceleration (a phenomenon which Aristotle certainly took seriously) must be analysed in terms of motion and speeds over periods of time, and/not in the more manageable shorthand of velocity at an **162**
instant. But this is not the root-issue. Unable to talk of speed at an instant, Aristotle has no room in his system for any such concept as that of initial velocity, or what is equally important, of the force required to start a body moving. Since he cannot recognize a moment in which the body first moves, his idea of force is restricted to the causing of motions that are completed in a given period of time. And, since he cannot consider any motion as caused by an initial application of force, he does not entertain the Newtonian corollary of this, that if some force F is sufficient to start a motion the continued application of F must produce not just the continuance of the motion but a constant change in it, namely acceleration.[40] It is the clumsy tools of Aristotelian dynamics, if I am right, that mark Zeno's major influence on the mathematics of science.

[40] He would have had another reason for rejecting Newton's account of acceleration, for that account holds good only in a vacuum, and Aristotle thought a vacuum impossible. But some of his followers re-imported the vacuum without abandoning the rest of the system.

II

PLATO

4

The Place of the Timaeus in Plato's Dialogues

It is now nearly axiomatic among Platonic scholars that the *Timaeus* and its unfinished sequel the *Critias* belong to the last stage of Plato's writings. The *Laws* (including, for those who admit its claims, the *Epinomis*) is generally held to be wholly or partly a later production. So, by many, is the *Philebus*, but that is all. Perhaps the privileged status of the *Timaeus* in the Middle Ages helped to fix the conviction that it embodies Plato's maturest theories. 79

I want to undermine that conviction by questioning the grounds on which it is commonly based and by sharpening the paradoxes it imports into the interpretation of Plato. No one familiar with Platonic scholarship will claim that these paradoxes could not be explained away, given enough ingenuity. But I think that, once they are seen in aggregate, the cost in such ingenuity should seem quite exorbitant.

This discussion is preliminary to any assessment of Plato's later work. It tries so far as possible to avoid large and controversial interpretations of any dialogue and to canvass a few manageable issues on common ground. Its thesis could have been supported otherwise, by showing how the *Parmenides* and its successors gain in philosophical power and interest when they are read as following and not as paving the way for the *Timaeus*; here I want only to find grounds for this approach. And it defers what I take to be proof that the changes of view here ascribed to Plato square with and sometimes elucidate the comments of Aristotle.

The evidence of style

Campbell's pioneer studies in Plato's style[1] were open to attack, partly for their reliance on Ast's *Lexicon*[2] and their uncritical deductions from the statistics of rare and unique words, partly for their assumption that the *Timaeus* and *Critias* could be taken *en bloc* with the *Laws* as Plato's latest

[1] L. Campbell, *The Sophistes and Politicus of Plato* (Oxford 1867), introd.; essays in *Republic* (ed. B. Jowett and L. Campbell), vol. 2; *CR* 10 (1896), 129-36.

[2] Campbell and Lutoslawski, Raeder and Constantin Ritter have at different times written as though, even if Ast does not list all occurrences of a word, he does name all the dialogues in which it occurs; this is quite false (cf., for example, p. 71 n. 32 below). He does not even list all Plato's words. (D.F. Ast, *Lexicon Platonicum* (Berlin 1835, repr. 1908).)

writings. And Campbell's pupil Lutoslawski,[3] though he attempted a comparison of the *Timaeus* and *Laws*, still assumed a stylistically uniform *Laws* as the terminal work.[4] He also forgot in practice that, where a dialogue such as the *Timaeus* is unique in its technical range, the originality of its vocabulary cannot be used as a mechanical test of dating. And he discovered, after compiling his much-quoted tables on the opposite principle, that the opportunity for the occurrence of more or fewer stylistic pointers in a work bears no proportion to its volume. His admission that only equal amounts of text should have been compared (p. 185) had the effect of largely invalidating
80 his own and most earlier and/ later attempts to order the dialogues by relative affinities of style. Stylometrists ignored the warning. But cases arose in which Campbell and Lutoslawski were compelled to exercise their discretion. Their statistics left the *Theaetetus* beside the *Protagoras* (C.) or before the central books of the *Republic* (L.), the *Phaedrus* seemed later than the *Philebus* (C.), the *Critias* earlier than the *Timaeus* (L.). The effect was, reasonably, to discredit mechanical stylometry until it narrowed its field: it was seen to be applicable only to those formal and linguistic features which were wholly independent of the topic and chosen manner of treatment.[5]

The new search for neutral criteria produced L. Billig's analysis of the rhythms of Plato's clausulae.[6] He found that 'the *Timaeus* has nothing to do with the rhythms of the *Sophist* digression, the *Politicus*, the *Philebus* and the *Laws*. Rhythm puts its composition earlier than that of all these works,'[7] And in this he confirmed Kaluscha's earlier study in the same field.[8] Raeder[9] and Taylor[10] drew attention to the finding; Cornford ignored it, but saw a safe stylistic test in the avoidance of 'illegitimate' hiatus.[11] Yet this avoidance gives no rule of thumb for ordering, say, the *Timaeus* and *Theaetetus*. That it is not an automatic test is tacitly admitted by nearly all stylometrists in dating

[3] W. Lutoslawski, *The Origin and Growth of Plato's Logic* (London 1905), ch. 3.

[4] This was the sheet-anchor of stylometrists who were not content with such broad groupings of the dialogues as that accepted by A.E. Taylor (*Plato, the Man and his Work* (London 1926), 19). Yet there is no external or internal evidence which proves that the *Laws* or even some section of it was later than every other work: cf. pp. 81-2 below.

[5] Here the attempts of Schanz, Dittenberger, and Constantin Ritter to measure the relative frequency of synonyms were theoretically sound. But a study of the *Phaedrus* (cf. pp. 67-8 below) proves that Plato adopted the 'late' synonyms in passages of elevated style earlier than elsewhere. In fact, when Plato is said to be dropping one synonym for another he is commonly borrowing from poetry (Campbell, *Rep.* ii, 50-1), and to find these borrowings either in speeches for whose poetic vocabulary Socrates apologizes (*Phdr.* 257a5) or in a work 'in Inhalt und Form mit der Poesie wetteifernd' (Wilamowitz on the *Timaeus*) is obviously not the same thing as finding them in dialogue proper.

[6] *J. Philol.* 35 (1920), 225-56.

[7] p. 250. The distribution of end-rhythms in the *Tim.* closely matches that in the middle and early dialogues. Thus the rhythms which are dominant (65-85 per cent.) from the *Soph.* digression onwards total 45.6 per cent. in *Tim.*, the same in *Crito*, and 2-3 per cent. below in (for example) *Phd.*, *Rep.* 6 and 10.

[8] W. Kaluscha, *Wiener Studien* 26 (1904), 190.

[9] H. Raeder, *Platons Epinomis* (Copenhagen 1938), 13, n.1.

[10] A.E. Taylor, *A Commentary on Plato's Timaeus* (Oxford 1928), 4-5.

[11] F. Cornford, *Plato's Cosmology* (London 1937), 12, n.3; cf. now R. Hackforth, *Plato's Phaedrus* (Cambridge 1952), 3; J.B. Skemp, *Plato's Statesman* (London 1952), 238.

the *Phaedrus* before the *Theaetetus* and *Parmenides* even though the former already shows, as the latter do not, a 'striking rarity of hiatus'.[12] (It clinches the point to construe this as a passing compliment to Isocrates.) And the *Timaeus* is essentially an essay, a 'conscious *tour de force* of style' (Shorey) where the carelessness of conversation has no place; it may well have been a later decision to adopt such ornaments in writings which make serious use of the dialogue form. (Such warnings patently apply rather to an idiom like the shunning of hiatus, which requires a decision on the writer's part, than to one such as the emergence of dominant prose-rhythms which – as Billig proved for Plato, at least (p. 242) – does not. And we shall see that the rhythms are unaffected by the transition between easy and elevated diction.)

Moreover, I shall try to show why, after an exercise in essay style, Plato/
should revert in the *Theaetetus* and the opening debate of the *Parmenides* to a **81**
conversational form more reminiscent of the early dialogues. For I argue that the *Timaeus* and its sequel or sequels were designed as the crowning work not of the latest dialogues but of the *Republic* group. The project was abandoned from dissatisfaction with certain basic theories, and in the first works of the critical group Plato dropped the confident didacticism of the *Timaeus* to make a fresh start on problems still unsolved. Thus we at once account for the four major characteristics which Taylor singles out as allying the *Timaeus* with Plato's latest writings.[13] The lack of dramatic conversation and the recessive role of Socrates and his scepticism, the predominance of positive teaching and of the periodic essay style, all alike are marks of the doctrinaire assurance with which Plato set himself in the *Timaeus* to expound the system he had constructed. And just as the disappearance of these devices signals the renewal of Plato's doubts, so their readoption in the *Sophist* and its successors marks a new period of assurance which contains his maturest thought. Similarly with many affiliated devices, such as the lack of hesitant and 'subjective' replies (*emoige, dokei moi*, etc.) investigated by Siebeck and Ritter. Such features are not, what they are artlessly taken to be, neutral aids to the ordering of the dialogues. They depend directly on the aims and methods of work in hand.

This point can be proved. For it can be shown that, at a date much earlier than that now assigned to the *Timaeus*, Plato could on occasion adopt an elevated style which by the orthodox tests[14] tallies closely with that of the *Timaeus*: namely, the style of Socrates' speeches in the *Phaedrus*.[15] There is no need to repeat the broad contrasts between these and the dialogue proper (e.g. the elimination of Socrates' personality, on which Stenzel insisted); but

[12] Fr. Blass, *Die attische Beredsamkeit* II^2 (Leipzig 1887-98), 458. By Janell's count the figure for the *Phdr.* is little more than half that for the *Parm.* (23.9 and 44.1 per page of Didot, respectively).

[13] *Comm.*, 4.

[14] For which cf. esp. C. Ritter, *Untersuchungen über Platon* (Stuttgart 1888), 2-33, 56-9 (with corrections in *Platon*, I (Munich 1910), 236-7), 70, n.1; Th. Lina, *De praepositionum usu platonico* (Diss. Marburg 1889), 12; Campbell, *Rep.* ii, 53-5. But these critics draw no distinctions within the *Phdr.*, and sometimes we shall correct their totals.

[15] Lysias' speech, which I shall not consider, tallies by present tests with the dialogue proper.

consider the following contrasts of detail.[16] In the speeches *ontôs* has ousted *tôi onti* (5/0: in *Tim*: 9/1), while in the dialogue *tôi onti* is ubiquitous save where at 260a3 its clumsy repetition is avoided by *ontôs*. In the dialogue *peri* c. gen. still exceeds the equivalent *peri* c. acc. (65/22), *isôs* exceeds *tacha* (11/4), and *heneka* exceeds *charin* (8/5); but not in the speeches (10/11, 0/1, 2/2: in *Tim*. 88/116, 0/1, 13/7). Of another group of 'late' forms the speeches show not only *kata dunamin* and *eis* (*hêmeteran*) *dunamin* (as *Tim*. does) but *hôs dunaton* (as it does not), and echo the rare *kath' hoson dunaton* of *Tim*. 90c; of these the dialogue proper has *eis dunamin* once. The proportion of *de ge/de dê* in the dialogue is 5/8, but in the speeches 0/10 and in *Tim*. 1/24 – a figure otherwise unapproached save in works comparable in form, *Symposium* (1/7) and *Apology* (0/5). *Kathaper*, except for the poetic interlude of the cicadas (259a), is confined to the speeches, where its ratio to *hôsper* (3/5) is over four times that for the whole work. (This is less than in *Tim*., but in other 'late' forms the speeches not only surpass *Tim*. but carry the dialogue with them, e.g. in the complete ousting of *schedon ti* by *schedon* and the frequency of the Ionic dat. pl.) There is further, as Campbell showed, the massing in the speeches of tragic,
82 religious and medical expressions/ often coinciding with those of *Tim*. and *Crit* (C. gives some twenty instances peculiar to this group); and Campbell's instances of late periphrasis (*hê tou thaterou phusis, to tês anaplanêseôs*) are echoed in *Phdr*. (*hê tou kallous phusis* 254b, *to tês mnêmês* 250a). Other such echoes are *pantêi pantôs, pasan pantôs* (246a, 253c). The same conclusion is confirmed by other figures, e.g. for certain uses of *te* and for expressions confined to the dialogue proper (*ti mên; ge mên, dêlon hoti/hôs*, etc.). No one would use these data to argue that the speeches were written later than the dialogue (and no one should have used them indiscriminately to post-date the whole work). What they prove is that, when Plato was still writing dialogue having very close affinities with the *Republic* and *Theaetetus*, he could write uninterrupted prose having equal affinities with the *Timaeus*. This distinction is not touched by the fact that he was not yet prepared to shun hiatus thoroughly in a work of which two-thirds was dialogue (though, equally, in such a work he now refused to give it free rein). What is of quite different importance in this connexion is that the speeches do not interrupt the graph of end-rhythms in the *Phaedrus*. The test of rhythm sustains its claim to neutrality.

Billig went on to ear-mark the few indexes of style other than end-rhythms which seemed to him to have the required neutrality, and his suggestions tell for my thesis.[17] That thesis (to repeat) is that, while the *Timaeus* and *Critias* undoubtedly follow the *Republic* and possibly follow the *Phaedrus*, they precede the 'critical' group which begins with the *Parmenides* and *Theaetetus*. And on

[16] Ritter's figures, after large corrections in *Platon* and articles in Bursian's *Jahresbericht*, remain untrustworthy: e.g. in *Phdr*. he underestimates cases of *kata/eis dunamin* (2 excluding 257a3), *hôs dunaton* (1), *poteron* and *potera* before a vowel (2, 1), *eipon*, etc., in rel. clause (2), *de dê* (18).

[17] e.g. in the coining of adjectives in *-ôdês* and *-eidês* the *Tht*. and *Parm*. are characteristic of the late dialogues, and the *Tim*. of the middle period (Lutoslawski, 115). Of Billig's other criteria some are discussed above and one, the greater frequency of *peri* after its noun, is not a late form (cf. Lutoslawski, 131-2: in the *Rep*. it is much higher than in the *Tim*. and as high as in the *Soph*. and *Pol*.): B. may have confused this with the predominance of *peri* c. acc. over *peri* c. gen.

the strength of the present discussion and of some clues of diction still to be noted[18] it seems fair to claim that this reordering tallies well with the admissible evidence of style.[19]

Now for the paradoxes of orthodoxy. In discussing them I follow the order of the critical group.

Paradeigmata in the Parmenides

At one stage of the earlier argument in the *Parmenides* (132c12-133a7) Socrates defines *methexis*, 'participation', in terms of *homoiômata*, 'likeness', and *paradeigmata*, 'paradigms'. Parmenides has no trouble in proving that, if participation in some character *A* is to be construed as resemblance to some *paradeigma* in respect of *A*, then, since resemblance is symmetrical, both *paradeigma* and *homoiôma* must exhibit *A* and hence *ex hypothesi* resemble a further *paradeigma* in that respect. And so on, in the relation between Forms and particulars given in the *Timaeus* (e.g. 29b, 48e-491, 50d1, 52a, 52c). So commentators, hoping to reconcile a late *Timaeus* with a Plato who saw the point of his own arguments, have laboured to show that the *Timaeus* theory was immune (or at worst thought to be immune) to the objections raised in the supposedly earlier work. But their attempts have failed./

Taylor's contention (after Proclus)[20] that the *paradeigma* and *homoiôma* were not related symmetrically by *homoiotês*, 'similarity', was refuted by Hardie,[21] and since it combined a logical fallacy[22] with a disregard for the evidence[23] there was no excuse for its repetition by Cherniss.[24] Cherniss also **83**

[18] Cf. pp. 71, n. 32; 82, n. 76 below.

[19] [Owen wished to add at this point a discussion of L. Brandwood, *The Dating of Plato's Works by the Stylistic Method*, Ph.D. Thesis, University of London, 1958, which points to serious problems in the use of stylistic evidence made by H. Cherniss in his reply to this paper ('The Relation of the *Timaeus* to Plato's Later Dialogues', *AJP* 78 (1957), 225-66)-Ed.]

[20] 'Parmenides, Zeno and Socrates', *PAS* 16 (1916), 234-89; *Plato's Parmenides* (Oxford 1934), 26.

[21] W.F.R. Hardie *A Study in Plato* (Oxford 1936), 96-7.

[22] That of arguing as though, because the relation between copy and original is not simply resemblance, it does not *include* resemblance; for if it is included Parmenides' regress follows at once. The most one could maintain on Taylor's lines is that, if to predicate *X* of *A* is to assert that *A* is not only like but copied from a Form, then (by definition of 'Form") it is a contradiction to predicate *X* of the Form that *A* allegedly resembles in respect of *X*. But then no such resemblance between *A* and the Form can be maintained, nor *a fortiori* can *A* be the Form's copy; so this serves Parmenides' ends by wrecking the *eikôn-paradeigma* account of predication. But the evidence is against this line of argument (see next note).

[23] e.g. (i) such uses of the *paradeigma* terminology as at *Rep.* 501b where the legislator is a painter with his eye on the *theion paradeigma*, 'divine paradigm', and able to make a direct comparison between sitter and portrait (cf. *Phd.* 76e2); (ii) the fact that on the old theory of Forms the property represented by the Form was predicated without qualms of the form itself: Justice just, Holiness holy (*Prot.* 330c-e), Largeness large (*Phd.* 102e5), where the predicate-expression is used unambiguously of Forms and particulars, as is proved, for example, by *scholêi mentan ti allo hosion eiê ei mê autê ge hosiotês hosion estai*, 'There could scarcely be anything else holy, if holiness itself were not holy' (*Prot.* 330d8); (iii) Aristotle's use of the premiss that the *logos* was common to Forms and particulars (e.g. *Meta.* 997b10-12; *EE* 1218a13-15). So Plato did

argued[25] that in the *Republic* (597c) and the *Timaeus* (31a) Plato used a regress argument of the type in question (the 'third man') in order to establish the uniqueness of a Form, and hence, since both these dialogues postulate *paradeigmata* and *eikones*, 'likenesses', that Plato thought the argument applicable to relations between Forms but not to those between Forms and particulars. But this is a confusion which seems to arise from the indiscriminate use of the label *tritos anthrôpos*, 'third man' (some of the heterogeneous batch of arguments it covers do not even employ an infinite regress: cf. Alex. *in Meta.* 84. 7-21). For neither in the *Republic* nor in the *Timaeus* does Plato use a regress of *similarities*;[26] his premiss is simply that of the *hen epi pollôn*, 'one over many', which is (as Parmenides' interrogation of Socrates shows) neutral as between the resemblance-account of *methexis* and others. So neither argument shows or requires any awareness of Parmenides' point that, since resemblance is symmetrical, on this version of predication the same account which is given of the particular's participation in the Form must be extended to the Form.

(On this faulty foundation Cherniss built another proof of Aristotle's dishonesty.[27] Aristotle was accused of citing such regress arguments as valid against the old Forms[28] without mentioning that Plato had, or supposed he had, rebutted them. But the reason why Aristotle is as silent as Plato himself on this vital answer is just that no answer existed.[29])/

84 Ross agrees that the apologists have failed and that Parmenides' objection goes home.[30] But, by accepting the lateness of the *Timaeus*, he falls on the second horn of the dilemma. He is forced to suggest that in the *Timaeus* the defeated version of *methexis* is retained as a 'metaphorical way of describing the relation'; but his own argument refutes this. For in discussing the scope of *eikôs logos*, 'likely account', in the *Timaeus* he rightly says that 'in general for his metaphysics, Plato would claim that it is true. That for which he disclaims anything more than probability is not his metaphysics but his cosmology';[31] and he recognizes that the metaphysics of the *Timaeus*, save for

---

not suppose the paradeigmatic function of the Form of *X*, any more than its being *monoeides*, 'unique', or *aïdion*, 'eternal', to rule out the assertion of resemblance between Form and *eikôn* in respect of *X*. And this position is not modified in the *Tim.* Hence Parmenides' regress is the exactly appropriate criticism of the theory.

24 *Aristotle's Criticism of Plato and the Academy* (Baltimore 1944), 297-9.

25 ibid., 295-7; cf. O. Apelt, *Beiträge* (Leipzig 1891), 52-3.

26 In the *Tim.* the resemblance of *eikôn* to *paradeigma* is introduced to prove not the uniqueness of the Form but that of the *ouranos*, 'universe', given that of the *panteles zôion*, 'the perfect living thing'.

27 *ACPA*, 293.

28 e.g. *Meta.* 990b17, 991a2-5, 1032a2-4.

29 As to the answer which Cherniss constructs for Plato, certainly Plato later concluded that the *eidos* should be regarded as '*being* that which the particular *has* as an attribute' (*ACPA*, 298) – the necessary type-distinctions are forced by Parmenides' first regress (132a1-b2) and sketched in *Tht.* 156e, 182a-b; but to expound *methexis* in the idioms of resemblance and copying is just to show that one has not yet grasped these type-distinctions.

30 *Plato's Theory of Ideas* (Oxford 1951), 89, 230-1.

31 ibid., 127.

the Demiurge, centres in the description of *paradeigmata* and the receptacle (*hupodochê*) and its contents (50c-52c) – a description to which the resemblance of Forms and particulars is integral. Moreover, the distinction between *eikôs muthos*, 'likely story', and unshakeable truth is explained wholly by reference to the relation of the physical *eikôn* to its Model (29b-d). The explanation (and with it the pointed use of *eikôs*) is annulled if at the time of writing Plato regarded any talk of *eikones* in this connexion as a mere metaphor which on his own showing could not be pressed without generating absurdities.

In fact, Plato does not again introduce such *paradeigmata* to explain predication:[32] in the *Politicus* (277d-278c) he emphasizes a different and important function of the expression *paradeigma*; and in the *Philebus* (15b-17a) he either leaves the nature of *methexis* an open question or, as I think, implies a different analysis.[33] The reasonable solution of the puzzle is to regard the *Timaeus* as preceding the *Parmenides* and as inheriting from the middle-period dialogues a fallacy which Plato subsequently exposed./

Genesis and ousia **85**

The *Timaeus* distinguishes absolutely between *to on aei, genesin de ouk echon*, 'that which is always and has no change', and *to gignomenon men aei, on de oudepote*, 'that which always changes and has no being' (27d-28a); that is, it

[32] Ross (*PTI*, 228-30) has collected occurrences of the idioms by which the relation between Forms and particulars is described in the dialogues. From his data he infers that 'there is a general movement away from immanence towards transcendence' (sc. towards the *paradeigma*-idioms). But his list does not bear this out. Of the dialogues taken to follow the *Phdr.*, the *Tim.* is alone in using the *paradeigma*-idioms, and uses them exclusively and almost exhaustively. *Tht.* 176e3-4 is no exception (as Ross agrees, 101), for the context (the 'digression') is strongly metaphorical, and the twin *paradeigmata* cannot be *ta ekei*, 'things in the other region', because the 'godless most miserable thing' at least has no place in the 'realm pure of evils' which is the soul's proper habitat (177a5). Ross does not note the following points: (*a*) the special term *noêsis* used to describe knowledge of the *paradeigmata* seems to be confined to the *Rep.* and *Tim.*, except for its occurrence at *Crat.* 407b4 and 411d8 where the particular form is required by the etymology. Since such knowledge was a dyadic relation between minds and Forms, it seems likely that the old expression was shelved when the *Tht.* had proved (199c-200c) that knowledge and error were not a matter of bare recognition and misidentification. (*b*) The term *homoiôma*, introduced in the *Phdr.* myth and *Parm.* and subsequently often used for *eikôn*, etc., is not found in the *Tim.*, which here too confines itself to the vocabulary of the *Rep.* (e.g. *aphomoiôma* seems to be peculiar to these two works). But the word occurs in *Crat.* 434a (Ast omits this, so it has eluded Campbell and Lutoslawski).

[33] Contrast with the refutation of the *paradeigmata* the less intimidating arguments brought against the so-called 'immanence' version of *methexis* (*Parm.* 131a4-e5). In the *Phil.* (15b) it is these arguments alone that are quoted as needing an answer if the *monades*, 'monads', are to be saved. Professor Skemp (*P.St.*, 238) thinks that, since *to dêmiourgoun*, 'the producer', is explicitly located in the fourfold classification in *Phil.* 23c-27c, the *paradeigmata* cannot have been superseded either. The plain fact, whatever one makes of it, is that this classification of *panta ta nun onta en tôi panti*, 'all things that are now in the whole', does make room for the *aitia*, 'cause', and does not make room for *paradeigmata*: I do not quote this on behalf of my position, but it scarcely tells against it.

'treats *genesis* [coming to be] and *ousia* [being] as simple incompatibles'.[34] It reaffirms this incompatibility by advocating that the expression *esti*, 'is', be reserved for pronouncements about *aïdios ousia*, 'eternal being', and (by implication) that *gignetai*, 'comes to be', be left to do duty in statements of contemporary empirical fact (37e-38b). So it has taxed commentators to say why this principle is to all appearances jettisoned in the *Laws* and its immediate predecessors.[35] But the common plea that such departures show merely a venial looseness of language[36] fails, for they are the exact consequence of new arguments in the late dialogues.

First, the *Theaetetus* states and explodes the thesis that *genesis* excludes *ousia*. By a convention which echoes that imposed on contingent statements in the *Timaeus*, Plato eliminates *einai* in favour of *gignesthai* in all contexts (*Tht.* 157a7-c2; cf. *Tht.* 152e1 with *Tim.* 27d6-28a1). And then by using the distinction between change of quality and change of place he shows that this convention produces absurdities. Some have wanted to believe that Plato is at this point trying to establish the thesis of the *Timaeus*: namely that, although *gignetai* alone is appropriate to contingent statements, there must be some entities (viz. the Forms) to whose description only *esti* is appropriate.[37] If Plato had drawn this conclusion from his argument it would have been a sheer blunder,[38] but he does not draw it. He is saddled with it to save the *Timaeus*. What he plainly points out is that if *anything* (and anything in this world, not the next) were perpetually changing in all respects, so that at no time could it be described as being so-and-so, then nothing could be said of it at all – and, *inter alia*, it could not be said to be changing. If an object moves, we can say what sort of thing is moving[39] only if it has some qualitative stability (182c9-10); conversely, to have complete qualitative flux ascribed to

[34] Taylor, *Comm.* 32. Taylor says that the *Tim.* maintains this incompatibility 'from first to last' in sharp contrast to the *Phil.* theory of *genesis eis ousian*, but contradicts himself in a note on 31b3 by importing an allusion to the *Phil.* and so leaving the *Tim.* inconsistent on a key-doctrine; he is corrected by Cornford ad loc. (*PC*, 42, n.1). The *Tim.* does not in fact (and does not promise to) adhere always to the special usage proposed in 37e-38b and discussed in this section: naturally, since (as Plato came to see) its adoption is ruled out by logical absurdities. The point is that if he had seen this when writing the *Tim.* the proposal made in 37e-38b would never have been made.

[35] *Laws* 894a5-7, *Phil.* 26d8, 27b8-9, 54a-d (cf. Aristotle, *PA* 640a18), *Soph.* 248a-249b, *Parm.* 163d1-2, and passages discussed above. *Phil.* 59a and 61d-e are not parallels to the *Tim.* disjunction, because the *Tim.* says not only (as the *Phil.* does) that some things exist without changing but (as the *Phil.* does not) that some things change without existing; this step, the outcome of the *Republic*'s muddles about existence, is not entailed by the commonplace distinction between *hôsautôs onta aei*, 'things which are always the same', and *gignomena (mê bebaia*, etc), 'changing (unstable) things,' etc.), and it is this which is refuted in the *Tht.*

[36] Cf. A. Diès, *Philèbe* (Budé, Paris 1900), xxviii-xxix.

[37] e.g. Cornford, *Plato's Theory of Knowledge* (London 1957), 101; Cherniss, *ACPA*, 218, n.129.

[38] Cf. R. Robinson, *Phil. Rev.* 49 (1950), 9-10.

[39] *hoia atta rhei ta pheromena*, 182c10: this argument defeats the lame plea of the *Tim.* (49d-e) that even if we cannot say *what* any mere *gignomenon* is we can describe it as *to toiouton* (cf. *Tht.* 152d6). In a similar argument the *Crat.* makes the point so explicitly ('If it is always slipping out from us, is it possible to say of it rightly, first, that it is that thing, then that it is such a thing?' 439d8-9) that this alone would vindicate its place in the critical group.

it, a thing must have location. Nor can any quality of the object, such as its
whiteness, be/ claimed as a subject of this unqualified change: any change **86**
here would be *metabolê eis allên chroan*, 'change to another colour', and to apply 'whiteness' to a colour-progression is to deprive it of determinate sense (182d2-5). So no description of any process is possible if we can say only that its constituents are changing from or to something and never that they are something (cf. *Tim.* 37e5-38a2, where it is allowed to say only what a *gignomenon* was and will be; the white Queen offered Alice jam on the same terms).

Notice that Plato does not say, as he is reported to say, that knowledge is not perception because the objects of perception are always wholly in flux. He says that the attempt to equate knowledge with perception *kata ge tên tou panta kineisthai methodon*, 'according to the doctrine that everything is changing', fails because that *methodos* is (not false for some things, but) nonsense about anything. His instances are drawn from the everyday world, not from the world of Forms. And on the strength of this he goes on to ascribe *ousia* to objects of perception (185a, c, 186b ff.) and thereby to demolish the equation of perception and knowledge independently of the theory of flux.[40]

I omit arguments in the *Sophist* and *Philebus* which help to supersede the assimilation of *ousia* and *genesis* to a pair of incompatible qualities. But one other is worth mention. The *Parmenides* introduces (and for its own ends misemploys) the Megarian thesis that any process of change is analysable in terms of a series of particular states of affairs, each obtaining at a different time and none being itself a process (152b1-d4). It is validly deduced from this that to the descriptions of the component states of affairs the process-word *gignetai* will be inappropriate and that *esti* is indispensable to some statements of contingent fact (152c6-d2). Now this is Plato's theory, if the analysis of perception in the *Theaetetus* is his; for sensible change is there atomized into a succession of *aisthêta*, 'objects of perception', with correlated *aisthêseis*, 'perceptions' (*Tht.* 156a-157c, 182a-b) and it is correspondingly argued, and made a basis of the perception theory, that a person undergoing change is rather a series of persons (159b-c, e) having no term as long as the change continues (166b-c). (True, in temporarily amalgamating this with the theory of general flux Plato talks of reimporting change into the atoms of change. But this patently self-defeating step is cancelled with the defeat of the *rheontes* (the flux theorists), and before that the right theory is kept very carefully in view: cf. 160b5-6, 8-10, 166c6.)

However, this atomistic theory could consistently be denied to be Plato's. But the first argument certainly cannot. It suffices to defeat the disjunction of *genesis* and *ousia* in the form propounded by the *Timaeus*, and Plato, unlike his commentators, does not resuscitate it.

[40] Cornford, misconstruing the previous argument, can naturally make nothing of the fact that this final refutation hinges on the *ousia* of *aisthêta*. He is reduced, first to seeing an ambiguity in *ousia*, finally to making the argument turn on the *denial* of *ousia* to *aisthêta* (*PTK*, 108-9).

Eudoxus

It is commonly agreed that by 368 at latest Eudoxus had brought his school to Athens, and that it was probably at this period that he answered Plato's challenge by producing his pioneer contribution to the mathematical theory of astronomy.[41] Hence it is a familiar puzzle why, if the *Timaeus* is late, Eudoxus' hypothesis has had no effect on its theories. Taylor cited this
87 peculiarity in/ defence of his thesis that the dialogue was a philosophical archaism.[42] No one has given the simpler explanation that the *Timaeus* was written before Eudoxus' theory was produced (and so quite possibly before the *Theaetetus*, which is now by common consent dated a little after 369). Yet the sole essential difference between the astronomy of the *Timaeus* and that represented by the simple model described in the Myth of Er seems to be that the *Republic* does not provide for the obliquity of the ecliptic.[43] However we expound the 'contrary force' of *Tim.* 38d4, the expression embodies Plato's continued failure to meet his own challenge ('On what assumption of uniform and ordered motions could we save the appearances concerning the motion of the wandering bodies?') For whether the point of it is to ascribe all apparent variations in planetary speed and direction to intermittent voluntary action on the part of the planets[44] or merely to record, without explaining, such variations on the part of Venus and Mercury in particular,[45] the introduction of the Contrary Power is no substitute for an explanation in terms of 'uniform and ordered movements'.[46] Where Plato failed to meet his own requirements, Eudoxus came near to succeeding. Yet his hypothesis is ignored by that 'best of astronomers' Timaeus.

The 'wanderings' of the five minor planets are 'incalculable in number, and marvellously varied'[47] (*Tim.* 39d1-2), a phrase in which Cornford seems (inconsistently with his main position) to detect a reference to Eudoxus' theory.[48] But for these planets Eudoxus required only twenty component motions (or in effect twelve, since two are shared by all) – a number for which

[41] Apollodorus sets his *floruit* in 368-365. The theory was in any case presumably published before he left Athens for the final task of legislating for Cnidus (DL 8.88), and this in turn must be some years before his death in 356-353. Cf. J. Harward on *Ep.* 13. 360c3 (*The Story of the Platonic Epistles* (Melbourne 1920), 234).

[42] *Comm.*, 211.

[43] As this implies, if *illomenên* at *Tim.* 40b8 signifies a motion I accept Cornford's account of it as compensatory rotation (*PC*, 130-1).

[44] Cornford, *PC*, 106-12.

[45] Taylor, *Comm.*, 202.

[46] In fact it represents part of the source of Plato's complaint against empirical astronomy in *Rep.* 530a3-b4 – a passage which clearly prefigures the *Tim.*, and not only in introducing 'the artificer of the universe'. Equally, it explains why Plato's astronomy throughout depends for its precise exposition on the manipulation of an orrery (e.g. *Tim.* 40d2-3).

[47] πλήθει μὲν ἀμηχάνῳ χρωμέναι, πεποικιλμέναι δὲ θαυμαστῶς, Eudemus ap. Simpl. *in De Caelo* 292b10 (488. 20-24, cf. 492. 31-493. 32).

[48] *PC*, 116.

plêthos amêchanon, 'incalculable number', would be an absurdly strong expression even in Cornford's weakened version ('bewildering in number').[49] If, on the other hand, we construe the 'wanderings' as all those apparent anomalies which Eudoxus' supplementary motions were later designed to explain (a clear inference from 40b6: 'turning, and wandering in such ways'), it is tempting to find Plato's later acknowledgement of Eudoxus' solution in the vexed passage of *Laws* 7 (821b-822c) which rejects all celestial 'wanderings'.[50] Some critics find nothing here to contradict the *Republic* and *Timaeus*. So they can point to nothing which Plato might have learnt in later years ('not young, not long ago'). I am inclined to locate the discovery, not indeed in the whole of what is maintained there, but in the implication that the other planets need no more be supposed to 'wander', in the sense of showing arbitrary variations in speed and direction, than the sun and moon themselves.

The alleged dependence of the Timaeus on the Sophist

So far we have been chiefly concerned with the probability that the *Timaeus* preceded the *Parmenides* and *Theaetetus*. Now, following the order of the late/dialogues, we turn to the recent counter-claim that at two points the **88**
Timaeus presupposes the argument of the *Sophist*.

1. Concerning the psychogony of *Tim.* 35a Cornford has maintained, with less reservations than Grube[51] or Cherniss,[52] that 'the *Sophist* (as the ancient critics saw) provides the sole clue to the sense of our passage'.[53] Such arguments for dating can cut both ways: e.g. Cornford has to appeal to the *Timaeus* to support his account (or expansion) of the perception-theory in the *Theaetetus*[54] and of the description of mirror-images in the *Theaetetus* and *Sophist*.[55] But in any case the claim cannot be allowed. Cornford can hardly have supposed that Plato's readers had to await the *Sophist* in order to be informed that any *eidos* existed, maintained its identity, and differed from others (cf. *Phd.* 78d5-7, *Symp.* 211b1-2, *Rep.* 597c) or that existence, identity,

[49] Cornford in this connexion wrongly quotes the number 27 (which includes the motions of sun, moon, and stars); but even 27 is no *plêthos amêchanon*.

[50] It is sometimes said (e.g. by Professor Skemp, *The Theory of Motion in Plato's Later Dialogues* (Amsterdam 1967), 79) that the *Tim.*, like the *Laws*, condemns the description of the planets as *planêta*, 'wanderers'. This is not so. It says merely that they are so called (*epiklên echonta 'planêta'*, 38c5-6) and goes on to define the 'wandering' (40b6). Cf. Simplicius *in De Caelo*, 489. 5-11.

[51] G. Grube, *CP* 27 (1932), 80-2; *Plato's Thought* (New York 1964), 192.

[52] *ACPA*, 409, n.337.

[53] *PC*, 62. The parenthesis hardly deserves refutation. If such 'ancient critics' as Xenocrates and Crantor ever attended to the *Sophist* in constructing their divergent interpretations, it was notoriously not their 'sole clue': cf. Taylor, *Comm.*, 112-15. Xenocrates' importation of motion and rest was presumably grounded in the *Tim.* itself (57d-e), and attempted to reconcile the *Tim.* with the definition of *psuchê* given in the *Phdr.*

[54] *PTK*, 50 and n.2: cf. especially his introduction of 'visual fire' and 'fiery particles' which 'interpenetrate and coalesce'.

[55] *PTK*, 124, n.2; 327, n.2.

and difference could be distinguished from each other (this is of course assumed throughout the *Parmenides* and occasionally stated, e.g. at 143b in the case of existence, difference, unity). Yet this is all that he borrows from the *Sophist*.[56] The distinction between divisible and indivisible *ousia* is explained by reference to the descriptions of *eikones* and *chronos*, 'time', in the *Timaeus* and the contrast between *hapla*, 'simples', and *suntheta*, 'complex things', in the *Phaedo*.[57] On the indivisibility of Identity and Difference he is reduced to 'conjecture'[58] – naturally, for there is no enlightening contrast to be found in the divisibility of 'the nature of the different' in the *Sophist* (257c-258a) which cannot be accommodated within the disjunction of the *Timaeus*. The *Timaeus* employs an older and simpler schema: the 'divided nature of the different' which is contrasted with the 'undivided' is 'what occurs in connexion with bodies', and Cornford admits that the *Sophist* does not discuss divisibility of this order.

Consequently I cannot see that Cornford's exposition takes anything from the *Sophist* which is original to the argument of that most important dialogue, or which could not be gathered from such an earlier passage as that in the *Republic* (454a-b) which makes 'the ability to divide according to forms' a mark of dialectic and ascribes it to a failure in dialectic that 'we didn't in the least consider what sort of difference and sameness we were using in our definition, and where it aimed'. And, on the other hand, it is noteworthy that, in a highly elliptical context[59] and a dialogue whose ellipses are seldom supplied elsewhere, Plato subsequently offers so full an explanation of this stage of the soul-making (*Tim.* 37a-c). To go beyond this and pronounce the indivisible Existence, Identity, and Difference 'Forms', as Cornford does, is to manufacture the difficulty (which he ignores) that their role in the psychogony then breaks the law laid down for all Forms in *Tim.* 52a2-3.[60]/

89 2. Perhaps we can settle the order of the *Sophist* and *Timaeus* in the course of rebutting a further claim. Discussing the account of *logos* in the world-soul (*Tim.* 37a-c), Cornford remarks that the passage 'can only be understood by reference to the *Sophist*. There all philosophic discourse is regarded as consisting of affirmative and negative statements about Forms.'[61] Now this argument would carry weight if the *Timaeus* anywhere presupposed the analysis of negation in terms of difference offered in the *Sophist*. But it does not. It mentions only assertions of identity and difference (37b, 44a), and in this respect shows no advance on the passage quoted earlier from the *Republic*.

[56] *PC*, 59-66.

[57] *PC*, 62-4, 102. It might have been glossed by the *Phdr.* myth (247c-e) in which the knowledge that represents 'the being that really is' is contrasted with that which is 'different in every different one of those things that we now call beings'.

[58] *PC*, 65-6.

[59] Cf. the determining of harmonic intervals in the world-soul and the mathematical idioms in *Tim.* 31c4, 36c5-7.

[60] I think Plato may have seen conclusive reasons for excluding *paradeigmata* of existence, identity, and difference before he saw the general objection to making the Forms *paradeigmata*: then the readmission of existence, etc. as *eidê* in the *Sophist* would mark the revised function of the *eidos*. But this falls outside the present paper. In the *Tim.* Plato does not commit himself and should not be committed by his commentators.

[61] *PC*, 96.

So it is at least misleading to gloss *logos ho kata tauton alêthês* (37b-d) as 'discourse true in either case, whether the judgments are *affirmative or negative*'.[62]

This in itself shows only that in the *Timaeus* the analysis of negation given in the *Sophist* is not presupposed,[63] not that it had not yet been worked out. But this further point can also be proved. For the tenet on which the whole new account of negation is based, namely that *to mê on estin ontôs mê on*, 'what is not really is *not*' (*Soph.* 254d1), is contradicted unreservedly by Timaeus' assertion that it is illegitimate to say *to mê on esti mê on*, 'what is not is *not*' (38b2-3); and thereby the *Timaeus* at once ranks itself with the *Republic* and *Euthydemus*. Cornford tries to excuse this, but his plea miscarries. He has to say that at *Tim.* 38b2 *to mê on* means 'the absolutely non-existent, of which, as the *Sophist* shows, nothing whatever can be truly asserted'.[64] But what the *Sophist* argues is that any attempt to give this use to *mê on* (we could say, to treat *on* as a proper adjective) leads directly to absurdities, and that *in the only sense which can consistently be allowed to mê on* it is wholly correct to say *to mê on esti mê on*.[65] And this formula is echoed insistently and always without the reservation which would be required on Cornford's interpretation.[66] So the *Timaeus* does not tally with even a fragment of the argument in the *Sophist*. That argument is successful against exactly the Eleatic error which, for lack of the later challenge to Father Parmenides, persists in the *Timaeus*.

Second thoughts on government

1. At the start of the *Timaeus* Socrates alludes to a number of theses canvassed in the *Republic*. They are to be developed and illustrated by Critias in the sequel (*Tim.* 26c-27b). Some critics, perplexed at the omission of other doctrines found in the *Republic*, have guessed at an implied discontinuity in the argument of the two dialogues instead of insisting, as Plato does, on its continuity. They forget, firstly, that Plato repeatedly takes care to quote the words/ of the *Republic*;[67] secondly, that the *Timaeus* describes the doctrines it **90**

[62] *PC*, 95, n.1.

[63] 'Timaeus always talks of the *mê on* in the old undiscriminating fashion familiar to us from the fifth book of the *Republic*' (Taylor, *Comm.*, 32).

[64] *PC*, 98, n.4.

[65] To try to give it the former use is to try to say what is 'unsayable and inexpressible and inexplicable' (238c10); correspondingly, 'When we speak of what is not, it seems, we are not speaking of what is contrary to what is, but only of what is different' (257b3-4). For a further refutation of Cornford's account of the *Sophist* see A.L. Peck, 'Plato and the *megista genê* of the *Sophist*', *CQ* 2 (1952), esp. 35-8. Though I think Dr. Peck's positive thesis mistaken (viz. that the *Soph.* has primarily the local virtue of beating certain sophists on their own ground), I take it to be at least partly prompted by the very real problem why the *Soph.* differs markedly from the *Tim.* in its terminology and interests (cf., for example, op. cit., 39, 53). My own answer to this will be evident.

[66] *Soph.* 258c2-3, *Pol.* 284b8, 286b10.

[67] Cf. Rivaud's notes on *Tim.* 17c-19a; he does not remark *Tim.* 18b3 = *Rep.* 419a10 or the deliberate use of *sunerxis* for the State marriages (a word apparently confined to *Rep.* 460a9 and *Tim.* 18d9).

takes over as *kephalaia*, 'headings', of Socrates' talk on the previous day and that in the *Politics* (1264b29-1265a1) Aristotle summarizes the conclusions of the *Republic* in exactly the way adopted in the *Timaeus*, explaining the selection by saying that the rest of the dialogue consists of 'digressions and a discussion of the Guardians' education'. And Plato also calls the central books a digression (*Rep.* 543c5). With this emphasis on continuity in mind, then,[68] we can try to connect the abandoning of the *Critias* with the fact that certain doctrines which the *Timaeus* takes over from the *Republic* as a basis for its sequel are rejected outright in the *Politicus*. For the moment we shall set on one side what is said in the *Laws*.

First, some special theses. The *Timaeus* (18b) repeats the prescription of the *Republic* (417a) that the Guardians must have no gold or silver or private property. Breach of this law in the *Republic* marks immediate degeneration from the perfect constitution (547b-548b). But against this the *Politicus* insists (four times in two pages, to show that this is novel doctrine: 292a, c, 293a, c-d) that whether the true ruler has any wealth is wholly irrelevant to the question whether his is the best possible government. Correspondingly, the system of marriages for the Guardians (*Rep.* 457c-465c, echoed in *Tim.* 18c-d), which was said to stand or fall with the abolition of private property (*Rep.* 464b-c), is abandoned by the philosophic statesman in the *Politics* (310a-311c). Its nearest analogue is the complete elimination of normal marriage and parenthood, by other means, in the non-historical time-cycle of the myth (271e8-272a1), whither Plato also banishes the lack of private property. Nor can these discrepancies be patched by saying that in the *Politicus* Plato argues only that the abolition of property – and, by implication, of families – is not to be taken as *defining* the best government, though it is, in a weaker sense, still a necessary condition of it. Plato does indeed insist that it is not a *horos*, 'defining mark', of right rule, but what he now denies is that it is a necessary condition at all: this is proved (quite apart from the myth, to which I shall return) not only by the present context (e.g. 293a-b, if a doctor worthy of the name can be rich so can the statesman), but by the suggestion of different and more familiar arrangements for property and the marriages of rulers under a scientific government (310a-311c).

But, more important, Plato now jettisons the general principle on which these detailed prescriptions depended: namely the assumption that legislation, provided it does not become embroiled with minutiae, can be final.[69] In

[68] As to dramatic date, surely the reason why the *Tim.* could not be set after the *Rep.* (i.e. two days after the Bendidea) is just that when writing the earlier work Plato had not yet formulated the plan of the later and therefore had not seen the need to introduce any speaker of Timaeus' powers among either Cephalus' guests or Socrates' (presumed) auditors next day. Hence a further recital had to be invented. To infer from this that 'the design of the [*Timaeus*] trilogy is completely independent of the *Republic*' (Cornford) is to invert the natural inference.

[69] Barker's paradox, that the *Republic* is 'uncompromisingly hostile to law' and that this hostility is relaxed in the *Politicus* (*Greek Political Theory*³ (London 1947), 271), hardly needs refutation. The *Republic* does not repudiate any 'system of law'; it contends only that continuous piecemeal legislation and litigation will be eliminated 'if only god allows them to preserve the laws we have just explored' (425e), since then the Guardians will know 'what laws must be made'. Even if the laws of the *Republic* were 'unwritten ordinances', the *Politicus* censures

the/*Republic* there is no question of changing the original broad laws laid 91
down by Socrates, e.g. those governing the living-conditions and marriages of the Guardians and the ordering of their education. Earlier, the Guardians are permitted merely to obey the laws and 'imitate' them in details of interpretation (458c); later, when there is no longer (as once in 414b) any need or hope of duping them with the Noble Lie, their powers are commensurate with those of the original legislator solely in as far as they now understand why the laws must be maintained (497b7-d2) and must be supreme (519e1-2). Correspondingly, the prime virtue of Critias' model State is that of Sparta, fine laws (*Tim.* 23c6, 24d4), and it is Socrates' laws which are taken over as the basis of that best city (e.g. *Tim.* 23e5). But this whole doctrine of sovereign and immutable laws, asserted in the *Republic* and inherited by the *Timaeus* and its sequel, is denounced in the *Politicus*. No art (such as statesmanship) can lay down a permanent and universal rule (294b). The scientific ruler will be independent of legislation (294a-301a *passim*), and if for convenience he enacts laws, he is liable to discover that those which were the best possible in past circumstances need to be changed (295b-296a). Only inferior constitutions require laws binding on all members of the State, and such laws must be written records of what is at some time prescribed for the best State (297c-e).

The conclusion is in sight that the *Timaeus*, since it adopts without comment these superseded theories, was written before the *Politicus*; but there are two more steps required to reach it. And in countering the first objection we shall find independent support for our view.

2. It has been argued that the propositions quoted from the *Politicus* do not apply at all to human statecraft. On this interpretation, what the myth in that dialogue teaches is that the ruler with knowledge and independent of the laws is not a human possibility or matter for 'serious political theory',[70] so in the latter sphere, for all that Plato says, the *Republic-Critias* constitution may still rank first. But this is demonstrably a misreading of the *Politicus*,[71] where the argument moves as follows. The initial definition of the statesman as a kind of shepherd of men is pronounced unsatisfactory; it is inferred that by mistake some other pattern of kingship has been defined. The mistake is illustrated by the myth, which brings to light these objections: (*a*) The king and statesman of the present time-cycle (viz. the historical as opposed to the ideal) must be distinguished from the divine shepherd of the other cycle: only the divine shepherd is worthy of the original definition, but he is 'higher than a king' (274e10–5a2, 275b4-c1). And (*b*) the earlier descriptions of the statesman as

---

immutability in written and unwritten alike (295e5); but in fact it is only the regulations (*nomima*) that seem minor that will not have written legislation (*Rep.* 425a-b). No punishment for crime is considered because Plato concentrates on the Guardians, whose crimes will disrupt the constitution and make punishment unavailable and unavailing. If it is true of this state that 'its government is the result of its nature' (op. cit., 204), it is conversely true that its nature is the result of the education prescribed by laws which are irrevocable (424b-d).

[70] Taylor, *PMW*, 397.

[71] Probably under the influence of *Laws* 4. 713a-714a, on which see n.77 below. For another refutation of Taylor's interpretation see J.B. Skemp, *P.St.*, 52.

ruling the whole State must be clarified and amended (275a2-5). The objections are respectively met by (*a*) replacing *trophê*, 'nurture', by *epimeleia*, 'care', in the definition and (*b*) analysing the human ruler's *epimeleia* to distinguish it from other functions in the State. The conclusion at once
92 follows that the true statesman/ independent of laws who subsequently appears in the dialogue is a 'kingly man who has wisdom (*phronêsis*)' (*anêr meta phronêseôs basilikos*, 294a8): unlike the divine shepherd of the myth, he is a human possibility.[72]

Campbell saw Pythagoreanism in the political theories which are contrasted, under the guise of the divine shepherd, with Plato's own current doctrine.[73] But his evidence is late, and we can come nearer home. When Socrates wishes to see his state illustrated in the lives and actions of philosophers and statesmen (*Tim.* 19e5-6), Critias without qualms establishes it under the guidance of 'divine shepherds' (*Crit.* 109b6-c). Then (*a*) if the *Politicus* follows and corrects the *Critias*, it can be read as arguing that the very appropriateness of the *Republic*'s institutions to a Golden Age should have removed them from a study of statesmen. And Critias' introduction of the gods and their instrument 'persuasion' (109c3) has merely the purpose it seems to have – that of avoiding the difficulties (already envisaged in *Rep.* 500d-501a, 540d-541a) of establishing by authority a State based on consent.

But (*b*) if the *Critias* follows the *Politicus*, there can be only one inference from Critias' reference to divine shepherds. His whole discourse must then be devoted to illustrating the negative thesis that the institutions taken over from the *Republic* are not a matter of human political theory at all (and this not in the sense that they are a *paradeigma en ouranôi*, 'model in heaven', as the ideal *human* State may be, but that they are a radically inappropriate model for men). No one, I imagine, would defend this paradox. But two other points make it intolerable. First, it makes Critias' promise to talk of things mortal and human (107d7-8, taking up Socrates' request) a pointless fraud. Next, Critias takes the distribution of the earth among various gods as the setting for his state (109b1-2); and the *Politicus* not only relegates this setting to the ideal time-cycle but denies that under these conditions there would be any state at all (271d4-6, 271e8).

3. This weakens in advance a last objection, but it deserves independent discussion. It could be said that in the *Laws* Plato reverts to political theories having a closer affinity with the *Republic*, and hence that the *Timaeus* and *Critias* may equally have been written after the reversion. Now it is easily shown that the *Laws* as a whole embodies no such reversion, and that its

[72] The possibility is not cancelled by the concession that men do not credit it and that at present no such natural autocrat is to be found (301c-e). At this point Professor Grube's analysis breaks down (*Plato's Thought*, ch. vii). Against Barker he rightly points out that the *Republic* never supposes, what the *Politicus* affirms, that 'the best laws, even those enacted by the philosopher-king himself, are inevitably imperfect' and that law is a *deuteros plous* (second-best) (*Plt.* 300c2). But he thinks that now the philosopher-king has risen 'so high [sc. above law] as to join the gods' (281), and is consequently puzzled that 'the final definition of statecraft seems to imply the philosopher's knowledge all over again' (p. 284).

[73] *Politicus*, intro., xxi-xxvi.

inconsistency on a cardinal issue reflects the changes in political theory sketched above.

In *Laws* 4 (715c) it is laid down categorically that the ruler must be 'most faithful to the established laws': here the continuity with the *Republic* is still direct and unbroken by the argument of the *Politicus*. (Contrast, for example, the assertion in 715d, that no State can hope for salvation unless the law is 'master of the rulers and rulers are slaves of the law', with *Plt.* 294a: 'the best thing is for power to lie not with the law, but with the kingly man who has wisdom'.) Curators of the law must also be legislators in order to fill any lacunae, but they must remain guardians of the law (*nomophulakes*) (770a6, cf. *Rep.* 458c2-4): no question here, as in the *Politicus*,/ of inevitable revision and **93**
repeal.[74] But in Book 9 (875c-d) there is the first clear echo of the *Politicus* argument in the present sequence of the *Laws*.[75] There it is suddenly conceded that order and law are second-best and that knowledge (*epistêmê*) and understanding (*nous*) should not be subject to them; but that, since the latter commodities are found 'pretty well nowhere', the inadequacies of legislation must be tolerated. Note that previously the 'best state', without reservation, has been that whose laws are fixed and supreme: e.g. in 5. 739a-e the first city (as contrasted with the second best, which is shown in more detail) is that whose laws prescribe a thoroughgoing communism; this is at once the best state and the best laws, and Plato calls it the paradigm of a state (cf. *Rep.* 472d, 592b). Moreover, such legislation is the direct result of power in the hands of a man possessing wisdom and shrewdness (711e-712a), whereas in the *Politicus* (294a) it is independence of such permanent and universal laws that marks the kingly man who has wisdom. On the other hand, the sole difference of view between the passage in *Laws* 9 and the *Politicus* seems to be that, whereas the *Politicus* suggests that a ruler with knowledge may well be found (e.g. 293a2-4, 297b5-c2), the *Laws* implies that the search has been and will probably continue to be a failure.

Thus what enters the *Laws* as a paradigm of a state becomes before the end a *deuteros plous*. And if Book 9 imports an internal change of theory which reflects the emergence of new arguments in the *Politicus*, either of two explanations may be given. It may be that the *Laws* as a whole is Plato's latest work and that in it he designed to modify and reconcile political theories which he had advanced at different times. In that case the material is present but (what is evident on other counts too) the work is unfinished. The *Timaeus* and *Critias* show no signs of this late intention. On the other hand, it is arguable that the writing of the *Laws* was concurrent with that of the various

[74] Taylor seems to be right in saying that 'we are apparently to think of the authorities of [Plato's] "city" as needing less than a generation for the experience which would justify them in declaring their institutions definitely inviolable' (*The Laws of Plato* intro., xxxii).

[75] There is perhaps another in 12. 945b-948b where certain political abuses described in *Plt.* 298e-299a are eliminated by arrangements for the election and scrutiny of magistrates. In 6. 773a-c the marriage of complementary characters recommended in *Plt.* 310a-311a is independently defended. On 4. 713a-714a see p. 82, n.77 below.

late dialogues[76] and that Plato transferred arguments from them to the *Laws* without returning to make the necessary revision of earlier passages in the
94 work.[77] But however the/ chronology of the *Laws* is decided, our point is made that the dialogue embodies no consistent reversion to the political theories of the *Republic* and that, on the other hand, we shall go astray if we deny the direct continuity with the *Republic* which is stressed in the *Timaeus* and *Critias*. These three dialogues know nothing of the hope (whether inspired by Dion or Dionysius or a new analysis of art) that a State may be saved by the supremacy not of immutable laws but of a wise man above the law.

Conclusion

I hope I have proved that in metaphysics and cosmology, in logic and politics, the *Timaeus* and *Critias* belong to the middle dialogues and ignore salient arguments and theories developed in (or, in the case of Eudoxus' hypothesis, concurrently with) the later 'critical' group. No one doubts, I suppose, that the *Timaeus* represents the culmination of a period of growing confidence, a time in which Plato came to think himself ready to expound an ambitious system of speculations. The misfortune is that this crowning work has been tacked on to the latest dialogues, with which it disagrees largely in interests, methods, and conclusions. Its place is at the end of the *Republic* group (allowing a sufficient interval of time for Plato to have developed and coordinated the contributory theories). Just as the tripartite soul is taken over and given a physiological basis in the *Timaeus* (44d, 69c-72d), so the *analogia* of the Divided Line is repeated and made a basis of the metaphysics (28a, 29c), the *paradeigmata* are put to the service of the Demiurge, the astronomy of the

[76] Suggested by Taylor, Diès, Field, and Ross, *inter alios*. There is no direct evidence that any part of the *Laws* was written after every other dialogue. The work certainly followed the *Republic* (Aristotle, *Pol.* 1264b28). But Diogenes' remark that it was left on the wax does not certify even that it occupied Plato to his death, much less that nothing else was written at the same time. (Who would argue that the works which Descartes or Leibniz left in manuscript must have been their last?) The connexion of the preludes with Plato's work at Syracuse (*Ep.* 3. 316a) does not show that the technique first suggested itself to him there or in the year 360 (Taylor, *PMW*, 464-5; cf. J. Burnet, *Greek Philosophy* (London 1914), 301. But note that in the *Tim.* (29d5) the contrast between prelude and law has the musical connotation found in the *Rep.* (531d8), not the later legal sense). Taylor arbitrarily and inconsistently assumes a 'block' *Laws* in arguing that, if *Laws* 4. 711a-b (describing as if from personal knowledge the powers of a tyrant, which the wise legislator may hope to harness) should be dated after Plato's last return from Syracuse, '*the work* must therefore belong to a date later than 360'; (*Laws*, intro., p. xii). In any case (*a*) the optimism of the passage hardly accords with Taylor's dating and (*b*) the personal experience (of a tyrant's power to shape a State for good or evil) could clearly have been gained earlier.

[77] This would more easily explain the form of a myth in *Laws* 4. 713a-714a which bears a superficial similarity to that in the *Politicus*. The moral wrongly imported by Taylor into the *Plt.* (namely that the ideal ruler independent of laws is not an historical possibility) is in fact the moral of the allegory in the *Laws*, which can be regarded as a briefer and less sophisticated version corrected, in the light of later political theories, by the *Pol.* For whereas in *Laws* 4 the 'divine shepherd' and the supremacy of law are presented as a simple disjunction (713e-714a) and law is itself the *dianomê nou* (714a2), the *Plt.* insists on the *tertium quid*, the independent ruler with *nous* and *phronêsis*. And in the *Laws* this possibility does not seem to be entertained before Book 9.

Myth of Er is developed and refined, and a quasi-historical illustration of the *Republic*'s political doctrines is undertaken. (So, too, with details: the *Republic*'s proof of the uniqueness of any Form is given a second hearing.) And this provides us with more cogent reasons than those usually given for the abandoning of the *Critias* and the non-appearance of its sequel (supposing a sequel is promised in *Crit.* 108a-c). Doubtless, if a third member of the group was planned, much of the material for it may now be found in the *Laws*. But we need not suppose that Plato – after repeatedly insisting on his practice of selecting from the available subject-matter (e.g. *Tim.* 89d7-e3, 90e3-6) – was merely bewildered into shelving his project by the abundance of this material.[78] We can suggest now that some or all of the changes of theory outlined in this paper induced him to turn aside and make the fresh start recorded in the *Parmenides* and *Theaetetus*.

The ordering of the *Timaeus* and *Phaedrus*, whose affinities so far outweigh their discrepancies, cannot be determined by arguments of the sort that I have tried to find. There are, however, some pointers. For instance, it seems that an apologia for the abandoning of the *Critias* may be found in the *Phaedrus*, with its novel denial of stability to any written work and its condemnation of the man who 'has nothing more valuable than his own past writings and composi-/tions which he has spent time turning and twisting, **95**
welding, and censoring' (278d8-e1). There is no hint of this revulsion in what the *Timaeus* and *Critias* have to say about types of *logoi* (29b-d, 1078a-e); and if the *Timaeus* group was abandoned through dissatisfaction with some now veteran theories, the refusal to waste time 'welding and censoring' gains point after the abandonment but sounds oddly if it comes between the *Republic* and its avowed successor.

Again, there is Plato's apparent inconsistency on the nature of discarnate soul. The *Timaeus*, as from our argument we shall expect, combines the tripartite psychology of the *Republic* with the immortality of *nous* taught in the *Phaedo* (cf. *Rep.* 611b9-612a6): it excludes passions and appetites from the 'deathless principle of the soul'. But this is seemingly contradicted in the *Phaedrus* (246aff.) and the *Laws* (897a). However, we avoid the conclusion that Plato 'wavered to the end' between these alternatives[79] if we set the *Phaedrus* after the *Timaeus* (and the resulting account of Plato's final views seems to be confirmed if Jaeger and Nuyens are right, as against Themistius, in denying that in the *Eudemus* Aristotle confined immortality to *nous*). Within the same field there are other pointers. Those who accept Aristotle's literal exposition of the 'creation' in the *Timaeus* can of course argue that the doctrines of that dialogue exclude the definition of soul as self-moving and so without a beginning (*Phdr.* 245c-d). But even if we follow Xenocrates here, doubts remain. It is not merely that no mention of the definition occurs in the *Timaeus* (for what is sometimes taken for an oblique reference to it in 46d-e may well contain only its raw material). It is rather that, firstly, when Plato does mention self-motivation, he denies it to plants in the same breath as he

[78] Cf. Cornford's development of Raeder's suggestion, *PC*, 6-8.

[79] Hackforth, *Plato's Phaedrus*, 75.

ascribes soul to them (77b-c: contrast, for example, *Phdr.* 245e4-6); that is, he seems to use self-motivation (*kinêsis huph' heautou*) in an everyday sense innocent of any special doctrine. And, secondly, it does not seem that any attempt to reconcile the disorderly motions in the *Timaeus* with the doctrine that soul is the principle of motion has yet won general credit. But these hints do not add up to a reasonable certainty. In particular, they are weaker than arguments of the type I have so far tried to find because they do not exhibit a precise error or inadequacy correlated with a subsequent precise correction.

On the other hand, I trust the earlier arguments may arouse enough faith to remove one mountain and deliver our interpretation of the critical dialogues from the shadow of the *Timaeus*. It is time, I am sure, to be quit of such ancestral puzzles as that of inserting the Paradigms into the more sophisticated metaphysic of the *Philebus*, and to leave the profoundly important late dialogues to their own devices.

5

Notes on Ryle's Plato

In 1939 Gilbert Ryle broached his apparently inexhaustible cask of new 341
thoughts on Plato. He argued in a paper and a book-review in *Mind* that the *Parmenides* was 'an early essay in the theory of types.'[1] He found the same interests active in the *Theaetetus* and *Sophist*, other late dialogues which have philosophical and dramatic ties with the *Parmenides*. A year or so earlier, in 'Categories,' he had paid Aristotle a modified compliment, but his Aristotle was in essentials one of those already established in the literature. He has been understood to say that in those days it looked as though Aristotle had been, for the time at any rate, pretty well surveyed while Plato still called for exploration. But there is more than that to the interest that brings him so often back to Plato. In his studies of the late dialogues it became almost an alliance. Here are some comments, inadequate thanks for the illumination and excitement that have resulted. They centre in Ryle's discussion of the dialogue which Russell in *The Principles of Mathematics* called 'perhaps the best collection of antinomies ever made.'[2]

Russell's description of the *Parmenides*, like the diagnosis I quoted from Ryle,
was evidently meant for the sec-/ond and last part of the dialogue 342
(137c-66c).[3] Certainly there are unsolved paradoxes enough in the first part. Zeno's are merely sketched for Socrates when he tries to spell out his theory of Forms. But the systematic collection of antinomies on a large scale begins with the exercise in dialectic that Parmenides carries out in the second part. And it is immensely systematic. Many commentators from antiquity on have flagged after the early stages and offered correspondingly lop-sided interpretations. Ryle was not among them, and I imagine I have his sympathy for the obvious counter-move I must try later: drawing a map of the

[1] G. Ryle, 'Plato's *Parmenides*', *Mind* 48 (1939), 129-51 and 302-25; review of F.M. Cornford, *Plato and Parmenides*, *Mind* 48 (1939), 536-43. The paper, but not the review of Cornford, was reprinted with an Afterword (1963) in *Studies in Plato's Metaphysics*, ed. R.E. Allen (New York, 1965), and page-references to this and other papers prefaced by '*SPM*' will be to this collection.

[2] *Principles*, 355. He also (357) accepted Plato's argument from the proliferation of unity and being discussed in the last pages of this paper as proof of an infinite class, but gave this up with apparent regret in the *Introduction to Mathematical Philosophy*, 202-3, as conflicting with the theory of types.

[3] 'The dialogue': Ryle has recently (e.g. *SPM*, 145) come to think the *Parmenides* a patchwork of parts from different dates. On this see the Additional Note, p.103 below.

argument. But maps can be one-sided in other ways.

Broadly, the deductions in this part of the dialogue fall into four groups or stages, I-IV, and each stage into two movements, A and B. (For brevity I use these headings rather than Ryle's: Plato of course used none. So IA starts at 137c, IB at 142b, IIA at 157b, IIB at 159b, IIIA at 160b, IIIB at 163b, IVA at 164b and IVB at 165e.) One movement in each stage (the 'positive' movement) professes to prove, and the other (the 'negative') professes to disprove, both members of various pairs of antithetical predicates of one and the same subject. In I and III the subject of the antinomies is *hen* or *to hen*, 'One' or 'the One' or 'Unity' according to the predilection of translators: I am inclined to prefer either of the first two versions for a reason that Ryle gives for preferring the third, viz. that Parmenides has undertaken to speak of one of Socrates' Forms, but pending comment I shall use them indifferently. In II and IV the subject of the paradoxes is everything other than One or Unity.

The first two stages are represented as starting from one hypothesis and the other two as starting from the contradictory of that hypothesis. Assuming
343 that Plato does/ not, as some think, equivocate on this point, his hypothesis in I and II is that One *is* and in III and IV that One *is not*: for the present, with a caveat, I shall follow Ryle here and write the easier English 'exists' and 'does not exist.' The caveat is that some of the arguments (notably in IIIA, 162a-b) turn on the fact that Greek has only one verb at this date for 'be' and 'exist.' And this need not make for bad philosophy: it is part of Plato's *tour de force* in the *Sophist* to isolate a number of puzzles which for us cluster about non-existence, without marking off an 'existential' sense of the verb.[4]

Plato allows two small anomalies in his scheme. The first stage has an appendix (IC, 155e-57b) on the paradoxes of instantaneous change. And in the first but not in the later stages the negative movement precedes the positive. The reason for the later ordering is no doubt mere economy: once the subject of a negative movement is shown generally incapable of carrying predicates, it is enough to refer back to the positive antinomies for all the pairs of laboriously established predicates that are now denied it. The reason for starting with the negative movement in I is probably connected, on the other hand, with some broader functions that Plato means to assign to the dialogue. Dramatically he seems to place it at the head of a group containing the *Theaetetus, Sophist* and *Statesman* (as well as perhaps the *Cratylus* and *Philebus*),[5] and as an introduction to that group it might be expected to play two roles: that of marking where previous theories are suspect or superseded, and that of broaching a set of problems with which its successors will be
344 concerned. At any rate these two tasks seem to be/carried out, with some overlapping, by its first and second parts respectively; the overlap is inevitable since the new problems are largely the result of pressing dissatisfactions with

[4] Cf. M. Frede, 'Prädikation und Existenzaussage'. *Hypomnemata* Heft 18 (Göttingen 1967), and my 'Plato on Not-being', below, Chapter 6.

[5] The dramatic sequence of *Theaetetus, Sophist,* and *Statesman* is fixed (*Tht.* 210d, *Soph.* 216a-b, *Plt.* 257a-b); the place of the *Parmenides* in the sequence is suggested, less certainly, by *Theaetetus* 183e-84a.

the old theories. So the deductions of the second part begin with a negative movement because the general effect of that movement is to show the bankruptcy of one way of dealing with unity which had been characteristic of the theory of Forms brought up by Socrates in the first part (129a-e; cf. *Rep.* 525e). Just as a dyer's sample of vermilion might be a piece of cloth having that and no other colour, so it had been thought that in a higher world unity could be represented by a Form so paradigmatically unitary as to have no sort of plurality in it at all. The notion was helped by identifying the Form with the number 1 (*Rep.* 525e). How can 1 be another number of anything? but then how can it even be defined by any conjunction of properties? The question belongs to the lumber-room of philosophy partly because the movement IA was, *inter alia*, the necessary clearing-operation.

It is this network of deductions that was designed, in Ryle's view, to show by *reductio ad absurdum* part of the difference between two sorts of concept. In the nature of the case Plato could not have had labels for them; in Ryle's labelling they are the 'formal' concepts, such as unity and existence, and 'proper' or 'specific' and generic' concepts such as squareness and largeness. 'When we treat a formal concept as if it were a non-formal or proper concept, we are committing a breach of "logical syntax". But what shows us that we are doing this? The deductive derivation of absurdities and contradictions does, and nothing else can. Russell's proof that, in his code-symbolism, φ cannot be a value of x in the propositional function φx is only another exercise in the same genre as Plato's proof that "Unity" cannot go into the gap in the sentence-frame " ... exists" or " ... does not exist".'

The logical apparatus of Ryle's discussion is recogniz-/ably that of **345**
'Categories' and some of his post-war writings. The logical forms which interest philosophers are ascribed to propositions (and not, as in an earlier paper, to 'facts'), and concepts are assigned to different types which answer broadly to different roles in the formation of propositions: formal concepts 'are not subject or predicate terms of propositions but rather the modes of combining terms' (itself an echo of Russell). One and perhaps the main job of philosophers is to expose forms of speech that, without falling into blatant nonsense, misrepresent the logical powers of the concepts they employ. As a statement of grammar, ' "Unity" cannot go into the gap in the sentence-frame " ... exists" or " ... does not exist" ' would be false. Ryle takes it to be a statement of 'logical syntax' proved by Plato. He does not of course think that Plato argues in the formal mode. So what does he take the proof to consist in?

Here there are two points at which one would like him to have said more.

First, he speaks more than once of both the hypothesis 'Unity exists' and its contradictory as *entailing* the families of contradictions that they severally breed. As an analogy he cites Russell's use of the so-called Vicious Circle paradoxes to show that '$\varphi(\varphi\hat{x})$' is ill-formed. But he does not, of course, offer to show that Plato's antinomies follow from their first premisses as directly as those which Russell collected to argue the need for a theory of types. On Ryle's own survey of the *Parmenides* there seem to be many other premisses

and assumptions intervening in the plot. The reader is left to wonder whether these interventions are systematic or perhaps just random – as they might be expected to be, for example, on Robinson's thesis that Plato 'is genuinely failing to notice the extra premisses as such.'[6] But the answer, I think, is that they are systematic. They are so arranged that the conflicts between them are
346 the nerve of Plato's argument. If I can/ establish this, there will be closer analogies to Plato's strategy to be found in the classes of puzzle that Ryle discusses in 'Dilemmas.'

More particularly, unity is a paragon of a formal concept and Parmenides picks out One or Unity as the subject of his hypotheses. So once more the alerted reader might hope to be shown just where and why the antinomies come from miscasting unity in a non-formal role – even if other paradoxes can be seen to come from a comparable miscasting of other concepts. But the comments with which Ryle intersperses his summary of the argument play coy to this expectation too. He is ready to suggest that the starting-point of the argument in IA is illegitimate because 'Unity exists' and 'Unity is unitary' are both 'bogus sentences.' But the reason he notices for rejecting the first sentence is that it couples 'exists' with what is supposed to be a proper name, so this is a mistake about 'exist' compounded with another about abstract nouns. (Thereafter, particularly on IIIA-B, he notices similar misuses of 'exist' as 'signifying a quality, relation, dimension, or state, etc.') The reason he suggests for calling the second sentence bogus is that it treats a universal as one of its own instances. (But if unity *were* a universal, would it not have to be one of that odd subset that instantiate themselves? Russell still thought so in *Principles*. Back to this later.) His only other detailed comment on the mistreatment of unity is: 'We may suspect that the argument [of IA] presupposes that unity is a quality.' So it does indeed: as I have said, it argues as though unity could preclude plurality as one colour precludes others. Still, extracting paradoxes from the miscasting of a non-quality as a quality is not enough to show (or show awareness) that it is a formal concept in Ryle's sense. The same miscasting was possible with any of that favoured set of incomplete predicates which seem to have provoked Plato to invent Forms as quasi-ostensive samples for them because the world, understandably, offers
347 no such samples. The set, as any reader/ of the *Phaedo* and *Republic* V-VII and the first part of the *Parmenides* well knows, is a logical mixed bag including *large, heavy, equal, double, hard, just,* and *beautiful* and their contraries and cognates as well as *one* and *many* and *similar* and *dissimilar*. And the miscasting not only could be but surely had been made. The Forms answering to these predicates seem to have had, among their other duties, that of being just those privileged (and logically impossible) samples in which the attributes behave as qualities.[7] When Socrates at *Parm.* 129b6-c3 says he will be astonished if the Form of unity can be shown to be plural or the Form of plurality shown to be unitary, he is arguing from the same assumptions as when he lays it down in *Phaedo* 102d6-103a2 that neither the Form of largeness nor even its proxy

[6] R. Robinson, *Plato's Earlier Dialectic*[2] (Oxford 1953), 274.
[7] *SPM*, 303-8.

largeness in the individual can be or become small. Parmenides wrings a paradox from the latter claim in *Parm.* 131c-e, and most of IA together with the start of IB can be taken as addressed to the former. There is nothing in this, central as it is to Plato's emancipation from old confusions, to show a recognition that unity must be handled quite differently from those overt or covert relatives and grade-concepts that fill up his list.

Is this to say that Ryle has no evidence for his thesis? Of course not. There are arguments, perhaps too obvious for him to have singled out, that seem designed to show the absurdity of treating Socrates' oneness as another property co-ordinate with his pallor or smallness. The two chief candidates will be interviewed later. Still it will be a question how far they can be read as proofs, even in a suitably philosophical sense of 'proof.' That Plato is at grips with the logic of formal concepts here and in other late dialogues seems to me certain, and this certainty was established by Ryle. But an interest in proving the necessary distinctions does not seem to lie central to the strategy of the *Parmenides*. As I shall represent it, the method/that Plato explores with such **348**
enthusiasm is tailored not to the constructing of proofs but to the setting and sharpening of problems, and problems of a characteristically philosophical stamp. It is the first systematic exercise in the logic of aporematic and not demonstrative argument.

We shall get no further in this direction without the map I promised at the start. Here it is, as accurate as I can make it on this scale but with no claim to completeness.[8] It will help to fill Ryle's silence on the first point, for it tries to mark out, and locate conflicts between, the (or a representative majority of the) cardinal theses on which Plato's antinomies turn. I number the key-assumptions as Plato introduces them, trying to confine myself to those he expressly recognizes; though I have sometimes allowed myself a more general and abstract formulation when he cites only the particular application, and in doing so used forms not available to him. But in using letters in a way which had not yet become part of logic I preserve his ambiguities: on occasion 'S is P' will cover identities as well as predications, and there are no type-restrictions on the terms. To mark one of those conflicts between theses which seem to me to be the nerve of his argument, I shall put the sign '#' before the reference to some thesis which rejects or otherwise undermines the thesis under discussion.

Finally, to avoid encumbering the map, I relegate to a note the definitions and divisions that are introduced and not subsequently challenged in the argument.[9]/

[8] In an earlier version it has been refined and enlarged in theses by David Bostock and Malcolm Schofield, and I print it partly in the hope that it will prompt further efforts in the same field.

[9] In IA he defined 'whole' (137c, cf. *Theaetetus* 205a, Aristotle, *Phys.* 207a9-10); 'round' (137e, cf. *Epistles* vii 342b and Euclid's improvement in *Elements* i def. xv); 'straight' (137e, cf. Aristotle, *Top.* 148b27 and contrast Euclid, i def. iv); 'like' and 'unlike' (139e, 140a, and thereafter unchallenged, cf. 147c; but see *Protagoras* 331d-e, *Philebus* 13d); 'equal' and 'unequal' (140b-c, designed to cover incommensurables); 'coeval' (140e). IB takes these definitions over and adds one of 'contact' 9148e, adopted and reshaped by Aristotle, *Phys.* 226b18-27b2). IC defines

349 *I. If One exists, what can be said of it?*

1A (137c-42a) is negative in its conclusions. In addition to the definitions mentioned, its deductions depend primarily on nine premisses.

(1) 137c: *The One is one and not many* [# the opening argument of 1B and, for a reason to be given directly, # (15)]. From this it is deduced that the One cannot have parts or members or be a whole.

(Very likely (1) depends on a confusion between the identifying and predicative uses of 'S is P': One is not the same as Many and so is not many of anything. Let us call this the I/P confusion. It is surely one source of the so-called 'self-predication assumption' which characterizes the theory of Forms both in earlier dialogues and particularly in Socrates' account of the theory in *Parm.* 128e-30a. It will be challenged by the schema in (15), which distinguishes identity from participation, but the effect of (15) will in turn be spoilt by (16).)

(2) 137d: *The limits or extremities of anything are parts of that thing* [#(11)]. From this, together with the last conclusion, stem the proofs that the One cannot have limits, shape, or position./

350 (Throughout the deductions, save for those concerned with progress and regression in time, mathematical interests are obvious. Recall that the Form of unity had among its other duties that of representing the cardinal number 1. Here the geometrical application to points is evident, and Aristotle makes it explicit in *Phys.* 212b24-25 (cf. 209a7-13). Arguing that points cannot have a location because they cannot have a perimeter is part of Plato's 'war against points' (Aristotle, *Meta.* 992a19-22).)

(3) 139e-40a and ?138c, 139c: *If anything has more than one character or attribute these pluralize the thing* – or, as it is put in 1B, 142d, they are *parts or members* of the thing. The attributes in question are unrestricted in type: they include unity, identity, existence, in fact anything distinguishable by the criteria in (4) below.

(A minor question is when this premiss is introduced. It does not occur explicitly until 139e-40a. But some think that from it, together with the conclusion given under (1), stem the proofs that the One cannot (a) change in quality or even (b) be identical with, (c) differ from or be (d) like or (e) unlike itself or anything else. On the other hand, and by way of showing how tentative this mapwork must be in detail, it is arguable that (a), and (b) and (c) with their derivative (e), depend only on the I/P

'combination' and 'dispersion,' 'assimilation' and its opposite, and 'increase,' 'diminution,' and 'equalization' (156b). In addition, from IA on Plato assumes the equation between having a location and being contained in something which is standard in Greek philosophy (138a, cf. Zeno B 5, Gorgias B 3, and Aristotle's analysis in *Physics* IV 1-5). As for divisions, IA distinguishes 'shape' into 'round' and 'straight' (to which IB, 145b, adds 'mixed'), and 'change' (*kinêsis*) into 'change of quality' and 'motion' (138b-c, cf. *Tht.* 181d: there is an illegitimate conversion of one of the disjuncts in IIIA, 162e, and IIIB, 163e, though previously the division was given correctly in IIIA, 162d).

confusion: thus (a) anything changing character is taken to lose its identity (138c), and (b,c) whatever is (identical with) One is not (not even predicatively) anything else, such as same or different (139c-d). But (d) is expressly represented as depending on (3) and so, in retrospect, are (b) and (c) (139e-40a). This still leaves (a) as dependent on the I/P confusion. In any event the argument for (b) imports a criterion of non-identity that finds an echo in IIB and IIIA and *Sophist* 255a-c.)/

(4) 139d: *If the statement that S is P differs in truth-value* (or, in the form in which 351
it is assumed in IB, 142b-c, *differs in sense*) *from the statement that S is Q, then P is different from Q*. (Note the extension of this in IIIA, 160c: if the statement that S is P differs in sense from the statement that T is P, even when 'P' stands for 'non-existent,' then S is a different thing from T. All such assumptions seem to be applications of the general view of words as names which appears in (17), but Plato does not draw the connection.) From the conclusions already listed under (3) it is further argued that the One is not equal or unequal to anything and that it has no temporal attributes.

(5) 138d: *Changes* (more strictly, *movements to a place*) *take time: to describe S as becoming P is to describe something temporally intermediate between an initial and a final state* [# the argument under (22), which trades on the possibility of describing the initial and final states as 'p' and 'not-p' or vice versa]. From the conclusions listed under (2) it is argued that the One cannot move in one place, and then from (1) and (5) it is shown that the One cannot change place either.

(The character of one of the negative movements is becoming clear. Again Aristotle makes the application to geometrical points explicit, at *Phys.* 240b8-41a6.)

(6) 141b: *If* (*when*) *X is becoming different from Y, it cannot be the case that Y is different from X: otherwise X would already be different from Y and not merely becoming so*. Hence it is argued that, if X is becoming older than itself, it is also becoming younger than itself. But from the conclusions under (3) and (4) the One can have neither this temporal property nor that of remaining coeval with itself; hence it does not exist in time.

(Formally (6) is an argument, but I give it as a premiss. The implicit but unexpressed premiss is/
(6*) *If S is becoming P it cannot yet be P* 352
and this is challenged by (19) in the parallel context in IB.)

(7) 141d-e: *What exists exists in time* (more exactly, *Whatever is or becomes, is or becomes at some time past present or future*). From this and the conclusions under (6) it is argued that the One does not exist (more exactly, is not in any way, is not *anything*).

(8) 141e: *If S is P, then S is or exists*. (Cited here in the particular form 'If the One is one, the One is,' but in its general form the premiss recurs in IIIA, 161e, and IIIB, 163e, and it is challenged by IIIA in an argument based on

the considerations under (4).) From this and the conclusion under (7) it follows that the One is not one (or not One).

(It is worth remark that even this premiss, like its predecessor, does not prove Plato's recognition of a separate existential sense of the verb 'to be.' Arguably, the logic of (8) appeared to him nearer to that of 'If Smith lies to one person, Smith lies.')

(9) 142a: *What does not exist can have nothing related to it* [# the argument under IIIA]. From this and the conclusion under (7) it follows that the One cannot be named and that there can be neither speech nor knowledge, perception nor idea of it at all.

IB (142b-55e) is positive and its deductions depend primarily on premisses (10)-(20) together with some from IA, viz. (1), (3), (4), (6), (7), (8), and the converse of (9). Two of these inherited premisses, (1) and (6), are challenged in the same movement. The opening arguments have no fresh premisses:

353 142b-43a: By (4), if the One exists its existence is not/ the same as its unity; hence, by (3), unity and existence are pluralizing parts of the one [#(1)]. But the same is true of each part in turn. (Here, in ascribing unity to each part, the argument seems to anticipate premiss (10); and in ascribing existence to whatever is unitary it seems to rely on (8).) Hence the One is a whole with infinite parts, and unity and existence are infinitely distributed.

143a-44a: Furthermore, if the One and its existence are differentiable they exhibit difference, which (seemingly by reliance on (4) again) is distinct from either of them. The sums and multiples of these three generate all numbers.

(10) 144c: *What is not one is nothing at all* (more strictly, *if a part were not one part it would be nothing*) [#(23)]. From this it is argued that any part of a plurality is one, that anything divisible is divisible into some number of parts, and generally that any number is a number of units.

(Here starts one of the trains of paradox which show the anomalous behaviour of unity as judged by that of squareness or heaviness. The opening arguments of IB, and the premiss (10) which they import, claim that we cannot 'abstract from' the unity or existence of a subject because unity and existence must always be reimported in talking of whatever parts or members are left. In giving a thing's properties we cannot systematically discount unity as we can systematically discount shape or weight. This is what (23) will try to challenge.)

(11) 144e-45a: *A whole contains, and so limits, its parts* [#(2), #(13)]. From this and the conclusions under (9) and (10) it is argued that the One is limited as well as unlimited.

(Here comes another trouble over unity, the unity of any limited set. The
354 effect of (11) is to upset (2) by/ making the limit or limiting factor external to, and not part of, what is limited. Trouble is coming with (13).)

(12) 145b: *If X is limited X has spatial extremities.* Hence the One has shape.

(For the importing of spatial terms cf. (14) and its temporal analogue in (7).)

(13) 145c: *If X has parts X is identical with the aggregate of those parts* [#(11)]. From the conjunction of (11) and (13) come the proofs that the One, qua parts, is contained in itself, qua whole; and also (reversing the roles) that it is not contained in itself. From this in turn flow many of the later conclusions, as that it is in contact with itself and that it is both larger and smaller than itself.

(Premisses (11) and (13) say, respectively, that the whole is an extra element over and above its parts, and that it is nothing more than the parts. In the analysis of syllables in *Theaetetus* 203e-5a these possibilities are given as an exhaustive disjunction and not, as here, as a conjunction. The disjunction as in turn superseded in the *Sophist* 252e-53c, on which more below, and Aristotle puts the moral in its simplest form in *Meta.* 1041b11-27: a syllable is a whole which is neither a heap of elements nor an extra element.)

(14) 145e: *What exists must be somewhere*, sc. (the standard treatment of location in Greek philosophy) *must be in something.* From this and the conclusions under (13) it is argued that the One must be both in itself and in another; and that, qua 'in itself,' it is always 'in the same,' and qua 'in another,' it is always 'in something different.' From this, by way of a flagrant fallacy of relations, it is deduced that the One is static and moving and, later, that it is different from itself./

(The fallacy is that 'in the same,' which began by meaning 'in the same **355**
thing as itself,' is tacitly reconstrued as meaning 'in the same thing as that in which it previously was'; and 'in another' is successively construed as meaning 'in something other than itself,' 'in something other than that in which it previously was,' and 'in something other than that in which it now is.' Nor does Plato stop labouring the fallacy here, and this becomes a test-case for those who think him oblivious to all the component fallacies in the argument. The same misuse of 'same' and 'other,' together with the I/P confusion, provides the later argument that nothing can be different from anything; and it was a comparable fallacy in IA that engendered confusions over 'getting older than oneself' and 'staying coeval with oneself.' In the *Sophist* 259c-d Plato is severe on those who commit the fallacy and produce superficial paradoxes by failing to complete the predicates 'same' and 'other.')

(15) 146b: *Anything is related to anything in one of three ways: (a) by identity or (b) by difference or (c) as part to whole or whole to part.*

(The part-whole relation is exemplified in the sequel by 'partaking of unity' or, what comes to the same, 'being in a way (i.e., for present purposes predicatively) one' (147a). So here identity seems to be distinguished from predication. But the effect is spoilt by (16) which reimports, for negations at least, the I/P confusion.)

(16) 147a: *What is not one is related to One by (b) and not by (a) or (c).* Hence things that are not one have no unity of any sort [#(10)]; and from this,

together with the conclusions under (10), they are argued to have no number at all.

(The argument is that being not X excludes being X in any way whatever:
356 the negation is construed as deny-/ing that the subject is X both in the identifying and in the predicative sense of the words. So here is the I/P confusion again; it is cleared up in the *Sophist* 256a-b, but here Plato forces the issue by the challenge that is coming in IIA. Meantime the present argument is reinforced at 147a by an appeal to (1), which reappears yet once more at 148e-49a.)

(17) 147d: *Words are names, and to repeat a word is to name the same thing twice.* Here 'words' (*onomata*) covers at least all those general terms for which Plato had postulated Forms: thus it is argued that, in 'A is different from B and B is different from A,' the two occurrences of 'different' name a thing that A and B have in common, and thus their difference makes them alike.

(The most general Greek expression for 'word' also means 'name,' but (17) is not just a muddle reflecting this fact. It embodies the logical or semantic atomism which had shown itself in earlier writings and which probably underlies the assumptions in (4). Ryle has often argued, I think rightly, that Plato manages to recognize this linguistic model and reject it; later I shall suggest that the decisive rejection takes place when the *Sophist* moves beyond the disjunction of (11) and (13). Meantime the view in its simplest form faces the puzzle set by IIIA and IIIB jointly: even non-existing things can apparently be mentioned and distinguished from others.)

(18) 150a-d: *Smallness is small, largeness is large, etc.* (In detail: if smallness were itself equal to or larger than anything, it would be '*doing the jobs of largeness and equality, and not its own*'; and if there were no smallness in anything else, 'there would be nothing small *except smallness.*') This is put to proving that nothing but largeness can exhibit largeness, nothing but smallness smallness, etc./

357 (Here, explicitly and even flamboyantly introduced, is the 'self-predication' assumption which some believe that Plato was unable to recognize as a premiss of some paradoxes in the first part of the dialogue, including the notorious Third Man (132a-b). He applies it here to the very concept – largeness – which had been exploited in the Third Man, and uses it to produce still more outrageous consequences. Even if Aristotle had not recorded for us the Academy's recognition and formulation of the assumption it would take some determination to think of Plato as still reduced to 'honest perplexity' by his inability to see that largeness cannot be a large thing.)

It is now deduced from (7) that the One exists in time, and from (6) and the conclusion under it that the One is getting not only older but younger than itself.

(19) 152c-d: *If X is becoming Y, then at any 'present time' in the process X is (and not: is becoming) Y* [#(6), and esp. #(6*)]. The premiss is formulated quite generally and then applied to 'becoming older' (152c6-d4): if the One is growing older then at any present time it is older. (Unluckily but idiomatically this is expanded into 'older than itself,' and used to argue that the One is also

younger than itself, but this extra fallacy of relations does not affect the main point of the conflict between (19) and (6*): see the comment below.) Subsequently, by an extension of (5) to cases of coming-into-existence, it is argued that the One is both older and younger, and neither older nor younger, than the others. And further paradoxes are wrung from the idea of becoming relatively and asymptotically older and younger.

(Premiss (19) is plausible when applied to 'X is in the process of becoming older (or taller)'; (6*) is plausible when applied to 'X is in the process of becoming an octogenarian (or six feet tall).' In *Philebus* 23c-27c Plato brings out part of the difference between these two sorts of filling, saying that the second but not the/ first sets a terminus to the becoming. **358**
Aristotle profited from Plato's distinction in his own account of *kinêsis* and *energeia.* I take Plato to be pressing the need for such a distinction by setting up (19) as a challenge to (6), and the distinction once grasped is lethal to the simple dichotomy of 'being' and 'becoming' that Plato had inherited. Roughly, becoming is incompatible with being in (6) and entails being in (19): everything depends on the question, 'Becoming *what*?')

(20) 155d: *What exists has (or can have) other things related to it.* By this converse of (9), the One can be named and spoken of and there can be knowledge, perception, and thought of it.

IC (155e-57b) is a joint appendix to IA and IB, using some conclusions from each but dropping others. It adopts those given under (1), (8), and the opening arguments of IB, but tacitly drops that under (7) on which the conclusion under (8) depends.

(21) 155e: *If S is both P and not P it is P at one time and not P at another.* From this together with the various contradictions listed for the One, it is argued that the One undergoes various forms of change from P to not-P or vice versa.

(Here, by another I/P confusion, being both P and not-P is construed as a matter of existence and non-existence. On these terms (21) can be invoked to evade all contradictions, including that on which (24) will depend.)

(22) 156c: *There is no time in which S can be neither P nor not-P.* Hence any change, construed as a transition from P to not-P or vice versa, takes no time: it occurs at 'the instant.'/

(Premiss (21) depends on the law of contradiction, (22) on the law of **359**
excluded middle; but the excluded middle seems not to apply to descriptions of 'the instant.')

II. If One exists, what can be said of everything else?

IIA (157b-59b) is positive. It depends chiefly on premiss (23), together with (10), (15) and the converse of (1) (which thus foreseeably becomes an equation). But the inherited premiss (10) is challenged in the same movement.

157b: Things other than the One are not the One (and in this sense are called 'not one,' cf. 158c). So, by an appeal to the converse of (1), they must be distinguished from the One itself by forming a whole containing parts or members; and by (10) and the conclusions under it, each part must have unity by 'partaking in the One.'

> (Here it seems initially that the argument wants to cut loose from the restrictive interpretation of 'not one' given in (16). That interpretation reimported the I/P confusion into negation by pretending that the options given under (b) and (c) in (15) were mutually exclusive. Here, things other than the One are carefully said to be 'not *the* One' before this phrase is replaced in 158c by 'not one.' Vain hope. The next move in the argument rejects (10) and the conclusions under it, and the puzzle is restored.)

(23) 158c: *If anything is related to the One by neither the first nor the third of the options under (15)* – i.e., neither is nor even exhibits unity – *it must be mere unlimited plurality* [#(10)]. Now considered in themselves ('at the time they are starting to partake of the One,' or 'abstracted in thought') the things other than the One answer to this condition and hence are bare plurality. In this way they
360 are unlimited as well as (in virtue of the/ unity that accrues to them) limited; and from these contraries all others are made to flow.

> (See the comment under (10). (23) and its dependent arguments propose an answer to the question 'What can be said of anything in abstraction from its unity?' as though this had the logic of 'What was he before he became a greengrocer?' or 'What sort of thing is it, apart from its shape?' (10) claimed in effect that the abstraction is impossible; and in particular, the hopeful answer that what is left is a kind of bare plurality runs against the conclusion under (10) that any plurality is a plurality of units, a conclusion repeated in IIB.)

IIB (159b-60b) is negative and relies wholly on premisses already introduced. The One and the things other than the One form an exhaustive disjunction. By the conclusion under (1) it is argued that the two camps cannot be related by (c) in the schema at (15), and evidently they cannot be related by (a) either; so the other things are isolated from all unity. If IIA were right, quite a lot could still be said of them. But IIB reverts to the conclusion under (10), that any plurality is a plurality of units; so these things other than the One are not plural either [#(23)]. They have neither number nor limit nor any enumerable properties whatever.

III. If One does not exist, what can be said of it?

IIIA (160b-63b) is positive and relies on premisses already introduced or, in the case of (4) and (8), on more or less questionable extensions of them. By the extension of (4) noted under that premiss, it is argued that even a non-existent One can be known and mentioned and distinguished from other things; hence it has various properties and stands in various relations. Yet, by

(8), if it does not exist it must lack properties and relations, from which it follows that it cannot have equality with any-/thing; and hence, by a fallacy 361
of negation which underlay another argument in IB (150d), it is deduced to be unequal to anything.

(The fallacy is the assumption that if something lacks a given predicate it must have some other of a family of incompatible predicates which includes the first. Perhaps the double use of 'not,' to signify both bare negation and this loaded variety, is acknowledged in *Theaetetus* 183b – though not, I think, in *Sophist* 257b.)

But now, by an extension of (8), the One must exist if only to *be* non-existent. From its existence and non-existence are deduced its mutability and other characteristics.

(But the detail of the argument makes it clear how far Plato is here from saying unambiguously that S must exist in order to have non-existence. Otherwise he would also be claiming that S must be non-existent qua *not being* non-existent. 'To be' and 'not to be' are run in harness here as in the *Sophist*, and that dialogue tackles its problems about not-being without giving up either the hard-won subject-predicate model for statements or the treatment of '... is ...' and '... is not ...' as a two-place predicate.)

IIIB (163b-64b) is negative and relies on premiss (24), together with (9).

(24) 163c: *What does not exist cannot also 'in some sense exist'* [≠ the general argument of IIIA]. Hence, by (9), nothing can be said or known, etc., of the One.

(A beneficial truth about existence? But in the Greek the factotum verb 'to be' is still in play. So Plato may be calling attention once more to a misuse of negation that began in (16) and will still exercise him in the *Sophist*: the assumption that what is not X, in some sense or respect, is not X at all. He may just be anxious/ to discredit the notion that *not to be* is *not to be* 362
anything.)

IV. If One does not exist, what can be said of everything else?

IVA (164b-65e) is positive and relies on premisses already introduced together with the relational fallacy described under (14).

If the others are other, by (9) they cannot be other than the One; so they are other than each other. But if so they must be supposed, or must seem, to have plurality and hence, by the conclusion given under (10), they must be deemed to have number, unity, and the dimensional properties inferred from these in IB.

(IVA reinforces IIIA, arguing that even if the One does not exist it must figure in discourse and conjecture, however mistaken. IVB, like IIIB, replies by an appeal to premiss (9).)

IVB (165e-66a) is negative and relies wholly on premisses previously introduced. By (10) and the conclusions given there, any plurality is a class of units; and by (15) and the conclusions drawn from it in IIA any unit must partake in the One. But by (9) this connexion is now impossible, nor can the One be introduced in any connexion whatever. So nothing can be said of the others at all; hence nothing exists.

Now for some morals. Two negative conclusions will help clear the way for the positive.

Sometimes the antinomies have been diagnosed as an exercise in ambiguity. The key-hypotheses *hen ei estin* and *hen ei mê estin* have been thought to vary in sense between any two antithetical movements, and for a given movement the sense is to be gathered from the supporting premisses. But one
363 thing our map shows is that the/ premisses which supposedly fix the sense for one movement commonly turn up in its twin as well. And some of them are both used and challenged in the same movement.[10] Again, the antinomies are sometimes branded as a professional lampoon or a school primer of fallacies. But the map makes it easier to see how often the premisses are the very assumptions which Plato puts to serious work in other dialogues of his maturity.[11]

Ryle rejected such attempts to diminish the seriousness of the work. But since a budget of unresolved paradoxes cannot be meant to expound positive doctrine, he saved the work's seriousness by reading it as a direct *reductio ad absurdum* of both one hypothesis and its contradictory – a project nearer to Kant's paradoxes than Russell's. It might be replied that in the *Sophist* Plato still seems content to have formal concepts as the subject of such hypotheses; but more recently Ryle has proposed a very late date for the second part of the *Parmenides* which would avoid this objection.[12] Even so, the map seems to show Plato far less single-minded than such a *reductio* would make him. And in particular it shows that throughout the deductions he recurs to one
364 favourite strategem,/that of setting up a conflict between a pair of premisses or between one premiss and a thesis derived from others. And these various conflicts do most to generate the major contradictions between and within movements and stages of the argument; and they are serious. They set, without solving, problems that exercise Plato in other late dialogues.

[10] The premiss (1) is used in IA and IB (and their appendix IC), and again in IIA and IIB. (3), (4), (5), (6), and (7) are used in IA and IB, and (2) after its entry in IA is implicitly subsumed under (13) of IB. (8) is used in IA and IB and again in IIIA and IIIB. (9) is used in IVA and IVB, and its use in IA is echoed by its converse in IB. (10) is used in IIA and IIB and again in IVA and IVB. (15) is used in IIA and IIB. Premisses both used and challenged in the same movement are (1) in IB, (10) in IB and again IIA, (11) and (13) and (16) in IB. And (5), which is used in IA and IB, is challenged in their appendix IC.

[11] The premiss (1) is used in *Soph.* 245a and (2) in *Soph.* 244e. (3) is used, implicitly, at any rate in *Tht.* 157b-c, 209c; (4) in *Soph.* 255a-c; (6), or the unexpressed (6*) given under it, in *Tim.* 27d-28e, with which cf. *Tht.* 182c-83b and *Soph.* 248a; (8) in *Soph.* 255e-56a, cf. 256e; (9) in *Soph.* 237c-39b; the disjunction of (11) and (13) in *Tht.* 203e-5a; (18) in the 'self-predicational' treatment of the Forms criticized in *Parm.* 131c-32b and later (cf. 134b6-7); (20) in *Soph.* 238a, and (24) in *Soph.* 239b.

[12] See the Additional Note, p. 103 below.

Here are examples: I believe a more detailed map would show others. (i) The confusion between identity-statements and predications which had beset the earlier metaphysics is brought out, with especial reference to negations, by the conflict between (16) and the argument drawn from (10) in IB and IIA, and teased out in the *Sophist* (250ff. and esp. 256a-b). (ii) Puzzles which we for some purposes can, as Plato could not, label as puzzles of non-existence, and which are taken up and transformed in *Sophist* 237b-63d, are set here by confronting (9) with the extension of (4) used in IIIA. (iii) The veteran assumption that 'being' and 'becoming' mark two different states characterizing different worlds (an assumption which the *Timaeus* appears to be trying to modify from within, without ever finally breaking the shell) is called in question by the conflict between (6) and (19), a conflict that Plato stresses by connecting it with the particular notion of 'growing older'; and the conflict and the dichotomy are sufficiently demolished by the distinction in the *Philebus* noticed under (19). (iv) The conflict between (10) and (23) is another example of the same strategy: I reserve it for a later page. (v) An abstract puzzle about the relation of a whole to its parts is set by the juxtaposition of (11) and (13). In a more concrete version (but one which is said to have quite general application, *Tht.* 204a2-3) these same premisses reappear as a disjunction in the *Theaetetus* argument to which I referred under (13). It is worthwhile following this train of argument a little further into familiar territory, for it marks Plato's emancipation from the atomism noticed under (17) and, what is more/ to my purpose, it shows how the **365**
Parmenides sets without solving problems which Plato elsewhere offers to solve.

The *Theaetetus* (201dff.) and the *Sophist* (253a, 261d) use Plato's favourite analogy of letters and syllables to illustrate the complexity of whatever can be known and explained, and therewith the complexity of what must be said to explain it. In the *Theaetetus* (202e-6b) Socrates tries to argue this complexity away. He urges that a syllable is either just the letters that compose it or a separate single entity produced by their juxtaposition; so knowing a syllable is either just knowing each letter or knowing the new incomposite, and either way the knowledge is just of simple objects and not of complexes. After all, he pursues, the whole business of learning letters is the effort to pick out each one by itself (206a). But when the *Sophist* takes up the analogy (252e-53a) it points out that a syllable is (not an aggregate of pieces and not an extra piece, but) a nexus of constituents of different types fitted together in certain ways; and the knowledge of letters exercised in spelling is not just an ability to tell the letters apart but the knowledge of how they can be legitimately combined and how, in virtue of their different powers of combination, they differ in type. The *Philebus* (18c) points one moral: no letter can be learnt in isolation from the rest. And the *Sophist* argues that it is like this with our knowledge of the 'forms' or concepts which give our words meaning, and with our knowledge of the words themselves: they too cannot be learnt in isolation, they too are marked off by their powers of combination into different types (253a, 261d). Speaking is not stringing nouns together, and learning to speak is not, as the *Cratylus* had implied, a piecemeal business of correlating atoms of the world

with atoms of language. This is a familiar enough train of argument;[13] my
366 excuse/ for recalling it here is that the quandary from which it sets out in the *Theaetetus* is typically set as a conflict of theses in the *Parmenides*.

Anyone who stresses, as I have, the plurality of philosophical interests that Plato engineers into these paradoxes must ask why he tries to give some unity to the business by the architectural scheme I sketched earlier. Here is part at least of a reply. At the start of the antinomies (135d-36c) Parmenides promises that the ensuing exercise in dialectic will be an application and extension of Zeno's methods. And Zeno's hand can surely be seen in the deductions from one hypothesis, the fresh starts in the trains of argument, the consequent clusters of contradictions or seeming contradictions. But what of the extension of the argument from one hypothesis to its contradictory, and from the subject of the hypothesis to everything else; and above all what of those conflicts between theses that I have made the focal points of the enterprise?

The Zeno we need is, of course, Plato's Zeno: a defender of Parmenides who wrote one book consisting wholly of arguments against plurality (*Parm.* 127e-28e). Whether Plato's interpretation was accurate is immaterial here and undecidable anyway. Some years ago I proposed a scheme which would allow the extant arguments of Zeno to be grouped into such a book.[14]

Plato does not think Zeno proved his case and does not represent himself as taking over a method of proof. To use an anachronism, it is not the shape of the vault but the use of the buttresses that he means to acknowledge and
367 adopt. To begin with he has seen that Zeno, arguing/ against all those who naïvely suppose the world to contain a plurality of things, proceeds by offering his opponents options. Either the kind of division that produces the alleged plurality is of a sort to end after a finite number of steps or it can be continued for an infinite number, and then on this second option either it reaches some limiting indivisibles or it can never be finished; and Zeno professes to wring an absurdity from each of these possibilities. If this is so (and I am taking my old scheme as a working assumption), such a method of trying the alternatives explains not only the variations that Plato plays on his hypothesis but other devices he adopts in the later dialogues, such as the use of logical division that he defends in the *Philebus*: division prevents hasty generalizations about a class from some unrepresentative sub-set.

But his acknowledgment to Zeno goes deeper than this. Zeno seems often to overpress his paradoxes by joining in one conclusion the consequences of more than one option – as when he says that the members of a plurality must

[13] There is no space to discuss Ryle's attractive suggestion ('Letters and Syllables in Plato', *Phil. Rev.* 69 (1960), 431-51, answered by D. Gallop, 'Plato and the Alphabet', *Phil. Rev.* 72 (1963), 364-76) that when Plato speaks of letters he means not the separate written characters but the 'abstractable noise-differences' which cannot be produced separately. Even if Plato means to be understood phonetically, the analogy of notes and chords that he conjoins with that of letters and syllables (*Tht.* 206a-b, *Soph.* 253a-b, *Phil.* 17a-c) suggests that he does not have Ryle's moral in mind.

[14] See above, Chapter 3.

be 'so small as to have no magnitude yet so large as to be boundless.' Yet these conjunctions are not arbitrary, just because each of the conflicting options is (or is made by Zeno to seem) plausible in its own right. Suppose *per impossibile* that the division of any magnitude is pushed as far as it will theoretically go, then the end-products can have no magnitude (else divisions can still be made) yet must have some magnitude if the thing divided is not to vanish into nil components; and from this he goes on to extract the conjunction already quoted. Similarly – there is a copybook example in the paradox noticed under (v) of the previous section – Plato manufactures contradictions both within and between the movements of his argument by treating both parties to one of his conflicts as forming one logical conjunction, just as at the end of the dialogue (166c) he collects all the preceding inimical conclusions into one contradiction. The training in dialectic that he acknowledges to/ Zeno, and illustrates in his own **368**
antinomies, is a training in the presentation of conflicts between theses each of which seems cogent in its own right. He neither adopts nor proposes any general training in the resolving of such conflicts.

Still, even if proofs are not Plato's central interest in the *Parmenides*, does he not incidentally manage to prove some differences between unity (and therewith all numbers, according to the arguments under (10)) and common properties such as size and colour?

1. Surely this is the moral of the collision between (10) and (23). He seems to be pointing to that logical indispensability that he claims for unity in the *Philebus*: its character of being presupposed by all forms and subjects of discourse (15d4-8, 16c9, 19b6). He does it by exploring the embarrassments we run into if we try to describe any subject or congeries of subjects that has no unity and cannot be resolved into parts having any, something that happens not to be or contain one of anything at all. He proceeds as though this were a project as straightforward as describing a subject that lacks some shape or size; and then he proposes an answer that, in the fashion of the dialogue, is made to seem unavoidable under (23) and impossible under (10).

Yet here too the conflict is plainer than the moral to be drawn from it. For one thing, it is not clear that his argument allows him to mark off unity from, say, relative size and weight. The question he professes to answer under (23) is, What can be generally true of things which are coming to have but do not yet have any unity? (Cf. 158b5-9.) But consider the predicate 'large,' which he takes to be typically applicable to whatever is larger than something else (not necessarily larger than a standard object or than the average of some class). A comparable puzzle seems to arise if we ask, What can be true of something which is coming to have but does not yet have any/ largeness? For **369**
the answer seems to be that it cannot then have any size at all, yet the question implies that it is of a type to have some size or other. Let us look for an argument that does force a distinction between 'large' and 'one,' that diverse pair that had for so long rubbed shoulders in the theory of Forms.

2. Given a certain view of Plato's grasp of the issues, there is a brace of arguments that seem to force just this distinction. And they are evidence of that distribution of duties between the two parts of the dialogue that I suggested earlier. It is in the first part that, in the view of many including Ryle, Plato brings out a fallacy that had pervaded his earlier statements of the theory of Forms. He had, in Ryle's words, spoken as though universals could be instances of themselves; and he now proves, by ascribing largeness to itself, that to credit anything with both functions generates a regress, in this case a regress of largenesses that turns the supposedly single Form into an unlimited class (*Parm.* 132a-b). Notice that the regress does not depend on mistreating largeness as a quality: it is equally effective whether or not the relational nature of the attribute is recognized. That Plato was able to isolate the mistake which lies at the root of this and other troubles in the context is, I think, put beyond question by premiss (18) and the arguments under it: I refer to my note there.

Now there is a comparable regress in the second part of the dialogue, making use this time of the 'ingredience' model of predication that appears in premiss (3); and it seems designed to show the recalcitrant behaviour of such putative properties as unity and being. In IB (142b-43a) Plato argues that if unity is a part or property of something (in this case, the One) it is *one* of the thing's parts and there *is* such a part; and the same is true of the thing's being. So both unity and being have the parts or properties of unity and being, which
370 in turn have both/ parts, and so *ad infinitum.* But suppose Plato to have recognized the point of his first regress, namely that the common run of a thing's properties are not to be assigned to themselves; then here is a dilemma. Either he must say that unity and being cannot be component properties of anything on the same terms as its colour and size, or he must rule that unity canot be said to be unitary or being to be. But the second alternative will not readmit them as component properties of anything, for Plato is ready to argue that any component is *one* part and there *is* such a part. He seems to be marking off the sort of concept – identity and similarity and some others as well as unity and being – that will appear as 'common' in *Theaetetus* 185c4-d3 and as the ubiquitous vowel-connectives of *Sophist* 253a4-6, c1-3, concepts which must be reintroduced in describing their own behaviour as in talking about anything else (e.g., 255d9-e6, 257a1-5).

Does this settle the question? Only for those who take Plato to have come to grasp the difference between largeness and anything large, and for those others who think him incapable at any time of that confusion. There are some who still think he never saw the distinction, and the review of their reasons would take us far outside the *Parmenides.* Their Plato is a grimmer and more baffled man than Ryle's, and more baffled on these issues than Plato's immediate colleagues and successors.

What positive conclusions Plato wants to be drawn from his nexus of conflicting arguments is perhaps, like the song the Sirens sang, a question not beyond all conjecture. It seems to me more conjectural than the programme I have ascribed to him. But whether he is trying a prentice hand at a highly

sophisticated kind of proof, or constructing a frame within which to set and tie together puzzles about a remarkable family of very abstract concepts, Ryle's chief point is made. These are the concepts and the problems with which Plato will so often/ be concerned henceforth, and Ryle was the first to turn 371
the eyes of Plato's modern readers in this direction.

Additional note

Recently Ryle has come to believe that the two parts of the *Parmenides* must have been written at different times and without the initial intention of combining them in one dialogue. For 'while Part I is in Oratio Obliqua, Part II, apart from one initial "he said" [sc. 137c4], is in Oratio Recta.' (*SPM,* p. 145). Let us tease this out. First, the words ascribed to the disputants are given throughout in direct speech. Secondly, the report of the conversation in which these quoted words occur is put in the mouth of Cephalus, who was unluckily not present at it; so Plato makes him give it in the form 'Antiphon told me that Pythodorus told him that Socrates said ...' But of course Plato can't keep this up even in the first Part: over and again there is a straightforward 'Socrates (or Zeno or Parmenides) said ...' (*ephê* used of one of these characters at least 13 times, in addition to 3 *eipen* which of course may be a misreporting of an original *eipein*). Moreover, as in the *Republic* and other dialogues, there are stretches of dialogue without an intervening 'he said' (e.g., 134a6-d3), and these come most naturally when the argument is being jabbed ahead and broken only by words of assent. Once the interlocutor fades into total insignificance, in Part II, the 'he said's equally drop out of sight. But, thirdly, Ryle has a special theses in view. Most of the dialogues, including the parts of the *Parmenides,* were in his eyes written with a view to dramatic presentation. So the first part could be assigned to one actor reading 'Cephalus' while the second asked to be distributed between 'Parmenides' and 'Aristotle,' and two different dramatic dates would be involved. This general thesis of Ryle's I shall not discuss; but the imagination labours at the thought that the second part, with its unremitting complexities and its cowed interlocutor, was designed to be absorbed and enjoyed at one or more dramatic readings. This new twist to the/ suggestion that the thing 372
was planned as an academic joke comes implausibly from the man who argued best for its total seriousness. In any event it was Plato who patched it together for his own purposes, and those purposes I have been trying to make clear.

6

Plato on Not-Being

223 Platonists who doubt that they are Spectators of Being must settle for the knowledge that they are investigators of the verb 'to be'. Their investigations make them familiar with certain commonplaces of the subject for which, among Plato's dialogues, the *Sophist* is held to contain the chief evidence. But the evidence is not there, and the attempt to find it has obstructed the interpretation of that hard and powerful dialogue. The commonplaces that I mean are these:

In Greek, but only vestigially in English, the verb 'to be' has two syntactically distinct uses, a *complete* or *substantive* use in which it determines a one-place predicate ('X is', 'X is not') and an *incomplete* use in which it determines a two-place predicate ('X is Y', 'X is not Y'). To this difference there answers a semantic distinction. The verb in its first use signifies 'to
224 exist' (for which Greek in/Plato's day had no separate word) or else, in Greek but only in translators' English, 'to be real' or 'to be the case' or 'to be true', these senses being all reducible to the notion of the existence of some object or state of affairs; while in its second use it is demoted to a subject-predicate copula (under which we can here include the verbal auxiliary) or to an identity-sign.[1] Plato's major explorations of being and not-being are exercises in the complete or 'existential' use of the verb. And, lest his arguments should seem liable to confusion by this versatile word, in the *Sophist* he marks off the first use from the verb's other use or uses and draws a corresponding distinction within the negative constructions represented by *to mê on*, 'not-being' or 'what is not'.[2] For the problems which dominate the

* Delivered in shortened form as an Arnold Isenberg Lecture in Philosophy at Michigan State University in March, 1967. The lecture took up an older promissory note (*New Essays on Plato and Aristotle*, ed. Bambrough (London 1965), 71 n. 1, below, Chapter 15) which was accepted in its original form by G. Vlastos ('A Metaphysical Paradox', *Proc. Am. Philos. Ass.* 39 (1965-66), 8-9). The bones of the argument were taken from a larger stew of many years' standing, familiar to seminars at Oxford and Harvard; I wish I could now distinguish the many cooks. But mention must be made not only of clarifications already published by members of those seminars but of unpublished benefactions. In the first class fall J.M.E. Moravcsik, 'Being and Meaning in the *Sophist*', *Acta Philosophica Fennica* 14 (1962), 23-78; W.G. Runciman, *Plato's Later Epistemology* (Cambridge 1962); and most recently M. Frede, 'Prädikation und Existenzaussage', *Hypomnemata* 18 (1967), 1-99, and J. Malcolm, 'Plato's Analysis of *to on* and *to mê on* in the *Sophist*', *Phronesis* 12 (1967), 130-46: the last two came too late for me to do more than signal agreement in these notes. In the second class, the treatment of *kath' hauto – pros heteron* on pp. 128-9 was, I think, first suggested by a conversation with R.G. Albritton; it was reached independently by Frede.

[1] For the broad treatment of the verb see LSJ s.v. *einai* and recent versions of the Oxford and Webster dictionaries s.v. 'be'; for the application to Plato see e.g. I.M. Crombie, *An Examination of Plato's Doctrines* (London 1962), vol. 2, 498-9.

[2] P. Shorey, *What Plato Said* (Chicago 1933), 298, asserted that in the *Sophist* Plato 'laid the

central argument of the *Sophist* are existence-problems, so disentangling the different functions of the verb 'to be' is a proper step to identifying and resolving them.

Since the following arguments were put together most of these commonplaces have come under fire.[3] Consequently here the fire/can be 225
confined to one arc, the interpretation of Plato and particularly of the *Sophist*. The general syntactic claims will not come into question: we can accept a distinction between the verb's complete and incomplete uses provided we are wary of confusing the first with elliptical occurrences of the second – and this is no longer a matter of syntax (p. 127, below). The *Sophist* will turn out to be primarily an essay in problems of reference and predication and in the incomplete uses of the verb associated with these. The argument neither contains nor compels any isolation of an existential verb. Yet the problems about falsehood and unreality which it takes over from earlier dialogues do seem to be rooted in what we should call existence-puzzles, so it will need to be explained why they present themselves here in such a way as to lead to a study of '... is ...' and '... is not ...'.

The argument from nothing

Let us begin, as Plato begins his own discussion of not-being, with Parmenides. That philosopher had written (B2.7-8): 'You could not distinguish, nor could you express, *what is not*.' Which of its roles is the verb 'to be' playing here? Given the conventional choice it was natural to plump for the existential role. Not because the verb carries no complement – it is noteworthy that scholars have been ready here to detect an unmarked lacuna after the verb. The better reason was that Parmenides goes on to equate 'what is not' with 'nothing'.[4] It would be absurd to think that because a thing is not such-and-such – not blue, for example, – it is therefore nothing at all; but it is natural enough to equate what does not exist with nothing. No

---

foundation of logic' by, inter alia, 'explicitly distinguishing the copula from the substantive *is*'; A.E. Taylor, *Plato, the 'Sophist' and the 'Statesman'*, ed. Klibansky-Anscombe (London 1961), 81-2, claimed that Plato 'has definitely distinguished the "is" of the copula from the "is" which asserts actual existence' and further that 'he has ... discriminated the existential sense of the "is" from the sense in which "is" means "is the same as", "is identical with" '. So, with variations, F.M. Cornford, *Plato's Theory of Knowledge* (London 1935), 296; J.L. Ackrill, 'Plato and the Copula', *JHS* 77 (1957), 2; Crombie, op. cit., 499; Moravcsik, op. cit., 51.

[3] On the general account of the verb see C. Kahn, 'The Greek Verb "To Be" and the Concept of Being', *Foundations of Language* 2 (1966), 245-65, who notes the difficulty of making a firm syntactical distinction between the 'absolute' and 'predicative' constructions and then argues against taking the first as 'existential'. Vlastos, in 'A Metaphysical Paradox' (n. * above) and 'Degrees of Reality in Plato', *New Essays on Plato and Aristotle*, 1-19, holds that Plato's theory of *ontôs onta* is concerned with grades not of existence but of reality, and explores a sense of '... is real' which reduces it to the two-place predicate '... is really (sc. unqualifiedly or undeceptively) ...'. That the *Sophist* marks off an existential sense of *einai* has been queried by Runciman, op. cit., ch. 3, Kahn, op. cit. 261; and now Frede and Malcolm, op. cit.

[4] Diels-Kranz, *Vors.*[13] 28B8.7-13, cf. 6.2 with 7.1.

mermaid exists: nothing is a mermaid. Hence no doubt the pleasing entry in my desk copy of Webster's Dictionary: 'Nothing: something that does not exist'.

Discontent about the philosophical interpretation of the verb 'to be' has often focussed on this reading of Parmenides. How can he be pinned to one use of his favourite verb when he slides so unwarily between different uses? For he argues first that a thing cannot be at one time but not at another (B8.6-21), and then takes himself to have shown that it cannot change at all, i.e. cannot be *anything* at one time which it is not at another (B8.26-28). The
226 objection can be met in this form,[5] but it returns in others.[6] We need/not pursue it: our interest in Parmenides is just that the equation of *what is not* with *nothing* has often seemed to settle the matter. For when Plato takes over Parmenides' topic he adopts this equation, so here too the question has seemed, by default, to be settled. The *Republic* echoes the familiar argument, 'How could anything that is not be known?' (477a1), and adds a little later: 'Properly speaking, that which is not must be called not one thing but nothing' (478b12-c1). It seems only to be emphasising Parmenides' equation when it speaks of 'what is not *in any way*' and 'what *utterly* is not' (477a3-4, 478d7). And the equation with its attendant phraseology is repeated when Plato returns to the topic in the *Theaetetus* (189a6-12) and the *Sophist*
227 (237c7-e2).[7] So it seems that/ in these contexts he is expressly concerned with the possibility of speaking and thinking about what does not exist. Peipers, listing what he took to be the occurrences of the 'existential' verb in Plato, remarked: 'haec nota communis est: in omnibus animo obversatur oppositio *eius quod est et nihil* (*tou ontos et tou mêdenos*).'[8]

[5] As perhaps in 'Eleatic Questions', above, Chapter 1 n. 45.

[6] Thus Kahn, op. cit., 251, represents the verb as in effect an assertion-sign, engrossing the 'existential' and 'predicative' uses; and M. Furth, in 'Elements of Eleatic Ontology', *JHP* 6 (1968), 111-32, argues ably that such a 'fused' use of the verb would not itself commit Parmenides to fallacy. Many points in Furth's paper bear on my contentions here.

[7] Notice that in *Tht.* 188e-89a the move from 'what is not' to 'nothing' is argued, not assumed: F(something) - ~F(nothing) -F(one thing) - F(a thing that is), hence F(a thing that is not) - F(nothing). In the manipulation of the same counters at *Rep.* 478b-c it is assumed: F(something) - ~F(nothing) - F(one thing), but F(a thing that is not) - F(nothing) - ~F(one thing), hence F(something) - ~F(a thing that is not). Whether it is argued or assumed in the *Sophist*'s opening puzzle depends on the sense of 237c-e and ultimately 237d6-7. Tht. has just agreed that, since 'what is not' cannot be said of *what is*, it cannot be said of *something* (237c10-d5); and the ES [Eleatic Stranger] then says, *either* 'Do you agree to this because you look at it in this way, that a man who speaks of *something* must speak of *one thing?*' (so e.g. Diès, Fraccaroli, Taylor). The second is attractive because it takes the argument forward from a proposition already agreed, that what is not cannot be something: it deduces from this that what is not cannot be even one thing and hence is nothing, and the latter proposition thus becomes a corollary and not an assumption of the argument. But the reading assumes a deviant *hoti*-construction with (*sum*)*phanai*, which has no parallel in Plato (*Phd.* 64b3-4, wrongly adduced by Ast et al. as the single exception, is not one: the verb governs not *hoti* ... but *eu eirêsthài* ... *hoti* ...). Back then to the first construction: the ES asks why Tht. agrees that what is not cannot be something, and offers an elliptical argument for it which uses our proposition as an assumption: F(something) → F(one or more things) {but F(nothing) → ~F(one or more things)}, hence F(nothing) → ~F(something); {*but F(what is not) → F(nothing)*} hence F(what is not) → ~F(something).

[8] D. Peipers, *Ontologia Platonica* (Leipzig 1883), 16.

This conclusion in turn lends a sense to another step in Plato's argument. He contends, in the *Theaetetus* (189a10-12) and the *Sophist* (237e1-6), that thinking or speaking of what is not is simply not speaking or thinking at all, and then in the *Sophist* (238d-39a) he turns this contention on itself and brands the very expressions 'what is not' and 'what are not' as ill-formed inasmuch as they pretend to pick out one or more subjects of discourse. What can this mean but that he now denies sense to any attempt to speak of what does not exist? Thus Cornford contrasted later attempts to find 'non-existent things like chimaeras' an entrée into discourse, and summed up: 'This is all (Plato) has to say about a problem that has troubled modern logicians who have discussed the thesis that "whatever is thought of must in some sense be" '.[9]

As it stands, this is an ambiguous thesis. I may tell you (a′) 'The elves interrupt my typing', when there are no such creatures, or (a″) 'De Gaulle means to bribe Britain into the Common Market', when there is no such project; I may warn you (b′) 'The creatures named in (a′) don't exist' or (b″) 'The project reported in (a″) doesn't exist', and thus in different ways challenge the truth of (a′) and (a″); and in turn I may comment on the sense but not the truth of these last sentences and say (c) 'Any one uttering (b′) or (b″) is speaking of what does not exist'. All these sorts of utterances, and others too, will fall under the rubric 'speaking of what does not exist'. Faced with such a division a defender of the established view would probably say that the *Theaetetus* is content to leave the problem of falsehood in its traditional form: it assimilates the falsehood in (a″) to the failure of reference in (a′), but it assumes without question the significance of such expressions as 'what is not'; whereas the *Sophist* turns to challenge the very use of these expressions. So it seems that/ in the *Sophist*, if not before, Plato expressly **228**
discounts negations of existence as unintelligible.

This reading of the argument is generally coupled with the assurance that the *Sophist* represents *assertions* of existence as wholly respectable. Cornford has his own version of this conjunction: 'Every Form exists; consequently "the non-existent" has no place in the scheme, and we have ruled out that sense of "is not" '.[10] This suggests that it was a decision to talk about nothing but Forms which induced Plato to find a discussion of the status of Chimaeras unintelligible. Whether or not Cornford meant this travesty of the argument, he can at least be counted as subscribing to the common view that Plato divides positive statements of existence from their negative counterparts and welcomes the first but disbars the second.[11] There is still room for dissension

[9] op. cit., 208.

[10] ibid., 296.

[11] But there is a striking incoherence in Cornford's account. After saying that the existential sense of 'is not' has been 'ruled out' (296) he goes on to write as though this sense had been not excluded but positively vindicated: he speaks of 'the preceding demonstration that "is not" has two senses – "does not exist" and "is different from" ', and even of Plato's showing that 'the thing that is not' does not *always* [my italics] mean 'the non-existent' (298-9). Thereafter in translating and explaining 262c3 he reimports the sense 'does not exist' without caveat (305 and

within this common view: some of its adherents offer Plato the hospitable thesis that 'existence is a predicate of everything whatever' or 'is necessarily/
229 all-inclusive', in a sense which will readmit Cornford's Chimaeras.[12] Still the foundation holds firm. Plato in the *Sophist* has isolated a complete use of the verb 'to be', that in which it determines a one-place predicate and signifies 'to exist', and within this use he rejects negative constructions with the verb as breeding intolerable paradox. Whether Chimaeras benefit from the distinction is a matter for scholarly debate. They and their like rear no head in the dialogue from start to finish.

This familiar reading of the *Sophist* runs into such troubles that no amount of ingenious patching now seems to me able to save it. I shelve other considerations for the moment and mention two drawn from Plato's own account of his strategy.

The prospect of joint illumination

First, Plato nowhere suggests, and by implication he consistently denies, that he has found a use of the verb 'to be' in which only its positive occurrences have significance.

At the end of the long review of perplexities in 236d-50e, the Eleatic Stranger says: 'Now that both being and not-being have turned out equally puzzling, this in itself (*êdê*) offers the hope that if one of them can be made out to a greater or less degree of clarity the other can be made out to the same degree' (250e5-51a1). Being and not-being have been steadily coupled in this way in the preceding arguments (241d6-7, 243b7-c5, 245e8-46a2) and they are similarly coupled in what follows (254c5-6, 256e2-3, 258a11-b7, and 262c3, of which more on p. 133 below). After volunteering this prospect of joint illumination it would obviously be perverse to represent a positive use of the verb as luminous but reject the negative as wholly dark. Nor would the perversity be lessened if Plato had argued, as some of his interpreters do, that although the complete or 'existential' use of the verb makes sense only in its

---

ibid. n. 1: see p. 133 below). On 295 n. 1 (cf. 208) he concedes that at 238c '*to mêdamôs on*, "the simply non-existent", was dismissed as not to be spoken or thought of'; yet he at once dilutes this to the claim that 'there are no *true* statements saying that any *Form* does not exist' (my italics again). What is said in 238c is that *to mê on* as there construed is flatly unintelligible; what is said in 257b is that *whenever* (not, as Cornford, 'when') we speak of what is not we do not mean a contrary of what is (*hopotan to mê on legômen ... ouk enantion ti legomen tou ontos*) – this latter phrase representing, by Cornford's own admission, the *mêdamôs on* of 238c (locc. citt.). This unfounded reading of the *Sophist* he subsequently applied to the interpretation of the *Timaeus* 38b2-3 (*Plato's Cosmology* (London 1937), 98 n. 4), and a rejoinder of mine (above, Chapter 4) which resumed the objections here set out was dismissed by an American scholar as 'brushing aside Cornford's attempt' (H.F. Cherniss, *JHS* 77 (1957), 18), although the scholar neither quoted nor apparently grasped the objection. He then felt able to retrieve 'is non-existent' as a 'more probable' interpretation of *to mê on* at *Tim.* 38b and yet claim that this agreed with the *Sophist*.

[12] cf. Runciman, op. cit., 65-6; Moravcsik, op. cit., 41; *contra*, W. Kamlah, 'Platons Selbstkritik im Sophistes', *Zetemata* 33 (1963), 23 n. 1.

positive form there is a *different* use or uses marked out in the dialogue in
which negation comes into its own.[13] The hope/ offered by the ES is that any 230
light thrown on either being or not-being will equally illuminate the other.
And since he then sets himself to justify expressions of the form 'A is not' only
when they can be completed into 'A is not B',[14] it is an incomplete use of the
verb that we can expect to find vindicated in positive constructions too.

Let us call this assumption, that the one cannot be illuminated without the
other, the 'Parity Assumption' or, for short, 'PA'. It has obvious affinities
with the recommendation at *Parmenides* 135e8-36a2. And it governs the ES's
next proposal. 'Suppose on the other hand that we can get sight of neither:
then we shall at any rate push the argument through, as creditably as we
may, between both of them at once' (251a1-3). Since Campbell there has
been general agreement on the sense of the words,[15] and no one is likely to
explain the talk of pushing between being and not-being as a proposal to hold
them apart and save only one. What is envisaged is that both may remain
incomprehensible, and then the argument/ must get clear of both Scylla and 231
Charybdis. (The project of dispensing with the verb 'to be' was after all an
occupational temptation in Greek philosophy: witness *Tht.* 157b1-3 and
Aristotle, *Phys.* 185b27-28.) So the PA is maintained. Logically it is the proper
assumption, historically it is the appropriate reply to Parmenides.[16] It tells
directly against the common view of Plato's strategy. Some holders of that
view have thought to see a way round it, but this can be blocked in the course
of setting out another difficulty.

[13] Thus it will not do to suggest, as Moravcsik does (op. cit., 27-8), that when Plato says that we are now in as much confusion about being as about not-being (250d5-e7) he means that the confusion about not-being is a puzzle about *existence* whereas the confusion about being is due to conflating the *other* uses of 'is' (27 n. 1). It is in the lines immediately following those quoted by Moravcsik that Plato suggests that light thrown on the one will bring corresponding light to the other (250e7-51a3). Moravcsik thinks that the perplexity about being is introduced in 250a-e and not in the preceding 242b-49e because he takes the latter passage to be proving important theorems about existence. Yet one line of argument which would be integral to these 'proofs' (243c-44b) is represented by the ES as identical with that which generates the puzzle in 250 (249e7-50a2). As for the ES's supposed interest in proving existence to be indefinable, what he proposes however tentatively at 247e3-4 is a *definition* of *einai*, and not, as Cornford said (op. cit., 238) and many have repeated, a 'mark' (*aliter* 'symptom', 'attempt to characterize', etc.). What he says, on the most natural interpretation, is 'I lay it down, as a *horon horizein* the things-that-are, that they are *nothing but* power'. Moreover the context (247d2-e6) shows that he is improving on the materialists' attempt to *horizesthai ousian* (246b1), where Cornford rightly renders the verb as 'define'. For *horos* = 'definition' see e.g. *Phdr.* 237d1 (cf. c2-3), *Plt.* 266e1, 293e2; and of course the *horoi*, esp. 414d.

[14] This at least is common ground to those divided by the issue discussed on pp. 113-17 below.

[15] L. Campbell, *The 'Sophistes' and 'Politicus' of Plato* (Oxford 1867), 136. Cornford (op. cit., 251) objects that on this reading *hama* is redundant (251a3), and proposes to understand *amphoin* quite otherwise: 'we will force a passage through the argument *with both elbows at once*', a curiously irrelevant appeal to violence which leaves the *hama* far more nakedly redundant. The *hama* reinforces Plato's point: if both being and not-being stay intractable we must get clear of both at once.

[16] Whose project was, after all, to discount 'is-not' and retain 'is'; and his arguments are not to be met by distributing different senses of the verb between the two expressions, cf. nn. 5-6 above.

Negation and contrariety

A second trouble for the received view is that Plato does not say that his problems about not-being come from understanding 'being' in a certain way; he says that they come from understanding 'not' in a certain way. On his showing, they are to be resolved, not by giving up a particular sense of the verb in negative constructions, but by giving up a confusion about negation.

Twice in setting his puzzles about not-being – once in each of the lines of argument projected in 236e1-2 and followed in the subsequent pages – the ES gets his respondent to agree that what is not is the *contrary* of what is.[17] The sophist's teaching has been branded counterfeit and false. So, in the Greek idiom which is under scrutiny, he professes to deal in what is, but instead he retails and speaks of what is not (or of 'things that are not', by contrast with 'things that are'); and this is innocently equated with the contrary of what is.
232 When the ES comes to solve the paradoxes he picks on/ this as a cardinal mistake. When a negation-sign is affixed to the verb 'to be' the expression no more signifies some contrary of being than the negation-sign in 'not large' compels that expression to mean the contrary of large, i.e. small (257b1-c4). He returns to the point in his summing-up (258e6-7). So – and I shall accumulate more evidence for this later, for it is often tacitly denied – his argument is one from analogy. (In fact it is of the pattern subsequently explained in *Statesman* 277d-78e under the title of 'example', *paradeigma*.) It illuminates a troublesome case by a tractable parallel: it draws a comparison between affixing a negative to the verb 'to be' and affixing one to a predicate such as 'large'.[18] Within the comparison the sense of the negated terms is not called in question. What it is designed to explain is the role of the negation-sign itself.

Here again, then, Plato's diagnosis of his perplexity does not square with the usual view. But we have only the skeleton of an argument until we have

[17] 240b5, 240d6-8: the puzzles are those of deceptive semblances and of falsehood, respectively. In the first statement of the puzzles (236e1-2), *alêthes* does duty for *on* in the problem of falsehood but not in that of semblances; in the development of the puzzles (cf. 240b5, 240d6-8) it is vice versa. Plato tries to assimilate the two lines of argument (pp. 123-4 below), so both appeals to a 'contrary of what is' are met by the reply in 257b3-c4, 258e6-59a1. Campbell, (op. cit., 96) rightly saw *tanantia tois ousi* as anticipating *tounantion tou ontos* of 256e6; Cornford (op. cit., 212 n. 1) wanted to distinguish them and thereby to allow Plato's final account of falsehood to recognize 'things which are *contrary* to the facts'. But Plato's account (263b7-12) insists on the formula *ontôn hetera* and defends it by harking back to the argument of 256e-57a, which heralded the contrast between difference and contrariety.

[18] 'Whenever we speak of *not* being we don't mean some *contrary of* being; we just mean *different*. – How? – Just as whenever we call something not large: do you think then we mean *small* by our words, any more than we mean *middling?* – Surely not.' Need it be pointed out that this passage does *not* say that 'not large' means '*either* middling *or* small', and hence does not introduce a new account of 'not', and of 'different', in terms of incompatibility? It says that 'small' has no more claim to be what 'not large' means than 'middling' has. Incompatibility has no place in Plato's explanation of falsehood either: see n. 30 below.

explained the diagnosis, and this calls for two preliminary points to be made clear. First, I have represented Plato as concerned with affixing negatives to parts of sentences and not, as later logic accustoms us to expect, to whole sentences. This is clear from the text and needs no argument. But I have also spoken of negating the verb 'to be' and not only, as in Plato's illustration, of attaching a negative to the expression *on*, 'being'; and this needs explanation. 'Being' catches much of the Greek word's variety of use: it shifts between participle and collective noun and abstract noun in a way disheartening to philosophers. But in this context it is a participle. Plato is discussing the negating of predicates: he is comparing what it is to describe something as 'not large' with what it is to describe it as 'not-being'. And the preceding lines 256d11-57a6 show that this participial or predicative use can be taken to represent other uses of the verb in which/ 'not' can be attached to it: to **233** describe any thing or things as 'not-being' is just to say that it 'is not' or they 'are not'.[19] After all, the point of Plato's comparison is to clarify the perplexity about speaking of *what is not* or of *things that are not*. The verb is put in participial form here because Plato wants to draw a clear analogy with the negating of another predicate 'large', but it is the negating of 'is' and 'are' that he is out to explain.

Moreover it is the incomplete '... is ...' whose negation interests him. For the same preceding lines show that 'is/are not' and 'not-being' are being treated as fragments of predicates drawn from sentences of the form 'A is/are not B' or phrases of the form 'not being B'.[20]/

[19] For the purpose of this and later notes it will be useful to set out the relevant passage 256d11-e6. 'So it must be possible (a) for not-being to be, (b) in the case of change and moreover (c) in respect of all the kinds. For in respect of all of them the nature-of-difference renders each one (d) different from being, and so leaves it not-being; and thus we shall be right to describe them all, on the same terms, (e) as not-being and (f) on the other hand – since they partake in being – as being, and to say that they are ... Consequently, (g) for each of the forms *being* is multiple and *not-being* is countless in number.' The 'not-being' which appears in the singular in (d) is put into the plural in (e) and answered by the plural 'being' in (f), which is itself explained by 'that they are' (in *oratio obliqua*); so in these phrases 'being' is the participle going proxy for finite uses of the verb. Moreover, since 'not-being' has been explained in the preceding lines 256d5-8 as equivalent to 'different from being', and (d) takes up this equation, 'different from being' must also be understood as applying to any subject that is said *not to be*. There is a crux here. In the preceding argument change has been shown to be different from *rest*, from *the different*, and finally from *being* (255e11-14, 256a3-5, 256d5-8); and in these proofs of non-identity it is natural to take 'being' and the other terms as nouns, the names of abstract entities. Yet 256d-e is introduced as the immediate corollary of this passage, and the key-expressions can hardly have shifted their roles so profoundly. I shall not pursue this problem beyond pointing out that the proofs of non-identity have consisted in showing the non-substitutability of *predicates* (252d6-10; 255a4-5; 255b8-c3; and on the interpretation given below, 256c8-d7), and that what 'being' must be in 256d-e is a *predicate*. Notice too that the conclusions in 256d-57a are said to apply to *all* forms, including 'being.'

[20] See n. 19. When the *not-being* of (a) reappears in (g) it is said to be countless in number in the case of each form, and this is evidently to say that each form *is not* indefinitely many others. But (g) is presented as a conclusion of the preceding argument, in which change was expressly differentiated from just four other forms; so where has the ES pointed out the availability of this vast range of fillings for 'not-being ...' or 'is not ...'? In (c), I think. Commonly (b) and (c) are rendered 'in the case not only of change but of all the other kinds'. But one would then expect the same preposition *epi* to cover (b) and (c); more importantly, the preposition used in (c) is repeated

234 This being so, it will make for better understanding of Plato's comparison if it is reformulated by way of a distinction which Aristotle took up in his logic (*Int.* 19b19-20, *APr.* 51b5-10). It must be remembered that in Greek the negation-sign is commonly prefixed to the verb, but that it can be shifted to precede and modify other parts of the sentence. Aristotle accordingly distinguishes (I) 'this not-is white' from (II) 'this is not-white'. The moral he draws from his dinstinction is unclear,[21] but Plato's point can be clarified by it. For, as applied to Aristotle's examples, I take his comparison to come to this: that in (I) the negative modifies the verb and so imports the notion of not-being, while in (II) it modifies the adjective and so imports the notion of not-white; and that just as in (II) the effect of the negative is not to produce an expression meaning the contrary of the negated term – calling a thing 'not white' does not relegate it to the other extreme, black – so in (I) saying that it 'not is' does not relegate it to another extreme from being. Thereby he clears the way for his stronger conclusion. 'Not large' does not *mean* 'small' any more than it *means* 'middling', 'not white' does not mean 'black' any more than it means 'grey'; but of course things that are not large or not white may be small or black just as they may be middling or grey. The conclusion he is leading to is that in one case this latter option is not open. With the verb 'to be' the negative construction not only does not mean the contrary (which is what the analogy was designed to show) but cannot even be applied to anything in the contrary state. For Plato, or his speakers in the dialogue, can find no intelligible contrary to being or to what is (258e6-59a1). But, he
235 insists, this breeds no confusion in the notion of speaking of what is/ not. Those who try to justify the notion by searching for such a contrary, and equally those who make capital of the failure to find one, have just mistaken the sense of the negation.

This, then, is what remains to be explained in his diagnosis: the claim that there cannot be anything in a contrary state to being. His meaning is not hard to see, but one clue to it fails. Earlier in the dialogue change and rest were described as 'contrary' and 'most contrary' to each other (250a8, 255a12, b1), but it is debatable what relationship he means to hold between them. Most commentators have taken him to be denying just that the two are identical and that either is predicable of the other.[22] But these negative conditions seem to be satisfied not only by the pair large and small, which are his examples of contraries in 257b6-7, but by large and middling; and middling is his example of what is not large without being the contrary of large.

More light can be found in the treatment of large, middling and small at

---

a few lines later (255a4-5) to introduce not the subject of 'is not' but the various complements for which it is true of the subject. So the argument is this: it has just been shown that change *is not* certain other kinds, and this can be generalized for the complement 'all other kinds', since the difference between *any* kind (*hekaston, sumpanta*) and any other can be established. Any 'differs from being, in respect of any other'.

21 Cf. J.L. Ackrill, *Aristotle's Categories and De Interpretatione* (Oxford 1963), 143-4.

22 Thus Grote, *Plato*^{3} (London 1875), vol. 2, 444; Taylor, op. cit., 53; *contra*, Moravcsik, op. cit., 43-7.

Parm. 161d1-2. Here he exploits the familiar Greek idea of a middle state between contraries as containing something of both extremes.[23] What is middle-sized is not large, but it avoids smallness by having in it something, in a broad sense some proportion, of both large and small. And this is his point in the *Sophist*: to ascribe not-being to any subject – that is, in this context, to use 'is not' or some negative construction with the verb 'to be' in describing it – does not preclude ascribing some proportion of being to it – that is, saying that it 'is' so-and-so. Indeed, in the case of being, the negation turns out to be applicable only to subjects in the middle state, For Plato's analogy does no more than resume his previous arguments. The attempt to speak of what is not as *nothing*, a subject which is not anything at all, has broken down (237b-39b). Thereafter it has been shown, for some specimen 'kinds' of the highest rank, that there must be many things that each of them is as well as a still larger number that each is not (256e2-7),[24] and this is later assumed to hold good of all subjects of discourse (263b11-12). So those who take the negation of 'is' to import some contrary of being are those who try, hopefully or polemically, to construct a subject which for every predicate F is not F. This gives the correct/ sense to the expression 'is not *in any way*' which we **236**
noticed (Cornford's 'the totally non-existent' seems unintelligible), and relevance to the ES's reply that any subject 'is in many ways as well as not being in many others' (259b5-6, cf. 237b7-8, 260d3).[25] What he has shown, in short, is that a subject must be identified and characterized as well as differentiated; and for Plato this presents itself as an exercise in the incomplete use or uses of 'is'.[26]

The reductive thesis

Before interim conclusions are drawn, there is an objection to be met. Perhaps Plato does not wish to exploit an analogy between the variant elements in the sentences (I) and (II) which we borrowed from Aristotle. Perhaps his whole object in 257b1-c4 is to reduce (I) to (II) without remainder.

This reduction appears, unargued and at full strength, in Mr. Crombie. 'The view that negation signifies not "the opposite" but "the different" is the view that all statements assert that their subject partakes in existence, the function of negation being to locate the subject in some region of existence other than that part of it specified by the negated term. We might put this by saying that "not" is logically hyphenated, not to the copula, but to the rest of

[23] Cf. e.g. *Rep.* 478e1-5.

[24] On this difference in number cf. pp. 127, 131 below.

[25] 'But if "X not-is" is elliptical in this way, surely a subject can exhibit the contrary of being: a black thing unqualifiedly-not-is white for instance.' In respect of white the black thing has the partial not-being which marks the lack of some attribute, to whatever degree; it cannot, in virtue of its relation to any predicate, have the total not-being which marks the lack of all attributes.

[26] Or in the vowel-form 'being', one of the connectives which bring other forms into combination (253c1-2).

the predicate; and that is what Plato almost does say in 257c when he speaks of "not" signifying the opposite of the words to which it is prefixed and then goes on to take examples such as "not large".'[27] A footnote tries to make amends: 'One cannot say that Plato actually makes the point which I say he almost makes, for the copula commonly is one of the words to which the "not" is prefixed.'[28] Commonly indeed: the point is that it is so prefixed in *this* passage, both to the copula and to its proxy the participle. But let us shelve difficulties for the moment and notice how this reading of Plato's argument offers a way round the Parity Assumption./

237 Those who think that Plato is preoccupied with an existential sense of 'to be' in which the verb cannot be intelligibly negated might well claim, on these terms, to acknowledge the PA. They might agree that, when we are led to expect a joint illumination (or joint eclipse) of being and not-being, it is the same concept of being that we can expect Plato to illuminate in positive and negative statements; but then, with one proviso, they might claim this to be just the concept represented by their non-negatable verb. The proviso is that in negative statements the negation-sign is to be understood as detached from the verb and attached to one of its complements. Rewrite 'A isn't (sc. not-is) a greengrocer' as 'A exists as a non-greengrocer', and both assumptions seem to be saved. True, so far as Plato's argument is concerned the verb must now give up its connection with a one-place predicate. It must be read as '... exists as ...' in negative statements and so, if even lip-service is to be paid to the PA, in positive statements too. But then we shall find that the one-place predicate was always a red herring. And in settling for the syntactically incomplete use as the existential verb this interpretation does avoid the absurdity (which I believe no commentator has entertained) of suggesting that A's failure to be a greengrocer is a sort of *non*-existence for A.

This reductive thesis will not do. Plato means his analogy and is ready to leave the negation-sign annexed to the verb but, as he hopes, disarmed. But before seeing the thesis founder we must salvage what is true in it. It is true and important that, in the pages before Plato introduces his analogy, he has been showing on what terms something can be described as 'not-being' and has done so by proving the thing *different from*, and so *not*, various other things. He has confined his operations to certain 'greatest kinds' or, in practice, to the predicate-expressions representing these kinds, and he has proved their non-identity mainly by the experiment of substituting the predicate-expressions in context.[29] Subsequently, when he moves on from such negations of identity to considering falsehood in predicative statements, he builds on this earlier account of 'not-being' as grounded in difference-from-some-X. 'Theaetetus flies' says what-is-not about Theaetetus because what it says of him, viz. ... *flies*, is *different from* all the predicates he does have – or, in the
238 locution that 263b echoes from 256e, different from 'the/ many things that

[27] op. cit., vol. 2, 512.
[28] ibid., n. 1.
[29] Cf. n. 19 above.

are with respect to him'.[30] So difference-from-some-X always is, or is contained in, the grounds on which Plato admits any subject as 'not-being'.

But it is never a ground on which he proposes to transfer the negative construction from the verb. The subject 'must be described as different from other things and consequently, in respect of all those other things, it *not-is*. for in *not-being* them it is its own single self but at the same time *not-is* all those countless others' (257a1-6, taken up more emphatically in 259b1-6: the subject, treated as representative of all the others, is Being or What-is). By such arguments he tries to show that 'not-is' calls for completion, and on what terms the completion is to be supplied. But he never professes to cut his knots by relieving his key-verb of its negation-sign. Otherwise his argument would be over by 257a instead of culminating, as it does, in the carefully-worked analogy of 257b-59b. And its conclusion would be different and, considered as a device for saving existence-propositions and disarming their negations, a distinct anticlimax.

Before mounting some larger objections to the reductive thesis it is worth noticing how it gets illicit help from Cornford's version. He renders the ES's warning at 257b9-c3 correctly enough: 'So, when it is asserted that a negative signifies a contrary, we shall not agree, but admit no more than this: that the prefix "not" indicates something different from the words that *follow* – or rather from the things designated by the words pronounced *after* the negative' (my italics). Yet throughout the context he translates *to mê on* by 'what is not', reversing Plato's ordering of the last two words. So the innocent reader is led to suppose that Plato is concerned not at all with the negation-sign as preceding and hence modifying the verb but only with its role in such sentences as (II).

But Plato's interest in his analogy is proved by more than the text that Cornford misdepicts. For we have seen, first, that he has a/ stronger **239**
conclusion in view: 'not-X' not only does not *mean* 'contrary-of-X' but in one case, that of the verb 'to be', cannot even be applied to a contrary, since no subject can be intelligibly relegated to a state contrary to being. But if 'not-being' is always to be recast in the form 'being not-X' there will be plenty of contraries to being. Finding them will be merely a matter of finding a contrary to the negated term. When *not-being* is *being not-large*, *being small* is the desiderated contrary.

Further, it is the analogy between negating 'being' and negating such terms as 'large' and 'beautiful' that governs the next stretch of the argument (257c5-58c5). The ES observes that 'not beautiful' and 'not large' each mark off a real class on the basis of a particular difference: the first marks off what

[30] This remains the simplest interpretation, requiring no shift in the sense of 'different' such as is sometimes found in 257b (cf. n. 18 above). To be sure, if it were taken as a rule for verifying or falsifying statements it would make falsification an interminable business, but this is not its function. If X is not beautiful, all X's predicates fall into the class different-from-beautiful introduced at 257d4-e11. (For 'nature-of-the-beautiful' in this passage as equivalent to the predicate '(the) beautiful' and not to the abstraction 'beauty' cf. 257a9 'the nature of the kinds' = 'the kinds' and similar periphrases at *Rep.* 429d, *Phdr.* 248c, etc.)

is other than beautiful, the second what is other than large.[31] He generalizes this for an indefinite range of values of 'not X' (258a4-10); and then he applies
240 the generalization to the case of 'not-being' (258a11-b3).[32]/ The pattern of argument is brought out clearly in his conclusion (258b9-c3): 'We must have the nerve then to say that not-being certainly is something with its own nature, just as we agreed that large is large and beautiful is beautiful, and the same with not-large and not-beautiful: *in just the same way*, not-being *too* has turned out to be, and is, not-being – *one* sort of thing to be counted among the many sorts of things that are' (cf. 260b7). The being or reality ascribed here to sorts and classes will be taken up later. Our present business with the argument is that it shows Plato still pursuing his parallel. It is the effect of attaching a negation-sign to the verb 'to be' that he wants to explain, and he is still explaining it by analogy with, and not by reduction to, the negating of any grammatical complements the verb may carry.

So the non-negatable use of 'to be' is nowhere in view, and the Parity Assumption is not diluted to accommodate such a use. Our interim conclusion stands firm: Plato's account of his strategy tells directly against two theses basic to current views of the dialogue. The one is that he wants to signal a sense of the verb in which it cannot be straightforwardly and intelligibly negated; the other is that he represents his troubles about not-being as due to taking the verb in a certain sense rather than (as in fact he does) to taking the negation in a certain sense. In short, there is no hint that any sense of the key-verb must be dropped or modified between positive and negative constructions, or between the opening puzzles and the subsequent explanations. What then of the commentators' existential verb? Plato's clarifications of 'not-being' are a study in the syntactically incomplete

[31] At 257e2-4 *allo ti* is often construed as the interrogative *nonne*, but a question answering another question does not need such a prefix (e.g. 257d6-7) and the sentence does not then lead directly to the conclusion in 257e6-7, that 'not beautiful' represents a contrast between two things-that-are: so the antithesis must be *allo ti tôn ontôn – pros ti tôn ontôn*. Again, it is often assumed that what not-beautiful is 'marked off from' (*aphoristhen*) is the same as what it is 'contrasted with' (*antitethen*), which leaves a pointless repetition; what it is marked off from is the whole class *different* under which it falls (cf. 229c1-3, 231b3-4, 268d1-2; so too 257c11); what it is contrasted with is *beautiful*. Thus 'One of the things that are, marked off from a given class (the different) and moreover contrasted with one of the things that are (the beautiful) – is this what the not-beautiful turns out to be? ... So the not-beautiful turns out to be a contrast between one thing that is and another thing that is.' I have shifted between the predicate-expression 'beautiful' and the class-description 'the beautiful': for the not-beautiful to be is for it to be marked out by a particular difference, viz. from the beautiful, and this comes to more than saying (though it certainly includes saying) that the sense of the predicate 'not beautiful' is given by this difference: Plato is also assuming that the predicate has application (cf. pp. 130-1 below).

[32] Since he is still concerned with the effect of negating the verb we are not to supply *moriou* with Campbell at 258b1: that is the reductive thesis. Similarly at 258e2 *hekaston* is better taken with *morion* (cf. 257c11: so Diès *et al.*) than with *on* (Campbell), but interposing *hekaston* between article and noun is poor practice. Accordingly I accept the *hekastou* of all MSS. (Stallbaum's often-repeated claim that Simplicius 'preserved the correct reading, *hekaston*' is quite misleading: *Phys.* 238.26 reads *hekaston* but the first transcription at 135.26 has *hekastou*). The sense here is: 'that part of the different which is contrasted with the being of any subject is not-being': 'X is ...' expresses X's being, and the negation of this imports that part of the different which is contrasted with X's being. For some complement, X is different-from-being ...

'is', and so long as the reductive treatment of the negation-sign was taken to be part of his strategy it was possible to read the 'is' as 'exists'. But it is not part of his strategy; he does not offer to detach the negative from the verb it modifies, only to show grounds for its attachment and bring out its sense by parallels. And I assume without more argument that no one will read these exercises in 'not-being' as an attempt to explain the *non*-existence of motion and rest and the other kinds. So the concept of being that he takes himself to
be elucidating here is/ not that of existence. By Parity, it cannot be an **241**
existential sense of 'to be' that he means to isolate and explain in positive constructions either. If the Chimaera rears its head in the dialogue, it is in the shape of the familiar interpretation from which we set out. It is time to reconsider our original reason for accepting that interpretation: the equation of 'what is not' with 'nothing' in Plato's puzzles, which persuaded us that by 'what is not' he here meant 'what does not exist'.

The subject Nothing

(a) Plato equates 'what is not' with 'nothing'; (b) 'nothing' is equivalent to 'what does not exist'. Can either claim be upset?

1. Perhaps too much weight was put on (a). The ES sets out his puzzles about not-being in five stages, and of these only the first makes any play with 'nothing'. But the first is the puzzle of falsehood in its old form, using 'what is not' without suggesting that its very use is logically incoherent. That suggestion is argued through the second and third stages, but by that time 'nothing' has left the scene. So the equation plays no part in the argument it was used to interpret.

This objection fails, but it is prompted by a distinction of the first importance. I discuss it by way of making that distinction clear.

Briefly and provisionally, the stages of the ES's puzzle are as follows; I shall come back to the assumptions which control them later. (i) 237b7-e7 is a version of the familiar paradox.[33] 'What is not' stands for nothing, hence speaking of what is not = speaking of nothing = not speaking at all. (So, if speaking falsely is speaking of what is not, there is no such speaking as false speaking; but the application is not made here.) (ii) 238a1-c11 tries for conclusions that have *what is not* as their express subject. Since what is not cannot have any actual attributes, it cannot have any number nor therefore be one or many of anything, yet to speak or think of it we have to refer to it in the singular or the plural; so it eludes our references and cannot be spoken or thought of. But by this reliance on the material mode (ii) undermines itself. (iii) 238d1-239c8 points out that according to (ii) the argument and conclusion of (ii) cannot be consistently formulated. If it proves anything,
it/proves that no subject of discourse can be introduced under the description **242**
'what is not' or 'what are not'. So the ES's inquiry has no subject and threatens to vanish without trace.

[33] But the version already contains the seeds of a transformation, cf. p. 119 below.

The remaining two stages (239c9-240c6, 240c7-241b3) bring no new arguments for the incoherence of 'what is not'. With them the strategy shifts, in a way reminiscent of the second part of the *Parmenides*, from negative arguments terminating in philosophical frustrations and silence to a positive display of contradictions which must somehow be swallowed if sense is to be made of counterfeits and falsehoods.[34] These are not our present business.

What is the connexion between (i) and the two stages which follow it? First, it is obviously not the job of (ii) to challenge (i) in the way that (iii) upsets (ii). No doubt (i) deserves challenge: it interprets its thesis, that 'what is not' stands for nothing, simply as allowing the substitution of 'nothing' for 'what is not' while keeping both expressions in use.[35] So it seems open to the charge of attempting what it claims to be impossible – speaking of what is not. But (ii) also keeps 'what is not' in use and indeed makes its role as a referring expression central. Its claim to deal with the 'very basis of the argument'[36] means that it picks out *what is not* as its formal subject, where (i) had framed its conclusion in terms of *speaking of what is not*. About this subject it seems to argue for much the same conclusion as that which (i) had reached by its equation between 'what is not' and 'nothing'.

But if (ii) does not challenge (i), it does not seem to build on it either: and this is what suggests that (i) is merely superseded in the argument. (ii) leaves the important equation in silence, and (iii) follows suit: it makes no play with 'nothing' and concentrates its attack on (ii). The effect is to make (ii) and (iii) appear a self-contained pair, providing between them all the material for the *Sophist's* new problem: the problem, namely, whether sense can be made of
243 those expressions 'what is not' and 'what are not' which/ had been so artlessly used in describing and debating falsehood. (ii) introduces them as carrying a reference, (iii) replies that on (ii)'s interpretation of them no reference has been made. This is what prompts the notion that the treatment of the key-verb which leads to the impasse in (iii) is not to be explained by drawing on (i). 'To be', as any account of the dialogue shows, is a versatile source of mischief; in (i) the ES pays respect to one veteran puzzle which can be got from negating the verb, and it is common opinion that this is a puzzle about non-existent subjects of discourse. But if it is quietly shelved in stating the new paradox, we need not assume this or its solution to turn on an existential use of the verb. And if such a switch of sense seems violent, the objector has a defence. After all, the conventional interpretation requires Plato to drop the existential sense of 'what is not' between the puzzles and the solution. It is only an improvement on this to suggest that the sense is dropped in the course of the puzzles and before the substantial problem is set at all.

I said that this objection would serve to introduce a major distinction. What it grasps or half-grasps is that the argument which culminates in (iii)

[34] In the *Sophist*, unlike the *Parmenides*, these stages lead to the positive proposal to disarm the paradoxes (241d1-242b5). This seems the correct moral to draw for the *Parmenides* too.

[35] 237e4-6 is not of course a recommendation to drop the expression 'nothing', but a claim that speaking of nothing is not speaking at all.

[36] *Peri autên autou tên archên,* sc. *tou logou* (cf. 237e7): at 233e1-3 Theaetetus fails to understand *tên archên tou rhêthentos* because he does not understand the subject of discussion, *panta*.

has transformed the old perplexity about speaking of what is not: that it is an anachronism to read the *Sophist* as answering the *Theaetetus*' problem in the *Theaetetus*' terms. Even the *Euthydemus* and the *Cratylus*, which debate the possibility of falsehood expressly in terms of fitting words to the world, use such locutions as 'what is not' without ever asking whether *these* are capable of coherent use.[37] The *Sophist* by contrast proceeds on the view that if and only if we can understand the proper use of 'what is not' and some related expressions, we shall understand – understand philosophically – the situations those expressions are commonly invoked to explain. When it turns to query the tools which had been taken for granted in constructing the old puzzles, it carries the mark of Plato's maturity. It ranks with, and because it offers solutions it goes beyond, the study of 'participation' in the *Parmenides*.

It is also true that the first stage of its argument reads in part (237e1-6) like a mere echo of the old puzzle. If speaking of what is not is speaking of nothing, it is not speaking at all: why? The *Theaetetus* has already supplied one analogy
(188e3-89a14): seeing/ nothing is not seeing, hearing and touching nothing **244**
are not hearing or touching (188e2-89a14).

Beyond this the objection miscarries. No doubt (i) ends by settling for a version of the old paradox, with the key-expressions still unassailed; but it begins by asking the *Sophist*'s question, and the answer it gives controls the following stages. 'Suppose one of this company had to give a serious and studied answer to the question, *what is the proper application of the name "what is not"*? Of what thing and what sort of thing should we expect him to use it, and what would he point out to his questioner?' (237b10-c4, recalled at 250d7-8).[38] And the answer, that 'what is not' = 'nothing', is only verbally absent thereafter. It is surely this equation that (ii) is designed to reinfore by its independent proof that what is not cannot be one or more of anything (238a5-b5). The puzzle is converted into one about reference when (ii) deduces that, since what is not (i.q. nothing) does not give us even one thing to mention, it is unmentionable (238b6-c10). And it is the incoherence of this conclusion, and therewith of the original answer, that is shown by (iii).

So the first of the two claims stands firm. The equation with 'nothing' cannot be dislodged from the puzzles. We must shift to the second: the claim that 'nothing' is equivalent to 'what does not exist' or, more exactly, that Plato could not set and solve puzzles about the former without supposing that his puzzles were about the latter. We have a distinction in hand now that will defeat this second conjunct.

2. Let us try adapting a Platonic argument to show that the non-existent is not the same as nothing. If I talk or think of centaurs I am not talking or thinking of nothing, for then I should not be talking or thinking at all. If I tell Theaetetus he has taken wing I speak of a non-existent flight, but not of nothing. Plato's discussion of 'is not' in the *Parmenides* (160b6-161a5, countered at 163c2-d1) suggests that he has an approximation to this

[37] The *Cratylus* at 429d, unlike the *Euthydemus*, uses *mê to on* (and not *to mê on*) *legein*, but the other expression is implied by 385b10.

[38] A syntactically confused text; but the sense is not in question.

distinction in view. But as a help to grasping his intentions in the *Sophist* it is open to objection, and it is worth distinguishing objections from two different points of view. One, to put it broadly, is that of the *Theaetetus,* the other is that of the *Sophist.*

The form of the puzzle which is found in the *Theaetetus* seems to depend on
245 obliterating just this distinction. Speaking of something/ is not distinguished from saying something, and the speaking is compared to seeing or touching, as though the words had content to the extent that they made contact with the actual situation (189a3-10). In falsehood the speaker does not touch anything: where there should be the flight ascribed to Theaetetus,[39] there is no such object for the words to hit. There are primitive assumptions about language in Plato which reinforce this view from a consideration of words rather than of speakers. Words are given their purchase on the world by being used to name parts of it, and names, or the basic names to which others are variously reducible, are simple proxies for their nominees.[40] Thus falsehood at its simplest, for instance in the presence of the falsifying situation, becomes as vacuous as calling 'Stetson!' when Stetson is not there, or pointing at vacancy.[41] These assumptions have been too often studied in Plato to need expansion here, and I take them to be modified at an essential point in the *Sophist.* In due course I shall argue (pp. 133-6 below) that the modification does not make use of an existential sense of 'to be': it does not need an existential sign. But there is no blinking the fact that for us Plato's puzzle in the *Theaetetus* seems to consist just in the non-existence of what falsehoods speak of, and that this is apparently what he expresses there by the phrase 'speaking of nothing'.

Now the *Sophist.* Is it true that if I talk or think of nothing I do not think or
246 talk at all? I seem to be able to do the first without/ ceasing to talk, for I have just done it: I have been asking whether *nothing* is to be identified with *what does not exist.* To meet the *Theaetetus* puzzle we needed a distinction between the case in which there isn't anything being talked about and that in which what is talked about is a fictitious animal or an imaginary situation; now we seem to need a distinction between the case in which there isn't anything being talked about and that in which there is something that is talked about, viz. nothing. Let us for the moment, with Plato's leave, assume these

[39] Or perhaps the flying Theaetetus or the fact-that-Theaetetus-flies: the original puzzle notices no such distinctions, but the suggestion that the false statement says what-is-not *about* something (*Tht.* 188d2, 9-10) implies that what is missing is the flight. This squares with the implication of *Tht.* 190b2-4 that if X is beautiful and I call it ugly what I do is misidentify the *beautiful*; what misfires is the predicate-word 'ugly'. For an interesting attempt to reimport Theaetetus-flying, on the strength of a construction with some verbs of perceiving (though not with 'touching', and not with verbs for saying or believing), see D.R.P. Wiggins' paper 'Sentence Meaning, Negation, and Plato's Problem of Non-Being', in *Plato I*, ed. G. Vlastos (Garden City 1970), 268-303. See too Furth's discussion, op. cit., 123-4.

[40] Thus e.g. *Tht.* 201e1-202b5 and the thesis pursued in *Cra.* 391a-428e.

[41] At *Cra.* 429eff. Socrates accepts the 'Stetson' analogy and offers to vindicate falsehood on these terms, but in effect he does so by distinguishing the conditions for making a reference (looking towards, pointing, etc.) from the actual use of the name; I shall argue that the *Sophist*'s final account of falsehood is a more sophisticated version of this distinction (pp. 134-5 below).

distinctions: let us say that we can speak of mythical centaurs or chimerical flights (which I think Plato does not wish to deny), and that we can also speak of nothing without ceasing to speak (which I take him to be denying). How shall we show that these do not come to the same thing?

Well, we can describe our centaurs. They have hooves, not fishtails; they are made of flesh and blood, not tin; and they are fictitious, not found in Whipsnade Zoo. Similarly with the flying done by Theaetetus: it can be described, and indeed must be if we are to know what we are rejecting as false. But suppose we are asked to describe the *nothing* that we have been talking about: then there seems to be no description at all available for it. It is not (to put an instance) a horse, for it can't be added to another horse to make two of them. In discourse the function of 'nothing', like that of 'nobody' and 'nowhere' and 'never', is just to indicate that there isn't as much as one of whatever it may be. This is a point that Plato drums home for his *what is not* when he equates it with *nothing* in the *Republic* (478b) and in stage (i) of the *Sophist*'s perplexity, and (ii) reinforces it. It can seem an unremarkable point or, as Plato makes it seem in the *Sophist*, astonishing and indeed unintelligible. It is unsurprising if we reflect that expressions such as 'nothing' were coined to block gaps that would otherwise be filled by references to one or more of whatever sort of thing is in question. It becomes baffling if we insist that if Nothing can be spoken of it must conform to the rules for those subjects of discourse that it is designed to displace: that is, if we ask Plato's question, 'What is the application of this name, "what is not"? Of what and of what sort of thing should we expect a man to use it?' and then identify What is not with Nothing. For this is to require that if Nothing is to be mentionable it must establish its credentials as a logical subject, identifiable and describable: we must be able to say that it is a so-and-so, and which so-and-so it is. Yet the more we miscast Nothing/ as such a subject and **247**
ignore its role as a subject-excluder, the more we run into those paradoxes flagged by Plato and after him by Frege and Quine.[42] We find ourselves unable to say, not only that it is one or more of anything, but what it *is* at all (238e5-39a2).

Plato's question, then, sets strong conditions for reference. Naturally it produces (anyhow temporary) bafflement when it is applied to Nothing. The word seems to flout the basic requirements of accidence: a singular term, framed to exclude singular reference. But if this were the sole claim of the paradox on philosophers' interest it could long ago have been stored with the other phlogiston of the subject. 'Nothing', we could say, is only parasitically singular, taking the size of the gap it blocks; it dissolves into 'not even: one thing'. If in consequence its role in the language cannot be explained as a name or description under which references can be made, so much the more reason for seeking other models of explanation. But in fact the paradox has no

[42] *Frege: Translations*, Geach and Black (Oxford 1955), 83: 'The answers "never", "nowhere", "nothing" ... to the questions "when?", "where?", "what?" ... are not proper answers but refusals to answer, which have the form of an answer'. They are not of course refusals either; merely designed to show that there is no answer.

independent importance in Plato's argument. His aim is to show that when 'what is not' is correctly understood the *Sophist*'s question *can* be answered. The impression that it cannot is produced by identifying, as the sophist tries to, 'what is not' with 'nothing'; and I have argued that Plato's subsequent diagnosis makes it certain, for the *Sophist* at least, how he wants to understand this identification. It introduces not a special sense of the verb but a special mistake about negating it. It comes to equating 'what is not' not with 'what does not exist' but with 'what is not anything, what not-in-any-way is': a subject with all the being knocked out of it and so unidentifiable, no subject. As the scope of the negation is cleared up, so it becomes clear that anything can and must 'be many things as well as not being many others'. The answer to the *Sophist*'s question – the original question, let me insist: not an impostor smuggled in by switching the sense of the verb – is not 'nothing' but 'anything whatever considered as differentiable from other things'. And the answer (or part of the answer) to the sophist's puzzle about falsehood is that his diagnosis imports an unintelligible term: but not the term on which the commentators pitched.

248 How much or little do these considerations prove? They prove, I think, that it is possible to raise puzzles about Nothing without confusing them with puzzles about non-existence. They show that the *Sophist*'s question brings these puzzles to the fore of the discussion so as to lead naturally to that study of subject-predicate syntax and of the connective '... is ...' which Plato does undertake. They leave the way open to the sole interpretation I can find which squares with the evidence already canvassed and does not accuse Plato of grossly missing or misrepresenting his own strategy.

And they leave Plato's argument a piece of successful pioneering in its chosen territory and not a lame attempt to evade a problem about non-existence by, in Cornford's phrase, 'ruling out' an accepted sense of a word in one construction. Teachers of logic generally spend time explaining how substitution-instances are supplied for the constituents of the formulae (Fa) and (Ra,b) before they introduce $((\exists x)Fx)$ or $((\exists G)Ga)$ or any expressions for individual existence. Nor do they mention existence among the requirements for the terms of such elementary propositions. Plato's study is earlier than formal logic and concerned with far more than the construction of formulae, but it can be read as the earliest exercise at the level of those initial explanations. It is essentially preliminary to, and not based on, the isolation or construction of the difficult notion 'exist'.

Before following out this suggestion it may be as well to make one disclaimer. I am not arguing that Plato never, or never in the *Sophist*, uses the verb *einai* in such a way that 'exist' is a natural English translation. No doubt he does. What I hope to show is that the central arguments and explanations become broken-backed if they are read as containing an implicit or explicit separation of such a sense of 'is' from others. But so far the interpretation leaves a good deal of unfinished business. I proceed to detail what seem the main difficulties it faces and then, as best I can, to meet them.

Existence reimported

(1) It can be argued on the following grounds that the problem set in the central section of the dialogue can be solved only by isolating an existential use of the verb.

The sophist, unless he is that mere sophist whom Dr. Peck regarded as deserving only treatment in kind,[43] might well feel that a/ substantial child **249**
has gone with the bath-water. Given greater articulateness he might complain that it is all very well to save the locution 'speaking of what is not' by proving it capable of carrying an intelligible reference at the point where the sophist's translation of it is not. But how was he ever induced to suppose, or to try to say, that false speaking is speaking about a non-subject? Surely because what it speaks about does not exist because there just is not the correlate in the world for the false words to express?

And the ES's puzzles recognize this existential concern. They have been under-described until all the assumptions and problems are set out. In particular, consider the assumption on which (ii) relies to prove that what is not is nothing, i.e. not one or more of anything. It lays it down (238a7-9, c5-6, cf. 241b1-3) that something that is cannot be attached to what is not, and interprets this to mean that what is not cannot have any of the attributes that are, such as number. What is this but the hatstand model of predication: actual hats cannot be hung on non-existent pegs?

Again, stages (iv) and (v) await description. The sophist has been denounced for offering only semblances of the things he claims to purvey, and making false claims in doing so (cf. 236e1-3). So he both purveys, and states, what is not instead of what is. But in both cases this contrast between what is and what is not can be made problematic. (iv) (239c9-40c6) discusses semblances, and its language (esp. the recurrent *alêthinon* in 240a7-b8) makes it natural to interpret the verb 'to be' here as 'to be real'. What distinguishes a semblance of A from A itself? Well, A is real, the semblance is not (in fact 'in no way real, the *contrary* of real'). Yet surely it really is what it is, a semblance? A real unreal, then, which upsets the incompatibility of what is and what is not which we seemed to assume in denouncing the sophist. (v) (240c7-241b3) discusses falsehoods. False thinking is thinking that what is, is not (in fact is 'the contrary of what is'), and vice versa; but this diagnosis has to mention what is not as though it had being (241b1-2). Or, to supply the usual interpretation, it professes to refer to just that non-existent state of affairs which the man with false belief supposes to exist.

'To be real', 'to exist': such a confusion is one which Plato has the terminology to avoid, for 'real' can be turned by the word *alêthinon* as it is in (iv), and this word does not naturally go proxy for other uses of the verb 'to be'. Instead Plato seems to do what he can to strengthen the confusion,

[43] A.L. Peck, 'Plato and the *megista genê* of the *Sophist*: a reinterpretation', *CQ* n.s. 2 (1952), 32-56: my 'sophist' is no doubt a fiction but represents positions that (*pace* Dr. Peck) Plato takes seriously and tries to meet.

250 stretching the same formula to/ cover the paradoxes of both (iv) and (v) (240c3-5, 241b1-2, d6-7) and ultimately reducing the problem of unreality to that of falsehood (264c10-d5). The conflation can be left as a puzzle to those who believe that in his metaphysics Plato must and can readily divide reality from existence.[44] It does not weaken the point I have to meet. The picture of the argument just given seems to show that its assumptions and problems do not hinge on the connective '... is ...' which carries no expressly existential sense but serves as copula or identity-sign. The senses of the verb that seem to be required are those conventionally associated with the one-place predicate '... is'. So it is surely this use of the verb, in which it signifies existence or reality, that Plato must pick out for scrutiny if he is to dissolve his puzzles about not-being.

The same moral can be drawn from the puzzles about being which succeed them (242b-250e); for now an enquiry is broached into the number and nature of real things (242c5-6). We have seen that the two lines of perplexity are linked in 250e5-6. So it is the same use of the verb that asks to be picked out and clarified here.

(2) Next, it will be argued that not only Plato's problems but his positive conclusions compel him to distinguish this use of the verb. For (a) it is surely the existence (or else the reality) of change for which he is contending in 248e6-249b3, and which he thereafter assumes (250a11-12, b9, 254d10, 256a1). And (b) it is surely the existence (or reality), first of the not-beautiful and not-large, and then of what-is-not itself, which is the burden of the argument in 257d12-258e5. And finally (c) there is the explanation of falsehood itself (261d-263d). It seems common doctrine that here he 'assumes that, whatever statements are about, if they are about anything they are about something that exists'.[45] Is not this, after all, the moral of the exercise: that to speak falsely is not to make the vain attempt to mention what does not exist, but rather to mention something that does exist and ascribe to it real properties which are however different from the real properties it possesses? Is not this his way of satisfying the 'hatstand' assumption which controls stage (ii) of the first puzzles?/

251 (3) That Plato does expressly mark off the existential use of the verb which his reasoning should force him to recognize has been argued in this way.[46]

First, he seems prepared to distinguish two *incomplete* uses of the verb, that in which it couples subject and predicate ('this is fragile') and that in which it marks an identity ('that is Socrates'). The section of the dialogue in which the distinction is drawn is introduced by a puzzle to which it is directly relevant (251a5-c2). Some opsimaths have failed to understand how one thing can have various appellations, for instance how anything can be called not

[44] Vlastos, in the papers named in nn. * and 3 above. Since Plato here conflates 'to be' with 'to be real' and since Vlastos takes the second in Plato to mark a two-place predicate distinct from existence, the interpretation I shall propose can be read as a corollary of his thesis.

[45] Moravcsik, op. cit., 41.

[46] Most explicitly by J.L. Ackrill, op. cit., 1. Disagreement with Ackrill's express conclusion, that Plato wants to mark off different senses of 'is', does not at all carry disagreement on his substantial issue, that Plato succeeds in distinguishing predications from statements of identity.

only a man but good; and the common and plausible diagnosis of their confusion is that they have mistaken the different predications for different and competing statements of identity.[47] The appropriate distinction is then made in 256a7-b4. The ES proposes to explain how we can say that a thing is F and yet is not F, when by the first arm of the statement we mean to ascribe an attribute to it and by the second we mean to deny that it is identical with the attribute ascribed. His explanation is that in the first case the thing 'partakes of F' whereas in the second it 'shares in (i.q. partakes of) difference which severs it from F'. These formulae are not expressly proffered as analyses of the verb 'to be'; still it seems reasonable to infer that Plato regards the verb in its copulative use as requiring the analysis 'partaking of ...', but in its identifying use as requiring the analysis 'partaking of identity relatively to ...' (or, in the negative form discussed by the ES, 'partaking of difference relatively to ...').

If this is so the context seems to give us yet a third way of analys-/ing or 252
paraphrasing out the verb. At 256a1, for instance, the ES remarks that 'change is, by *partaking in being*' (*esti dia to metechein tou ontos*). Since this formula did not occur in the previous analyses and since unlike the others it seems to make '... is' a one-place predicate, it arguably should represent a third sense of 'to be'. What can this be but the existential sense?

(4) Finally, the existential meaning appears to be marked off once more at 255c8-d8, where the ES is distinguishing being from difference. 'I think you agree that there are two ways in which we speak of "things that are": in some cases we call them so in their own right (*auta kath' hauta*), in some cases we call them so with reference to other things (*pros alla*); but "the different" is only ever so called with reference to something different (*pros heteron*). This would not be the case if being and difference were not quite distinct things; if difference partook of both characters as being does, the class of different things would sometimes contain a thing that was different but not relatively to something different from it.' It is commonly said that here Plato is representing being as both 'absolute' and 'relative', while difference is only 'relative';[48] and that what he means is just that, while the description of a thing as 'different' is always an incomplete description, awaiting some further reference to complete it, the description of something as 'being' or as 'what is' does not in one use of that expression call for any completion. And this latter use, the use in which one can say of something that *it is* and leave it there, is

[47] To this it is irrelevant whether 'man is man' and 'good is good' are the sole legitimate forms of statement in their object-language or whether these are the sole forms admitted in their meta-language to justify some analysis (e.g. atomistic) of their object-language. It is irrelevant too (though important for other issues) whether they had any grasp of such distinctions (cf. G. Prauss, *Platon und der logische Eleatismus* (Berlin 1966), 184). What they reject, wittingly or unwittingly and on some level of discourse, is predication: 'they do not allow anything to be called another thing by sharing in the other's character' (252b9-10).

[48] For the list of those who have said so, from Wilamowitz on, see now Frede, op. cit., 22; he could have gone back to Campbell op. cit., 152. An old comment of mine to the same effect (below, p. 172 n. 25) has been taken as supporting evidence by Moravcsik and Runciman *inter alios*, and pp. 125-30 below, are addressed to them by way of apology. The comment was retracted in the paper mentioned in n. *, p. 104 above.

surely the existential use.

So far as I know, and as forcefully as I can put them, these are the considerations which have led scholars to ignore the troubles attending any version of the established interpretation. I must try now to show that they are misleading. Of the four heads of argument, (1) and (2) profess to prove that Plato could not help but notice the importance to his discussion of picking out an existential sense of the verb 'to be'. (3) and (4) profess to show that he
253 ex-/pressly made this distinction. So (3) and (4) make the stronger claim, and I take them first.[49]

The explicit distinction

(*3) The appeal to the expression 'partaking in being' can properly be met by the reminder that Plato also uses 'partaking in not-being' (*metechein tou mê ontos*, 260d7; *koinônein tou mê ontos*, 260e2-261a1) and plainly does not mean this to signify non-existence or mark a one-place predicate.[50] But without reliance on Parity the same point can be proved of the positive expression. When it occurs in the *Parmenides*, for instance, it is evidently not pre-empted for existential being.[51] And (lest this be set down as another chicanerie of the *Parmenides*) we can bring it home to the *Sophist*. That the phrase can be used of that connective '... is ...' which I have alleged to be at the heart of Plato's investigation is proved by 259a6-8. The ES sums up his argument about the Different: it 'partakes in being, and is by virtue of that partaking – but not the thing of which it partakes but something different'. The verb in the last clause must be supplied from its predecessor, and the verb supplied is the incomplete 'is'. (To be sure, the reductivists hoped to save an existential sense for the incomplete 'is' without engaging Plato in a study of denials of existence. But their thesis depended on displacing the negative, and that is a past issue.)

Now consider the formula 'partaking in being' as it occurs at 256a1. It is embedded in a stretch of reasoning (255e8-256e6) whose results are summarized, with the help of the same formula, at 256d11-e6. The reasoning was sketched under (3): it consists in showing, for various general terms P, that with a certain proviso a specimen subject (in this case, Change) can be
254 said both to be P/and not to be P. The proviso is that the pattern of analysis of 'This is P' varies in the two cases: in Plato's examples, the positive statement is predicative and the negative is a denial of identity. The ES concludes: 'So not-being necessarily *is* in the case of change, and with respect to all the kinds,[52] for with respect to them all difference makes each one

[49] They have now been ably debated by Frede, op. cit., 55-9 and 12-29, but I retain my own replies as making a few different points of controversial interest.

[50] What it does mean to say that *logos* partakes in not-being is obscure until *logos* is replaced by *to legomenon* (much as *kinêsis* and *stasis* had to be replaced in the non-identity proofs by *kineitai* and *hestêke* or *kinoumenon* and *hestos*, 250c6-d2, 252d6-10). *What is said*, in a falsehood, *is not*: that is, about some subject one says what is not in the sense explained above (p. 114, and n. 30 above).

[51] Among many occurrences note 141e7-14, 161e3-62b8, 163b6-d1, e6-64a1.

[52] On the interpretation of this see nn. 19-20 above.

different from what is, and so makes it what is not. Hence it is in just the same way that we can correctly describe them all as "not being" and on the other hand (since they partake of being) say that they "are" and describe them as "being" ... So,' the ES goes on, 'in the case of each of the forms, the being is multiple and the not-being is countless in number.'

'The being is multiple, the not-being is countless': I shall come back to this distinction in number, but a little must be said of it now. Briefly, the ES has been arguing concerning a specimen subject that it is, predicatively, many things, but that it is not identical with these things. So it *is not*, as a matter of identity, all those things which it *is* predicatively. But in addition to this it is not, as a matter of identity, countless things which it is also *not* predicatively. (Greed is one of the things which change is not identical with, but neither is it a possible attribute of change.) So if 'This is P' is understood predicatively and 'This is not P' is understood as a denial of identity, there are countless more things that anything is not than that it is. That the ES has been dividing the positive and negative occurrences of the verb in this way seems clear enough, and I shall suggest a reason later. Meantime the distinction does not affect our argument. The use of the verb 'to be' on which the ES rests his conclusion is the connective use, distributed between identity and predication. So he can fairly claim that 'it is in just the same way (*kata tauta*, i.e. by finding an appropriate complement) that we can correctly describe them all as "not-being" and – since they partake of being – as "being".' And to clinch his meaning the ES at once refers to the multiple being and countless not-being of any of the forms he has been discussing. He means that (as Cornford's version paraphrases it) 'there is much that each *is* and an indefinite number of things that it *is not*'.

So to extract any express recognition of a substantive or existential use of 'is' from this passage would not square with the argument. The formula 'partaking of being' is not used to mark this distinction in the summary of the
discussion at 256e3 (or therefore/ in the preceding lines 256d8-9). Nor, as we **255**
saw, is it so used in 259a6-8. It cannot therefore have this task in the argument's opening move at 256a1. Whether the words 'change is' are read as a fragment of the preceding 'change is different from rest' (255e11-12)[53] or as elliptical for 'change is with respect to something' (i.e. is instantiated, the converse of participation: 256e5, 263b11-12, and p. 131 below), fragmentary or elliptical they surely are in Plato's view.

'Partaking in being', then, is not pre-empted for ascribing unqualified being to any subject. But once it is put in this way no reader of Plato should cavil. Participation was shaped as a technical device to meet just those cases in which a thing is qualifiedly P but also qualifiedly not P.[54] Consider the uses of 'partaking' in our context: each thing is different, by partaking in the form of difference (255e4-6); each is identical, by partaking in identity (256a7-8); and each thing is, by partaking in being. The question remains

[53] cf. Frede, op. cit., 56-7.
[54] See below, Chapter 9.

what something differs from, what it can be identified with, and, quite generally, what it is.

A particularly illuminating parallel is the treatment of unity in the *Parmenides*. There (129c4-d2) Socrates explains how he can be both one and many: he is many parts, and in this way partakes in plurality; he is one man, and thus partakes in unity. It would be absurd to suggest that Plato views these partakings as endowing Socrates with some kind of unqualified unity and plurality: on these terms, Socrates would still be the subject of a contradiction and Zeno's paradoxes could never be cleared up. In other words, Plato does not represent the situation as analysable into 'Socrates is one & Socrates is many & Socrates is human & Socrates has parts'. To say that Socrates is one and many is to say something elliptical, not to isolate two independent conjuncts from a longer conjunction: 'one' and 'many' are completed by specifying 'in what respect and in what relation' (*Rep.* 436d).[55] Similarly, then, with participation in being and not-being.

(*4) The second argument for presenting Plato with the explicit distinction
256 of existence from other sorts of being can be more/quickly met.[56] In 255c12-d7 he does indeed draw a distinction between different uses of the verb 'to be'; but these are almost certainly its incomplete uses, in statements of identity and of predication.

First, when the ES marks off difference from being he does not say, as the commentators make out, that to call X 'different' is to give a *relative* or *incomplete* description of X (*pros ti*). He says that it is to give a description which must always be filled out by reference to something *different from X* (255d1, 7). By contrast, when we describe things as 'being' (i.e. say that they are) it is only in some instances that what we say must be completed by reference to something other than the subject (*pros alla*, 255c13);[57] in other instances things can be said to be 'themselves in their own right' (*auta kath' hauta*, 255c12-13). Now it is in predication that the complement of the verb 'to be' imports something different from the subject: on this the ES hangs a major argument at 256a3-c10, and it was of course a thesis basic to the theory of Ideas.[58] In identity-statements, on the other hand, the expressions which flank the verb cannot designate different things; indeed in this context they seem to be regarded as typically of the form 'A is A' (254d15, 257a5, 259b3-4).

Secondly, the language with which the ES makes his contrast at 255c-d

[55] This gives added point to Parmenides' query whether Socrates wants a Form of Man, and to Socrates' hesitation (*Parm.* 130c1-4): for to admit this *would* seem to commit him to analysing 'I am one man' as 'I partake in unity and I partake in humanity'. In fact it does not: the essential incompleteness of 'one' and 'many' and 'same' and 'different' and 'is' and 'is not' is well brought out by paradoxes in the *Parmenides* (e.g. 146d5-e4, 147a3-8, 161e3-162b8), and for them the original model of participation holds good.

[56] Cf. Frede, op. cit., 12-29. See also 'Additional Note' at the end of this chapter.

[57] That Plato does not mean to distinguish between *heteron* and *allo* here (Deichgräber *apud* Frede, 12 n. 1) is proved by 256c5-6, 257a1, 257b4 and 10, and in the essential anticipation at 252b10, c3.

[58] It is a premise of the Third Man paradox, Alex., *Metaph.* 84.21-85.12.

(*kath' hauto* ... *heteron, allo*) has already been introduced, at the start of this section of the argument, to mark the distinction between identity-statements and predications. The opsimaths whose theory commits them, wittingly or unwittingly,[59] to leaving only the first sort of statement standing, are said to 'debar anything from sharing in the condition of another and so being called that other' (*mêden eôntes koinôniai pathêmatos heterou thateron/prosagoreuein,* 257
252b9-10); and then in producing the identity-statements that are essential to stating their case they are said to couple the expressions *einai* ... *chôris* ... *tôn allôn* ... *kath' hauto* (252c2-5). So the commentators who gloss our passage by the distinction between *kath' hauto* and *pros ti* or *tini* in the *Philebus* (51c) or the *Theaetetus* (157a-b) have looked too far afield and brought back the wrong dichotomy.[60]

Thirdly, it is this interpretation that explains, as the older one cannot, why the ES needs a different argument (255b8-c7) to distinguish being from *identity.* For 'same' is a grammatically incomplete predicate, no less than 'different'; what makes the argument inapplicable to it is just that it cannot be supposed to mark a relation between different things (cf. 256b1).

Fourthly, the ES at 255c10 introduces his distinction between uses of 'to be' with the words 'I think you agree' (and not, as translators on the received interpretation generally feel impelled to turn it, 'I think you will agree'). Why assume that he already has Theaetetus' assent? Simply because he has just followed his review of the opsimaths' theory with an argument to show their mistake (252d-254d): predications are possible and necessary, even though in abstract contexts it takes philosophical expertise to determine what can be predicated of what. And Theaetetus has agreed: predication is as necessary as identification.

This plea, that the distinction be read as arising from its context, can be made broader. Just as it is the division of identification from predication that the ES needs to settle the opsimaths' confusion, so it is this that he requires to explain the general paradox about being which precedes it (249c10-250e4: see p. 132 below) and to disarm the paradoxes which follow (255e8-256c10, cf. 259b8-d7). The division that is not made, and not relevant to these problems, is one between a complete or existential use of 'to be' and an undifferentiated parcel of incomplete uses.

There is another moral to be drawn from these answers. Even in performing the valuable and essential task of disentangling predicative and identity-statements which carry the verb 'to be',[61] Plato can hardly have seen his project as that of displaying different/ senses of the verb. His 258
comments upon its syntax are taken to mark out the different tasks, or different possibilities of combination, of a single undifferentiated form, being. For if (*3) shows that the expression 'partaking in being' is not used to identify a special sense of the verb it becomes the less likely that the other

[59] Cf. n. 47 above.

[60] The distinction as here interpreted also leads naturally to Aristotle's division between *to kath' hauto legomenon* and *to heteron kath' heterou legomenon.*

[61] The brunt of Ackrill's argument, op. cit.

expressions quoted in (3) are meant to paraphrase the verb in other senses; no such role is claimed for them in the text (256a10-b4).[62] And the matter seems to be clinched by the argument just discussed. If Plato took himself to be distinguishing senses of 'being' he would surely have to conclude from his reasoning in 255c8-d7, that he had managed to distinguish difference from only one of the concepts falling under that name, i.e. from the sort of being which is *not pros allo* (or, on the older interpretation, *pros ti*). One proof that being remains for him a unitary concept is that he concludes directly to his distinction between being and difference.[63]

In the *Sophist*, then, Plato does not (in Shorey's words) 'explicitly distinguish the copula from the substantive *is*'. Does his argument nevertheless compel him to set apart an existential use of the verb?

The paradoxes

(*1) Consider again the assumptions which govern Plato's puzzles about not-being (236d-241b), and his treatment of those assumptions. The paradoxes are represented as all in various ways dependent on one veteran and protean hypothesis, that *being can have no connexion with not-being* or, more at length, that what-is-not cannot be in any way and what-is cannot not be in any way (cf. 241b1-2, d6-7). Understandably, in view of its ambiguity, the hypothesis takes various forms: in (i), that 'what is not' cannot designate anything that is (237c1-7); in (ii)-(iii), that an attribute that is cannot be attached to a subject that is not (238a7-9, c5-6); in (iv), that it is paradoxical
259 that what really is not (or is not real)/ should really be (or be a real) anything at all (240b12-c3, Badham's text); in (v), that it is paradoxical, in the case of believing what is not, that what is believed should also have being (241a3-b3). In addition, (i) assumes the identity of what is not with nothing,[64] and (iv) and (v) take what is not to be the contrary of what is (249b5, d6-9).

I believe it will be agreed that Plato's understanding of these skeletal assumptions must be gathered from his subsequent treatment of them. On this point the traditional interpretations seem curiously ambivalent. There is an evident wish to retain the second assumption, construed as meaning that only existent subjects can have actual attributes (see (2c) on p. 124). Otherwise the assumptions are regarded as an intractable set of dicta about non-existence which Plato drops in favour of some innocuous ones exploiting

[62] Indeed, 256a11-b4 (where the supposedly central verb 'to be' is merely left to be understood from the previous sentence) is more easily read as offering different analyses of 'the same': in 'change (is) the same' it signifies 'partaking in the form Identical', in 'change (is) not the same' it signifies 'the form Identical'. If *ouch homoiôs eirêkamen* (256a11-12) promises paraphrases these are the readier candidates, but a phrase that often promises paraphrases in Aristotle must not be assumed to in Plato (cf. p. 136 below).

[63] It remains the vowel-form, being (n. 26 above); but I cannot here pursue the conceptual distinctions embodied in the 'communion of forms' or the role of *methexis*.

[64] Cf. n. 7 above.

a different sense of the verb 'to be'. But neither of these reactions is Plato's. He offers to *contradict* them all, to refute them and prove their negations (cf. *ton elenchon touton kai tên apodeixin*, 242a7-b5). He takes them (though he cannot yet allow himself the luxury of the word) to be, straightforwardly and sense unchallenged, false.

Thus the first is contradicted by showing that, given the appropriate complements, 'what is not' and 'what is' must be applicable to the same things (256e2-7) and indeed to any subject of discourse (263b11-12). The third, i.e. the claim that 'real' and 'unreal' do not cohabit, can evidently be rebutted in the same manner, and the ES's formulation of the reality-puzzle (240b9-13) seems tailored to this solution: the semblance is not the real original but it certainly is the real semblance.[65] But in the end he simply reduces the problem of unreality to that of falsehood (264c10-d5).

Nor, of course, is the second assumption smuggled out of this general rebuttal. It is contradicted by the same passages which prove the contradictory of the first. What is not (sc. not so-and-so) must nevertheless have attributes that are – viz. 'are with respect to it', are its attributes (256e5-6, 263b11-12). On these terms an attribute can evidently be said both to be and not to be, belonging to some subjects but not others: the incomplete 'is' in one more role, introduced (but not paraphrased) to mark a relation just the converse of participation./

Here, however, there is a complication which helps to explain the course of **260**
Plato's argument. Some forms – being, identity and difference *imprimis* – can be attributed to anything whatever. So how can these be said 'not to be' with respect to any subject? Well: they can, provided this is understood as a denial of identity. This I take it is why Plato, discussing these all-pervasive concepts, is ready to explain the 'multiple being' which belongs to a subject in terms of the predicates which are true of it, but turns to non-identity to explain its 'countless not-being' (cf. p. 127 above). And it is why, when he shifts to such unpervasive attributes as flying and sitting, this asymmetry seems to be quietly given up: the not-being of these attributes is extended to the case in which they are not truly predicable of some subject (263b11-12). But the tacit extension is not a slip: no doubt Plato feels entitled to adapt his analysis to these cases on the ground that non-identity is still central to it. If flying 'is not with respect to Theaetetus', the non-identity holds now between flying and any and all of the attributes which do belong to Theaetetus, which 'are' for him (pp. 114-15 above). And thus he prepared his ground for contradicting the assumption used in (v) to extract contradictions from falsehood. The man who speaks or thinks falsely does after all and without paradox ascribe being to what is not, or not-being to what is: he counts among X's attributes one which 'is not with respect to X', i.e. which differs from any of X's attributes; or he counts among attributes of the second class one which 'is with respect to X'. The distinction seems to be that between positive and negative falsehoods, and Plato deals expressly only with a falsehood of the first class

[65] On this as an element in Plato's standard view of reality see Vlastos, op. cit. (nn. 3 and 44 above).

(263a1-d5); but his language implies that he is ready for the others (240e10-241a1; cf. *apraxian* [non-action] 262c3).

There is no need for more words on the remaining assumptions, that what is not is *nothing* and is *contrary to what is*. The sophist is nowhere advised that his puzzles over not-being and falsehood employ a special concept of being or a sense of the key-verb which will not stand negation. He is instructed in the proper scope of, and safeguards on, the 'is' and 'not-is' that he mismanaged. He will look in vain for any recognition here of the baffling unavailability of what false statements try but fail to mention.

Let us leave him unassuaged for the moment and notice that the subsequent paradox about being (242b6-250e4) is equally ill-adapted to
261 forcing a recognition of 'exists' as a distinct sense of/ 'is'. As the ES forecast, the accounts of 'is' and 'is not' go hand in hand.

This section of the dialogue is designed to culminate in a paradox (the *aporia* of 250e1-2) whose diagnosis is generally agreed.[66] It depends on confusing identity-statements with predications. This is why the ES moves at once to the opsimaths (251a5-c6) and proposes to give one answer to both difficulties (251c8-d2). On the way to his problem he has shown that previous attempts to characterize being (or 'what is' and 'what are') were unduly restrictive: those who say that being is a plurality or else that it is only one thing, that it is corporeal or that it is immutable and non-perceptible, are all rebuked for leaving something out of the inventory (242c4-249d8). Thus he reaches a proposal (A) that seems to leave nothing out: 'being is whatever is changed and (whatever is) unchanged' (249d3-4). He comments that the disjunction 'changed-unchanged' is surely exhaustive (250c12-d3), and in fact any other exhaustive dichotomy would serve the paradox equally well. For now he repeats an argument which saw service earlier against the pluralists: being is neither change nor rest – it is this different thing, being (250c3-4). And this is at once restated (B) in the form: 'by its own nature being neither rests nor changes' (250c6-7). So (A) seems to be in conflict with (B).

It is commonly agreed that (B) is proved by an illicit move from 'X is not identical with either Y or Z' to 'X is not characterized by either Y or Z'; and that subsequently the ES blocks this move by distinguishing identity-statements from predications and showing, for some ubiquitous predicates (being, identity, difference), that a subject which is not identical with one of these still cannot help being characterized by it. So this problem is set and solved as an exercise in the logic of identity and predication, not of existence. True, commentators have hoped to find Plato arguing positive truths about existence in his prefatory review of older theories of being.[67] Given his general strategy in the section, such truths could be no more than

[66] Even when existence is thought to be the topic of the introductory pages: n. 13 above.

[67] On this see J. Malcolm, op. cit., who finds no existential sense of the verb distinguished in it; and notice that Plato takes no care in these pages to restrict the verb in its critical appearances to one grammatical role. It varies from adverb to connective and from these to roles in which no explicit complement is supplied.

parenthetical. For my part I doubt that Plato is/ pressing even such 262
parenthetical doctrine on the reader: it is enough to read this study of 'things that are (or are not)' against the *Parmenides*' study of 'things that are one (or not one)' for the essentially elliptical character of these descriptions to be clear. Plato's arguments about being are, what he represents them to be, prefatory to a paradox. What they show (at best) is the incoherence of certain claims that, for some favoured value of F, *to be* is just *to be F*. They lead to the proposal that *to be* is *to be either or both F and not-F*; and thus they set the scene for the puzzle described above.

The approach to falsehood

(*2) In the ES's scheme, the being of an attribute such as change or not-being carries at least the requirements that it be unproblematically identifiable and instantiated. That is, to say that 'it is' promises two sorts of completion: that it is A, 'having a nature of its own', and not B (cf. 258b8-c3); and that it is 'with respect to' other things C, D ... (p. 131 above). Similarly with any subject of attributes: to say that 'it is' is to face the *Sophist*'s question 'Is what and what sort of thing?' What then of the requirement, supposedly fundamental to Plato's final analysis of true and false statement (261c6-263d4), that the subject of any statement must exist?[68]

Evidently the requirement can no longer be defended as satisfying the 'hatstand' assumption discerned in stage (ii) of the puzzles. The ES has contradicted the assumption governing that stage, and in such a way as to show that it was not understood as existential. But consider the analysis itself.

What is striking is that, while Plato insists that a statement must be *about* (or *of*, or must *name* or *belong to*) something, he does not use the verb 'to be' in any existential sense to bring out the nature of this thing. He says that a statement must be about *something* (262e5) and not *nothing* (263c9-11), and he has spent a long argument explaining the terms on which the first but not the second can be made a subject of discourse; but when he uses the verb in this connexion he speaks of the subject as 'what is or what is not' (262c3). This last phrase has understandably troubled the defenders of the received view: they have tried to deny that it applies to the subject of a statement, and even construed it as making a broad distinction between positive and negative assertions.[69] But the context defeats/ them. Plato is arguing that any 263
statement requires the coupling of a subject- and predicate-expression. Without marrying some such expression as 'a lion' to one of a different family such as 'runs', it is not possible to declare 'the action or non-action or being of what is or what is not' (*oudemian praxin oud' apraxian oude ousian ontos oude mê ontos*, 262c2-3). Just as 'action or non-action or being' characterizes what the

[68] Moravcsik, op. cit., 41.
[69] ibid., 63 n. 1; cf. Campbell, op. cit., 173 ad loc.

predicate-expression contributes,[70] so 'what is or what is not' picks out the contribution of the subject-phrase.[71] Plato wants to provide for such subjects as 'the not-beautiful' (or 'what is not beautiful') as well as for 'the beautiful' ('what is beautiful'). Otherwise he would have disallowed some of his own conclusions as candidates for a truth-value. As it is, when it is most important for the received interpretation that he should pick out the subject by an existential use of the verb, it is the connective 'is' and its negation that he leaves entrenched.[72]

It remains to show how the sophist's puzzle is finally diagnosed within this scheme of concepts, which lacks or ignores an expression for 'exist' and makes no attempt to isolate such a 'kind' or 'form' as existence. The *Theaetetus*' analogy between speaking and seeing or touching is not recalled: that was only a symptom.[73] What is taken up is the premise from which the *Euthydemus* started its paradoxes about falsehood, that things (*pragmata*) can be spoken of only by expressions which belong to them. The ES accepts this – too hospitably – in the form that any statement having a truth-value must belong to something, viz. to what it is 'of' or 'about', the *pragma* that it 'names' (cf. 263a4-5, 262e12-13). Let me call this relation between a statement and what
264 it is about the/'A-relation', and notice two points in Plato's treatment of it. First, he illustrates but does not offer to analyse it: evidently he assumes that it has been elucidated by the whole study of subject-predicate relations which he now recalls in the dictum 'There is much that is with respect to each thing and much that is not' (263a11-12). Secondly, it becomes clear from 262e12-263a10 (esp. 263a4-10) and c5-d1 that he takes the intuitively plausible view of the relation: he holds that 'Theaetetus sits' and 'Theaetetus flies' are both about just one thing, Theaetetus. There is no suggesting that they are about (or name, or belong to) *sitting* or *flying*. Of course statements about sitting and flying are possible, including some which are equivalent to those just quoted: 'Sitting is with respect to Theaetetus', for example. But from what Plato says it seems that these are not the same statements: they would not be characterized as being about the same subject (262e5-6).[74]

It is this A-relation, then, that gives the sophist the connexion he demands

[70] And the 'being' cannot be represented by the traditional interpretation as existence without committing Plato to explaining in the sequel how existential statements can be false but significant. On the whole phrase, Apelt, *Sophista*, ad loc.; on *ousia*, n. 72 below.

[71] So Diès, 'ni action, ni inaction, ni être, soit d'un être, soit d'un non-être', and Taylor, 'the action, inaction, or being of anything that is or is not'.

[72] The *ousia* of 261e5 is of course the 'being' studied in the preceding arguments: the texts cited in n. 51 above prove that it is not confined to existential contexts, and the other occurrences in the *Sophist* can be explained on the same terms.

[73] Such non-intensionally transitive verbs as 'hitting' and 'kicking' seem equally appropriate to conveying the sophist's demand for a verbal contact between statement and situation. On one view that (some) verbs of perception are especially important to the analogy, see n. 39 above.

[74] This brings out the irrelevance of representing Plato as meeting the sophist's puzzle by the explanation that 'Theaetetus flies' mentions (= belongs to, is of or about) two things, the falsehood consisting in mentioning together things not found together in fact; or of looking for some 'correlate' with which the false sentence as a whole makes verbal contact. The expressions used at 261e4-6 and 262e10-11 are innocuous preliminaries to the point insisted on in 262e5-6, 262e10-263a10, c5-11.

between the words and the actual situation described: the verbal contact, or the verbal 'belonging'. (It is what Austin called the demonstrative component in the statement; what is often called the reference.) The sophist is allowed his claim that if this relation does not hold, no truth or falsehood has been uttered. But then it is explained that he has exaggerated the scope of the relation. It is a necessary condition of both truth and falsehood, but it is not a sufficient condition of truth. The mere naming – even the stringing together of names (262a9-10) – does not 'complete the business' (*perainein ti*) or achieve a truth-value (262b9-c7): that comes only when something is *said about* what the statement is about,[75] and for this one needs to import an expression with quite another function, such as '... sits' or '... flies'. Once the place of 'what is not' in the diagnosis has been vindicated, it is in the/ A-relation that Plato **265**
seems to locate the residual mistake in the sophist's picture of falsehood. Falsehood had appeared an abortive attempt to mention something, like an unsuccessful effort to touch or to hear; and this confused the conditions for naming with the conditions for truth.

I need not dwell on this familiar and, I think, satisfactory account of Plato's reply.[76] My argument concerns the way in which the relation of aboutness is introduced. Doubtless it needs (and is currently receiving) harder analysis before it will carry any more ambitious study of statement-structure; but Plato's exploration of the ways in which something can be unparadoxically differentiated, assigned and denied attributes, is a necessary and for his purpose an adequate introduction. The requirement that the subject should exist is neither: witness the insoluble and irrelevant query whether he wants to make room for centaurs.

'But the requirement that the statement should be about *something* and not *nothing* just is the requirement that the subject should exist; for Plato, *to be* is *to be something*,[77] and surely this is an account of existence.' Two last remarks on this.

I have tried to characterize the scheme of concepts within which Plato studies 'nothing' and its twin, 'something', as possible subjects of discourse. For such a study of subject-predicate structure an account of existence is

[75] That the *peri* in 263b4-5 is to be coupled with the *legei* and not merely with the *onta hôs estin* is certified by 263d1 and generally by the requirement that the *logos* must be *tinos* or *peri tinos* (262e5-6, 263a4).

[76] But since I have implied that it is novel with the *Sophist* I must notice the unitarian suggestion that the solution is already recognized in the *Euthydemus* (284c) and *Cratylus* (385b), which characterize true speaking as speaking of things that are, as they are, and false speaking as speaking of things that are, as they are not. The first half of the conjunction is echoed in the *Sophist* (263b4-5). But (i) the description of falsehood is not echoed in the *Sophist* – understandably, since it is at least ambiguous and its ambiguity is used to generate unresolved paradoxes at *Euthd.* 284c-e, 285e-286b. (ii) The echo of the truth-description in the *Sophist* has a quite different sense: the *Euthd.* makes it clear that the 'things that are' are subjects of the statement (see examples in 284d-e) whereas in *Soph.* 263b4-5 they are equally clearly predicates; and the sense in which a predicate 'is (or is not) with respect to' a subject has had to be established earlier (256e5-6, recalled here at 263b11-12).

[77] In the earlier passage cited in n. * on p. 104 I used the expression '*to be* is *to be something or other*' in describing Plato's theory, and now think this unperspicuous for reasons given here. The familiar idiom *einai ti* is of course used in the *Sophist* (e.g. 246e5) as elsewhere in Plato.

neither a presupposition nor a part; but it might well be a further outcome,
266 much as a logic without existen-/tial presuppositions can be made to yield a formula for individual existence.[78] This is, I think, what it became in Aristotle's metaphysics. But notoriously Aristotle complains of Plato for not taking this step, for ignoring the consequent distinction of senses in 'is' and remaining content with his unitary concept, being.

As for the equation '*to be* is *to be something*,' the negation of 'to be something' is 'not to be anything' or 'to be nothing', which Plato holds to be unintelligible; and then it would follow from the equation that 'not to be' makes no sense. But Plato recognizes no use of the verb in which it cannot be directly negated. He holds indeed that *to be in no way at all* is a merely paradoxical notion; but he argues with all possible emphasis that this is not the legitimate negation of *to be*. To discount this is to fall into the embarrassments of the traditional account: to saddle Plato with an argument which first sets puzzles about non-existence, then offers to refute the
267 assumptions on which the puzzles depend, and finally backs down/ and recommends that direct negation be prudently reserved for other uses of the verb 'to be'.

Additional note
(see n. 56 above)

The preceding argument (255b8-c7) distinguishes being from identity, and since it discusses being without specifying any complement for the verb 'to be' it is often understood as dealing expressly with existence. But it follows the argument of 255a4-b6, in which change and rest (C and R) are distinguished from identity and difference on the ground that, while both C and R can be called either identical or different, C cannot be said to rest nor R to change. Thereafter being is distinguished from identity on the ground that C and R can both alike be said to be, but not said to be identical (*tauton*). Throughout both arguments the complements to 'identical' and 'different' are left unspecified. So in the first argument the ascription of identity to C and R is tacitly understood as meaning that C is identical *with C*, and R *with R*, while in the second it is tacitly understood as meaning that they are the same *as each other*. (The use of the singular *tauton* as a joint predicate in 255c1 helps the shift, but is itself illegitimate: the counterpart predicate from the verb 'to be' would be *on*, which cannot be a joint predicate at all.) What the arguments show, if anything, is that for some subject in whose description 'the same' and 'different' can properly occur (sc. with some undeclared complement), neither expression can be replaced in the description by 'changing' or (in the alternative case) by 'at rest'; and that, for some subjects in whose joint description 'being' can properly occur, that expression cannot be replaced by 'identical' (again with some undeclared complement). Patently the argument

[78] J. Hintikka, 'Studies in the Logic of Existence and Necessity, I: Existence', *Monist* 1 (1966) 55-76.

loses none of its force if we write: 'for some subject in whose description "being" can properly occur (*with some undeclared complement*)'; the argument systematically discounts complements.

7

Plato on the Undepictable

349 This unavoidably brief and inadequate salute to Gregory Vlastos was written on the occasion of his retirement from Princeton. Here, as no more than a token of the gratitude and affection due him, is another view of one piece of argument in his favourite philosopher.

There is a passage in Plato's *Statesman* which has lent itself to quotation by unitarians of both camps. (Unitarians are those who hold that Plato maintained his middle-period theory of paradigm-forms in the face of all objections; they divide broadly into those who think he did so because he had undivulged answers to the objections, and those who think he did so because he had not decoded the objections he himself helped to retail.) Divorced from their context, the lines 285d9-86a7 have commonly been cited to show that in this late work Plato still assumed without argument that the participant in any Form was related to that Form as a likeness (or, more strongly, a copy) to its original. True, on this reading of the passage it carried the caveat that some Forms, and those 'the greatest and most valuable,' had no satisfactory perceptible likenesses. But this was not counted as an embarrassment, for a similar warning seems to be issued in the *Phaedrus* (250a5-e1), and it does not deter Plato there from crediting any form with earthly likenesses (*homoiômata, eikones*) even when there is no illumination in the likenesses and the nature of the Form can be made out from them only with difficulty, 'the instruments being dark and the men to do it few' (250a6-b5). Still there was a residual embarrassment to be brushed aside. The words in the *Phaedrus* occur in that 'mythic hymn' (265c1) for whose 'rather poetical language' Socrates feels constrained to apologize at the end (257a4-6), and which he calls 'in other respects a game' when he chooses to preserve from it for technical use only the
350 methods of collection and division/ it employs (265d8-66d2). Certainly neither the tripartite soul nor the theory of paradigms which bulked so large in the mythic hymn plays the least part in the subsequent proposals for a practical psychology of rhetoric. So it is easy to sympathize with the unitarian's relief that no such apologies are made in the *Statesman*.

They are not, I argue, because they would be irrelevant. Read in context the passage says nothing of the paradigm-metaphysics. It makes a sound philosophical point in plain terms.

The Eleatic Stranger (henceforth the 'ES') is conducting an enquiry into statesmanship – or kingship, as he often calls it. He has just suggested (285c4-d7) that the enquiry is like a school spelling exercise: its chief aim is not to spell out the one thing, statecraft, but to make the group generally better at spelling – better dialecticians, that is, on any subject proposed. Still less,[1] he says, would any man in his senses do for its own sake what they have just done by way of illustration: construct a laborious definition of wool-weaving.

He goes on:

> But here is something that I think most people overlook. In the nature of the case[2] some things have perceptible likenesses which are easy to grasp,[3] and which can be readily shown to an enquirer, when he asks to/ have the things **351**
> explained and you want an easy way of pointing them out without the trouble of explaining. But with the greatest and most valuable things this is not so. These have no image clearly made for men[4] which you can display to your enquirer and bring within range of any of his senses so as to give any tolerable satisfaction[5] to his mind. That is why we must practise the ability to give and to follow explanations of anything whatever. For it is by explanation and by nothing else that the non-bodily things, the finest and greatest, are plainly displayed: and all we are now saying is said for the sake of these. But in every case it is easier to practise on the lesser, not on the greater.

For brevity, let us call the text just translated 'P'.

[1] ἦ που … γε, 285d8, 'And *certainly* no man …'; a fortiori, cf. J.D. Denniston, *The Greek Particles* (Oxford 1934), 281. Not 'Exactly, for …' (Skemp).

[2] On πεφύκασιν, 285e1, see pp. 142-3 below.

[3] The mss. at 285d10-e1 read τοῖς μὲν τῶν ὄντων ῥᾳδίως καταμαθεῖν αἰσθητικαί τινες ὁμοιότητες πεφύκασιν. (i) For αἰσθητικαί edd. read αἰσθηταί (*Tim.* 61d1 is insufficient to show that the first can have the sense of the second: contrast Taylor's rendering ad loc. with that in his note on 37c1, *A Commentary on Plato's Timaeus* (Oxford 1928)). (ii) ῥᾳδίως καταμαθεῖν. Since Schleiermacher some scholars have accepted Heusde's emendation (subsequently retracted by himself) of ῥᾳδίοις for ῥᾳδίως, evidently troubled by the infinitive construction. Others have translated the ms. without comment, some (like Heusde later) connecting the phrase with τοῖς τῶν ὄντων, some more recently (e.g. Campbell, Taylor) connecting it with the ὁμοιότητες. Valuable comments of Professors Mourelatos and Whitman have helped to make it seem likelier that the ms. should be kept, and that the infinitive should be attached to the ὁμοιότητες much as καθίζεσθαι and κατακλιθῆναι are to πόα at *Phdr.* 229b1-2 (cf. K.-G. II, p. 3 Anm., and p. 11.29-31 for other near-parallels; on the *Phdr.* text Stallbaum remarks that the infinitives are connected with the noun 'ad notionem veluti explendam atque consummandam, unde saepenumero finis et eventus nascitur significatio,' and de Vries agrees). πεφύκασιν is not of course to be read as governing the infinitive in its usual sense but as having the construction of εἰσίν, ὑπάρχουσιν (cf. e4-5). It remains exceptional that the infinitive should precede the substantive it amplifies, but the contrast (μέν … δέ, d10-e4) between 'some things' and 'the greatest and most valuable things' is more direct and arguably more pertinent than that between 'some things easy to understand' and 'the greatest and most valuable things.' The decision does not affect the argument of the paper.

[4] πρὸς τοὺς ἀνθρώπους εἰργασμένον ἐναργῶς, 286a1-2; see p. 143 below.

[5] ἱκανῶς πληρώσει, 286a4: not of course 'satisfy in a satisfactory way'; ἱκανῶς is a modifier. The satisfaction derived from the εἴδωλον as against the λόγος is only up to nursery standards: see p. 143 below.

The context: 277a-87a

1. The last sentence of P goes most of the way to marking the context in which it is to be read. It would be opaque or irrelevant if we did not know that the ES is still defending his excursus into wool-weaving, the 'lesser' parallel by which he promises to clarify the social inter-weaving he is going to require of the statesman.[6] That excursus reaches back to 277d, where he begins to explain the nature and importance of philosophical examples such as weaving; he compares them to the shorter and easier syllables in which a child can reidentify letters that cause it trouble in spelling longer and harder words (277d-78e). In terms of this analogy, the longer and harder syllable they have to spell out is statesmanship, the short and easy one they will take as an example is wool-weaving; just what the common 'letter' or 'letters' may be that the ES hopes to find in both can be left for the moment undecided. Accordingly some pages are given up to a dissection of weaving (279a-83a). They are of a tedium little relieved by the suspicion that Plato is playing some lexicographical jokes,[7] and the tedium moves the ES to defend the length of
352 his illustration. There/ are two ways of measuring, he protests (283c-87a):[8] was his excursus just longer than some others or was it *too* long by some appropriate standard? His apologia catches the infection, and runs through P and down to 287a.

I shall argue shortly that Plato has other devices to mark the internal unity of this train of argument. Meantime this much is clear: in reading P we are expected to have immediately in mind a context reaching back to 277d. But it goes back for another essential half-page, to 277a3, for it has a prelude.

2. Before 277a the ES has been engaged in the direct attempt to define statesmanship by methods of generic division, to which he returns in 287b. The first result of this attempt was to equate the statesman with (I repeat J.B. Skemp's summary) 'the art of the collective nurture of living creatures which are tame, live on the land, have no horns, do not interbreed with other creatures, walk on two legs, and have no feathers.' Some of our dissatisfaction at this is voiced by the ES. It represents the ruler as a kind of shepherd or herdsman; and even when the model is revised to avoid this comparison it gives us no help in distinguishing the true ruler from other functionaries in the state. So the ES starts by telling a story addressed to the first of these complaints. It is designed to mark off the human statesman from the 'divine shepherd' of a golden age in which the signs of time run contrary to ours. The moral is imported into the definition: the statesman must be required to

[6] 279a1-b5, cf. 305e8-6a3.

[7] See J.B. Skemp's note on 280e4 (*Plato*'s Statesman, trans, and comm. (London 1952)).

[8] At 284d1-2 the ES forecasts that the distinction made here will sometime be needed πρὸς τὴν περὶ αὐτὸ τἀκριβὲς ἀπόδειξιν. Whether this is a promise of the *Philebus* 23e ff. remains an open question, though the language of 283d7-9 strongly suggests it.

provide not nurture but merely some care (276d1-2) for his consenting featherless bipeds.[9] And at this outcome the ES becomes understandably restive, and turns to supplementing the direct method by an appeal to the *paradeigma*, or instructive parallel, which takes him into wool-weaving.

He introduces this new turn by saying that he and his hearers have been like sculptors who rush at their work and then have to waste time revamping.
'In fact our explanation is like a picture[10] which/ gives a tolerable outline but **353**
hasn't yet got the clarity that comes with pigments and the blending of colours. – Still,' he goes on, 'any living thing[11] is more suitably shown by verbal explanation than by painting or any handiwork, if you have people able to follow the explanation. The others are better shown it by handiwork' (277b7-c6).

So at the start of our context we are told: explain where you can, where you have hearers able to follow you; otherwise depict or use models. Later in P we are warned: the most important things cannot in any case be depicted or modelled, they can only be explained. The 'clarity' which a picture can carry in the earlier lines (*enargeia*, 277c3) is echoed later in the 'clarity' which can mark the fashioning of some images for men (*enargôs*, 286a2). The 'explanation' that is contrasted with the depicting or modelling in both passages is *logos* (*lexis kai logos* at 277c4). If we have the context in mind it can hardly be doubted that when Plato speaks in P of perceptible likenesses and images fashioned in a clear way for men he means to be understood literally, not in theory-laden metaphors.

3. Moreover this device, of returning to an earlier theme with a major amendment, is characteristic of our context: indeed it is Plato's way of marking the internal unity of the passage. (The external pointers to its unity need no emphasis: at 277a the ES begins his diversion from the direct pursuit of a definition by generic division, at 287a-b he announces his return to it.) Briefly, Plato allows the ES three major issues in the context. One is the contrast between explaining and depicting or modelling; that, I have argued, is recalled and amended in 285d9-86a7. The second is the analogy between spelling and dialectical analysis; that is similarly recalled with a new proviso in 285c4-d6. The analogy had suggested that identifying letters in a simpler combination was just an aid to their detection in a harder word, but that misrepresents the chief point of such exercises, whether in spelling or in dialectic; the aim is to make better spellers or better dialecticians in general. The third is the distinction between 'longer' and 'too long' in 283b-85c. That too returns with a caveat (286d4-87a6). There are different standards by
which 'too long' can be/ judged, including those of pleasure or speed, and **354**

[9] Further on this argument see 'The Place of the *Timaeus*', above, Chapter 4.

[10] ζῷον: 'picture' at 277c1, 'living thing' at 277c4; just what point Plato intends by the double use of the word here remains obscure, though the general connection between the senses seems plain. Even when an artefact, a ζῷον need not be a picture: cf. *Rep.* 514b-15a where stone and wooden figures can be either ἀνδριάντες or ἄλλα ζῷα.

[11] See n. 10 above.

now at the reprise the ES proposes the one standard he thinks appropriate, derived from the method of enquiry itself.

So by this device too the context marks the continuity of argument from 277a.

The language of P

But does not the language of P itself tell against this plain and literal reading? Must we not construe the 'perceptible likenesses' (*aisthêtai homoiotêtes*) and the 'image clearly made for men' (*eidôlon pros tous anthropous eirgasmenon enargôs*) as technical vocabulary of the paradigm-metaphysics, applicable generally to the contents of the physical world and not just, as our context suggested, to such human artefacts as pictures and models? Indeed we must, if some translators are to be followed. It can be shown, first that we need not, then that, on the evidence of P, we should not.

The crucial expressions occur at 285d-e and 286a. At 285d10-e1 Plato writes *tois tôn ontôn rhaidiôs katamathein aisthêtai tines homoiotêtes pephukasin*, which a recent English translation turns into 'Likenesses which the senses can grasp *are available in Nature* to those real existents which are in themselves easy to understand.[12] At 286a1-2 Plato speaks of an image as *pros tous anthrôpous eirgasmenon enargôs*, and in the same translation this appears as 'work *of nature* clear for all to look upon.' In the second passage the words I have italicized are a gratuity of the translator. In the first they mislead the English reader about a familiar Greek construction. Here I must follow the ES and risk tedium in stating the obvious.

The verb *pephukenai* governing a dative, with or without a dependent *einai* in view, does not have the sense of 'to be available in Nature' if this is understood as excluding human artefacts; and how else is the English reader to understand it, especially in conjunction with that unfounded 'work of nature'? In *Laws* IV 723b-d it is said that in legislation every *logos* has its *pephukos prooimion* (c3-4) and that in general this holds good for all *aismata* (songs) and *logoi* (*pephuke* (*prooimia*) *einai pasin*, d2). Patently this does not imply that either in legislation or in music the preludes are 'works of nature' or 'available in Nature' if that precludes their being man-made. The preludes
355 embody an *entechnos/ epicheirêsis* (722d5) and require a *sunthetês* (722e3), however naturally suitable they may be to the particular law or melody.[13] So too in the *Cratylus* (389c-d) the fact that there is a *phusei hekastôi pephukos organon* does not of course imply that tools are not manufactured.[14] There is

[12] J.B. Skemp (n. 7 above). Prof. Skemp translates Heusde's ῥᾳδίοις (see n. 3 above); that is immaterial to my argument here.

[13] The latest English translator, T.J. Saunders, renders πεφυκὸς προοίμιον by 'appropriate introduction' and πέφυκε προοίμια εἶναι πᾶσιν by 'they all have introductions in the nature of the case.'

[14] The point is unaffected by Socrates' equation of the 'naturally right tool' with an εἶδος to be discovered and embodied in the materials. That shows at most that there are Forms (in some sense) of artefacts (in the ordinary sense).

no need to go beyond Plato for other evidence, such as the familiar uses of the same verb in connection with human skills at *Phdr.* 277a4, *Rep.* 341d7.

So nothing in the language of P requires us to read, or entitles us to translate, the 'image clearly made for men' and the 'perceptible likenesses' as referring to something other than the human artefacts introduced earlier. Needless to say, Plato is ready elsewhere to describe the contents of the physical world quite generally as artefacts of an exalted kind, products of divine artifice (as earlier in this dialogue, 269d, 270a, in the course of the myth; cf. *Rep.* 530a4-7, 597b-d, *Tim.* 28a ff., *Soph.* 265b-66d, *Laws* 903b-d). In these other contexts Plato makes the extension of ordinary usage very clear. The language of P does not require it; and the context, as we have seen, tells against it. But in fact the language of P tells against it too.

The image that cannot be produced for the 'greatest and finest things' is described as *pros tous anthrôpous eirgasmenon enargôs* (286a1-2); that is, it is *fashioned* (1) *for* or *with a view to men* (2) *clearly* or *in a clear way.* The distribution of the words makes it highly unnatural to read *pros tous anthrôpous* as merely qualifying *enargôs*, so as to yield the weaker translation 'with clarity, so far as concerns men' (or 'by men's lights,' etc.). There is clarity in the work; and it is made with a view to men, addressed to men's purposes.[15] Now where Plato speaks of the physical world in general as a collection of divine artefacts men are themselves among the artefacts (e.g. *Soph.* 266b2-4) and they are made for the sake of the universe, not it for them (*Laws* X903b-c). To this *Timaeus* 46e-47e is no exception:/ men are given sight, speech and hearing to enable **356**
them to conform their own intelligences to the regularities of the universe; it was not made for their benefit. So the hand that is immediately responsible for the *eidôlon* of P is likelier to be man's than God's.

So much for the sense of our passage and its context. Where a student cannot follow an explanation of weaving, say, or those other crafts that Plato describes as being represented in paintings[16] – he can be introduced to the sense of the words by pictures and models. Doubtless that procedure was at home in Plato's schoolrooms as in ours. To be sure, this can be only an elementary introduction; it gives a 'tolerable' satisfaction,[17] and the word echoes the earlier 'tolerable' outline that still awaited filling in (*hikanôs*, 277c2, 286a4). Just what Plato takes it to lack must be considered shortly. Meantime he issues a warning: the most important things cannot be taught even to nursery standards from pictures and models (I shall say, for short, that they are not 'depictable'). They are, in the appropriate sense, 'bodiless'; with them the enquirer must hope to find or follow an explanation such as the ES proposes to give of statesmanship.

[15] The second point is well taken in the latest edition of Jowett, 'designed for men's instruction,' though I think the first is lost by translating ἐναργῶς as 'obviously' (I have called attention to the probable echo of 277c3). Diès comes close enough with 'images créés pour en donner aux hommes l'intuition claire,' and in his note on 286a rightly refers back to 277c (*Platon, Politicus* (Paris 1941), 47 n.2).

[16] *Rep.* 598b-c.

[17] cf. n. 5 above.

Objection

But, it may be said, could not Plato's contrast be as well made in terms of the paradigm-metaphysics? If something is depictable, surely it has 'perceptible likenesses' in the special vocabulary of that theory, and if not, not? The choice between the plainer and the more weighted interpretation seems immaterial.

Two points in reply. First, it is important if true that the argument of our context does not import that metaphysics – not just for the controversial benefit of taking a plank from unitarianism, but because we shall not now be diverted into treating Plato's contrast as a piece of apparatus within a theory, accessible to criticism only by way of a critique of that theory.

A second reply has implications that I can only sketch here. Briefly, to suppose that these two interpretations come to the same thing is to discount a piece of realism for a myth that satisfied empiricist philosophers until well after Russell. The myth was to suppose, concerning at least the great majority of words, that where these were not taught via other verbal constructions they
357 must be learnt by 'osten-/sive definition,' viz. by introducing the words in the immediate presence of the objects they supposedly stood for. Of the many difficulties in this amiably simple picture only one need be noticed here: it might be called the Schoolmaster's Objection. When a pupil cannot follow the verbal explanation of 'X' it is highly unlikely that there will always be actual samples of X on hand to show him – or indeed that it would be safe or very clarifying if there were. In P Plato insists that there is no difficulty at all (*ouden chalepon*) in producing the requisite 'perceptible likenesses.' What can be produced *ad lib.* in such circumstances, as Plato is apt to remark elsewhere (e.g. *Rep.* 596b-e, *Soph.* 234b5-10) and as any teacher or producer of trade catalogues or scientific manuals knows, are pictures of the sort of entity in question. Of course a picture or model of a lion is not in vital respects as enlightening as the live beast.[18] But it is understandably common practice, in conveying some grasp of an expression 'without the trouble of explaining,' to use some picture or model as coming more readily to hand as well as being more tractable and, for that matter, likelier than some random circus sample to represent a desirable norm of lionhood (cf. *Rep.* 472d).[19]

This is not of course to suggest that a learner might acquire his basic vocabulary merely from an acquaintance with pictures and models of what the words more directly apply to. Nothing in the contrast that Plato draws in P implies that paradox. Even in the middle dialogues, where he represents the confused majority of men as confined to a world of pictures and reflections, he equips them with a vocabulary that seems to have been independently

[18] Though Aristotle, thinking of the material picture rather than what it can be taken to portray, arguably overpressed this contrast, e.g. at *PA* 640b29-41a6.

[19] This said without prejudice to the demotion of the graphic arts in *Rep.* X 597e ff. Plato knows well enough the pitfalls in teaching by pictures.

acquired.[20] Still it is worth recalling how similar to pictures were the 'impressions' or 'sense-data' which figured so largely in the teaching-situation imagined by the empiricists. The relation of the learner to such data was notoriously passive: interfere with them, try to manipulate or dismantle them in the hope of more enlightenment, and the impression or datum was at
once replaced by another. So too with pictures: the picture interfered/ with **358**
becomes a different picture. (Of course there is a margin of vagueness here, and just this margin was transferred to those veteran problems concerning the identity of a sense-datum.) The use of pictures in teaching is at the back of the empiricist's mind. It is at the front of Plato's.

Common letters

To return to our text. It is plain from 277e-79b that the 'longer and harder syllable' to be spelt out is statesmanship and the 'shorter and easier' is wool-weaving. It is less plain, as P develops the contrast, that it is wool-weaving that can be depicted and statesmanship that cannot; but that can hardly be in doubt. It is the *megista* that cannot be depicted, and we have already met statesmanship as a *megiston on* where wool-weaving was called *smikrotaton* (278e7-8, 279a7-b2) – the contrast that is evidently recalled in 286a7-b2. When the ES represents all that he is saying as aimed at the undepictable *megista* (286a5-7) but denies that he is concerned just with statesmanship (285d4-7) his point is that the specimen analysis of statesmanship will aid the group in analysing other hard and undepictable subjects, not that statesmanship is not itself one of these.

True, there are two other characters in the plot – those many-sided skills that Plato calls Combining and Separating, *sugkritikê* and *diakritikê* – that are called *megala kata panta* (282b6-7). But their status, we shall see, is not to be captured by the simple dichotomy depictable-undepictable.

So far, then, Plato's interest in the inadequacy of teaching by pictures can be seen as taking a step beyond some assumptions familiar from the *Republic* as elsewhere. In *Rep.* X 596a-601b he had introduced painting in order to compare it with dramatic poetry and particularly the work of Homer. A painter who depicts a cobbler or a carpenter, knowing nothing of their craft, can deceive children and simpletons who see the likeness at a distance into thinking they see a real carpenter or cobbler (598b-c). They judge merely from the colours and shapes (601a). And this, by analogy, is what Homer does too. We ought to question his credentials, not perhaps concerning the other arts he writes of but certainly concerning those *megista te kai kallista*, wars and generalships and the governance of states and the education of men (599b-d).

So here there are ways of speaking even about such *megista* as/
statesmanship which Plato is ready to compare with painting. The analogy **359**

[20] cf. the prisoners at *Rep.* 515b, possessed of a vocabulary but mistaking the reference of the words (Adam's text of 515b2-4 and notes, vol. 2, pp. 90-1, 179-80).

between painting and language is a favourite with him; it is pressed uncritically in the *Critias* (107b-d), explored vigorously and critically in the *Cratylus*. Our own context starts at much the same point in 277a-c by assimilating a story about kingship to sculpture and painting. But then it adds that telling is always better than picturing or modelling; and finally it warns that in explaining the most important things there is no picture at all available to meet even nursery standards of instruction. That is certainly a step forward; it helps to break the seductive analogy. But it is not the most remarkable suggestion in the context.

The ES has explained that his use of the weaving-analogy is comparable to identifying letters in easier combinations as an aid to finding them in harder; in applying his analogy he speaks of 'the long and hard syllables of *things*' (*tas tôn pragmatôn makras kai mê rhaidious sullabas*, 278d4-6). What then is the 'letter' or 'letters' common to the things weaving and statecraft, the 'same likeness and nature' (278b1-2, the 'same form' (278e8), the 'same enterprise' (*pragmateia*, 279a8)?

After 305e2-6a3, if not before, there can be no doubt. The common element is Combining or Interweaving. It is put to work first in the analysis of wool-weaving, later in that of the social interweaving required of the king or statesman, whether this is the intertwining of the military, judiciary and forensic classes (cf. 305e2-6) or, as the ES finally argues, the interbreeding of aggressive and gentle strains in the citizens (306a-11c). At 282b6-7, where it is called *sugkritikê,* its counterpart is *diakritikê,* Separating; and the ES says 'These two arts we have found to be important in all fields' (*megala tine kata panta hêmin êstên techna*). But where did we find this out? Well, in 281a weaving was distinguished as a sort of *sumplokê* from combing or carding, which is *tôn sunestôtôn kai sumpepilêmenôn dialutikê*; and between them these two kinds of operation exhaust all departments of wool-working. That might be all that is implied by *kata panta* here. But in fact the arts of combining and separating have seen ambitious use in the *Sophist*, the *Statesman*'s dramatic precursor, and the reader is expected to have the argument of that dialogue in mind (cf. *Plt.* 284b7-9). In *Soph.* 226b-c Separation is itself introduced by examples (*paradeigmata*) drawn from menial operations such as carding and spinning, much as Combination is in the *Statesman*; and then it is taken to cover, *inter*
360 *alia*, the separating of men from various sorts of physical/ and mental ills (226c-31b). Thereafter the verb is reimported to describe the skill of the dialectician in distinguishing the concepts he investigates (253e1, cf. 253d1-3). Just as he must be able to distinguish them, so he must be able to combine them or see their connections. The counterpart verb *sugkrinein* is not assigned to this task, but other words of the same class (*sunagein, sunaptein*) are used in describing the ability to see which concepts can be coupled in significant discourse; and in the same argument the verb that carries the weight in the last pages of the *Statesman*, *sumplekein* (306a2, 309b7, 311b7), appears as a verbal noun (*Soph.* 259e5-6). Thereafter, by what is represented as an extension of the analogy with spelling, the same verb of combination is used to describe the coupling of syntactically complementary expressions in any true or false statement (*Soph.* 262c5-d4).

Versatile twins, indeed. Faced with the many uses that Plato finds for Combination and Separation in the *Sophist*, and with the still further applications of them in the *Statesman*, the reader is likely to complain that he has been introduced not to a pair of concepts but at the least to a family of them. True, the *Sophist* recognizes that Separation can be divided into different sorts or kinds (226a-31b), and no doubt Combination can be parcelled out in the same way. But wool-weaving and statesmanship will be sorts of Combining; and the *Statesman* is emphatic that when these are spelt out the identical element Combining will be found in both. How can Plato picture this as a single element?

The reader's doubt can be sharpened. Combining is an element in wool-weaving, which is depictable; and it is an element in statesmanship, which is not depictable. Is Combining itself, we may innocently ask, something that can be learnt (at least to nursery standards) from pictures, or not? We recall Frege's contempt in the *Grundlagen* for a theory in which numbers sometimes appear as physical properties and sometimes not. Aristotle surely had these arguments of Plato's in view when he insisted that the elements of perceptible and of imperceptible things must be different elements (e.g. *Meta.* 993a7-10).

The simplest reply to this objection is that the question whether Combination and Separation are depictable or undepictable cannot arise within the conceptual framework of the *Statesman.* For the dichotomy of depictable-undepictable is drawn within the range of things that can be explained, that have a *logos*; and to explain them is to articulate them into
their elements, like spelling a word into its/ letters. But in this analogy **361**
Combination (and, we may assume, Separation) is a letter, not a spellable.

There is more to it than this, however. To learn what weaving is from pictures and models alone is precisely not to be able yet to produce or follow the *logos* in which the concept is spelt out. At most, no doubt, it enables the learner to say 'weaving' when confronted with the activity or when mentioning it in contexts where ignorance of its correct analysis will not defeat the reference. But to be introduced to weaving in this way is not to be introduced to the master-concept, Combination, at all; the recognition of that awaits the kind of explanation that goes beyond picture-teaching. To the extent that weaving is depictable, what is depicted cannot be Combination itself.

Plato's interest in analogies drawn from pictures and picturing pervades his work. It plays a major part in his metaphysics, his theory of language, even his account of false pleasure (*Phil.* 39b-40c). It is tempting to think that in P he is once more turning to picture-analogies. He is not: he is saying something of lasting interest about picturing itself and what can be pictured.

III

ARISTOTLE

8

Aristotle: Method, Physics and Cosmology

Aristotle's father served as personal physician to Amyntas II of Macedon, 250
grandfather of Alexander the Great. Aristotle's interest in biology and in the use of dissection is sometimes traced to his father's profession, but any suggestion of a rigorous family training in medicine can be discounted. Both parents died while Aristotle was a boy, and his knowledge of human anatomy and physiology remained a notably weak spot in his biology. In 367, about the time of his seventeenth birthday, he came to Athens and became a member of Plato's Academy. Henceforth his career falls naturally into three periods. He remained with the Academy for twelve years. Then, when Plato died in 347, he left the city and stayed away for twelve years: his reason for going may have been professional, a dislike of philosophical tendencies represented in the Academy by Plato's nephew and successor, Speusippus, but more probably it was political, the new anti-Macedonian mood of the city. He returned in 335 when Athens had come under Macedonian rule, and had twelve more years of teaching and research there. This third period ended with the death of his pupil, Alexander the Great (323), and the revival of Macedon's enemies. Aristotle was faced with a charge of impiety and went again into voluntary exile. A few months later he died on his maternal estate in Chalcis.

His middle years away from Athens took him first to a court on the far side of the Aegean whose ruler, Hermeias, became his father-in-law; then (344) to the neighboring island Lesbos, probably at the suggestion of Theophrastus, a native of the island and henceforth a lifelong colleague; finally (342) back to Macedon as tutor of the young prince Alexander. After his return to Athens he lectured chiefly in the grounds of the Lyceum, a Gymnasium already popular with sophists and teachers. The Peripatetic school, as an institution comparable to the Academy, was probably not founded until after his death. But with some distinguished students and associates he collected a natural history museum and library of maps and manuscripts (including his own essays and lecture notes), and organized a program of research which *inter alia* laid the foundation for all histories of Greek natural philosophy (see Theophrastus), mathematics and astronomy (see Eudemus), and medicine.

* In the *Dictionary*, this article was followed by a bibliography compiled by Professor Owen, which he did not wish reproduced here. There followed an article by another author on Aristotle's natural history and zoology. – Ed.

Recent discussion of his intellectual development has dwelt on the problem of distributing his works between and within the three periods of his career. But part of the stimulus to this inquiry was the supposed success with which Plato's dialogues had been put in chronological order, and the analogy with Plato is misleading. Everything that Aristotle polished for public reading in Plato's fashion has been lost, save for fragments and later reports. The writings that survive are a collection edited in the first century B.C., allegedly from manuscripts long mislaid: a few items are spurious (among the scientific works *Mechanica, Problemata, De Mundo, De Plantis*), most are working documents produced in the course of Aristotle's teaching and research; and the notes and essays composing them have been arranged and amended not only by their author but also by his ancient editors and interpreters. Sometimes an editorial title covers a batch of writings on connected topics of which some seem to supersede others (thus *Physics* VII seems an unfinished attempt at the argument for a prime mover which is carried out independently in *Physics* VIII); sometimes the title represents an open file, a text annotated with unabsorbed objections (e.g., the *Topics*) or with later and even post-Aristotelian observations (e.g., the *Historia Animalium*). On the other hand it cannot be assumed that inconsistencies are always chronological pointers. In *De Caelo* I-II he argues for a fifth element in addition to the traditional four (fire, air, water, earth): unlike them, its natural motion is circular and it forms the divine and unchanging substance of the heavenly bodies. Yet in *De Caelo* III-IV, as in the *Physics*, he discusses the elements without seeming to provide for any such fifth body, and these writings are accordingly sometimes thought to be earlier. But on another view of his methods (see below, on dialectic) it becomes more intelligible that he should try different and even discrepant approaches to a topic at the same time.

Such considerations do not make it impossible to reconstruct something of the course of his scientific thinking from the extant writings, together with what is known of his life. For instance it is sometimes said that his distinction between 'essence' and 'accident', or between defining and nondefining
251 characteristics,/ must be rooted in the biological studies in which it plays an integral part. But the distinction is explored at greatest length in the *Topics*, a handbook of dialectical debate which dates substantially from his earlier years in the Academy, whereas the inquiries embodied in his biological works seem to come chiefly from his years abroad, since they refer relatively often to the Asiatic coast and Lesbos and seldom to southern Greece. So this piece of conceptual apparatus was not produced by that work: when Aristotle tries to reduce the definition of a species to one distinguishing mark (e.g. *Metaphysics* VII 12, VIII 6) he is a dialectician, facing a problem whose ancestry includes Plato's theory of Forms, but when he rejects such definitions in favour of a cluster of differentiae (*De Partibus Animalium* I 2-3) he writes as a working biologist, armed with a set of questions about breathing and sleeping, movement and nourishment, birth and death.

The starting point in tracing his scientific progress must therefore be his years in the Academy. Indeed without this starting point it is not possible to understand either his pronouncements on scientific theory or, what is more important, the gap between his theory and his practice.

The mathematical model

The Academy that Aristotle joined in 367 was distinguished from other Athenian schools by two interests: mathematics (including astronomy and harmonic theory, to the extent that these could be made mathematically respectable), and dialectic, the Socratic examination of the assumptions of mathematicians and cosmologists. Briefly, Plato regarded the first kind of studies as merely preparatory and ancillary to the second; Aristotle, in the account of scientific and philosophical method that probably dates from his Academic years, reversed the priorities (*Posterior Analytics* I; *Topics* I 1-2). It was the mathematics he encountered that impressed him as providing the model for any well-organized science. The work on axiomatization which was to culminate in Euclid's *Elements* was already far advanced, and for Aristotle the pattern of a science is an axiomatic system in which theorems are validly derived from basic principles, some proprietary to the science ('hypotheses' and 'definitions,' the second corresponding to Euclid's 'common notions'). The proof-theory which was characteristic of Greek mathematics (as against that of Babylon or Egypt) had developed in the attempt to show why various mathematical formulae worked in practice. Aristotle pitches on this as the chief aim of any science: it must not merely record but explain, and in explaining it must, so far as the special field of inquiry allows, generalize. Thus mathematical proof becomes Aristotle's first paradigm of scientific explanation; by contrast, the dialectic that Plato ranked higher – the logical but free-ranging analysis of the beliefs and usage of 'the many and the wise' – is allowed only to help in settling those basic principles of a science that cannot, without regress or circularity, be proved within the science itself. At any rate, this was the theory.

Aristotle duly adapts and enlarges the mathematical model to provide for the physical sciences. Mathematics, he holds, is itself a science (or rather a family of sciences) about the physical world, and not about a Platonic world of transcendent objects; but it abstracts from those characteristics of the world that are the special concern of physics – movement and change, and therewith time and location. So the nature and behaviour of physical things will call for more sorts of explanation than mathematics recognizes. Faced with a man, or a tree, or a flame, one can ask what it is made of, its 'matter'; what is its essential character or 'form'; what external or internal agency produced it; and what the 'end' or purpose of it is. The questions make good sense when applied to an artifact such as a statue, and Aristotle often introduces them by this analogy; but he holds that they can be extended to every kind of thing involved in regular natural change. The explanations they produce can be embodied in the formal proofs or even the basic definitions of a science (thus a lunar eclipse can be not merely accounted for, but defined, as the loss of light due to the interposition of the earth, and a biological species

can be partly defined in terms of the purpose of some of its organs). Again, the regularities studied by physics may be unlike those of mathematics in an important respect: initially the *Posterior Analytics* depicts a science as deriving necessary conclusions from necessary premises, true in all cases (I 2 and 4, but later I 30) the science is allowed to deal in generalizations that are true in most cases but not necessarily in all. Aristotle is adapting his model to make room for 'a horse has four legs' as well as for '2 × 2 = 4.' How he regards the exceptions to such generalizations is not altogether clear. In his discussions of 'luck' and 'chance' in *Physics* II, and of 'accident' elsewhere, he seems to hold that a lucky or chance or accidental event can always, under some description, be subsumed under a generalization expressing some regularity. His introduction to the *Meteorologica* is sometimes cited to show that in his view sublunary happenings are inherently irregular; but he probably means
252 that,/ while the laws of sublunary physics are commonly (though not always) framed to allow of exceptions, these exceptions are not themselves inexplicable. The matter is complicated by his failure to maintain a sharp distinction between laws that provide a necessary (and even uniquely necessary), and those that provide a sufficient, condition of the situation to be explained.

But in two respects the influence of mathematics on Aristotle's theory of science is radical and unmodified. First, the drive to axiomatize mathematics and its branches was in fact a drive for autonomy: the premises of the science were to determine what questions fell within the mathematician's competence and, no less important, what did not. This consequence Aristotle accepts for every field of knowledge: a section of *Posterior Analytics* I 12 is given up to the problem, what questions can be properly put to the practitioner of such-and-such a science; and in I 7, trading on the rule 'one science to one genus', he denounces arguments that poach outside their own field – which try, for instance, to deduce geometrical conclusions from arithmetical premises. He recognizes arithmetical proofs in harmonics and geometrical proofs in mechanics, but treats them as exceptions. The same impulse leads him to map all systematic knowledge into its departments – theoretical, practical, and productive – and to divide the first into metaphysics (or, as he once calls it, 'theology'), mathematics, and physics, these in turn being marked out in subdivisions.

This picture of the autonomous deductive system has had a large influence on the interpreters of Aristotle's scientific work; yet it plays a small part in his inquiries, just because it is not a model for inquiry at all but for subsequent exposition. This is the second major respect in which it reflects mathematical procedure. In nearly all the surviving productions of Greek mathematics, traces of the workshop have been deliberately removed: proofs are found for theorems that were certainly first reached by other routes. So Aristotle's theoretical picture of a science shows it in its shop window (or what he often calls its 'didactic') form; but for the most part his inquiries are not at this stage of the business. This is a piece of good fortune for students of the subject, who have always lamented that no comparable record survives of presystematic research in mathematics proper (Archimedes' public letter to

Eratosthenes – the *Ephodos*, or 'Method' – is hardly such a record). As it is, Aristotle's model comes nearest to realization in the systematic astronomy of *De Caelo* I-II (cf. e.g. I 3, 'from what has been said, partly as premises and partly as things proved from these, it follows ...'), and in the proof of a prime mover in *Physics* VIII. But these constructions are built on the presystematic analyses of *Physics* I-VI, analyses that are expressly undertaken to provide physics with its basic assumptions (cf. I 1) and to define its basic concepts, change and time and location, infinity and continuity (III 1). *Ex hypothesi* the latter discussions, which from Aristotle's pupils Eudemus and Strato onward have given the chief stimulus to physicists and philosophers of science, cannot be internal to the science whose premises they seek to establish. Their methods and data need not and do not fit the theoretical straitjacket, and in fact they rely heavily on the dialectic that theoretically has no place in the finished science.

Dialectic and 'phenomena'

Conventionally Aristotle has been contrasted with Plato as the committed empiricist, anxious to 'save the phenomena' by basing his theories on observation of the physical world. First the phenomena, then the theory to explain them: this Baconian formula he recommends not only for physics (and specifically for astronomy and biology) but for ethics and generally for all arts and sciences. But 'phenomena', like many of his key terms, is a word with different uses in different contexts. In biology and meteorology the phenomena are commonly observations made by himself or taken from other sources (fishermen, travellers, etc.), and similar observations are evidently presupposed by that part of his astronomy that relies on the schemes of concentric celestial spheres proposed by Eudoxus and Callippus. But in the *Physics* when he expounds the principles of the subject, and in many of the arguments in the *De Caelo* and *De Generatione et Corruptione* by which he settles the nature and interaction of the elements, and turns Eudoxus' elegant abstractions into a cumbrous physical (and theological) construction, the data on which he draws are mostly of another kind. The phenomena he now wants to save – or to give logical reasons (rather than empirical evidence) for scrapping – are the common convictions and common linguistic usage of his contemporaries, supplemented by the views of other thinkers. They are what he always represents as the materials of dialectic.

Thus when Aristotle tries to harden the idea of location for use in science (*Physics* IV 1-5) he sets out from our settled practice of locating a thing by giving its physical surroundings, and in particular from established ways of talking about one thing taking another's place. It is to save these that he treats any location as a container, and defines the place of X as the innermost static boundary of the body surrounding X. His definition turns out to be circular:/ moreover it carries the consequence that, since a point cannot lie **253**
within a boundary, it cannot strictly have (or be used to mark) a location. Yet we shall see later that his theories commit him to denying this.

Again, when he defines time as that aspect of change that enables it to be counted (*Physics* IV 10-14), what he wants to save and explain are the common ways of *telling* the time. This point, that he is neither inventing a new vocabulary nor assigning new theory-based uses to current words, must be borne in mind when one encounters such expressions as 'force' and 'average velocity' in versions of his dynamics. The word sometimes translated 'force' (*dunamis*) is the common word for the 'power' or 'ability' of one thing to affect or be affected by another – to move or be moved, but also to heat or to soften or to be heated, and so forth. Aristotle makes it clear that this notion is what he is discussing in three celebrated passages (*Physics* VII 5, VIII 10, *De Caelo* I 7) where later critics have discerned laws of proportionality connecting the force applied, the weight moved, and the time required for the force to move the weight a given distance. (Two of the texts do not mention weight at all.) A second term, *ischus*, sometimes rendered 'force' in these contexts, is the common word for 'strength', and it is this familiar notion that Aristotle is exploiting in the so-called laws of forced motion set out in *Physics* VII 5 and presupposed in VIII 10: he is relying on what a nontechnical audience would at once grant him concerning the comparative strengths of packhorses or (his example) gangs of shiphaulers. He says: let A be the strength required to move a weight B over a distance D in time T; then (1) A will move $1/2\ B$ over $2D$ in T; (2) A will move $1/2\ B$ over D in $1/2\ T$; (3) $1/2\ A$ will move $1/2\ B$ over D in T; and (4) A will move B over $1/2\ D$ in $1/2\ T$; but (5) it does not follow that A will move some multiple of B over a proportionate fraction of D in T or indeed in any time, since it does not follow that A will be sufficient to move that multiple of B at all. The conjunction of (4) with the initial assumption shows that Aristotle takes the speed of motion in this case to be uniform; so commentators have naturally thought of A as a force whose continued application to B is just sufficient to overcome the opposing forces of gravity, friction, and the medium. In such circumstances propositions (3) and (4) will yield results equivalent to those of Newtonian dynamics. But then the circumstances described in (1) and (2) should yield not just the doubling of a uniform velocity which Aristotle supposes, but acceleration up to some appropriate terminal velocity. Others have proposed to treat A as prefiguring the later idea not of *force* but of *work*, or else *power*, if these are defined in terms of the displacement of weight and not of force; and this has the advantage of leaving Aristotle discussing the case that is central to his dynamics – the carrying out of some finite task in a finite time – without importing the notion of action at an instant which, for reasons we shall see, he rejects. But Aristotle also assumes that, for a given type of agent, A is multiplied in direct ratio to the size or quantity of the agent; and to apply this to the work done would be, once more, to overlook the difference between conditions of uniform motion and of acceleration. The fact is that Aristotle is appealing to conventional ways of comparing the strength of haulers and beasts of burden, and for his purposes the acceleration periods involved with these are negligible. What matters is that we measure strength by the ability to perform certain finite tasks before fatigue sets in; hence, when Aristotle adduces these proportionalities in the *Physics*, he does so with a view to showing that the strength required for keeping the sky turning for all time would be immeasurable. Since such celestial revolutions do not in his view have to overcome any such resistance as that of gravity or a medium we are not entitled to read these notions into the formulae quoted. What then is the basis for these proportionalities? He does not quote empirical evidence in their support, and in their generalized form he could not do so; in the *Physics* and again in the *De Caelo* he insists that they can be extended to cover 'heating and any effect of one body on another', but the Greeks had no thermometer nor indeed any device (apart from the measurement of strings in harmonics) for translating qualitative differences into quantitative measurements. Nor on the other hand does he present them as technical definitions of the concepts they introduce. He simply comments in the *Physics* that the rules of proportion require them to be true (and it may be noticed that he does not frame any of them as a function of more than two variables: the proportion is always a simple relation between two of the terms, the others remaining constant). He depends on this appeal, together with conventional ways of comparing strengths, to give him the steps he needs toward his conclusion about the strength of a prime mover: it is no part of the dialectic of his argument to coin hypotheses that require elaborate discussion in their own right.

It is part of the history of dynamics that, from Aristotle's immediate successors onward, these formulae were taken out of context, debated and refined, and finally jettisoned for an incomparably more exact and powerful set of concepts which owed little to dialectic in Aristotle's sense. That he did not intend his proportionalities for such close scrutiny/ becomes even clearer **254**
when we turn to his so-called laws of natural motion. Aristotle's universe is finite, spherical, and geocentric: outside it there can be no body nor even, therefore, any location or vacuum or time (*De Caelo* I 9); within it there can be no vacuum (*Physics* IV 6-9). Natural motion is the unimpeded movement of its elements: centripetal or 'downward' in the case of earth (whose place is at the centre) and of water (whose place is next to earth), centrifugal or 'upward' in the case of fire and (next below fire) air. These are the sublunary elements, capable of changing into each other (*De Generatione et Corruptione* II) and possessed of 'heaviness' or 'lightness' according as their natural motion is down or up. Above them all is the element whose existence Aristotle can prove only by a priori argument: ether, the substance of the spheres that carry the heavenly bodies. The natural motions of the first four elements are rectilinear and terminate, unless they are blocked, in the part of the universe that is the element's natural place; the motion of the fifth is circular and cannot be blocked, and it never leaves its natural place. These motions of free fall, free ascent, and free revolution are Aristotle's paradigms of regular movement, against which other motions can be seen as departures due to special agency or to the presence of more than one element in the moving body. On several occasions he sketches some proportional connection between the variables that occur in his analysis of such natural motions; generally he confines himself to rectilinear (i.e. sublunary) movement, as, for example, in *Physics* IV 8, the text that provoked a celebrated exchange between Simplicio and Salviati in Galileo's *Dialoghi*. There he writes: 'We see a given weight or body

moving faster than another for two reasons: either because of a difference in the medium traversed (e.g. water as against earth, water as against air), or, other things being equal, because of the greater weight or lightness of the moving body.' Later he specifies that the proviso 'other things being equal' is meant to cover identity of shape. Under the first heading, that of differences in the medium, he remarks that the motion of the medium must be taken into account as well as its density relative to others; but he is content to assume a static medium and propound, as always, a simple proportion in which the moving object's velocity varies inversely with the density of the medium. Two comments are relevant. First, in this as in almost all comparable contexts, the 'laws of natural motion' are dispensable from the argument. Here Aristotle uses his proportionality to rebut the possibility of motion in a vacuum: such motion would encounter a medium of nil density and hence would have infinite velocity, which is impossible. But this is only one of several independent arguments for the same conclusion in the context. Next, the argument discounts acceleration (Aristotle does not consider the possibility of a body's speed in a vacuum remaining finite but increasing without limit, let alone that of its increasing to some finite terminal speed); yet he often insists that for the sublunary elements natural motion is always acceleration. (For this reason among others it is irrelevant to read his proportionalities of natural motion as an unwitting anticipation of Stokes's law.) But it was left to his successors during the next thousand years to quarrel over the way in which the ratios he formulated could be used to account for the steady acceleration he required in such natural motion; and where in the passage quoted he writes 'we see', it was left to some nameless ancient scientist to make the experiment recorded by Philoponus and later by Galileo, of dropping different weights from the same height and noting that what we see does not answer Aristotle's claim about their speed of descent. It was, to repeat, no part of the dialectic of his argument to give these proportionalities the rigour of scientific laws or present them as the record of exact observation.

On the other hand the existence of the natural motions themselves is basic to his cosmology. Plato had held that left to themselves, i.e. without divine governance, the four elements (he did not recognize a fifth) would move randomly in any direction: Aristotle denies this on behalf of the inherent regularity of the physical world. He makes the natural motions his 'first hypotheses' in the *De Caelo* and applies them over and again to the discussion of other problems. (The contrast between his carelessness over the proportionalities and the importance he attaches to the movements is sometimes read as showing that he wants to 'eliminate mathematics from physics': but more on this later.)

This leads to a more general point which must be borne in mind in understanding his way of establishing physical theory. When he appeals to common views and usage in such contexts he is applying a favourite maxim, that in the search for explanations we must start from what is familiar or intelligible to us. (Once the science is set up, the deductions will proceed from principles 'intelligible in themselves'.) The same maxim governs his standard way of introducing concepts by extrapolating from some familiar, unpuzzling

situation. Consider his distinction of 'matter' and 'form' in *Physics* I. He argues that any change implies a passage between two contrary attributes – from one to the other, or somewhere on a spectrum between the two – and that there must be a third thing to make this passage, a substrate which/ changes but survives the change. The situations to which he appeals are those **255**
from which this triadic analysis can be, so to speak, directly read off: a light object turning dark, an unmusical man becoming musical. But then the analysis is extended to cases progressively less amenable: he moves, via the detuning of an instrument and the shaping of a statue, to the birth of plants and animals and generally to the sort of situation that had exercised earlier thinkers – the emergence of a new individual, the apparent coming of something from nothing. (Not the emergence of a new *type*: Aristotle does not believe that new types emerge in nature, although he accepts the appearance of sports within or between existing types. In *Physics* II 8 he rejects a theory of evolution for putting the random occurrence of new types on the same footing with the reproduction of existing species, arguing that a theory that is not based on such regularities is not scientific physics.) *Ex nihilo nihil fit*; and even the emergence of a new individual must involve a substrate, 'matter', which passes between two contrary conditions, the 'privation' and the 'form'. But one effect of Aristotle's extrapolation is to force a major conflict between his theories and most contemporary and subsequent physics. In his view, the question 'What are the essential attributes of matter?' must go unanswered. There is no general answer, for the distinction between form and matter reappears on many levels: what serves as matter to a higher form may itself be analyzed into form and matter, as a brick which is material for a house can itself by analyzed into a shape and the clay on which the shape is imposed. More important, there is no answer even when the analysis reaches the basic elements – earth, air, fire, and water. For these can be transformed into each other, and since no change can be intelligibly pictured as a mere succession of discrete objects these too must be transformations of some residual subject, but one that now *ex hypothesi* has no permanent qualitative or quantitative determinations in its own right. Thus Aristotle rejects all theories that explain physical change by the rearrangement of some basic stuff or stuffs endowed with fixed characteristics. Atomism in particular he rebuts at length, arguing that movement in a vacuum is impossible (we have seen one argument for this) and that the concept of an extended indivisible body is mathematically indefensible. But although matter is not required to identify itself by any permanent first-order characteristics, it does have important second-order properties. Physics studies the regularities in change, and for a given sort of thing at a given level it is the matter that determines what kinds of change are open to it. In some respects the idea has more in common with the field theory that appears embryonically in the Stoics than with the crude atomism maintained by the Epicureans, but its chief influence was on metaphysics (especially Neoplatonism) rather than on scientific theory. By contrast, the correlative concept of *form*, the universal element in things that allow them to be known and classified and defined, remained powerful in science. Aristotle took it from Plato, but by way of a radical and very early

critique of Plato's Ideas; for Aristotle the formal element is inseparable from the things classified, whereas Plato had promoted it to independent existence in a transcendent world contemplated by disembodied souls. For Aristotle the physical world is all; its members with their qualities and quantities and interrelations are the paradigms of reality and there are no disembodied souls.

The device of extrapolating from the familiar is evident again in his account of another of his four types of 'cause', or explanation, viz. the 'final', or teleological. In *Physics* II 8 he mentions some central examples of purposive activity – housebuilding, doctoring, writing – and then by stages moves on to discerning comparable purposiveness in the behaviour of spiders and ants, the growth of roots and leaves, the arrangement of the teeth. Again the process is one of weakening or discarding some of the conditions inherent in the original situations: the idea of purposiveness sheds its connection with those of having a skill and thinking out steps to an end (although Aristotle hopes to have it both ways, by representing natural sports and monsters as *mistakes*). The resultant 'immanent teleology' moved his follower Theophrastus to protest at its thinness and facility, but its effectiveness as a heuristic device, particularly in biology, is beyond dispute.

It is worth noting that this tendency of Aristotle's to set out from some familiar situation, or rather from the most familiar and unpuzzling ways of describing such a situation, is something more than the general inclination of scientists to depend on 'explanatory paradigms'. Such paradigms in later science (e.g., classical mechanics) have commonly been limiting cases not encountered in common observation or discourse; Aristotle's choice of the familiar is a matter of dialectical method, presystematic by contrast with the finished science, but subject to rules of discussion which he was the first to codify. This, and not (as we shall see) any attempt to extrude mathematics from physics, is what separates his extant work in the field from the most characteristic achievements of the last four centuries. It had large consequences for dynamics. In replying to Zeno's paradox of the flying arrow
256 he concedes Zeno's claim that nothing can be/ said to be moving at an instant, and insists only that it cannot be said to be stationary either. What preoccupies him is the requirement, embedded in common discourse, that any movement must take a certain time to cover a certain distance (and, as a corollary, that any stability must take a certain time but cover no distance); so he discounts even those hints that common discourse might have afforded of the derivative idea of motion, and therefore of velocity, at an instant. He has of course no such notion of a mathematical limit as the analysis of such cases requires, but in any event this notion came later than the recognition of the cases. It is illuminating to contrast the treatment of motion in the *Mechanica*, a work which used to carry Aristotle's name but which must be at least a generation later. There (*Mechanica* I) circular motion is resolved into two components, one tangential and one centripetal (contrast Aristotle's refusal to assimilate circular and rectilinear movements, notably in *Physics* VII 4). And the remarkable suggestion is made that the proportion between these components need not be maintained for any time at all, since otherwise

the motion would be in a straight line. Earlier the idea had been introduced of a point having motion and velocity, an idea that we shall find Aristotle using although his dialectical analysis of movement and location disallows it; here that idea is supplemented by the concept of a point having a given motion or complex of motions at an instant and not for any period, however small. The *Mechanica* is generally agreed to be a constructive development of hints and suggestions in Aristotle's writings; but the methods and purposes evident in his own discussions of motion inhibit him from such novel constructions in dynamics.

It is quite another thing to say, as is often said, that Aristotle wants to debar physics from any substantial use of the abstract proofs and constructions available to him in contemporary mathematics. It is a common fallacy that, whereas Plato had tried to make physics mathematical and quantitative, Aristotle aimed at keeping it qualitative.

Mathematics and physics

Plato had tried to construct the physical world of two-dimensional and apparently weightless triangles. When Aristotle argues against this in the *De Caelo* (III 7) he observes: 'The principles of perceptible things must be perceptible, of eternal things eternal, of perishable things perishable: in sum, the principles must be homogeneous with the subject-matter.' These words, taken together with his prescriptions for the autonomy of sciences in the *Analytics*, are often quoted to show that any use of mathematical constructions in his physics must be adventitious or presystematic, dispensable from the science proper. The province of physics is the class of natural bodies regarded as having weight (or 'lightness', in the case of air and fire), heat, and colour and an innate tendency to move in a certain way. But these are properties that mathematics expressly excludes from its purview (*Metaphysics* XI 3).

In fact, however, the division of sciences is not so absolute. When Aristotle contrasts mathematics and physics in *Physics* II he remarks that astronomy, which is one of the 'more physical of the mathematical sciences', must be part of physics, since it would be absurd to debar the physicist from discussing the geometrical properties of the heavenly bodies. The distinction is that the physicist must, as the mathematician does not, treat these properties as the attributes of physical bodies that they are; i.e. he must be prepared to explain the application of his model. Given this tie-line a good deal of mathematical abstraction is evidently permissible. Aristotle holds that only extended bodies can strictly be said to have a location (i.e. to lie within a static perimeter) or to move, but he is often prepared to discount the extension of bodies. Thus in *Physics* IV 11, where he shows an isomorphic correspondence between continua representing time, motion, and the path traversed by the moving body, he correlates the moving object with points in time and space and for this purpose calls it 'a point – or stone, or any such thing'. In *Physics* V 4, he similarly argues from the motion of an unextended object, although it is to be

noticed that he does not here or anywhere ease the transition from moving bodies to moving points by importing the idea of a centre of gravity, which was to play so large a part in Archimedes' *Equilibrium of Planes*. In his meteorology, explaining the shape of halos and rainbows, he treats the luminary as a point source of light. In the biological works he often recurs to the question of the number of points at which a given type of animal moves; these 'points' are in fact the major joints, but in *De Motu Animalium* 1 he makes it clear that he has a geometrical model in mind and is careful to explain what supplementary assumptions are necessary to adapting this model to the actual situation it illustrates. In the cosmology of the *De Caelo* he similarly makes use of unextended loci, in contrast to his formal account of any location as a perimeter enclosing a volume. Like Archimedes a century later, he represents the centre of the universe as a point when he proves that the surface of water is spherical, and again when he argues that earth moves so as to make its own (geometrical) centre ultimately coincide with that of the
257 universe. His attempt in *De Caelo* IV 3 to interpret this in terms/ of perimeter locations is correct by his own principles, but confused.

This readiness to import abstract mathematical arguments and constructions into his account of the physical world is one side of the coin whose other face is his insistence that any mathematics must be directly applicable to the world. Thus, after arguing (partly on dialectical grounds, partly from his hypothesis of natural movements and natural places) that the universe must be finite in size, he adds that this does not put the mathematicians out of business, since they do not need or use the notion of a line infinite in extension: what they require is only the possibility of producing a line n in any required ratio with a given line m, and however large the ratio n/m it can always be physically exemplified for a suitable interpretation of m. The explanation holds good for such lemmata as that applied in Eudoxus' method of exhaustion, but not of some proportionalities he himself adduces earlier in the same context or in *De Caelo* I. (These proportionalities are indeed used in, but they are not the subject of, *reductio ad absurdum* arguments. In the *De Caelo* Aristotle even assumes than an infinite rotating body would contain a point at an infinite distance from its centre and consequently moving at infinite speed.) The same concern to make mathematics applicable to the physical world without postulating an actual infinite is evident in his treatment of the sequence of natural numbers. The infinity characteristic of the sequence, and generally of any countable series whose members can be correlated with the series of numbers, consists just in the possibility of specifying a successor to any member of the sequence: 'the infinite is that of which, as it is counted or measured off, it is always possible to take some part outside that already taken.' This is true not only of the number series but of the parts produced by dividing any magnitude in a constant ratio; and since all physical bodies are in principle so divisible, the number series is assured of a physical application without requiring the existence at any time of an actually infinite set of objects: all that is required is the possibility of following any division with a subdivision.

This positivistic approach is often evident in Aristotle's work (e.g. in his analysis of the location of *A* as the inner static boundary of the body surrounding *A*), and it is closely connected with his method of building explanations on the familiar case when he argues that infinite divisibility is characteristic of bodies below the level of observation. His defense and exploration of such divisibility, as a defining characteristic of bodies and times and motions, is found in *Physics* VI, a book often saluted as his most original contribution to the analysis of the continuum. Yet it is worth noticing that in this book as in its two predecessors Aristotle's problems and the ideas he applies to their solution are over and again taken, with improvements, from the second part of Plato's *Parmenides*. The discussion is in that tradition of logical debate which Aristotle, like Plato, called 'dialectic', and its problems are not those of accommodating theories to experimentally established facts (or vice versa) but logical puzzles generated by common discourse and conviction. (But then Aristotle thinks of common discourse and conviction as a repository of human experience.) So the argument illustrates Aristotle's anti-Platonic thesis that mathematics – represented again in this case by simple proportion theory – has standing as a science only to the extent that it can be directly applied to the description of physical phenomena. But the argument is no more framed as an advance in the mathematical theory itself than as a contribution to the observational data of physics.

Probably the best-known instance of an essentially mathematical construction incorporated into Aristotle's physics is the astronomical theory due to Eudoxus and improved by Callippus. In this theory the apparent motion of the 'fixed stars' is represented by the rotation of one sphere about its diameter, while those of the sun, moon, and the five known planets are represented each by a different nest of concentric spheres. In such a nest the first sphere carries round a second whose poles are located on the first but with an axis inclined to that of the first; this second, rotating in turn about its poles, carries a third similarly connected to it, and so on in some cases to a fourth or (in Callippus' version) a fifth, the apparent motion of the heavenly body being the resultant motion of a point on the equator of the last sphere. To this set of abstract models, itself one of the five or six major advances in science, Aristotle makes additions of which the most important is the attempt to unify the separate nests of spheres into one connected physical system. To this end he intercalates reagent spheres designed to insulate the movement of each celestial body from the complex of motions propelling the body next above it. The only motion left uncancelled in this downward transmission is the rotation of the star sphere. It is generally agreed that Aristotle in *Metaphysics* XII 8 miscalculates the resulting number of agent and reagent spheres: he concludes that we need either fifty-five or forty-seven, the difference apparently representing one disagreement between the theories of Eudoxus and Callippus, but on the latest computation (that of Hanson) the/figures should be sixty-six and forty-nine. The mistake had no effect on **258**
the progress of astronomy: within a century astronomers had turned to a theory involving epicycles, and Aristotle's physical structure of concentric nonoverlapping spheres was superseded. On the other hand his basic picture of

the geocentric universe and its elements, once freed from the special constructions he borrowed and adapted from Eudoxus, retained its authority and can be seen again in the introductory chapters of Ptolemy's *Syntax*.

Conclusion

These arguments and theories in what came to be called the exact sciences are drawn principally from the *Posterior Analytics, Topics, Physics, De Caelo* and *De Generatione*, works that are generally accepted as early and of which the first four at least probably date substantially from Aristotle's years in the Academy or soon after. The influence of the Academy is strong on them. They are marked by a large respect for mathematics and particularly for the techniques and effects of axiomatizing that subject, but they do not pretend to any mathematical discoveries, and in this they are close in spirit to Plato's writings. Even the preoccupation with physical change, its varieties and regularities and causes, and the use of dialectic in analyzing these, is a position to which Plato had been approaching in his later years. Aristotle the meticulous empiricist, amassing biological data or compiling the constitutions of 158 Greek states, is not yet in evidence. In these works the analyses neither start from nor are closely controlled by fresh inspections of the physical world. Nor is he liable to think his analyses endangered by such inspections: if his account of motion shows that any 'forced' or 'unnatural' movement requires an agent of motion in constant touch with the moving body, the movement of a projectile can be explained by inventing a set of unseen agents to fill the gap – successive stages of the medium itself, supposed to be capable of transmitting movement even after the initial agency has ceased acting. In all the illustrative examples cited in these works there is nothing comparable to even the half-controlled experiments in atomistic physics and harmonics of the following centuries. His main concerns were the methodology of the sciences, which he was the first to separate adequately on grounds of field and method; and the meticulous derivation of the technical equipment of these sciences from the common language and assumptions of men about the world they live in. His influence on science stemmed from an incomparable cleverness and sensitiveness to counterarguments, rather than from any breakthrough comparable to those of Eudoxus or Archimedes.

9

A Proof in the Peri Ideôn

In his lost essay *Peri Ideôn* Aristotle retailed and rebutted a number of 103
Academic arguments for the existence of Ideas.[1] Several of these, together with Aristotle's objections to them, are preserved in Alexander's commentary on I 9 of the *Metaphysics*. The first object of the following discussion is to show the sense and the provenance of one, the most complex and puzzling, of these surviving arguments. For several reasons it seems to deserve more consideration than it has yet had.[2] 1. Its length and technicality make it singularly fitted to illustrate the sort of material on which Aristotle drew in his critique. 2. Moreover, Alexander reports it by way of amplifying Aristotle's comment that, of the more precise arguments on Ideas, *hoi men tôn pros ti poiousin ideas, hôn ou phamen einai kath' hauto genos*, 'one group produce ideas of relatives, of which we say there is no in-virtue-of-itself (non-relative) class' (*Meta.* 990b15-17 = 1079a11-13); and the condensed and allusive form of this remark and its immediate neighbours in the *Metaphysics* can be taken to show that here Aristotle is epitomising parts of his *Peri Ideôn* that are independently known to us only through his commentator. We shall not understand the objection if we misidentify its target; and another purpose of this discussion is to show that the objection is not the disingenuous muddle that one recent writer labours to make it. 3. But Alexander's report of the argument is a nest of problems, and the same recent writer brands it as almost incredibly careless. To this extent, the success of our explanation will be a vindication of the commentator. But on all the heads of this discussion I am well aware that much more remains to be said.

[1] The issue of *JHS* in which this article originally appeared was a Festschrift for Sir David Ross. Further discussion of this argument from the *Peri Ideôn* will be found in 'Dialectic and Eristic,' this volume, Chapter 12.

[2] It has been discussed by L. Robin (who first assigned it to the *Peri Ideôn*), *Théorie platonicienne des Idées et des Nombres* (Paris 1908), 19-21, 603-5, 607; H. Cherniss, *Aristotle's Criticism of Plato and the Academy*, I (Baltimore 1944), 229-33, esp. n. 137; and Wilpert, *Zwei aristotelische Frühschriften* (Regensburg 1949), 41-4, each of whom knew only Robin's discussion; and Suzanne Mansion, 'La critique de la théorie des Idées dans le *Peri Ideôn* d'Aristote', *Revue Philosophique de Louvain* 47 (1949), 181-3, esp. n. 42. I shall refer to these writings by the author's name.

The proof

In the authoritative text of Alexander[3] (which, with a minor emendation of Hayduck's,[4] Sir David Ross prints on pp. 124-5 of his *Fragmenta Selecta Aristotelis*) the specimen argument that produces *ideas tôn pros ti* is given as follows.

> I. When the same predicate is asserted of several things not homonymously (*mê homônumôs*) but so as to indicate a single character, it is true of them *either* (*a*) because they are strictly (*kuriôs*) what the predicate signifies, e.g. when we call both Socrates and Plato 'a man'; or (*b*) because they are likenesses of things that are really so, e.g. when we predicate 'man' of men in pictures (for what we are indicating in them is the likenesses of men, and so we signify an identical character in each); *or* (*c*) because one of them is the model and the rest are likenesses, e.g. if we were to call both Socrates and the likenesses of Socrates 'men'.
>
> II. Now when we predicate 'absolutely equal' (*to ison auto*) of things in this world,[5] we use the predicate homonymously. For (*a*) the same definition (*logos*) does not fit them all; (*b*) nor are we referring to things that are really equal, since the dimensions of sensible things are fluctuating continuously and indeterminate. (*c*) Nor yet does the definition of 'equal' apply without qualification (*akribôs*) to anything in this world.
>
> III. But neither (can such things be called equal) in the sense that one is model and another is likeness, for none of them has more claim than another to be either model or likeness.
>
> IV. And even if we allow that the likeness is not homonymous with the model, the conclusion is always the same – that the equal things in this world are equal *qua* likenesses of what is strictly and really equal.
>
> V. If this is so, there is something absolutely and strictly equal (*esti ti autoison kai kuriôs*) by relation to which things in this world, as being likenesses of it, become and are called equal. And this is an Idea. (Alexander, *Meta*. 82. 11-83. 16 Hayduck.)

I shall refer to this report of the argument in the *Peri Ideôn* as P. Its gist, if not its detail, seems clear. What is allegedly proved, for the specimen
104 predicate 'equal', is a doctrine familiar/ from several Platonic dialogues: things in this world can carry the predicate only derivatively, by virtue of

[3] The A of Bonitz and later edd. The version of the commentary in L and F excerpted in Hayduck's apparatus is later in origin (Hayduck, *Alexandri in Meta. Commentaria*, pref. viii-ix and ix, n. 2). It modifies the text of our passage in a clumsy attempt to evade the difficulties discussed below, pp. 167-9. (But notice that, where A uses Socrates and Plato as examples, LF at first uses Callias and Theaetetus, reverting then to those in A.) On Robin's attempt (loc. cit.) to assign LF equal authority with AM see Wilpert, n. 38, Cherniss, n. 137.

[4] cf. p. 173 n. 28 below.

[5] 'We': not of course the Platonists, who make no such error, but generally the unwary or unconverted to whom the argument is addressed. The objector envisaged at *Phaedo* 74b6-7, and Hippias (*Hipp. Maj.* 288a and 289d), see no objection to using *auto to ison* and *auto to kalon* of sensible things.

resembling a Paradigm that carries it in its own right. The comparison with the *Phaedo* 73c-75d is especially obvious. Both arguments assume that *auto to ison* describes something, and prove that what it describes is no physical thing. But already one characteristic of the author of our argument is clear. As we shall see, he is substantially faithful to his sources in Plato: but he takes pains to sharpen the logical issues they involve. As it stands in P, his proof depends on what must be intended as an exhaustive analysis of the ways in which a predicate can be used without ambiguity.[6] Now it is Alexander's report of this analysis that has perplexed his readers. For it seems plausible to say that the author of the proof cannot have regarded the sort of predication illustrated in I(*c*) as non-homonymous, in the sense initially given to that expression in I, and on the other hand that he cannot have regarded that which is illustrated in I(*b*) as non-homonymous in the sense of that expression required in II; so that the description of these sorts of predication as non-homonymous must be a confusion in P. To lay these doubts is to take a long step towards understanding the argument and establishing the reliability of P.

Criteria of synonymy in Aristotle and Plato

The difficulty in I(*c*) seems both logical and historical. We may say 'That is a man' without ambiguity when pointing to each of two flesh-and-blood men. Or (in a very different case) we may say it when pointing to each of two pictures, and what we say has the same sense of both pictures: in that respect we are still speaking unambiguously. But we are inclined to add that now we are not using the predicate in the same sense as in the first case; otherwise we should be mistaking paint and canvas for flesh and blood. Moreover this is Aristotle's view, and his examples suggest that he has our argument in mind.[7] Yet, as it stands, I(*c*) says just the opposite. The analysis seems to have distinguished cases (*a*) and (*b*) in order to assert with all emphasis that a combination of them in (*c*) imports no ambiguity at all.

The later version of the scholium (n. 3 above) takes a short way with the difficulty, reclassifying I(*c*) as a case of homonymy. Robin (loc. cit.) tried to wrest this sense from the original text; Wilpert (loc. cit.) rejected the attempt

[6] *mê homônumôs* in the Aristotelian sense but not, as we shall see, using Aristotelian criteria. Some will detect the influence of Speusippus in P.I, noticing that in it the vehicles of homonymy and its opposite seem to be not things but words, and that this is held to be characteristic of Speusippus by contrast with Aristotle (E. Hambruch, *Logische Regeln der plat. Schule* (Berlin 1904, repr. N.Y. 1976) 27-9, followed by other scholars including P. Lang, *De Speusippi academici scriptis* (Bonn 1911, repr. Hildesheim 1965), 25-6. Hambruch contrasts Aristotle, *Cat.* 1a1-12, with Boethus's account of Speusippus in Simplicius, *Cat.* 38.19). Quite apart from doubts about the tradition represented by Boethus, it is clear that Aristotle's usage is far from being as rigid as Hambruch supposes (see e.g. *A. Post.* 99a7, 12, *Phys.* VII, 248b12-21: H. neglects such passages in detecting a book of Speusippus behind *Topics* I 15). Moreover in P. III the *homônuma* are things, not words. All that we can say is that P reflects a general academic usage.

[7] *PA* 640b35-641a3, *De An.* 412b20-2, and on the traditional interpretation *Cat.* 1a1-6 (cf. Porphyry, *Cat.* 66.23-8, followed by later commentators, and see earlier Chrysippus fr. 143 (von Arnim). But *zôion*, the predicate cited, is ambiguous in a more ordinary sense: LSJ[8] s.v. II).

but regretted the anomaly. Yet the problem is fictitious. The logical issue can only be touched on here. The fact is that, although the difference between I(*a*) and I(*b*) predication does show an ambiguity of an important type, this is not the sort of ambiguity that can be exhibited by the methods of Aristotle and the Academy.[8] It no more proves that the predicate-word has two paraphrasable meanings than the fact that I can point to a portrait and say 'That is Socrates' proves that Socrates had an ambiguous name. This is true, but it is doubtful whether it is the point that our author is making. For the wording of I(*b*) suggests that in its derivative use the predicate *is* to be paraphrased otherwise than in its primary use (i.e. in terms of 'likeness'), though this difference of paraphrase does not constitute an ambiguity. Similarly we shall find (pp. 176-8 below) that the argument of II can be construed as allowing, with one proviso, that a predicate can be used unambiguously of several things even when the *logos* of that predicate differs in the different cases; the proviso is that that different *logos* shall have a common factor. (In the cases distinguished in I this factor is the primary definition of 'man', and in II it is the definition of *to ison auto.*) If this interpretation is correct our specimen of Academic argument contains an obvious parallel to Aristotle's admission of a class of *pros hen kai mian tina phusin legomena*, 'things said in relation to one thing and a single nature', which are in a sense synonymous (*Meta.* 1003a33-1003b15, cf. *EE* 1236a15-20, and n. 38 below).

But Aristotelian parallels are irrelevant to showing the reliability of P. What matters is that the analysis in I would misrepresent its Platonic sources if I(*c*) were *not* a type of unequivocal predication. This is implied by the reference in *Rep.* 596-7 to a bed in a picture, a wooden bed and the Paradigm Bed as *trittai klinai* 'three beds' (even when, as in P.I, only one of these is 'really' what the predicate signifies); and more generally it is implied by such
105 dicta as that nothing can be just/ or holy or beautiful if the corresponding Form is not so.[9] These utterances have no sense unless the predicate applies without difference of meaning to model and likeness alike,[10] and they are

[8] For a connected discussion I can refer now to P.T. Geach, 'The Third Man Again', *Phil. Rev.* 65 (1956), 74.

[9] See e.g. the instances cited by Vlastos, 'The Third Man Argument in the Parmenides', *Phil. Rev.* 63 (1954), 337-8. But Vlastos obscures the point by saying 'any Form can be predicated of itself ... *F*-ness is itself *F*'. The very fact that Plato could assume without question that *auto to megethos* is big (e.g. *Phd.* 102c5, cf. *Parm.* 150a7-b1 and 131d), whereas in English such an assumption about *bigness* makes no sense, should give us qualms at rendering the title of the Form conventionally in such contexts by an abstract noun (Vlastos' '*F*-ness'). V.'s formula misleads him into assimilating the two regresses in *Parm.* 132-3. If the first can (but with reservations) be constructed as confusing bigness with what is big, the second requires only that the Form should *have* the character it represents. If the first forces a choice between two possible functions of a form, the second reduces one of these to absurdity.

[10] This is unaffected by the fact that the Forms are standards. 'That is a yard long' has a different use when we are speaking of the standard yardstick and when we are speaking of other things (Geach, loc. cit.), but this does not entail that 'yard' has two meanings. Aristotle commonly treats the Forms as *sunônuma* with their images (cf. *de Lin. Insec.* 968a9-10, *hê d'idea prôtê tôn sunônumôn*, 'the idea is the first of the things that are synonymous'). The objection considered in *Physics* VII 4, that *sunônuma* need not be *sumblêta*, may well stem from the attempt to safeguard this thesis from the 'Third Man'.

integral to the doctrine that things in this world resemble the Forms. The author of our proof found the latter doctrine in his chief source (*Phd.* 73c-4c) and remarked that it is illustrated there by the relation between Simmias and Simmias *gegrammenos* (a drawing of Simmias) (73e), and in paragraph I he tried to do no more than put his original into precise logical shape. We recall Jaeger's suggestion that Aristotle did this very service to Plato in the *Eudemus*. But we had better defer any conjectures on the authorship of our proof.

to ison auto and to ison

A second puzzle turns on the three occurrences in P of the keyword 'homonymous'. P.I distinguishes three possible cases in which a predicate can be used *mê homônumôs*, which is shown by paraphrase to mean 'not ambiguously'. But P.II then seems to contend that the predicate 'equal' is used *homônumôs* of things in this world, although the explicit conclusion of P as well as the evidence of the dialogues on which P is based prove that such predication would be subsumed under I(*b*). Lastly, P.IV puts the case that the likenesses carry the predicate *non*-homonymously with their model, which squares with I but seems incompatible with II. In fact P.II seems the misfit; and again the later version in LF takes the short way, replacing the *homônumôs* of II with *sunônumôs ou kuriôs de* ('synonymously, but not strictly so') so as to bring the predication in question clearly under I(*b*). Robin's version of the argument (loc. cit.), which covertly reduces it to a *petitio principii* and contradicts the provisions of I, has been criticised by Cherniss (loc. cit.). Mlle Mansion (n. 42) has seized the important fact that P.II is concerned not with *to ison* but with *to ison auto*, but I have not understood her claim that the argument is a *reductio ad absurdum* and I do not agree that IV is an interpolation. Wilpert has not considered the problem.

Cherniss has propounded a singular solution (n. 137). He holds that *homônumôs* cannot be used in the same sense throughout P; and accordingly he claims that in II it is introduced without warning in a *Platonic* sense, such that the Platonic *homônumôs* is compatible with the 'Aristotelian' *mê homônumôs* in I (which he at once denounces as a 'careless summary' by Alexander of his source). The Platonic sense is identified as 'having the common name and nature derivatively'. So far, the effect is exactly that of the verbal change in LF. But he is then faced with the *mê homônumon* in IV. On his interpretation this cannot contradict the other occurrences of the expression, yet he cannot plausibly let himself say that it is a return to the 'Aristotelian' sense 'in the midst of the argument'. Consequently he has to provide a different Platonic sense, equally unadvertised by Alexander, whereby *mê homônumon* in IV signifies that 'the image is not *of the same class as* the model'; and this in order that the use of *homônumôs* in the first 'Platonic' sense shall be compatible with the use of *mê homônumon* in the second 'Platonic' sense and both of these compatible with that of *mê homônumôs* in the original 'Aristotelian' sense. In face of this it is easy to sympathise with his suspicion that the *mê* in the third occurrence must be an interpolation.

On the canons of this interpretation I have something more to say, but not

until we have reviewed the problem. A closer reading of the text seems sufficient to dissolve it. For what is maintained in II is that *to ison auto* would be predicated homonymously of things in this world; and *to ison auto* is expanded in V into *autoison kai kuriôs* (sc. *kuriôs ison,* cf. IV: *kuriôs kai alêthôs ison*). Thus the question broached by II is just whether *ison* can be used *kuriôs* of things in this world, i.e. as a case of the non-derivative predication illustrated in I(*a*); and the answer is that, except by a sheer ambiguity, it cannot be so used.[11] But this conclusion is perfectly compatible with the conclusion in IV and V that *ison without* this qualification can be predicated/
106 unambiguously of a group including physical things, i.e. that physical things can be called equal by the *derivative* sort of predication shown in I(*b*). The arguments in II are designed solely to prove that, if 'equal' keeps its proper sense, nothing in this world can be called 'strictly' equal.[12] III proves the corollary, that no group of things on earth can be called equal even as a case of mixed, I(*c*) predication (which would entail that something in the group *was kuriôs ison*). What is not even considered in II and III is whether physical things can be called equal wholly derivatively, as in I(*b*).

Now IV is concessive in form[13] and what it concedes is just this third possibility. (Its form does not of course mean that it is surrendering any part of the argument. It is concessive because it forestalls an objection: the objection that the talk of ambiguity in II is misleading and may be taken to apply to *ison*, not *to ison auto.*) And, in fact, I(*b*) predication is the only possibility still open to us if we are to keep any unity of sense in our everyday ascriptions of equality. But copies entail models, and this conclusion requires that *to ison* is predicated *kuriôs* of something *not* in this world, of which this world's instances of equality are likenesses.

But, finally, IV is only a concessive parenthesis, and it implies (*aei hepetai*) that the same result would follow from II and II alone. So it does: for II maintains that when we talk of what is *kuriôs ison*, what we are referring to (unless the expression is being used ambiguously) cannot be anything in this world. It follows that, unless we call everyday things equal in some sense unconnected with the first, they must be so called derivatively. And since this conclusion is explicitly drawn in V, II, III, and V form a complete argument.

So the form of P is clear and its use of the terminology introduced at the start is, as we might expect, consistent. But it is worth noticing two other considerations which are jointly fatal to Cherniss's account. The gross

[11] Instead of asking in set terms whether 'equal' can, without ambiguity, be predicated *strictly* of such things, II seems to introduce the compound predicate 'strictly equal' and ask whether this can, without ambiguity, be predicated of such things. This comes to the same thing (in fact the distinction is too hard-edged for the Greek), but it helped to seduce the author of LF into the absurd notion that the compound predicate *autoison* could properly be used, in a derivative sense, of earthly things.

[12] It may be said (I owe the objection to D.J. Furley) that the argument in II(*a*) is designed to rule out I(*b*) predication as well as I(*a*), since even I(*b*) would presumably require an identical *logos* in the various subjects. But in that case the conclusion of II would contradict V, as well as being a thesis foreign to Plato and never attacked by Aristotle; moreover the difference of *logoi* does not entail ambiguity since, as we shall see, they all have a common factor.

[13] Cf. Alexander, *Meta.* 86.11-12 Hayduck.

carelessness of which he accuses Alexander is out of character; he has not remarked that, when the commentator does introduce *homônumos* in the non-Aristotelian sense, he takes pains to explain the ambiguity.[14] Moreover, apart from all particular questions of interpretation (but see nn. 16, 20), the evidence adduced by Cherniss for the existence of his 'Platonic' senses of *homônumos*[15] has no tendency to prove his point; and the reason for this is worth emphasis. Plato does use *homônumos* fairly frequently. It seems clear that he does not use it in the technical Aristotelian sense of 'equivocal'. Sometimes (as at *Tim.* 52a, *Parm.* 133d, *Phd.* 78c) it is *applied* to cases of what Aristotle would doubtless call synonymy. But it does not for a moment follow that the expression *meant* for Plato what is meant by Aristotle's *sunônumos*, any more than it follows that because 'soldier' can be applied to all bombardiers, 'soldier' means 'bombardier'. Elsewhere the same word is used of things that plainly do not have the same *logos tês ousias.*[16] This should entail for Cherniss that Plato's use of the word was ruinously ambiguous, but of course it was not. As Plato uses it, what it means, its correct translation, is 'having the same name'; and the argument never requires more than this of it (cf., for instance, the versions of Cornford). The mistake recurs in Cherniss's further comment that 'for Plato *homônumos* when used of the relationship of particulars and ideas meant not *merely* "synonymous" in Aristotle's sense. The particular is *homônumon*, not vice versa, because it has its name and nature *derivatively* from the idea.' Yet elsewhere the word is used of an ancestor *from* whom the name is derived[17] and elsewhere again where there is no derivation either way.[18] Nor does Plato reserve any special meaning for the metaphysical contexts Cherniss has in mind.[19] The fact is that when he thinks it necessary to say that particulars are like the Form in nature as well as name he says so explicitly (*homônumon homoion te, Tim.* 52a5) and when he wants to say that they derive their names from the Forms he says that too (*Phd.* 102b, 103b, *Parm.* 130e).[20] The second 'Platonic sense' of the word rests on the same basis.[21]/

But why labour this point? Because the thesis in question seems a **107**

[14] Alexander, *Meta.* 51.11-15, 77.12-13. Cf. ps.-Alex. *Meta.* 500.12-35, 786.15.

[15] Cherniss, n. 102, citing A.J. Taylor, *Commentary on Plato's Timaeus* (Oxford, 1928) 52a4-5.

[16] *Laws* 757b; cf. *Phil.* 57b, which Cherniss (loc. cit.) misconstrues as saying that 'the different mathematics, if *homônumon*, are a single *technê* when the point is that although they are *homônuma*, it would be wrong to infer that they are one *technê* (57d6-8).

[17] *Rep.* 330b, *Parm.* 126c.

[18] *Prot.* 311b

[19] That Aristotle, who certainly knew that particulars were 'called after the Ideas' (*Meta.* 987b8-9), did not recognise a sense of *homônumos* in these contexts such that 'the particular is *homônumon tôi eidei* and not vice versa' must be proved for Cherniss by *Meta.* 990b6, which reports that the Form is *homônumon* with its particulars: here Cherniss is ready to find 'Plato's sense of the word' (n. 102).

[20] *Not* however *Parm.* 133c-d, which Cherniss has misread (loc. cit.): it is not the Ideas that are referred to as *hôn hêmeis metechontes einai hekasta eponomazometha*, 'partaking in which we call each of them by their names' but the 'likenesses-or-what-you-may-call-them' in this world. Since the particulars are nevertheless said to be *homônuma*, to the Forms, this sentence alone, if he still takes it as seriously, explodes his thesis.

[21] And a misreading of the text cited, *Phil.* 57b, cf. n. 16 above.

particularly clear application of one general principle of interpretation, and this principle underlies a well-known theory of the 'unity' (in the sense of fixity) of Plato's thought, to which Professor Cherniss is the distinguished heir. It is often observed that arguments for this theory assume that an expression in one context must carry a special sense determined by its application in quite another setting.[22] And no doubt some of the things to be said in this paper do not square well with that doctrine.

kath' hauto and pros ti

So far, P keeps our confidence. It remains to discuss it as a digest of Platonic argument and a target of Aristotle's criticism.

On the face of it, P distinguishes two sorts of predicate: those such as 'man', which can be predicated *kuriôs* of things in this world [I(*a*)], and those such as 'equal', which even when they are used unequivocally of such things can be predicated of them only derivatively [II-V]. To all appearance it seeks to provide forms for predicates of the second class by contrasting them with those of the first; and we shall see this impression confirmed by other evidence and by the detail of the argument. This distinction Cherniss tacitly suppresses in his précis of P,[23] and he is accordingly able to find 'no reason to suppose that the argument ... was not also meant to establish the existence of Ideas in the case of *all* common predicates'.[24] He suggests no reason for this rewriting, unless it is (what is in any case no justification) that the similar argument in *Phaedo* 74-5 is said to apply to all things *hois episphragizometha to 'auto ho esti'*, 'on which we set the seal of the "that which is" ' (75c-d). But to assume that this includes all predicates whatever is to beg the same question. The predicates actually cited there as examples – *ison*, 'equal', *meizon*, 'greater', *elatton*, 'less', *kalon*, 'beautiful', *agathon*, 'good', *dikaion*, 'just', *hosion*, 'holy' – are all of the restricted type to which the argument of P applies; in the relevant respect they are all, as we shall see, the logical congeners of 'equal' and not of 'man'.[25] Moreover, the same distinction, which is essential to the

[22] I can refer now to Vlastos, op. cit., 337, n. 31; cf. R. Robinson, *Plato's Earlier Dialectic*² (Oxford 1953), 2-3.

[23] Cherniss, 230. To do this he omits the illustrations of the three types of predication in P.I. Yet (*a*) without the illustrations the analysis is merely formal and without explanatory force; (*b*) that the predicate cited in the first paragraph of Alexander's source was not *ison* and was not a 'relative' term is implied by Alexander's remark that at any rate the proof *goes on* to deal with *ison*, which *is* relative (83. 23-4); and (*c*) in any case the illustration from portraits cannot be excised since it comes from the Platonic source (p. 169 above). This in addition to the considerations adduced in the following pages.

[24] Cherniss, n. 186.

[25] Similarly those given to illustrate similar formulae at *Phaedo* 76d, 78d, *Rep.* 479a-d. The one passage in which Plato seems unequivocally to require a Form for every predicate (*Rep.* 596a) cannot be ingenuously cited by any critic wedded to the 'unity of Plato's thought' since (even if *Parm.* 130 is brushed aside) taken literally it contradicts *Politicus* 262a-3e and incidentally leaves Aristotle's criticism of the *hen epi pollôn*, 'one over many' argument valid for every negatively defined predicate (*Meta.* 990b13: cf. Alexander and Ross *ad loc.*). Readers other than those *stasiôtai tou holou* are likely to find the comment of D.J. Allan in a review of H. Cherniss, in *Mind* 55 (1946), 263-72, at 270-1, sound and to the point.

argument of P and its sources, is the basis of Aristotle's criticism of these arguments. That criticism gives the rest of our discussion its starting-point and conclusion.

It has come to be agreed that Aristotle's objection to the arguments which 'produce Ideas of relatives' (*Meta.* I 9, 990b16-17, cf. p. 165 above) is not of the same form as those preceding it in its context. He is not arguing that such proofs as that reported in P can be used to establish Ideas that were explicitly rejected by the Platonists. He is saying that their conclusions contradict a logical principle accepted by the Academy; and the commentary of Alexander enables us, I think, to identify the principle in question. (But Sir David Ross is one scholar who would not agree with this identification (*Aristotle's Metaphysics* (Oxford 1924), ad loc.), and in this he is followed by Wilpert.) Namely, Aristotle in this and the following sentence of his critique is turning against the Platonists their own dichotomy of *kath' hauto* and *pros ti*:[26] a dichotomy inherited from Plato and evidently regarded as not only exclusive but exhaustive, since the school of Xenocrates maintained it against the needless elaboration of Aristotle's own categories.[27] Aristotle is objecting that such a proof as P sets up a 'non-relative class of relatives', a *kath' hauto genos tôn pros ti*, and that 'we say' that there is no such class.

The first thing to remark is the wide sense carried by the Academic *pros ti* when measured by more familiar Aristotelian standards. This seems to have eluded Alexander: hence, perhaps his reference to P as proving *ideas kai tôn pros ti*, 'ideas of relatives as well' where Aristotle says only *ideas tôn pros ti* 'ideas of
relatives':[28]/ he seems to have seen that the proof applies, not certainly to all 108
predicates, but to many that fall outside the Aristotelian category. (He reassures himself with the reflection, and the *goun* seems to prove it his own, that 'anyhow the example used in the proof *is* relative' – sc. in the orthodox sense: *Meta.* 83. 23-4.) In any case he is betrayed by his surprise when in the next sentence of the *Metaphysics* Aristotle argues from the priority of *arithmos*, 'number', to the priority not of *to poson*, 'quantity', but of *to pros ti*, 'relation' (990b19-21). Here Alexander reports what is certainly the correct explanation (*pas arithmos tinos estin*, 'every number is *of* something', *Meta.* 86. 4-5; cf. Aristotle, *Meta.* 1092b19, and *Cat.* 6a36-7: *ta pros ti legomena*, 'things said in relation to something' are, *inter alia*, *hosa auta haper estin heterôn einai legetai*, 'all those things that are said to be just what they are *of* other things'). We know that *ton arithmon ontos einai*, 'number is *of* something that is', was an Academic premiss: Alexander, *Meta.*, 78.16). But not content with this, he attempts to

[26] Alexander, *Meta.* 83. 24-6, 86. 13-20. The relevance of this dichotomy was pointed out by D.G. Ritchie against Henry Jackson: cf. James M. Watson, *Aristotle's Criticisms of Plato* (London 1909), 32.

[27] *Soph.* 255c-d, *Philebus* 51c, cf. *Rep.* 438b-d, *Charmides* 168b-c, *Tht.* 160b. Xenocrates, fr. 12 (*Heinze*) = Simplicius, *Cat.* 63. 21-4. I am not concerned here with the development and supplementation of this dichotomy in the early Academy, which has been the subject of recent studies. The subsequent conflation of the Platonic 'categories' with the Aristotelian, e.g. in Albinus (R.E. Witt, *Albinus and the History of Middle Platonism* (Cambridge 1937), 62-7), may derive from Aristotle himself (*EN* 1096a19-21).

[28] Alexander, *Meta.* 83. 17, 22, 85. 7. But the text of 82. 11 (*ho men ek tôn pros ti kataskeuazôn ideas logos*) should not be emended, for this comes from the *Peri Ideôn* and not from Alexander.

interpret the anomaly away (86. 11-13);[29] an attempt at once refuted by the amplification of the argument in *Metaphysics* XIII 1079a15-17, which makes it wholly clear that Aristotle does intend here to subsume number under *to pros ti* as a general class contrasted with *to kath' hauto*.

Nor are the sources of such a classification in Plato far to seek. In *Republic* VII (523a-525a) numbers are classed with such characteristics as *light* and *heavy, large* and *small*, on the score that our senses can never discover any of them *kath' hauto*, in isolation (525d10): in perceptible things they are inseparable from their opposites.[30] For, as Socrates argues in the *Parmenides* (129c-d), what is one of something is any number of something else – one man is many members. We may say, for convenience, that 'one' as we ordinarily apply it to things is an *incomplete* predicate and that, accordingly as we complete it in this way or that, it will be true or false of the thing to which it is applied. Now the same is true, or Plato talks as if it is true, of all those predicates which in the *Republic* and earlier works supply him with his stock examples of Ideas; and conspicuously so of the logical-mathematical and moral-aesthetic predicates for which the young Socrates unhesitatingly postulates Forms in *Parmenides* 130b-d. In this world what is large or equal, beautiful or good, right or pious, is so in some respect or relation and will always show a contradictory face in some other.[31] As large is mixed with small (*Rep.* 524c), so just and unjust, good and bad, in having commerce with bodies and action[32] have commerce with each other (*Rep.* 476a4-7[33]); and in an earlier context Plato argues that such seeming contradictions are to be resolved by specifying those different respects of relations in which the antagonistic descriptions hold good (436b-7a). Notice how various such specifications will be: some of Plato's predicates are concealed comparatives ('large') or can be forced into this mould ('beautiful' in the *Hippias Major* 288b-9c), some are more overtly relational ('equal'[34]), some are neither

[29] *pace* Wilpert, 109, who cannot think that Alexander would allow himself such an interjection. But see Mansion, n. 79, Cherniss, 301-2.

[30] *Enantia*, in a sense that includes any *prima facie* incompatibles (e.g. different numbers).

[31] With *Rep.* 479a-b, cf. 331c and 538d-e and P. Shorey, *Republic* (London 1930) vol. 1, 530, n. *a*.

[32] 'actions': but Plato seems to have in mind *types* of action (refs. in last note; cf. *Dissoi Logoi* 3. 2-12). The *Symposium* (180e-1a) makes the necessary distinction but here, as elsewhere, seems a step beyond the *Republic*.

[33] The debate on this passage has doubtless lived too long, but the natural sense is surely that given above. The *koinônia* of the opposites with each other is a characteristic of those 'manifestations' in the physical world which seem to make a plurality of the Form; this is the only sort of pluralisation in question in the passage (cf. 476b, 479a-b), and any attempt to read back the *koinônia tôn genôn* of the *Sophist* into this text simply fits the argument too loosely. Plato is talking in terms of pairs of opposites – the unity of a Form is proved by contrasting it with its opposite, and the same *logos* is said to hold good of the rest (476a) – but the corresponding pluralisation that is marked by the reconciling in one object of such a pair of opposites has nothing to do with the *Sophist*. Good and bad cannot 'communicate' in the *Sophist* sense (*Soph.* 252d). Cf. rather the *krasis pros allêla*, 'mixture in relation to one another' of *Tht.* 152d7 and, with due reserve, *On Ancient Medicine* 15.

[34] Yet, as many have said, for Plato at this time equality and other relations are attributes of the individual. (It is worth recalling that *ison* could be used to mean 'of middle size' and in this

('one'); we have to ask what X is larger *than*, what it is a certain number *of*, what it is equal *to*.[35] Later in the *Philebus* (51c), Plato is ready to say that even of physical things some can be *kala kath' hauta*, 'beautiful in virtue of themselves' and not merely *kala pros ti*, 'beautiful in relation to something', but (although what is said of pleasure at *Rep*. 584d seems a first move towards this) there is no such admission in the *Republic*.

Notice, too, that Plato's treatment of these incomplete predicates makes no essential use of the idea of physical mutability, often though that idea recurs in the characterising of the Forms. Here, it is with the compresence and not the succession of opposites that he is expressly concerned.[36]

With these predicates Plato contrasts others of which 'finger' is an example. A finger can be/ seen *kath' hauto*: sight never reports it to be at the **109** same time not a finger (*Rep*. 523d). This predicate, then, breeds no contradictions that have to be resolved by specifying *pros ti*. And the same is evidently true of 'man', and of 'fire' and 'mud': all those predicates for which the young Socrates is unready to admit Forms.[37] That something is a finger is a matter on which sight is competent to pronounce (523b, 524d), and it is characteristic of the sorts of thing to which Socrates refuses ideas that they are just what we see them to be (*Parm*. 130d). The *Phaedrus* reapplies the distinction (263a: cf. *Alcibiades* I, 111-12) when it argues that men disagree not on the use of 'iron' or 'stone' but on that of 'good' or 'right' – or, we can add, on that of 'one' or 'similar'; for Zeno's logical puzzles, like the moral antinomies of his successors, were built on such incomplete predicates, and the *Parmenides* of itself would suffice to show that these two classes of problem lie at the root of Plato's earlier theorising. If we hope to resolve such disagreements by reference to some unexceptional standard, we shall find that the world which contains unambiguous samples of fire and fingers contains no comparable cases of goodness or similarity or equality *kath' hauto*. If we persist, our unambiguous Paradigms must be located elsewhere, in a *noêtos topos*, 'intelligible place'.

Plainly, the exclusion of Forms of such non-relative predicates as 'man' is

---

use is not overtly relational.). Geach's conviction (*Studies in Plato's Metaphysics* (London 1965) 269) that Plato must have thought of any case of equality, including the Form, as a pair of related terms cannot be justified by the bare *auta ta isa*, 'the equals themselves' of *Phaedo* 74c1. Geach writes that the Form 'has to consist of *two* equals, or there wouldn't be equality at all'; Aristotle in the *Peri Ideôn*, discussing the same line of thought in Plato, said 'What is equal must be equal to something, so the *autoison* must be equal *to a second autoison*' (Alexander, *Meta*. 83. 26-8), and whatever we think of Aristotle's methods of polemic *this* would have been absurd if Geach were right. See p. 176 below.

[35] The argument of *Phaedo* 74b-c is probably better-construed on these lines, taking the *tôi men* ... *tôi d' ou* of 74b8-9 (despite the then misleading dative in 74c1) as neuter and governed by *isa*. This at any rate seems to be the sense that the argument in P makes of its chief source (pp. 177-8 below). Otherwise it turns directly on relativity to different observers (cf. *Symp*. 211a4-5).

[36] *hama* 'at the same time', *Rep*. 524e2, 525a4, 523c1 and d5, *aei*, 'always' 479b8, *tauta onta*, 'being the same', cf. *Phd*. 74b8 with *Parm*. 129b6 and *Phd*. 102b-c.

[37] *Parm*. 130c-d. Parmenides' explanation of Socrates' choice, that he rejects Ideas of *geloia*, 'ridiculous things', is applied only to mud, hair, and dirt (130c5). In any case it is a diagnosis of motive and not a characterisation of the reasons that Socrates could have offered.

not characteristic of later dialogues nor even of the last book of the *Republic*. A greater preoccupation with mutability (as in the *Timaeus*) would naturally suggest that in a further sense *all* predicates are incomplete in their earthly applications, for all apply at one time and not at another. This point is already expressly made in a dialogue marked by that preoccupation, the *Symposium* (210e-211a), and the principle which could suggest it is already enunciated in the *Republic* (436b). So doubtless the argument of P, which ignores this extension of the theory, isolates one strand in Plato's thinking which in his earlier work at least he took small care and had small motive to distinguish sharply or to reconcile with others. The same is true of other arguments collected in the *Peri Ideôn*. But what seems beyond serious question is that the earlier accounts of Forms are dominated by a preoccupation with incomplete predicates, in the narrower sense given to that expression.

Man, fire, and *water* seem to have remained stock Academic instances of *ta kath' hauta legomena* by contrast with *ta pros heteron*, 'things (said) in relation to something different' or *ta pros ti*,[38] and there is small doubt that the broad distinction sketched above between complete and incomplete predicates in Plato lay at the source of the Academic dichotomy as well as of some major arguments for Ideas. The so-called *Divisiones Aristoteleae* preserved by Diogenes Laertius define *ta kath' heauta legomena* as *hosa en têi hermêneiai mêdenos prosdeitai* and *ta pros ti legomena* accordingly as *hosa prosdeitai tinos hermêneias*(67 Mutschmann). Now it seems plain that the same distinction underlies the argument of P. For this explanation of *ta pros ti* recalls the argument of II(*c*) that the definition of 'equal' does not apply without further specification, *akribôs*,[39] to anything in this world. To explain why one thing is called equal (and here again we have to note that equality is treated as an attribute of the individual thing) is to specify another with whose dimensions those of the first tally. And II(*a*) seems only the other face of this coin, for different cases of equality will require the *logos* to be completed in different ways.[40] [II(*b*) seems to add the rider that, since the dimensions of sensible things are constantly fluctuating, even to say 'having the same size as A' is to use a description without fixed meaning.] But even in Alexander's possibly

[38] Hermodorus apud Simpl. *Phys*. 247. 30 ff., Diogenes Laertius 3. 108, Sextus Empiricus *adv. math*. 10. 263.

[39] = *haplôs*, 'without qualification', opposed to *kata prosthesin*: cf. *A. Post*. 87a34-7, *Meta*. 982a25-8 and 1078a9-13, *EN* 1148a11.

[40] Or the sense may be that different cases involve specifying different measurements; but this would leave the senses of *logos* in II(*a*) and II(*c*) unconnected. And II(*c*) may mean just that nothing is equal without being unequal too. But, besides robbing Aristotle's reply of its immediate point (p. 178 below), these interpretations neglect a parallel of thought and language in the *Eudemian Ethics*. In the discussion of three types of friendship in *EE* VII 2 it is said that one *logos* does not fit all the cases (1236a26), but the *logos* of friendship in the primary sense (*kuriôs*) is an element in the *logoi* of the rest (1236a20-2: 'the rest' are here of course species and not, as in P, individuals). For whereas friendship in the strict sense is to choose and love a thing because it is good and pleasant *haplôs*, friendship in its derivative senses is to do this because it is good *pros ti* or pleasant *tini*. In other words a definition that fits primary friendship without qualification (*haplôs* = *akribôs* in P. II(*c*)) needs to be completed to give the *logoi* of the derivative cases. So in P: the similarity of language is very striking.

condensed version it is clear that II(*a*) and II(*c*) are not duplicates and that their sequence is important. For the point of II(*a*) is that the specification of various correlates can be no part of the meaning of 'equal' if it is not merely ambiguous, and the point of II(*c*) is that when the common core of meaning is pared of these accretions it no longer characterises anything in this world.

Such arguments apply only to predicates which in their everyday uses are, in the Academic sense, relative. They follow Plato in deducing the existence of Ideas from the perplexing behaviour of 'equal' (or *mutatis mutandis* of 'beautiful' or 'good') when this is measured against such unperplexing expressions as 'man'. To this II(*b*) alone might seem an exception, for it can be read to imply (what it certainly does not say) that phenomenal things are continually changing in all/ respects and so not *kuriôs* the subjects of any **110**
predicates. But such an interpretation would be the death of P. It would contradict P.I, and it would leave the detail of P.II inexplicable, since the special arguments of II(*a*) and II(*c*) would be at once redundant – logically outbidden. Further, it would leave Aristotle's identification of such arguments as producing 'Ideas of relatives' unaccountable. For it seems to be true of all the proofs to which he refers in this context that they produce such Ideas, *inter alia*,[41] so that he can only mean to characterise a further class of argument concerned directly with *ta pros ti*.

A non-relative class of relatives

The author of our proof is substantially faithful to the class of Platonic arguments he presents but here again he is anxious to sharpen a logical issue. What the dialogues describe as an appeal to an intelligible Paradigm is seen, in practice, to be the application of a correct definition (e.g. *Euthyphro* 6e). It is in terms of definitions that P is framed. To say that nothing on earth affords an unexceptionable Paradigm of equality is re-phrased as saying that to nothing on earth can the definition of 'equal' be applied, pared of irrelevant accretions. Now this re-phrasing brings out, more clearly than Plato's words, the crucial point at which Aristotle directs his objection – and any success in explaining his reply must stand in favour of our interpretation of the argument. Where a Paradigm is required for a predicate that is incomplete in its ordinary use it must indeed be (as the argument of P faithfully shows) a Standard Case, exhibiting rather than being the character it represents. But more: it seems that the Form, and the Form alone, must carry its predicate *kath' hauto* in the sense given by the dichotomy. *Auto to ison* is indeed equal, but how can we without absurdity ask to what it is equal? It cannot be equal to everything or to nothing (both would engender paradoxes), and it cannot be equal to some things but not others (which would re-import just the compresence of opposites that the Form was invented to avoid: *Parm.*

[41] *Meta.* 990b11-17. The proofs *kata to hen epi pollôn*, 'according to the one over many', and *kata to noein ti phtharentos*, 'according to thinking of something that is no longer there', do so because they are logically unrestricted in scope. For the *logoi ek tôn epistêmôn*, 'arguments from the sciences', see Alexander *Meta.* 79.13-15.

129b-130a). The incompleteness which so embarrassingly characterises 'equal' in its ordinary applications cannot, it seems, characterise it when it designates the Form. This is the natural sense of Socrates' warning that the 'equal' he is to discuss is not 'stick equal to stick or stone equal to stone but just *equal*' (*Phd.* 74a), and it is the main point of the argument in P that unless 'equal' is merely ambiguous the core of meaning common to all its uses must apply to something *akribôs* or, as Aristotle puts it in the *Metaphysics*, *kath' hauto*. One aim of the second part of the *Parmenides*, I take it, is to find absurdities in a similar treatment of 'one'. It is the extreme case of Greek mistreatment of 'relative' terms in the attempt to assimilate them to simple adjectives.[42]

This is the point on which Aristotle fastens, and his rejoinder is not the simple deception that Cherniss reads into it.[43] It is developed in more than one place. In the *Metaphysics* he is content to observe that such arguments construct a 'non-relative class of relatives', i.e. a class of non-relative instances of relatives. They require that any essentially incomplete predicate shall in *one* application behave as though it were complete – yet the Academy's use of the familiar dichotomy recognises no such exceptions (see the *Sophist* 255c-d). Alexander reports what is in effect the same objection: nothing can be equal that is not equal to something; but this entails that *to autoison* is equal to another *autoison*, and thus the Form is duplicated (*Meta.* 83. 26-8). But even without this corroboration we could be sure of Aristotle's sense. In chapter 31 of the *De Sophisticis Elenchis* he says: 'We must not allow that predications of relative terms (*tôn pros ti legomenôn*) mean anything when taken out of relation (*kath' hautas*), e.g. that "double" means something apart from "double of half" merely because it is a distinguishable element in that phrase ... We may say that by itself "double" means nothing at all; or, if anything, certainly not what it means in context' – and this rebuts the treatment of 'equal' in P and its sources as applying synonymously to earthly things and to the Form. If 'equal' does not behave as tractably as 'man' in this world, that does not entail that there is another world in which it does: the use of 'equal' is *irreducibly* different from that of 'man'.

The consequence attacked by Aristotle is, I think, implied by the Platonic arguments on which the proof in P relies. But did Plato clearly contemplate the consequence in framing the arguments? That is surely doubtful. It would be easy to overlook it in the case of an asymmetrical relation such as *double-of-half*, where the absurdity of having to give the Form a twin in order to supply it with its appropriate correlate does not arise. And Plato's very use of *kath' hauto*, by contrast with the Academic usage that grew out of it, shows the weakness; for in characterising a case of X as *kath' hauto* he evidently means rather to exclude the opposite of X than to exclude the relativity which gives entry to an opposite (*Parmenides* 128e and 129d, *Republic* 524d: notice that
111 the solution of/contradictions by specifying *pros ti* and *kata ti* is broached in quite a different context of the *Republic*). Nor is the latter exclusion the only

[42] cf. Cornford, *Plato and Parmenides* (London 1939), 78, n. 1, and for a later parallel R.M. Martin, *Philosophy and Phenomenological Research* 14 (1953-4), 211.

[43] Cherniss, 279-85.

means to the former, for where the Idea is overtly or covertly a comparative it can as well be represented as *superlatively* X, X in comparison with everything; so that here the predicate would retain its 'relative' character even when used of the Idea. Between these alternatives the treatment of *auto to kalon*, 'the beautiful itself', in *Symposium* 210e-211a seems to be ambiguous. But 'equal' and 'one' are not so amenable: their purity is not preserved by making them, in strict analogy, equal to or one of everything. The proof in P does not seem to be mistaken about the implications of its source.

Yet it brings out those implications with a new clarity, and in doing so it plays very neatly into Aristotle's hands. This fact, and the obvious concern of its author with logical reformulations, suggest that here at least we should be incautious in treating our records of the *Peri Ideôn* as a source of fresh information on Academic arguments about the Ideas. It looks as though Aristotle may be responsible for the representative proof that he produces for refutation. This is not indeed wholly plausible, for by characterising such proofs as *akribesteroi*, 'more exact' (*Meta.* 990b15) Aristotle presumably means to commend his opponents and not himself for the logical care with which the proof is developed. And the argument of P is not a mere (even disingenuous) *réchauffé* of extant Platonic arguments, but a new structure of argument in its own right. But is this reason enough to dismiss the suspicion?

10

Logic and Metaphysics in Some Earlier Works of Aristotle

163 Much of Aristotle's early work in logic sprang from the practice and discussions of the Academy in Plato's lifetime. This is a commonplace, but I have tried to illustrate it here by evidence which throws an unfamiliar light on the development of some of Aristotle's most characteristic theories. The commonplace itself is not to be confused with a narrower thesis about the origins of the theory of syllogism: on that well-worn issue I have nothing to say here. I have confined myself to another part of Aristotle's logical studies, namely that part which shaped his views on the nature and possibility of any general science of *to on hêi on* ('being *qua* being'), any inquiry into the general nature of what there is. Here his major issues were problems of ambiguity, particularly the ambiguity that he claimed to find in 'being' or *to on* as that expression is used in the different categories. And his problems were shared by his contemporaries in the Academy. By opposition and by suggestion they helped to form the logic that underlay First Philosophy.

There is a justly famous picture of Aristotle's development to which I must try to relate my argument. According to this picture, Aristotle remained for many years after Plato's death wedded to the project of constructing a 'Platonic' mistress-science of metaphysics. Only later, as this Platonic period fell further behind him, did he turn to concentrate his attention on the
164 departmental sciences. When he wrote *Metaphysics* IV, no less than when he had written the *Protrepticus* and the *Eudemian Ethics*, he could still see himself as the 'Erneuerer der übersinnlichen Philosophie Platons' (although by now he had reformed his inheritance to the extent of discarding the transcendent Forms, and so leaving only God as the object of the study). But – according to this same account – in *Metaphysics* IV a new interest has crept in beside the old. For now Aristotle tries to find room for a second and very different inquiry under the old rubric of 'First Philosophy', an inquiry that is not 'Platonic' but essentially Aristotelian: the general study of being, *tou ontos hêi on*.[1]

The evidence I have to discuss does not wholly square with this account. It seems to show that when Aristotle wrote *Metaphysics* IV he had returned to,

[1] W. Jaeger, *Aristotle*², tr. R. Robinson (Oxford 1948; first German ed. Berlin 1923), chs. viii and xiii: 'reviver of Plato's supersensible philosophy', 339.

or newly arrived at, a belief in the possibility of a general metaphysics after a period in which he had denounced any such project as logically indefensible and castigated Plato and the Academy for pursuing it. It was in this period that for reasons of logic he confined his interest to the special sciences (of which theology was one). It was in this period that he wrote, *inter alia*, the whole or the most part of the *Organon*, the *Eudemian Ethics*, and the polemic against the Academy; and his attitude at the time to a Platonic mistress-science must surely be gathered from that polemic at least as much as from his continuing interest in the special science of theology. Seen in this perspective the kind of inquiry that is introduced in the fourth book of the *Metaphysics* looks more like a revival of sympathy with Plato's aims (or what Aristotle took to be those aims) than like a new departure from them.

Ambiguity and the attack on metaphysics

'In general', says Aristotle in *Metaphysics* I 9, 'it is fruitless to look for the elements of all the things there are without distinguishing the different senses in which things are said to be' (992b18-24). This interest in ambiguity was shared by others in the Academy. Speusippus as well as Aristotle set up **165**
criteria for synonymy and homonymy.[2] And we can hear a general debate behind the remark in the *Sophistici Elenchi* that, while some cases of homonymy deceive no one, some seem to elude even the experts, since they often quarrel over such words as 'one' and 'being': some hold that the words have a single meaning in all their applications, others refute the Eleatics by denying this (182b13-27). Aristotle was one of those who denied this. In his view, *to be* was *to be something or other*: for a threshold, he says, 'to be' means 'to have such and such a position', for ice it means 'to have solidified in such and such a way'.[3] And, at the level of greatest generality, to be is to be either a substance of some sort or a relation or a quality or a member of some other category. There is no general sense to the claim that something exists over and above one of the particular senses.

That this dispute over the ambiguity of 'being' and 'one' took some of its impetus from the *Parmenides* and the *Sophist* can hardly be doubted. That it was more than a lexical diversion is proved by many of Aristotle's major arguments, and particularly by those which, like the objection already quoted, were aimed at the Platonists. One of the most remarkable of these forms part of the polemic against the Academy in the first book of the *Eudemian Ethics*.[4] In it Aristotle argues that, since 'being' and 'good' have

[2] Boethus apud Simplic., *Cat.* 38.19-39.9, 36.28-31 (cf. E. Hambruch, *Logische Regeln der plat. Schule* (Berlin 1904, repr. N.Y. 1976), 27-9).

[3] *Meta.* 1042b25-8, cf. *De An.* 415b12-15. This is not to deny the distinction between *einai ti* and *einai haplôs*. For the essential link see e.g. *Meta.* 1028a29-31, *A.Pst.* 73b5-8 and n. 16. To be *haplôs* is to be a substance, for substance is what a thing is *kath' hauto*.

[4] I find myself unpersuaded by arguments brought against the substantial authenticity of the *Eudemian Ethics* (e.g. recently by Schaecher, *Studien zu den Ethiken des Corpus Aristotelicum* II,

166 different senses in the different categories, there can be no unitary science of either being or the good;[5] and he adds later that a science can study only some *idion agathon*, 'special good' (1218a34-6) – or, by implication, some *idion on*, 'special being'. It is a conclusion to make any reader of the *Metaphysics* or the *Nicomachean Ethics* rub his eyes. True, the *Eudemian Ethics* does not deny all connexion between different types of good, or the sciences that study them: like the *Nicomachean*, it orders the humanly achievable goods in a hierarchy of means and ends (1218b10-25). And it is also true that the *Nicomachean Ethics* still retains the old argument against any general science of the good.[6] But the *Nicomachean Ethics* adds the redeeming afterthought that *all* the uses of 'good' may be connected either by affiliation to some central use or else by analogy,[7] and of this there is no hint in the *Eudemian*. So in the earlier work
167 when Aristotle argues that each thing seeks its own separate good he cites the eye which seeks vision and the body which seeks health (1218a33-6), but in the *Nicomachean Ethics* he uses such examples to point the analogy between different uses of 'good' (1096b28-9). And there is another, related difference whose importance will become clearer as we proceed. The *Eudemian Ethics*

Paderborn 1940). The passages in *EE* where older critics discerned the tidying and supplementing hand of an editor tell the other way. The man who wanted the throat of a crane is given his name and patronymic in *EE* (1231a17) but not in *EN* (1118a32): no editor ferreted out this piece of news – it was dropped between the two works. Similarly though less obviously with the quotation from Heraclitus (*EE* 1223b22-4, *EN* 1105a7-8). And the more schematic treatment of *prohairesis* and *orexis* in *EE* (1223a26-7, 1225b22-4) is not an editor's improvement on the looser account in *EN* (1111b10-12) but the plan presupposed by that account. As will appear, the inferences that I draw from the polemic in *EE* could equally be drawn from texts in the Corpus whose authenticity is beyond quibble. But this too confirms the bona fides of the *Eudemian Ethics*.

[5] 1217b25-35. Aristotle does not use the word 'homonymy' here, as he does of 'being' and 'one' in the *Topics* passage quoted above and as he does when he reconsiders the present argument in the *Nicomachean Ethics* and *Metaphysics* (see below). He says that 'being' and 'good' are *pollachôs legomena* (said in many ways), an expression which is also used in the *Topics* passage and which in the early logic comes to the same thing. If a *word* is *pollachôs legomenon* then it is a case of homonymy, requiring different definitions in different uses (*Top.* 106a1-8): the only *pollachôs legomena* which are not cases of homonymy are not words but ambiguous *phrases* (110b16-11a7). Gradually Aristotle came to explore a way in which a word could be *pollachôs legomenon* but avoid mere homonymy, but we shall see that in the present argument he does not consider this possibility. *Homônumia* I have rendered conventionally and for brevity's sake as 'ambiguity': on another occasion it may be shown why this is less apt than the clumsy 'plurality of meanings', and how the distinction throws light on Aristotle's metaphysics, but the point is not relevant here.

[6] *EN* 1096a23-9 = *EE* 1217b25-35, *EN* 1096a29-34 = *EE* 1217b35-1218a1.

[7] 1096b26-9. 'Relative to one' (*pros hen*) and 'derived from one' (*aph' henos*) are not generally distinguished (cf. *GC* 322b31-2, *EE* 1236b20-1 & 25-6); they must not be confused with the 'adding and subtracting' of *Meta.* 1030a27-b4. Nor must they be confused with the 'by analogy' which Aristotle though not his commentators contrasts with them: see pp. 192-3 below. It may be noticed that the new concession in the *Nicomachean Ethics* does not in fact affect the shape of Aristotle's ethics. He gives an extra paragraph to reconsidering the possibility that there is a 'universal' sense of good or a good that is capable of separate and independent existence, but concludes that these are irrelevant for his purpose since he is concerned with what is humanly achievable. In *EE* and *EN* the humanly achievable goods are ordered in a hierarchy terminating in *eudaimonia*, happiness, and this is defined, firmly in *EE* and with qualifications in *EN*, by a relation to one good that is not *prakton*, something that can be achieved, namely God.

prefaces its polemic with a warning: the topics to be discussed belong necessarily to another inquiry, one that is in general more dialectical (*logikôteras*), for it is this (sc. dialectic or 'logic') and no other science that deals with arguments which are both general and destructive.[8] But the *Nicomachean Ethics* softens those general and destructive arguments with its own constructive suggestion about the senses of 'good', and then comments that precision on this question must be left to *another philosophy* (1096b30-1). Commentators have rightly identified this other philosophy with the type of inquiry introduced in *Metaphysics* IV, a general metaphysics whose first object is to mitigate the ambiguity of words which have different uses in the different categories by showing that all their senses have one focus, one common element.[9] So we can say, tentatively: In the earlier ethics a word such as 'good' which is used in different categories is ambiguous, and the analysis of such ambiguities falls to dialectic. In the later ethics the ambiguity is circumvented, and this circumvention is the work of **168**
metaphysics.

Still more surprising than the intransigence about 'good' in the *Eudemian Ethics* is the corollary that there can be only departmental sciences of being. This runs flatly counter to the argument of *Metaphysics* IV, VI, XI[10] where Aristotle contends that 'being' is used not homonymously but even, in a way, synonymously (*tropon tina kath' hen*), since all its senses can be explained in terms of substance and of the sense of 'being' that is appropriate to substance. To explain what it is for there to *be* qualities or relations one must explain what it is for there to *be* (in a prior sense) substances having qualities and relations. And from this Aristotle concludes at once that there *is* a single science of being *qua* being, and this is universal in scope and not another departmental inquiry.[11] There is nothing new in the suggestion that at one time Aristotle restricted First Philosophy to a single department of reality; but it would be hard to find better evidence for it than this polemic in the *Eudemian Ethics*, which shows both that the restriction was deliberate and

[8] 1217b16-19. For the identification of *logikon* and *dialektikon* see T. Waitz, *Aristotelis Organon* vol. 2 (Leipzig 1846), 353-5. *Top.* 105b30-1 seems to divide them if it implies (as perhaps it does not) that 'logical' problems, like 'physical' and 'ethical', can be handled either dialectically, *pros doxan*, or scientifically, *kat' alêtheian*. Here (a) Aristotle may mean that, inasfar as the common principles (which are in virtue of their generality 'logical premisses') are employed in this or that science and take their use from the science (*A.Pst.* 76a37-40), their function is understood *kat' alêtheian* only by the particular scientists. Or (b) we may compare *Top.* 162b31-3 which says that the account of *petitio principii* given there is merely *kata doxan*, but the account *kat' alêtheian* can be found in the *Analytics* – viz. in *A. Pr.* II 16, where the treatment is distinguished from that in the *Topics* merely by using the formal theory of the syllogism. Thus the distinction corresponds to that in *A.Pst.* 84a7-9, b1-2, between *logikôs* and *analutikôs*. On either interpretation, 'logical' problems and 'logical' techniques are wholly general. 'Logical' problems can be but need not be handled by 'logical' techniques. And 'logical' techniques are dialectic.

[9] Hence Alexander's mention of good as well as being among *pros hen legomena* in his commentary on *Meta.* IV (242.5-6).

[10] Nothing in my argument requires the authenticity of *Meta.* XI. See now A. Mansion, *Rev. Phil. de Louvain* 56 (1958), esp. 209ff.

[11] 1003a21-b19, 1026a29-32, cf. 1028a34-6, 1045b29-31, 1060b31-1061a10, 1061b11-12.

why it was so.[12] True, if this were the sole evidence it might be suspect. Its singularity might reinforce those doubts about the authenticity of the *Eudemian Ethics* which are noticed elsewhere in this chapter.[13] But it is not unique, and we need only take it as a clue in our hands to find other evidence
169 which would by itself compel the same conclusion.

In sum, then, the argument of *Metaphysics* IV, VI seems to record a new departure. It proclaims that 'being' should never have been assimilated to cases of simple ambiguity, and consequently that the old objection to any general metaphysics of being fails. The new treatment of *to on* and other cognate expressions as *pros hen kai mian tina phusin legomena*, 'said relative to one thing and to a single character' – or, as I shall henceforth say, as having *focal meaning* – has enabled Aristotle to convert a special science of substance into the universal science of being, 'universal just inasmuch as it is primary'.[14]

Now it is time for some caveats. I am not saying that when Aristotle wrote the *Eudemian Ethics* he was not yet acquainted with the idea of focal meaning. He was, and his use of that idea persuaded von Arnim that he must already have evolved the whole argument of *Metaphysics* IV.[15] But this is a mistake. Von Arnim overlooked the passage that we have considered. Aristotle does indeed use the idea of focal meaning in the *Eudemian Ethics*: he applies it to his stock example 'medical' and then in detail to 'friendship'(1236a7-33). But he has not seen its application to such wholly general expressions as 'being' or 'good'. When he uses it he takes pains to explain it, and it is characteristic of his earlier work – the work of a young man fond of schematic argument – that the explanation he gives in the *Eudemian Ethics* is far more clearcut than the arguments in the *Nicomachean Ethics* and the *Metaphysics* which rely on the same idea (*EN* 1156b19-21, 35-1157a3). A word such as 'medical', he says, is not univocal – it has various definitions answering to its various senses, but one of these senses is primary, in that its definition reappears as a component in each of the other definitions. If to be a medical man is to be XY, to be a medical knife is to be of the sort used by a man who is XY (1236a15-22). This is the pattern of reductive translation that Aristotle later applies to 'being'[16] and to

[12] Jaeger defends the suggestion but ignores this section of the *EE*, which conflicts with his account of Phronesis in that work: there, according to him (*Aristotle*, 239), it is still Platonically regarded 'as ruling over all the sciences (*kuria pasôn epistêmôn*, *EE* 1246b9) and as the most valuable knowledge (*timiôtatê epistêmê* [no ref.])', and 'this is clearly opposed to the *Nicomachean Ethics*'. But the sense in which it is *kuria pasôn* is given in *EE* 1218b10-25 (esp. 12-13), with which cf. *EN* 1094a26-7; and the sense in which it is *timiôtaton* is given in 1216b20-5, cf. *EN* 1103b26-9. Margueritte and Léonard have pointed out that *phronêsis* is used in an 'Aristotelian' as well as a 'Platonic' sense in *EE*, and in the latter sense generally in noticing the views of others: it is noteworthy that the former sense seems to occur first in the polemic (1218b13-14, where it is bracketed with *politikê* and *oikonomikê*), and thereafter predominates.

[13] nn. 4 and 17.

[14] 1003a23-4, 1026a30-1, cf. 1064b13-14. Obviously I am concerned here only with the device by which A. converts a science of substance into a science of *to on hêi on*, not with the quite different reasons for which he selects theology as the pre-eminent science of substance.

[15] *Eudemische Ethik und Metaphysik*, Akad. der Wiss. in Wien (1928), 55-7.

[16] In *Meta.* IV 2, but the account raises a small puzzle. Where he might be expected to say that all the subordinate senses of *on*, 'being', must be defined in terms of a primary sense of that expression, what he says is that all senses of *on* must be defined in terms of *ousia*, 'substance', just

those other expressions, such as 'one' and 'same' and 'opposite', which have a use in all categories but a primary use in the first (*Meta.* 1004a23-31, cf. 1018a31-8). But in the earlier work that ambitious application is still to seek. What is more, in the analysis of friendship we are warned against supposing that if one sense of the word is *primary* it is therefore *universal* (*EE* 1236a22-9); and this is another warning that the Aristotle of *Metaphysics* IV and VI, anxious to minimise the contrast between synonymy and focal meaning, will need to retract or reformulate. **170**

Logical priority, natural priority

There is another objection to be met before we can move to other evidence. So far I have suggested that in its polemic against the Academy the *Eudemian Ethics* takes no account of the logical analysis of 'being', and the consequent possibility of a single general science of being, that is proposed in parts of the *Metaphysics*. But in the same context the *Eudemian Ethics*, like the *Nicomachean*, recognises not only a difference in the senses of 'good' as it is used in the different categories but also a general order of *priority* among different types of good (*EE* 1218a1-15, *EN* 1096a17-23). Now it is natural to assume that these types of good correspond to the senses of 'good', and hence that the priority in question is just the priority of the first category. And if this assumption is allowed, then surely the *Eudemian Ethics* must be presupposing the argument of *Metaphysics* IV and VI which professes to show how the other categories are logically subordinate to the first? Once grant this, and there is a dilemma which is either way fatal. For either the inconsistency between these two works on which I have laid such stress is an illusion, or the *Eudemian Ethics* was written in full awareness of the analysis proposed in the *Metaphysics* and nevertheless contradicts the inference drawn from it in that work, namely that there can be a single science of being. On this latter alternative, the *Eudemian Ethics* must be a later production and presumably not the work of **171**
Aristotle at all.[17]

We might challenge the first move in this objection. For both in the *Eudemian* and in the *Nicomachean Ethics* the argument from priority is quite distinct from that which alleges an ambiguity and exploits the theory of

---

as all senses of 'healthy' must in terms of 'health': a formulation which makes no provision for the *priority* of one sense of *on*. But he then talks as though he had provided for that priority; and the explanation is plain – *on* in its primary sense *is ousia* (cf. 1028a29-31. The formulation in VII-IX is far clearer: with VII 1 cf. IX 1, 1045b27-32).

[17] Perhaps this alternative can be strengthened. It has been suggested that the rejection of any universal science was characteristic of the Peripatos in the first generation after Aristotle, because Theophrastus in his fragment on metaphysics observes that 'being' has more than one sense and that our knowledge of beings must be correspondingly departmental (8b10-20, 9a10-11, 23-b1). Generally speaking (*schedon*), says T., all knowledge is of *idia*, special fields (8b20-4). But here the parallel to *EE* goes astray. T. is careful to correct his overemphasis on the fragmentation of knowledge (8b24-7): it is also the task of science to aim at generality, and this may produce a subject-matter which is identical not in kind but simply by analogy.

categories. It seems doubtful whether the original form of the argument from priority involved the categories at all; in the Eudemian version they are not mentioned (1218a1-15), and in the Nicomachean the mention of them is at once superseded by the older Academic dichotomy of *kath' hauto*, '*per se*', and *pros ti*, 'relative', to which the categories were a more elaborate rival.[18] Still, let us suppose that the priority in question is the priority of the first category. This does not in the least entail that Aristotle had already reached his analysis of the *logical* priority of substance, the analysis which is propounded in *Metaphysics* IV and which depends directly upon recognising the focal meaning of 'being'. For logical priority – priority in *logos* or definition – is only one of the kinds of primacy that Aristotle eventually comes to claim for substance (*Meta.* 1028a32-b2). Another kind is 'natural' priority, a more primitive notion which Aristotle evidently took to be the older of the two since he fathers it on Plato and says that in a way the other types of priority were named after it (*Meta.* 1019a1-4). *A* is *naturally* prior to *B* (*proteron kata phusin, kat' ousian*) just in the case that *A* can exist without *B* and not *vice versa*; and it is plain that, just as this simple priority does not entail the more sophisticated kind, neither does the recognition of the first in a given case require recognition of the second. Thus a stock example of natural priority was the sequence points, lines, planes, solids; yet the Academy seems to have regarded this relation as allowing either the defining of the posterior terms by
172 the prior, or the converse, or neither.[19]

Now the sole type of priority that is expressly invoked in our passage of the *Eudemian Ethics* is natural priority (1218a4-5). At the start of the polemic the Idea of the Good has been said to be prior to other good things just in the sense that its annihilation would involve the annihilation of the rest but not *vice versa*.[20] It is true that the Idea is also said to be that by reference to which other things are *called* good (1217b12-13, cf. *Meta.* 987b7-9); but the striking fact is that neither here nor in his other critiques of the Forms does Aristotle take this formula to imply that the definition of 'good' or any other predicate *differs* when the word is applied to the Idea and when it is applied to the participant.[21] That is to say, at this stage or in this context he does not consider the idea of focal meaning or the associated notion of *logical* priority at all; and it is these ideas, and not any older and vaguer account of the primacy of substance, that later enable him to evade his own polemic and circumvent the ambiguity of 'being'.

So the objection fails and we can get on.

[18] 1096a17-23; Simplicius, *Cat.* 63.21-4.

[19] Posterior defined by prior, *A.Pst.* 73a34-7, *Meta.* 1077a36-b2; prior by posterior, *Top.* 141b19-22 (Plato? cf. *Meta.* 992a21-2; but also Aristotle, *Top.* 158a31-b4, 163b20-1); neither, *Meta.* 992a10-18 (Speusippus? cf. the contrast between *pros hen* (relative to one thing) and *ephexês* (in serial succession), *Meta.* 1005a10-11). At *Meta.* 1077a36-b11 Aristotle insists that logical does not entail natural priority (cf. 1018b34-7).

[20] 1217b10-16, a standard paraphrase of the criterion of natural priority; cf. de Strycker in *Aristotle and Plato in the Mid-Fourth Century*, ed. I. Düring and G.E.L. Owen (Göteborg 1960), 89.

[21] *EE* 1218a10-15, *EN* 1096a35-b5, *Meta.* 1040b32-4, 1079b3-11; cf. the final section of this paper.

Ambiguity and metaphysics in the Organon

Elsewhere we can see the search for focal meaning, by contrast with the simple detection of homonymy, taking on interest and importance for Aristotle. When he elucidates some cardinal expression by displaying some of its senses as elaborations upon a primary sense, his technique marks a major advance on the Socratic search for definitions. He employs it occasionally in the physical writings[22] and in the Lexicon, *Metaphysics* V, sometimes with the **173**
air of an afterthought.[23] In a special form it comes to dominate the psychology. Aristotle is already beyond one pitfall in the Socratic method when he argues in the *Topics* that, since 'life' is used in different senses of plants and of animals, it is wrong to attempt a general definition of the word: what we need is a separate definition for each form of life (148a23-36). But he is beyond the *Topics* when he says in the *De Anima* that, while we cannot be content with a general account of soul, neither can we stop at giving separate definitions of the various types of soul. Our explanation must show how these types are ordered, the posterior potentially containing the prior (414b25-415a1). Here there seem to be quite conscious parallels with the language of the *Metaphysics*: with soul as with being, it is the primary sense of the word that shows what is common to all the senses (415a23-5), and it is only what is denoted by the word in its primary sense that can have 'separate' existence (413a31-b10). But at the same time there are large differences in the two uses of focal meaning, and we are not concerned here with the psychology. The example raises other problems that lie on our way. The *Topics* is a commonplace book whose compiling and subsequent enlarging may have stretched over a considerable period. Is it reasonable then to say, as I have said in this instance, that in his later concern with focal meaning Aristotle is 'beyond the *Topics*'? Or, as I shall argue, that he is beyond the *Organon* as a whole?

Consider first what signs there are in these works of general interest in focal meaning, disregarding the special use that Aristotle finds for the idea in *Metaphysics* IV. In the *Topics* he quotes various examples which will later serve as standard cases of *pros hen legomena*.[24] But here they seem to be treated merely as cases of ambiguity ('good', for instance, is bracketed with *oxu*, 'sharp', 'acute', which is used in different senses of notes and knives and angles). Robin dismissed this treatment as 'une expression insuffisante et peu **174**
exacte de la doctrine d'Aristote':[25] perhaps he thought its inadequacy a sign

[22] *Phys.* 222a20-1, significantly not in 260b15ff.; *GC* 322b29-32.

[23] 1016b6-9, 1018a31-8, 1019b35-1020a6, 1020a14-32 (cf. *Cat.* 5a38-b10), 1022a1-3, 1024b17-1025a13. But for an apparent echo of the later metaphysics cf. 1017a13-22.

[24] 'Healthy', 106b33-7, 'good', 107a5-12 (cf. von Arnim, op.cit., pp. 55-6), 'being' in the different categories, 103b20-39. It is interesting that 'medical', which gave A. his first illustration of focal meaning in *EE*, does not appear.

[25] L. Robin, *La Théorie platonicienne des idées et des nombres* (Paris 1908), 153, n. 171; cf. Alexander, *Meta.* 241.21-4.

of the negative aims of the *Topics*. But the destructive side of the dialectic has been very much exaggerated, and it is at least as likely that Aristotle had not yet evolved the general 'doctrine' for which Robin was looking. At any rate, whether or not he had already met the notion of focal meaning (a question we shall face later) and whether or not that notion is implied or foreshadowed in some other passages of the *Topics*,[26] the work gives no sign that he attached any importance to it. When he recognises a third possibility beside bare synonymy and homonymy, the possibility is 'metaphor' (with, as a fourth case, something 'worse than metaphor'), and there is no attempt to explain metaphor by focal meaning.[27] And there are revealing passages such as the discussion of a problem in the fifth book. The problem depends on the possibility of assigning a predicate both to a primary subject and to other things which are 'called after' that subject (134a18-25), and it would be solved by calling in focal meaning – that is, by allowing the predicate different but connected definitions in its different uses. But, though he seems at one point on the verge of this solution (134a32-b1, cf. 145a28-30), Aristotle treats the predicate as a simple unit throughout and merely enjoins the speaker to say whether the expression is being applied to its primary subject or not (134b10-13). This simple treatment takes on a special significance in his attacks on the Ideas, for he recognises that the Platonists' use of the prefix *auto* or *ho estin*, 'absolute' or 'what [really] is', is just such an attempt to pick out the Idea as the primary subject of a predicate; yet here too he does not suppose that such a prefix entails any variation in the *logos*, the definition of the predicate (cf. p. 186, n.21 above). For him the Idea is 'first of a synonymous set', naturally but not logically prior to its participants.[28]

175 Nor does focal meaning find formal recognition in the class of paronyms which is introduced in the *Categories* and recognised in the *Topics*, for the definition of paronyms is merely grammatical. It shows, not how subordinate senses of a word may be logically affiliated to a primary sense, but how adjectives can be manufactured from abstract nouns by modifying the word-ending.[29] Plainly the *Categories* does not and could not make any use of this idea to explain how the subordinate categories depend on the first. Nor does it use focal meaning for that purpose (2b4-6). If focal meaning can be seen in the *Categories* it is in the analysis of some category – clearly enough in the definition of quantity (5a38-b10), far more doubtfully in the account of

[26] Materials for it seem to be present but unused in 106a4-8, 106b33-7, 114a29-31, 117b10-12, 124a31-4, 134a32-6, 145a28-30.

[27] 139b32-140a17. (I cannot find that any supporter of a widely accepted reconstruction of the *Protrepticus* has discussed this passage, which denounces as 'worse than metaphor' any attempt to describe law as measure or image of things naturally just.)

[28] *Lin. Insec.* 968a9-10, Aristotelian though not by Aristotle.

[29] cf. J. Owens, *The Doctrine of Being in Aristotle's Metaphysics*[2] (Toronto 1963), 51 and 330, nn. 19-21. But the idea was apparently extended, *Phys.* 207b8-10 (and cf. the connexion with *para ti legesthai*, 'being so called by virtue of a relation to something', W.D. Ross, *Aristotle's Metaphysics* (Oxford 1924), vol. 1, 161). In the *Categories* its function is to provide a simple tie between adjective and abstract noun (corresponding respectively to that which is 'predicated of' and that which is 'present in' a given subject) so that both can be treated in the same category.

the two uses of 'substance' (2b29-37, 3b18-21) – but not in that logical ordering of different categories and different senses of 'being' which lies at the root of the argument in *Metaphysics* IV.

This point can be strengthened and generalised, and then it is fundamental. Whether or not Aristotle did think at the time of writing the *Topics* (and the *Categories*, if he wrote that work) that focal meaning held some interest for philosophers, neither there nor in the rest of the *Organon* is there any hint of the use to which the idea is put in the fourth book of the *Metaphysics*. There is no room in the picture for a general science of 'being *qua* being'. Rhetoric apart, the sole discipline that Aristotle recognises in these works as dealing with material that is common to all sciences and all fields of discourse is dialectic;[30] and dialectic lays no claim to the title of First Philosophy. In its relation to the sciences it is a preliminary technique for clarifying and hardening those ideas in current use which they can take over
and put to more accurate work.[31] The common principles that it investigates **176**
have a different use in the different sciences and the different categories (*A.Pst.* 76a37-40, 88a36-b3) – here is an inescapable parallel to the treatment of 'being' and 'good' in the *Eudemian Ethics* – and the uses of such a principle are connected only by 'analogy' (76a38-9). Certainly, this analogical connexion is itself an admission that words and formulae which are shared by all fields of discourse are not for that reason baldly equivocal; but it does not explain why this is so, and we shall see later how far it is from implying that systematic connexion of meanings by which *Metaphysics* IV disarms the same ambiguity. It does nothing to show the possibility of a general science of 'being and the necessary characteristics of being', which takes the common axioms of the sciences as part of its subject-matter just because those axioms hold good of being *qua* being. Once Aristotle thinks he has established this possibility, he can claim a new importance for dialectical techniques by embodying them in the new science.[32] But no such science is in view in the *Organon*.

Yet commentators anxious for the unity of Aristotle's thought have managed to see the later metaphysics in the logical texts. They have descried it in the *Sophistici Elenchi* when Aristotle explains that dialectical argument is

[30] *Top.* 101a36-b4, cf. *Rhet.* 1358a2-32; and texts discussed in the next paragraph. Finding no other room for a general metaphysics in the *Organon*, E. Poste (*Aristotle on Fallacies; or, The Sophistici Elenchi* (London 1866), 212) proposed to regard it as 'more or less completely identical' with dialectic. His problem was correct: there is no room for it.

[31] As in much of the *Physics*, for instance. 'Physicam dialecticae suae mancipavit' (Bacon).

[32] As in the defence of the law of contradiction in IV 4. Cf. VII 4, where dialectic (*to logikôs zêtein*) is auxiliary to the philosophical argument, the first showing 'how we should speak' and the second 'how things are' (1030a27-8): but 'it doesn't matter in which of the two ways one puts it' (1030b3-4), i.e. the tenet that 'be' and therefore the question *ti esti*, 'what is it?', have their primary use in the category of substance can be shown either by dialectic ('adding' and 'subtracting', 1030a21-7, pointing out elliptical uses of 'be' in the subordinate categories) or by the philosophical analysis of 'being' as a *pros hen legomenon* (1030a34-b3). (I cannot comprehend why Cherniss renders *logikôs* at 1030a25 as 'a mere verbalism' ('The Relation of the *Timaeus* to Plato's Later Dialogues', *JHS* 77 (1957), 21); 1029b13 if nothing else would have shown that the word describes Aristotle's own method in the chapter.)

not confined to a determinate class of objects, does not prove anything, and – the critical phrase – is not *hoios ho katholou*, 'like universal reasoning' (172a11-13). What is this universal reasoning (ask the interpreters, from pseudo-Alexander to Jean Tricot) but the universal science of being
177 announced in *Metaphysics* IV? Yet in the very next lines Aristotle flatly denies that all things can be brought under the same principles, and a little later he says in the same vein that the common ideas with which dialectic deals do not form a positive subject-matter: they are more like negative concepts (*apophaseis*, whose claim to a common genus Aristotle denied from the *De Ideis* onwards).[33] Waitz saw that in this context the 'universal' method with which dialectic is contrasted can only be that which is explained in the *Posterior Analytics*, the method of the special sciences whose subject-matter is defined by 'universals that are not equivocal'.[34] Alternatively, if we are to see a reference to general metaphysics in the phrase, it must be glossed by that passage in the *Posterior Analytics* where Aristotle distinguishes the special sciences not only from dialectic but also from 'any science that might try to give universal proofs of the common axioms, such as the law of excluded middle' (77a26-31). Here too the commentators from John Philoponus onwards have caught the scent of *Metaphysics* IV. Yet Aristotle held consistently that the common axioms are *amesa*, 'immediate', and cannot be proved; at best, as in the fourth book of the *Metaphysics* itself, they can be recommended by dialectical methods (*Meta.* 1006a11-18). So the science that Aristotle has in mind here cannot be one of his own making. On the contrary, as Ross saw, it is what he repudiates: 'a metaphysical attempt, conceived after the manner of Plato's dialectic (sc. as that is represented in the central books of the *Republic*), to deduce hypotheses from an unhypothetical first principle'.[35] So too when Aristotle says, a little earlier in the *Posterior Analytics*, that one science cannot prove the theorems of another and (almost in the same breath) that geometry cannot prove the general principle that the knowledge of contraries is a single knowledge (75b12-15): *if* (as interpreters unwarrantably assume) he is thinking here of some other science as professing to prove such general principles, it is the *Republic* and not the *Metaphysics* that gives him his model. And this is a model for philosophy that he rejects as wholly misconceived.

178 Just as it is a Platonic metaphysics that he has in view when he denies that the common axioms can be proved, so it is with this target in mind that he rejects the possibility of deducing the special premisses of any given science (76a16-25). Such a proof, he says, would devolve on a mistress-science, *kuria pantôn*. We need not dwell on the struggles of Zabarella and others who read this as a reference to Aristotle's own general metaphysics and then have to explain away the plain repudiation of any such procedure in the text before them. The inquiry described in *Metaphysics* IV is not mentioned in the

[33] 172a36-8, cf. Alex. *Meta.* 80.15-81.10; *Top.* 128b8-9, *Meta.* 1022b32-1023a7.

[34] Waitz, *Organon* ii p.551-2, *A.Pst.* 73b26-8; cf. 85b15-22 on the need for univocity in the scientific universal.

[35] Ross ad loc.: *Aristotle's Prior and Posterior Analytics* (Oxford 1949), 543.

Organon; nor is it hidden in Aristotle's sleeve. In contexts such as those we have considered it must have been noticed if it had already established itself, and there is no sign of it.

The nature of the texts makes the argument from silence a strong one, but it can be corroborated by comparing these passages that we have just considered with a later echo of their argument. For the straightforward conclusions of the *Analytics* reappear in the *Metaphysics* in quite another guise: they have become problems which must be resolved if any general science of being is to be possible. The *Analytics* had argued against any attempt to prove the common axioms of all the sciences and, on connected grounds, against any attempt to prove the special principles of a given science. Both arguments reappear in *Metaphysics* III, but both have been relegated to the preliminary *aporiai* or puzzles of the subject (997a2-11, 15-25) – just as the reason which was given in the *Eudemian Ethics* for rejecting a single science of being turns up again in the *Metaphysics* merely as another difficulty to be circumvented (1003a33, 1060b31-5). The conclusion seems inescapable. The arguments against any universal science which are collected and to some extent disarmed in the *Metaphysics* were – at least in some important instances – first formulated when Aristotle thought them conclusive, namely when the polemic against the Academy was at its height and when the sole model of general metaphysics that Aristotle had in view was some form or version of Platonic dialectic. Any such would-be universal science, he then believed, must commit two logical crimes. It must aim at giving wholly general proofs of matters proprietary to particular sciences, and it must ignore the ambiguity of 'being' and all those ubiquitous words with which it tried to define its own **179**
subject-matter. Later, when he introduces his own programme for a general metaphysics, he deals differently with these two objections. The first he is ready to accommodate. The new enterprise is not cast in the form of a deductive system and it does not dictate premisses to the special sciences. Instead of general proofs it undertakes general analyses of the use of those same ubiquitous words and formulae: but here it runs against the second objection. And what gives the new departure its impetus and its character is just that Aristotle has now seen, in the concept of focal meaning, a way of defeating that objection.[36]

[36] Proved by the place assigned to it at the start of the argument in IV (and cf. VII 4, where it is the focal analysis of 'being' that distinguishes the philosophical from the dialectical treatment of the problem: n. 32). It is this device that enables Aristotle to make the last and most important qualification to the old principle that one science deals with one sort of object (Alex. *Meta.* 79.5-6), a principle qualified first by Socrates' claim that the same science deals with contraries (*Symp.* 223d, *Rep.* 333e-4a); then extended to all opposites, to means and ends, and finally to all *sustoicha*, 'coordinates' (*Top.* 109b17-29, 106a1-8, 110b16-25, 164a1-2, cf. *Phys.* 194a27-8). But none of these previous extensions had infringed Aristotle's thesis that the objects of a science fall inside one *genos* (*A.Pst.* 87a38-b4).

Analogy and focal meaning

I hope the picture emerges of a fairly clear stage in Aristotle's thought. In his logic he tended at this time to work with the simple dichotomy of synonymy and homonymy; apparently he saw little if any importance in that *tertium quid* for which he was gradually to find such notable uses. In metaphysics this simple scheme enabled him, as part of his critique of Plato and the Academy, to deny the possibility of any universal science of being. This denial was framed without provision for the system he was himself to propose in *Metaphysics* IV, VI and VII. True, he already held a theory of categories in which priority was ascribed to substance, but this priority was of an older Academic vintage which did not involve focal meaning. So it did nothing to mitigate the ambiguity that Aristotle claimed to find in 'being'.

The same polemic against a universal science figures largely in *Metaphysics* I 9. Here too an important weapon is the claim that the Platonists have neglected questions of ambiguity, and here too Aristotle seems to overlook focal meaning. Thus he maintains that if the Platonists had recognised the ambiguity of the expression *ta onta* ('beings') they would have seen the futility
180 of looking for the elements of all the things there are, for only the elements of substances can be discovered (992b18-24). This does not formally contradict the argument of the fourth book, but it is out of tune with the claim that a general inquiry into the elements of the things that are is legitimate and that those who had engaged in such an inquiry were on the right track (1003a28-32). It contrasts too with the argument in *Metaphysics* XII that all things can be said to have the same elements 'by analogy' (XII 4, esp. 1070b10-21). But now it is time to take up an earlier promise and show that these two pronouncements, in IV and XII respectively, are by no means equivalent, despite the immemorial tendency of commentators to describe the theory in IV as 'the analogy of being'.[37]

The claim of IV that 'being' is an expression with focal meaning is a claim that statements about non-substances can be reduced to – translated into – statements about substances; and it seems to be a corollary of this theory that non-substances cannot have matter or form of their own since they are no more than the logical shadows of substance (1044b8-11). The formulation in terms of 'analogy' involves no such reduction and is therefore free to suggest that the distinction of form, privation and matter is not confined to the first category (1070b19-21). To establish a case of focal meaning is to show a particular connexion between the definitions of a polychrestic word. To find an analogy, whether between the uses of such a word or anything else, is not to engage in any such analysis of meanings: it is merely to arrange certain

[37] G. Rodier (*Aristote: Traité de l'âme* (Paris 1900), vol. 2, 218) draws the distinction excellently, but misconstrues Aristotle's definition of the soul as relying on analogy, not focal meaning.

terms in a (supposedly) self-evident scheme of porportion.[38] So when Aristotle says in *Metaphysics* XII that the elements of all things are the same by analogy, the priority that he ascribes to substance is only natural priority
(1071a33-5) and he does not recognise any general science of being *qua* **181**
being.[39] There is no mention of *pros hen legomena* in XII, and none of analogy in IV. And when he says in the *Analytics* that each axiom has as many uses as there are sciences and kinds of beings, his concession that these uses are connected by analogy is no substitute for the later claim that the axioms hold good of being *qua* being and are therefore to be studied by the single science described in IV. It is IV, not XII, that moves decisively beyond the old polemic, the denunciation of any general inquiry into the 'elements of things' which is still audible in *Metaphysics* I.

That polemic turned on the neglect or suppression of the idea of focal meaning at a point where Aristotle later set great store by its use. Neglect or suppression: but which? We cannot take Aristotle's candour here for granted; but what we think of it will depend on what we can make of some earlier traces of the idea in the Academy.

The Academy on focal meaning

There is nothing new in the complaint that when Aristotle attacks the Academy he ignores focal meaning. A familiar example of this omission is the dilemma that he forces on his opponents in *Metaphysics* I 9: either it is a mere equivocation to use the same word of both the Form and its participant, or else they must carry their common name synonymously and so be specifically alike (991a2-8 = 1079a33-b3). Notoriously, the penalty for taking the second option was the regress which the Academy called the 'third man': the Form 'Man' and the individual man can now be treated as a single class whose existence entails that of a further Form 'Man', and so *ad infinitum*. To this dilemma Aristotle's critics retort that if only he had allowed the Platonists the benefit of his own *tertium quid*, focal meaning, the argument would
collapse. For suppose Socrates is called 'man' in a sense neither identical with **182**
nor merely different from that in which the Form is so called, but derivative from that sense: then the regress cannot get started. If the existence of a class of X-dependent things entails that of an X-thing, this by no means shows that

[38] See e.g. *Meta.* 1093b18-21, *EN* 1096b28-9. The idea of proportion is central to analogy (*Meta.* 1016b34-5), even when the terms are not fully stated because they are obvious (beings are the same by analogy because as one use of 'being' is to substance so another is to quantity, etc.).

[39] 1069a36-b2, cf. Jaeger, *Aristotle*, 220-1. I am concerned only with cases in which Aristotle came to think focal meaning a better explanation of some 'systematic ambiguity' than analogy. I do not imply either (a) that he supposed focal meaning would explain every case of analogy or (b) that where he adopted a focal analysis he consequently rejected the weaker description in terms of analogy as false or improper. 'Analogy' would still be the safest general way of characterising the logic of a word whose senses were interconnected but not confined to one genus, as in *Meta.* 1016b31-1017a3, a chapter of V which also uses focal meaning to analyse 'one' (1016b6-9).

the existence of a class of X-dependent things and one X-thing entails that of another thing that is X.

This neglect of focal meaning is aggravated by an argument that appears only in the version of the polemic that is preserved in *Metaphysics* XIII. There Aristotle suggests, as he does nowhere else, that the Platonists may wish to vary the definition of the predicate so as to distinguish its use when it names the Idea from its use in other contexts (1079b3-11). But the variation he has in mind is merely the incorporation of *ho esti*, 'what [really] is', when the predicate is used of the Idea;[40] and this does not touch hands with focal meaning. It is no more than the warning-index which the *Topics* recommended in such cases (134b10-13, cf. p. 188 above). The absurdities that Aristotle wrings from it here could not have been wrung from the analysis that he is accused of suppressing.

But now perhaps we have the material for a defence. Aristotle, we may argue, was not suppressing that analysis: it is just that his criticisms of the Academy were framed in that earlier period when he habitually worked with the bare dichotomy of synonymy and homonymy. It was not until later, when the heat of the debate was past, that he came to recognise the third possibility and explore it on his own account. And there perhaps the defence might rest – if only there were not evidence that the Academy was already familiar with focal meaning, and that Aristotle must have known this.

We need not turn to the *Lysis* for this counter-evidence. Since Grote's chapter on that dialogue, scholars have hailed its argument for a *prôton philon*, 'primary dear thing', as the source of Aristotle's analysis of friendship in the *Eudemian* and *Nicomachean Ethics*,[41] and the Eudemian version is probably the first and clearest exposition of focal meaning in the Corpus. No doubt
183 Aristotle wrote it with the *Lysis* in mind; but the logical device which is the nerve of the Eudemian argument is not to be found in Plato's dialogue. What Plato says is that things which are loved for the sake of something else are merely *called* dear, and only that for whose sake they are loved is really dear (220a6-b3). But the relationship between these orders of dear things, which Plato expresses by saying that the first are *phila heneka philou*, 'dear on account of something dear', is not logical but psychological; he is concerned, not with a nexus of meanings, but with the valuing of means to an end.[42] Far more damaging to Aristotle, at first sight, are two other texts. The first seems to show that he himself had already made use of focal meaning in developing a substantially Platonic theory; the second implies that the use of that idea in expounding the theory of Forms was common doctrine in the Academy. This is the evidence that makes his neglect of the idea elsewhere look like a piece of eristic, and the stage of logical puritanism that I have pictured seem the result not of innocence but of malice.

[40] Reading with Shorey *ho esti* in 1079b6 for the *hou esti* of MSS (so too Ross, Jaeger).

[41] *Lysis* 218d-220b. Grote, *Plato*^{3} (London 1888), vol. 1, 525 note *a*, followed by Joachim, Jaeger et al.

[42] Esp. 218d-219b. The essential word *heneka*, 'on account of', takes on another sense at 220e4 still further removed from the notion of focal meaning.

The first evidence occurs in Jaeger's reconstruction of the *Protrepticus*.[43] Not only do the familiar extracts from Iamblichus make use of the old notion of natural priority current in the Academy;[44] they are equally at home with the suggestion that a word may have two senses (*dittôs legomenon*) of which one is primary (*kuriôs, alêthôs, proteron*) and the other is defined in terms of the first.[45] And the author bases a major argument on this latter kind of priority. He contends that, even when a word is used in its primary sense of A and in its derivative sense of B, still a comparison can be made between A and B in **184** the very respect that is marked by the ambiguous word. For *mâllon* can signify 'in a stricter sense' as well as 'to a greater degree'; and thus what is good in an absolute sense can be called *more* good than what is so in a relative sense, and what is actually alive (this being the primary sense of the word) more alive than what is potentially so (57, 6-23). Now this claim is contradicted by the more rigorous doctrine of other seemingly early works of Aristotle. More than once he insists that, if one thing can be called more X than another, the predicate must apply to them both in exactly the same sense.[46] And in this contrast the *Protrepticus* seems to show its background, for the convention that what is *really* X is also *superlatively* X is characteristic of Plato.[47] Plato had ignored or exploited the ambiguity in *mâllon*, and when the author of the *Protrepticus* propounds a Platonic *argumentum ex gradibus*, he accordingly seeks to safeguard his argument by recognising the ambiguity but treating it as harmless. Only by minimising it can he go on to argue that the man who is superlatively alive knows that which is superlatively exact and intelligible; for the first superlative and the second correspond to different senses of *malista*. Admittedly, this is an ambiguity which Aristotle himself takes no pains to clear up in some important passages of the *Topics*, [48] and with which he seems to struggle awkwardly at one point in the *Categories* (3b33-4a9). But later in that work, and in the other texts I have just cited, he seems to see its dangers and so to reach his own standards of logical rigour; whereas in the argument

[43] It is not necessary to find Platonic Ideas in the texts Jaeger reclaims from Iamblichus (as I, for one, cannot) in order to feel that the mid-fourth century would be a natural date for the *Protrepticus*. The identity of the recipient and the apparent connexion with the *Antidosis* suggest that the work was a pamphlet designed to invade Isocrates' field of patronage in Cyprus, and a particularly promising time for this would be when Isocrates was embarrassed by the medising of the Evagorids shortly before or during the mid-century anti-Persian revolt in the island (after which Pnytagoras, an Evagorid with a better record than Evagoras II, seems to have kept the throne of Salamis). If Themison represented a pro-Macedonian reaction this would explain the claim of the later Cypriot Themison to the friendship of Antiochus II and the title 'Macedonian' (Athen. 7. 35). It would also, of course, explain Aristotle's connexion with him.

[44] Iamblichus, *Protrepticus* 38.10-14 Pistelli (= Aristotle, fr. 5 W & R).

[45] op.cit. 56.15-57.6 (= Aristotle, fr. 14 W & R).

[46] *Phys.* 249a3-8 (the early seventh book), *Cat.* 11a12-13, cf. *Pol.* 1259b36-8.

[47] Cf. *Top.* 162a26-32. Familiar instances are the equivalence of *ontôs onta*, 'really real', and *mâllon* or *malista onta*, 'more' or 'most real', and such arguments as that in *Republic* IX which proves that the philosophically just man has a life which not only is 729 times more pleasant than that of the unjust man but also contains the only real or most real pleasure (587d12-e4).

[48] Esp. the treatment of topics of 'more or less' in II 10, V 8, and of the comparison of goods in II 1.

preserved by Iamblichus, Aristotle – if he is its author – is still occupied in constructing a logic for theories that were part of his inheritance.[49]

185 So, without querying Jaeger's reconstruction of the text, we could claim that it does nothing to discredit Aristotle. If this were all, his subsequent silence on focal meaning could be excused: its interest for him would be cancelled by second thoughts about the argument he had constructed with it. If a word has a primary and a derivative use then it is ambiguous, and the *Protrepticus* had tried to blink this plain fact. And later, if his analysis of the meaning of such words had been an original contribution to the logic of an old theory, he would surely have the right to file it away with other promising but non-performing ideas, and ignore it in his debate with the Platonists.

But this defence is spoilt by other evidence. The idea was not his to file away. It had already been introduced in defence of the theory of Forms, and his opponents' use of it had been recorded by Aristotle himself. For it is to be found, I think, fully-formed, in the most complex and remarkable of those arguments for the Ideas that Alexander of Aphrodisias has preserved from Aristotle's lost essay on the theory.[50] The argument, according to Alexander, is a sample of those which Aristotle describes in the *Metaphysics* as producing Ideas of *ta pros ti*, relatives (*Meta.* 990b16 = 1079a12). It begins by distinguishing different uses of a predicate such as 'man'. We may say 'That is a man' when pointing to a creature of flesh and blood, or we may say it when pointing to a painting of one. The uses are different, but the difference does not amount to homonymy: for in both cases we are referring to the same *phusis*, 'character' – only in the second case the reference is indirect, and what we now mean by 'a man' is '*a likeness of* a man' (where 'man' in its first sense reappears as one element in the meaning). And then it is argued that whenever we call anything in the physical world 'equal' our use of 'equal' bears the same relation to some primary use of the word as the second use of 'man' bore to the first. The definition of 'equal' in its primary sense (*ison auto*, 'absolutely equal', *ison kuriôs*, 'strictly equal') does not fit any mundane case
186 of equality *akribôs*, without modification: like the definition of 'man' in the portrait-case, it must be supplemented in such secondary uses. (The argument seems to show that, for 'equal', the supplement required is the specification of something *to which* or *in respect of which* the particular mundane equality obtains – a supplement which will vary from case to case, and which is not required in the primary use of the word when, as the argument concludes, it stands for a Form.) In all this there are striking parallels of thought and

[49] But one difficulty deserves notice. It might be suggested (though to my knowledge it has not been) that the baffling reference which Stewart wanted to excise from *EN* VIII 2 ('for [friendship] admits of the more and the less, as do things different in species. We have discussed these matters previously', 1155b14-16) relates to and agrees with the argument in the *Protrepticus*. But Aristotle's 'previously', *emprosthen*, seems always to refer to an earlier context in the same work (cf. Bz. *Index* 244a5-8). It seems impossible to find a wholly apt context in *EN*, though A. may have in mind the general treatment of vices and virtues as constituted by degrees of some feeling or behaviour (so now Dirlmeier).

[50] Alexander, *Meta.* 82.11-83.17. For a fuller discussion of this argument I must refer to 'A Proof in the *Peri Ideôn*', this volume, Chapter 9.

language with Aristotle's own accounts of focal meaning, particularly that which is given in the *Eudemian Ethics*.[51] And, if this is so, it seems to be the damning evidence against him. After this, his insistence that the Idea and its participant are either partners to an ambiguity or parents of an infinite regress must rest on an indefensible suppression of the third possibility propounded by his opponents.

But this picture in turn, I think, is false.

In the first place, we have no evidence whatever to show that focal meaning had been invoked at any stage as a *general* answer to the 'third man'. The academic proof in which we have just found it does not apply to all the types of predicate for which at one time or another the Academy set up Ideas. It neither says nor implies that when any predicate whatever is used of things in this world its use must be analysed in the way in which the proof analyses that of 'equal'; on the contrary, it says that 'man' is used of physical things in its primary as well as its secondary sense, and its reason for denying this of 'equal' is precisely the point in which 'equal' differs from 'man', namely its *relativity*: in the everyday use of the words, nothing on earth can be unqualifiedly equal in the way that Socrates is unqualifiedly a man. This is why in the *Metaphysics* Aristotle distinguishes the sort of proof which produces Ideas of relatives from those which involve the 'third man' (990b15-17 = 1079a11-13). If predicates such as 'man' are to have Ideas, they at least cannot shelter from the regress behind a proof which finds focal meaning in *every* mundane use of the predicate: for no such proof has been given. Accordingly focal meaning plays no part in the other, more general arguments for Ideas that are retailed by Alexander. Aristotle could treat the 'arguments from the sciences', for instance, as proving, not as much as their
authors hoped, but at least the existence of universals (*koina*) in his sense **187**
(Alexander, *Meta.* 79.15-19); and certainly he did not believe that 'man' is to be defined differently when it is used of Socrates and when it names the universal, i.e. the species (*Cat.* 2a19-27, 3a33-b9, *Top.* 122b7-11, 154a15-20). The same considerations explain why, before launching his simple dichotomy of synonymy-or-homonymy against the Ideas, Aristotle takes care to eliminate by an independent (and provokingly obscure) argument all Ideas other than those answering to substance-words, such as 'man' (990b22-991a8). If focal meaning had not been and could not consistently be used as a general asylum from the regress, he can be excused for not casting it in that role.

This explanation of his silence goes some way, but not far enough. For the fact remains that the author of the Academic proof had illustrated focal meaning by analysing a description which applied both to an original and to a portrait; and the relation between original and portrait (or a more generic relation of which this is one species) had been used quite generally by Plato to illustrate the connexion between any Idea and its participant. So the possibility of extending the focal analysis to all predicates and all Ideas must surely have occurred to the Academy, and accordingly should have figured in

[51] cf. 'A Proof,' p. 176 n. 40 above.

Aristotle's polemic. Moreover, if his silence in that context can be explained, how to account for his apparent failure at this time to see any value in the device for his own work? One reason for his refusal to allow the Platonists this general refuge seems clear. He did not think that any commensurately general argument had been given (any argument, that is, that embraced all predicates and not merely relatives) for the proposition that the contents of this world are portraits or copies of other, transcendent entities. Taken in this unrestricted form the theory of Paradigms and Copies seemed to him to rest on the assumption that something worked as a copyist in making the world; and this was not argument, merely metaphor (991a20-3).

But there seems to be another reason why Aristotle's polemic does not take more notice of the device on which his opponents' proof depends; and it is also, and more importantly, a reason why he did not yet see its value for his own work. It is that, to all appearance, he thought the analysis by which the
188 Academic author had introduced and illustrated focal meaning a sheer mistake. The example preoccupied him: over and again in his writings he cites the case of a predicate which is applied both to an original and to a picture or statue; but always – even in works which elsewhere make good use of focal meaning – he cites it simply to illustrate homonymy.[52] His reason for doing so is clear and unvarying. An eye or a doctor, a hand or a flute, is defined by what it does; but an eye or a doctor in a painting cannot see or heal, a stone hand or flute cannot grasp or play. So when they are used in the latter way, 'eye' and the other nouns must be used homonymously. And Aristotle, who allows that ambiguity is a matter of degree (*Phys.* 249a23-5, *EN* 1129a26-31), nowhere suggests that *this* homonymy is redeemed and brought nearer to synonymy by the sensible resemblance which, in his view, forms the sole connexion between the eye or doctor in the painting and its fleshly counterpart. That resemblance, be it noted, is not only the result of conscious imitation but is expressly invoked to define one sense of the predicate on trial: yet that Aristotle meant to reject the Academy's example of focal meaning seems to be confirmed by his own examples. After citing 'healthy' and 'medical', he adds merely that other words which behave in this way could be found (*Meta.* 1003a33-b5); but if he had allowed his opponents' claim he could have referred to an inexhaustible class of predicates – all those, namely, which can be applied to things both in and out of pictures.[53]

Now on the general point at issue Aristotle seems to be right. If focal meaning is to count as a convincing extension of synonymy – if, from his later point of view, it is to carry the weight of argument he lays on it – then it is not a strong enough condition of focal meaning that the bearers of a predicate should exhibit some physical resemblance and that this resemblance should

[52] *PA* 640b29-641a6, *De An.* 412b20-2, *Meteor.* 390a10-13, *GA* 726b22-4, *Pol.* 1253a20-5, and on the conventional interpretation *Cat.* 1a1-6 (but for *zôion gegrammenon*, 'painted animal' cf. *Mem.* 450b21 & 32, *Pol.* 1284b9).

[53] No such claim is implied by *GC* 322b29-32 even if this is read (as e.g. by Fr. J. Owens) as saying that *any* word has a number of senses and is used either homonymously or focally; but Joachim's version is surely correct (*Aristotle on Coming-to-be and Passing Away* (Oxford 1922), 141).

be used to define one sense of the predicate. (Consider the word 'collar'. Among its meanings, according to the Pocket Oxford Dictionary, is **189**
'collar-shaped piece in machines'. But there is no substantial connexion between this and its more familiar meaning. It would be absurd, for instance, to claim that no one could understand the engineer's use of the word without understanding the more familiar use; yet it is a claim analogous to this that Aristotle wants to make in *Metaphysics* IV in respect of 'being' and 'one' and other *pros hen legomena*.[54] Without this the notion of focal meaning would be of small use to him.) But if such resemblance is not a strong enough condition, what is? When Aristotle himself comes to specify the criteria of focal meaning he is at once too narrowly scholastic and too hospitable. He calls for precise definitions which exhibit a particular formal connexion – *logoi ek tôn logôn*,[55] one definition contained in the rest; yet his criterion would admit the Academic example that elsewhere he seems to reject. But this is not, I am sure, the inconsistency of a controversialist. Aristotle has not solved the problem of defining focal meaning fully and exactly so as to give that idea all the philosophical power that he comes to claim for it: he has given only the necessary, not the sufficient, conditions for its use. But there is no reason to think that this problem can have a general answer. Aristotle's evasion of it may come from the conviction that any answer would be artificial, setting boundaries that must be endlessly too wide or too narrow for his changing purposes. The concept of a word as having many senses pointing in many ways to a central sense is a major philosophical achievement; but its scope and power are to be understood by use and not by definition.

To conclude. On the evidence, Aristotle seems to have been unlucky in his early brushes with focal meaning. If the contexts in which we have just seen it are to be assigned to his years in the Academy, he would regard it as an **190**
ill-defined device for which false claims had been made in some Academic arguments, his own and other people's, which on other grounds he had come to reject. The general disregard of it in his criticism of the Platonists was not forensic guile, and the neglect of it in some of his own earlier philosophising was not the price of guile. Perhaps the attack on the Ideas and on any general metaphysics of being encouraged him to treat ambiguity as a matter of black and white. Yet it seems to have been this same debate which gave him the method of analysis that finally freed him from his own objections. It was by suggestion, then, as well as by opposition, that the Academy helped to form the logic of those different inquiries which at different times took on the title of First Philosophy.

[54] To say this is not to confuse priority *tôi logôi*, in definition, with priority *têi gnôsei*, for knowledge. As Ross remarks (*Metaphysics* 161) the first is one form of the second in *Meta.* 1018b30-2 and entails it in 1049b16-17. In *Meta.* IV Aristotle plainly assumes that his focal analysis of 'being' shows that understanding the primary sense of the word is indispensable to understanding the rest. When in VII 1 he distinguishes the two kinds of priority he is not contradicting this but making quite another point (1028a31-b2): substance is said to be 'prior for knowledge' in the sense that the *ti esti* (what is it?) question, *in any category*, is the most informative; when he wants to show that this question has its primary use in the first category he falls back once again on the focal analysis of 'being' (1030a34-b7).

[55] *Meta.* 1077b3-4: on this crabbed text see Ross's note.

11

The Platonism of Aristotle

125 Eight years ago, in a memorable Dawes Hicks Lecture to this Academy,[1] Sir David Ross spoke of Aristotle's development as a philosopher. One theory of that development he singled out as having established itself in the fifty years since it appeared. It was pioneered in this country by Thomas Case and in Germany, with great effect, by Werner Jaeger. It depicts Aristotle, in Sir David's words, as 'gradually emerging from Platonism into a system of his own'. Aristotle's philosophical career began in the twenty years that he spent learning and practising his trade in Plato's Academy, and it ended in the headship of his own school. So it is tempting to picture him first as the devoted partisan, then as arguing his way free of that discipleship.

'Platonism' has become a familiar catchword in references to this theory. Case and Jaeger used it, and I have kept it in my title. Probably my argument will be reported as maintaining that we have been looking for Aristotle's Platonism in some wrong directions and proposing other directions to follow. But a warning is called for at the start. The catchword 'Platonism' will carry no independent weight in the argument. It is too often taken on trust, and too riddled with ambiguity to be trusted. Lest this seems to you either extravagant or truistic let me show its importance for the matter in hand.

Before you and I joined in a systematic search for Platonism in Aristotle – and this is a project far beyond the scope of one lecture – we should, if we knew our business, try to reach some understanding on Plato's own philosophical progress and achievements as well as on what Aristotle took those achievements to be. Then we should have to settle, at least *ambulando*, what kinds of agreement or sympathy with Plato were relevant – whether we were looking for affinities in large programmes as well as in special problems, for instance, in arguments and methods as well as in conclusions. Case and Jaeger both endeavoured to explain what they understood by 'Platonism'.
126 But/curiously little attention seems to have been paid to their answers to the questions I have just sketched. What Jaeger means by 'Platonism' differs at important points from what Case means, and this fact has not been advertised by those who hail them as co-founders of one theory. And what Jaeger means by the word commits him to giving a very odd answer to our questions: it

[1] W.D. Ross, 'The Development of Aristotle's Thought', *Proceedings of the British Academy* 43 (1957), 63-78. Reprinted in *Aristotle and Plato in the Mid-Fourth Century*, ed. I. Düring and G.E.L. Owen (Göteborg 1960); and in *Articles on Aristotle*, I, ed. J. Barnes *et al.* (London 1975).

depends upon a theory of Aristotle's procedure which is both radical to his interpretation and, I think, mistaken. Clearing up the mistake will be a first step towards some positive conclusions. That it has excited so little comment seems largely due to the muffling effect of the blanket-word 'Platonism'.

Aristotle's debts

Aristotle remained a member of Plato's Academy for nearly twenty years. He joined it as a student when he came to Athens about the time of his seventeenth birthday, and when Plato died in the spring of 347 he left the city. Thereafter, according to Jaeger, he gave up his practice of publishing works in which he wrote simply as the philosophical partisan of Plato. Those twenty years were to be the longest time he spent in Athens, and there can be no doubt of their importance either for Aristotle or for Plato himself. For Plato they seem to have been a time of immense activity, in which political disappointments were far outweighed by philosophical achievements. He wrote, *inter alia*, the *Theaetetus* and the *Parmenides*, the *Sophist* and the *Statesman* and the *Philebus*, dialogues in which he showed a new preoccupation with philosophical method and with what his successors classified as problems of logic. These were the years in which logic was born in the Academy; the dialogues must have partly fomented, partly reflected the impulse towards that subject which seized Speusippus and Aristotle and their contemporaries, and sent them seeking criteria for synonymy and homonymy and settling the rules of definition and division. So Jaeger was right to say, at the beginning of his study of the subject, that if we are to understand Aristotle's relationship with Plato it is on this period of the Academy and of its founder's career that we must concentrate.

Yet of those later dialogues, and of the whole context of logical discussion in the Academy which Aristotle records in his *Topics*, Jaeger had disappointingly little to say. During these years, he insisted, Aristotle was a faithful spokesman of Plato's theories. The proof was to be found primarily in fragments of the pupil's writings that could be dated to the last five or six
years/ before Plato died. But the Plato that Jaeger detected behind some of **127**
these fragments was the Plato of the *Phaedo* and the *Symposium* and the *Republic*, dialogues which on Jaeger's own view were already classic when Aristotle reached Athens and already under fire in the Academy long before the fragments in question were written. Some of this fire came from Plato himself, in the *Parmenides* and *Sophist* and *Philebus*; some of it can be heard in Aristotle's handbooks of Academic debate, the *Topics* and *De Sophisticis Elenchis*. Yet in the *Eudemus*, a dialogue which Aristotle wrote after the death of a friend in 354 BC, Jaeger discovered the theory of Forms and the view of personal immortality which had been propounded in the *Phaedo*; and he himself held that neither of these survived without change or challenge in Plato's later writings.

Still worse, Aristotle wrote a dialogue, the *Sophist*, which Jaeger dated to the time of his dependence on Plato and (in default of any direct evidence) held to have been just as faithful in conforming to Plato's dialogue on the same name as the Eudemus was faithful to the *Phaedo*. Yet Plato's *Sophist* contains a powerful attack on the metaphysics of the *Phaedo*.

So this feature of the 'Platonism' that Jaeger discerned in Aristotle's lost works certainly called for comment, namely the hospitable impartiality of his metaphysical borrowings. The problem need not exercise those unitarians who suppose that Plato never changed his mind or conceded an objection. Case may have been one of these, so far as Plato's published writings are concerned, though he held that during Aristotle's membership of the Academy Plato turned to other theories which are not represented in the dialogues. But Jaeger, like most later scholars, was no unitarian. He represented his account of Aristotle's development as an overdue attempt to do for Plato's pupil what had already, and successfully, been done for Plato. So the supposed jackdaw borrowings cried for some explanation.

The explanation that Jaeger found was striking. He divided Aristotle's philosophical theories from his studies in logic and philosophical method, and claimed that in the Academy the second proceeded quite independently of the first. He appealed to fragments of the *Eudemus* to show that Aristotle worked out much of his logic, and in particular his account of substance and the categories, without letting himself recognise that it implied the rejection of important parts of Plato's metaphysics as that had been developed in, for instance, the *Phaedo*. Later, after Plato's death, he was to press this
128 implication at every turn. But/ so long as he was under Plato's spell he was content to take his conclusions from his master's writings and to draw on his own logic merely to provide these with new and sharper arguments.

So the answer to those questions we raised about 'Platonism' is clear and surprising. 'Platonism' becomes a matter not of arguments but of theorems, not of philosophical method but of doctrinal conviction. Aristotle 'was already a master in the realms of method and logical technique at a time when he was still completely dependent on Plato in metaphysics'; and Jaeger concludes that 'this dependence was obviously rooted in the depths of Aristotle's unreasoned religious and personal feelings'.

If this were true it would explain more than Aristotle's supposed readiness at this time to draw doctrine from any part of Plato's work. It would certainly explain that; for 'unreasoned religious and personal feelings' can accommodate a good deal of inconsistency, so long as they are not made answerable to 'method and logical technique'. But it would also explain the relative neglect of Aristotle's logic in Jaeger's impressive sketch of his philosophical progress. Thomas Case could appeal to Plato's analysis of true and false statements in the *Sophist* in order to explain the 'Platonism' of some of Aristotle's early moves in logic. But here his difference from Jaeger is fundamental. For Jaeger the Platonism is not to be sought in the logic.

At the same time Jaeger's explanation put a premium on a certain method of interpretation, a method to which Jaeger himself allowed little force when he turned to Aristotle's extant works. If doctrines are to be removed from their parent arguments and taken for independent agents, they need other means of identification. The readiest method then of picking them out in other philosophical contexts is by the occurrence of particular idioms and turns of phrase which accompanied their appearance in the original, canonical, context. This popular device is exploded by Aristotle's own writings. There is a set of idioms in which he is accustomed to portray Plato's theories, and when he does so he is liable to denounce the idioms as vacuous or misleading. They include the expressions 'idea', 'paradigm', 'participation', 'the one beside the many'. But elsewhere in his work they turn up, clean and ready for use, where the context shows that they carry no reference to the rejected theories.[2]

This preamble may serve to show that the word 'Platonism'/ is not to be **129**
taken without scrutiny as a key on the interpreter's ring. But it leads to a more substantial point. The divorce that Jaeger thought he had made out between the logical and metaphysical partners in Aristotle's early philosophising was fictitious. There is no good evidence for it, and strong evidence against it. And the evidence against it is positive support for the different approach that I shall sketch later. Let us start at the negative pole of this argument.

Categories and Forms in the Eudemus

The topic of Aristotle's lost dialogue, the *Eudemus*, was the immortality of the soul. It was not one of those dialogues in which Aristotle is reported to have introduced himself as a speaker, so some scholars have urged that we cannot be sure whether a given view derived from the work would have been endorsed by its author. But the argument with which we are concerned does not call for this scepticism. It can safely be credited to Aristotle, not because it reinforces an argument in Plato's *Phaedo* but because in his later work *De Anima* Aristotle is still attacking the same theory against which our argument is levelled.

The theory under attack is that the soul, the principle of life, is nothing but a 'harmony', that is to say a proper co-ordination of elements in the body. When the co-ordination breaks down the life and therefore the soul is at an end. In the *Eudemus* Aristotle is said to have countered this by saying: 'Harmony has a contrary, disharmony. But soul has no contrary. So the soul is not a harmony' (fr.7, Ross; Philoponus, *In De An.* 144. 22-5). Another authority fills out the arguments: 'Soul has no contrary, *because it is a substance*' (fr.7, Ross; Olympiodorus, *In Phaed.* 173. 20-3). This expansion is one of the pivots on which Jaeger's interpretation turns. He recognises that it is almost certainly a gratuity from the commentator, Olympiodorus, who puts similar stuffing into other Aristotelian and Platonic arguments in the same context. But in this case Jaeger thinks that the expansion merely brings out an implication that was present though tacit in the original. For if Aristotle said

[2] 'Idea', Bonitz, *Index Arist.* 338b34-48; 'paradigm', *Phys.* 194b26, *Meta.* 1013a27, *Top.* 151b20-1; 'participate', Bonitz, op.cit., 462b36-43; 'one beside the many', *A.Pst.* 100a6-9, Alexander, *In Meta.* 79, 16-17.

that soul has no contrary he must have had in mind the proposition which appears in the *Categories*, that substance has no contrary. White has a contrary, black; in Aristotle's account of the categories this is enough to prove that white and black are not substances. They are qualities, or species of
130 quality. Man is a species of/ substance, and there is no logical contrary to man. So, if Aristotle's argument in the *Eudemus* presupposes that the soul is a substance, it presupposes the analysis of substances *vis-à-vis* other categories that is proprietary to Aristotle's logic.

But now for the other arm of Jaeger's interpretation. In the *Phaedo*, and again in the fifth book of the *Republic*, Plato had proposed his own candidates for the title of *substance* or *ousia*, namely the Forms. In the *Phaedo* he gives as examples of such Forms the Equal, the Beautiful, the Good, the Just, the Greater, the Less. All of these have contraries, and in the *Republic* he expressly argues to the unity of a Form from its having a contrary, and seems to say that the same argument holds good of all Forms (*Phd.* 75c; *Rep.* 475e-476a). So these Forms cannot satisfy Aristotle's definition of a substance. Nor does Aristotle think that Plato is using the word 'substance' simply in a different sense from his own: he consistently reproves Plato for putting up candidates for the status of substance which fail to meet the basic requirements for that grade. So it is unsettling to find Jaeger arguing, as the other limb of his account of the *Eudemus*, that in that dialogue Aristotle accepted the theory of Forms as it had been formulated in the *Phaedo*. It is by combining these two theses that he is able to conclude that at this time Aristotle was wholly dependent on Plato for his metaphysics but quite independent of him in his logic, namely in his theory of categories. He does not seek to palliate, nor even expressly recognise, the paradox that in Aristotle's view this would commit him to accepting a class of substances which is expressly debarred by the logic he deploys. For my part I find this degree of philosophical *akrasia* incredible.

Fortunately, we need not believe it. Neither arm of Jaeger's interpretation holds firm. That the doctrine of the *Categories* had been worked out during Aristotle's years in the Academy seems to me certain, and I shall try to show how it came about. But given that doctrine, there is no inference from the statement that the soul has no contrary to the presupposition that the soul is a substance in Aristotle's sense. For the *Categories* lays it down that the lack of a contrary is characteristic not only of substances but of the members of various other categories: all quantities, some qualities, some relatives. The argument works very well as it stands: it operates by a simple appeal to a distinction in current usage, and this is wholly appropriate to the form of dialogue that Aristotle is writing: possibly a piece of consolation literature, certainly not a systematic treatise./

131 It remains a question whether, and if so in what sense, the soul was argued to be a substance in the *Eudemus*. Evidently Aristotle wrote the work with the *Phaedo* in mind: part of the discussion was concerned with the possibility of the soul's existence before and after its incarceration in the body, a possibility for which his mature psychology leaves no room. On the other hand, part of the discussion is said by Simplicius to have depicted the soul as a 'form' (*eidos ti*), a use of the word which is familiar enough in the mature psychology but

makes small sense within the Platonic theory of Forms.[3] In brief, the evidence is too equivocal to saddle Aristotle himself at this date with a theory that the soul is a separate substance transiently and painfully housed in a body; and even if it were not, it would not commit him, as Jaeger claims in the second arm of his interpretation, to postulating Plato's transcendent Forms for the disembodied soul to contemplate. Jaeger himself allows that the lost dialogue 'On Philosophy' seems to have given a sympathetic hearing to the first theory but rejected the second, and it would be natural for Aristotle to hold them apart: the immortality of the soul was a matter of tradition, the theory of Forms a philosopher's invention. When Aristotle discusses the views of 'the many and the wise', it is the second party that gets the shorter shrift.

What evidence then is there that the Forms of the *Phaedo* still haunt the *Eudemus*? There is a mythological description of the soul's passage from Hades, in which the soul is said to forget 'the sights yonder',[4] but comparison of other texts from the same source shows that these 'sights' were probably not the desiderated Forms but merely Styx and Lethe and the conventional paraphernalia of the underworld. What part this and other myths played in the dialogue we cannot tell, but plainly they are not to be confused with metaphysical argument. Nor again can Aristotle's beliefs be deduced from a report discovered in the Arabian philosopher al-Kindi, to the effect that Aristotle discussed an anecdote in which the soul of a Greek king departed to contemplate 'souls, forms and angels'.[5] The myth of Plato's *Phaedrus* must stand behind the anecdote, but what use Aristotle made of the myth is not on record.

I shall not pursue this hunt for the Platonic Forms into the fragments of
Aristotle's *Protrepticus*, where Jaeger thought to find/ them. The fragments **132**
have been well beaten in recent years, and the quarry was not there. What evidence remains? Aristotle set up to teach rhetoric in the Academy in rivalry to Isocrates. Worse, he seems to have tried to capture some of Isocrates' own field of political patronage in Cyprus. Henceforth he was a fair target for Isocrates' school. A historian of the fourth century AD records that one of Isocrates' pupils wrote against Aristotle and remarks, with astonishment, that Aristotle was attacked as representative of Plato's best-known theories and in particular of the theory of Forms. But the more we learn of the conventions of ancient rhetoric the less weight there seems to be in this evidence. It is matched by the polemic of another contemporary, Euboulides, in which Aristotle was accused of destroying his master's writings and being absent at his master's death;[6] these charges too seem to have been first levelled at Plato and then ritually transferred to his pupil, much as in comedy and public and forensic oratory the misdemeanours of the parent or patron were visited

[3] fr.8, Ross; Simplicius *In De An.* 221. 28-30; cf. *Meta.* 1077a32-3 and H. Cherniss, *Aristotle's Criticism of Plato and The Academy* (Baltimore 1944), 506-12.

[4] fr.5, Ross; Procl. *In Remp.* ii, 349, 13-26; fr.4 in context, Procl. *In Tim.* 323. 16-44.

[5] fr.11, Ross; cf. *Select Fragments*, trans. Ross, p.23.

[6] See I. Düring, *Aristotle in the Ancient Biographical Tradition* (Göteborg 1957), 374.

on the dependent.[7] Such a polemic is not even evidence that the polemicist did not know Aristotle's own views, though in itself this is likely enough.

Still it may be felt that philosophical piety would be the natural posture for Plato's pupils and associates, at least during the great man's lifetime. We know that it was not; the best of the others, Eudoxus and Speusippus, challenged and tried to reform the theory of Ideas. Nor would simple acquiescence be encouraged by those later dialogues in which Plato subjected his own earlier metaphysics to an unsentimental appraisal. The debates charted in Aristotle's *Topics* are enough to prove that his criticisms of Plato would not estrange him from the rest of that argumentative school. More positively, it can be shown that Aristotle's own account of substance and the categories, so far from being the autonomous growth required by Jaeger, was born and bred in these controversies of the Academy. So far from seeming reconcilable with the theory of Forms it presupposed and was evolved from a celebrated criticism of that theory.

Before turning to this point it may be worth while entering two disclaimers. First, there are of course many signs of Plato's influence to be found in Aristotle's early works, including the fragments of his lost writings, other than the putative signs I have been questioning. To some of these I have called attention elsewhere; others, notably in Aristotle's cosmology, have
133 often/been discussed.[8] Nothing in my argument makes against the importance of detecting and exploiting these clues in interpreting Aristotle. I have been concerned only with one, the most celebrated and influential, account of Aristotle's 'Platonism', and with a curious thesis on which that account turns. And I have been questioning this not from the joy of battle but because, as I shall try to show, it obstructs the use of genuine clues to Aristotle's philosophical progress.

Next, in saying that Aristotle's logic was bred of discussion in the Academy, I do not imply that it was a donation from his colleagues. There used to be a myth, promoted by Burnet and Taylor, that the theory of categories was a commonplace of the Academy, derived from scattered hints in Plato's writings. This myth was exposed, not simply by the obvious lack of system in the supposed hints, but by the fact that no other Academic known to us endorsed the theory and that Xenocrates, Plato's self-appointed exegete, denounced it as a pointless elaboration and went back to a simpler distinction derived from Plato's dialogues. Nor again do I mean that Aristotle's logic had come to full maturity before Plato's death. The division of the categories, and probably the general theory of the syllogism, had been worked out by then; but Aristotle continued to review and develop these doctrines in his later work. The same is true of his theory of definition and, more generally, his theory of meaning. What is beyond question is that these theories were developed in practice and not as an independent exercise. The theory of definition was modified to keep pace with the work of a biologist who had

[7] See W. Süss, *Ethos* (1910), 247-54.

[8] Recently by F. Solmsen, *Aristotle's System of the Physical World* (Ithaca 1960); I. Düring, 'Aristotle and the heritage from Plato', *Eranos* 62 (1964).

once held that a definition could be reduced to a single differentia and then found himself, when he set out to define any natural species, faced with a set of competing criteria. The theory of meaning, of synonymy and homonymy, was enlarged to allow a value to philosophical inquiries which had been earlier denounced as trading on an equivocation. At every stage Aristotle's logic had its roots in philosophical argument and scientific procedure: it would be an anachronism to think otherwise. So what arguments lie at the root of his early account of substance and the categories?

Substance and the criticism of the Forms

Aristotle brings a great variety of arguments against the theory of Forms, and the variety reflects the faces and phases of/ that theory as well as Aristotle's **134**
shifting interest in it. But the objection to which he recurs most often is that which the Academy dubbed 'the Third Man'. It makes an ambiguous appearance in Plato's *Parmenides*, and it was set out schematically in Aristotle's early essay *On Ideas*.[9] It is the argument behind Aristotle's stock complaint that when Plato invented his Forms he made a mistake about predicates: he took any predicate-expression to stand for some individual thing instead of for some sort of thing (e.g. *SE* 178b36-179a10; *Meta.* 1038b34-1039a3). Thereby, Aristotle held, he committed two faults: he failed to explain how we use predicates to classify and describe actual individuals, and he cluttered the scene with other individuals which were fictions.

Here it is important to be clear on Aristotle's use of 'predicate' and 'predication'. If I say 'Socrates is old' or 'Socrates is a man', what I predicate of Socrates is not old age or manhood but simply *old* or *man* – or, in English, *a man*. Its linguistic expression must be an appropriate filling for 'Socrates is ... (or is a ... or is a kind of ...)'. Greek lacked, what English enjoys, an indefinite article; and Greek philosophers had not come to see the cardinal importance of quotation marks, or of the clumsier devices that served for such marks. But though this sometimes clouds the interpretation of what Aristotle says about predicates it does not blunt the point of his objection to Plato.

The point is this. Plato is accused of misconstruing the logic of such a statement as 'Socrates is a man' by making two incompatible assumptions about it. He thinks (*a*) that what is predicated, in this case *man* (not the expression but what it stands for), is always something different from the subjects of which it is predicated; for if it were identical with its subjects these would become identical with each other. Plato is a man, Socrates is a man: if these statements have the form of '$a = c, b = c$', a will be b and Plato will be Socrates. But also Plato thinks (*b*) that what is predicated is itself a subject of that same predicate; for it seems undeniable even if truistic that *man is man* or *a man is a man*. We can borrow the indefinite article and recast the point. Plato had said: 'When I call *A* a man and *B* a man, what does this common label

[9] *Parm.* 131e-2b (the argument in 132c-133a with which later writers conflated it is a different objection); *De Ideis* fr.4, Ross; Alexander *In Meta.* 84. 21-85, 12.

"a man" stand for? Not for the individual subject I apply it to, else it would stand indifferently for any such subject; but *A* and *B* cannot both be the
135 single common thing we are after. So/ "a man" stands for some third thing.' But then, it is objected, *ex hypothesi* this third thing is *a man*. And thus we have three men where we began with two, and by similar manipulations we can generate a fourth and fifth *ad infinitum*.

The two premisses (*a*) and (*b*) set out by Aristotle were recently rediscovered and entitled the Non-identity Assumption and the Self-predication Assumption. I am not now concerned with the fairness of the objection that Aristotle bases on them, only with the moves by which he constructs a theory of predication that is immune to the paradox. There is a familiar and somewhat reach-me-down diagnosis of the Third Man regress, to the effect that it showed the error of construing every predicative statement as relational – of analysing 'Socrates is a man' as mentioning two objects and reporting some relation between them. Plato had said: 'There is Socrates, and there is Man, and we have to determine the connection between them: participation, resemblance, or whatever'. No doubt Aristotle has seen something of this when he accuses Plato of taking the predicate-expression to signify a 'this' instead of a 'such-and-such', an individual instead of a sort or kind. But for two reasons he could not propound this as a final diagnosis. One is that he is scarcely clearer than Plato on the nature of relations. He has no words for 'relation' in the modern sense, and his nearest approach to the idea is in fact a survey of incomplete or relative predicates such as *father, slave, bigger* (as in *Cat.*7; *Meta.* V 15). The second and more important reason is that he came to think his first short reply – that what is predicated of an individual is not another individual – as much of an over-simplification as the theory it was meant to rebut. His own positive account of the matter, and therewith his first move towards a new theory of predication and the categories, came when he considered which of the two premisses of the regress must be given up, and characteristically refused to give one general answer. For the question assumes that one account will hold good of all predicates, and Aristotle tried to show that this was false.

He countered it by drawing a sharp contrast between two sorts of predicate. One sort is represented by 'man', the other by 'white': these remained his favourite illustrations. 'Man', he points out, is used in the same sense whether we use it to describe Socrates or to speak of the kind or species under which Socrates falls. For suppose we ask what man is: the answer to this general
136 question (say, 'a featherless biped') will be equally applicable to/ the particular man Socrates. But with 'white' it is different. To say that Socrates is white is to say that he is coloured in a certain way; but if we go on to ask what white is, we shall have to say, not that white is coloured in a certain way, but that white is a certain colour. In the *Categories* Aristotle puts this contrast by saying that when we use 'white' to describe someone or something we cannot predicate of our subject the *definition* of white; we can predicate only the word 'white'. But when we call someone 'a man' we can go on to predicate of our subject the definition of man (2a19-34). Elsewhere he puts it by saying that a man cannot be *what white is* (e.g. *A.Pst.* 83a28-30;

Meta. 1007a32-3).

With the Third Man in view the moral of this is obvious. There is one sort of predication that does not seem to imply the Self-predication Assumption: white is not white in the sense in which Socrates is white. But there is another sort, represented by the predication of *man,* which for convenience I shall call 'strong predication'; and this sort does seem to imply this Assumption.

If this is so we can expect Aristotle to tolerate the Non-identity Assumption in the first case but to repudiate it, on pain of a regress, in the second. And this he does: not indeed in the early *Categories*, which resorts to an older way of disarming strong predication, but in other works which build on the *Categories*. The first sort of predication, he says, is one in which the subject is something *different from* the attributes ascribed to it ('one thing is said of another', 'it is something different [from white] which is white' etc.). But the second is one in which there is no such difference: *man* is just what Socrates is. 'Man' and 'white' remain his stock examples (*A.Pst.* 83a24-32; *Meta.* 1030a3-5, 11).

The *Categories* is at an early and interesting stage of these ponderings on the Third Man. It has seized the difference between the two sorts of predicate, but it has not yet swallowed all the implications. It is still at the stage of disarming strong predication by the old plea that 'man' does not stand for any individual thing. So it can still speak of such a predicate-expression as standing for something different from its subject (3b10-19, 1b10). And thereby it avoids the embarrassments into which Aristotle is later due to fall when he decides to reject the Non-identity Assumption outright in such predications. Some of the perplexities of *Metaphysics* VII stem from this rejection: for it leads him to argue that, if we take any primary subject of discourse and say just what it is, we must be producing a statement of/
identity, an equation which defines the subject. And this in turn helps to **137**
persuade him that the primary subjects of discourse cannot be individuals such as Socrates, who cannot be defined, but species such as man.[10] In the *Categories*, on the other hand, the primary subjects are still the individual horse or man or tree. Aristotle seems at this early stage to be much more hostile than he later becomes to Plato's treatment of the species as a basic and independent subject of discourse. So it becomes tempting to think of this element in *Metaphysics* VII as a return to, or a renewal of sympathy with, Plato. Perhaps it is, but it is the outcome of pressing a powerful objection to Plato's theories. It is a philosophical position, hard-won and (as Aristotle insists) hard-beset. If this is Platonism there is nothing of pious discipleship in it.

To return to our division of predicates. We have already enough evidence to prove that Aristotle's criticism of Plato led him to draw some distinctions in his account of predication. It is not yet enough to prove that that criticism lay at the root of his theory of predication and the categories. If Aristotle had

[10] That this is one thesis that Aristotle takes seriously in *Meta.* VII needs no arguing: it is already afoot when 1030a6-14 is read with VII 6. How much of it survives the argument of the later chapters is another matter.

left his contrast here it would have remained both parochial and perplexing. Its importance came from his use of it to make a far more radical distinction. Namely, it enabled him to divide all the predicates of any individual into two groups: those which hold good essentially or *per se* of their subject, as *man* does of Socrates; and those which merely happen to be true of their subject, as *white* does of Socrates. What Socrates happens to be is what he could also cease to be without ceasing to exist: after such descriptions of the subject it makes sense, even if it is false, to add 'but only sometimes' (*Top.* 102b4-26; cf. *A.Pst.* I 22, *Meta.* V 30 and VI 2). But it would be absurd to say that Socrates merely happened to be a man. If Socrates were still in existence it would be the same man in existence, whatever had happened to his colour or shape. So *man* is the kind of predicate that shows what the individual is, whereas to call Socrates 'white' is (as Aristotle can finally put it, after reflecting on the Third Man) to introduce something different from the subject, a colour that happens to belong to or be found in Socrates (as in the stock descriptions of accidental predication, 'one thing is said of another', 'it is something different [from *F*] which is *F*' etc.).

Now notice one consequence of drawing the contrast in this way. We have
138 given pride of place to the *noun* 'white' over the/adjective, and this primacy of the noun was engineered by stressing the question *what white is*. The same result follows when the noun and the adjective differ in verbal form: it is 'brave' that is derived by change of inflection from 'bravery' and not vice versa, according to Aristotle in the *Categories* (1a11-15), for to say '*X* is brave' is to invite the question what bravery is; and thus again the situation comes to be represented as the presence of bravery in *X*. But with 'man', Aristotle says, it is different. Yet why not perform the reduction here too? Granted, as Aristotle points out, we cannot say 'there is man (or a man) in Socrates' as we can say 'there is bravery in Socrates'. But – shelving other objections to this curious test of status – why not coin one more abstract noun, say 'humanness' (since 'humanity' and 'manhood' have been pre-empted for other jobs), and let this replace 'man' in the first sentence? Why not 'there is humanness in Socrates'? And then, for all this criterion shows, being a man will be just as much something that merely happens to be true of Socrates as being brave or white. All alike will be attributes present in a Socrates who remains *ex hypothesi* different from them all.

It is not hard to piece together Aristotle's answer. It is no accident that there are predicates like *man* which form no abstract noun in current use. Not all predicate-expressions can be analysed as introducing attributes which are merely present in some individual; for there must be an identifiable individual to possess or contain them, i.e. a subject identifiable on different occasions as the same *so-and-so*, as Socrates is identifiable as the same *man*. To say baldly that something is 'the same' is, in Aristotle's view, to say something that either has no determinate sense or else requires different interpretation for different sorts of subject. So the distinction holds firm between what the individual is, as a matter of strong predication, and what else may turn up as an attribute in the individual.

Now it is notoriously this distinction that Aristotle takes as the basis of the

general theory set out in his *Categories*. Reflection on the Third Man had thrown up two morals. One was that to say 'Socrates is a man' is to mention one individual and not two. But this would remain nebulous until more light was thrown on the idea of an individual. So Aristotle asked: What is it to distinguish a particular *X* from *X*-in-general? Can one answer to this be found to cover all values of *X*, particular virtues or times or places as well as particular men? In the *Categories* he tackled these questions by applying the second moral derived from the/ Third Man, the distinction we have just **139**
made out between what can be said of the individual as a matter of strong predication and what attributes may turn up in the individual.

By manipulating the first arm of the distinction Aristotle contrives to distinguish individuals from the species and genera under which they fall; in strong predication the predicate-expression never introduces an individual, always a species or genus. And then by using the second arm he is able to cross-divide these partitions so as to mark off substances from non-substances. A substance can never turn up as an attribute in some other subject in the way that, for instance, a colour or a virtue does. Meditation on the Third Man has borne fruit. And the anti-Platonic provenance of the whole account is further certified by the examples that Aristotle gives of substance in the 'strictest, primary sense': mutable things such as a man or a horse, able to house contrary attributes at different times, but never identical with the contraries they house. The substance itself – the mutable man, or horse, or tree – has no contrary. When Jaeger borrowed this proposition from the doctrine of the *Categories* he was drawing upon a logical system that could not have been constructed before Aristotle had rejected the classical theory of Forms.[11]

This is enough to upset our confidence in the 'Platonism' postulated by Jaeger. But in lifting us off a false trail it puts us upon a true one. Aristotle's philosophical relationship to Plato had better be plotted, not by cutting off his studies of logic and method from his philosophical and scientific thinking, but by watching the interplay of the two in the Academy. So let us take Aristotle back again to his seventeenth birthday and ask: what philosophical interests, and what associated methods, could a new student expect to find in the Academy if he joined it in 367? To this the dialogues of Plato's middle period, together with the evidence of Aristotle and his pupils, give a sufficiently clear answer.

The Academy: the autonomy of the sciences

Briefly, the student could expect to find two major and conflicting interests at work. Plato had professed to reconcile them,/ and the nerve of Aristotle's **140**

[11] Jaeger himself held that the *Categories* in its present form is not an early work by Aristotle, but he took its doctrines to be both early and Aristotelian. His reasons for doubting the authenticity and earliness of the work (or at least its first nine chapters) were weak (*Aristotle*², tr. R. Robinson (Oxford 1948), 46 n.3).

early work is his exposure of the conflict.

In the first place the Academy housed a great deal of activity in exact science which played no part in, for instance, the rival school of Isocrates. Greek mathematics had made huge progress since its beginnings in the sixth century. Arithmetic, impeded by a clumsy notation and bewildered by the discovery of irrationals, was becalmed; but geometry flourished. Already in the three-quarters of a century before the founding of the Academy so many theorems had been (at least notionally) proved that it became a question how to connect them in a family tree – that is, how to axiomatise the science by isolating the fewest independent assumptions from which these and further discoveries could be validly derived. This project held the attention of Plato and the Academy and issued in more than one handbook of mathematical 'elements'. Two generations later Euclid is said to have built his own canonical system of Elements on the work done in Plato's circle. Here Aristotle would meet the principal mathematicians of the day, resident or visiting; and there is some thin evidence, often quoted, that the best of them, Eudoxus, was deputising for Plato when Aristotle arrived.

So when in the first book of the *Posterior Analytics* Aristotle sets out what he takes to be the general logical structure of a science it is naturally to mathematics and especially to geometry that he looks for his model. His picture of a systematic science probably belongs to his Academic years or shortly after, and its debt to mathematics is a commonplace; but the debt is general and not particular. It is in devising and adapting the details that he shows his hand.

Thus it is mathematics that provides him with the expository (or what he often calls 'didactic') form in which the science is to be cast. In nearly all the surviving productions of Greek mathematics traces of the workshop have been systematically removed; proofs are found for theorems which were certainly first reached by other routes. It is mathematics too that shows him the anatomy of such a science: knowledge is demonstrable, save when it is of the sort presupposed by all demonstration, and demonstration calls for an axiomatic system in which theorems are derived by valid forms of argument from principles basic to the science. It may have been mathematics that gave him his division of these principles into hypotheses, definitions, and general rules of inference. But it is when he goes beyond his mathematical brief,
141 setting himself to analyse the logical form of the proofs and the/ nature and derivation of their ultimate premisses, that the philosophical interest of his account begins. The theory of syllogistic argument is his own, and he has obvious difficulty in fitting a mathematical proof into this form (*A.Pr.*48a29-39). His long discussions of definition in the second book of the *Posterior Analytics* are designed partly to show how the mathematical model is to be adapted to the procedures and explanations of natural science (cf. e.g. *A.Pst.*94b8-95a9 with *Meta.* 996a21-b1).

Indeed if one considers the influence of the mathematical model on his other writings it is this remaking of the ingredients that seems to matter, far more than the general recipe for a science. The recipe plays small part in his scientific and philosophical inquiries just because it is not a model for inquiry at all but for subsequent exposition of the results of inquiry. Nevertheless there remains one point at which the influence of the favoured science on Aristotle's philosophising was radically important.

The drive to axiomatise mathematics and its branches had one implication which Aristotle seems to have pressed far harder than his contemporaries: it was a drive for autonomy. The domestic economy of one field of knowledge was to be settled by fixing its frontiers. The premisses of the science were to determine what questions fell within the mathematician's competence and, not less importantly, what questions did not. Thus a cardinal section of *Posterior Analytics* I is given up to the problem of what questions can be properly put to the practitioner of such-and-such a science. Other parts of the work, trading on the rule that one science studies one class of objects, denounce arguments which poach outside their own field – which try, for instance, to deduce geometrical conclusions from arithmetical premisses. Even when an axiom is applied in both arithmetic and geometry the formula has a different use in each science: the analogy between them may be recognised, but for Aristotle 'analogy' is compatible with the formula's retaining not even the most generic identity of sense. He allows that sometimes one science may take over and apply the arguments of another; but these are the exceptions. The impulse throughout the first book of the *Posterior Analytics* is towards establishing what he later calls 'exact and self-sufficient sciences' (*EN* 1112a34-b1).

It is the same impulse that leads him to map the field of knowledge into its departments and sub-departments.[12] Such/mapwork was not his prerogative **142**
in the Academy; Plato among others took a hand in it, as an exercise in generic division. But for Aristotle the rationale was supplied by the hard-won independence of the axiomatic system; and this ran quite counter to Plato's interests and apparently to those of his contemporaries, including Speusippus (cf. Diog. Laert. 4.2, but the sense of this remains uncertain). When in the *Posterior Analytics* Aristotle presses for 'universality' in the theses of a science he means just that *within the given science* the premisses should have a given form: the subjects should be classes and not individuals, and the predicates should hold true necessarily of all and only the members of the subject class (73b25-74a3). Plato had tried to engage his colleagues in a very different search for universality. The second strand that we have to trace in Aristotle's early philosophising is his rejection of this attempt.

The Academy: dialectic

Under Plato mathematics could not be the sole or even the primary concern

[12] Even in the well-known fr.5*a* of the *Protrepticus*, or rather in that version of the fragment which E. de Strycker proved to contain the original argument (in *Aristotle and Plato in the Mid-Fourth Century*, 76-104), what is remarkable is not so much the parallel which Aristotle sets up between an ethical and a physical argument as the care with which he distinguishes the two and assigns them to separate sciences.

of the Academy. The *Republic* had argued for a grounding in the exact sciences as a valuable propaedeutic to philosophical inquiries, valuable because philosophy deals chiefly with a world of Forms which is not the physical world, and the numbers and exact figures and angles treated in mathematics are themselves evidently not physical objects but part of the furniture of the non-physical world explored by philosophers. But, though valuable, the mathematical sciences were not in Plato's view the highest form of inquiry; and his prime reason for demoting them is just the drive for independence which so impressed Aristotle. Mathematicians, Plato complains, argue from hypotheses which they do not step back to explain or justify. But, he goes on, there is one form of inquiry which is designed to examine people's assumptions, in mathematics or in morals or wherever: the inquiry or family of inquiries that Plato calls 'dialectic'. This alone is qualified to play governess to all the departmental sciences and to aim, by contrast with them, at a synoptic account of reality. Earlier, in the *Euthydemus*, Plato had claimed that any mathematician in his senses would hand over/
143 his discoveries to the dialectician to use; later, in the *Philebus*, 'dialectic' is still the name of a master-science which takes precedence in 'truth and exactness' over mathematical studies. A student as impressed as Aristotle by the mathematicians' drive for autonomy would have to take a stand on these issues. He would hardly be put off by the solemn recommendation in the *Republic* that young men under thirty should not be taught dialectic. Whether or not the Academy offered him any training in the subject there was enough evidence at hand to show what Plato had meant by dialectic, enough written evidence on which to assess his claims. So what, on the evidence, would these claims come to?

Dialectic at its simplest is what Socrates and other speakers do most of the time in Plato's earlier dialogues. Someone asks, 'What is courage?' or, 'Can we be taught to be good?' And various answers are tried out and either brought to grief by Socratic arguments or else, supposing they can be defended from the inquisition, accepted at least provisionally as true. The propositions handled in the argument are the stock material of philosophical discussion, generally matters of common conviction or usage, sometimes the minority views of intellectuals. Aristotle in his own account of dialectic calls them 'things accepted by all men or by the majority or by the wise'.

With time, as Plato becomes more self-conscious over his methods, the devices at the speaker's command become more sophisticated. The objections turn decreasingly on trapping an opponent into self-contradiction, increasingly on serious paradoxes of the sort developed in the *Parmenides*, *Theaetetus*, and *Sophist*. There is a new insistence on the risks of over-simplification. The old Socratic hunt for the unitary definition of some general idea gives way to the attempt, reinforced by the use of generic division, to show that such an idea embraces a family of specifically different and sometimes contrary ideas. In the *Theaetetus* Socrates is still insisting as strongly as he had in the *Meno* on seizing some highly generic concept, such as knowledge or virtue, in a single definition, discounting the various forms that knowledge or virtue can take. Later, in the *Philebus*, he warns his

interlocutor against generalising irresponsibly about pleasure or wisdom before he has meticulously listed and compared the varieties of both. And the same insistence on considering all the possibilities bearing on a topic produces the recommendation in the *Parmenides* to work out the implications of denying as well as of asserting a hypothesis, and to work them/ out for other things as **144**
well as for the formal subject of the hypothesis. Significantly, Parmenides addresses his recommendation to the young Socrates, who had been dashing into the business of defining Goodness and Beauty and Justice without any adequate training for the job. The faults of over-simplification against which Plato is now producing his safeguards are the faults of Socrates in the earlier dialogues. It is Socrates, or Plato the Socratic, who had generalised hastily from a few favoured instances, Socrates whose trust in the telling counter-example has led him to trust the would-be telling example. Now Plato is taking precautions.

Many of these safeguards were introduced in dialogues which appeared during Aristotle's years in the Academy. All reappear in his own dialectical exercises. The impulse behind them is central in his own thinking: his standard complaint against other philosophers is that they over-simplify. Like Plato, they rely on one model of predication to explain predicates of very different types. Or they fail to realise that the same state of affairs can usually be explained in many different ways (Aristotle reduces them to four). Or they try, like Plato's Socrates, to manufacture a single definition for an expression that can be shown to have many senses: we shall come to an important example of this shortly. So it is tempting to suggest that here, at least, and in another sense than Jaeger's, Aristotle shows himself a Platonist. The methods which come to bulk large in Plato's later dialogues are Aristotle's methods. But in the circumstances we are not entitled to this claim. What may be part of the Platonism of Aristotle may equally be part of the Aristotelianism of Plato.

In any event Aristotle accepts dialectic on these terms and codifies its procedures in the *Topics*, not merely as a device for intellectual training or casual debate but as essential equipment in constructing the sciences. Yet, as he insists, the material of dialectic remains common convictions and common usage, not the self-evident truths which his admiration of mathematics persuades him are characteristic of science. Nor are the methods of dialectic confined to systematic deduction. So how could Plato claim more certainty and exactness for such discussions than for geometry? In outline the reply seemed clear, though the detail varied with time. Dialectic took its authority from its proprietary connection with the Forms. Its successes were neither arbitrary nor confined to corrigible personal agreement because it was the sole method competent to identify and map those/ stable realities of which **145**
Plato in his middle dialogues had argued the physical world to house only deceptive reflections.

So when Aristotle came to the Academy there would seem to be two principal strands in Plato's large claims for dialectic. One was the thesis that above the special sciences struggling for autonomy there stands a quite general survey of what there is, a master-science without whose authorisation the work of the rest is provisional and insecure. The other was the theory, or theories, of Forms. Aristotle came to think that dialectic itself was competent to undermine both these claims. Recent controversy over the question whether he was a 'Platonist' in his earlier years has focused on his handling of the second claim. We have said enough of that. The originality of his position in the Academy will be clearer if we consider his rejection of the first.

Return or advance?

This is a twice-told tale[13] and I need not dwell on it before discussing its moral for our inquiry. Aristotle in his earlier works turned two principal arguments against Plato's master-science. One was drawn from his own model of a science. A master-science, he urged, must set out to prove the premisses of the others, that is, to establish by deduction from its own quite general axioms the requisite special truths on which the departmental sciences were based. But no such proof can be given. Nor can any general proof be given of the rules of inference applied in these sciences, such as the law of excluded middle. If Plato had attended to the actual procedures of those disciplines whose independence he deplored he would have been saved from this piece of logical *naïveté*.

The other argument was one more accusation of over-simplifying. There cannot be a single synoptic science of all existing things because there is no such genus as the genus of existing things; and one, though not the only, reason for this is that the verb 'to exist' (strictly, the verb 'to be' in its existential role) is a word with many senses. For a cat to exist is for it to be alive, and alive in more ways than a vegetable. For a patch of ice to exist is for it to be, *inter alia*, hard and cold; when it ceases to be these things it melts and
146 ceases to exist. At the most general/ level, for a substance to exist is one thing, for a quality to exist is another, for a quantity it is yet another. Plato had not drawn these distinctions when he engaged in his hunt for the common elements or principles of all existing things (*stoicheia tôn ontôn*). He was the dupe of one multivocal word.

When we turn to *Metaphysics* IV and VI all is changed. There is, after all, a single and universal science of what exists. If those who looked for the elements of all existing things were on the track of this science, their enterprise was respectable. In the previous book of the *Metaphysics* Aristotle has made a good deal of the first objection to any such general science; now that objection is quietly dropped. The new science is not an axiomatic system; and lest it seem curiously like those non-departmental inquiries which Aristotle had previously dubbed 'dialectical' or 'logical' and branded as unscientific, dialectic is quietly demoted to one department of its old province so as to leave room for the new giant (cf.1004b17-26 with *SE* 169b25 etc.). It

[13] The evidence for what follows is discussed in 'Logic and Metaphysics in Some Earlier Works of Aristotle', above, Chapter 10, and 'Aristotle on the Snares of Ontology', below, Chapter 15.

is the second objection to the programme that is triumphantly disarmed. The verb 'to exist' is not to be dismissed as a mere source of puns: the simple dichotomy 'univocal or multivocal, synonymous or homonymous' is not sophisticated enough to catch such a word. It is, certainly, a word with a great range of senses, but these senses are systematically connected. They can be sorted into one which is primary and others which are variously derivative from the first. The primary sense is that in which substances, the ultimate subjects of reference in all discourse, exist; and this sense will reappear as a common element in our analyses of the existence of non-substances such as colours or times or sizes. Their existence must be explained as the existence of some substance or substances having them as attributes. Given an understanding of this reduction, an inquiry into substance will be an inquiry into all existence.

So the search for the 'elements of existing things' is reinstated, and it is tempting to say that in his metaphysics Aristotle has come back to Platonism rather than moved from it. But, again, 'Platonism' in what sense? The old questions must be pressed. Certainly Aristotle seems prepared to represent his broad programme as conceived in the tradition of Plato's metaphysics, and certainly the methods by which he begins to carry it out are descended from Plato's dialectic and not from the axiomatic systems which he had taken for a model in the departmental sciences. This is why he can inaugurate it by arguing dialectically for logical axioms which, as he has always insisted,
cannot/ be axiomatically proved without begging the question. But what lies **147**
at the heart of the new enterprise, including the discussion of the axioms, is Aristotle's analysis of substance. And that analysis is not intelligible except as the product of his criticism of Plato.

It may be argued, on the other hand, that the device by which he turns an inquiry into substance into a survey of all that exists is a conscious debt to Plato or to the partisans of Plato's metaphysics. For the idea that an expression has *focal meaning*, that is to say that it has a primary sense by reference to which its other senses can be explained, seems to have been first clearly set out and exploited in an argument for Plato's Forms. The argument was retailed by Aristotle in his essay On Ideas (*De Ideis* fr.3, Ross; Alexander *In Meta.* 82. 11-83. 17), and that essay is earlier than the earliest criticisms of Plato in our text of the *Metaphysics.* But then it becomes a puzzle why Aristotle took so long to appreciate the value of this device. True, the illustration of it in the original argument was one which he evidently found unacceptable. He had to work out his own examples, and he pitched on the expressions 'medical' and 'healthy' as favourite illustrations. It is medical skill that is called 'medical' in the primary sense; a medical knife is a tool required for the exercise of that skill, and so forth. But dissatisfaction with the original illustration scarcely explains, what the evidence shows to have been the case, that Aristotle was at one time content to work with the simple dichotomy 'univocal or multivocal' and saw little if any virtue in the *tertium quid.* It may then seem plausible to suggest that, as he renewed his sympathy with Plato's metaphysical programme, so he came to see new virtue in a technique that had been evolved in support of that programme.

This explanation will not do. Aristotle's appreciation of focal meaning seems to have increased steadily in his work, as can be seen from an analysis of the strata in his philosophical lexicon, *Metaphysics* V. And for this a different explanation suggests itself. There are two very different impulses in his philosophy which do not naturally mesh together. In the use of focal meaning he found himself, with increasing confidence, able to mesh them.

One of these we have already seen. He is occupationally sensitive to expressions with more than one meaning. In the Academy he and Speusippus worked out methods of showing the different senses carried by a single word,
148 methods which come down/ finally to finding a different paraphrase for the word in its different roles. For Aristotle, this is one more expression of the conviction that he shared with J.L. Austin, that 'it is an occupational disease of philosophers to over-simplify – if indeed it is not their occupation'.

But when he turns to the positive business of explaining one of his own key-terms, a different method comes in view. Now he is liable to start from some special, favoured situation of use. Given this starting-point there are likely to be uses of the expression which do not match up to the favoured conditions, and with these uses he deals in various ways. Sometimes he discounts them; sometimes he stretches and weakens his description of the basic situation to cover them; finally he sees a better way of accommodating such deviant forms.

These manoeuvres can be readily illustrated. The first is familiar from his reply to Zeno's paradox of the flying arrow.[14] He cheerfully concedes Zeno's claim that nothing can be said to be moving at an instant, and insists only that it cannot be said to be stationary either. He is so preoccupied with the requirement that any movement must take a certain time to cover a certain distance (and, as a corollary, that any stability must take a certain time but cover no distance) that he discounts any talk of motion, and therefore of velocity, at an instant. He takes no account of the fact that in Greek, as in English, one can ask how fast a man was running when he broke the tape, i.e. at an instant. Yet he could have accommodated this derivative use of expressions for motion and velocity admirably by recourse to focal meaning, and his failure to do this spoilt his reply to Zeno and bedevilled the course of dynamics.

The second manoeuvre can be seen in his analysis of change in the first book of the *Physics*. In the fourth and fifth chapters of that book he argues that any change implies a swing between contrary attributes – either from one to the other, or somewhere on a spectrum between the two. In the sixth and seventh chapters he argues that there must be something to make the swing, that is, something which changes but survives the change. His first illustrations show the typical situation from which he argues: something expanding or contracting, or something that is light turning dark. But he stretches his analysis of this situation to cover an instrument going out of tune, the building of a house from a jumble of bricks, the shaping of a statue

[14] *Phys.* 239a23-b9, 30-3; cf. 'Zeno and the Mathematicians', above, Chapter 3.

from unformed/ bronze; and in the process the two basic ideas, of a *contrary* **149**
and of a *subject*, are also inevitably extended. A contrary attribute may now be a nameless state of affairs which is identified only by its lack of the positive marks which could, in some sense of 'could' which Aristotle proposes to explain, have been present. He cites as examples the unsculptedness of bronze, the disorder of bricks that could be a house. The idea of a subject is similarly enlarged to take account of situations which are not at all a matter of contrary states succeeding each other in some separately identifiable subject. Among such situations he mentions the birth of a plant or an animal. The subject, the 'matter', is no longer required to secure its identity by satisfying some categorical description, answering to some such classification as 'a man' or 'a tree'; for the man and the tree are the outcome, and not the residual subjects, of such processes as these. So, with each step away from the original situation, something seems to be dropped or weakened: some condition for the central or typical use of the expressions concerned.

I am not saying that this is a bad procedure: it is a familiar and valuable procedure. Without it we could not speak as we do of the feelings and thinkings of other kinds of animal than men. I cite it to illustrate Aristotle's inclination to start from the favoured case in explaining some important expressions and then move outwards.[15] But there are hazards. In the second book of the *Physics* Aristotle argues that natural processes have as much right to be explained in terms of ends and purposes as the products of any skilled artificer. The reader acquiesces when he points out that we speak of spiders spinning their webs or swallows building their nests 'for a purpose', but he starts to squirm when Aristotle goes on: 'As one proceeds in this way step by step one can see that with plants too things happen for some end – leaves are grown to shade the fruit, roots are sent down to get moisture.' As he proceeds step by step, Aristotle progressively disengages our talk of purposive behaviour from the idea of having skills or being able to think out steps to an end, and it
is not clear where the process is to stop. Now we/ hanker for Aristotle's other **150**
approach, the readiness to detect and delimit the different senses of one multivocal expression. It is a relief, and an achievement, when he marries this second technique to his interest in setting out from some central, paradigm situation of use. They are wedded in the concept of focal meaning, and we need not talk of Platonism in order to explain Aristotle's steadily increasing appreciation of this fertile device.

'Platonism', to be sure, is a slippery term. But we might have looked in many other directions for signs of Plato's influence on Aristotle and, given due care, brought home the booty. We took this direction because the others, in physics and psychology for instance, have been and continue to be well

[15] There is a wealth of other instances. One of the best known is his description of the terms in the syllogism. In all figures of the syllogism he calls the predicate of the conclusion the *larger* or *major*, and the subject of the conclusion the *lesser* or *minor*; but these descriptions and his explanations of them (*A.Pr.* 26a21-3), are appropriate only to the first figure. Similarly with his description and explanation of the middle term (25b35-6). See W. and M. Kneale, *The Development of Logic* (Oxford 1962), 68-71; G. Patzig, *Aristotle's Theory of the Syllogism* (1st German edition 1959; English translation by J. Barnes, Dordrecht 1969), ch.3.

explored, whereas in logic and metaphysics the hunt seemed to get off to a false start. So long as the logical and metaphysical strands in Aristotle's thinking were taken to be initially separate, his progress in both became unintelligible.

It seems possible now to trace that progress from sharp and rather schematic criticism of Plato to an avowed sympathy with Plato's general metaphysical programme. But the sympathy is one thing, the concrete problems and procedures which give content to Aristotle's project are another. They are his own, worked out and improved in the course of his own thinking about science and dialectic. There seems no evidence of a stage in that thinking at which he confused admiration with acquiescence.

12

Dialectic and Eristic in the Treatment of the Forms

In Professor de Vogel's absence from the Symposium it fell to me to introduce 103
her paper.[1] The following remarks were a contribution to the same discussion. I did not undertake to represent her, having seen that I could not satisfy the rules for such performances given at *Topics* 159b27-35. Nor for the most part did I address myself to the detail of her argument. It seemed more useful to introduce some issues for which the scope of her paper had left little or no room. But one of these issues is so critical for her method of inquiry, as well as for other Aristotelian studies, that I have taken it as a peg for my discussion.

I. The theory

When Professor de Vogel ransacks the *Topics* (under which title I shall include the *Sophistici Elenchi*) for evidence of Aristotle's attitude to Plato's doctrines, she treats the arguments and analyses which seem to be endorsed in that work as serious and candid expressions of a philosophical view. One hears nothing of the possibility that Aristotle is teaching an art of wrestling with all comers, let alone that this may be wrestling with no holds barred. In other words Professor de Vogel does not take up the suggestion that in his dialectic Aristotle thinks himself, in common with any other practitioner, entitled to put up arguments on either side of a case without thereby committing himself to what he defends. Nor, *a fortiori*, does she move against the thesis that 'the essential feature of Dialectic as Aristotle conceives it' is 'the conflict of two minds each taking advantage of the misconceptions, short-comings, and blindness of the other' (G. Grote, *Aristotle* (London 1872), ii. 101-2). In the same vein as Grote Professor H.F. Cherniss contended that 'the purpose of the method justifies any treatment of the thesis which may
enable the dialectician to discomfit his/ opponent' (*Aristotle's Criticism of Plato* 104
and the Academy (Baltimore 1944), i. 18). Grote developed one damaging corollary: dialectic, whatever Aristotle may protest to the contrary, is no

[1] C.J. de Vogel, 'Aristotle's Attitude to Plato and the Theory of Ideas, according to the *Topics*', in *Aristotle on Dialectic: the Topics*, Proceedings of the Third Symposium Aristotelicum, ed. G.E.L. Owen (Oxford 1968), 91-102.

more than eristic, the verbal jockeying that he professes to disdain (op. cit. 93-106). Cherniss drew another: the 'dialectical fence' illustrated in the *Topics* is not concerned with the accurate presentation or serious rebuttal of any philosophical doctrine (op. cit. 18). Let us call this attempt to reduce dialectic to eristic the 'reductive thesis'. If it is true, Professor de Vogel's enterprise miscarries from the start.

So do some larger enterprises which do not enjoy Professor Cherniss's affection. Outside the *Topics* Aristotle makes great use of dialectical procedures in his examinations of Plato and other thinkers. If those procedures allow '*any* treatment' of a thesis under fire, it becomes idle to study such discussions either as independent sources or as responsible criticism of the views treated. One consequence will be the discrediting of Aristotle's insistent and impressive attempts to map his own position in the context of other thought. Another will be to make it more plausible that Aristotle's own cardinal ideas cannot have been gained from a dialectical survey of other philosophers. He may claim, indeed, that the road to the first principles of every science lies in dialectic (*Top.* 101a34-b4), and imply that the theory of categories itself can be established only by this method (*A. Pr.* 43a37-39);[2] but a dialectic that aims simply at the discomfiture of an opponent by any device can hardly show a great philosopher's ideas in the making. And thus those ideas come to be taken as always preceding and standing behind the dialectical discussions in which they appear: preconceptions, their role in dialectic confined to the supplying of ammunition or the suggesting of a line of attack.[3]

105 These further consequences of the reductive thesis would not/follow without one assumption which is freely made by commentators from Alexander onward.[4] It is that those reviews of extant theories and beliefs which commonly preface and accompany Aristotle's theorizings are, wholly or partly, dialectical in method. The assumption needs defending, for this dialectic is not cast in the form of the yes-or-no question-match whose stratagems are plotted in the eighth book of the *Topics*, and whose importance and antecedents have become clearer in recent studies, such as those of Paul Moraux and Gilbert Ryle.[5] But it does answer to the major requirements of

[2] *Kata doxan*, i.e. dialectically, as in Alexander's second explanation (*in A. Pr.* 293. 6), cf. 65a37, *Top.* 105b30-31. That the categories are in question is shown by comparing 43a36-37 with *A. Pst.* 83b12-17. On the better-known claim at *Rhet.* 1355a8-10 that the study of 'all syllogism' belongs to dialectic, see refs. in Moraux, 'La joute dialectique', *Aristotle on Dialectic*, 311 n.4.

[3] Thus Aristotle's notion of substance is taken to provide both 'the point of view' from which he tends to interpret the theory of Ideas (Cherniss, op. cit. 220) and his 'chief weapon' in attacking it (ibid. 315), just as his treatment of Academic divisions 'presupposes his own theory of the relation of genus to differentia' (ibid. 41). On the priority of Aristotle's doctrine of substance to his criticisms of Plato Cherniss finds an unlikely ally in Werner Jaeger (*Aristotle*[2], trans. R. Robinson (Oxford 1948), ch. iii); I have argued to the contrary in 'The Platonism of Aristotle' (above, Chapter 11).

[4] e.g. Alex. *in Top.* 29. 17-32. 4, on Aristotle's claim that the method of reaching the first principles of the sciences is 'proprietary or specially appropriate to dialectic', *Top.* 101b2-3.

[5] *Aristotle on Dialectic*, 277-311 and 69-79 respectively. For my problem see 307-11, and for another move in its solution cf. Ryle's 'digests of actual elenctic disputations' (73).

dialectic set out in the first books of the *Topics* and elsewhere. It does, that is, argue deductively and inductively from *endoxa*, the convictions and the usage of 'the many or the wise' (*Top.* 100a25-b23, 105a10-19), and of these it is ready to upset some (though not all or most) in the course of argument (162b16-22, 24-27). Its problems are substantial and controversial (104b1-17) and the solutions, unlike their premisses, cannot be truistic or matters of general agreement (104a6-7). Commonly it sets out by raising difficulties (101a34-36). And, as against one inference drawn from the reductive thesis, it does aim (as I tried to show elsewhere for part of the *Physics*: see below, Chapter 13) at finding and fixing the basic truths and concepts of sciences which cannot, on pain of a regress or a *petitio principii*, establish these for themselves (101a36-b4). But what is the connexion between these familiar and beneficial procedures and the question-and-answer duel?

In the *Prior Analytics* (24b10-13) Aristotle seems to recognize both as dialectic but to draw a sharp line between them. 'For the man who is putting questions', he says, 'the dialectical *protasis* is an asking (sc. an invitation to choose one) of a pair of contradictories. For the man who is reasoning to a conclusion, it is an assumption of that which is accepted and accredited.'[6] This makes it look as though in the first kind of dialectic, the question-match, any premiss must be tolerated since the respondent may/ opt for either p or **106**
not-p (cf. *A. Pst.* 72a8-10, 77a31-35, *Int.* 20b22-24); but in the second kind it must be a *phainomenon kai endoxon* ('accepted and accredited') (contrast the first, where it seems to be merely good policy to claim that what one says is *sunêthes kai legomenon*, 'familiar and what is said', *Top.* 156b20-23). In the first the argument starts from an asking (*erôtêsis*), in the second from an assumption (*lêpsis*). So it becomes tempting to say that it is the first sort of dialectic that is no more than eristic, ready to make the most of whatever premiss is granted it, and that its cut-throat manoeuvres need not transfer to the second.

But Aristotle does not speak of two species of dialectic, here or elsewhere. The passage is designed merely to mark off two senses of '*protasis*', both of which occur in Aristotle's account of dialectical exercises, though only one was formally introduced at *Top.* 101b29-32. Briefly, the dialectician does ask his yes-or-no questions, called *protaseis*; he asks until he gets the concessions he needs, concessions which must, if the argument is to be dialectical, be *endoxa*. These too, recast in the form of propositions not questions, are called *protaseis*, and he must 'secure' them and not 'assume' them: to understand *lêpsis* in our present text it is as well to recall how the parent verb *lambanein* occurs nearly a score of times in *Topics* VIII 1 alone.

So Aristotle takes no pains to distinguish what seem to be two forms of dialectic; rather he tries to assimilate them. Just as he can represent an inquiry of the second sort as a colloquy with dead thinkers (*Meta.* 987a2-3),

[6] *Dialektikê de (protasis) punthanomenôi men erôtêsis antiphaseôs, sullogizomenôi de lêpsis tou phainomenou kai endoxou.* The distinction between *lêpsis*, 'assumption', and *erôtêsis*, 'asking', was drawn earlier (24a24), where dialectic was confined to *erôtan*, 'to ask'.

so, on the other hand, he can claim that the question-match is strictly dialectical only when there is collaboration and a common aim, not a competition which only one can win (*Top.* 161a33-b5).[7] But this way of saving the unity of dialectic, and with it the larger consequences of the reductive theory, will not comfort the exponents of that theory. The requirement that dialectic should be co-operative and not contentious runs plainly in the face of the claim that 'the purpose of the method justifies any treatment of the thesis which may enable the dialectician to discomfit his opponent'.

Where, then, does Aristotle profess any such 'purpose' for dialectic? The
107 evidence that Cherniss adduces for his dictum/does not support it.[8] And the distinction between dialectic and eristic is one to which Aristotle comes back time and again: eristic employs methods and materials of argument to which dialectic must not stoop.[9] Still it may be that when he comes down to brass tactics he relaxes this prohibition. Some would say that the relaxation is conspicuous in the eighth book of the *Topics*. In that book he moves from codifying the logic of the dialectician's arguments to suggesting means whereby those arguments can be slid under the guard of a stubborn opponent; and the means include talking so as to distract the respondent's attention from the essential premisses and structure of the argument.[10] Yet here too Aristotle insists that the argument must be valid and that these further devices, just to the extent that they are bred of controversy, are not dialectical or not good dialectic.[11] Certainly dialectic is not denied the use of false premisses. It argues from men's convictions, and these can be false (162b27, *Rhet.* 1402a33-34). And, while it is possible to derive true conclusions from false premisses (*Top.* 162a8-11), it is also always possible that 'for purposes of training and testing' or of 'testing and inquiry' (159a25, 33, 161a25) the dialectician will have to maintain a false thesis (161a24-33). But such arguments, where they do not serve as a *reductio ad impossibile* (162b16-22), are branded contentious because they aim at an unco-operative respondent.[12] Amid the duelling rules of the eighth book the professed aim of dialectic remains where Socrates would have set it: co-operative argument, concerned to solve problems and not to obstruct their solution (161a37-b1, 161a13-15).

[7] So even *erôtan* comes to mean 'assume', e.g. 42a39 (where Alexander equates it with *lambanein*; Waitz ad loc., 'petere ut aliquid concedatur, etiam sine interrogatione'); 77a36-41.

[8] He documents it by a reference to *Top.* 159a18-24 (op. cit. 18), without appearing to notice the force of the *tôn dia tên thesin anagkaiôn*, 'what is necessitated by the thesis', at 159a20 (cf. *A. Pst.* 75a22-27). Elsewhere in the context he cites 100a18-21, yet here Aristotle specifies the two requirements which jointly distinguish dialectic from eristic (cf. 100a25-27, 29-30, b21-101a4); and 105b30-31, where the *pros doxan*, 'addressed to opinion', contrasted with *kat' alêtheian*, 'conforming to truth', relies on the same earlier explanation (100a27-b25). For an illuminating recurrence of *kata doxan*, 'conforming to opinion', cf. p. 222, n. 2, above.

[9] *Top.* 100b23-1a4, 108a33-37, 112a9-11, 159a30-37, 161a23-24, 33-b5, *SE* 171b6-34.

[10] 155b3-7a5: notice the *krupsis*, 'concealment', *kruptein*, 'conceal', *kruptikôs*, 'in a concealed manner', in 155b23, 26, 156a7-8, 13-14, 157a6, 163b34-35.

[11] Not dialectic, 161a23-24, 33-34; bad dialectic, 161b3, 161a17-19.

[12] *Hoi toioutoi tôn logôn*, 'arguments of this sort', 161a25-26, i.e. those described in 161a17-24.

So much for Aristotle's claims. But his preaching on dialectic may point one way and his practice quite another. What matters is to dissect the practice, with an eye for chicanery but without/ a predisposition to believe **108**
that by the rules of the game there must be chicanery to be found. As a sample of the practice recommended by Aristotle, then, let us reconsider the arguments in the *Topics* which are, or have been thought to be, critical of Plato's theory of Ideas.

II. The practice

It will be useful to have some distinctions. Given any Platonic Idea, at least two and possibly three very different sorts of thing can be said of it. (A) Certain things will be true of it in virtue of its status as an Idea, e.g. that it is immutable. These predicates (call them 'A-predicates') will be true of any Idea whatever. (B) Certain things will be true of it in virtue of the particular concept it represents: these (call them 'B-predicates') are sometimes held to fall into two radically distinct groups. (B1) There are predicates which can be applied to the Idea in virtue of the general logical character of the concept for which it stands: thus it will be true of Man that it is, in the scheme of Xenocrates and the Academy, *kath' hauto* 'in virtue of itself', and not *pros ti* 'in relation to something', or *pros heteron* 'in relation to something different',[13] and in Aristotle's scheme that it is (or is an Idea of) substance and not quality, etc.[14] (B2) Other predicates belong to the Idea because, regardless of philosophical disagreements over types or categories of concept (the B1-predicates), they are simply accepted as serving to define the particular concept in question. Man, for instance, is two-footed and an animal. For the purpose of this argument the distinction between B1 and B2 will not matter; and this is just as well, for it is tied to the disputed distinction between 'categories' and 'classes'. Philosophers have been exercised by the question whether the categorial predicates falling under B1 are merely one sort, perhaps the most general sort, of the classificatory predicates found under B2.[15] Whether Aristotle himself recognized any major distinction between them is equally disputable. He implicitly denies such a difference when he treats/ the categories as merely the highest genera of the individuals falling **109**
under them, but he seems to suggest one when he speaks of substance and perhaps of quality in the *Categories* as though these were not genera at all.[16] But, as luck will have it, we shall need only the contrast between A-predicates

[13] Simplicius *in Cat.* 63. 21-24, *Divisiones Aristoteleae* apud Diog. Laert. 3. 108: 'A Proof in the *Peri Ideôn*', above, Chapter 9. I should no longer count *Sophist*, 255c-d among the Platonic sources of this distinction: 'Aristotle on the Snares of Ontology', below, Chapter 15, n. 2.

[14] For the application of the categories to the Ideas cf. *Meta.* 990b22-29 (with Alexander ad loc., 88. 5-17) and *SE* 178b36-179a10, discussed below.

[15] A discussion and partial bibliography in John Passmore, *Philosophical Reasoning* (London 1961), ch.7.

[16] Highest genera, as in the phrase *genê tôn ontôn*, etc., Bonitz, *Index*, 378a35-39. But in the *Categories* Aristotle says (*a*) that the genus of a substance is predicated in exactly the same sense of

on the one hand and some variety of B-predicate on the other.

It seems plain that if Aristotle can show that an Idea possesses contradictory predicates *within* one of the brackets described, he will have produced a paradox that is prima facie valid: e.g. if he can show that, on the level of A-predicates, an Idea as such must be both mutable and immutable (as he holds that on Eudoxus' interpretation of the Ideas it must be). On the other hand, it seems plain that if he professes to show a contradiction, not between predicates from the same bracket, but between predicates from different brackets, his paradox will be suspect: for prima facie there seems to be no contradiction in saying that man is mobile but the Idea of man is immobile, or that man is by definition mobile but, *qua* Idea, immobile. Let us call paradoxes of the first sort *one-level* paradoxes, and those of the second sort *two-level* pardoxes, and look at the one-level paradoxes first.

III. A-predicates

(1) 113a24-32. The statement that the Ideas exist in us (says Aristotle) entails contradictions: for the allegedly immobile Ideas will also be mobile, since whatever we contain moves with us when we move (*kinoumenôn hêmôn*
110 *anagkaion kai ta en hêmin panta/sugkineisthai*); and, though supposedly accessible only to thought, they will also be perceptible, since the form in the individual (*hê en hekastôi morphê*) is recognized by means of sight.

The objection, as Alexander recognized (*in Top.* 189. 10-12), has nothing to do with the suggestion treated in *Parmenides* 132b-c that the Ideas are thoughts in the mind, *noêmata en psuchais*: *pace* Professor de Vogel, it would be absurd to equate a *noêma* with the visible *morphê en hekastôi*. The target is Eudoxus and his adherents, against whom the first arm of the same objection was levelled in the *Peri Ideôn* (Alexander, *in Meta.* 98. 21-24). And since Aristotle is criticizing a special interpretation of the Ideas there is no immediate relevance in Cherniss's comment that the topic 'indicates a method ... of overthrowing Platonic definitions by developing the inconsistency between transcendent idea and immanent universal, for Aristotle does not allow any distinction between them *on the part of the Platonists*' (op. cit. 10, my italics). His reference to a further application of this 'method' in 148a14-22 is to a two-level paradox, and therefore not our present business.

Is Aristotle's argument unfair? If anything can be said against it, it is that his own theory of universals seems to be open to the same objections, and that in evading them he modifies or denies the assumptions of the present argument in ways which he might charitably have allowed Eudoxus. Thus at one point Aristotle too requires that forms and attributes (*eidê kai pathê*) shall not move or change although their possessors do so (*Phys.* 224b5-7, 11-16), yet at another he concedes that they can be said to change place in the sense that they are present in things which do so (*houtô metabeblêke ton topon hoti en hôi huparchousi metaballei*, 211a22-23). By the first of these propositions he may mean simply that universals must not change in that respect in which they

determine a particular type of change – that a colour, for instance, cannot itself change colour though it may shift in place. If so he is not maintaining a theory of wholly immutable universals of the sort that he ascribes to Eudoxus and the Academy, and the paradox does not touch him. But more probably he thinks himself protected by the distinction drawn in *Physics* 211a17-23 (cf. ps.-Plutarch, *Plac.* 899b, Simplicius, *in Cat.* 218. 19-21). Universals cannot be said to move in their own right (*kath' hauta*), and if they are said to move *per accidens* this is in a sense still weaker/than that in which any physical part of **111**
the moving body does so.[17] But, if this is an escape-clause, why not concede it to Eudoxus? Here, as in other examples, three lines of explanation suggest themselves. (*a*) It may be that the criticism of Eudoxus was formulated before Aristotle's own account of universals was worked out. This, even if true, can be discounted: the *Peri Ideôn* which contained the criticism seems also to have contained Aristotle's explanation of his own *koina* (Alexander, *in Meta.* 79. 17-19), and in any event both are still in play in the *Topics*. (*b*) Aristotle's silence may be claimed for the reductive thesis. (*c*) The natural explanation seems to be that Eudoxus is not presented with Aristotle's distinctions simply because they are Aristotle's, and as such constitute a different thesis. There is no compulsion to present another philosopher with theories he did not formulate (*Top.* 159b27-35).

So too with the second arm of the objection. Aristotle may cover himself by noting that the universal is perceptible only *per accidens* (*Meta.* 1087a19-20), or by distinguishing between perceptible and intelligible forms and trying to find a place for both (*De An.* 432a4-6); but whatever the saving force of these distinctions, there is no call to father them on Eudoxus.

(2) 178b36-179a10. The Third Man, not discussed by Professor de Vogel. The version of the paradox implied by the text, as many commentators since Grote have seen, is probably not the argument supplied by pseudo-Alexander ad loc. (*in Soph. El.* 158. 20-26)[18] but the familiar objection which Alexander

---

its species and of the individuals in the species (3b2-9), yet (*b*) that *substance* is predicated 'most strictly, primarily, and especially' of the individual, and only on reduced terms of species and genera (2a11-19). By proposition (*a*) he can protect the inference 'Socrates is a man, man is an animal, so Socrates is an animal': on the univocity of the major term cf. *A. Pst.* 85b9-10, 15-16, 18-22. But what of the corresponding inference 'Socrates is a man, man is a substance, so Socrates is a substance'? It seems to be disallowed by (*b*), which Aristotle feels compelled to accept in order to avoid the Third Man regress which comes of treating species as individual substances. If the *Categories* had employed the quantifiers which appear in the *De Interpretatione*, this inference too could have been saved – but then there would be no temptation to saddle 'substance' with different senses: 'Socrates is a man, *every* man is a substance, so Socrates is a substance.' As for *poiotês*, 'quality', its analysis as a *pleonachôs legomenon*, 'said in many ways', (8b26) and the effect of this on its claims to be a genus remain as debatable as they were for Alexander and Simplicius (Simpl. *in Cat.* 220. 5-228. 3).

[17] *Quaerit* Verbeke, is not *Phys.* 211a17-23 applicable only to *sumbebêkota*, 'accidents', since the only examples given are *leukotês*, 'paleness', and *epistêmê*, 'knowledge' (22)? *Respondeo*, *epistêmê* and *thermotês* 'heat', are also the examples for the argument embracing *eidê kai pathê*, 'forms and attributes', in 224b12-13, and there is no obvious reason to restrict the escape-clause to *pathê*.

[18] His version of the Third Man is a replica of that reported in Alexander, *in Meta.* 84. 7-14, and would naturally be explained as copied from that commentary (so Cherniss, op. cit. 290 n. 194) but for the evidence that the latter text, and the paragraph which follows it (84. 16-21), are

reports from the *Peri Ideôn* (*in Meta.* 84. 21-85. 3). The A-level contradiction/
112 on which it depends is that of construing any Idea both (*a*) as a predicate distinct from anything of which it is predicated and yet (*b*) as itself a subject of the predicate in question.[19] In his account of the argument in the *Philosophical Review* 63 (1954) Vlastos christened these the 'Non-Identity Assumption' and the 'Self-Predication Assumption' respectively, and held that the failure to disentangle them explained the failure of Plato to locate or come to grips with the difficulty. But the Academy did disentangle them, and Aristotle's report of the argument in the *Peri Ideôn* is the record of their success.[20]

I defer comment on this notorious argument to another time. A battery of recent studies has confirmed, what few would question, that it is not a piece of eristic malpractice but a central and serious objection to Plato's theories.[21] Cherniss remarks that 'in the *Sophistici Elenchi* Aristotle refers to [it] as to a well-known sophistical argument' (op. cit. 293); but in calling it a sophism *para to schêma tês lexeôs*, 'due to the form of the utterance', in this passage Aristotle makes it clear that it is so only when used against those who do not, as in his view the Academy did, treat the predicate as itself an individual subject of predicates (179a3-10). That he did not himself see it as a debater's dodge is proved by his own theory of predication and the categories, which was framed with the same familiar objection in view.[22]

---

interpolations in the commentary whose date is unknown (as Cherniss himself recognizes, ibid. 500-1). To the identification of the commentator on the *SE* I have nothing to contribute save a possible connexion with the manuscript tradition represented by Waitz's CcuT: he seems to be the only commentator to use 'Hipponicus' as a stock name (167.29), and the name otherwise appears only in u and less often in CcT as a variant for the 'Coriscus' of other manuscripts (173b38, 175b19-22, 176a7 – but here it would naturally be suggested by the proximity of 'Callias'–, 178b39-179a1, 181a10).

[19] *Ei gar allos ho (anthrôpos ho) katêgoroumenos hôn katêgoreitai, kai kat' idian huphestôs, katêgoreitai de kata te tôn kath' hekasta kai kata tês ideas ho anthrôpos, estai tritos tis anthrôpos.* 'If (a) the man predicated is different from those things of which it is predicated, and exists in its own right, and (b) man is predicated both of the particulars and of the form, there will be a third man.'

[20] Vlastos has to claim that Aristotle 'did not *see* what was thus within his grasp'. Otherwise (op. cit. 339 n. 36) Aristotle 'would have argued to even better effect' from the Self-Predication Assumption that 'the Forms which are predicable of the particulars *qua* particulars (e.g. perishableness, change, mortality) have predicates incompatible with their predicates *qua* Forms'. Aside from any doubts on the credentials of some of these 'Forms' (they are produced by 'Parmenides' at 136b, after his drubbing of the old Paradigms; but *Phaedo* 105 seems to entail a Form of Death at least), Aristotle's awareness of 'what was within his grasp' should be sufficiently proved for Vlastos by the general argument at *Top.* 148a18-21 that it is contradictory to define any Idea in terms of acting and being acted on; for these attributes were taken by the 'Friends of the Forms' to be properties of all *genesis*, 'becoming', and no *ousia*, 'being', (*Sophist* 248b7-9). In any event Aristotle not only spells out the implications of Self-Predication (*Top.* 154a16-20), he expressly accepts the assumption himself where in his view the non-Identity Assumption does not apply, i.e. where the formula gives the *ti esti*, 'what is it' (*A.Pst.* 83b17-19).

[21] See the bibliographies in Vlastos's paper cited above and in Strang's shrewd study of the argument, 'Plato and the Third Man', published with Rees's reply in *Proc. Arist. Soc.*, suppl. vol. 37 (1963), 147-76, repr. in *Plato I*, ed. G. Vlastos (Notre Dame 1978), 184-200.

[22] 'The Platonism of Aristotle', above, Chapter 11.

IV. B1-predicates 113

(3) 181b25-34. Relative expressions are never to be explained as simple adjectives: 'We must not allow that predications of relatives mean anything when taken out of relation.'[23] The passage does not mention Ideas, and consequently is not discussed by Professor de Vogel; but it embodies a criticism of Plato which reappears in *Metaphysics* I 990b15-17 (= XIII 1079a11-13) in the condensed formula 'Of the more exact arguments, one group produce ideas of relatives, of which we say there is no non-relative class.'[24] The pattern of argument for the Ideas that Aristotle is criticizing is reported from the *Peri Ideôn* by Alexander (*in Meta.* 82. 11-83. 16), and the commentator brings out clearly the force of Aristotle's objection (83. 26-28). The Academic argument tries to prove the existence of an Equal, *autoison*, which is not equal *to anything*: in Academic terminology, it treats the Idea as equal *kath' hauto* and not *pros ti* or *pros heteron.* Thus for any relative predicate the argument professes to adduce one example – the Idea – which is *non*-relative, and so it sets up a 'non-relative set of relatives' (*kath' hauto genos tôn pros ti*, with which cf. the *tôn pros ti legomenôn kath' hautas katêgorias* of *SE* 181b26-27). And this, Aristotle says, 'we do not admit'. Relative predicates are incurably relative: hence the *Peri Ideôn* argued that the Equal must after all be equal to something, yet this something can be nothing but a second Idea of Equal, which is absurd (Alexander, *in Meta.* 83. 26-28).

'Relative', in the Academic sense which it carries in this argument, extends beyond the Aristotelian category to cover all incomplete predicates, 'predicates which require completion if they are to be applied unambiguously to things in this world' (Strang): that is, it covers not only 'equal' but 'good', 'large', 'one'. I have discussed them and the arguments built on them elsewhere, and Mr. Strang has carried the discussion further.[25] Here it is enough to point out that the contradiction set up by Aristotle between *kath' hauto* and *pros ti* is a valid one-level contradiction between B1-predicates, and not the invalid two-level opposition with which Cherniss wished to saddle Aristotle (op. cit. 283). Cherniss contended that the sense of *kath' hauto* required in this criticism is not that in which it is the logical twin of *pros ti* but that in which it is 'applied to the mode of existence of the ideas. In the latter/ 114
case the phrase means absolute self-subsistence ... The dialectical objection of Aristotle depends on the substitution of the ontological for the logical sense of *kath' hauto.*' This is to discount both the evidence from the *Peri Ideôn* and the amplification of Aristotle's criticism given in our passage. The charge of malpractice misfires.

[23] *Phaneron hôs ou doteon tôn pros ti legomenôn sêmainein ti chôrizomenas kath' hautas tas katêgorias.*

[24] *Eti de hoi akribesteroi tôn logôn hoi men tôn pros ti poiousin ideas, hôn ou phamen einai kath' hauto genos ...*

[25] 'A Proof in the *Peri Ideôn*', above, Chapter 9; Strang, 158-62.

There remains one ground of suspicion which can be met now. The Academic proof of an *autoison*, 'equal itself', was demonstrably framed with the argument of *Phaedo* 73e-75a in view, and so no doubt was Aristotle's rejoinder. But at one point in that argument Plato refers to the Form of equality as *auta ta isa*, 'the equals themselves', putting the Form's usual title into the plural (74e1); and so he does with the Forms of likeness and unlikeness in the *Parmenides*, calling them *auta ta homoia* and *ta anomoia* (120b1-2). That he is referring to a Form by these locutions, and not, as Burnet and many later scholars have suggested, to some quite different perfect instances of equality or similarity, is certified by the economy of the argument and has become common ground to its interpreters. But then why the plural? Geach proposed an interpretation which would entail (though he did not note this implication) that Plato had anticipated Aristotle's comment. 'Equal' is indeed incurably relative; so for Plato the Paradigm of equality must be 'a pair of absolutely equal things'.[26] But if this was known to be Plato's view, then Aristotle's objection, however appropriate to the proof laid out in the *Peri Ideôn*, would be a wilful misrepresentation of Plato himself. The credit of dialectic stands in question again.

Later interpretations of the same texts have tried to avoid Geach's inference while preserving the insight that Plato's plural is meant to name a Form. They have hardly measured up to that remarkable plural.[27] But consider the context. In the *Phaedo* Socrates is trying to show that a predicate-word such as
115 'equal'/ stands for something in its own right, something different from the sticks and stones to which we apply it; though of course he does not speak of the word but just of what it (supposedly) stands for. This he calls 'the equal itself', *auto to ison*, and the definite article together with its reinforcing *auto* has a clear force in the context. Socrates begins by saying 'We agree, I take it, that there is an *equal*' (*phamen ti einai ison*, whose ambiguity he at once tries to resolve): 'I don't mean a stick [equal] to a stick or a stone to a stone, but something different from all these: just the equal by itself.' So the word 'equal' is first introduced without the article; then we are made to think of it in context, 'a stick ... to a stick'; and then we are told to discount the stick and concentrate just on the *equal*. It is as though Plato drew a ring round the word in its context and told us to think of *that*, pointing to it – except that, to repeat, he is concerned not with the word but with what it stands for. That is why he later substitutes for it the noun that we conventionally but proleptically translate 'equality'. More to the purpose, it is why he takes the

[26] P.T. Geach, 'The Third Man Again', *Philosophical Review* 65 (1956), 76: the Form 'has to consist of two equals, or there wouldn't be equality at all'.

[27] Vlastos, having first accepted Geach's view, now rejects it ('Additional Note' in *Studies in Plato's Metaphysics*, ed. R.E. Allen (London 1965), 291); he prefers to explain the plural by that generic use of the adjective which shifts easily between plural and singular, citing as instances *Gorgias* 454e-5a *Rep.* 520c, 538c. In none of these contexts, however, is the titular prefix of the Form pointedly introduced as it is in the *Phaedo*, and the plurals are naturally explained as pointing to such questions as 'What things are beautiful?'. Other scholars have compared the use of *ta tria* interchangeably with *hê trias*, e.g. at *Phaedo* 104e; but this is standard Greek usage, and the equation of *auta ta isa* and *autê hê isotês* is not.

predicate 'equal' out of context in whatever form it has just assumed, singular or plural. After introducing it in the singular, he goes on to speak of 'stones and sticks which appear equal to one but not to another' (74b7-9), and at once picks it out in its *plural* form (*tôi men isa phainetai, tôi d'ou ... ti de? auta ta isa ...*). So too in the *Parmenides* (*ei ... esti tôi metechein amphoin homoia te kai anomoia auta hautois, ti thaumaston? ei men gar auta ta homoia ... ê ta anomoia ...*). He is interested, not in the different forms in which the predicate may appear, but in that single Idea which we wittingly or unwittingly mention in calling one stick 'equal' to another or a pair of sticks 'equal' each to each. So Geach's special interpretation of the plural *auta ta isa* is not called for, and here too the credit of dialectic survives scrutiny.

V. B2-predicates

(4) 143b11-32. Suppose any genus is divided by negation, e.g. length is divided into length with breadth and length without breadth. Then, since by the law of excluded middle nothing can be neither A nor not-A, the genus itself must fall under one of these species and possess one of these differentiae. But this is absurd (cf. 121a10-19, 144a28-b3). It is absurd because this/
would entail either that every length necessarily has breadth, or that every **116**
length necessarily lacks breadth, whereas lengths may be of either sort. But, having said this, Aristotle recognizes that a genus correctly understood is not a proper subject for this application of the law of excluded middle: it is *a* number, and not the class Number, that must be either an odd or an even number, and *a* length that must either have or lack breadth. So the objection goes home only against the patrons of the Ideas who treat the genus Length as *a* length, a further individual answering to the same predicate as its mundane likenesses. The objection depends on this last assumption; and it is no eristic contrivance but the settled conviction from which the greater part of Aristotle's criticism of Plato sets out.[28]

So much for the one-level paradoxes. If I am right, they are honest and well-founded. It is the two-level arguments that arouse a more profound suspicion, and I turn to these forthwith. But the one-level contradictions have given us the main key to the rest.

VI. Two-level paradoxes

(1) 148a14-22. One test of a definition (says Aristotle) is to see whether it applies to the *idea*. Here Plato's definitions of animals fail, for they import the term 'mortal', yet mortal is what an Idea cannot be. And in general the same trouble awaits any definition that mentions a capacity to act or to be acted on, for the Ideas are held by their partisans to be immune from action and

[28] It is, of course, the ground not only of the Third Man but of the objection that Plato simply reduplicates the world he wants to explain, *Meta.* 990a34-b8 = 1078b32-1079a4.

change. Against these people, Aristotle adds, there is a use for arguments of this kind too. He harks back to this comment later (154a18-20).[29]

The predicates ascribing immutability and imperishability are A-predicates, those ascribing the contradictories of these are B-predicates. So by our earlier agreement the paradox is to be regarded as prima facie suspect. Indeed if it is valid how can Aristotle safeguard his own conclusions against it? He too believes that perishability must be mentioned in defining natural kinds, for it is an essential characteristic of its subject just as imperishability/
117 is of eternal things: on this very claim he builds a variant of the present objection in *Metaphysics* 1058b36-1059a10. He too holds that such definitions must mention the capacity for change (1036b28-32). Yet he insists that a form cannot be said to come into existence or perish or change (*Meta.* 1033b5-8, *Phys.* 224b11-16); so he too seems to think the two-level paradox harmless.

But consider this suspect paradox more closely. Man, we say, is two-footed; but Man is a universal (or, if you prefer, a class-concept), and universals do not have feet. The average man lives on the ground and not in a tree; the average man is an abstraction, and abstractions have no physical location. Why do such conjunctions not strike us as intolerable contradictions? Because, we might reasonably reply, one arm of the conjunction tells us what it is to be *a* man, and the other does not. To be *a* man is to be mortal, two-footed, a land animal; it is patently not to be an abstraction or a timeless universal. So the supposedly incompatible predicates operate on quite different levels and do not collide. In his own terms Aristotle can bring out the difference by insisting on the error of confusing the universal *man* with an individual of the species, and still more by requiring the quantifier 'Every' to be written in front of a formula such as 'Man is mortal': the prefix would obviously be absurd in front of 'Man is a universal'.[30] So for Aristotle the paradox need hold no threat.

But it is just at this point that in Aristotle's view Plato went most gravely astray. The same conviction that explained the last paradox is in point here: for Aristotle, to be a Platonic Idea of Man is to be *a* man: a transcendent paradeigmatic sample, to be sure, but a sample, logically on a par with other members of the class. And if to be a man is to be mortal, and to be an Idea is to be immortal, then in Aristotle's eyes the contradiction holds good against Plato. Moreover, when he says that against the Platonists there is a use for arguments 'of this kind too', he does not at all imply, as some interpreters
118 have thought, that with/ these opponents any manoeuvre is justified. He means that a paradox which carries no menace for most people becomes serious just on that theory which he thinks proprietary to Plato, the theory

[29] This later reference proves the correctness of the reading *pros toutous* at 148a21, as against the *pros toutois* which Alexander reads but queries.

[30] If Aristotle's discussion of *horoi* at *A.Pst.* 76b35-77a4 is a discussion of definitions (as commentators assume) and not of terms in propositions, definitions are said at 77a3-4 *not* to carry quantifiers. If so he must intend nominal definitions and not the explications of *ti esti* which serve as premisses in demonstration (*A.Pst.* 75a30-31, ii. 10). But his insistence here that *horoi*, unlike *hupotheseis*, are not even *protaseis* (premisses) (76b36) conflicts with the general account of definitions at 72a7-24 and suggests that here a discussion of *terms* has been imported into the text.

which 'separates' and individualizes the universal.

This, then, is the consideration which entitles him to treat A-predicates on the same footing with B-predicates when he is reviewing the Ideas, though not of course when he is expounding his own reformed theory of *eidê*. Whether he surrenders this entitlement in other passages concerned with the Ideas I shall ask later. First there is another two-level argument to be inspected, and the same consideration will carry us some way to understanding it; though not, as it turns out, the whole way.

(2) 146b36-147a11. A wish is a hankering after what *seems* good, though it may prove not to be good; a desire is similarly a hankering after what *seems* pleasant. But a Platonist is supposed to define an Idea only by reference to other Ideas (a principle which Aristotle recognizes for the definition of universals, as in *Metaphysics* VII 15). So real Wish can be related only to real Good, real Desire to real Pleasure. The Platonist must define Wish and Desire as having the really good and the really pleasant as their objects, and this is a mistake.

Here the reality which is taken to exclude mere seeming is an A-predicate carried *ex officio* by any Idea. The B-predicate is the seeming, the possibility of deception which characterizes things wished for and desired. How can the Platonist admit a real Apparent Good? But now the old way of justifying such paradoxes seems too thin. Give Aristotle his conviction that the Idea of X-ness is an X thing, and therewith his assimilation of the two-level to the one-level paradox. Still why should there not be an Idea of what is apparently good, namely a thing that has the real appearance of goodness? Why, that is, should the reality attach to the goodness rather than to the apparent goodness?

The question sounds, and in the nature of the case is, frivolous (but see Verdenius, p.38; *contra*, Düring, p.216).[31] It is frivolous because Aristotle regards the Ideas, with unimpeachable warrant from Plato, as Paradigms or standard samples of the attributes they represent; and there patently cannot be a sample whose total is to exhibit some variety of ostensibleness – or rather of flat deceptiveness, since this sample is *ex hypothesi* not the genuine article,
the really Good or really Pleasant. A conjuring/ trick is an excellent sample 119
of deceptiveness because it really is something other than it appears. But something whose function is to give the appearance of X-ness without being a real sample either of X-ness or of anything else which precludes X-ness is, as Aristotle calls it, absurd. What could show that it was merely X in appearance, except that it was Y in fact? So Aristotle can fairly claim that the kind of reality ascribed to the Ideas would prevent the prefix 'apparent' from occurring in any designation of an Idea. The two-level paradox is once more reduced to the valid one-level contradiction. Dialectic so far, not eristic.

There is a loose end to be tied in. Elsewhere Aristotle remarks that it need not matter whether the final cause is defined in terms of the good or the apparent good (*Phys.* 195a24-26 = *Meta.* 1013b26-28). He is not reneguing on

[31] W.J. Verdenius, 'Notes on the *Topics*', in *Aristotle on Dialectic*, 22-42; I. Düring, 'Aristotle's Use of Examples in the *Topics*', *Aristotle on Dialectic*, 202-29.

his argument in the *Topics*. What we wish for is good in the sense, but only in the sense, in which what we believe is true; namely that the man who believes p necessarily takes q to be a good thing. For to deny that p is true or that q is good is to show, barring evidence to the contrary, that one does *not* believe p or wish for q. But of course the wisher and the believer can be mistaken about their objects. In a later jargon, the good is the intensional object of the wish (cf. Alexander, *in Meta.* 352. 3-8), but the neutral observer's criterion of my wishes must still be what *seems* good to me (*Rhet.* 1369a2-4).

So far Aristotle's two-level paradoxes stand firm. Given one settled conviction about the nature of the Ideas he was justified in treating A-predicates on the same footing as B-predicates in these objections. But there are passages in which he seems to concede the Platonists the very distinction in predicate-levels which he here denies them. If this is so, it seems to threaten our defence. Let us see whether it is so, and whether the defence is threatened.

(3) 137b3-13. In testing the claim that P is a property of a subject S it is useful to consider the *idea* of S.[32] (*a*) To upset the claim, see whether P is predicated of the *idea* of S not *qua* S but simply *qua idea* – as for instance immobility can be ascribed to the *idea* of man ('Man-itself') simply *qua idea*, but not *qua* man. (*b*) Correspondingly, to defend the claim, see whether P is a property of the *idea* of S not *qua idea* but *qua* S – as, for instance, it is/
120 characteristic of Animal-itself to be a compound of soul and body, but characteristic of it *qua* animal and not *qua idea*.

Here, surely, the distinction between A-predicates and B-predicates is clearly in view. But there is room for dissension over what Aristotle does with it. It might be supposed, and I shall discuss the supposition in due course, that here he presents the Platonists with the distinction in working order, thereby discrediting the last two paradoxes we have reviewed. Cherniss, on the other hand, implies that a major element in the distinction is guilefully suppressed. He says (op. cit. 1-3): 'The relationship between idea and property on the one hand and between subject and property on the other is assumed to be identical, and this assumption requires the "analysis" of the idea into existential and essential moments and the dismissal of the former as irrelevant. The Platonic conception of the idea as the *identification* of essence and existence is silently denied.' This 'analysis' is therefore 'a conscious dialectical trick and Aristotle did not expect any *Platonist* to make use of it in either attack or defence'.

The references to 'existential and essential moments' do not shed the light that their author must have hoped. But Cherniss's point seems to be made by saying that in the propositions 'Man is a rational animal' and 'Socrates is a rational animal' the defender of the Ideas would recognize a radical difference of logical form: the first exhibits 'the relationship between idea and property', the second 'the relationship between subject and property'. This he asserts without argument, but the argument can be conjectured from other

[32] I transliterate ἰδέα in these lines without giving its name the honorific Platonic capital: the reason will appear later.

texts. In general, he would claim, where PQ is a set of defining or proprietary characteristics of Man, Plato and his adherents would not allow that 'Man is PQ' says at all the same sort of thing as 'Socrates is PQ'; for Socrates is a sample or specimen of PQ, but the Idea is the PQ of which Socrates is a sample: 'the idea *is* that which the particular *has* as an attribute' (op. cit. 298). On the other hand (though Cherniss does not draw out this implication), the same account cannot be given of the A-predicates which are ascribed to the Idea; for of these attributes – immobility, eternity, and the rest – the Idea can only be, in common with its fellows, one specimen among others.[33] But if this is so Aristotle is blanketing a major difference/ in the ways in which the **121**
Academy ascribed A-predicates and B-predicates to the Ideas. Moreover this difference, if it existed, would block my justification of the two-level paradoxes. For Cherniss implies that Plato could not be supposed by any serious student, even Aristotle, to have regarded the Ideas as samples or instances of the attributes they represent. But in Aristotle's defence I appealed to his conviction that Plato did understand the Ideas in just this way.

So much has been written in rebuttal or mere defiance of Cherniss's contention that the argument need not be drawn out here.[34] Vlastos observed that, if Plato had believed what Cherniss constructs for him, ' "Separation" would make no sense, and the Third Man Argument would be not only pure sophistry but so easily refutable sophistry that it would be impossible to understand why Plato takes it as seriously as he does yet leaves it unrefuted.' As a comment on one reductive method of interpretation the validity of this goes beyond the present case. But that case itself embodies one of the most debated questions in Platonic studies, and to beg it against Aristotle is not only to disallow the Third Man. It is to discount or interpret away the standard idioms of copying and resemblance in which Plato describes the relation between earthly things and Ideas, and in general it is to jettison the evidence, drawn not only from language but from the argument, that Plato took quite seriously his account of the Ideas as Paradigms or standard samples. On all this Aristotle's stand is firm and consistent, not at all a device to be taken up or dropped as the debate may require.

Supposing Cherniss wrong, however, Aristotle is not yet clear of suspicion. For, on the alternative reading of the present argument, he is not misrepresenting but fairly recognizing a distinction between A-predicates and B-predicates, and apparently conceding the same recognition to the partisans of the Ideas. Yet this is a distinction that the earlier two-level arguments seem to depend on obliterating. The first, for instance, required that no attribute should appear in the definition of an Idea if it conflicted with the standard prerogatives of Ideas. But the present argument seems to allow that an Idea such as Man may be mobile *qua* man, yet immobile *qua* Idea./

This same concession seems to be carried further in *Metaphysics* I **122**

[33] I do not discuss those Ideas which themselves represent A-predicates, e.g. the Idea of eternity (if there is one), for the paradoxes do not arise with these.

[34] Of the literature indirectly referred to on pp. 228-30 above, for instance, the papers of Vlastos, Geach, and Strang have this tendency.

990b27-34, where Aristotle tries to show that, 'according to necessity and the opinions held about the Ideas' (i.e. according to a valid dialectical argument from *endoxa*), there cannot be Ideas of accidents but only of substances. He draws a sharp distinction between the A-predicate, *eternal*, and a B-predicate: his example of the latter is *double*, but since the appropriate example turns out to be a substance-predicate I shall use *man*. Suppose then that Socrates partakes of the Idea, Man. Since Man is eternal, Socrates might be said to partake of eternal; but this would be participation *per accidens* and not in the strict sense. Socrates is a man, and patently is not eternal. Why does his eternity not follow from the premisses, as his being a man does? Because, says Aristotle, eternity is only an accident of man, i.e. not all or even most men are eternal (cf. *Meta.* 1025a14-15, 1065a1-3): in fact only one man, the Paradigm, is so. From this he infers that, strictly speaking, *no* predicate which is merely accidental to some class of substances can be partaken of. Otherwise eternity would have to come in with the rest. So there can be no Ideas of accidents.

The argument is crabbed and apparently invalid.[35] But what concerns us now is not its invalidity but the fact that Aristotle is allowing the Academy a distinction between different-level predicates which he seems to refuse them elsewhere. 'Participation' is the sieve which brings out the distinction: if something participates in an Idea, it is the B-predicates which come through to it, not the A-predicates. Yet Aristotle makes nothing of this difference of role in marshalling his other two-level paradoxes against the Ideas. His neglect comes to look like double-dealing.

But the reductivists should not take heart yet. This text from the *Metaphysics*, and the foregoing passage from the *Topics*, do nothing for their theory. The assumption which by implication Aristotle ascribes here to the
123 Academy is that one and only one/ man is eternal; and this does nothing to show how the eternity of *this* man can be squared with the mortality that belongs to any man by definition. Nor does the *Topics* passage give any clue to reconciling this man's immobility with the motion characteristic of men. And these contradictions are not mitigated by the plea that, if something participates in an Idea, it stands in *various* relations to the Idea's predicates (Aristotle's 'participation' and 'participation *per accidens*'), and therefore acquires some of them but not others. To give this reply any force it would have to be shown that these different relations entailed some relevant difference in the ways in which the Idea carried its predicates: that is, a difference which would show the two-level contradiction to be specious. But Aristotle, holding that the Platonic idea is *a* sample of man just as it is *an*

[35] Suppose (*a*) S partakes of D, (*b*) S and D are members of some class to which a further predicate P is accidental, (*c*) D is a P thing; then Aristotle can claim that these propositions do not jointly *entail* that (*d*) S partakes of P, but he has not shown that they *preclude* (*d*); and still less has he proved what he wanted, namely that (*d*) would be precluded by a conjunction of (*a*) and (*b*) with the different proposition that *S* is P. I cannot think this meets A.'s argument, yet no expansion known to me leaves it valid, and indeed the text can hardly be regarded, like the earlier part of the chapter, as deliberately stenographic.

Idea, can see no such relevant difference. The Idea, like the King of Balustan, is known to be mortal in common with its subjects but required to be immortal *ex officio*; and the subjects are expected to copy the first characteristic but not the second. For the Idea, like the King, the requirements remain an incurable contradiction.

This is enough to meet the challenge. Aristotle is fully entitled to use the Academy's assumptions at one point to involve them in further difficulties, as he does in the context from the *Metaphysics*, but at another to step back and prove contradictions in the assumptions themselves. It would be wrong, however, to leave the present passage of the *Topics* without noticing another more radical reply to the criticisms of Aristotle that scholars have built on it. There is a large and plausible assumption about the argument which is commonly made and which has so far remained without serious challenge. It is that the passage is concerned solely with the Platonic Ideas and that Aristotle's purpose in it is to admonish their adherents. This seems to me very possibly false.

Notice, to begin with, that the appeal to the *idea* is presented as valuable both in disputing and in establishing a property. If at the same time Aristotle were trying to dismantle the concept of *idea* on which this device depends he would be disabling his own claims for its value. 'But this is just what dialectic is – the supply and use of devices which are philosophically worthless but handy in a fight.' Even the hardiest reductivist might shrink from this reply, not just because it begs the question but because/ the price of begging it here **124**
is exorbitant: however devious one may want to believe Aristotle, it is just not credible that the very argument by which he recommends a dialectical manoeuvre is designed in the same breath to expose its failings.

The reason for supposing the passage to be directly concerned with the Platonic Ideas is the occurrence in it of language closely associated with Plato's theory: *idea*, and above all *autoanthrôpos*, 'man itself', and *autozôion*, 'animal itself'. Yet it is important to remember Aristotle's familiar attitude to such terminology. 'Those who assert the *ideas*' come under frequent fire, yet he himself constantly uses '*idea*' in the same sense as his own '*eidos*' (Bonitz, *Index*, 338b34-48). He complains that to call the Forms *paradigms* and say that other things *partake in* them is to talk vacuously, in poetic metaphors (*Meta.* 991a20-22); but he writes of his own forms as *to eidos kai to paradeigma* (*Phys.* 194b26 = *Meta.* 1013a27), and employs 'participation' as an important term of logic (Bonitz, *Index*, 462b36-42). He berates the Academy for admitting Forms *besides* the particulars (e.g. *A.Pst.* 77a5-7), yet he uses this very formula, *hen para ta polla*, of his own universals.[36] He denounces the prefix *auto*, which conventionally marks the designation of an Idea, as adding nothing to that designation except, perhaps, the indication that the Idea is an *eternal* sample of the predicate it carries (*Meta.* 997b5-12, *EN* 1096a34-b5). Yet he knows a use of this prefix in the Academy to pick out the universal even where

[36] *A.Pst.* 100a7, Alexander *in Meta.* 79. 16-19 (from the *Peri Ideôn*); cf. Cherniss *contra* Solmsen, op. cit. 77, n. 56.

its identity with the Idea is in dispute,[37] and elsewhere he distinguishes *autoepistêmê*, 'knowledge itself', as universal and therefore, in his own view, potential knowledge, from the Idea of knowledge which must be actual.[38] In general, then, Aristotle is ready on occasion to use Academic terminology for his own purposes, perhaps because it is familiar and in the context none of its special and objectionable connotations need come in question, perhaps because he takes himself, as with 'participation' and 'idea', to have improved and clarified the concepts behind the words. The present passage of the *Topics*
125 would read as a straightforward contribution of Aristotle's to the/ detection of properties if it were not for the echoes of Academic terminology; but elsewhere it would be absurd to construe all such echoes as showing that Aristotle was engaged either in polemic or in collaboration with the Platonists.

Aristotle illustrates his argument by observing that it is a property of *autozôion* to be a compound of soul and body. To Cherniss this mention of corporeality is 'itself an indication of sarcastic antagonism to the theory of ideas and expressive of the attitude that even for adherents of the theory the ideas as such are useless' (op. cit., 3). Düring calls it chicanery (*môkia*, 215). Yet here too the illustration is simply one which Aristotle himself accepts.[39] As I have argued, the verdict on Aristotle's candour and fairness in his treatment of Plato does not turn on the question whether the Ideas are under examination in this passage. But in fact Aristotle does not say, and need not be interpreted as hinting, that he is engaged in that old combat here.

I leave unexamined the curious argument at 162a24-34, whose point, as Professor de Vogel remarks, is not so much to discredit the Ideas as to show the vice of multiplying premisses *praeter necessitatem*. Nor can I pursue her into a survey of the many other arguments in the *Topics* which bear on some or other of Plato's views. Of these arguments those which criticize the Ideas are only a small part, and the scrutiny of them cannot go far to proving the general seriousness of Aristotle's dialectic or even its scrupulousness in handling one philosophical school. Still, if there were such a proof it would have to consist of such scrutinies. And so far as the evidence reviewed here is concerned, the conflation of dialectic with eristic seems to do small justice either to Aristotle's theory or, more important, to his practice. The reductive thesis has ground to make up if it is not to seem a better example of eristic than the evidence that is claimed for it.

[37] *Meta.* 1036b13-17, where *autogrammê*, 'line itself', means, as Bonitz says, simply 'ipsa natura et substantia lineae': the point holds good however the text is construed (Ross, *Meta.* II. 203; *contra*, Cherniss, op. cit. 567-8).

[38] *Meta.* 1050b34-1051a2, where the *autoepistêmê*, is the *katholou epistêmê*, 'universal knowledge', of 1087a10-25, as Cherniss remarks (op. cit. 344).

[39] *Pol.* 1254a34 (where for the sense of *prôton* cf. Bonitz, *Index*, 653a26-b7), *Pol.* 1277a6; cf. *Top.* 131a8-11.

13

'Tithenai ta phainomena'

The first part of this paper tries to account for an apparent discrepancy 83
between Aristotle's preaching and his practice on a point of method. The second part reinforces the first by suggesting a common source for many of the problems and methods found in the *Physics*.

I

There seems to be a sharp discrepancy between the methods of scientific reasoning recommended in the *Analytics* and those actually followed in the *Physics*. The difference is sometimes taken to lie in the fact that the *Posterior Analytics* pictures a science as a formal deductive system based on necessary truths whereas the *Physics* is more tentative and hospitable both in its premisses and in its methods. But this is too simple a contrast. It is true that for much of the *Physics* Aristotle is not arguing from the definitions of his basic terms but constructing those definitions. He sets out to clarify and harden such common ideas as change and motion, place and time, infinity and continuity, and in doing so he claims to be defining his subject-matter (*Phys.* III 1, 200b12-21). But after all the *Analytics* shows interest not only in the finished state of a science but in its essential preliminaries; it describes not
only the rigorous/ deduction of theorems but the setting up of the *archai*, the 84
set of special hypotheses and definitions, from which the deductions proceed. And the *Physics*, for its part, not only establishes the definitions of its basic concepts but uses them to deduce further theorems, notably in books VI and VIII. The discrepancy between the two works lies rather in the fact that, whereas the *Analytics* tries (though not without confusion and inconsistency) to distinguish the two processes of finding and then applying the principles, the *Physics* takes no pains to hold them apart. But there seems to be a more striking disagreement than this. It concerns the means by which the principles of the science are reached.

In the *Prior Analytics* Aristotle says: 'It falls to experience to provide the principles of any subject. In astronomy, for instance, it was astronomical experience that provided the principles of the science, for it was only when the *phainomena* were adequately grasped that the proofs in astronomy were discovered. And the same is true of any art or science whatever' (*A.Pr.* I 30, 46a17-22). Elsewhere he draws the same Baconian picture: the *phainomena* must be collected as a prelude to finding the theory which explains them. The

method is expressly associated with natural science (*phusikê*) and the natural scientist (*phusikos*),[1] and from the stock example in these contexts – astronomy – it seems clear that the *phainomena* in question are empirical observations.[2] Now such a method is plainly at home in the biological works and the meteorology;[3] equally plainly it is not at home in the *Physics*, where as
85 Mansion observes 'in general everything comes down to/ more or less detailed conceptual analyses – analyses often guided and illustrated by, rather than founded upon, empirical data' (*Introduction à la physique aristotélicienne*[2] (Louvain 1946), p.211). In this sense of '*phainomena*' it would be grossly misleading for Aristotle to claim that he is establishing the principles of his physics upon a survey of the *phainomena*. And there his critics are often content to leave the matter.

But in other contexts similarly concerned with methods of inquiry '*phainomena*' has another sense.[4] In the *Nicomachean Ethics* Aristotle prefaces his discussion of incontinence with the words: 'Here as in other cases we must set down the *phainomena* and begin by considering the difficulties, and so go on to vindicate if possible all the common conceptions about these states of mind, or at any rate most of them and the most important' (*EN* VII 1, 1145b2-6). Here Sir David Ross translates *phainomena* by 'observed facts', a translation evidently designed to bring Aristotle's programme into conformity with such passages as those already cited. But this can hardly be its sense here. For, in the first place, what Aristotle proceeds to set out are not the observed facts but the *endoxa*, the common conceptions on the subject (as the collocation of *phainomena* and *endoxa* in his preface would lead us to expect). He concludes his survey with the words 'these are the *legomena* (things said)' (VII 1, 1145b8-20), and the *legomena* turn out as so often to be partly matters of linguistic usage or, if you prefer, of the conceptual structure revealed by language (especially VII 1, 1145b10-15, 19-20). And, secondly, after this preliminary survey Aristotle turns to Socrates' claim that those who act
86 against their own conviction/ or what is best do so in ignorance, and says that this is plainly in conflict with the *phainomena* (*EN* VII 2, 1145b27-8). But he does not mean that, as Ross translates it, 'the view plainly contradicts the observed facts'. For he remarks later that his own conclusion about incontinence seems to coincide with what Socrates wanted to maintain (VII 3, 1147b14-15), and in reaching it he takes care to answer the question that he had named as a difficulty for Socrates, namely what kind of ignorance must be ascribed to the incontinent man (VII 2, 1145b28-9; 3, 1147b15-17). So Socrates' claim conflicts not with the facts but with what would commonly be said on the subject, and Aristotle does not undertake to save

[1] *PA* I 1, 639b5-10 with 640a13-15; *Cael.* III 7, 306a5-17.

[2] cf. further *A.Pst.* I 13, 78b39 with 79a2-6; *Cael.* II 13, 293a23-30; 14, 297a2-6; *Meta.* XII 8, 1073b32-8; Bonitz, *Index Arist.* 809a34ff.

[3] *PA* II 1, 646a8-12, referring to *HA* I 7, 491a7-14; *Meteor.* III 2, 371b18-22 with Olympiodorus' scholium (217.23-27, Stueve. Olympiodorus' reference to *GC* is to I 5, not II 8 as Stueve and Ideler think).

[4] There is a temptation to distinguish this sense as what *phainetai einai* by contrast with what *phainetai on*. But this overstates the difference; see pp. 242-4 below. Aristotle is ready to use *phainesthai* with the infinitive even of empirical observations; cf. *De An.* I 5, 411b19-22.

everything that is commonly said. He is anxious, unlike Socrates, to leave a use for the expression 'knowing what is right but doing what is wrong', but he is ready to show *a priori* that there is no use for the expression 'doing what is wrong in the full knowledge of what is right *in the given circumstances*'.[5] It is in the same sense of the word that all dialectical argument can be said to start from the *phainomena*.[6]

This ambiguity in *phainomena*, which was seen by Alexander (*Meteor.* 33.6-9), carries with it a corresponding distinction in the use of various connected expressions. Induction (*epagôgê*) can be said to establish the principles of science by starting from the data of perception (*A.Pst.* II 19,
100b3-5; I 18, 81a38-b9)./ Yet *epagôgê* is named as one of the two cardinal **87**
methods of dialectic (*Top.* I 12, 105a10-19) and as such must begin from the *endoxa*, what is accepted by all or most men or by the wise (*Top.* I 1, 100b21-3); and in this form too it can be used to find the principles of the sciences (*Top.* I 2, 101a36-b4). Similarly with the puzzles (*aporiai*). When the *phainomena* are empirical data such as those collected in the biology and meteorology, the *aporiai* associated with them will tend to be questions of empirical fact (*Meteor.* II 3, 357b26-30) or of the explanation of such facts,[7] or the problem of squaring a recalcitrant fact with an empirical hypothesis (*Meteor.* II 2, 355b20-32). In the discussion of incontinence, on the other hand, where the *phainomena* are things that men are inclined or accustomed to say on the subject, the *aporiai* that Aristotle sets out are not unexplained or recalcitrant data of observation but logical or philosophical puzzles generated, as such puzzles have been at all times, by exploiting some of the things commonly said. Two of the paradoxes are veterans, due to Socrates and the sophists (*EN* VII 2, 1145b23-27, 1146a21-31). The first of the set ends with the words: 'If so, we shall have to say that the man of practical wisdom is incontinent, *but no one would say this*' (not that it happens to be false, but that given the established use of the words it is absurd) (ibid. 1146a5-7). The last ends: 'But we say [i.e. it is a common form of words] that some men are incontinent, without further qualification' (ibid. 1146b4-5).

Now if the *Physics* is to be described as setting out from a survey of the *phainomena* it is plainly this second sense of the word that is more appropriate. Take as an example the analysis of place. It opens with four arguments for the existence of place of which the first states what *dokei* or seems to be the case (it
appeals to established/ ways of talking about physical replacement) (*Phys.* IV **88**
1, 208b1,5), the third states what certain theorists say (*legousi*: ibid. 208b26),

[5] *EN* VII 3, 1146b35-1147a10, 1147a24-b14. But Ross's translation of *phainomena* in the two passages I, 1145b3 and 2, 1145b28 is at any rate consistent and so superior to that adopted by most scholars from Heliodorus to Gauthier-Jolif, who see that at its first occurrence the word must mean *endoxa* (cf. Heliodorus *Paraphr.* 131.16, Heylbut) but suppose that at its occurrence 25 lines later it means the unquestionable facts (ibid. 137.29-30).

[6] *A.Pr.* I 1, 24b10-12; *Top.* VIII 5, 159b17-23. cf. *Phys.* IV 1, 208a32-34, where the *phainomenon* is the theory as contrasted with the facts (*ta huparchonta*). At *Cael.* II 5, 288a1-2; 12, 291b25; IV 1, 308a6; *PA* I 5, 645a5, it is the speaker's own view.

[7] *Meteor.* I 13, 349a12-14 with a31-b2; II 5, 362a1-13; *Long.* 1, 464b21-30; *GA* IV 4, 770b28-30 with 771a14-17; *HA* VI 37, 580b14-17.

the fourth quotes what Hesiod and the majority think (*nomizousi:* ibid. 208b32-3), and the remaining one relies on the doctrine of natural places which is later taken as an *endoxon.*[8] Of the *aporiai* which follow, one is due to Zeno, one is due to an equally rich source of logical paradoxes of which I shall say more in a later section, and all ultimately depend on the convictions or usage of the many or the wise. Nor are these arguments merely accessory to the main analysis: those of the *dokounta* which survive the preliminary difficulties are taken over as premisses for what follows.[9] 'For if the difficulties are resolved and the *endoxa* are left standing', as Aristotle says in both the *Physics* and the *Ethics*, 'this in itself is a sufficient proof'.[10] As for *epagôgê*, when it is used in the argument it proves to be not a review of observed cases but a dialectical survey of the senses of the word 'in'.[11]

By such arguments the *Physics* ranks itself not with physics, in our sense of the word, but with philosophy. Its data are for the most part the materials not of natural history but of dialectic, and its problems are accordingly not questions of empirical fact but conceptual puzzles. Now this reading of the work is strikingly reinforced, as it seems to me, when we recognise the influence of one other work in particular on the argument of the *Physics*. In a following section of this paper I shall try to show that in the *Physics* Aristotle over and again takes his start, not from his own or others' observations, but
89 from a/ celebrated set of logical paradoxes that may well have appeared during his own early years in the Academy. Far more than that over-mined quarry the *Timaeus*, it is the *Parmenides* which supplies Aristotle in the *Physics* not only with many and perhaps most of his central problems but with the terminology and methods of analysis that he uses to resolve them. But before turning to this evidence let us see whether we are yet in a position to explain the discrepancy from which we set out.

Can we appeal to this ambiguity in Aristotle's terminology in order to explain how such a generalisation as that quoted from the *Prior Analytics* could be taken to cover the methods of the *Physics*? By now the ambiguity seems too radical for our purpose. Even within the second sense of *phainomena*, the sense in which it is equated with *endoxa* and *legomena*, some essential distinctions lie concealed. For an appeal to a *legomenon* may be an appeal either to common belief about matters of fact (e.g. *EN* I 11, 1101a22-24) or to established forms of language (e.g. VII 1, 1145b19-20: 2, 1146b4-5) or to a philosophical thesis claiming the factual virtues of the first and the analytic certainty of the second (e.g. I 8, 1098b12-18). And the broader ambiguity between the two senses of the word was one which Aristotle himself had the means to expose. For when he wishes to restrict *phainomenon* to its first sense he calls it expressly

[8] *Phys.* IV 1, 208b8-25; 4, 211a4-6 with Ross's note on 5, 212b29-34 (*Aristotle's Physics* (Oxford 1936), 580).

[9] *Phys.* IV 4, 210b32-211a7. Thus for instance the common conception of place as a container which is not part of what it contains (1, 208b1-8; 2, 209b28-30) must be rescued from Zeno's puzzle (1, 209a23-6; 3, 210b22-7) by a survey of the senses of 'this is in that' (3, 210a14 ff.), and can then be taken as secure (4, 210b34-211a1).

[10] *EN* VII 1, 1145b6-7; *Phys.* IV 4, 211a7-11. The verb for proof in each case is *deiknunai.*

[11] *Phys.* IV 3, 210b8-9 (*epaktikôs skopousin*) with 210a14-24.

a *perceptual phainomenon* and distinguishes it from an *endoxon* (*Cael.* III 4, 303a22-23). And in the *De Caelo* it is this more precise form of words that he uses to describe the criterion by which the correctness of our principles in physics must ultimately be assessed (7, 306a16-17).

I think such considerations show that it is a mistake to ask, in the hope of some quite general answer, what function Aristotle assigns to *phainomena*, or to *aporiai*, or to *epagôgê*; for they show how the function can vary with the context and style of inquiry. But we have pressed them too hard if they
prevent/ us from understanding how Aristotle could have taken the formula 90
in the *Analytics* to apply to the *Physics* as well as to the *Historia Animalium*. If there is more than one use for the expression *phainomena*, the uses have a great deal in common. Thus for example it is not a peculiarity of *phainomena* in the second sense that they may fail to stand up to examination; for so may the *phainomena* of perception,[12] and within this latter class Aristotle is careful to specify only the reliable members as a touchstone for the correctness of physical principles.[13] As for his favourite example, astronomy, Aristotle knew (or came to realise) how inadequate were the observations of the astronomers (*PA* I 5, 644b24-28). And of the biological 'observations' many were bound to be hearsay, *legomena* to be treated with caution (e.g. *HA* II 1, 501a25-b1). Such *phainomena* must be 'properly established', ascertained to be 'true data' (*A.Pr.* I 30, 46a20, 25). In the same fashion the *endoxa* must pass the appropriate scrutiny, but in doing so they too become firm data.[14] Nor, if Aristotle associates the *phainomena* with experience (*empeiria*), as he does in the text from the *Analytics*, must it be supposed that his words are meant to apply only to *phainomena* in the first sense. *Endoxa* also rest on experience, even if they misrepresent it (e.g. *Div.* 1, 462b14-18). If they did not Aristotle could find no place for them in his epistemology; as it is, an *endoxon* that is shared by all men is *ipso facto* beyond challenge.[15]

Nor is it in the least surprising if Aristotle, writing in the tradition of Parmenides and Protagoras, tended to assimilate these different senses of
phainomena. For Parmenides, the/'mortal opinions' include not only the 91
supposed evidence of the senses but the common assumptions (and specifically the common use of language) which form men's picture of the physical world.[16] As for Protagoras, both Plato and Aristotle represent his theory as applying indifferently to perceptual phenomena and *endoxa* and use *phainesthai* in describing both these applications.[17] It is the same broad use of the word that is to be found in the formula from the *Prior Analytics*. In the *De Caelo*, it is true, Aristotle observes that it is the *phainomena* of *perception* by which we must

[12] *Cael.* II 8, 290a13-24 and especially *Meta.* IV 5, 1010b1-11. (On Protagoras cf. below.)

[13] *Cael.* III 7, 306a16-17: *to phainomenon aei kuriôs kata tên aisthêsin* 'the perceptual *phainomenon* that is reliable when it occurs', *not*, as Tricot translates, 'l'évidence toujours souveraine de la perception sensible': for *kuriôs* here cf. *Meta.* IV 5, 101b14-19.

[14] *Phys.* IV 4, 210b32-4, 211a7-11; *EN* VII 1, 1145b6-7.

[15] *EN* X 2, 1172b36-1173a1; cf. VIII 13, 1153b27-28; *EE* I 6, 1216b26-35.

[16] A conflation helped by talking as though data of perception were themselves arbitrary assumptions (B8. 38-41 DK). On the 'common uses of language' see B8. 53; B9; B8. 38.

[17] *Crat.* 386a1; *Meta.* IV 5, 1010b1, 1009a38-b2.

ultimately test the adequacy of our principles in physics (III 7, 306a16-17); but this is said of *phusikê* as a whole, a body of science in which the analyses of the *Physics* proper are preliminary to other more empirical inquiries and consequently must be justified, in the last resort, by their success in making sense of the observations to which they are applied. But this is not to say (and it does not commit Aristotle to supposing) that in the *Physics* proper the analyses either start from or are closely controlled by our inspections of the world. Nor in fact is he liable to consider his analyses endangered by such inspections: if his account of motion shows that any unnatural movement requires an agent of motion in constant touch with the moving body, the movement of a thrown ball can be explained by inventing a set of unseen agents to fill the gap (*Phys.* VIII 10, 266b27-267a20). The *phainomena* to which the *Physics* pays most attention are the familiar data of dialectic, and from the context in the *Prior Analytics* it seems clear that Aristotle's words there are meant to cover the use of such data. For in concluding the passage and the discussion in which it occurs Aristotle observes that he has been talking at large about the ways in which the premisses of deductive argument are to be chosen; and he refers for a more detailed treatment of the same matter to the
92 'treatise on dialectic' (*A.Pr.* I 30, 46a28-30). He/ evidently has in mind the claim made in the *Topics* that the first premisses of scientific argument can be established by methods which start from the *endoxa*.[18]

II

I turn to the part played by the *Parmenides*, and specifically by the arguments in which 'Aristotle' is the interlocutor, in shaping the *Physics*. Perhaps it is by misreading the *Physics* as a confused and cross-bred attempt at empirical science that critics have been led to look for its antecedents elsewhere and so to make excessive claims for its originality. So it is worth dwelling on this particular Platonic influence, partly for the light that it throws on the methods and interests of Aristotle's work, partly to call in question the claim that 'the discussions in books III-VI ... attack a series of problems for which there was little in Plato's teaching to prepare the way',[19] and partly to establish, if this needs establishing, that the *Parmenides* was not read by the Academy either as a joke or as a primer of fallacies.[20] What the positive aims of the dialogue may have been does not concern us: the present inquiry is a necessary preliminary to settling such questions.

[18] *Top.* I 2, 101a36-b4. Ross seems to mistake the sense of the *A.Pr.* text (46a28-30) when he writes: 'It is of course only the selection of premisses of *dialectical* reasoning that is discussed in the *Topics*; the nature of the premisses of scientific reasoning is discussed in the *Posterior Analytics*' (*Aristotle's Prior and Posterior Analytics* (Oxford 1949), 396). But in this passage Aristotle is concerned with finding the principles of scientific reasoning, and must be thinking of the claim made in the *Topics* to find such principles dialectically.

[19] Ross, *Aristotle's Physics*, p.9.

[20] In this respect what follows can be read as complementary to D.J. Allan 'Aristotle and the *Parmenides*', in *Aristotle and Plato in the Mid-Fourth Century*, ed. I. Düring and G.E.L. Owen (Göteborg 1960).

Consider the celebrated account of the point. It is Plato in the *Parmenides* who argues first that what is indivisible (namely the One, which cannot be plural and so has no parts) cannot have a location. For to have a location is to have surroundings, i.e. to be contained in something; and this is to be contained either in something other than oneself or in oneself. But to be contained in something other than oneself is to have a/circumference and to be in contact **93**
with that other thing at various points, and an indivisible thing cannot have various points of a circumference distinct from its centre. Nor can a thing without parts be contained in itself, for this would entail dividing it into container and contained, and no such division of it is possible. 'Hence it is not anywhere, since it is neither in itself nor in another'.[21] This concept of place as surroundings is normal in Greek philosophy, as the arguments of Zeno and Gorgias show (and in ordinary conversation, which has small use for plotting objects by Cartesian co-ordinates, it still is so). Aristotle took it over as an *endoxon* and made a more sophisticated version of it in the fourth book of the *Physics*. And one problem that he raises at the start of his argument depends on the assumption that if a point has any location it must be its own location, an assumption that flatly conflicts with the received view that place is a container distinct from the thing contained (*Phys.* IV 1, 209a7-13). Aristotle does not argue the assumption; plainly he is drawing on Plato's argument that an indivisible cannot be contained in something else, nor yet can there be any distinction within it between container and contained. And he concludes that a point cannot be said to have a location (*Phys.* IV 5, 212b24-25).

On the way to this conclusion, and as a preface to his general account of place, he lists the different senses in which one thing can be said to be in another (*Phys.* IV 3, 210a14-24), and follows this with an argument to show that a thing cannot be said to be in itself except in the loose sense that it may be a whole having parts present in it (210a25-b22).This sense is sharply distinguished from the 'strictest sense of all', that in which a thing is said to be in a place (210a24). Why does he spend so much time on this? Because/ of **94**
further arguments in the *Parmenides*. Having maintained, in the first arm of his argument about the One, that an indivisible cannot be contained in itself, Plato goes on in the second arm to reduce his subject to a whole of parts and so, by dubious steps, to reimport the notion of place. For (*a*) since the subject is in itself in the sense that all its parts are contained in it (145b6-c7), it is always 'in the same thing', i.e. in the same place and hence at rest (145e7-146a3); and (*b*) since the subject is not in itself, in the sense that as a whole it is not contained in any or all of its parts, it must be always in something else (145c7-e3) and so never at rest (146a3-6). Among other eccentricities, the argument clearly relies on (and I think is clearly out to expose) an ambiguity in the form of expression 'being in so-and-so': it shows that any sense of the phrase in which a thing can be said to be in itself cannot be the appropriate sense for talking of location, otherwise paradoxes result. Anaxagoras had traded on this ambiguity (*Phys.* III 5, 205b1-5), and no doubt Plato wrote with Anaxagoras in mind; but that

[21] *Parm.* 138a2-b6 (Burnet's lineation). The lack of shape and circumference is proved in 137d8-138a1.

Aristotle's arguments are framed primarily with a view to those of the *Parmenides* is shown by the fact that he mentions Anaxagoras' thesis not in this context but elsewhere and by the clear echoes of Plato's language in his own.[22]

Points, then, cannot have location. And it is Plato who first proves the corollary, that something without parts cannot be said to move. But his reason is not just that what has no location cannot be said to change location. It is that to move to a certain place is a process, and there must be some intermediate
95 stage of the process at which the moving body has/ arrived partly but not altogether (*Parm.* 138d2-e7). And it is just this argument that Aristotle in the *Physics* takes over and generalises, so that it applies to other forms of change besides locomotion (VI 10, 240b8-241a6). Again, Plato prefaces his proof that an indivisible thing cannot change place by showing that it cannot even rotate in one place, since rotation entails a distinction between a centre and other parts (*Parm.* 138c7-32); and with this in mind Aristotle prefaces his argument by noticing the case in which a point might be said to move if it were part of a rotating body, but only because the whole body, which has a distinct centre and circumference, can be said to move in the strict sense (*Phys.* VI 10, 240b15-20). Since it is often mistakenly said that Aristotle accepted the definition of a line as the path of a moving point,[23] it is worth stressing how thoroughly he accepts Plato's reduction of this idea to absurdity – a *reductio* which no doubt counted as part of Plato's 'war against the whole class of points' (*Meta.* I 9, 992a19-22).

Again, consider the account of a connected concept, continuity. In the *Parmenides* Plato defines 'contact' (*haptesthai*) in terms of 'succession' (*ephexês*) and 'neighbouring position' (*echomenê chôra*) (*Parm.* 148e7-10). These terms Aristotle takes up in the fifth book of the *Physics*. 'Contact' he defines as holding between terms whose extremities are together, i.e. in one and the same place;[24] an unhappy suggestion, since in themselves extremities can have no magnitude
96 and so no position. And then,/changing Plato's order of definition, he defines 'neighbouring' (*echomenon*) in terms of 'contact' and 'succession' (*Phys.* V 3, 227a6-7). From both accounts, it is clear, the same implication can be derived: Plato, by defining contact in terms of neighbouring *position*, and Aristotle, by defining it in terms of things having *extremities*, preclude the attempt to talk of a series of points as having contact with each other and so making up a line or any other magnitude. But this result only follows from Plato's definition if it is

[22] e.g. *Phys.* IV 3, 210a25-6 = *Parm.* 145d7-e1; *Phys.* IV 3, 210a27-9 = *Parm.* 145c4-7. Notice too that by *merê* here Plato means attributes of the subject, i.e. its being and unity and their derivatives (cf. 142d1-5); and that in the corresponding context of the *Physics* Aristotle corrects this use of the word by pointing out that attributes may be contained *kata merê* in the subject not as being *merê* themselves (which he rejects, *Cat.* 2, 1a24-5) but as being attributes of *merê* (*Phys.* IV 3, 210a29-30).

[23] e.g. by Heath, *Mathematics in Aristotle* (Oxford 1949), 117; he cites *De An.* 14, 409a4-5, where Aristotle is reporting someone else's theory. Of other passages which seem to imply this view *Phys.* IV 11, 219b16-20 can be read otherwise and *Phys.* V 4, 227b16-17 may represent an objector's view. But Aristotle does inconsistently credit points with location at *A.Pst.*, I 27, 87a36; 32, 88a33-4; *Meta.* V 6, 1016b25-6, 30-1, and perhaps with the possibility of being in contact at *Phys.* V 3, 227a27-30 (but this seems to depend on the un-Aristotelian thesis in lines 27-8).

[24] *Phys.* V 3, 226b23. 'Together' (*hama*) is defined in 226b21-22.

coupled with the argument that an indivisible thing cannot have position: and no doubt it was this that determined Aristotle to reform the definition so that the conclusion would follow directly from the simple premiss that a point has no parts or extremities. This reordering of the definition would not have served Plato's purpose, for in this particular chain of reasoning in the *Parmenides* he reserves the right to treat his subject as indivisible[25] without committing himself to the conclusion that it can therefore have no location. His definition allows him to talk of an indivisible thing as having contact with something else, and when he proves that it cannot have contact with itself it is on other grounds than the mere lack of location (*Parm.* 148e10-149a3). As a result his proof is valid for all things and not merely for indivisibles. But it is plain that his definition of contact, taken together with his denial of location to indivisibles, produces exactly the conclusions which Aristotle draws from his own definitions at the beginning of the sixth book of the *Physics* (1, 231a21-b10), namely that there is no sense in saying that lines are collections of points in contact. It was in the *Parmenides* that Aristotle found not only the general approach to his problem but the special ideas in terms of which he treats it.[26]/

There is another point in these contexts at which Aristotle corrects Plato. **97**
For Plato, contact requires *immediate* (*euthus*) succession in the contiguous terms, and this immediacy he explains by saying that they must occupy neighbouring positions (*Parm.* 148e7-10). But a little later he explains this requirement in turn by saying that there must be no third thing between the two terms (149a6); and Aristotle is anxious to find room for this condition too in his definitions. He cannot use it to define 'neighbouring', since he has another definition of that concept in view; so he uses it to define 'successive' (*Phys.* V 3, 226b34-227a4), and in doing so he adds an important qualification: there must be nothing between the terms *of the same kind as themselves* (*Phys.* V 3, 227a1; cf. VI 1, 231b8-9). If A B C are consecutive sections of a straight line, *C* cannot follow *ephexês* after *A*, but it evidently can do so if *B* is merely a point. In correcting Plato here Aristotle may have in mind the treatment of limits in one passage of the *Parmenides* as parts of a thing, logically comparable with what lies between them (137d4-5); but this is a treatment that Plato's own argument enables Aristotle to reject.

There is an embarrassing wealth of examples of this influence in the *Physics*, and I shall not bore you with them all. But one group is too important to omit. We saw earlier that, in arguing that an indivisible thing cannot move, Plato (and Aristotle after him) treated movement as a process taking time and having intermediate stages. As Aristotle would say, it is a continuous change, divisible into parts which are themselves changes taking time. But later in the *Parmenides*

[25] *Parm.* 147a8-b2; but earlier in the same movement he has treated it as divisible into parts and continues to do so later.

[26] Another such term in the same context is *chôris* (*Parm.* 149a5), taken over and defined by Aristotle. And there are other reminiscences of Plato's treatment of these ideas. One is the comment at *Phys.* I 2, 185b11-16, which Aristotle admits to be irrelevant to the argument in hand. Why does he introduce it? Because he has just mentioned continuity, and this reminds him of Plato's argument in this connection that, since the parts can be distinguished from the whole, the whole can have contact with itself (*Parm.* 148d6-7, 148e1-3).

Plato argues that if a change is construed as the passage from not-*A* to *A* the
98 change must be instantaneous; for there is no time/ in which a thing can be neither *A* nor not-*A*, neither at rest (for instance) nor in motion.[27] And this introduction of changes which are not processes is carefully prepared by some earlier arguments. Twice – once in each of the first two chains of argument about the One – Plato discusses the logic of growing older. In the first argument (141a6-c4) he considers it as a special case of becoming different; and he argues that if *X* is becoming different from *Y* it cannot be the case that *Y* already is different from *X*, since otherwise *X* would already be different from *Y* and not merely becoming so. All that follows from '*X* is becoming different from *Y*' is another proposition about becoming, '*Y* is becoming different from *X*'. The conclusion is applied forthwith to the particular case, to show that if *X* is becoming older than itself it is at the same time becoming younger. But on a later page the same example is taken up again (152a5-e3). Now Plato argues that at any moment during the process of growing older the subject must *be* older; at any stage of becoming different, the thing must already be different. For to say that it is becoming different is to say something about its future as well as its present; but so far as the bare present is concerned, it must already be something that it was becoming, given that the process of change is under way at all. Thus the argument relies heavily on the law of excluded middle: either the changing thing is already different, or it is not. If it is not, the process of change is not yet under way. And if it is, then the old conclusion, that from '*X* is becoming different from *Y*' we can infer only what *X* and *Y* are becoming and not what they are, breaks down. The old conclusion relied on inserting a *tertium quid* between '*X* is different' and '*X* is not different', namely '*X* is becoming different', something temporally intermediate between the first two; but such a *tertium quid* is ruled out by the law of excluded middle. Yet it is just this law that leads to the problem of instantaneous change with which we began; for Plato
99 goes on to argue that/ if there is no time in which a thing can be neither *A* nor not-*A*, neither still nor moving, it baffles us to say when it makes the change from the one to the other (156c1-7). When it changes from rest to motion it cannot be either at rest (for then the change would be still to come) or moving (for then the change would be past). Yet the change is not to be talked away: 'if a thing changes, it *changes*'.[28]

Here then is the problem, and the whole context of argument, taken over by Aristotle. It is generally held that Plato's purpose was to show that there can be no *period* of time during which a thing is neither *A* nor not-*A*, and consequently that the change from one to the other must occur at a moment of time.[29] But Aristotle evidently thought the puzzle more radical, and I think he was right.

[27] *Parm.* 156c6-7; the whole context is 155e4-157b5.

[28] *Parm.* 156c7-8: 'But it does not change (*metaballei*) without changing'. Cornford (*Plato and Parmenides* (London 1939), 200, n.2) mistakes the sense, insisting that the statement is 'intelligible only if we suppose that Plato shifts here from the common use of *metaballein* for "change" in general to the stricter sense of "transition" or passing from one state to another'. What Plato means is like our truism 'business is business' – i.e. it mustn't be taken for anything else or explained away. He would probably regard Aristotle as explaining such changes away.

[29] Cornford goes so far as to call it a 'businesslike account of the instant' (ibid., 203).

For by the same law of excluded middle not only is there no period but there is no point of time at which a thing can be neither *A* nor not-*A*. At any rate, whether Aristotle is enlarging or merely preserving Plato's problem, he gives it considerable space in the *Physics*. He agrees that some changes take no time at all (VIII 3, 253b21-30, cf. I 3, 186a13-16). Among other instances he cites the recovery of health, which is 'a change to health and to nothing else' (VIII 3, 253b26-28); in other words, although the process towards recovery may take time, the actual recovery is simply the change from not-*A* to *A*.[30] In any process
of change to a given state there will be a similar completion of/ the change, and **100**
this will take no time (VI 5, 235b32-236a7); the argument at once recalls Plato's discussion of the transition from movement to stillness. Later, in the eighth book, Aristotle faces the problem squarely. It will not help, he argues, to postulate a time-atom between the period in which something is not white and the subsequent period in which it is white, with a view simply to providing a time for the change to occur from not-white to white. For one thing, time-atoms cannot be consecutive to periods of time or to other time-atoms, just as points cannot have contact either with lines or with other points. Moreover the suggestion would set a regress on foot. For when we have postulated one time-atom to house the change from not-white to white, there will be another change to be accommodated in the same way: the change from changing to being white (VIII 8, 263b26-264a1). In brief, Aristotle takes the puzzle to show that it is a mistake to look for a special time-reference such that the subject is then neither white nor not-white. The primary moment at which the subject becomes (or, as Aristotle prefers to say, has become) white is the first moment at which it is white.[31] And, given this moment, it becomes improper to talk of the last moment at which the subject was *not* white, for the two moments would have to be consecutive (VIII 8, 264a3-4). Equally, given a last moment of stability there cannot be a first moment of change (VI 5, 236a7-27). And Aristotle, having thus saved the situation and the law of excluded middle, can take over without qualms the moral of Plato's second
analysis of growing older: namely that at any time/ during the period in which **101**
a thing is becoming different, it has already completed a change and to that extent is different from what it was (VI 6, 236b32-237a17).

His reply to Plato's puzzle has side-effects on other discussions. To underline the paradox, Plato had called all change from not-*A* to *A* 'sudden' change (*exaiphnês*; 156d1-e3). Aristotle restores the word to its proper use: it is used of what departs from its previous condition in an imperceptibly short time (IV 13, 222b14-16). But all change, he adds, involves departing from a previous

[30] Ross explains it otherwise; but for the treatment of *hugiansis* (recovery) as the limit of a *kinêsis* (process) cf. *Meta.* IX 6, 1048b18-23.

[31] ibid., 263b9-26, 264a2-4; cf. the earlier argument in VI 5, 235b32-236a7. The solution of Plato's puzzle given in *Physics* VIII 8 is more trenchant than the earlier reply in VI 9 (240a19-29): there Aristotle suggested that even between not-*A* and *A* a *tertium quid* could be inserted, namely when the subject is neither *wholly not-A* nor *wholly A*; but this is easily defeated by reformulating the contradictions as 'wholly *A*' and 'not wholly *A*'. Just as the reply to Zeno which is given in VI 9 is admitted to be inadequate in VIII 8 (263a15-18), so the reply to Plato's puzzle given in VI 9 is superseded in the same later chapter.

condition; and his motive for adding this is clear. He has in mind that because of this characteristic Plato had tried to reduce all change to sudden change, and he implies that this was a misleading extension of the word's use. There is nothing physically startling in most changes and nothing logically startling in any of them.

There is no need to go on. It might indeed be objected that the evidence does not necessarily show that Aristotle was indebted to the *Parmenides*; both Plato and Aristotle may have been drawing on a lost source. These problems were surely discussed in the Academy,[32] and the Academy in turn must surely have drawn on earlier arguments, in particular those of Zeno and Gorgias. The general purposes of this paper would be as well served by such a theory, but it cannot account for the intricate correspondence that we have seen in our two texts. Gorgias' part in the matter is guesswork: the evidence for his sole adventure into abstract thought has been contaminated, probably beyond cure, by traditions to which both the *Parmenides* and the *Physics* contributed. Of Zeno luckily we know more; we know that Plato does echo some arguments of
102 Zeno,/ but that he transforms them radically for his own ends.[33] The *Parmenides* was not a historical anthology, and when Aristotle's words and ideas coincide closely with those of the dialogue he is under the spell of a work of astonishing brilliance and originality. A work, moreover, of logic or dialectic, not in the least a piece of empirical science; and the *Physics* is in great parts its successor.

This is not to say, of course, that Aristotle would call his methods in the *Physics* wholly dialectical. He, and his commentators on his behalf, have insisted on the distinction between 'physical' and 'dialectical', or 'logical', or 'universal', arguments; and no doubt some of the reasoning in the *Physics* falls within the first class. Yet even if the distinction were (as it seldom is) sharp and fundamental in sciences where a knowledge of particular empirical fact is in question (e.g. *GA* II 8, 747b27-748a16), we need not expect it to be so in such an inquiry as the *Physics*. This is clear from the one major example of the contrast that is offered in the work, the dialectical and physical proofs that there can be no infinite physical body.[34] The dialectical proof is evidently distinguished by

[32] We know for instance that others had tried to define continuity (*Phys.* III 1, 200b18-20), though they did not make use of the nexus of ideas common to Plato's and Aristotle's treatments of the subject; hence Aristotle can take over their definition at the start of the *Physics* (I 2, 185b10-11) before producing his own revision of Plato's account.

[33] The Arrow underlies *Parm.* 152b2-d2, and the argument of B1 and 2 in Diels-Kranz (the resolution of a thing into its fractions without ever reaching ultimate units) underlies *Parm.* 164c8-d4 and 165a5-b6. I have not been convinced by H. Fraenkel's interpretation of B3, nor therefore by his claim that it underlies the last-mentioned passages of the dialogue: see 'Zeno of Elea's attacks on plurality', *American Journal of Philology* 63 (1942), 6, 198-9 = *Wege und Formen*[3] (Munich 1968), pp. 203, 227-8. Fraenkel is also inclined to see the Arrow behind *Parm.* 145-6 (art.cit., p.13, n.33 = *Wege und Formen*, 210, n.1), where others will more readily detect Anaxagoras (cf. p.120 above); and he sees B4 behind *Parm.* 156c-d (ibid., pp. 11-13; pp.207-9). He says all that is necessary for my purpose when he observes that in such echoes 'Plato modifies the argument and ... transfers it, as it were, to a higher order'.

[34] *Phys.* III 5, 204b4-206a8. There is a second use of the same distinction (unnoticed by Bonitz, op.cit., *logikôs*) at VIII 8, 264a7-9, and here too it proves elusive. The 'logical' arguments can hardly be marked by their generality (the 'more appropriate argument' at 246b1-2 itself

the fact that it proves too much:/starting from a definition that applies to 103
mathematical as well as to physical solids, it reaches conclusions that apply to both sciences.[35] Yet immediately after his promise to turn to physical arguments Aristotle produces a proof that no complex body can be infinite, and this proof shares the characteristics of its predecessor. It relies partly on quite general definitions of 'body' and 'infinite' (204b20-21), partly on a treatment of the ratio between finite and infinite terms which could be formulated quite generally,[36] and which in fact is later given a different application to speed and resistance (IV 8, 215b10-216a11); and partly, perhaps, on the argument against an infinite number of elements which occurs in the first book and relies largely on quite general premisses (III 5, 204b12-13; I 6, 189a12-20). Certainly there are other arguments in the context which seem to depend on special empirical claims, such as the unfortunate hypothesis of natural places.[37] But the impulse throughout the work is logical, and the restriction of its subject-matter to movable bodies and their characteristics does not entail a radical difference of method from other logical inquiries. It makes for better understanding to recall that in Aristotle's classification of the sciences the discussions of time and movement in the *Parmenides* are also physics.

---

applies to kinds of change other than movement) nor the 'physical' by their reliance on the special theorems of physics (the 'logical' also may do this, 264a24).

[35] *Phys.* III 5, 204b4-7; cf. Ross's notes on 204b4, 204b6.

[36] ibid. 204b11-19: a particularly clear case of the artificial restriction of a general theorem of proportion so as to bring it within 'physics'.

[37] *Phys.* III 5, 205a10-12; but for the treatment of this too as an *endoxon*, see n.8 above.

14

Inherence

97 Often in the *Categories* and once in the *Topics* Aristotle draws a distinction between *being in a subject* and *being said*, or *predicated, of a subject* (*Cat.* 1a20-b9, 2a11-14, 2a27-b6, 2b15-17, 3a7-32, 9b22-24; *Postpred.* 11b38-12a17, 14a16-18; *Top.* 127b1-4). Elsewhere he makes no use of the distinction, at least in this form. Once in the *Categories* he blankets it under the formula *belonging to something* (11b38-12a17). But it has earned a good deal of attention, and there is a fashionable dogma about it that I should like to nail. Hints of the dogma can be seen in older writers such as Porphyry and Pacius. Its modern exponents are Ross, *Aristotle*, p. 24 n.1; Jones, *Phil. Rev.* (1949), 152-70; and most recently Miss Anscombe in *Three Philosophers*, pp. 7-10, and Mr. Ackrill in *Aristotle's 'Categories' and 'De Interpretatione'*, pp. 74-5, 83, 109.

For a start let us mark out an area of agreement. Set aside the question whether Aristotle thinks of a predicate primarily as an expression, or as what an expression stands for, or as both indifferently: let us for grammatical convenience have predicates in quotation marks and reserve the right to shift on occasion into the material mode. Then it is generally agreed that for 'X' to be predicable of Y, in the sense required by the *Categories*, it must be proper to say 'Y is X' (or 'is an X' or 'is a kind of X'). If Socrates is a man, what is predicable of him is 'man' and not 'manhood'; it would be absurd, or a stretch of language, to say that Socrates is (or is a kind of) manhood. (One sin of the old Oxford translation was in writing 'manhood' for 'man' at 3a12-13.) Jones is virtuous: 'virtuous' is his predicate, but what is *in* him is virtue (or, not to beg the later question, some virtue). If 'virtue' is to be predicated its subject must be not a man but a virtue, such as breviloquence.

Again it is agreed that for Aristotle this is only a necessary condition of predicability. It is not a sufficient condition, for Aristotle will not allow the designation of a primary substance to occur in the predicate-position. To say that the man with no shoes is Socrates is not to predicate (or, in the concessive phrase of *A.Pr.* 43a34-5, it is only to predicate *kata sumbebêkos*,
98 incidentally). Why not? Aristotle gives no rule. But his/ reason is commonly taken to be that to predicate of an individual is not to name or, in a strong sense, to identify that individual. It is to classify it or to bring it under some general description. I hope agreement goes as far as this.

Now in introducing his distinction Aristotle says: 'Some things are in a subject but not said of any subject. By "in a subject" I mean what (a) is in something not as a part, and (b) cannot exist separately from what it is in. For example, some particular linguistic knowledge is in a subject, viz. the mind, but it is not said of any subject; and some particular light colour is in a subject, viz. the body (for every colour is in a body), but it is not said of any subject' (1a23-29). *Leukon ti*, 'a particular light colour', not 'a particular white': people may forget or deny that there are different particular shades of white. *Leukon* covers all light colours as *melan* covers all dark colours: that is why the commonplace that all colours range between or are composed of *leukon* and *melan* (*Cat.* 12a17-19, *Phys.* 188b3-5, *De An.* 442a12-13) is sense and not the nonsense that translators usually make of it. In default of any single English equivalent for *leukon* I shall use 'pink'.

I take the point to be this. Compare the predicate 'animal' with the predicate 'colour'. 'Animal' is predicable of man, and 'animal' and 'man' are in turn predicable of Socrates the individual. His individuality is just that he, or his name, is not predicable of anything less general; and further, since he is an individual *substance*, that he is not found *in* any individual in the way that colours and shapes and sizes are found in their possessors. 'Colour', on the other hand, is predicable of pink, and 'colour' and 'pink' are in turn predicable of any particular shade of pink – any of those shades of which Aristotle is ready to prove that only a finite number is discriminated by sight (*Sens.* 445b20-446a20). Call the specimen shade 'vink'. Then vink is an individual in the category of quality, analogous to Socrates in the category of substance. (Miss Anscombe's claim that 'Aristotle never calls what exists in something else an individual, but reserves that term for substances', p. 8, repeated on p. 9, seems to come from a misreading of 1b6-9. Mr. Ackrill gives the usual and, I think, correct interpretation: 'Things that are individual and numerically one are, without exception, not said of any subject, but there is nothing to prevent some *of them* from being in a subject'.) The analogy is just that vink, or its name, is not predicable of any less general shade of colour. To say 'That shade is vink' is to name the shade, not to bring it under a wider class of colours: vink is a wholly determinate specimen of its class. (Of course/ 'vink' **99**
may have another use as a colour-*adjective* and can then be predicated, but predicated of coloured things and not of colours. Aristotle recognizes this in the case of *leukon*, 2a27-34, cf. 3a15-17. The use that concerns us is its use as the name of a colour – the use which Aristotle takes to be shown by its definition, 2a29-34.)

Similarly with the particular linguistic knowledge. (Ross's 'a particular piece of grammatical knowledge' is happier than Miss Anscombe's 'such-and-such grammarianship'.) 'Linguistic knowledge' can be predicated of its branches, such as the knowledge of French (or, if you like, the knowledge of languages having a certain degree of inflexion). And just as Socrates is a particular specimen of man and vink a particular specimen of the colour pink, so the knowledge that the third person plural present of 'voir' is spelt 'voient' is a particular specimen of the knowledge of French and more generally of linguistic knowledge. Nothing could fall under the general description 'knowledge that the third person plural, etc.', for the good reason that there is no such general description. The phrase picks out an item and not a branch of knowledge. Exercises and displays of the knowledge do not fall under it: Aristotle never subsumes the *dunamis-energeia* (or for that matter the type-token) distinction under the distinction of species and specimen.[1]

To say that vink is a particular colour is to say that it, or its name, cannot be predicated: it is not to say that it cannot be found in more than one subject. Any particular shade of colour is of course reproducible. Any bit of linguistic knowledge can of course lodge in more than one head. Aristotle does not for a moment contemplate denying this. His commentators saddle him with the denial, and this is the dogma I set out to examine.

If there is any evidence for the dogma it is a half-sentence in the *Categories*. Aristotle says 'By "in a subject" I mean what (a) is in something not as a part, (b) cannot exist separately from what it is in' (1a24-5). It is (b) that has seemed to entail the odd consequence, namely that the only item from any category that can be present in an individual subject, in the requisite sense of 'in', is one that is not only quite determinate but non-recurrent: a unit property in Russell's sense. For suppose that the hue of Smith's face could be found in Jones as well: then it *could* exist separately from Smith, and for that
100 matter it/ could exist without either of them. So to have condition (b) Smith's shade of purple must, logically must, be different from Jones's. Aristotle, to be sure, does not draw these corollaries. He does not conclude, as Stout did, that it must be misleading to say that Smith and Jones have just the same colouring: that at best they have irreducibly different colourings between which some philosophical relation of exact similarity obtains. But, whatever he says, the dogma commits him to holding that to identify any particular colour, or generally any individual other than a substance, involves identifying the individual substance which is its sole proprietor. And it commits him to something more surprising. It entails that any non-substance whose identification does *not* carry this condition, say the colour pink or the knowledge of Greek, can *not* be said to be in any individual subject at all (Ackrill, p. 74). Pink is in body but not in Smith's or any one else's body; for it can exist without Smith's body but not without body. General attributes are not in individuals, particular attributes are not in more than one individual.

This cannot be what Aristotle means. Let us list some objections and then look again at the words that seemed to entail the dogma.

First, then, Aristotle never explicitly follows, and often flatly contradicts, the rule he is supposed to have laid down. It is not just that he does not mention its implications. In the very passage in which it is supposedly introduced he gives 'in the soul' as the locus of both a particular linguistic knowledge and knowledge in general (1a25-26, 1b1-2). Here if anywhere it would seem important to distinguish the first subject from the second as being not merely in the soul but in a particular soul; but he does not do so either here or elsewhere. Nor is it open to a dogmatic to read 'in the soul' as either meaning or even implying 'in a particular soul', otherwise the second example is a mistake.

These are negative signs: what are the positive contradictions? When

[1] *Meta.* 1087a10-25 is another matter: for one interpretation which disarms it cf. H.F. Cherniss, *Aristotle's Criticism of Plato and the Academy*, I (Baltimore 1944), 340-8.

Aristotle remarks that an expression such as 'pink' is predicable of the body in which pink is present (2a29-34) he flouts the rule if he has particular subjects in mind, Smith's body as well as body. That he does is clear from the context in which he repeats the point (3a7-17); but it is put beyond question by the lines which follow the remark (2a36-b3). These lines deserve quotation, for by themselves I think they settle the issue. Aristotle draws a careful parallel between predication and inherence: ' "Animal" is predicated of man,
consequently "animal" must also be predicated of the particular man; for if/it **101**
were not predicated of any particular man it would not be predicated of man at all. And colour is in body, consequently it is in a particular body; for if it were not in any of the individuals it would not be in body at all.' With respect, it is mere despair to write off the second half of this as 'compressed and careless' or to represent Aristotle as merely '*speaking as if*, because colour is in body, colour is in an individual body' (Ackrill, p. 83). The unwanted consequence lies at the heart of Aristotle's parallel. And the parallel is subsequently taken for granted, e.g. at *Postpred.* 11b38-12a17, where Mr. Ackrill would prefer not to see the old distinction at all (p. 109).

Then there is the paradox of the breakdown of categories. The dogma says that each particular item in categories other than substance must be identified as the such-and-such quality (or quantity, or whatever) *of so-and-so*. The consequence is that members of the subordinate categories are seconded in one sweep to the category of relative terms. At any rate they satisfy Aristotle's criteria for relatives, including the last and strongest, quite as well as his own examples (8a35-8b15). According to him, *double* is relative because any particular double can only be known to be so by knowing just what it is the double of: and if one thinks of any large even number, doubts arise. But there are no doubts with the dogma: any particular colour (or size or shape, etc.) can only be known for the colour it is by knowing just what individual it is the colour of. Conceded, some such reduction may lie behind *EN* 1096a20-23, though I think the distinction there has another origin. But it is very odd that Aristotle should say nothing of it in the *Categories*, for instance when he argues that knowledge is relative but not the 'particular knowledges' which entitle their possessors to be called 'knowledgeable' (11a20-36). It can hardly be lurking behind the abrupt admission that something might fall under the category of relation as well as that of quality (11a37-38).

And there is the paradox of implication. If X is an individual, the statement that a particular Y (say a particular colour) is in X will not entail but actually preclude saying that Y without qualification is in X. You ask me what colour there is in Socrates' body: I reply meticulously 'Socrates' pink'. You may find this to some extent uninformative; but when I try to isolate the informative element for you I founder. If I say 'The colour in Socrates' body is pink', the dogma rules out what I say as ill-formed. Alternatively, 'pink' may be supposed to stand for a different colour with each different individual subject;
but Aristotle/ never suggests this (except perhaps at *SE* 165a10-13? Contrast **102**
Meta. 1006a31-b10), and he knew an argument that could be turned against it. It is an Academic argument reported by Alexander, pretty certainly from Aristotle's early essay *On the Ideas* (*Peri Ideôn*) (Alex. *in Meta.* 81. 12-18).

'When a man *denies* something of a number of things his denial must refer to something single: for in saying "man is not white (*leukos*!), horse is not white ..." he is not denying some separate thing of each of them – he refers to one and the same thing and this is what he denies all through, viz. *white*. If so, then a man who *asserts* something of a number of things must also be asserting one and the same thing and not something different of each of them: e.g. he asserts *man*, referring to one and the same thing. For what holds good of denying holds good of asserting too.' The argument is about predication, but it can readily be brought to bear on inherence. If I say you are one of the people in whose eyes there is no green I am not saying that your eyes lack the green proprietary to them: ex hypothesi there is no such green. Nor, therefore, does the contradiction of my statement mention any proprietary shade of green. The argument evidently applies to determinates as well as determinables and to other categories as well as quality.

Perhaps, indeed, it is when the dogma is extended to other categories that it becomes a joke: so that two things cannot be said to have the same particular size when they are both six feet tall, or cannot be said to occupy the same particular place at different times. Aristotle's account of place in the *Physics* rests squarely on the assumption that A can move into the identical place vacated by B.

Hence friends of the dogma slip from Aristotle's own examples to supplying him with others. Miss Anscombe relies on the idea of a particular *surface* (pp. 8-10): plainly my desk cannot be said to have the same (as against the same sort of) surface, or edges or corners, as any other. But just this is why Aristotle is exercised by the old question whether surfaces and other boundaries of a body should count as substances (*Meta.* 1002a4-14, cf. 1017b17-21); and why he treats surface as the primary subject in which there is colour (5b6-8, *Phys.* 248b22-23, *Meta.* 1002a16-17, cf. Bz. *Index* 282a30-32); and why finally such boundaries are given no niche in his account of the categories – they appear as the standard possessors of dimensional properties, but are not themselves such properties nor apparently anything else (4b23-24). What I can share with you or take over from you is an intriguing question: your aches? your limbs? your memories? But shapes and sizes and colours are not among these problematic items./

103 Give Aristotle his examples. What could persuade him or us that A's colour or knowledge of the past participle in French cannot be just the same as B's? He might have thought, as a matter of experience, that some difference is bound to reveal itself on a closer inspection. Some people believe, wrongly, that Plato argued on these lines in the *Phaedo*. But one who thought this would equally expect to find differences of colour within any one surface, and then the particularity of Socrates' pink is lost. More probably if Aristotle held the view his reasons were of another kind. Plato for instance had argued (*Tht.* 209b-c) that the snubness of Theaetetus' nose, and 'everything else that made up' Theaetetus, must be peculiar to him: how else could he be known for the individual he was? But Plato was mistaken, and Aristotle knew at least part of the mistake (*Top.* V 1, relative and temporary properties). And when we try to prop the dogma with other arguments we fare no better.

No one would defend it by the plea that I can talk or think of A's colour or knowledge of Greek without talking or thinking of B's: in this way one can as well prove that Shakespeare was not the author of *Cymbeline*. But some one might point out that A's colour (or size, or whatever) can change without any change in B's, however much they may have been said to be just the same colour at the start. Still this will not do. In this use 'A's colour' does not stand for any determinate colour: all that is said is that A can change colour, that from having one determinate colour it can come to have another. The first colour no more suffers change in the process than twelve o'clock changes when it gives way to later times. In any event, if Aristotle had such an argument in mind he would have suggested, around 4a14-15, that a particular colour could be both light and dark because the colour of a man's face can darken.

'But the particular purple on A's face may vanish (or, more pretentiously and less revealingly, cease to exist) when what is called just the same purple on B's face survives.' This too can be rephrased without loss: the same shade of purple may stay on one face when it has left another. And the legitimacy of the rephrasing shows how misconceived it would be to construe this on the model of 'One of these identical twins may die and the other survive'.

A last defence. A's knowledge of French is necessarily distinct from B's knowledge where 'A's knowledge of French' does duty for a noun-clause: the reason for A's appointment was *his* knowledge of (that he knew) French;
they're hanging Danny Deever for the colour of *his*/ hair. Yes, but Aristotle's **104**
leukon is the wrong word for this job, as 'white' or 'pink' would be in English. What we need is the *whiteness* of A, the *leukotês* which does not appear until 4b15. If you doubt this try substituting noun-clauses in 1a25-b3.

Aristotle tries none of these bad arguments for the dogma, and what he says elsewhere in the *Categories* rules it out. So the sentence on which it is alleged to rest calls for review. And on review it reveals its ambiguity. Aristotle says: 'By "in a subject" I mean what (a) is in something not as a part, (b) cannot exist separately from what it is in'. (The importing of '(a)' and '(b)' is of course mine, but not I think unfair: all the commentators known to me, from Porphyry and Simplicius on, distinguish the conditions in this way.) Commentators hasten to supply the concrete instance: there is some colour in Socrates, so condition (b) must be read as requiring that that colour cannot exist apart from Socrates. That is, to use a handbook idiom, they read both (a) and (b) as governed by the same quantifier: if Z is in some subject, in the prescribed sense of 'in', then there is an x such that Z is in x and Z is no part of x and Z cannot exist *apart from x*. But, condensed as Aristotle's formula is, it is open to another interpretation. It can indeed be read as saying 'Z is in something ... and Z could not exist without this thing to contain it', but it can equally well be read as saying 'Z is in something ... and Z could not exist without something to contain it'. That is, the phrase 'separately from what it is in' can be taken generally, in a way that is matched by the familiar phrasing of Aristotle's other complaints at Plato's separation of the universal. When Aristotle argues that the universal cannot exist separately from *the particulars* of which it is predicated (first perhaps in the diagnosis of the Third

Man in *Peri Ideôn*, Alex. *in Meta.* 84. 22-23, cf. 999a17-21, 1033b19-21, 1040b25-30), or when, still more reminiscently of our text, he objects that if the Idea is a substance it cannot exist separately from *that of which it is the substance* (991b1-3 = 1079b35-1080a2), these idioms ought to provoke the friends of the dogma. For the particulars of which 'man' is predicated are Socrates, Plato ... Smith; so by the original argument Aristotle must be implying that there could not be man if there were not Socrates or ... or Smith. But Aristotle knew quite well that there might have been men even without Socrates. And the grammatical singular in 'that of which it is the substance' does not, in this context anyhow, carry the suggestion that the Idea could not be the substance of more particulars than one (cf. 991a12-14,
105 992a26-27). To say that there could not be man apart/ from the particulars called 'men' is to say that man's existence entails that some (and perhaps more than one) individual is a man. To say that if the Idea of man is a substance it cannot exist apart from that of which it is the substance is to say that its existence requires (indeed consists in) the existence of at least one individual falling under the classification *human.* And to say that pink or a particular shade of pink cannot exist apart from what contains it is to say, as Aristotle always says against Plato, that something must contain it if it is to exist at all.

15

Aristotle on the Snares of Ontology

Aristotle's commonest complaint against other philosophers is that they 69
oversimplify. One oversimplification to which he is especially attentive is the failure to see that the same expression may have many different senses. And among such expressions there is one arch-deceiver against which he often issues warnings: the verb 'to be', '*einai*'. I shall discuss part of his attempt to unmask this deceiver, namely his account of the verb in what is ordinarily, and too sweepingly, called its 'existential' use.

I

Aristotle often remarks that the verb 'to be' has many uses, *pollachôs legetai to einai*. Sometimes instead of the infinitive '*einai*' in this formula he writes the participial noun '*to on*', which the Oxford translators conventionally render as 'being'; sometimes the same word in the plural, which the translators divorce from its singular counterpart by turning it into 'things that are' or, perhaps more intelligibly, 'existing things'. We have to get behind these opaque translations, and an obvious first step is to collect some texts in which Aristotle draws conclusions from the verb's alleged multiplicity of use.

In *Metaphysics* I (992b18-24) he says that because of this variety in the use of '*onta*' it is a mistake to engage in a general search for the *stoicheia tôn ontôn* ('elements of *existing things*', Oxford translation). In *Metaphysics* XIV (1088b35-1089b33) he argues this thesis at length (concerning 'existing things' or 'things that are',/O.T.). In the *Eudemian Ethics* I (1217b25-35) he 70
maintains that the same multiplicity shows that there can be no single comprehensive science of *to on* ('being', O.T.). In *Metaphysics* IV (1003a21-b16), resuming the same subject, he amends his claim: despite this multiplicity of use there *can* be a single comprehensive science of *to on* and *ta onta*, and those who looked for the elements of *ta onta* were very likely on the track of this science. There is a contradiction between these claims which is not our immediate business, though it is central to Aristotle's philosophical development and reflected in many other texts: I have discussed it elsewhere,[1] and it will make a brief appearance later. Our present interest in

[1] Logic and Metaphysics in Some Earlier Works of Aristotle', above, Chapter 10, hereafter called '*LM*'.

the texts is that they deal with the same topic, and that there is wide and reasonable agreement on what this topic comes to. In these contexts 'being' or '*to on*' means 'what there is' or 'what exists'. In Ross's version *Metaphysics* IV opens with the words: 'There is a science which investigates being and the attributes which belong to this in virtue of its own nature. Now this is not the same as any of the so-called special sciences; for none of these others treats universally of being as being. They cut off a part of being and investigate the attributes of this part: this is what the mathematical sciences for instance do.' Ross's commentary on the passage embodies the familiar interpretation from which I want to set out. Particular sciences deal only with some part of 'being', for they deal with part of what there is. Numbers are part of what there is, and mathematics deals with them; colours are another part, and mathematics does not deal with them. The same account makes sense of Aristotle's readiness to put '*to on*' into the plural and talk of a general enquiry into what there *are* (1003b15-16), into the elements of 'existing things' (1003a28-30). Ontology is, isn't it? an accredited field of philosophy, and what Aristotle has to say of 'being' in these contexts falls under ontology. If only it were so simple.

Still, this is a first, unwary step in the right direction. It steers us past an interpretation of Aristotle's words that would be proper in other contexts where he discusses the complex behaviour of the verb 'to be'. There is one obvious sense in which that verb, both in Greek and in English, does have
71 many uses, but our texts/ are not concerned with this sense. Namely, in some contexts it serves to couple subject and predicate, as it does in 'Arrowby is idle'; in others it serves as an identity sign, as it does in 'Arrowby is the Mayor of Margate'; in yet others it has (still provisionally speaking) the sense of 'exist', as it does in 'Arrowby is no more'. In the *Sophist* Plato had gone some way to disentangling the first two of these uses. I do not myself think he was equally successful with the third; he seems in the end content to assimilate it to (or to scrap it in favour of) the others. That is, he treats 'to be' and 'not to be' alike as incomplete or elliptical expressions which always call for some completion: *to be* is just *to be something or other*.[2] And if this is so his analysis becomes the direct parent of Aristotle's.

At any rate, whatever Plato's success in the venture, it is evidently a similar broad division in the uses of that verb that Aristotle is drawing in such passages as the seventh chapter of *Metaphysics* V where he marks off *to*

[2] Not arguable here, but the essentials are: (*a*) either 'to be' or 'not to be' is taken to be clarified just to the extent that the other twin is made clear (*Sophist* 250e-251a), and thereafter 'not to be' is found always to need some completion (258d-e); (*b*) the idiom 'partaking in being' can hardly be taken to mark off a use of the verb in which it needs no complement: see 256e and *Parmenides* 162a-b; (*c*) the contrast between *kath' hauta* and *pros heteron* ('in relation to something different') *onta* at 255c is probably not the contrast between complete and incomplete uses of the verb but between two incomplete uses, viz. in statements of identity and of predication: this explains the *heteron* (identification does not and predication does import a complement different from the subject); it explains why the same contrast is not used a little earlier to show the difference between *identity* and being; and it explains some Aristotelian terminology (e.g. *Posterior Analytics* I, 73b5-10).

kath' hauto on ('that which is in virtue of itself') from, among other things, *to kata sumbebêkos on* ('that which is incidentally'). But the same chapter shows that it is not these broad distinctions that he has in mind in the texts from which we set out. For he offers to take only one such general function of the verb and show that it harbours a certain multiplicity of use; and he identifies this multiplicity by saying that 'being' has *different uses in different categories* (1017a22-30). This is just what he says in our texts. In the *Eudemian Ethics*, for example, he argues that there cannot be a single comprehensive science of either 'being' or 'good' because these expressions signify sometimes a substance, sometimes a quality, sometimes a quantity, and so forth (1217b25-35). So the argument in our/ texts is confined to one general **72**
function of the verb; and this squares with the view that it is concerned with questions of existence. If the *Eudemian Ethics* is to query the possibility of any general study of *to on* in the sense of 'what there is' or 'what exists', it is in *this* sense that the verb 'to be' must be exposed as having not one but many uses.

(Let us just notice, and shelve for later comment, the expression '*kath' hauto on*' which Aristotle uses in *Metaphysics* V 7 to label the relevant sense of the verb. It sounds oddly in this connection, but it comes to the same thing.)

II

Now look back at the formula by which Aristotle makes his point, *pollachôs legetai to on*. For '*to on*' we shall try writing 'existence' or, to mark the role of '*on*' as a grammatical predicate, 'existent'. Aristotle, then, is saying that 'existent' has many uses. And in the *Topics* he makes it clear that to say that a word (as contrasted with a complex phrase or sentence) has many uses is to say that it is used *homonymously*.[3] Accordingly, he can remark in the *Sophistici Elenchi* (182b13-27) that some cases of *homonymy* escape even the practised eye, and illustrate the point by a dispute over whether 'being' and 'one' have many uses (*homônumian ... pollachôs legesthai*). 'One' is a word whose behaviour he often compares with that of 'existent': both are polygamous predicates, ready to marry subjects from any category; and 'one' reappears as a case of homonymy in *Physics* VII (248b19-21).[4] 'Good' is another of this rootless family, and 'good' is a prime example of homonymy in *Topics* I (107a4-17). No doubt these are early writings; later, notably in parts of the *Metaphysics* and *Nicomachean Ethics*, he tries to improve on his earlier account. But the improvement turns out to be a sophisticated variant on the/ idea of **73**

[3] In *Topics* I 15 the multiple use of a word is *homonymy* (106a21-2, 106b3-4, 106b8, 107a5, 107a11, 107b7 (where the homonymy that survives *en logois* is still that of a single word, *summetrôs*), 107b25, 107b31): the multiple use of a phrase or sentence ('the whole *logos*', 129b31-2, 130a9) is distinguished from homonymy in 110b16-111a7, and illustrated under the name of 'amphiboly' in 166a6-14. (But for a deviant use of 'amphiboly' cf. *Rhet.* 1407a32, 1407a37, 1435a33, 1461a26.)

[4] At 248b19 '*ei etuchen*', = '*isôs*' (T. Waitz, *Aristotelis Organon*, vol. 1 (Leipzig 1844), 302; on such idioms, ibid. 401 and cf. Aristotle's explanation, *Top.* 156b23-5).

homonymy,[5] and it will be unintelligible if we do not follow up these older clues. We have to begin by seeing why Aristotle was inclined to class 'existent' as a case of homonymy.

What he means by 'homonymy' is not seriously in doubt. Commonly, though not always, he uses 'homonymous' and 'synonymous' to describe not words but the things to which a word is applied. Thus in the *Categories* (1a1-11) he explains that two things (or kinds or thing) are called *syn*onymous if they both answer to some such name as 'animal', and if the *logos* which corresponds to the name, i.e. the appropriate definition or paraphrase, is the same in each case. They are called *hom*onymous if both answer to the name, but the appropriate *logos* differs in the two cases. By *logos* in such contexts he plainly does mean a definition or paraphrase: this is shown by the many examples in his logic. What it is for the *logos* to correspond to the name (*kata to onoma*) is not explained in the *Categories*, but elsewhere he vouchsafes that the *logos* can replace the name, that they have the same force, even that it makes no difference which one says;[6] and more cautiously that it is a necessary though not sufficient condition of the correspondence that they should mean the same.[7] (He does not state the conditions for identity of meaning.) In the sixth book of the *Topics* he tries to define the connection more rigorously. In his latest works he is still trying.

Whatever his dissatisfaction with the formal merits of his account – and it is, after all, a dissatisfaction still unassuaged in the current discussions of synonymy – it seems clear enough what is to count as a case of homonymy. 'Cape' is used homonymously in English, for if I say that what I am wearing is a cape and what I am circumnavigating is a cape, I can replace 'cape' at its
74 first occurrence with 'sleeveless cloak' and at its second with 'point/ of land jutting into the sea', and these replacements are not interchangeable. By the rule of the *Categories* Aristotle would say that the two things I called 'cape' are homonymous; elsewhere, by a natural shift, he would say that the word 'cape' itself is homonymous.[8] We shall find this second idiom more convenient. It is closer to English usage, and it avoids the difficulty that, on the other way of speaking, the same things may be both synonymous and homonymous in respect of the same word. Sea stories are a bore in one sense, a tidal wave is a bore in more senses than one.

(No doubt grammarians will say that in this example 'bore' is not one word

[5] Which for political reasons he calls not homonymy in *Meta.* IV, 1003a34 (cf. VII, 1030a34, *GC* I, 322b31), but elsewhere not *chance* homonymy (*EN* I, 1096b26-7) or not *total* homonymy (*EE* VII 1236a17): see IX below, and for details *LM* (above, ch. 10). Often he takes no notice of this modification of homonymy, treating homonymy as the sole complement of synonymy where single expressions are concerned (Bonitz, *Index Aristotelicus* 514a31-40).

[6] Replacement, 21a29, 49b5, 101b39-102a1, 130a39, 142b3, 147b14, 149a1-2; same force, 49b3-5; no difference, 147b13-15 (cf. 142b2-6); all these from the logical works.

[7] 92b26-34 and 93b35 (cf. *Meta.* VII, 1030a7-9 and 1030b7-12).

[8] He is not so clear on the distinction as this suggests; but the word is evidently the vehicle of homonymy in *Top.* I 15 (E. Hambruch, *Logische Regeln der platonischen Schule* (Berlin 1904, repr. N.Y. 1976), 28; P. Lang, *De Speusippi academici scriptis* (Bonn 1911, repr. Hildesheim 1965), 25), as it is in *A. Pst.* II, 99a7 and 12, and as it seems to have been for Speusippus.

but two. But the distinction did not occur to Aristotle and brings its own snags: vide Quine, *Word and Object*, p. 129.)

'Cape', then, is homonymous, a word with more than one meaning. Admittedly, Aristotle's account seems too restrictive to let in all the words that we should count as having more than one meaning, for we are seldom prepared to identify each of a word's meanings by finding a paraphrase for it. In some contexts 'time' can be replaced by 'a term of imprisonment', but it is notoriously less exponible in others. Yet, as though to meet this objection, Aristotle tells us to persevere in the search for the *logos* (*Top.* I, 106a1-8): it is a hard job with words such as 'one' and 'being' (169a22-5), but we shall see him engaged in it.

Here a substantial point arises. Aristotle's account of homonymy is often translated and discussed as an account of *ambiguity*. But in the commonest use of the word 'ambiguity' signifies a very different thing from homonymy, and we shall need to hold them apart. If we have to harden the edges of current usage a bit in the process, there is no harm in that.

We can adapt a contrast of Mr. Strawson's and say that ambiguity shares one characteristic with truth and exaggeration which homonymy does not share: it is a function not of expressions but of particular utterances, the datable uses of expressions. If any expression has more than one meaning, there need not be any ambiguity in my words when I use it. 'Bore' is
homonymous in/English, but if I tell you 'You are the greatest bore in **75**
England' you will see no saving ambiguity in what I say. On the other hand, suppose you tip the scale at twenty stone and I greet you with 'You are twice the man your father was'; then what I say is ambiguous, but its ambiguity does not come from the fact that any of the expressions I utter has several meanings as 'bore' has. You can, of course, accuse me of meaning more than one thing by my words, or you can ask whether I mean that you are twice as accomplished as your father or twice as heavy or whatever. But the fact that 'twice' can be completed in these various ways to show my meaning does not entail that 'twice' is a word with various meanings. So the occurrence of an homonymous expression is neither a sufficient nor a necessary condition of ambiguity.

This contrast deserves more space than our present purposes will allow it, but we can take it a step farther. To show that an expression has more than one meaning we must say what it means in a language; to show that an utterance is ambiguous we must say what a speaker means or might have meant by it. And the question, what I mean by my words, presupposes an answer to the question, what the words mean in the language. Typically, what I mean is a set of inferences that I intend a literate hearer to draw from my utterance; but you may miss my meaning without showing the least ignorance of the language or of the various senses carried by its homonymous words.

(Again the grammarians have their own different use for the contrast: vide J. Hintikka, *Inquiry* 2 (1959), 137.)

Aristotle has no word that answers exactly to 'ambiguity'. The closest is 'amphiboly', which stands for a characteristic of a whole phrase or sentence,

as 'homonymy' stands for a characteristic of a particular word.[9] He does not draw the contrast between them as a contrast between words and utterances, yet some of his examples of amphiboly seem clear cases of ambiguity: witness *SE* 166a6-7, where he draws on that rich mine of face-saving ambiguities, the Greek oracles. But he does not use the notion of amphiboly to throw light on the existential rôle or rôles of the verb 'to be'. He treats a statement about 'the knowledge of many things' as, in effect, a case of amphiboly (*Top.*
76 110b16-28), but he does not bring this device to bear on/ 'the knowledge of existing things'. He consistently regards the oddity of the verb 'to be' as the oddity of one word in its context.

III

At various places Aristotle says things which show how the verb 'to be' in its existential rôle or rôles can have many senses. He says in *De Anima* II (415b13, cf. *GC* 318b25, *EN* 1166a4-5) that 'for living things, to be is to be alive'. He generalises the point when he speaks of the 'being' of a thing (its '*ousia*' or '*einai*') as what is explicated by its definition, that is, by an account of the sort of thing it is (Bonitz, *Index Aristotelicus* 221a41-61). And he documents it in many places, and notably in the difficult second chapter of *Metaphysics* VIII (1042b15-1043a7). Setting aside for the moment one question of interpretation, we can read the argument as follows: Some things are distinguished from others by the way their materials are put together, by blending or tying or gluing or nailing, for example; some by their position, for instance, a threshold and a lintel; some by their time, such as dinner and breakfast; and some by a combination of such marks. 'Plainly, then, the word "is" is used in a corresponding variety of ways. A threshold *is*, in that it is situated thus and so: "to be" means its being so situated. And that ice *is* means that it is solidified in such and such a way.[10] Of some things the being will be defined by all these marks ... e.g. hand or foot ... For yet other things, to be is to be mixed, and not to be is the opposite ...'

To be, then, is always to be something or other: this comes naturally from the Greek idiom, a favourite of Plato's, which expresses 'A exists' as 'A is *something*'. (Nor does it run counter to Aristotle's distinction in other contexts between 'being something' and 'simply being': vide *LM* p. 181 n. 3 above). It
77 was, we/ conjectured, Plato's conclusion in the *Sophist.* But Aristotle is far more precise on the matter than Plato.

For one thing, while he is always ready to expand 'A is' (sc. 'A exists') into

[9] See n. 3 above.

[10] Ross's account of the passage in his edition (*Metaphysics* ii, p. 228) is more correct and consistent than his translation. There is no need in 1042b27-8 for Bonitz's *to krustallôi einai* ('what it is to be ice', an emendation which is carried farther by Jaeger's insertion in 1042b27); this technical phrase is based on the use of the verb in predication (contrast the non-technical dative in 1042b36 which parallels the genitive in 1042b28 and introduces an *existential* use of the verb). *to krustallon einai* ('to be ice') is to be understood existentially, like the comparable phrases in 1043a2-4: that ice *is*, means that it is solid (supplying *auton* ('it') by analogy with *auto* in the previous line).

'A is P' for some value of 'P', he rightly rejects the converse inference. It does not follow from every proposition of the form 'A is P' that 'A is' (*Int.* 21a24-8), otherwise we should have to infer the existence of the non-existent merely from its being thought about (*Top.* 167a1, 180a32-3). For another thing he tries to meet the objection that on such an analysis of 'existence' the concept of homonymy would run riot and become unworkable. It looks as though a new sense of the word will have to be conjured up for each sort of thing we want to talk about; but it is absurd to suggest that a word has not merely more than one sense but an unrestrictedly large number of senses (*Meta.* IV, 1006a34-b11). Aristotle's answer is the theory of categories. Ultimately, he holds, to be is always to be either a substance of a certain sort, or a quality of a certain sort, or a quantity of a certain sort – the list notoriously varies, but the nucleus remains stable and the number remains small (*A. Pst.* 83b13-17). For these categories are the most general headings under which other classifications are grouped. And of these general headings Aristotle is ready to prove two things. First, no category is a species of any other: substances are not a kind of quality nor qualities a kind of substance (e.g. *Meta.* 1024b15, 1070b3-4). Second, no category is a species of *being* or of *what there is*, for there is no such genus as *being* (e.g. 998b22-7). So it seems that the verb 'to be' in its existential rôle enjoys a number of irreducibly different senses. Indeed, even in one category the senses of the verb will vary from one sort of subject to another, as Aristotle's examples show; but within the category the senses will have something in common which a full paraphrase will bring out. For a shark, to be is to be a *substance* of some kind; and so it is for a shamrock.[11] What Aristotle wants to dispel is the myth that there is equally something in common to sharks and shyness on the plea that each of them is a *being* or/
existent or *thing* of some kind. There is no such genus as being (and 'thing', as **78**
Berkeley confided to his notebook, is 'an homonymous word').

Philosophers who remark that existence is not a predicate sometimes find support in Aristotle's argument that being is not a genus. But what Aristotle says is that 'to be' means 'to be so-and-so', and that the values of 'so-and-so' vary with the sort of subject we assign the verb. So it seems that if Aristotle does not treat existence as a predicate this is only because he treats it as a disjunctive set of predicates. Nor is he anticipating a celebrated argument of Kant when he argues in the *Metaphysics* (1003b27-30, 1054a16-18) that 'existent man' means no more than 'man'. To say that Quine is a man and exists is, perhaps, to say no more than that Quine is a man; but what assures Aristotle of this is not any conviction that 'existent' is not a predicate at all, but a conviction that in this context it is a redundant predicate (*epanadiploumenon*). 'Dead man' is strictly a contradiction (*Int.* 21a21-3), and to say that Quine is not only a man but in existence is to say that he is a man and living a man's life.

[11] The first examples I wrote were *chalk* and *cheese*, but by Aristotle's criteria these are not strictly substances. Nor in fact are the examples quoted from *Metaphysics* VIII 2, as Aristotle remarks (1043a4-5); but he adds that the argument can be transferred to substances proper. So I shall move fairly freely between the examples 'ice' and 'man'.

What is to be said for such an analysis? It does seem to shed light on one general function of the verb 'to be' which would commonly be labelled 'existential'. For when we say, ticking off the obituaries, that Arrowby is no more (or speak of him as no longer in existence or as having, like Wordsworth's Lucy, ceased to be), don't we mean that he no longer *lives*? Whereas, when we ask whether the rule against smoking in hall still exists, don't we mean to ask whether it is still *accepted* or *enforced*? English has an idiom that helps to mark off such existential dicta from others that will take our eye later: it lets us rephrase them with the predicate 'in existence'. In any language they have other marks: the predicate can be qualified by some adverbs of time – 'still', 'always', 'no longer' – though not necessarily, as we shall see, by others; and in different contexts we call on different predicates to contradict it – 'extinct', 'dead', 'dismantled', 'disused', and so forth. According to a rule of the *Topics* (106a12-22) this last point alone would suffice to prove the original predicate homonymous.

So Aristotle's analysis has a claim to be heard. (It is the analysis, I take it,
79 which Geach imports to explain Aquinas' use of/ '*esse*';[12] and he seems content with it.) 'Arrowby is no more' is a proposition in subject-predicate form. There is a first, familiar objection to this analysis: the objection is that Arrowby cannot be the logical subject of a proposition which tells us that there is no Arrowby for us to refer to. The reply, not less familiar, is that this objection confuses the reference of the name with the name's bearer. 'When Mr. N.N. dies, we say that the bearer of the name dies, not that the reference dies. And it would be nonsensical to say that; for if the name ceased to have reference, it would make nonsense to say "Mr. N.N. is dead" ' (Wittgenstein, *Investigations* I, § 40). The reply has been argued more than once by Mr. Geach, and there is no need to expand it; but it leaves a residual qualm. What are the credentials, it may be asked, of a 'predicate' which can continue or cease to be true of Mr. N.N., but apparently cannot come to be true of him? It makes sense to say of some individual A that A is still, or no longer, in existence; but what sense does it make to import another temporal adverb from the same class and say that A is not yet in existence? Surely this is to assume and in the same breath to deny that the name 'A' has yet been given a reference? Haven't philosophers often enough vented their suspicions of the predicate in a comparable case – the alleged progress of an event from futurity to presentness or from probability to fact? But after discussion I can see little force in this difficulty. For it seems that, just to the extent that I can be said to know that some individual (say a child) will come into existence, I can be said to refer now to that individual. Certainly it is always possible that my hopeful reference will be defeated by the course of events: the child may not be born. But in this case I could not be said to know that there would be such an individual. And putative references to present or past individuals can equally be defeated by insufficient knowledge. So Aristotle's neglect of this objection seems to be neither a mark against his theory nor – what is our

[12] P. Geach, 'Form and Existence', *PAS* 55 (1954-5), 263-4, 266-8; *Three Philosophers* (Oxford 1961), 90-2.

present concern – a difficulty for this interpretation of it. But we have other troubles of interpretation on our hands.

One such trouble is a problem that we shelved in discussing the argument of *Metaphysics* VIII 2. Following the natural and usual reading of that text we took it to be dealing with statements of the form 'So and so exists' (n. 10 above). To say of a piece of ice/ that it still exists is to say that it is keeping its **80**
solidity, to say that it no longer exists is to say that it has lost this solidity, i.e. melted. The notion of solidity is introduced here to give the relevant sense of 'exist' (1042b27-8). But a little later in the same chapter (1043a7-12) Aristotle uses this same solidity to give the sense of 'ice'. His point now seems to be that the statement that X no longer has such solidity would be a paraphrase, or part-paraphrase, *not* of the statement 'X no longer exists' (where X is our patch of ice), but of 'X is no longer ice' (where X might be the water in the pond). On the whole this interest in defining classificatory words such as 'ice' suits the purpose of the chapter better; but what relevance has it to the claim, made and repeated in the preceding lines, that the word 'is' is used in different senses? Grant that 'ice' has a different definition from 'wood', how can this have the least tendency to show that when 'exists' is coupled with these words it too calls for a different paraphrase?

(Here again echoes of current controversy beat in.[13] Controversy must wait its turn: at present our object is to understand.)

Let us call this the problem of the overworked paraphrase. It has connections with other resident puzzles, such as the equivocal behaviour of the words '*ousia*' and '*einai*', which serve Aristotle both as general expressions for 'being' and as special terms for the 'nature' of a thing which is shown by some classificatory label and set out in its definition. We shall try first one, and then another, general solvent on such difficulties, and it will be a piece of economy (as well as a way of keeping up suspense) to raise another problem first.

This further problem is that we have presented Aristotle with an analysis of existential statements which seems to apply only, if at all, to statements about individuals which have beginnings and ends, or at least careers, in time. For suppose we want to deny in general terms that ice exists: then on such an analysis our denial becomes not empirically false but self-contradictory. It turns into 'Ice is not solid' (or whatever else is taken for a defining characteristic of ice; if there are more than one, it becomes the denial that ice has at least one of these). With our particular, transient patch of ice the difficulty does not arise. To say that the ice on the pond is no longer solid, that it has melted, runs no more risk of/ sounding like a contradiction than **81**
our report of Arrowby's death; for present purposes, the two can be taken to have the same logical form. 'The ice on the pond' refers to an object, the object has melted: absurd to suggest that the reference melted with the object. But with the general proposition 'Ice is not solid', the logical form seems to be not 'S is not P' but 'Whatever is P (or P and Q and R) is not P';

[13] M. White, *Towards Reunion in Philosophy* (Oxford 1956), ch. 4; W.V. Quine, *Word and Object* (Cambridge, Ma. 1960), 131.

and this is a bald contradiction.

We can discount one escape route from this difficulty. It might be said: 'Ice is solid, or rather frozen, water. So surely Aristotle's analysis of "Ice does not exist" will be "*Water* is not (or, No water is) frozen", and this is no contradiction: it just happens to be false.' But this cannot be Aristotle's point, for the analysis would have no tendency to show, what he plainly asserts, that for a particular subject 'is' or 'exists' calls for a particular paraphrase. The analysis imports another subject – Aristotle will no more confuse the water with the ice that comes from it than he will confuse the seed with the individual tree that comes into existence. So nothing in the analysis counts as the requisite paraphrase, and the homonymy of 'is' remains unproven. In fact, such an analysis would be an application of the notion of amphiboly, not of homonymy at all. We must try other moves against our puzzles.

IV

The first and most obvious move is to make a virtue of necessity. Let us agree that the scope of Aristotle's analysis had better be restricted to statements about individuals and see what follows. We shall find before long that this move will not take us home, but it will bring us a long step forward.

For one thing, it seems to explain the overworked paraphrase. For suppose we set out to analyse the statement that the ice on the pond is no more: then on Aristotle's directions we shall cast around for the appropriate paraphrase of the verb 'is'. And to discover that paraphrase we must ask the general question, what is it to be ice? So to understand what 'is' or 'exists' means in our statement about the *individual* ice-patch is to understand what 'ice' means *in general*. This innocuous connection seems enough to explain Aristotle's easy transition from using a certain form of words in defining a common noun such as 'ice' to using the identical form of words in paraphrasing the
82 appropriate sense of 'is'. If ice is/ frozen water, to say that any particular bit of ice has ceased to exist is to say that it has ceased to be frozen water.

From this a modicum of light is reflected on other problems. One is the ambivalent behaviour, already noted, of expressions such as '*ousia*' and '*einai*'. When Aristotle introduces '*ousia*' in the sense of the essence or definable nature of a thing, and then says that the *ousia* is, in the words of the Oxford translation, 'the cause of each thing's being' (*aitia tou einai hekaston, Meta.* VIII, 1043a2-3; cf. *De. An.* II, 415b12-13), he is not taking an advance draft on the Ontological Argument. He means just that the definition of 'ice' goes to explain what it is for our particular ice-patch to be in existence. (To explain, not to cause: is it too late to complain of 'cause' as the translation of *aitia*?)

Again, recall the expression which Aristotle uses in *Metaphysics* V 7 to identify that general rôle of the verb 'to be' in which it carries different senses in the different categories. We took this rôle to be the (or an) existential use of the verb. Aristotle calls it *to kath' hauto on* (1017a7-8, 22-3), a phrase which can certainly be applied to existential statements (e.g. at *Int.* 21a28), but which he often uses elsewhere to mark another function of the verb 'to be', namely its use in definitions or in statements immediately derived from definitions. But perhaps we need not puzzle over which application of the phrase Aristotle intends in this chapter. For him it is one and the same enterprise to set up different definitions of 'ice' and 'wood' and to set up two different senses of 'exist'.[14]

Benefits flow from our restriction. Let us warm to its defence. Would Aristotle think his analysis much shaken by the fact that it makes better sense when it is restricted to the existence of individuals endowed with careers in time? Granted, it is one thing to say that the restriction clarifies the analysis, quite another to say that Aristotle saw the importance of the distinction. But doesn't he see this? He often says or implies that individuals have/ more 83
claim than universals to be classed as *onta*: at *Metaphysics* XII, 1071a21-2 he says flatly that the universal Man does not exist – particular men have particular fathers. And when he speaks of individuals (*kath' hekasta, atoma*) he must not be assumed, unless the context certifies it, to have only particular *substances* in mind. Just as his analysis of 'existence' is said to cater for all the categories, so the line between individual and universal can apparently be drawn in them all.[15] The distinction between a man and the species under which he falls is paralleled in another category by the distinction between the particular, transient pallor on a man's face and the general type of discoloration under which it falls. In any such pair it is the first member whose existence seems to be explained by Aristotle's analysis, just as it is the first whose claim to be called 'existent' Aristotle defends against Plato's preference for the second. So in *Metaphysics* XII 1070a22-4 he says: 'Health exists just when the man is healthy. The shape of the bronze sphere exists at just the same time as the bronze sphere. Whether anything of it survives afterwards is another question': and by 'health' here he seems to mean just the particular state of health of the individual.[16] For such health to exist is for it to have a temporal career comparable with that of the ice on my pond. It is an arrangement of bodily components, and the arrangement can fall into disrepair.

But the defence had better cool down. Already it seems to have suggested a falsehood.

[14] There are passages where Aristotle does seem to assign the *copulative* 'is' a different sense in different categories: a text such as *A. Pr.* I, 48b2-9 (cf. 49a6-9) suggests the explanation. 'A is B' can be turned into 'B belongs to A', and 'belongs to' has a different sense in different categories: why? Because for *red* to exist is for it to be a quality, so for *red* to belong to A is for it to be a quality of A; and the analysis would be different with predicates of substance or quantity, etc. This probably explains the odd lines 1017a27-30 in *Metaphysics* V 7.

[15] *Cat.* 1a23-1b9, *Top.* I, 103b27-39. I can see no grounds whatever for supposing that in the first passage an *individual* colour or piece of knowledge is one that *occurs in only one individual*. See 'Inherence', above, Chapter 14.

[16] R.G. Albritton, 'Forms of Particular Substances in Aristotle's Metaphysics', *J. Philos.* 54 (1957), 700.

V

It has suggested a falsehood if it is taken to imply that Aristotle wants to restrict existential statements to statements about particular men and icebergs and states of health. For of course Aristotle often makes and discusses existential statements on other levels, statements that mention only classes or universals. In the *Posterior Analytics*, for instance in I 76a31-6 and in the opening chapters of II, he discusses the rôle of such statements in any/
84 systematic science. But his discussion is oddly uncertain and confused, and a particular diagnosis of the confusion seems to suggest itself.

The *Posterior Analytics* knows that being is not a genus (92b14) and that 'existing things' are parcelled into categories (88b1-3). It is, on other grounds than the *Eudemian Ethics*, just as hostile as that work to the idea of a general science of *onta.*[17] It holds that a logical formula which can be put to work in many fields of enquiry has a range of uses which are connected only by analogy (76a37-40); and this might be taken to imply that 'exist' has a comparable range of uses, since it can occur in such formulae. But the *Posterior Analytics* does not say that 'exist' has a different sense for different kinds of subject. Instead, it draws a formal distinction between the question *whether A exists* and the question *what A is*, and even, at the start of one tangled argument, treats the second question as arising after the first has been settled (89b34-90a1). True, it amends this later: it contends that we can only be said to know of A's existence to the extent that we know what it is to be A (93a21-33). Still it does not offer to paraphrase 'exist' variously for different values of 'A'.

Here the defender of our restriction will leap in with an explanation. Aristotle's treatment of the matter here is uncertain, he will say, because Aristotle sees or half-sees that paradoxes arise if his analysis of 'existence' is applied to such general existential statements as those which concern him in the *Posterior Analytics*. But this is less than half the story.

Consider the samples of existential statement that Aristotle provides in this work. They are answers to such questions as *ei estin ê mê esti kentauros ê theos* (89b32): Is there a centaur? Is there a god? or, what comes to the same, Are there any centaurs, or any gods? Elsewhere he uses the concepts 'straight line', 'triangle', 'unit of number', in similar examples (76a34-5). So he is mentioning certain concepts and asking whether anything falls under them, or listing certain descriptions and asking whether anything answers to them.

Now such examples certainly illustrate one use of the verb 'to be' which is commonly called existential: in fact, it is the use most commonly so called at present. Equally plainly it is not the rôle in which we have been watching it so
85 far. It is the use which is/ rendered by 'il y a' or 'es gibt', and represented in predicate logic by the formula '$(\exists x)\ Fx$'. And, as that formula was designed

[17] See *LM*, p. 190 above.

to show, it is not in any sense a predicative use of the verb but a use which is parasitic upon all predicates. Distinguish it by two asterisks, and the use we have been discussing by one: then we can say that while Arrowby is in existence there is** at least one man still in existence, but if Arrowby dies there is** one man who is* no more. Given any form of statement in which the verb 'to be' (or any other verb) plays the part of a predicate, we can construct another in which the verb 'to be' takes on its non-predicative rôle. So to reconstrue this in turn as predicative would set us on a futile regress.

Aristotle nowhere distinguishes these two uses of the verb. So he is not in a position to say that his analysis of the different predicative senses of 'exist' applies to being*, but not to his present concern, being**. Does this, then, explain his hesitations over existential statements in the *Posterior Analytics*?

It is the beginning of an explanation, no more. No more, because we have made our distinction look obvious (and Aristotle look something of a fool for missing it) by a gross oversimplification. We talked as though being* found a place only in statements about individuals such as the transient man or ice-patch, and being** only in statements about universals or classes; but of these propositions the second is possibly false (this is a sleeping dog that need not be woken now), and the first is certainly false. Moreover, Aristotle recognised its falsehood. Let us clear this up.

It is plain that there can be some general statements of being*. If a man can die and cease to be, a tribe can become extinct; and if a specimen of monkey can continue in existence, so, in its own way, can the species. (Certainly Aristotle does not believe in the emergence or destruction of species; but he holds that what distinguishes a species from its members is that it has a continuous career in time, *GA* II, 731b31-5). Moreover, if existence* is a predicate (or set of predicates), we can expect Aristotle to take a quite precise view of the connection between singular and general statements of existence*. In his logic, as Mrs. Kneale remarks (*The Development of Logic* (Oxford 1962), 63), Aristotle regards 'singular and general statements as co-ordinate species of a genus. The copula and the predicate should have the same/ function in both.' Thus the statement 'Ice (still, or no longer) exists' **86**
will be related to our reports of the (continued or discontinued) existence of the ice on our pond just as the statement 'Man is carnivorous' is related to our reports of this or that man's diet. For man to be a carnivorous animal, just as for Plato to be so, is for man to be an eater of meat; and for ice to be in existence, just as for our ice-patch to be so, is for it to be frozen.

Now Aristotle recognises this parallel quite expressly in the *De Interpretatione*. He marks it by writing the quantifiers 'Every' and 'Not every', not only in front of the harmless predicative sentence 'Man is just', but in front of the *existential* sentence 'Man is' (19b15-35). Commentators for the most part skirt this fact in embarrassed silence, and if the verb 'is' had to be understood here as 'is**' rather than as the predicative 'is*' their discomfort would be justified. For it would be absurd to write such quantifiers in front of the statement that there are** men. The quantifiers themselves must be analysed in terms of being**: to say that *every man is just* is to say that *there are** no men of whom it is not true that those men are just*, but it would be vacuous to say, and nonsense to deny, that *there are*** no men of whom it is not true that there are*** those men*. When the verb is understood as a predicate comparable to the predicate 'is just', this bogy of absurdity is laid.

(G.E. Moore once argued that, whereas 'All tame tigers growl' and 'Most tame tigers growl' have a plain sense, 'All tame tigers exist' and 'Most tame tigers exist' do not. He was talking of being**. When he came to consider the possibility of giving the verb a predicative sense – as, for instance, when 'non-existent' is taken to mean 'fictional' – he qualified his thesis.)

We can take this point further. Aristotle commonly and naturally writes general statements of existence in the form 'Man exists', without supplying any such prefixes as 'Every' or 'Not every'. And if 'exists' is to be understood in the second of the two ways so far distinguished (as surely it begs to be, in those examples from the *Posterior Analytics*), the omission is, as we have just seen, right and proper. But suppose it to signify being*: then the parallel between 'Man exists' and 'Man is just' yields a different moral. For when 'Man is just' is used without any such prefix as 'Every', Aristotle is ready to supply a prefix: he takes the sentence to mean '*Some* (i.e. at least one) man is
87 just' (*Top./* III, 120a6-20, *A. Pr.* I, 29a27-9). And to say this is just to say that some statement of the form 'Socrates is just' is true: 'Some man ...' promises the completion 'Some man, namely Socrates ...'. By Aristotle's criteria the predicate '(is) just' will have exactly the same sense and function in these different statements, right down to the statement that begins with a proper name or some other designation of an individual.

We can expect Aristotle to apply this conclusion to 'exist' in its predicative rôle; and I take him to be doing this when he says 'Health exists just when the man is healthy' (*Meta.* XII, 1070a22). It is not enough to reflect, as we did some pages back, that by 'health' here he must mean just the particular, transient health of the individual. He is pointing a larger moral. His avowed target in the passage is Plato, and he is saying that for health to exist is not for there to be an immaterial and eternal Paradigm of Health, but just for the health of some (at least one) individual to be in existence. And for such a state of health to be in existence is, as we said earlier, for it to have a temporal career amenable to Aristotle's analysis of being*: states of health have their own ways of breaking down.

So if Aristotle can parcel out the senses of 'exist' among our reports of particular cases he can fairly expect the same partitions in the use of the verb to survive in the general propositions about existence that stand on their backs. Moving from one level of generality to the other will not induce him to disentangle being* from being** but, if anything, help to blur the distinction. And thus his well-founded hesitation over the function of such a statement as 'Triangle exists' in the *Posterior Analytics* will remain unresolved.

It needs no saying that the distinction he missed is a capital distinction. To predicate being*, in the appropriate sense of the word, of men or icebergs, is tacitly to presuppose that there are** men and icebergs for this predicate to apply to. Aristotle's failure to mark this difference is one, and perhaps the chief, factor in his more celebrated failure to analyse the existential presuppositions of all those forms of statement to which his system of logic applies. But such talk of 'failure' makes little sense when we are mapping the advances of a pioneer./

VI 88

So much for our hopeful restriction on the scope of Aristotle's analysis. What remains of it? Well, it remains true, on the argument so far, that the cases of existence with which he is primarily concerned when he pigeon-holes the different senses of 'exist' are particular cases, expressed in singular propositions: for we have seen how these singular propositions carry the general propositions on their backs. (Further to this see W. and M. Kneale, *The Development of Logic*, p. 31.) But having thus documented Aristotle's care for the particular, we must allow that the general propositions call for the same pattern of analysis. So the problem of the overworked paraphrase seems to be back on our hands. If ice is (*inter alia*) solid, 'solid' will do double duty. It will see service not only in defining 'ice' but in paraphrasing the verb 'to be' when it occurs in existential statements about ice. And whatever troubles come of this will not be allayed by our artless distinction between general statements about ice and singular reports of existence which mention the ice on the pond. There are general statements of existence too, and in these the verb will call for the same paraphrase.

But by now this is the ghost of a puzzle. Our trouble with the general statement that ice exists was just that, by this double application of the paraphrase, it became a truism and its denial became a contradiction. We had no such difficulty over the statement that the ice on the pond was still, or no longer, in existence (sc. still solid or now melted). A deposed Mayor is not a Mayor, but this does not prove it a contradiction to say that the Mayor of Margate has been deposed. And now we have seen how Aristotle can assimilate the general statement of existence to the particular. 'Ice exists' can be read as 'Some ice is still solid, etc.'; and this is no more of a tautology than the statement about a particular ice-patch which, in Aristotle's view, gives concrete filling to that general reference. In fact, our notion of generality was doubly naïve. To discover the relevant sense of 'exist' in these sentences is indeed to discover what 'ice' means in general; but this discovery, in its simplest form, consists in appealing not to a general statement about the ice in the world but to a definition, which is neither a particular nor a general statement about material ice but a third thing: it carries no quantifiers, and it asks/ not to be verified but to be understood (*A. Pst.* I, 76b35-77a4). 89

Now notice the price to be paid for laying this ghost. We shall have to construe any assertion of existence, singular or general, as signifying that the subject is *still* in existence; and we shall have to read a denial of existence as meaning that the subject is *no longer* (or perhaps *not yet*) in existence. This suits Aristotle's observations on the existence of health and of the shape of the bronze sphere, and his query whether such things survive the perishable individual (*Meta.* XII 1070a22-4). It works well for statements about extant natural kinds and characters, such as man, or health, or ice, where statements of being** can without discomfort be replaced by, or mistaken for, statements of being*, complete with quantifiers. But when we turn to other assertions of being** it becomes absurd to rewrite 'not' as 'no longer' or 'not yet'. It is absurd to interpret 'Centaurs do not exist' as referring to the dead or unborn members of some tribe. (And another example from the same context stands to refute anyone so disheartened by this that he reverts to an interpretation scouted at the end of section III. Shall we say, after all, that 'Centaurs don't exist' is a statement about something in the world, namely certain 'matter'; and that it says that this matter does not have the characteristics of a centaur, that flesh and blood is not horse-rumped and man-headed? Aristotle mentions gods in the same breath as centaurs, and gods have no matter at all.)

In the *Posterior Analytics* Aristotle avoids applying his analysis of being* to such statements of being**, but his avoidance never clarifies itself in a sharp distinction of the two. We offered to explain this unclarity by the consideration that *some* general statements of being** can be readily confused with statements of being*. To be sure, this consideration applies only to a range of favoured examples – to extant sorts and kinds, and classes with members; but in formal logic and philosophy and science it is these cases that preoccupy Aristotle, to the point where he is no longer concerned to resolve old uncertainties about the non-existence of centaurs or tragelaphs.

When Aristotle analyses statements of existence, in short, he is commonly preoccupied with cases of being*. But having said this we must cut the claim down to size by one last, large qualification. There is still a third kind of
90 statement which would usually be/ dubbed 'existential' and which plays an important part in Aristotle's argument. He seems as ready to supply a paraphrase of 'existence' in these new cases as when he is dealing with men and milestones; yet it would be absurd to explain these, on the lines laid down, as cases of being*. So we need to mark off a third existential use of the verb 'to be'.

VII

Aristotle sometimes asserts or denies the existence of things when (*a*) the denial could not sensibly be taken to signify that the things are no longer in existence, and (*b*) the assertion could not sensibly be taken to signify that at least one sample is still in existence. Such things are time, place, the void, the subject-matter of mathematics. 'At least one time, namely *now*, is still present'.) Yet when he discusses the existence of the objects of mathematics he undertakes to say in detail the sense in which they can be said to exist (*Meta.* XIII, 1077b12-1078a31). When he analyses the concept of place in the *Physics* he starts, on the recommendation of the *Posterior Analytics*, by distinguishing the question whether place exists from the question what place is, and treating the former question first (208a28-9); but the problems he raises have the effect of making the questions coincide (209a29-30), and the problems are accordingly lumped together as difficulties concerning the 'being' or *ousia* of place (210a12-13). He shows in what sense the existence of the void cannot be allowed (if it is equated with empty space), but also in what sense it can (as the necessary condition of motion, 217b27-8). How are such existential claims to be taken?

Suppose I ask 'Is there such a thing as centramine?' or, 'as a centaur?' or, 'as self-deception?' Then I may be asking, in linguistic ignorance, whether there is such a word (say 'centramine') in the language. I may be asking, in ignorance of some empirical fact but knowing the use of the expression, whether anything in the world answers to the appellation (such as 'centaur'). Or, thirdly, I may be showing philosophical perplexity: I may be taking for granted the ordinary use of the expression, and assuming, moreover, that its users would generally agree that something answers to it, but asking whether the accepted use/ of the expression (say 'self-deception') is logically coherent. **91**
I am asking whether it provides a description that can be applied without generating conceptual puzzles that would justify its rejection or radical reform.

With the first of these questions Aristotle has no concern (compare Plato, who ensures that his interlocutors can at least talk Greek: *Charmides* 159a, *Meno* 82b, *Alcibiades* I 111b-c). With the second he does show concern: this is a question about being**, and 'centaur' is Aristotle's example. But it is the third that is exemplified in his uncertainties over the existence of time or place or mathematicals. These uncertainties are developed in puzzles, *aporiai*, which seem to be forced on us by common beliefs (or by the contentions of other philosophers), and in particular by accredited uses of the suspect expression and other connected expressions.[18] They are consequently resolved by a clear and unparadoxical statement of what time is, or what mathematicals are. The philosophical query 'Does time exist?' is answered by saying 'Time is such and such' and showing the answer innocent of logical absurdities. And thus once again it becomes natural for Aristotle to speak of having shown the sense in which the subject does or does not exist (*Meta.* 1077b15-17, 1078b7-8, *Phys.* 217b27-8).

This account needs to be clarified if it is to be saved from the two major difficulties that threaten it. In the first place, it implies that to give a definition of A is tantamount to asserting that A exists: yet Aristotle himself insists elsewhere (*A. Pst.* II, 92b19-25) that no definition can entail the existence of what it defines. Secondly, it implies that to reject a particular definition of time is tantamount to denying the existence of time; but it is surely preposterous to think this, or to father the thought on Aristotle the codifier of dialectic.

It is not hard to see how in these contexts, and just in these, both difficulties lose their menace. The first is irrelevant because Aristotle assumes that he is analysing a concept in current use: if the notion of time can be shown to be coherent, no one (or only those with a conceptual axe to grind) will deny it application – deny, for instance, that noon today is a different time from noon yesterday. The second falls to a similar consideration. Aristotle is/

[18] See '*Tithenai ta phainomena*', above, Chapter 13.

92 at pains to show that his analysis is not an arbitrary redefinition of a term. 'One need not agree with the crowd in everything, but one must not desert or subvert the common and received use of words' (*Top.* VI, 148b20-2). His analysis is designed to preserve all or the most important part of common belief and usage on the subject: this explains the thorough (and supposedly exhaustive) review of the *phainomena* and *legomena* which introduces any such analysis.[19] So in a confident mood Aristotle may assume that to reject his analysis is in effect to drop the topic (indeed, to expel the topic from the language), and thus to leave the objector no means of agreeing with Aristotle's conclusion that there is such a thing.

Some may find it natural to translate Aristotle's questions in these contexts in the form 'Is so and so *real*?' Certainly the verb 'to be' in Aristotle does sometimes ask to be rendered by way of this slippery adjective. A contrast such as that drawn in the *Sophistici Elenchi* (170b8-11) between 'the X which *is*' and 'the X which *seems*' may even suggest that when Aristotle brands the predicate 'existing man' as a pleonasm (see section III above) he is thinking of what it is to be a *real* man, by contrast with some sham or half-baked or makeshift version. But this contrast would be too restricted for the context of argument. The notion of unreality has no part to play in most of the texts we have been trying to digest in this paper. If it comes in with this third kind of existential statement, it serves only to sharpen the difference between this kind and the other two.

VIII

There is no space to push this interpretation further, and not much to comment on the theory it reveals. But if we have got the general lines of it right the following observations seem pertinent.

First, there are indeed different existential uses of the verb 'to be' discoverable in Aristotle's writings: we have sorted out three of these, and no doubt there are others. But Aristotle, armed only with his device for paraphrasing the predicate (and neglecting other more apt and powerful weapons in his own arsenal, such as amphiboly), gives no express recognition to these distinctions. Sometimes his uncertainties betray the cracks in the
93 ground./ But his own contribution to the topic lies chiefly in those distinctions which his paraphrastic technique enables him to make.

Secondly, then, where that technique is most at home, viz. in dissecting the senses of the supposed predicate being*, the credentials of the predicate are suspect. One possible source of suspicion is the equivocal status of the subject when the predicate is not yet true of it; but perhaps this suspicion was sufficiently disarmed in section III. It seems to stem from a general scepticism about our knowledge of future existence. Another trouble is an anomaly that seems to infest any negation of the predicate: but this can be settled at once. The objection is this: Let *man* be defined, after Aristotle, as an animal that

[19] See '*Tithenai ta phainomena*', above, Chapter 13.

travels on two legs. You ask after my man Friday, and I tell you he is no more. Then on Aristotle's analysis what I tell you is that man Friday is no longer an animal that travels on two legs; but I might have told you this if he had had, and survived, an amputation of those members. And if ice is solid by definition, still there can be crushed ice. Now this is a puzzle, not about the suggested analysis of 'is' or 'exists', but about the sufficient and necessary conditions for applying some classificatory word such as 'man' or 'ice'. What the existence of crushed ice and legless men shows is that, while two legs or solidity may be a mark or characteristic of men or ice, they are not necessary conditions for applying the relevant classification – not, that is, if this would imply that 'crushed ice' is a contradiction like 'square circle'. If such examples show anything to the purpose they show that Aristotle's view of the relation between some classificatory word and its *logos* was at one time too simple, at least if that *logos* is taken to show the conditions on which the word is correctly applied. What they do not show is that there is a looser relation between 'exist' and its paraphrase in such contexts than there is between the relevant classificatory word and *its* paraphrase. If the latter is a predicate whose sense can be given in a certain form of words, so, for all that this objection shows, is 'exist'.

Other criticisms cut deeper. Grant that it is a different thing for a man to exist and for a sandal to exist; why should this imply that 'exist' has different senses, any more than 'work' must be taken to have different senses because it is one thing for a banker to do his work and another for a hangman to do his? Great numbers of words (it will be argued) are in one way or another specially/ dependent on the context for their particular force: pronouns and **94**
demonstratives; disguised relatives like 'big' and 'heavy' (and even those bricks of epistemology, colour-adjectives – remember blue Persians and red cabbages); many words for working and correspondingly for idling; and many *substantive-hungry* words, to use Austin's label, such as 'same', 'real', 'one', 'good'. It is not that Aristotle neglects these words: it is that he is apt, as in *Topics* I 15, to try them with the same key as words which are far less context-bound – words such as '*philein*', which in many sentences can mean either 'love', or 'kiss' (106b1-4), or '*onos*', which can mean either 'ass' or 'pulley' (107a19-21). It is just because these last expressions are relatively context-free (though notice that this freedom like others is always relative) that they are liable to generate ambiguity in use; and this is why the device of fixing their senses in advance by paraphrase is proper and valuable, and why we cannot allow them an indefinite range of senses. But we ought to be suspicious of the claim that 'good' or 'same' or 'one' has in the same way a number of senses that must or can be listed or taught or circumscribed. Lexicographers manage to resist the suggestion. And, as Aristotle often insists, 'existing' falls into the same bracket as 'one' and 'same' and 'good'.

This was a hare to be raised, not chased now. The same is true of a last questionable corollary of Aristotle's analysis, one by which he sets great store. It is that, since 'exist' has many senses, there is no class of *existing things* which will embrace men and miles and modesty. The same conclusion follows from his thesis that numerals, no less than 'exist', have different uses in the different categories (the fullest argument for this is *Metaphysics* X, 1053b25-1054a19); for this entails that one substance and one quality and one quantity do not make three of anything at all. It was on this contention that he rested his rejection of any general study of what exists; and it is accordingly this thesis that he has to disarm, though not to discard, when he comes in *Metaphysics* IV to set up his own general science of being.

Yet Aristotle is compelled to use conjunctions that his theory disallows. 'Given that there are substance and quality and quantity,' he starts unguardedly in the *Physics* (185a27-8); and he comments without qualms on the restricted number of categories in the *Posterior Analytics* (83b13-17). Nor in
95 fact do his arguments/ show such conjunctions to be illegitimate, for the kind of existence that is asserted here is being**, and to this his device of paraphrasing the predicate is irrelevant. But this distinction is one of which, as we have been saying, Aristotle does not show himself aware.

IX

A final point, from abundance of caution. It may still be objected that Aristotle's account of 'existent' as an homonymous predicate does not represent his most influential or characteristic view on the subject. For when he comes to set up his own general metaphysics of 'being' he founds it on the claim that the different senses of 'exist' in the different categories are systematically connected; and this leads him to deny that 'exist' is really homonymous (*Meta.* IV, 1003a33-b19). There is a similar reconsideration in his mature ethics when he allows that 'good' is after all not an instance of *chance* homonymy (*EN* I, 1096b26-7).

These developments are another story (see above, Chapter 10). The aim of this essay, all too sketchily achieved, was to chart the basic patterns of Aristotle's analysis of existence. For that purpose it is enough to say that his later theories do not in the least entail the discarding of these patterns. His disclaimer in *Metaphysics* IV is politic: he is announcing his own 'general science of being *qua* being', and it was on the homonymy of 'being' that he had earlier built his objection to any such enterprise. But when he now claims to detect a systematic connection between the senses of 'exist' he is not denying, but presupposing, the possibility of paraphrasing that verb differently when it is married to different subjects. No doubt in claiming that these senses have something in common – that the paraphrases have an important overlap – he has moved beyond mere, or 'chance', or (as the *Eudemian Ethics* puts it in another connection) 'total', homonymy. But more important than these labels is the fact that his own theories were worked out wholly within the framework of those techniques on which the analysis that we have been reviewing here relies.

16

Particular and General

We meet in pride and confidence to inaugurate the centennial session of our 1
noble Society. At least, it is the centennial if our predecessors were right to celebrate 1928-29 as the fiftieth session after our unambitious beginnings in April 1880. Those beginnings entitled us to call 1879-80 Year One, and you can compute the rest. To those who wish to know more of our origins I can best commend Wildon Carr's paper in the Proceedings for June 1929. The Society was then holding a Commemorative Dinner (excellent example) with Samuel Alexander in the Chair. From being an association first proposed by an analytical chemist, and with its first paper ('What is Philosophy?') read by a practising doctor, it had already become a society of professional philosophers. The presence by then of enough philosophers in the universities to make up most of our membership is something for which this Society must bear much of the responsibility.

The second rule of the Society at its foundation ran: 'The objects of the Society shall be the systematic study of Philosophy; first, as to its historic development; second, as to its methods and problems'. I suspect it is this division which explains (or is explained by) the programme of the earliest meetings. Of those 'a certain number of evenings were given to the reading of papers on particular philosophers, the others were given to the discussion of philosophical problems – Substance, Cause, Perception, etc., with their dependent ideas. On these occasions there was no introductory paper *but members came with definitions*' (Wildon Carr, my italics). On several grounds we can be glad to have shed those Gold Coast customs. For one thing, it would
seem absurd/ to us now that the pursuit of other philosophers' ideas should be 2
systematically divided from independent conceptual inquiry. Or, if it does not seem absurd, the arguments that follow will have been misconceived. For in proposing some ways of reading Aristotle and Plato I shall argue about reference and classification; and then in exploring some puzzles in the analysis of different sorts of change I shall start from problems in Aristotle. But one last prefatory note may be called for. If Aristotle figures in my argument, that is of course no special piety to our Founding Fathers. For the record: 'Dr. Burns-Gibson, in proposing the name of the Society had doubtless in mind Hegel's scathing remark on the English abuse of the term

* Meeting of the Aristotelian Society at 39 Belgrave Square, London SW1 on Monday 9 October 1978 at 7.30 p.m: the Presidential Address.

"philosophical" in applying it to meteorological instruments. It was, therefore, essential to find a name which would definitely prescribe the speculative character of the study which was to be the Society's ideal, and it seemed that this could best be secured by adopting the name of a philosopher eminently representative. There is only one such name in the history of philosophy', Wildon Carr concludes, 'and so we became the Aristotelian Society.'

I turn to the argument.

Conflicts in reference

Aristotle's most powerful and influential analysis of substance – that is, of the general nature of individuals – begins by requiring that a substance be both *a this* and *what-is-it* or *what-it-is, tode ti* and *ti esti* (*Meta.* VII, 1028a11-18). The phrases sound oddly, but they have familiar connotations for his readers and they have their modern counterparts. A *this* is always a member of a class as against the class (or sometimes a species as against its genus); a subject to which classificatory predicates can be applied. The question *what-is-it*, on the other hand, introduces a classification or, when it is available and when the question is pressed, a definition of something. The first label suggests that we are to look for *subjects* of predicates, and this condition on substance Aristotle repeats later. Substances are to be those subjects of discourse to which all our descriptions of the world must, at any rate when properly analysed in canonical form, make direct or indirect reference (1028a18-30, 1030a34-b3). The second expression suggests the search for conditions of identity. If we press it in the case of Socrates Aristotle insists that we shall not be able to
3 pro-/duce a definition proprietary to him (1039b27-40a7); the content of a definition cannot exhaust the identity of anything having matter in it (1037a27-b5), for that can only be one among others of a kind (1034a5-8) and it cannot be guaranteed to satisfy a definition uniquely or always (1040a33-b1, 1040a2-7). But what the question can and must produce in Socrates' case is an *eidos*, a form or species, a necessary condition for understanding his identity and his existence. 'It is impossible for the same thing to continue yet entirely change its species; the same animal, for instance, cannot be a man at one time but not at another' (*Top.* 125b37-39, cf. 145a3-12).

Much of the subsequent strategy of *Metaphysics* VII is to press the apparent recalcitrance between these two requirements on substance. It pursues the first in the direction of a subject which eludes all classification (VII 3) and then the second in the direction of an *eidos* which, because its identity is wholly and satisfyingly exhausted by a definition, threatens to become the chief subject of reference in its own right (VII 6 with its postscript at 1037a32-b7). But I do not see that Aristotle's end-strategy is to sacrifice one of these factors to the other and christen the survivor '*ousia*', 'substance'. The plot of *Metaphysics* VII and VIII is to hold the recalcitrants together in one focus. Nor is it, so far as I can see, to be content with pointing out different senses or uses of 'substance'. Aristotle has one target and his strategy is a pincer-movement.

Philosophers who try to explain how we succeed in naming or making some unique reference to a thing or a person find themselves subject to two strong and contrary inclinations. Before seeing their lineaments in Aristotle, and then taking up some problems in his account, let us look at them directly.

One inclination is to say that we cannot make such a reference at all
without knowing what or whom we are referring to; and that this requires us
to be able to say, on demand, what or whom we are referring to without
falling back on the name or designation we first used. I tell you I have just
visited Santa Sofia; you ask what or who that is; I tell you, tempering the
reply to your apparent interest, that it is a celebrated building I saw on my
travels. But I misjudged your curiosity; you ask *which* building? (I shall take
up the ambiguity of this question.) Perhaps I can tell you no more than that it
is the building now occupying/ the site of the church built by Theodosius in 4
415 and burnt down in 532. But that may provide sufficient as well as
necessary conditions of identity; it enables you, with due enquiry, to pick out
which building I referred to.

It is easy to think of this second reply as giving a meaning to the name 'Santa Sofia'. Within the conversation I have sketched it seems as pointless for you to challenge my description as it would be to challenge the explanation of a triangle as a plane figure with three interior angles. Notoriously Frege said that 'in the case of genuinely proper names like "Aristotle", opinions about their *sense* may vary. One sense of the name that one might suggest is "Plato's disciple and the teacher of Alexander the Great".' He surely did not think of the different descriptions that you and I have in mind when we use the same name of the same thing as making the name equivocal; the different senses are equally successful if they determine the same reference. Still the puzzle remains under what conditions such descriptions can become false, or be found false, of the subject, without disabling the reference they are supposed to determine. So later writers have sought to weaken the connection between the name and the descriptions: Searle for instance says that, while 'it is a contingent fact that Aristotle ever went into pedagogy', 'it is a necessary fact that Aristotle has the logical sum, the inclusive disjunction, of properties commonly attributed to him'. But it is not hard to weaken the connection further; and this is the contrary inclination I spoke of.

Consider the Spartan lawgiver Lycurgus on whom Grote spent over 100 pages of his *History of Greece*. He prefaced those pages by quoting with approval Plutarch's comment: 'Concerning the lawgiver Lycurgus we can assert absolutely nothing which is not controverted; there are different stories in respect of his birth, his travels, his death, and also his mode of proceeding, political as well as legislative: least of all is the time in which he lived agreed on.' And we can readily imagine an article in a later learned journal which begins: 'It has now been established by archaeological evidence that Lycurgus was not a human politician but a stone image revered by the Spartans and named after Apollo Lykoerges.' Should we object that this is not a discovery about Lycurgus but the mere introduction of a new subject?

5 Surely not. We should certainly expect the writer to ex-/plain how the stone image was, so to speak, transformed in the tradition into a supposedly historic personage – by loss of the image, reappearance as *daimon* and then hero, etc.; not an unfamiliar task for historians. But on such terms we should surely say that he had contributed to the continuing debate about Lycurgus.

Could we then, by this kind of erosion, discover that Lycurgus had none or only a thin remnant of the attributes traditionally claimed for him? One thing we could surely not discover: that he was a stone image who turned into a human lawgiver, or vice versa. Some *ti esti* must remain essentially true of that *tode*, some *what-is-it* of that individual, if we could find it; either he was a man, and when the man came to an end there was an end of that one, or he was a stone and when that crumbled there was an end of that one. That is as far as the passage I quoted from the *Topics* a page ago (125b37-39) will carry us. If we cannot always find sufficient conditions for identifying an individual, we can surely find such necessary conditions. But outside the logical works Aristotle himself takes us further.

Certainly we jib at supposing a man to turn into a stone image or vice versa, because no physical laws known or intelligible to us will explain the change and there is no profit in enlarging possible worlds by fairy physics. But men turn to ashes, eggs into birds, a pound of wood to another weight of coal; or, to quote the examples with which Aristotle faces these issues in his *Generation and Corruption* (I 4, 319b14-18), 'when nothing perceptible persists in its identity as a substrate, and the thing changes as a whole – as when the seed as a whole is converted into blood, or water into air, or air as a whole into water – such an occurrence is (not change of quality, but) the coming-to-be of one thing and ceasing-to-be of another' (Joachim's version modified). Still, as Aristotle insists, we are more inclined to describe any of these changes in terms of something that survives a transformation than to speak of it as a mere replacement of A by B. Replacement, as Aristotle assumes throughout his account of location in *Physics* IV, requires the pre-and post-existence of both A and B. But here, when we say 'In a hundred years this seed will be a full-grown oak' or 'Yesterday these ashes were a full-grown oak', we seem prepared to talk of just one thing undergoing a thorough chemical change.
6 Whatever scientific theory professes to explain such changes, that/ is no more for us than it was for Aristotle part of what we ordinarily mean by such utterances. (That is, it is no part of the dialectic which Aristotle represents as the essential preliminary to the sciences, aiming to clarify the common usage and convictions that the sciences offer a theory to explain.) In his account of matter Aristotle was not advancing another scientific hypothesis. In *Physics* I 5-9 he produces an explanatory scheme which admirably fits our descriptions of a man changing colour and then extends it to such troublesome cases as that of a seed turning into a tree; a philosophical, not a scientific exercise. But he does not there tackle the total chemical change that interests him in *Generation and Corruption*. In the *Physics* (191a7-13) he says: 'The underlying nature can be known by analogy. For as bronze is to statue or wood to bed, or the shapeless before it acquires shape to something having shape, so is the underlying nature to the individual and the being, the *tode ti* and the *on*.' But

we are not entitled to read this as suggesting that there is some ultimate matter which can only be understood by analogy with more familiar and controllable cases such as bronze or wood. In *Metaphysics* XII 4 he makes a similar suggestion with regard to the form or *eidos* that can be understood only by analogy with more familiar instances such as the shape of a statue. He means that there is no generic idea of *the form*, not that any given form cannot be very well identified. And for all that he says in *Physics* I he means the same of matter.

It is only when, as in *Generation and Corruption* (notably but not only II 1-5), he descends the chain of predication until he has pushed every term of classification or description into the predicate position, even the names of the chemical elements and their component characters, that he comes within sight of the basic mutable subject of *Metaphysics* VII 3, a subject retaining only some second- or third-order powers of change but carrying *in its own right* no positive classification. And even here he seems dialectically right. If we were in a position to say 'That (elemental) water turned into this (elemental) air' we should surely prefer, without prejudice to any scientific theory designed to satisfy the Eleatics, to speak of this once more as a modification in one subject. This air *was* that water.

Here, at any rate, are the two opposing inclinations tugging us/when we try 7
to explain how we can be sure of naming or making unique reference to some individual. One is to say that we must be able to support the reference with a description that amounts at best to a definition. The other is to say that any such description can be rejected – or, in the extreme case that interests Aristotle, can become false of its subject – without endangering the reference. Frege and in some contexts Russell followed the first inclination, Russell in other contexts and Kripke followed the second. Aristotle tried to hold them both in one focus.

Platonic ancestry

We are to plot Aristotle's pincer-movement and then consider some paradoxes in it that still await analyses of change. But first it is worth noticing some antecedents in Plato for the conflicting inclinations.

There is a familiar line of argument in the third quarter of the *Theaetetus* (189b-200c) which can be summarized without too much travesty as follows. How can I misidentify something I know, i.e. take it for something it is not? Well, I can misidentify Theaetetus even though I know him and know the man I confuse him with, when I see him and point him out at a distance. Yes, but how can I mentally misidentify what I know when there is no question of pointing and perceiving at a distance? 12 is one of the numbers I have to know in order to calculate. How can I mistake it for 11 and say '7 + 5 = 11'? Well, perhaps my knowledge of 12 is not actively in play; the bird is loitering somewhere else in my mental bird-cage. But my knowledge of 11 is active; I have *named* 11, grasped the bird in optimum conditions, yet taken it for what it is not. Ah, but (says Socrates' interlocutor) perhaps the bird that presented itself was an impostor, a bit of ignorance and not of knowledge. Very well: I grasped this imposter with which I am presumably as well-acquainted as with anything else in my mind. So how did I fail to identify it for what it was? And so on.

The strand I want to pick out from this tangled argument is the remarkably strong condition it requires for naming something when the possibility of picking it out by mere pointing is ruled out. In such cases the ability to make the reference requires an ability to identify, and this is taken to imply an inability to misidentify. How can Plato have thought this plausible enough to make a paradox turn on it?/

8 It is natural to find part of the answer in Plato's earlier metaphysics. (I shall enter caveats later.) Socrates standardly introduces his inquiries in earlier dialogues by the plea: Tell me what X is, or I shall not know how to answer questions about X. If he does not know what virtue is, he will not know whether it is teachable (*Meno* 71b, 86d, 100b, *Prot.* 360e); if he does not know what friendship is, he will not know whether he and Lysis and Menexenus are friends (*Lysis* 223b); if he does not know what Justice is he will not even know if it is a virtue or if it is beneficial (*Rep.* 354c). For Plato is concerned here with expressions such that people wholly conversant with the language could still disagree over their application: 'justice', 'friendship', 'beauty', 'virtue' (cf. *Phaedr.* 263a, *Alc.* I 111b-12a). There was no consensus of usage or opinion to invoke if one merely claimed to recognize justice when it occurred without being able to explain how it was to be recognized. There was no standard unarguable case to point to. (Aristotle was later to say, in the *Nicomachean Ethics* 1143b7-14, that this ability even in the case of virtues was important; old men wise in the world had an eye for virtue even if they could not explain or defend their verdicts; but Plato would have asked them to say what they found virtuous in the actions they praised and subjected their answers to the inquisition that Cephalus and Polemarchus face in the first book of the *Republic*.) Still less would Plato allow that any successful reference to such a Form could be made by merely importing its name into a discussion; there are familiar arguments in the *Republic* and *Hippias Major* designed to show that men just do not know what such expressions actually refer to. So there was good reason for requiring anyone who professed to be discussing justice to tell us just how he recognized that elusive character.

For Plato these conditions carried a strong corollary. He seems to have supposed that if I can say what justice is, for example, then I can know everything else about it; for he held, correspondingly, that if I am insecure or mistaken or open to counter-argument or counter-evidence on these other questions I do *not* know what justice is. Transfer this conviction to the *Theaetetus*, and there is a ready explanation for the assumption that if I know something, in the sense of being able to think or speak of it and so have it firmly before my mind, I cannot be mistaken about it and in particular cannot confuse it with anything else./

9 There are snags in drawing this parallel between the *Theaetetus* and the earlier metaphysics. For one thing in our passage Socrates does not speak of definitions or use the established jargon of the Forms. That is less important:

much of the *Theaetetus* is concerned to lay out and examine skeletons of arguments and assumptions that underlay Plato's earlier work. More important in the *Theaetetus* is that Plato is as ready to apply his argument to speaking or thinking of a particular man or horse as to speaking or thinking of numbers (195d6-e4) or of just and unjust, beautiful and ugly (188b7-10, 189c5-7, 190b2-8). This may remind us of the *Cratylus*, where Socrates proposes to unpack names into the descriptions that give them their sense and then applies his method indifferently to the proper names of individuals and to the names of virtues and vices, natural kinds, feelings and actions and processes. But the *Cratylus* exploits the familiar fact that Greek proper names are compressed descriptions (even compressed prayers, 397b) as well as the truism that proper names, unlike uniquely individuating references, can be shared. Neither interest shows in the *Theaetetus*.

We may cautiously decide that here – in the *Theaetetus* and the earlier metaphysics – are two different elements in Plato's inclination to press our first requirement on reference. But the shift between general and particular would not have convinced Aristotle that Plato was not still concerned with the scheme of arguments supporting his earlier metaphysics. For Aristotle's commonest objection to the Theory of Forms is that it confuses the general with the particular. It mistakes a *toionde* for a *tode* (or *tode ti*), a 'such' for a 'this'; in brief, it takes a common predicate to stand for an individual subject. It is a distinction to which Aristotle returns often and from many directions. In terms of this contrast (he sometimes uses the expressions otherwise) his theory of predication requires that the universal *toionde* be predicable of the individual *tode*, but the *tode* not be predicable of anything else. It requires too that the universal but not the individual can carry quantifiers (e.g. *Meta.* 1018a3-4). But while such contrasts can be drawn between two sorts of factor for the Academy's benefit, their interdependence must not be called in question. For Aristotle a *this* is always thought of as carrying a predicative complement. Just as he will have no *toionde* without a *tode* to substantiate it, so there is no *tode* without a completing/ *toionde*. And when he repeats the **10** familiar Third Man objection against the Academy's individualising of predicables, the kind of *toionde* that interests him most is equally clear. As his examples show (even at *SE* 178b36-39) the expression covers those classificatory predicates which answer the question *ti esti* – what is X? – by assigning the subject to its definable species or its genus.

It would be unfair to leave Plato prone to the first of the two conflicting inclinations I sketched earlier without noticing another context in which he discusses the conditions on which we can speak successfully both of general concepts and of particular individuals, without falling into the assumptions that beset the *Theaetetus*.

In the *Sophist* the Eleatic Stranger proposes that a sophist is one who professes to purvey a reality when what he purveys is counterfeit, and who claims to teach truths when what he teaches are falsehoods. Under both heads he can be said to speak of *what is not* or of *what are not*. Later Plato reduces these different accusations to the complaint that he teaches what is false (264c10-d5), and it is the explanation of falsehood in which the dialogue centres.

But the problem of falsehood is not allowed to rest at the point it had reached in the *Cratylus* (429e ff.) and the *Theaetetus* (188c9-89b3), where speaking of what is not had been compared to the vacuous gesture of touching or saluting what was not there to be so saluted or touched. The *Sophist* turns to challenge the very terms in which the old and puzzling diagnosis of falsehood had been couched. If we describe falsehood as 'speaking of nothing', our description is puzzling not because the speaking would then be vacuous; it is puzzling because such an expression as 'nothing' seems to have no intelligible use. Plato tries to establish this by pretending that if it had an intelligible use it could play the role of an ordinary subject. He asks what, and what sort of thing, a speaker could be expected to pick out by such an expression 'what is not' if we equate it with 'nothing' (237b10-c4, recalled at 250d7-8); and he unsurprisingly decides that no answer can be found. Whatever description or classification one contemplates, Nothing cannot be even one thing falling under that head. The strategy becomes clear: the major achievement of the dialogue thereafter is to show what logical
11 conditions must be/ satisfied by any genuine subject of discourse. I cannot myself see that he does, or should, single out existence as one of those conditions or spend argument on isolating an 'existential' sense of the verb 'to be'. What concerns him in the *Sophist* is rather the teasing out of the sorts of positively and negatively framed propositions that must be available from the start in introducing any subject of discourse at all. What is established for the first time in the *Sophist* is a matter of syntax, the distinction of subject and predicate – and that calls only for further investigations into the 'incomplete' uses of 'to be' that connect two flanking expressions. It is established, first by illustrating that there must be many things that hold good of the subject as well as uncountably many that must be denied it (256e2-6, generalized from forms to individuals at 263b11-12); then by showing that our entitlement to deny something of the subject rests wholly on the difference – bald difference, not as some have thought incompatibility – between what we deny of it and anything that holds good of it. The whole analysis that ultimately provides a justification of falsehood thus rests on two notions: that of what can be positively and truly said about the subject, and that of difference between predicates.

What the *Sophist* does not consider, since it is no part of its business to do so, is how the positive assertions about the subject serve to identify it. Indeed, so far as identifying is concerned it seems content to recognize only negative identifications of the simplest form, A = B; though in 255c8-e1 it may be distinguishing two classes of statement of which one states an identity in a form more interesting than that of A = A.

Thus in one context, the latest, Plato concerns himself with the question what it is to have a subject of reference, and discusses this in a way wholly acceptable to those who feel doubts about the strong requirements for identifying individual subjects that I associated with the first of the conflicting inclinations. Indeed his treatment of the issues would allow an analysis of even existential statements, both positive and negative, which

would bypass one reason found by recent philosophers for taking names in such statements to be disguised descriptions. For perhaps the existential statements can, at least for suitable predicates, be recast in subject-predicate form. At any rate this seems to have been Aristotle's way with them. For Socrates to be was for him/to be a substance of a certain sort, viz. a man 12
living a man's life; for him to cease to be was for him to be no longer alive in that way and therefore no longer a man (since for Aristotle a dead man, lacking human abilities, was not in any proper sense a man). Some such subject-predicate analysis of existential statements would still be open to anyone who accepted the exploration of subject-predicate distinctions in the *Sophist*.

In other contexts, Plato imports very much stronger conditions for individuating any subject of speech or thought; he requires some set of sufficient conditions to be acknowledged which amount in effect to a definition; and his arguments imply, whether in the end he believed this or not, that such conditions must equally be specifiable in individuating such particulars as Theaetetus.

Aristotle and the pincer-movement

The strategy of *Metaphysics* VII is to allow our two requirements on substance – on, in fact, our ordinary references to individuals – to pull the argument in opposite directions, and then to show that either direction single-mindedly pursued leads to an intolerable result.

Consider first the pursuit of the subject. I suggested earlier that the argument of *Physics* I need not be read as leading directly to the 'matter' of *Metaphysics* VII 3 that carries no classification in its own right, none whose loss it cannot survive. Nor certainly need the 'prime matter' of 1049a18-49b3. The proposal of such an ultimate subject belongs to *Generation and Corruption* 329a27-35. He has already said (e.g. 321b22-34) that when an animal grows, what grows is not strictly its flesh and bone but the hand or foot or some organic part; what is true of the flesh and bone is just that some has been added to it (or subtracted from it), but the hand has grown as a whole. He puts this by saying that the thing grows *qua* form and not *qua* matter; the flesh and bones are matter with a certain form, that of a hand; and the hand grows. And because, when a substance perishes, this can be thought of as certain matter losing the form it had – the materials that made up Socrates, for example, ceasing to be a man and retiring to other jobs – there is a greater tendency to think that a corpse still retains flesh and bones than to think that it still has a hand or an arm (321b29-32). Hands, like men, have characteristic powers and activities; dead samples do not deserve the name (e.g. *Parts of Animals* 640b30-41a5)./

This suggests that what can be said to survive the death of the man is just 13
the materials, the flesh and bones. But elsewhere, in *Generation of Animals* (741a10-11, 734b24-27, cf. 726b22-24), he denies this too. It is impossible for flesh, any more than for a face or hand or any other animal part, to exist if

there is not a percipient soul in it; neither a face nor flesh exists if it has no life, and once perished they can only be called flesh or face in another sense. After all, flesh and bone too have their proper powers and performances only in the live animal. So if we want to locate the matter which pre-exists and survives we have to go below these descriptions and get down to the chemical constituents. But there too, in Aristotle's view, the situation is restored. He consistently refuses to suppose the world constructed from elements that have no representatives in our everyday experience. Atoms in a void he professes to discount because their supposed nature and movements offend some mathematical and physical rules, but his deeper reason is surely that these are philosophers' constructions, and his whole method in physics is to systematize our everyday knowledge and ways of speaking about the world. Suppose then that we rest content with such familiar components as fire, air, water, earth, and suppose we postulate that they shall occur in a pure form in our chemical analysis of the world; still they seem (or are traditionally supposed) capable of turning into each other, fire to smoke to air, air condensing to water, water solidifying, earth producing the inflammables that fire absorbs. So we must once more give up any hope of securely classifying whatever underlies and supplies the continuity in the transformations.

This, I take it, is the line of argument that lies behind the suggestion in *Metaphysics* VII 3 that matter is the ultimate subject of all predicates but finally married to none. There is no *eidos* that it must instantiate in order to survive; and given that the *eidos* is essential to explaining the existence and continued identity of ordinary individuals such as Socrates, it is intelligible – though I suspect that it is part of the *reductio ad absurdum* that Aristotle is contriving – that he now says of matter 'its being is different from that of any of the categories' (1029a22-23).

His rejection of its claims to be substance on these terms is clear and impeccable. What we have isolated is no longer even a *this* with independent existence of its own (1029a26-28); it carries no marks of identity in its own
14 right, like Socrates or a table; it/ cannot be made or born, there is no characteristic way of manhandling or misusing it. In this etiolated form matter makes no second appearance in VII or VIII; the matter that reappears as a 'this' later is always, broadly speaking, material of a certain description – this bronze, these flesh and bones (1033a2, 1034a6, 1041b5-7). And VII 16 adds (1040b5-16) that when we introduce such material under the description of an element or even of the part of a living body – this fire, that hand – its unity and substantiality are still, so to speak, promissory, borrowed from the stronger classification we can find for it by bringing it under some higher *eidos* such as *man. This man* is still Aristotle's paradigm of individual substance.

In VII 3 the attempt to divorce the *tode* from its *toionde* has collapsed; so in VII 4 Aristotle starts to pursue the second of his two factors, the form or species that can be defined. There must, he argues in VII 6, be some things whose identity is wholly given by a definition (which are 'identical with their *ti ên einai*'), on pain of an infinite regress; and these things he is prepared to call subjects in their own right, *kath' hauta legomena* (1031a28). From the argument at 1031a19-28 we might suppose that he still has in mind individuals such as Socrates; for that argument, broken-backed as it is, turns on the assumption of an identity between a man and a white man, where it must be a particular man that is in question. But when the issue is resumed in 1037a33-37b5 it becomes clear that he does not. He is investigating the definable *eidos* that elsewhere he labels *toionde*.

Some scholars have been content to think that it is on this second candidate that he finally settles as his prime example of substance, and indeed that the book's argument to this effect is practically concluded by VII 15. But this interpretation faces very evident difficulties.

First, in VII 13 (1038b24-25, 1038b35-39a1, 1039a16) he repeats his insistence that a substance must be a *tode*, an individual subject; and in the same chapter he argues that no universal (*katholou huparchon*) or common predicable (*koinêi katêgoroumenon*) stands for a 'this' but only for a 'such'. To ignore this is to invite the regress of the Third Man (1038b34-39a3). The argument and the example seems enough to debar the form from representing in its own right the substance that Aristotle is trying to locate. Some years ago a valiant attempt was made to argue/ that what is debarred from the **15**
status of substance is not the universals as such but that which is universally predicated. The form to be sure is universal, inasmuch as it is definable (cf. 1035b34-36a1); but in virtue of its dominant role in determining the nature of the individual it is not to be regarded merely as a common predicate applying to subjects that are independently specifiable. The interpretation ran into textual difficulties; but it had the virtue of stressing the importance of the specific form in Aristotle's analysis. However, matter is carefully reintroduced in VII 16, with the moral I have sketched above; and in VII 17 it plays an essential part in the analysis of substance that I take to be Aristotle's real conclusion, once the strategy of trying to divorce the two factors is over. In the summary in VIII 1 (1042a32-b6) matter is fully restored, a candidate for the status of substance.

I have no space to follow the complexities and novelties of VII 17, but I need now take from it only two connected conclusions. One is that in trying to settle the conditions for speaking of substance we were looking for an explanation, and that if so our question must be of the form 'Why is (or, *anglice*, what makes) A B?' That is, our question must already distinguish two components, the subject (these bricks and stones, that body in whatever condition it may be) and the essential predicate which makes it what it is (a house, a man). We are asking then why the matter is (at the suitably high level of classification) what it is. And that is substance (1041b8; like Jaeger, I am tempted to doubt the phrase which Christ bracketed).

The other conclusion is that if we ask in general how an individual can be picked out as the individual it is – why 'a thing is itself' (1041a14) – none but a vacuous answer is forthcoming (1041a11-20; at 1041a14 read '*allôs*', 'fruitlessly' or 'in vain', for the '*allo*' of mss. and edd.) 'The fact is given' (1041a15-16); to be asked why A is A is to ask to be reassured on a reference whose security is presupposed by the very question. No doubt the individual can be distinguished by some accidental attributes (cf. *Top.* 128b16-21) of the

sort available only to mutable things having matter in them – trade, height, truthfulness, etc. – but such attributes produce paradoxes of identification (ibid. 104b24-28). If Aristotle had answered what he regards as too general a question, his answer would doubtless be that to know how to distinguish
16 particulars under the *toionde* is just to understand that/ *toionde*, to know how to count units under that species; and to understand that species is, at least inter alia, to know how specimens of it are to be distinguished. There is no other general answer.

Then suppose Aristotle faced with the question 'Just where, in the situation that most concerns you, the growth and existence of a man or a plant or the making of a statue, is the *ousia* located? Where is the real individual?' Will it be enough for him to reply 'It is not important which factor you pick on first, the "this" or the "such", provided you recognize the interdependence of the two and their different roles'? Emphatically not. He does indeed introduce the distinction in various ways in the long analysis of change and becoming in *Metaphysics* VII 7-9. But the effect is sometimes to obscure the analysis and generate paradoxes. These paradoxes we must now try to resolve.

Paradoxes of change

I list three puzzles in Metaphysics VII 7-9. The first two may seem venial inconsistencies on Aristotle's part, but the third has force and its resolution will help to resolve the others.

1. Early in VII 7 Aristotle says that a man or a plant is an example of 'things which we say are substances most of all' (1032a19-20, cf. 1034a4), and the phrase recalls the 'substance which is so called primarily and most of all' of the *Categories* 2a11-12. 'A man or a plant' is soon echoed in 'a plant or an animal' (1032a23), which translators (with the exception of Reale) standardly construe as specimen references to individuals ('an animal, e.g. Socrates'). So it seems that Socrates is still an example of substance in the prime sense of the word. Yet shortly afterwards, without more argument, Aristotle cites not concrete individuals but their form or essence as 'primary substance' (1032b1-2), and holds to this use of 'substance' in what follows (1033b17, 1034a31-32, cf. 1032b3-6 with 16; so still in VII 10, 1035b15 & 26 and esp. 22 & 29 where the substance is contrasted with the concrete particular).

2. In VII 8, 1033b19-24 (cf. 1034a6), Aristotle argues that the form is not an individual (*tode kai hôrismenon*) but a *such*, intrinsically predicative. Yet in the context he has regularly introduced the form as a *this* (not only 1033b12 &
17 19 but generally/ 1033a28-b19 construed, contra Ross, as concerned with the possibility of generating form, not matter. On this reading, the *this* that the bronze becomes is the form it acquires; making this-from-that or this-form-in-that is not to make *this* simpliciter, 1033a31-b5).

3. In VII 8, 1033b22-26, Aristotle says that what a maker makes (or is making) out of a *this* (e.g. this bronze) is a *such* (e.g. a sphere); but when once it is made (not *is being* made: cf. the *hotan gennêthêi* of 1033b23 with *hotan genêtai*, 1033a6; so *to gegonos*, 1033b15), it is a *this such*, e.g. a particular bronze sphere. But:
(a) in this context the form is the 'such', yet Aristotle denies that in making a such one makes a form (1033a28-b19, recalled in VII 15, 1039b26-27, and as something proved elsewhere in VIII 3, 1043b16-18);
(b) what can be meant by saying that a statue once made is a particular thing (*tode toionde*) but that what the sculptor is engaged in making from his material is a sort of thing? Isn't the statue he is making the same particular statue that finally stands in the studio?

The proposals for resolving the puzzles start by answering No to the last question.

Roughly and provisionally: a sculptor engaged in making a statue is not making some particular statue, even if the end-product is a particular statue; a seed in process of becoming a tree is not becoming a particular tree, even if a particular tree is the end-product. Yet what the seed is becoming or the bronze is being made into is indeed *a* tree or *a* statue; we do not produce the universal Statue or Tree (1033a28-b18, recalled later, cf. 3 (a)). When Aristotle in 1032a18-19 cites *a* man and *a* plant as prime examples of substance, the phrases have the logic of 'a statue' and 'a tree' in '... is making/becoming a statue/a tree'. And just as 'a statue' in such contexts is not to be taken as referring to some particular statue under an indefinite description, so 'the statue which ...' is not to be understood as referring to one under a definite description: one cannot be making *the sphere* which the bronze comes to be (1033a28-29, 33, b3-8, 11-17) when one is making the bronze into a sphere (a32-33)./

The paradoxical air of this may be cleared by considering its philosophical **18**
credentials before touching the exegetical dividends.

(a) The thesis is not a complaint about temporal restrictions on reference. It does not say that, if the process of becoming/making a Y is still under way, there is *not yet* a particular Y to be shown or christened – though later, all going well, we shall have a definite reference to write in to our process-report. (As though the problem were met by saying 'That seed is turning into a tree, namely ...' after many years '... *this* tree'.) The point must hold good equally for 'was becoming/making' in cases where the end-products already exist. If 'Bill is/was demolishing a statue' carries as part of its analysis the timeless $(\exists x)$ Statue x & Demolishing (Bill, x), 'Bill is/was making a statue' carries no such analysis.

This would be wrong if one accepted Vendler's claim (*Phil. Rev.* 66 (1957), 145): 'If I say of a person that he is running a mile or of someone else that he is drawing a circle, then I do claim that the first one will keep running until he has covered the mile and that the second will keep drawing until he has drawn the circle. If they do not complete their activities, my statement will turn out to be false.' For this would make the importing of a particular circle just as integral to the logic of 'I am drawing a circle' as it is to that of 'I am rubbing out a circle'. Elsewhere (p. 345 below) I argued: 'Suppose you interrupt me when I am drawing a circle and the circle is never finished; it cannot follow that I was not drawing a circle. For if what I was drawing was not a circle but the circle-fragment left on my paper, you did not interrupt my drawing'.

One difference (there are others) may be conceded between drawing a circle and making a statue or becoming a tree. In the latter cases process and product can overlap: an unfinished statue can be a statue, an unfinished circle is not a circle. Aristotle disregards the difference, even in house-building (*Phys.* 201b11-12), and there are artificial ways of avoiding it ('He's still working on the statue he made', 'It's become a tree but still growing'). It does not affect the point that statements of the form 'A is becoming/making a Y' do not carry in their truth-conditions or entailments any requirement that there must (timelessly) be some particular Y for A to become/make./

19 (b) Rejecting the latter analysis for such statements does not require us to read them as reporting purposes or purpose-like ends, e.g. to read 'making' as 'trying/meaning to make'. Such a reading would indeed justify our unwillingness to replace 'a statue' or 'a tree' in such contexts by a description true of the actual statue or tree that happened to emerge; and perhaps such cases are at the forefront of Aristotle's mind. But the analysis should also provide for unintentional developments or such deviations as Aristotle tries to accommodate at 1033b33-34a2.

(c) It is natural to say that, whereas 'I am/was demolishing a statue' invites the question 'Which statue?', with 'I am/was making a statue' the question does not arise or if it arises may have no answer. But this needs care.

It has been argued that if someone says 'Callias is a man' the question 'Which man?' would be pointless; yet patently this could not show that Callias is not a particular man. Suppose then that I am at a dog-show and anxious to sort out the names in my catalogue (I can't tell which are of dogs and which are of owners); then if you tell me that Callias is a man I shall still press the question, Which man is he? (In fact it is hard to think of circumstances in which 'Callias is a man' would be informative but the further questions would not collect more information.) By contrast, if I say that I have been making a statue this does not entitle you to expect that there is any answer to the question 'Which statue?' I can disallow the question by saying 'But, as usual, it came to nothing'. But in default of any answer to 'Which man is Callias?' the claim that Callias is a man would fail.

Again, it has been pointed out that even if the statue-making came to nothing I might have an answer to 'Which statue?' Statues were commissioned from several sculptors; my assignment was the statue of Jeremy Bentham for the Philosophy Library. But, first, the question of the right statue now arises. If I did produce a statue answering to the description there would be no room for the question whether I had produced the right statue, and even if I produced two or more statues competing for the

description there would be no room for the question which was the right one; but if I set out to meet a particular man and met one or more answering to his description, both questions could/ still be raised. Secondly, it remains in any 20
case true that given the truth of 'I was making a statue' it is a contingent matter that the question 'Which statue?' should have or lack an answer, and given the truth of 'I was demolishing a statue' this is not so. The logic of making/turning into an X is not parallel to that of demolishing/ceasing to be an X.

Now for some exegetical dividends. I take the puzzles in the order in which they were set out.

1. Aristotle says that whatever becomes, becomes or is becoming *something* (*ti*), e.g. in the category of substance a man or a plant; and a man or a plant is a prime example of substance (1032a13-15, 18-19). Give 'a man' and 'a plant' their proper use in such contexts and problem 1 does not arise: they carry no namely-rider such as 'viz. Socrates or Callias or ...' So Socrates is not a prime sample of substance. The question 'Which man?' does not arise or can be reduced to 'What sort of man?', something still general. To explain 'a man' here is to give a definition: what one defines is always a sort of thing (1036a27-28), and in such cases it is the form (e.g. 1035a21, 1035b34-36a1).

On this reading Ross also misrenders 1032a23 in taking 'a plant or an animal' as specimen references to individuals. Probably the text should be read: 'For that which is produced has a nature, e.g. *a plant* or *an animal*': the expressions pick out a 'nature', which is the 'nature called after the form' of 1032a24. (So Giovanni Reale, without pursuing the implications: 'ciò che si genera ha una natura: per esempio, la natura di pianta o di animale'.)

So too Ross seems to mistake 1033a27: Aristotle means, not 'something is produced, e.g. a sphere or a circle', but 'that which becomes becomes *something*, e.g. a sphere or a circle'; he goes on at once to say that the sphere (i.e. what the thing becomes) is not itself produced (1033a29-30). The point of lines 31-32 is surely that to make an individual sphere is to make it from something, e.g. bronze; but if we are then supposed to make the sphere which the individual becomes we need something further to make it from, and are on regress. In 'this bronze is becoming a sphere' we do not mention two individuals or make two mentions of one. By this line of argument the bronze becomes the *tode*; what 'a sphere' stands for is a *such, toionde* (1033b21-24, 1034a6, cf./ *Timaeus* 49d-e), and Aristotle argues that to construe it as 21
referring to an individual such as a Platonic Form (cf. 1033b20, 22 & 24-25) would produce an absurdity. I take it he means that then the individual which should emerge only at the terminus of the process would be otiose inasmuch as the sphere that something was becoming would already be an existing individual.

It can be shown that the argument of 1033a1-5 is in line with this explanation.

2. Problem 2 seems equally to dissolve. What the seed is becoming is

indeed a *this*, for (as we can say, though the Greeks could not) it is becoming *a* tree. But what it is becoming is not any particular tree, but a *such*; for the process is identified by saying what sort of thing the seed is becoming. Here the vocabulary of 'this' and 'such' seems patently too primitive a device to capture the point he is after. To conclude that the form is 'a this separable in *logos*' (VIII 1, 1042a29) is only a gesture at the odd compound of singularity and generality he has seen in '(a) tree'.

3. Problem 3(b) has been discussed. As for 3(a), the same simple vocabulary of general and particular seems to be behind the trouble. It is natural to assimilate the uses of 'a statue' in 'I am making a statue' and 'What is a statue?', given that neither mentions a particular statue and that the second is meant to elicit an explanation of the sort of thing I am described as making in the first. But to answer the question is to define a form, and if I am not making a particular statue I am not making a form either. Aristotle offers some palliative idioms: one makes the form in (1033a34) or into (1033b10) or even out of (1033b2-4, given the construction suggested under 3(b)) the matter, but it is better to introduce the verb 'to be' (1033b8-9): one makes it that the form is in the matter. He is struggling with the assumption that where 'a circle' does not refer to a particular circle it must name a form (1033b1-3).

If I am right, there are admirable insights in Aristotle's analyses of making and turning-into. But the apparatus of *tode* and *toionde*, particular and general, that he brings to the business is too primitive to illuminate them.

17

Aristotle on Time

Aristotle's discussions of time in the *Physics*, principally in IV 10-14, remain a 3
classic source of argument for philosophers and historians of science. His problems are often ours, and his solutions often enlarge our view of the problems. Through Augustine his arguments continued to exercise later philosophers such as Wittgenstein; through other post-Aristotelian schools and commentators they shaped the debates on the subject in pre-Newtonian science. Aristotle's chief concerns are the nature of the present, the reality of time, and the relations between time, space and motion that he evidently takes to show time both real and measurable.[1] So these are the issues in his argument on which I shall concentrate.

The issues are directly linked, but there is a methodological interest which may also help to draw the discussion together. I can best introduce this by recalling, briefly and with apology, some suggestions made elsewhere (above, pp. 216-19 and nn.). It is a commonplace that Aristotle is alert to philosophically important expressions which have more than one sense or kind of use, and critical of philosophers who innocently build on these without noticing the ambiguities they harbour. The fifth book of the *Metaphysics* is given up to exploring thirty such sources of ambiguity. But in a more positive mood, when he is pressing his own analysis of some key-concept, there is often a different impulse in his treatment of such expressions, and it does not readily mesh with the first. He is apt now to start his explanation from some particular, favoured use of the expression and deal in various ways with other sorts of use which do not seem to fit the primary case though they bear some relation to it. (This notion of primacy rightly exercised him (e.g. *Meta.* V 11, VII 1); we shall have examples to discuss later.) One way of dealing with
such recalcitrant uses seems to be to argue them away; another is to extend 4
and often to weaken his account of the basic occasion of use to accommodate them; a third, and perhaps the only one to deserve the name of a method, is to import a device or family of devices, sometimes now discussed under the rubric 'focal meaning', which enables him to marry his interest in the paradigm case with his interest in the plurality of an expression's uses by explaining other kinds of use in terms of one that he represents as primary.

[1] Since drafting these arguments I have seen a forthcoming paper on some of the same topics by Professor Fred D. Miller, Jr., and felt able accordingly to shorten mine at some points and push it further at others. (Professor Miller's paper has now appeared: 'Aristotle on the reality of time', *AGP* 56 (1974), 132-55).

The second of these ways does not concern us here: it can be illustrated from many texts such as the analyses of change and finality in the first two books of the *Physics*.[2] The others play substantial parts in Aristotle's analyses of time and motion; and I shall suggest that in fact the first is used where the third would be appropriate, and the third is used where the question of a primary use cannot properly arise at all. But such cavils on method are subordinate to understanding the argument. This is not primarily a study of method.

Motion at a moment

There is an important but still debated case where Aristotle seems so preoccupied with paradigm conditions of use that he rejects other uses of an expression – or, in this instance, of a family of expressions, the verbs of motion and rest. I mean his denial that there can be motion or rest at a moment, an unextended point of time.

(Some translators prefer 'instant' to 'moment'; that does not matter provided it is understood that Aristotle is talking of temporal points with no duration. What matters more is that the same Greek expression is the word for 'now' or 'the present'; but that connection, and the reason for it, will not concern us yet.)

Aristotle reasonably argues that any movement must be taken to cover some distance in some period of time; for movements differ in speed, and speed is a function of extended times and distances, one measured against the other. And an extended time is one in which different moments can be distinguished and ordered as earlier and later (*Phys.* 222b30-23a15). Not, of course, that he will allow a period to be regarded as merely a class or collection of the moments by which we can mark off subdivisions in it, any more than he will have a line built of points (231b6-10). Start, as Aristotle does, with the thought that points are produced by divisions of magnitude, and it comes to seem evident that however far such divisions proceed they will at any stage be finite in number and the points produced by them finite and separated by stretches which are the real factors of the magnitude. Still, if motion and velocity require some period of time within which different moments can be distinguished, one conclusion seemed to follow: there can be no talk of something moving, or therefore moving at any velocity, at one moment (234a24-31, recalled at 237a14, 239b1-2, 241a24-6). Nor yet can a body be said to be stationary at such a moment, as Zeno had argued;[3] for if movement entails being at different places at different moments rest surely entails being at the same place at different moments. If we consider only one moment neither description applies (239a26-b2).

[2] Cf. 'The Platonism of Aristotle', above, Chapter 11; 'Aristotle', above, Chapter 8.

[3] This is how Aristotle read Zeno's conclusion, and not merely as holding, as Ross suggests (*Aristotle's Physics* (Oxford 1936), 658) that the arrow is not moving (which Aristotle would accept, adding that it is not stationary either): see *Physics* 239b30.

Now the Greeks like ourselves could speak of a body as moving, and moving relatively fast or slowly, just when it reached a winning-post or overtook another body; and this, we may surely object, is to speak of movement as going on at a moment. Aristotle himself rejects Zeno's paradox that a slow runner pursued by a fast one 'will never be overtaken when running' (239b15-16, cf. 26-9). Our talk of a body as moving at a moment is common usage, preceding any mathematical theory of limits designed to accommodate it. No doubt it is in an important sense parasitic on descriptions of the body as moving over distances through periods of time, for our assessments of speed begin with these. To consider a body as moving with some velocity at a moment is to consider it as moving at some over-all speed or speeds during periods within which the moment falls.[4] We can allow too that 'moving' has a different sense or use in the two contexts; for we can ask how much ground the body moved over in a period, and we cannot ask this of its performance at a moment. But between the two uses there are familiar translation rules, rougher in ordinary discourse, sharpened in post-Aristotelian theories of mechanics. When Aristotle rejects the derivative use of such verbs he is rightly impressed, but unluckily over-impressed, by the requirements of the paradigm case in which motion takes so much time to cover so much ground. Hintikka has found another instance of the same tendency in Aristotle's unwillingness 'to speak of a possibility at an instant' (*Time and Necessity* (Oxford 1973), 162). His rejection of such ways of talking of motion and velocity, force and possibility at a moment, seems to have contributed to the final sterility of his mechanics (cf. 'Zeno and the Mathematicians', above, Chapter 3). Yet the author of the *Mechanica*, once ascribed to Aristotle and probably written not much later (cf. T.L. Heath, *Mathematics in Aristotle* 6
(Oxford 1949), 227), can resolve circular motion into two rectilinear components, tangential and centripetal (848b1-849b19), and make the remarkable suggestion that the relation between these components must be instantaneous and not maintained for any time at all; otherwise, so long as it was maintained, the resultant motion would be not circular but in a straight line (848b26-7). This and other constructions in the same author seem to be ruled out for Aristotle.[5]

But this objection to Aristotle itself faces objections. In pressing on him one difference in the sense or uses of verbs of motion we may have given too little weight to another. For there are two senses in which we might want to deny motion at a moment: we might want to deny that at any moment a body can *move*, carry out a journey from A to B; or we might want to deny that at any moment a body can *be moving* from A to B. In English the senses are divided between the non-continuous (perfective) and continuous (imperfective) forms of the verb; both are covered by the Greek present tense, though in past forms the difference can be marked. Now there is good sense in saying that a body

[4] 'Over-all', *d/t*, rather than 'average', which itself requires analysis in terms of momentary velocities and is therefore doubly general.

[5] Notice e.g. his refusal to assimilate circular and rectilinear motion in *Physics* VII 4 (248a10-249a25).

cannot move at a moment, for this is only to say that it takes time to make a journey. It would be a mistake to say that at a moment a body cannot be moving, in transit between A and B. But surely, it may be protested, it is the first point that Aristotle is making. And considerations can be found to strengthen the protest.

First, the phrase I have rendered by 'at a moment' is more literally translated 'in a moment'. That suggests that Aristotle is making the legitimate point: a moment is not the sort of time within which a journey can be carried out. On this view, he has grasped a mistake in Zeno's paradox of the Flying Arrow, the paradox he introduces immediately after denying motion or rest at a moment (*Phys.* 239a20-b9). In Aristotle's version of the argument – and we have none earlier – Zeno had held that at any moment in its path a flying arrow cannot cover more than its own length and hence (since, presumably, there is no room for movement then) is stationary (cf. n. 3 above). And what is true of it at each moment of its flight is true of it throughout, so the arrow is stationary throughout its flight. The second step of the argument, with its inference from the moments to the period, Aristotle attacks by saying that a period is not composed of moments (239b8-9, 30-3);[6] we gave some sense to this earlier and we shall meet it again. The first step he rejects by arguing that when there is no time for movement there is equally
7 no time to be stationary (239a35-b4). In both replies he can be interpreted as locating Zeno's mistake in treating moments as cripplingly short periods of time, too small to move in and only sufficient for staying in one place. He corrects it, on this reading, by arguing that what cannot move *in* a moment cannot stand still in a moment either. *Move*, carry out a journey; not *be moving*, for the question what if anything can be contained in a moment can only be sharply discussed in terms of the first. Again, he often insists that motion is from one place to another and from one point of time to another (e.g. 224a34-b2, *EN* 1174a29-b5); and this can be taken to show that when he speaks of motion he always has in mind an X that carries out the journey from A to B, not just an X in transit between these points. A little earlier in the *Physics*, for example (237a17-28), he argues that whatever has moved must have taken some time to do so, for it could not have journeyed from A to B in an instant.

Does the issue have a disappointingly verbal air? The brunt of the protest seems to be just this, that Aristotle's rejection of motion at a moment is

[6] T.M. Penner ('Verbs and the Identity of Actions', in *Ryle*, ed. G. Pitcher and O.P. Wood (New York 1970), 458) contends against some earlier arguments of mine that Aristotle 'has no *general* presumption against saying that if X was φ-ing throughout a period *p*, then at any moment *t* during *p* X was φ-ing' (or, we may add in view of Penner's argument, against the converse). 'It is just that this cannot be said with movement, or, more generally, with *kinêseis*' (the latter being Aristotle's word for all changes for which he takes movement in important respects as a model). So Penner holds that Aristotle would readily concede my point that if I am asleep at any and every moment of the afternoon I am asleep throughout the afternoon, and the converse; but this would not spoil his reply to Zeno, which is that where movement is concerned no such inferences lie between moments and periods, for sleeping is not a movement or *kinêsis* but what Aristotle calls an *energeia*. But by the tests proposed by Penner *being at rest* is also an *energeia*; and Aristotle denies that a body can be at rest at a moment.

misrepresented in English by casting it in the continuous forms of the verb; translate it into the non-continuous forms and it is simply valid. Offer Aristotle a choice such as the past tenses in Greek allow, and (it is implied) he will choose wisely, confining his rejection to the former way of talking. But what has this issue of surface grammar to do with mapping the emergence of an exact science? Well, everything, as the protester recognises. The question is whether Aristotle does, in theory if not always in practice,[7] discard *all* talk of motion at a moment – including (and, as it will turn out, primarily) such talk as goes better into our continuous tenses. By such a rejection – and it is of course an argued rejection, not a mere confusion drawn from an ambiguous Greek tense – he will equally debar himself from all talk of velocity and rest at a moment; and therewith debar himself from considering, as the author of the *Mechanica* can, the idea of a 'force' or 'strength' operating on a point whose resultant motion can be characterised only for that instant. So the protest deserves to be met.

First, so far from using the expression 'in a moment' to point a logical error, Aristotle takes it as an unexceptionable part of speech. He imports it earlier in his own argument in the *Physics* (234a24, 237a14), and in our context (239a35-b3) he says: 'In a moment it (sc. the moving body) is over against
some static thing,[8] but it is not stationary itself ... What is true of it in a **8**
moment is that it is not in motion and is over against something ...' Translators commonly write '*at* a moment', knowing that the Greek preposition *en* has other senses than that of containment, and they are right.

Further, on the appeal to Aristotle's general account of movement it is sufficient to recall the theorems about moving bodies that he has defended just before his criticism of Zeno. One is that what moves, or is moving, must already have moved (236b32-327a17). *Moves*, or *is moving*: which? Surely the second, for it would be unreasonable to maintain that whatever makes a journey from A to B must have travelled previously (that way a pointless regress lies), but reasonable to say that something currently engaged in making that journey must have already come part of the way.[9] So too with the logic of 'coming to a halt', which Aristotle treats in parallel with that of 'moving'. He argues that, given a period in which something is coming to a halt, it must be coming to a halt in any part of that time (238b31-239a10).[10] Read 'come to a halt' instead of 'be coming to a halt', and the claim becomes nonsense. So does the connected claim that a thing is moving when it is coming to a halt (238b23-9) if you substitute the non-continuous forms of the

[7] The corollary for rest is ignored at *Phys.* 236a17-18.

[8] I retain the *menon* of the mss. at 239a35-b1 against Prantl, etc.: what Aristotle says does not entail that the static body is static at that moment, and the repeated *men* is not needed.

[9] The point is generally well taken by translators and commentators, together with the equally important point that the perfect tense is (of course) perfective, 'have moved' and not 'have been moving'.

[10] The argument requires this, and not just that the object must come, or be coming, to rest in any arbitrarily late part of the time in which it is coming to rest. Any such time can itself be divided into others in any of which the coming to rest is proceeding quickly or slowly (238b26-30).

verbs. The point that 'the Greek present tense is generally imperfective' was made (and subsequently forgotten) by T.M. Penner in a recent paper.[11] For verbs of motion, at any rate, it holds good, and it explains much else in Aristotle's account of movement.[12]

In logic and in grammar, then, the defence fails. Aristotle can in theory allow no talk of motion proceeding at a moment. No doubt it might still be protested that the notion of an exact moment having no duration in time is only adumbrated, approached only asymptotically, in the common discourse from which Aristotle professes to set out in shaping the basic concepts of his physics.[13] Modern English can be more precise because it is heir to so much analytic thought on the issues, including Aristotle's. If Aristotle is refining a vaguer notion for technical use, he is surely entitled to stipulate conditions for its use. And if he discounts linguistic clues which lead to motion at a moment in order to safeguard clues which connect motion with periods, his dialectical method allows for that too.[14]

It is no reply to point to the resultant theory of mechanics, cumbrous and impoverished by comparison with the almost Newtonian insights of the
9 *Mechanica*. Quite apart from the question whether we yet have a 'theory' on our hands, it was already a major advance in the science to insist that movement and velocity must in any final analysis be treated as functions of distances and periods. Not all advances can be expected at one time, or the papers in this volume[14A] would not have been written. But there is another reply to the protest.

Elsewhere in his analyses of time and motion Aristotle several times uses a device, or family of devices, which would have let him exploit the linguistic clues he jettisons, even while recognising that any talk of motion and speed at some moment in a period must be explained (no doubt roughly at first) in terms of motion and speed over periods. If there are two uses of 'moving' here, Aristotle knows ways of analysing a secondary use in terms of a primary without either conflating them or discounting the first. His stock examples of expressions amenable to such treatment are 'medical' and 'healthy': it is medical science that is called 'medical' in the primary sense, for medical treatment and medical instruments are so called as being a product of that science or adapted to its exercise, and the explanation could not proceed in the opposite direction (e.g. *Meta*. 1003a33, 1060b36-1061a7). These are nursery

[11] Point made (Penner, op.cit., p.400); neglected in the argument manufactured for Zeno, p.459 ('At a moment no distance is traversed', etc.). To speak of 'Aristotle's claim that there is moving only if there is a movement' is either misleading, if it is taken to support this rewriting in the non-continuous present, or transparently acceptable if all it says is that to be moving requires that a movement takes place from some A to some B – even though to be moving from A to C does not require the movement from A to C to be completed.

[12] E.g. (i) the use of imperfect tenses as proxies for the present in *Phys*. 231b30-232a2, (ii) Aristotle's unreadiness to use the present tense in saying that A *becomes* B at a given moment rather than to say that it then has become or earlier was becoming B (e.g. *Phys*. 263b26-264a1).

[13] Owen, '*Tithenai ta phainomena*', above, Chapter 13.

[14] Thus *EN* 1145b2-5: if all the common conceptions on a topic cannot be vindicated, we must defend most and the most commanding.

[14A] [Sc. the volume where this chapter originally appeared: see p.xi.]

examples, but (in reply to the protester) when Aristotle puts such patterns of analysis to larger use in his philosophy, he is often trying to put a harder edge on ideas implicit in common speech. It is hard to deny that an entrée could have been found here for motion at a moment.

Yet when he does use such analyses in his treatment of time and motion we shall find other difficulties arising. Once try to mark off different uses of a key-expression and put them in some order of dependence, and it becomes a question how the primary use is picked out and what sort of primacy is being claimed for it. Let us turn to these troubles.

The primary use of 'now'

One example of the kind of analysis just sketched is his review in *Physics* III of uses of 'infinite' (which in this context signifies *infinitely divisible*, divisible into parts which are themselves always further divisible). He writes (207b21-5): 'The infinite is not one and the same sort of thing in the case of distance and of motion and of time. The term has a primary use and another dependent on it. Motion is called infinite because the distance covered by the motion is called so ... and the time is so called in virtue of the motion.' Notice the **10**
ordering, on which we shall find Aristotle putting much weight later: first the application to spatial magnitude, then derivatively to the motion which traverses it, then, by a further explanatory step, to the time taken. In his treatment of time in the next book of the *Physics* he repeats the claim (219a10-14, b15-16), substituting 'continuous' for 'infinite' (which in effect comes to the same thing); and then he argues from this[15] that the expressions 'before' and 'after' are also used primarily of spatial distinctions and only secondarily, 'by analogy', applied to movement and thence in turn to time (219a14-19).[16] At this stage of the argument I cite these only as illustrations of what Aristotle evidently regards as a valuable (though flexible, and perhaps too hospitable) form of analysis. The results must be questioned later, and that questioning is better approached by considering yet another example of the same technique.

In *Physics* IV 10-14 Aristotle gives much discussion to the character of *now* or *the present*. When he takes himself to have settled its character he says (222a20-4): 'This is one way we speak of *now*; it is another now we speak of when the time is near to that first now. We say "He is going to arrive now" because it's today that he's going to arrive, and "Now he arrives" because it's today he came; but not "Now the events in the Iliad have taken place" or "Now the end of the world" – not because the time stretching to these events (sc. from the present) is not continuous, but just because they are not near.' Not near, that is, to the primary now: but what is the primary use of 'now'?

[15] I read *dê* = 'therefore' with Ross at 219a14: cf. his synopsis of the argument, *Aristotle's Physics*, 386.

[16] 'Analogy' covers but is normally wider than the asymmetrical relation of prior-posterior between different uses of an expression that is at issue here. Cf. 'Logic and Metaphysics in Some Earlier Works of Aristotle', above, Chapter 10.

In the set of puzzles with which Aristotle introduces his discussion of time he argues: How can time exist, except at best in some reduced and obscure sense? For part of it is past and exists no longer, part of it is to come and exists not yet; and between them this pair exhausts the whole of time and any particular stretch of it (217b32-218a3). If we object that this discounts the now, the present time lying between past and future, Aristotle counters with an argument that the now is no part of time; for (i) any part must serve to measure the whole of which it is a part, and (ii) time is not composed of nows.[17] But when a thing with parts has no part of it currently in existence, it does not exist itself (218a3-8).

The premises (i) and (ii) should show us something of what Aristotle understands by 'now', but they are surely debatable. How is time not composed of nows? Take all the times that ever have been or are or will be
11 present and that is surely all the time there could be: 1975 is present, 1974 was, 1976 will be, and so on, each year having its turn. So too with premiss (i): the present year can surely serve as a measure of time, inasmuch as (e.g.) a decade is just ten times its length. But, other objections apart,[18] it becomes clear that Aristotle will not have 1975, or any other period, as an instance of the now, the present he is trying to explain. For a few lines later (218a18-19) he says: 'Let it be taken that one now cannot be next to another, any more than one point can be next to another'. So the instances of *now* or *the present* that he is prepared to accept seem plain, and his later discussion bears this out. They answer, we may say (as he could not), to such time-references as '1200 hours 18 May 1974' *provided* this is somewhat artificially understood as fixing a point of time without duration. For on this understanding there is theoretically no *next* time-reference of the same order: however close we call our next reference, provided it has some finite value in the same system some period of time must have elapsed between the two within which a still closer reference could have been called. The spatial analogue is indeed the point.

But why should a point of time seem a satisfactory value of *now* rather than a present period such as 1975? So far from explaining this, our premisses (i) and (ii) merely presupposed it. But Aristotle's argument is not far to seek. It lies in the comment that past and future time together will be found to exhaust any period whatever (218a1-2). It is a line of reasoning that recurs in the Sceptics and perhaps most famously in the eleventh book of Augustine's *Confessions*. The present century, Augustine observes, is a long time. But is the whole century present? No, for we are living now in one year of it, and the others are past or to come. And so on down, through days and minutes, shedding whatever can be shed into the past and the future until we are left at last with the durationless present moment which has no parts to shed.

Here is trouble indeed. The present is like the point, and lines are not collections of points.[19] But we are not required to tackle the fairy-tale task of

[17] On the implications of this cf. n.6 above.

[18] There are older arguments alleging the lacking of parallel between measurements of space and time and based on the possibility of transporting a rigid measuring-rod in space but not in time. Aristotle does not discuss this issue, and the rigid transportable measuring-rod has become an anachronism.

[19] They can of course be treated as classes of points for many purposes, e.g. for the inference

building lines out of points, for there are countless lines in the world that can be drawn and shown and used to measure other lines. When we use the edge of the ruler, it is of no use to know that the twelve-inch mark is to the right of the one-inch mark, or to wonder how many points to the right it is. Distance cannot be measured in points alone. But then how to measure times, when Aristotle's argument leaves us with no lines in time present, only present
moments? And apparently all we can know of these is that one is earlier or **12**
later than another, which is no more than knowing that the twelve-inch mark is to the right of the one-inch mark. Augustine was so exercised by this that he supposed that what we measure in time is a kind of proxy time-stretch held in our memory. Others such as Marcus Aurelius drew morals: each of us lives only in this instantaneous present. The morals may be excellent, but the argument is insufficient. Aristotle evidently thought his paradoxes could be evaded even though he retained his account of the primary use of 'now'.[20]

The retrenchability of 'here' and 'now'

Let us start by considering a way of avoiding the first step into these paradoxes, and then look at Aristotle's way of retrieving the reality and measurability of time. Consider 'here' as the spatial counterpart of the temporal demonstrative 'now'. It is not an exact counterpart, as Dummett and others have pointed out,[21] but for the present argument it is close enough.

When Kingsley Amis entitled a book 'I like it here', it was not hard to find what he intended by 'here'. It became apparent from the disaffection he showed for those living beyond a certain perimeter – in fact, the English coast; and he might well have wanted to narrow that perimeter too. The compass of his 'here' was settled by what he took to lie outside. The same holds good of 'now'. If we are told, once more, that we live now in an Age of Anxiety or an Age of Violence we shall be clearer on our informant's meaning if we find him, for example, relegating the Boxer Rebellion to the past tense and providing for the future by saying that if certain détentes follow quickly he will retract his observation as spoken too late or too soon. Such dismissals into the past or the future are all we usually require or assume in taking ourselves to understand a claim about the present. Of course there are certain semantic rules that must not be broken except in artificial situations: I must not as a rule relegate the whole year 1975 to the past or the future tense when I am speaking in that year for instance. But within the application of such

---

sketched in n.6 above. Aristotle's principal objection relies on the Zenonian argument (p. 296 above) that, on any common rule of division, no exhaustive division of a magnitude into points can be completed.

[20] There is a question here: given that the paradoxes are not systematically and directly answered in the sequel, how and when were they prefaced to the argument? Compare the question how the paradoxes of *Metaphysics* III were given their present place.

[21] M.A.E. Dummett, 'A Defense of McTaggart's Proof of the Unreality of Time', *Phil. Rev.* 59 (1960), 500.

rules it remains true that what a speaker counts as present can be seen from what he counts as past or future or both; and the Greeks were as flexible in
13 this as we are. When Plato talks of the order of nature that obtains *now*, he shows the scope of his 'now' by contrasting the present with a pre-historic past age in which the order was reversed (*Politicus* 273e).[22] What a speaker consigns to the past or future – subject to those semantic rules – depends on his immediate purposes and subject-matter (as well as, no doubt, on his training and culture). That is why it can vary, as it familiarly does, from utterance to utterance.

This is troublesome to one like Aristotle who aims to bring uniformity into the linguistic procedures taken over by a science. But if 'here' behaves in this respect like 'now', it is tempting to find a counterpart to Aristotle's paradox about 'now'. Suppose I tell you 'It's all public land here', and you ask 'What do you mean by *here*? Just this field, or more?' Repeating 'here', with whatever emphasis and gestures, is useless. What will help will be to specify land and landmarks that lie inside and others that lie outside the borders of whatever my spatial demonstrative was meant to cover. Given an interest in a smaller stretch of land or a different interest in this one (say, the placing of a rare plant), the scope of my 'here' could have been narrowed by counting more things into the surroundings, to left or right or beyond. There is no one reason for setting the frontier closer or farther: the demonstrative carries no privileged reference to a measure of ground that could not for another purpose be narrowed. Let us say, for short, that 'here' is retrenchable.

But then it might be argued that, understood strictly, 'here' cannot be taken to pick out any stretch of ground. For if there is no stretch such that part of it could not equally be countered as *here* and the rest consigned to the surroundings, there is no reason to stop at any of these arbitrary and dwindling frontiers in trying to determine what really answers to 'here' on any occasion of using it to make a spatial reference. What really answers to it is of course something within which no relegations to left or right or beyond are possible. In its paradigm use, 'here' must on any occasion pick out a point of space. Given that use it can be allowed, derivatively and on sufferance, to indicate any stretch of land containing or (I parody Aristotle's account of 'now') near to that point.

As an account of our use of spatial demonstratives this is absurd. In settling the scope of the statement 'It's all public land here', we had no need (and probably no time or technique) to come to an agreement on the identifying of some unextended spatial point. To understand 'here', as to understand 'now', the idea of retrenchability for different purposes is essential, and that of picking out an unextended point is not.[23]

14 This would be a sufficient answer if the pseudo-paradox about 'here' were a

[22] *Politicus* 270d6-e1 does not say or imply that in some sense the order of time was reversed in that other age; even if it did, the point would not be affected.

[23] Of course one can imagine, under artificial conditions, a situation in which my utterance of 'now' or 'here' will pick out a point of time or space for my hearer. Suppose the chronometer set up to start just when I start to say, 'Now I see him pass the starting-point': I could not say it without being able to say, 'Now he is running fast'.

sufficient parallel to Aristotle's paradox about 'now'. But there is an asymmetry that seems to tell against it, and no doubt this is why Aristotle does not extend his temporal paradox to space. Past and future, we are inclined to protest, are not comparable to left and right and yonder, just because what *can* be counted on any occasion as past *is* then irretrievably past: it is not up to the speaker to retrieve it by deciding, within certain semantic conventions, what he will then count as past and hence as present. With space it is otherwise: what is counted as lying to the left for one purpose can on the same occasion be included in the central ground for another purpose, for all such options remain open in a space all of whose parts remain accessible. No doubt an observer falling ineluctably like an Epicurean atom in one direction might think of any fixed landmarks he had passed (if there were such landmarks) as irretrievably above or behind. Spatial logic might then match temporal logic. And, conversely, there have been attempts to give sense to the suggestion that progression in time could have more than one direction, like movement in space. But, as things are, the asymmetry seems undeniable so long as we stay within the confines of 'here' and 'there' and 'now' and 'then'.

There are difficulties in this argument; but I cannot pursue them here beyond asking whether Aristotle is entitled to such a reply after some further arguments we have yet to examine about spatial and temporal order. Those arguments we shall meet when we come to consider how Aristotle tries to vindicate the reality of time in the face of his paradox. But there is another issue to be considered first.

The now and the moment

In the opening discussion of motion and rest I made much use of the notion of a moment which occupies no stretch of time. In discussing Aristotle's treatment of 'now' I have made more use of it. In the first discussion I warned that the same Greek expression which is translated 'moment' in some contexts is the normal Greek for 'now' or 'the present'. Someone impressed by the argument from retrenchability might argue: what Aristotle says of 'now' makes poor sense of that expression, but good sense of our talk about
moments. Is it not, after all, the idea of a moment that Aristotle in his **15**
discussion of time is trying to explain? Perhaps by Aristotle's day the expression has acquired a conventional sense in philosophical contexts which depends on discarding the presentness and stressing the momentariness of a *now*. After all, he refuses to be upset by the paradox he retails. He does not directly confront the argument that, if all present time is momentary, all we have as materials from which to build time is a class of moments which by their nature cannot serve as building materials. In *Physics* IV 11 (219a10-b2) he sets up a parallel between the distance covered by a moving body, the movement that it performs, and the time taken by the movement. He remarks there (219a25-30, 220a14-21) that, just as between any two points on the ground there must be a distance which is not a collection of points, so between any two nows some time must elapse which is not composed of nows.

Read 'moments' for 'nows', and the claim becomes recognisable and valid. In fact, we may feel, it is better served by casting it in those tenseless forms of speech which allow us to treat of moments as standing in a linear order of earlier and later without either explicitly or implicitly importing a reference to the present or its concomitants the future and the past.[24] Science needs the bedrock of the first, not the shifting sands of the second.

The suggestion would be a mistake and an anachronism. Aristotle does not discuss the nature of moments in abstraction from the idea of the present. His paradox about the unreality of time plainly has teeth only if it is understood in his terms, as contrasting a present that exists with the non-existent past and future, not as making the perverse suggestion that there are only moments and not days. Nor, and here I agree with Hintikka, is he near to grasping the idea of tenseless statements; Parmenides and Plato came closer.[25] In his other arguments on time the word for 'now' brings together what seem to us two distinct concepts, that of the moment and that of the present. When he speaks of the lapse of time as marked by different nows in an order of earlier and later (219a26-30), we think of moments. When he speaks of the now as progressing through time in a way comparable to that of a body progressing through a movement, collecting different descriptions according to the stage it has reached (219b22-33), we think of the present as something continuously overtaking such successive moments and leaving them in the past. When he claims to show how the now is perpetually different yet
16 perpetually the same, since on the one hand there is a succession of nows (219b13-14, cf. 219a25-9) yet on the other there is the one progressing now (219b22-8), we cannot think of him as distinguishing the two concepts but rather as conflating them.

How then are the two wedded in the one expression? And how far was the divorce managed by Aristotle's successors?

In reply to the first question we might hazard that, once Aristotle had argued himself into the belief that in its strictest use 'now' must always denote a present moment, the word became for him, by a natural extension and in default of any technical Greek equivalent, the stock expression for any moment. Such extensions of usage are common enough with him (cf. 'The Platonism of Aristotle,' this volume, pp. 216-19 and nn.). We might alternatively father Aristotle's 'now' on Zeno, recalling the account of the Flying Arrow in which the arrow is stationary at any *now* of its flight (239b7, 32). Neither reply is enough. Aristotle's version of the Arrow, even if we could reconstruct the text with certainty, may be a recasting in his own terms of what he takes to be Zeno's point. And there is a fuller and more secure precedent for Aristotle's usage, one in which we can see 'now' being tailored for its philosophical use, and one which must have shaped the recasting of Zeno's argument if any such recasting took place. I mean an argument in that

[24] *Generalized* references to future, present and past go without remainder into this form: cf. Nelson Goodman, *The Structure of Appearance* (Cambridge, Mass. 1951), 298-99.

[25] Hintikka, *Time and Necessity*, ch. iv; Owen, 'Plato and Parmenides on the Timeless Present', above, Chapter 2.

treasury on which Aristotle drew so extensively for his own *Physics*, the second part of Plato's *Parmenides*.[26] Given the importance of Zeno in that dialogue I have no doubt that his paradox stands behind the argument, but I shall not debate the extent of the debt.

Plato is coining puzzles from the logic of growing older (*Parm.* 152a-e). Nothing will be lost for our purposes by replacing his special subject 'the one' by a neutral 'X', or by omitting arguments which offer to show that if X is becoming older it is also becoming younger.

The reasoning Plato puts into Parmenides' mouth is this:

> Whenever in this process of becoming older X is at the time that is *now*, between *was* and *will be*, then X *is* older. After all, in its journeying from the past to the future it is not going to skip the now. So whenever it coincides with the now, at that time it stops becoming older: at that time it is not becoming, but just is, older. For if it were moving on it could never be caught by the now: what characterises something moving on is that it is in touch with the future as well as the now, letting go of now and laying hold of the future and carrying out a change between the two. But then, given that nothing in process of change can by-pass the now,[27] it stops becoming on any occasion when it is at the now, and **17**
> then is whatever it may be becoming.[28] So it is with X: whenever in the process of becoming older it coincides with the now, forthwith it stops becoming: then it *is* older.

Then (152e1 ff.) Plato generalises this to cover X's whole career. 'Moreover the now always accompanies X throughout its existence, for whenever X is it is *now*. So X always *is* older, not just becoming so.'

Generally it is poor practice to isolate any argument in the *Parmenides* from the network of paradox that it serves, but this has a special interest for us. It shows 'now' being groomed for its Aristotelian part. First Plato maintains that *now* X cannot be becoming so-and-so, and only is so-and-so: if it is getting older, or moving to the left, it cannot be engaged in the business now; now it can only be older or further to the left. And then he argues that this conclusion can be generalised for the whole of X's career: whatever holds good of X must hold good at some time that is then present, a time that is then properly called 'now'.

The second arm of the argument seems innocuous. It generalises on the uses of one temporal demonstrative, at the price of one kind of referential opacity; but the possibility of such generalisation is already assumed in the first arm. Plato does not go on to say that sooner or later every time becomes a present time, or that a time only exists when it is present. Otherwise he might have been vulnerable not only to some of McTaggart's paradoxes but

[26] For the documentation cf. Chapter 13 above.

[27] F.M. Cornford, in *Plato and Parmenides* (London 1939), 187, translates the 'by-pass' (*parelthein*, 152b7) by 'it can never *pass beyond* the present', suggesting that Plato means that it cannot break out of the present. What Plato means is that it cannot avoid or side-step the present.

[28] Cornford (loc. cit.) translates here as 'whatever it may be that it was becoming', a possible imperfectival past sense of the participle but not relevant to the argument, which is to show that for a chosen X ('older') if *a* is becoming X, then at any given present time *a* just is X.

to a dilemma of Aristotle's (*Phys.* 218a14-18). For when does a moment cease to be present? Not at the time of its own occurrence, nor at any later time; for the first requires it to stop when it is still present, and the second requires it to linger to a later moment and so stretch into a period of time. The dilemma is artificial, depending on treating a moment as something with a career in time and not as itself an element of time. But Plato does not court this difficulty. Nor does he pursue, what this second arm of his argument suggests, the Aristotelian image of the present as progressing through time. He avoids the language which presents Aristotle with another paradox (218b13-18). For Plato the nonsense-quotation, how quickly the present proceeds on its path, does not arise.[29]

It is the first arm of the argument, then, that carries the load. Why cannot we say that X is growing older, or the arrow is flying, now? Because, Plato argues, such descriptions make tacit reference to the future as well as the
18 present. It could not be the case that X is becoming older unless at some later time X will be older than it now is; it could not be the case that the arrow is moving unless it will later be in some place other than where it is now. Otherwise the flight is at an end, the business of growing older is finished. So if we are to say only what is true of the subject now, we have to eliminate this future component from our description. The arrow is now in just the place it occupies, X just is older. The second is Plato's example, and it seems ill-chosen; for if X is now older, it is older than it was, and this implicit reference to the past should be excluded together with references to the future. *Now* X is just whatever in time it happens to be. But Plato uses the Greek idiom 'X is (or becomes) older *than itself*', and this obscures the point as well as furnishing him with other paradoxes.[30]

What more is there in Plato's argument than we found summarised (surely because it was now too familiar to spell out) in Aristotle's? Nothing, so far as I can see. But here is Aristotle's 'now' in the making. Its retrenchability is discounted by shedding from its scope whatever can be relegated to the future (and, Aristotle adds, to the past). So 'now' becomes a paradigm way of referring to a moment, and the way is open for Aristotle to extend it to all moments. But only by considering them all as becoming sooner or later present, in the sequence future-present-past. The word never came to signify the 'moment' of the translators or of our detensed text-books in physics. It kept its connotation of time present, the sense on which the arguments of Plato and Aristotle were built.

So the two senses, that of the moment and that of the present, stay wedded in the one expression, and we have to turn to our second question: was the appropriate divorce arranged later in Greek philosophy? I think it was, but the evidence has been sometimes misread.

[29] C. Strang ('Plato and the Instant', *PASS* 48 (1974), 63-79) draws other inferences from the text translated, together with an earlier reference to time as moving on (152a 3-4) – a reference at once replaced by an innocuous description of the subject as 'proceeding temporally' (not, *pace* Mr. Strang, as 'keeping pace with time'). His interpretation is not adopted here.

[30] Principally those paradoxes which concern its becoming younger as well as older (*Parmenides* 141a-d, 152a-b).

Consider what Chrysippus the Stoic is reported to have maintained about time present. According to Plutarch (*Comm. Not.* 1081c-82a), his contribution to the topic consisted chiefly in three theses. First, there is no such thing as a shortest time (1081c); secondly, the now is not something indivisible (ibid.); thirdly, any part of present time can equally be taken to be past or future (1081d-82a). Here, surely, is our retrenchable present. Elsewhere in their physics the Stoics were ready enough to admit indivisibles: they insisted, as Aristotle had before them (and to the scandal of Plutarch), that contact between bodies is not the juxtaposition of some smallest possible parts or volumes of those bodies, for there are no such volumes; contact is a function **19**
of surfaces without depth or of points without magnitude (1080e-81b). But they were clear that such indivisibles were not the model on which to explain our use of 'now'.

Although I cannot be sure that the Stoics have our point clearly in view, I am sure that they once had less than justice from one of their most persuasive sponsors, Samuel Sambursky. In *The Physical World of the Greeks* (London 1956), 151, he had this to say concerning the third thesis credited to Chrysippus: 'This formulation, with its definition of the present as the centre of a very small, but still finite, portion of time, is clearly an attempt to comprehend the elements of time as finite "quanta" and not as extensionless points. The present thus becomes, so to speak, an "atom of time", or, to use the language of the calculus, a differential of time.' A little later he said: 'So great was the desire of the Stoics to give a clear answer to the paradox of the arrow, that these bitter opponents of the atomic hypothesis and ardent champions of continuum and no compromise had to have recourse to an "atomic" solution.'

But not only is atomism in general just as repugnant to Stoic physics as Sambursky recognises, the suggestion that 'now' is always or primarily used to identify some time-atom is incompatible with the first two of Chrysippus' propositions and, as soon as it is reconsidered, with the third. Sambursky's belief that even for Chrysippus the use of our temporal demonstratives must ultimately reduce to a reference to just one sort of time-element – if not moments, then atomic times or real infinitesimals of time – seems to be one more sign of the spell that Zeno's Arrow or its interpreters cast on philosophy. It is this spell that Chrysippus seems anxious to break.

Priorities and parallels between space and time

We left Aristotle in the grip of his paradoxes. Only the present is real, yet the present is never a stretch of time and time must consist of successive stretches, not of unextended moments. Moreover time is a function of change (218b21-219a10), but nothing can be changing at a present moment. How can time be real? Yet later Aristotle claims to have said of time both that it is and what it is (222b27-9). How does he break free?

His reply is that there could not be a present moment *without* time, any
more than there could be time without a now (219b33-220a1). He argues it **20**

by developing a detailed analogy between temporal and spatial structure. Just as there cannot be points without lengths that they divide and join, so there cannot be temporal points – 'nows' – without periods that terminate in such points, and specifically the stretches of time past and time future that meet in them (220a9-11, 222a10-12). The idea of a now that is not the boundary of a period is vacuous, and the idea of a period that is merely a collection of boundaries is absurd. Indeed, to notice that some time has elapsed is just to notice such a temporal boundary, and remark that something is true now that was not true at another moment once called 'now'. Both nows are limits of a period housing a change, and the change has taken time (219a22-b2). And if the change is of a certain sort, a regular and continuously repeated motion, time can be measured. Aristotle's ideal chronometer is of course the cycling of the astronomical system (223b12-224a2).

He is anxious to allow that the analogy between points and present moments is not complete. When we pick out a spatial point that divides a line, we can say, 'This point is the end of segment A' and then, indicating the same point, 'This point is the beginning of segment B'; but temporal points do not loiter to be picked out twice in this way (220a12-18, cf. 222a13).[31] It is not the most questionable element in his analogy, as we shall see.

The outcome is that, so far from shedding the past and future as unreal, the present cannot do without them (222a10-12). It might seem indeed that without his spatial analogy Aristotle already had sufficient grounds for this conclusion, for his arguments and those of the paradox-mongers he wants to disarm are in an important sense general: they are meant to apply to *any* present time, and so assume an inexhaustible range of different values for the variable. Hence his question whether the now of which we speak is always one thing (our inescapable fellow-traveller, as he seems to represent it later, collecting different descriptions from one stage of its progress to another) or always different. From this he might even have come to recognise those detensed forms of statements we desiderated earlier (cf. nn. 24 and 25 above). But he did not; and the generality in question was not his reason for reclaiming the past and future as co-adjutants to the present. His reason was the parallel he worked out between the logics of space and of time.

Before looking harder at that parallel one point seems worth making. With
21 the past and future restored, there seems to be no reason to shy at uses of the present tense (or therewith of the hospitable 'now') to describe occurrences or states of affairs that take time, even if the present is finally a mere point of time. To the extent that the analysis of such descriptions imports a reference to periods or points of time lying beyond the present moment, the reference can be divided between the past and the future. That is the option left open by Plato's argument in the *Parmenides*, where the reality of past and future is not called in question, and it seems to be the option Aristotle would adopt. Yet it generates a curious regress of analysis. Suppose we analyse 'X is walking to Tring this afternoon' as 'X is *now* at some place *p*, and until now X has been

[31] This seems the most direct interpretation of his argument and appears to agree with Ross's 'we must in thought pause over the point, as it were' (*Aristotle's Physics*, 602).

walking to *p* this afternoon, and after now X will be walking this afternoon from *p* to Tring'. Then we must provide some comparable analysis for the components relegated to the past and future tenses, for they go proxy for some present-tense statements that are true at some time before or after our now. More nows (in Aristotle's sense) must accordingly be introduced, and once more the time-stretches and their contents that we want to provide for are dismissed into the before and after, perpetually eluding us like Alice's jam. The readiest way of avoiding the regress is of course to reject at the start the analysis in terms of a *now* without duration. But is the regress noxious? Yes, if it is made an epistemological argument. If the identification of some now is the prerequisite of understanding any talk about a period containing that now, our understanding cannot get started. And just that requirement on our understanding of nows and periods seems to be maintained by Aristotle (219b28-33).

Let us come to the spatial parallel by which Aristotle assures himself of the reality of stretches of time and thereby of past and future. He introduces it near to the start of his positive account of time (219a10-21), after arguing that a lapse of time can neither be any sort of change nor yet occur independently of any change. It cannot be the first, for any change is a change in this thing or at that place, and time cannot be localised in this way: it is common to all things and places that share it (218b10-13). Moreover time does not go, as changes go, quicker or slower, for 'quick' and 'slow' are determined by, and not properties of, the passage of time (218b13-18). But neither can there be time without change. Here his first reasons are questionable: he argues (218b21-9a10) that we do not *notice* that time has passed unless we notice at **22**
least some mental change in ourselves; and later (223a21-9) he even suggests that there could not be time if there were not a mind capable of counting off and measuring time, even if there were some change going on which would otherwise supply material for the counting and measuring. It is no comfort that he prefaces this last suggestion with an argument that any change entails time, since it can proceed more or less quickly (222b30-223a4). What we need is an argument that any time entails change. For that conclusion his reason seems to be that we do not recognise time if we do not recognise a change we can measure by it. The reason is not enough, and later mechanics dispensed with it.

Still, grant that though time is not change it can always be plotted against change. Aristotle asks us to think of three lines and evidently draws them on his blackboard (an anachronism: it would have been a whiteboard). One represents the distance covered by a movement, the next represents the movement over that distance, and the third represents the time taken by the movement. Call them 'D', 'M' and 'T', as he does not. About these lines he argues two things. First, they are parallel in structure, all three being continua having parts which can be correlated, so that each of them can be measured by its neighbour: time by motion and vice versa, motion by distance and vice versa (220b14-32). Moreover we can take a particular point on M (b′) as representing the moving body at that stage of its movement and correlate it with the appropriate spatial and temporal points (b, b″) on D and

T (219b12-220a21).[32]

a	b	c	D
a′	b′	c′	M
a″	b″	c″	T

Secondly (and this is the stronger claim, though it comes first in his analysis), spatial order is somehow basic to the others: the structure of D prior to that of M, and that in turn prior to the structure of T. 'Since the moving object is moving from something to something' (e.g. from a to c in our diagram), 'and since every magnitude is a continuum, the movement answers to[33] the magnitude: movement is a continuum because magnitude is a continuum. And time is so because movement is so, for we always take the
23 amount of time that has elapsed to correspond to the amount of the movement. Thus (cf. n.15 above) *before* and *after* are found primarily in location, where they depend on position; and since they are found in the magnitude' (sc. D) 'necessarily they are found in movement too, by analogy with those there' (sc. the before and after in D). 'But in turn *before* and *after* are found in time, because the one always answers to the other' (sc. time to movement).[34] This claim of priority (219a10-19) he recalls later (220b24-8), cf. 219b15-16, 220a9-11). It is the last example we shall meet here of the pattern of analysis we desiderated in his treatment of motion at a moment, and found present but questionable in his account of 'now'. Here too its use is questionable.

As a preliminary question, what sort of priority or basicness has he in mind? Elsewhere, and notably in *Metaphysics* V 11, he distinguishes some main uses of 'prior' and 'posterior' (cf. pp.308-9 above). It is worth notice that he gives spatial order an earlier place in his account than temporal order (1018b12-19): that suits his analysis in the *Physics*, but it reverses the explanation in the post-predicaments of the *Categories*, if these are his work (14a26-9). But, more important, he distinguishes between what came to be called ontological and epistemological priority. Sometimes, as here, he brings 'priority in definition' under the second head (1018b32-3), sometimes he distinguishes the two more sharply (1028a34-b2); once (in our context, 1019a11-14) he implies that the epistemological is a kind of extrapolation from the ontological, the priority 'by nature and substance'. But the distinction holds firm. If A is prior to B 'by nature', then A can exist without B but not B without A. If A is prior 'for knowledge', the understanding or explanation of B requires that of A, and not the converse. There are different ways of understanding and explaining, and this priority can accordingly go different

[32] At 219b19 I read a comma after *auto,* and *hê* for *ê* before *stigmê*: Aristotle says 'the point (on my diagram) is (to be taken as) either a stone or something of the kind'.

[33] The verb is *akolouthein*; Hintikka (*Time and Necessity*, 43-7) makes a case for reading it in some contexts as expressing either compatibility or equivalence, but here as usually it does not stand for a symmetrical relation.

[34] *Physics* 219a19, *thâterôi thâteron*: 'The one to the other', not 'each to each'; Simplicius and the Loeb version have it right here, the Oxford and Budé, wrong.

ways (1018b30-1019a1); what matters for present purposes is that the epistemological priority does not entail the ontological, nor vice versa (cf. pp. 185-6 above).

Aristotle might have believed that there could be space but no movement over it; but then it could not be measured (220b28-32), and this he rejects. He might even have believed, for the brief span of one argument we noticed earlier (223a21-9), that there could be movement without time; but this too he consistently rejects elsewhere (e.g. 222b30-223a4, 232b20-3). Ontological priority is not what interests him here. He wants to show that spatial order is
conceptually basic to the rest, that by starting from this we can explain the **24**
order of movement, and at another step the order of time, without circularity – i.e. without importing into our explanations the things they were meant to explain. The enterprise fails. But enough remains of his parallel between space and time to make an argument for time's reality.

He argues first that, since the distance D is a continuum, so is the movement M over D; and since M is, so is T, for the time taken varies with the extent of the movement (219a12-14). Already we feel a qualm. The parallel between D and T relied, for a first step, on the parallel between D and M: the size and divisions of the movement corresponded directly to the size and divisions of the ground covered. But the time taken does not correspond equally directly to the ground covered, for speed can change. To bring the M/T parallel into line with the D/M parallel, we shall have to say that *at a given speed* the greater distance requires both a greater movement and, in the same ratio, a greater time; but this is to reimport the notion of speed, which employs the idea of time as well as of distance. The qualm can be met by giving up the requirement of a direct ratio between M and T or between D and M, and therewith the simple model of measuring one by its neighbour. Perhaps all we need to retain of the argument is the suggestion that (to put it roughly) further on in space is further on in the movement, and so further on in the time. But this is just the claim that spatial order is basic to the rest, and that claim seems untenable.

Spatial before-and-after is relative to some more or less arbitrarily chosen position on a line (cf. *Meta.* 1018b12-14). Thus on D, b is before c relatively to a if and only if ac contains ab but ab does not contain ac. Similarly b is before a relatively to c, because ac contains bc but bc does not contain ac. Now if temporal order is to be explained by the order of motion on such a line as D, evidently the motion must have a direction: for instance, on M, b′ must precede c′. But can this direction be derived from the spatial before-and-after we have just defined, without importing just the temporal priority we meant to explain? Evidently not. We might define a direction *abc for D, by saying that ac contains ab but ab does not contain ac; but of course we could on the same terms define the direction *cba. It is of no use to think we have given the movement a temporal direction by saying that it is on a line for which the spatial direction *abc can be defined, for the opposite direction can equally be defined for that line. It is just as useless to suppose we have given it such a
direction by saying that the body moving on abc may move over ab without **25**
moving over ac but not vice versa – hoping thereby to indicate that by moving

from a towards c it may reach b but not c. For this is compatible with its moving from b to a. And if we try to sharpen the condition by specifying where on the line the movement begins or ends, our explanation of temporal order becomes immediately circular. Spatially the movement can take either direction, temporally it can take only one. Just this was what prompted the earlier qualm about our appeal to retrenchability.

If Aristotle hopes to show spatial order conceptually prior to temporal order, the attempt fails. But does this spoil the general parallel between space and time by which Aristotle hopes to meet the paradox of time's unreality? Surely not, for the gist of that was that in both cases there cannot be points without the stretches they join and bound. The moment 5:30 and the period from 5:30 to 6 are interdependent. Time is left with periods which are, in Aristotle's sense, 'measures' of time. What he says of this goes admirably, as we can put it now, into a tenseless language of moments and durations. But it does not meet the paradox that at any real present the measurable stretches of time are behind or in front of us; that, as Marcus Aurelius holds, 'each of us lives only this momentary present' – with the possible comfort he derives from this, that dying is no loss since we cannot lose a past or future that is not real now.[35]

[35] *Meditations* vii 27, ii 14; both references I owe to Professor Miller's paper (n.1 above).

18

Aristotelian Mechanics

Students of this field may be forgiven for the impression that a species of cold war persists in it. It seems worth another attempt to resolve the disagreement, or at least to change its temperature. The first move is to distinguish the parties by referring to some classic modern studies.

The parties

Historians of science are familiar with the practice of extracting passages from Aristotle's physical writings for comparison with later work in mechanics. Occasionally some doubt is expressed about the value of this practice for understanding Aristotle; but as a way of assessing his influence, as distinct from his aims and methods, it has come to seem indispensable. Its ancestry goes back at least to Strato and it has played its part in later reforms in the subject. So the qualms tend to be stifled. Thus Drabkin felt it necessary to preface his fine 'Notes on the Laws of Motion in Aristotle'[1] with the warning that the texts he wanted to discuss could properly be understood only as parts of a larger 'metaphysical system';[2] but thereafter he felt free to present the so-called laws as 'mathematical equations' and to salute Aristotle's achievement in 'applying mathematics to physical phenomena, and in making certain abstractions which such treatment requires, e.g. in neglecting, as irrelevant, differences in the bodies moved other than weight (and, by implication, shape), and in considering the medium perfectly homogeneous, which it never is in nature, and in defining force quantitatively in terms of the effect produced'.[3] Of this definition he said conventionally that it made force proportional to 'average velocity' and not to acceleration, which would have promoted an 'incomparably superior theory'.[4] (He might have recognized 'over-all velocity' as preferable to 'average', which is a function of instantaneous speed not available to Aristotle.) But with this reservation he could congratulate Aristotle on 'having joined to the deductive and mathematical analysis of Platonic science a realization that the validity of a

[1] I.E. Drabkin, *American Journal of Philosophy* 59 (1938), 60-84; hereafter *NLM*.
[2] *NLM*, 61.
[3] I quote the later version in *A Source Book in Greek Science* (*SBGS*), ed. M.R. Cohen and I.E.Drabkin (N.Y. 1948), 203 n.1; cf. *NLM*, 65.
[4] *NLM*, 69, 70 n.21.

science of nature is ultimately tested by empirical observation', and in particular for showing, in his treatment of such observations, 'an appreciation of the importance of abstraction'.[5]

These verdicts, repeated and sharpened in the influential *Source Book in Greek Science,* probably represent for many students the orthodoxy of the subject. They stand in a tradition which can be seen in many earlier writers (represented in Ross's introduction to Aristotle's *Physics*, 26-33) and which is resumed in such later studies as Heath's *Mathematics in Aristotle* (144-6). But they stand in sharp contrast with other modern studies of Aristotle's physics such as those of Augustin Mansion and Friedrich Solmsen.[6] These take small stock of the pronouncements on weight and power, time and distance on which the first assessments rest. When Solmsen notices one such passage in the *Physics* he sets it aside with the comment: 'The fame or notoriety which these doctrines of inverse ratio have acquired stands itself in inverse ratio to their importance in Aristotle's own system.' Beyond this he mentions only two such texts out of many in the *De Caelo* and allows them no weight in his interpretation of the work.[7]

There must be something more to be said on both sides. The questions we are to discuss are evident from the claims already quoted. Does Aristotle in his physical writings practise a technique or techniques of 'abstraction' connected with the use of mathematical explanations? Does he apply these to empirical observations? And does he thereby give a quantitative definition of force, in some sense sufficiently like that familiar in later mechanics?

Abstraction and mathematical models

Beyond question Aristotle was deeply impressed by the mathematics that he found in progress in Plato's Academy. The pattern of a scientific system that is set up in the first book of the *Posterior Analytics* is derived from, even if it does not exactly reflect, mathematics and in particular geometry.[8] And a feature that Aristotle commonly praises in mathematics is its pursuit of abstraction. 'For things which are subject to change', he says in *Metaphysics* XIII, 'there will be arguments and sciences which treat them not as changing things but just as solids or again just as planes or as lines, and again either as divisible or as indivisible – and in this case either as indivisible things having position or just as indivisible'.[9] A science is more exact, he continues, 'if it takes no account of magnitude, than if it takes account of it; most exact if it discounts

[5] *NLM*, 82-3.

[6] W.D. Ross, *Aristotle's Physics* (Oxford 1936); T.L. Heath, *Mathematics in Aristotle* (Oxford 1949); A. Mansion, *Introduction à la physique aristotélicienne*[2] (Louvain 1946); F. Solmsen, *Aristotle's System of the Physical World* (Ithaca 1960).

[7] Solmsen, 137-8 and n.82, 260 n.23.

[8] See e.g. Heath, 53-7. That the syllogism does not capture mathematical deduction is a commonplace, and that Aristotle wishes to extend his scheme to generalizations that unlike the mathematical allow of exceptions is evident from e.g. *A.Pst.* I 30.

[9] *Meta.* XIII 3, 1077b27-30.

change, otherwise most exact if it studies the primary sort of change (motion) ... So too with harmonics and optics: these study their subjects not *qua* sight or sound but *qua* lines and numbers, which are attributes proper to sight and sound. The same is true of mechanics ... Each subject is best studied by doing what the arithmetician and geometer do, setting up as separate what is not separate'.[10]

Already this seems to take us to a level beyond the abstractions praised by Drabkin. Indeed we seem to see the familiar preliminaries to schoolbook mechanics. The proposal to treat a physical body for some scientific purposes as indivisible recalls many definitions of a material particle as a body such that 'for the purposes of our investigation the distances between its different parts may be neglected' (Clark Maxwell, quoted by Ramsey).[11] The association of such indivisibles with positions in space recalls Hertz's account of the particle as a means of associating a given point in space at a given time with a given point at any other time.[12] But if Aristotle is promising any such sophisticated treatment of bodies in motion we shall expect it to play a substantial part in his theories of the physical world. In face of the objections we shall confront later, we must look for confirmation in his general physics and his meteorology, his astronomy and his biology. And there does seem to be such confirmation.

I have discussed elsewhere the argument in *Physics* IV 11 by which Aristotle professes to show that our descriptions of time are dependent on our descriptions of motion (or, more generally, of change), and these in turn dependent on our descriptions of the path traversed by the moving body.[13] It involves making out a correspondence between three continua, the lines representing time, motion and distance, and in particular between points on these lines. What answers to the body is the 'now' on the time-line, i.e. the indivisible moment of present time.[14] So the body is the material analogue of a point in time or space. On the traditional reading of the text he says that what keeps its identity in the change is 'a point or a stone or any such thing'; with a minimal change of text he says that the moving thing which turns up at different times keeps its identity – 'for the point (in the diagram) is (sc. represents) a stone or any such thing' – though its description varies with its location.[15] The same account recurs in the next book, when Aristotle discusses motion in terms of a point moving from place to place; he is discussing an objection, but this is not the part of the objection to which he takes exception.[16]

The same abstract model reappears in his meteorology. In the third (and securely authentic) book of the *Meteorologica* he explains why the halo round any heavenly body is circular, and for this purpose treats the luminary as a

[10] 1078a11-23.
[11] *Dynamics* vol. 1 p.25, art. 4.13.
[12] *Principles of Mechanics*, trans. D.E. Jones *et al.* (London 1899, repr. N.Y. 1956), c. 1 def. 1.
[13] 219a10-220a11; cf. 'Aristotle on Time', above, Chapter 17.
[14] 219b15-25.
[15] 219b19.
[16] 227b16-17.

point-source of light.[17] So he does when he considers it as occupying a succession of different positions, in his discussion of the shape of the rainbow.[18] Other examples in the astronomy of the *De Caelo* will occupy us later; turn now to the biology. There he returns over and again to the question of the number of points at which a given type of animal moves.[19] These 'points' are in fact the man joints of the body,[20] and Aristotle might be taken to be using the word here without reference to its role in mathematics: elsewhere, for instance, he uses it of the speck or dot which marks the first appearance of the chicken's heart in the egg.[21] But in the *De Motu Animalium* he makes it wholly clear that he has a mathematical model in mind,[22] and goes on to point out the difference between the model and what it is designed to elucidate: the mathematical point is strictly indivisible and motionless and not, like its physical counterpart, divisible into one fixed and one moving element. A little later he drives the distinction home by castigating some theorists who fail to observe it. They ascribe a certain power to the poles of the heavens; but these are mere points without magnitude, and such things have no substantial existence.[23] The moral seems clear: provided the physical interpretation of the abstractions can be supplied and the differences noted, provided they are not misconstrued as descriptions of a higher, Platonic world (as Aristotle always construed that), they are indispensable tools.

It is worth comparing the same representation of the moving body as a thing with position but no magnitude that characterizes the essay *Mechanics* which once carried Aristotle's name. (In fact, as Duhem and others have shown, it is a systematic development of some suggestions found in his writings though inconsistent with others, and is probably not much later in date.) At the start of the work the theory of the lever is reduced to that of the balance, and this in turn brought under the study of circular motion. 'No two points on the same radius travel at equal speed: the point further from the fixed centre always travels faster, and we shall see that this has many surprising consequences for circular motion'.[24] The consequence of this approach appears in some later passages; it is the effect of a given 'strength' or 'force' on the velocity of a *point* that is in question.[25] It is noteworthy that neither the author of the *Mechanics* nor Aristotle himself (with one possible exception that I shall notice later) eased the transition from moving bodies to moving points by importing the idea of a centre of gravity, which was to play

[17] *Meteor.* III 3, 373a4-5 with 16-17. *Sêmeion* here has its geometrical sense of 'point' and not (as commentators have seen) its astronomical meaning of 'sign' (sc. constellation).

[18] *Meteor.* III 5, 375b20-21; 375b30 (body at first rising), 376b28-377a1 (body clear of horizon).

[19] *HA* 490a26-b1, *PA* 693b8-15, 696a11-16, *IA* 704a9-12, 707a16-23, 707b5-27.

[20] *HA* 490a31-32, *PA* 698a16-b1, 702a22-31.

[21] *GC* 321b14, *HA* 561a11-13, *PA* 665a34-b1.

[22] *MA* 1, 698a21-b1.

[23] *MA* 3, 699a20-25.

[24] 848a11-19.

[25] e.g. 849b19-21.

so powerful a part in Archimedes' essay on the *Equilibrium of Planes*.[26] But in other respects the *Mechanics* is in advance of Aristotle, for instance in resolving circular motion into two components, one tangential and one centripetal.[27] In doing so it makes the remarkable suggestion that the proportion between such components is not maintained for any time at all: otherwise, for so long as it is maintained, the resultant motion will be in a straight line.[28] Here, then, the idea of a point having motion and velocity is supplemented by the idea of its having a given motion or complex of motions at a moment and for no time at all. And even in discussing relative speeds in terms of *points* on a radius the *Mechanics* is more lucid and explicit than the texts of the *De Caelo* which seem to prompt the thesis.[29]

Yet in another way the astronomy of the *De Caelo* clears the ground for the mathematical model of motion that Aristotle uses elsewhere. That model requires, subject to the caveats noticed earlier, that locations shall be given by points and not by perimeters enclosing a volume, although this formally conflicts with Aristotle's analysis of place in *Physics* IV 4-5. Now this idea of unextended location seems integral to the account that Aristotle gives in the *De Caelo* of the movement of the universe and the elementary bodies in it. The centre of the universe is a place towards which not only earth but water falls. Aristotle, like Archimedes a century later, represents this place by a point when he proves that the surface of water is spherical.[30] So he does when he discusses the behaviour of earth. He distinguishes the geometrical centre of a body (the 'centre of magnitude' or 'centre of location') from the superior or dominant part of it, such as the heart in the animal; he may want to eliminate any Pythagorean question of the intrinsic value of different places in discussing the natural fall of earth.[31] But then if we consider only geometrical centres the question arises: is the midpoint to which earth falls the centre of the universe or the centre of the earth? As things are, the two coincide; but Aristotle insists that earth would make for the middle of the universe whether or not there were earth there already, just as fire would move toward the circumference.[32] And he accordingly treats this centre as a point which must ultimately coincide with the midpoint of the body that moves to it.[33] Sometimes indeed he disparages the centre as a place that can be fixed derivatively, by reference to the circumference;[34] but within the circumference itself he is ready to locate two other fixed points, the poles, and

[26] It was probably his invention; Hero's reference to one Posidonius (*Mech.* 1. 24) is probably to the Apamean and not (*pace* Heath, *A History of Greek Mathematics* (Oxford 1921), ii p.302) to some predecessor of Archimedes who discussed centres of gravity.

[27] 848b1-849b19, cf. Heath, *Mathematics in Aristotle*, 229-35.

[28] 848b26-27.

[29] *Cael.* II 8, 289b15-6, 34-290a5, and cf. generally I 4-5 271b26-273a6. But this is not always explicit in the *Mech.* either; cf. 848b3-10, 35-6, and Heath's comments, *Mathematics in Aristotle*, 230-1.

[30] *Cael.* II 4, 287b4-14.

[31] *Cael.* II 13, 293b4-13.

[32] *Cael.* II 14, 296b6-18.

[33] 297b4-14.

[34] *Cael.* II 13, 293b11-14; but the exact converse in I 6, 273a10-13.

discuss which of them lies above the other.[35] Point-locations, then, are integral to the cosmology.

(Simplicius thought that in speaking of the middle of the earth Aristotle was introducing the idea of a centre of gravity,[36] but Aristotle's expressions are too vague to bear him out.)

This may seem a tedious accumulation of evidence for a truism. Is it not plain enough that in his physical writings Aristotle makes conscious and serious use of mathematical models in which the moving body or its parts can be represented – subject always to the caveats given – as an unextended body occupying different points of space at different times? There were two reasons for starting with it. Without it the claims made by the first party to the cold war that Aristotle employs adventurous techniques of abstraction in his physics would have, so far as I can see, no initial plausibility: the evidence they cite has no weight in itself. Briefly, they locate the abstractions on the wrong level. And without these preliminaries we could not assess the opposition's claim that 'the use of mathematical concepts, propositions and methods in Aristotle's physics is incidental rather than essential'.[37] I take the issues in this order. Where repetition of some older arguments seemed unavoidable I have tried to supplement the material and document it more fully.

Laws of motion

In the passage quoted at the beginning of this paper Drabkin is in effect putting forward a weaker (and therefore, one might suppose, a more defensible) thesis about mathematical abstraction in the physics than those suggested in the last pages. The texts he refers to are taken to show that Aristotle 'removes from consideration, as irrelevant', not the extension of bodies but differences between them other than weight and 'by implication' shape. They are also taken to show that he discounts irregularities in the medium, and that by way of such eliminations he achieves a quantitative definition of force in terms of the effect produced. The texts fall into two classes, concerned respectively with natural motion and with forced motion requiring an external agency. It is the latter that Drabkin treats first, and it is in connection with these that he makes his claims about the importance of abstraction, both in the earlier paper and in the *Source Book in Greek Science*.[38] So we may start from these.

The passages on which he relies are taken out of four contexts, two in the *Physics* (VII 5, VIII 10) and two in the *De Caelo* (I 7, III 2). His comments and translations show that he takes them all to be concerned with stating 'a law of

[35] *Cael.* II 2, 285b8-11.

[36] Simplicius *in De Caelo* 543.21-24 Heiberg.

[37] Solmsen, 260 n.23.

[38] *NLM*, 62-3, 65 (the passage from *Phys.* IV 8 introduced on p.66 does not belong to the discussion of forced motion); *SBGS* p.203 and n.1.

proportionality connecting the force applied, the weight moved, and the time required for the force to move the weight a given distance'. Yet in two of the four contexts (*Phys.* VIII 10, 266a13-b24, *Cael.* I 7, 274b34-275b3) there is no mention of moving weights except in the interpretation offered; in both Aristotle expressly says that he is talking of 'heating or sweetening or throwing or making any kind of change',[39] 'heating or pushing or affecting or changing in any way'.[40] The word *dunamis* that Drabkin translates 'force' signifies accordingly just the power to produce any of these effects. And a third context seems to undermine the suggestion that Aristotle is pressing for a quantitative definition of *dunamis*. In this passage (*Phys.* VII 5, 249b30-250a28) Aristotle states some proportional connections between the *dunamis*, the object of change, and the time and distance traversed. He applies them first to the movement of weights, but goes on at once to insist that just the same conditions govern all changes of quality – even though, as he is careful to point out, such changes are a matter of the intensive 'more or less' and not of extensive quantity at all.[41] Only in the fourth of the contexts (*DC* III 2, 301b1-16) is Aristotle directly concerned with weight and its relation to *dunamis* and velocity. As for the other variables considered by Drabkin, in none of these passages dealing with forced motion is any medium mentioned, let alone stipulated to be homogeneous – as Archimedes for example does stipulate the homogeneity of fluid media at the start of his essay *On Floating Bodies*.[42] Nor is there any reference to the shape of what is moved.

So if *dunamis* can be said to be defined here (and we shall come back to this) it is defined not quantitatively but so as to cover any alteration in any quality. If it is then defined 'in terms of the effect produced', this is no more than Plato had done for the same expression in the *Republic*.[43] To be sure, Aristotle typically starts his explanatory schemes from some primary, favoured use of a concept, and (as he argues e.g. in *Physics* VIII 7) for him locomotion is the primary form of change. But in our contexts he is deliberately general. A power, as he explains elsewhere,[44] is a power to do or suffer X, or (derivatively) to resist the doing or suffering of X, and it is identified by establishing conditions in which X is done – whether X is sweetening or heating or throwing or whatever.

Where then can we find special reference to the shape of the moving body and the density of the medium? These appear, not in Aristotle's account of forced motion, but in what he says of natural motion; and in associating them with the first Drabkin is evidently taking an advance draft on the second.[45] Yet here too his claims for a deliberate practice of abstraction will

[39] *Phys.* 266a26-28.

[40] *Cael.* 275a2-3.

[41] 250a28-b7; cf. the preparatory remarks in 249b23-26, and generally VII 4.

[42] Postulate 1, 'Let it be taken that a fluid is of such a character that, of its parts which lie evenly and are continuous, that which is subject to the less pressure is driven out by that which is subject to the greater' (ii 318.2 Heiberg).

[43] *Rep.* V 477c-d.

[44] Esp. *Meta.* V 12, 1019a15-21; IX 1, 1046a9-31.

[45] He quotes from *Phys.* IV 8, 215a31-215b12 within the discussion of forced motion, *NLM*, 66.

hardly bear scrutiny. He divides the texts bearing on natural motion into three groups, and he takes these as respectively illustrating the following three theses:

(1) 'Of two bodies of different substances but of equal volume and alike in shape, both falling through the same medium from the same point, the heavier will fall more quickly and the ratio of the velocities will be the ratio of the respective weights. The reason for the greater speed of the heavier body is that it is better able to divide the medium.'
(2) 'Of two bodies of the same substance, alike in shape but differing in volume, both falling through the same medium from the same point, the larger volume will fall more quickly and the ratio of the velocities will be the ratio of the respective volumes, or, what in this case amounts to the same thing, of the respective weights.'
(3) 'Of two bodies of different substance, of different volume but of the same shape, both falling through the same medium from the same point, the heavier will fall more quickly and the ratio of the velocities will be equal to the ratio of the respective weights of the bodies – not weights per unit of volume, but total weights.'[46]

Now it is a fact that all the texts adduced in support of these so-called laws in Aristotle are concerned specifically with motion and not, like those discussed earlier, with all kinds of change. It is also a fact, which deserved remark, that the texts in the second and third groups[47] make no mention of shape at all, and further that those in the third group say nothing about difference of 'substance' (by which Drabkin means material constitution); in fact all are compatible with supposing the bodies compared to be of the same substance, and one positively requires it.[48] In general, the texts from these last two groups simply remark that speed is proportional to weight or lightness (or, in the case of bodies of the same substance, to size). One of them mentions a medium other than air, but not so as to contrast its effect on velocity with that of other media.[49] Where then does Drabkin find those references to the state of the medium and the shape of the body which go to fill out the laws he credits to Aristotle? They come from the texts given to illustrate the *first* proposition, or rather from the single context from which those texts are taken.[50] It is this passage, I suspect, which first occurs to anyone writing on the proportionalities of natural motion in Aristotle, and Heath argued that it is the passage to which Simplicio and Salviati refer in a famous argument in Galileo's *Dialogues*.

In *Physics* IV 8 Aristotle is trying to show that there can be no motion in a

[46] *NLM*, 75-76.

[47] (I have slightly amended some references.) Second group, *Cael.* I 8, 277b3-5, II 13, 294b4-6, IV 2, 309b12-15; III 5, 304b13-19; IV 1, 308b18-19, 27-28. Third group, *Phys.* IV 8, 216a13-16, *Cael.* I 6, 273b30-274a2; II 8, 290a1-2; III 2, 301a28-32.

[48] *Cael* II 8, 290a1-2 (of the relation between heavenly bodies and their circles).

[49] *Cael.* II 13, 294b4-6 (of earth falling in water).

[50] *Phys.* IV 8, 215a24-216a21.

vacuum. At the start of one of many arguments to this effect he says: 'We see a given weight or body moving faster for two reasons: either because of a difference in what it moves through (e.g. water or earth or air); or, the other things being equal, because of a difference in the moving body due to greater weight or lightness'.[51] He deals separately with these two factors. Under the first head, difference in the medium traversed, he remarks that not only the relative density but the relative velocity of the medium must be taken into account; and then in the first section of his argument he explores this connexion between the medium and the speed of passage.[52] In the second place he turns to examine the connexion between velocity and weight, and says again that it holds 'other things being equal'.[53] The MS text is disputed at this point, but Ross is clearly right in saying that Aristotle does not specify even here what the 'other things' are. He makes no mention of the shape of the falling body until this occurs to him almost as an afterthought in the last lines of the argument.[54] There is a passage in his writings in which he does take this factor seriously, the last chapter of the *De Caelo*; but even there he is concerned only with the difference between flat bodies and others, and his problem is simply why the first type of body floats on liquid better than the second.[55]

Where in these texts does Aristotle anticipate the proviso of Archimedes and discount internal variations in a medium or require it to be 'perfectly continuous and homogeneous'? Nowhere that I can see. He simply draws a broad and obvious contrast between the main types of media, and he says that the speed of fall of a given body will be greater in air than in water, in proportion as air is thinner than water. Nor can I share the comfort taken by some historians in quoting Stokes's Law, and saying that Aristotle's account of natural motion is at any rate vindicated for the steady terminal velocities of bodies falling in viscous media;[56] for Aristotle often observes that in natural rectilinear motion there is constant acceleration.[57] On the other hand, when he discusses forced motion he does contemplate constant speeds, as his formulae show;[58] but these are the cases in which he makes no mention of the resistance of a medium, doubtless because he now wants to generalize about all kinds of change and not only movement. The nearest he comes to it is in his discussion of the power of a grain of millet to move the air it falls through, which he oddly adduces as illustrating a point about forced motion;[59] but for this very reason he treats the air not as a medium to be traversed or divided but as an example of the object moved.

There is more to be said of Aristotle's different treatments of natural and

[51] 215a25-29.
[52] 215a29-216a12.
[53] 216a14; see Ross, *Physics*, 591.
[54] 216a19.
[55] *Cael.* IV 6, 313a16-21.
[56] e.g. Stephen Toulmin and June Goodfield, *The Fabric of the Heavens* (London 1961), 99.
[57] *Cael.* I 8, 277a27-33, b5; *Phys.*V 6, 230b24-25; VIII 9, 265b12-14.
[58] *Phys.* VIII 10, 249b30-250a9, discussed below.
[59] *Phys.* VIII 10 250a19-25.

forced motion when we come to our other questions. But what we have just seen might shake our confidence in the conscious and systematic pursuit of abstraction ascribed to Aristotle, at least so long as we are confined to the evidence just reviewed. The supposed laws of motion, with their recurrent stipulations on size and shape, medium and substance, seem to be an artificial conflation from very different contexts, helped by the device of construing silences as conscious abstractions. And this is surely how the other party to the cold war does regard them. To read these latter texts as aiming at the suggested equations would take the eye of faith. But perhaps the eye could be sharpened by the other evidence from which we set out, texts which expressly recognize different levels of mathematical abstraction in the treatment of moving bodies and others which, subject to proper caveats, make use of geometrical models of a higher degree of abstraction than the supposed equations which treat bodies not as unextended but as extended solids having shape and size and weight, subject to force and encountering resistance.

Now it is not enough for the opposition to deride this thin transference of plausibility. They may well question, concerning the particular ratios of speed to resistance propounded in the fourth book of the *Physics*, 'whether the more "precise" doctrines of our section have not been devised *ad hoc*'.[60] But they wish to go above this and suggest 'that the use of mathematical concepts, propositions and methods in Aristotle's physics is incidental rather than essential'.[61] So they must be addressed to the texts from which we began, and it is within the licence of Aristotelian dialectic to invent some arguments for them.

The opposition

First, they may say, it is beyond question that Aristotle praises the abstractness of mathematics. But this is surely just the point at which he contrasts mathematics with physics. Plato had constructed the physical world of two-dimensional and apparently weightless figures: when Aristotle attacks this he says flatly that 'the principles of perceptible things must be perceptible, of eternal things eternal and of perishable things perishable: in sum, the principles must be of the same kind as the subject-matter'.[62] So whatever use Aristotle makes of mathematical constructions in his physics must be adventitious and not an integral part of the science.

Again, it can be allowed that the pattern of a science set up in the *Posterior Analytics* is taken largely from the mathematics of the day. But what impresses Aristotle in that mathematics is not the value of drafting its special procedures into other sciences – there are other difficulties as well as that of adapting the proofs to syllogistic form – but the beneficial results of the drive to axiomatize

[60] Solmsen, 138.
[61] Solmsen, 260 n.23.
[62] *Cael.* III 306a9-11, cf. *A.Pst.* I 7-9; Solmsen, 262-5.

the subject. This drive had been under way for the better part of a century[63] and it enjoyed the patronage of Plato and the Academy.[64] What Aristotle wants is to secure for any science, so far as possible, the kind of autonomy that this one science and its branches have achieved. Each field of enquiry, insofar as it can be systematically taught, is now to declare its special assumptions, the hypotheses and definitions from which it argues and which define its frontiers.[65] The province of physics is the class of natural bodies regarded as having some weight and heat and hardness and size, and an innate tendency to move in a certain way. But it is just these properties that mathematics excludes from its purview. 'This is how the mathematician studies abstractions', says Aristotle in the *Metaphysics*: 'he eliminates all such perceptible things as weight and lightness and hardness and its opposite, as well as heat and cold and all other perceptible contrarieties. He leaves only what is quantitative and continuous'.[66] As for the notion of a mathematical body moving, that is a fiction.[67]

Moreover (continues the opposition), when Aristotle in the middle books of the *Physics* sets about defining his subject-matter by analysing the basic concepts of the science – change, time and place, the infinite and the continuum – he expressly excludes the mathematical models we were considering earlier from the proper field of physics. Thus the definition of place (*topos*) in the fourth book is said to rule out the assigning of a location to any point.[68] The account of movement two books later precludes any description of an indivisible thing as moving.[69] Both these conclusions are part of Aristotle's large debt to Plato's *Parmenides*,[70] and they are echoed elsewhere in his works.[71] And the *De Caelo* drives home the wedge between physics and mathematics by pointing out the absurdity of crediting a point with weight or density or any property that calls for an extended subject.[72]

Need the abstractionists give way to these general protests? No. In the first place, Aristotle's division of sciences is not absolute. Sometimes he allows a less abstract science to borrow from a more abstract – as, within mathematics, theoretical harmonics takes over the theorems of arithmetic.[73] Mathematics is certainly not physics; but when Aristotle contrasts the two in the second book of the *Physics* he argues that astronomy, which is one of 'the more physical of the mathematical sciences', must be part of physics, for it would be absurd if the physicist were debarred by the nature of his subject

[63] Cf. Heath, *Euclid's Elements* i, pp.116-17.
[64] Plato's views are discussed in Solmsen, *Die Entwicklung der aristotelischen Logik und Rhetorik* (Berlin 1929), 92-107.
[65] *A.Pst.* I 7 and 10.
[66] *Meta.* XI 3, 1061a28-33.
[67] *MA* 1, 698a25-26.
[68] *Phys.* IV 5, 212b24-25.
[69] *Phys.* VI 4, 234b10-20, 10 240b8-241a6.
[70] Cf. '*Tithenai ta phainomena*', above, Chapter 13.
[71] *De An.* I 4, 439a1-3, *GC* I 2, 316b5-6.
[72] *Cael.* III 1, 299a11-b14.
[73] *A.Pst.* I 13, 78b32-79a2, cf. I 7, 75b14-17, 9 76a9-15, 22-25.

from discussing the geometrical properties of the sun and moon, for example.[74] The distinction at this point between the physicist and the mathematician is just that the former must treat these properties as what they are, the attributes of physical bodies, while the latter can neglect this connexion between mathematics and the world.[75] To say this is just to require that the physicist must be prepared to explain the *application* of his model; and this we have seen Aristotle ready to do, for instance in his account of animal movement in the *De Motu*, by pointing out those features of the physical situation which the model discounts.

In this connexion the argument that when Aristotle is doing physics he will not allow a point either location or motion calls for more consideration. It is true that in the fourth book of the *Physics* he equates the location of an object with the frontier within which it lies, or, more exactly, with the innermost static boundary of the body that surrounds it;[76] and a point is not the sort of thing that lies within frontiers. Indeed if it had frontiers it could not be distinguished from them; so Aristotle briefly plays with the paradox that a point must be identical with its own location.[77] He solves it characteristically by showing that in no strict sense of the words can a thing be described as its own container.[78] On the strength of this appeal to linguistic usage he rules that a point cannot have a location.[79]

But there is more to it than this. Given that only a physical body can be located in the strict sense, still Aristotle allows that other sorts of thing can be located indirectly, by reference to the body with which they are primarily associated.[80] In the fourth book of the *Physics* points are not promoted to this latter class; but the sixth book allows that a point can be said to move provided this statement is translatable in terms of a moving body which contains the point – just as a man in a boat can be said to move because he has a certain relation to the moving boat.[81] So here too it seems that a moving body can be represented by the motion of some point (say its forepoint or midpoint), provided always that this can be translated back in terms of actual bodies and real surroundings.

Aristotle knew of course that in geometry points must be assigned locations and spatial relations – of a kind. Usually he calls such a location a *thesis*,[82] and distinguishes it from the *topos* or place of a physical object by claiming that the latter is not merely relative to some other arbitrarily chosen object or objects[83] but, given the present order of the universe, absolute or else defined by reference to some absolute location: for instance, there is just one fixed

[74] *Phys.* II 2, 193b22-30; cf. Ross ad loc., *Physics* 506-7.
[75] 193b31-35, 194a7-12.
[76] *Phys.* IV 4, 212a20-21.
[77] *Phys.* IV 1, 209a11-12.
[78] *Phys.* IV 3, 210a14-b22.
[79] *Phys.* IV 5, 212b24-25.
[80] *Phys.* IV 4, 211a17-23.
[81] *Phys.* VI 10, 240b8-20.
[82] e.g. *A.Pst.* I 32, 88a33-34, *Meta.* V 6 1016b25-26.
[83] *Phys.* IV 1, 208b22-25.

place to which earth falls freely.[84] So to give a physical interpretation to a network of *theseis*, to anchor them in the physical world, one must give a location that is not merely a *thesis* but fixed independently of other relative positions; and to do this, Aristotle thinks, one must directly identify the surroundings of some object.

(The trouble into which this analysis of location brought him is another story. One symptom of it is a confused attempt in the fourth book of the *De Caelo* to represent the centre of the universe as a location in the sense defined, i.e. as the boundary of some container.[85] The less restrictive treatment of such locations which we noticed in the second book of the *De Caelo* is probably later.[86])

This is enough to prove that Aristotle is not theoretically debarred in his physics from the use of mathematical models at various levels of abstraction. Given the lifeline – the interpretation, which will vary in kind from case to case – all is preserved. There remains the central objection that these appeals to mathematics are not integral to the argument; and to this the answer is a review of all the relevant contexts. Here I may summarise the results of such a review.

Briefly, these uses of more abstract geometrical proofs or models quoted earlier from Aristotle's physics and meteorology, biology and astronomy, were chosen partly because they were essential to some major argument; and by 'essential' I mean that they are not reinforced by other arguments of the same power or precision. As for the proportionalities of motion, it seems to be the case that when those which govern *forced* motion are introduced they play a similarly essential part. They have this role in the eighth book of the *Physics*, when Aristotle is showing that the infinite power of a Prime Mover cannot be housed in a finite body;[87] in the third book of the *De Caelo*, when he is showing that weight (and, in his sense of the word, lightness) is a property of all physical bodies;[88] and in the first book of the same work, when he is showing that an infinite body could not act or be acted on.[89] In the last context it is particularly noteworthy that when Aristotle offers a separate reinforcing argument he calls it *logikôteron*, more dialectical and less apt to the special science.[90] In one other passage, at the end of the seventh book of the *Physics*,[91] the proportionalities are not put to work; but this is because the book is unfinished. They were intended for the same context as that in which they now appear, and play their essential part, in the eighth book.[92]

[84] *Phys.* IV 1, 208b8-22.

[85] *Cael.* IV 3, 310b1-15. He remarks that (a) the place of anything is the boundary of what contains it and (b) bodies are contained by the centre and circumference of the universe, each evidently regarded as a separate location (cf. 10-11).

[86] On this dating cf. Solmsen, *Aristotle's System*, 297-303.

[87] *Phys.* VIII 10, 266a13-b24.

[88] *Cael.* III 2, 301b1-16.

[89] *Cael.* I 7, 274b34-275b3.

[90] 275b12.

[91] *Phys.* VII 5, 249b30-250a28.

[92] *Phys.* VIII 10, 266a12-b27.

The proportionalities of natural motion are another matter. In most cases they seem to be dispensable from the argument – as they are, for instance, in the fourth book of the *Physics*, when Aristotle is making his many-weaponed attack on the concept of a vacuum.[93] The one context in which they play a vital part is one in which they are coupled with those governing forced motion.[94]

This further contrast between the treatments of natural and forced motion should not surprise us. Natural motion, at least for the four sublunary elements, is always acceleration: Aristotle is clear on this.[95] But acceleration is a topic to which his approaches are notoriously brief and cautious. Witness the care with which he excludes any change of speed from his discussion of forced motion (we shall come to this directly), and witness, by contrast, his failure even to mention acceleration in those scattered texts from which writers have compiled his laws of natural motion. It was left to his successors to quarrel over the way in which those laws could be used to account for the acceleration which he held to be characteristic of such cases.[96] Perhaps this explains his unwillingness to base a major argument directly on such formulae. It is enough for our purpose that Aristotle does build some substantial arguments in his physical writings on those other proportionalities which he takes to govern forced motion.

So the opposition must give up a good deal of ground. They must allow that some major conclusions in Aristotle's physics are based on premisses which rely on mathematical operations, and that he does, at least in the case of some more abstract arguments which discount the extension of the moving body and its physical location, take care to signal important differences between the mathematical model and the class of concrete situations to which it is applied. And this is the best and so far as we have seen the only argument for supposing that in setting out the equations of forced and natural motion Aristotle also took himself to be dealing with abstractions and tacitly, though never explicitly, framed the proportionalities with all those reservations about the uniformity of the medium and the shape of the body which are claimed on his behalf.

Having given up some ground the opposition must surely cavil at this thin inference. For, in short, the level is now not abstract enough: setting up simple connexions between a man's strength and the speed of his work is a far cry from invoking a geometrical formula to explain the phenomena. Even if we confine ourselves to those contexts in which Aristotle is talking not of all kinds of change but of movement, the supposed quantitative definition of force seems to be no more than an appeal to conventional ways of assessing the strength of a gang of dockers, or to the common assumption that if you want to double a horse's maximum load you must harness another of equal strength to the cart. At the risk of some repetition we must return to those familiar proportions.

[93] *Phys.* IV 8, 215a24-216a21.

[94] *Cael.* III 2, 301a20-b17.

[95] Cf. n.57 above.

[96] Cf. Simplicius *in De Caelo* 264.20ff. Heiberg.

The proportionalities of forced motion

The claim that in his account of forced motion Aristotle sets out to *define* some concept of force or power might be defended by pointing to another contrast between the treatments of forced and natural motion. His observations on natural motion, and on the part played in it by differences in weight and medium, are typically introduced by the claim that 'we see' so-and-so to be the case,[97] that the alternative 'plainly does not occur',[98] that 'as things are' this is so,[99] that to deny this is to 'contradict the *phainomena*'.[100] By contrast his account of the role of *dunamis* or *ischus* in forced change (in which contexts the expressions are often translated as 'force') is typically introduced by a stipulation: 'Let it be taken that ...'.[101] There seem to be no comparable stipulations in the first set of texts, and no such appeals to observation in the second, except in one case to limit the scope of the stipulation.[102] This does make it look as though Aristotle wants, not perhaps to define 'force' (in the *Metaphysics* and elsewhere he does define *dunamis* quite generally for all kinds of change),[103] but at any rate to set up axioms which will govern its occurrence as a variable in the theory of forced motion.

But consider these axioms. They are found at greatest length in the seventh book of the *Physics*, where Aristotle is compiling notes towards a proof of the existence of a Prime Mover. The book seems to have been intended originally as the third and last part of an essay *On Change*, but it was left unfinished (much of it in two versions whose interrelations deserve more comment), and replaced by the more systematic argument which now appears as the eighth book of the *Physics*.[104] In the last chapter of the seventh book Aristotle lays it down that, if A moves B over a distance D in a time T, then A will move a half of B over twice that distance in the same time, and over the original distance in half the time; and a half of A will move a half of B over the original distance in the original time.[105] In the course of these remarks A is called a 'power' or 'strength' (*dunamis, ischus*) and B is called a 'weight'. There is a further proposition, to the effect that A will also move B half the original distance in half the original time: this may be either part of the premisses or a further corollary. If it is the former it amounts to an express proviso that the speed remains uniform; if it is the latter, it shows that the same assumption is made tacitly.[106]

[97] *Phys.* IV 8, 215a25, 216a13, cf. *Cael.* III 5, 304b13.
[98] *Cael.* II 13, 294b4-5.
[99] *Cael.* I 8, 277b3.
[100] *Cael.* IV 2, 309b25-27.
[101] *Phys.* VIII 10, 266a26-28, *Cael.* I 7, 275a4-10, 32-b2.
[102] *Phys.* VII 5, 250a12-19.
[103] See n.44 above.
[104] Cf. Ross, *Physics*, 15-19, Solmsen, *Aristotle's System*, 191-3.
[105] *Phys.* VII 5, 249b30-250a9.
[106] 250a5. With Bekker's punctuation it is a corollary; with that of Bonitz and most later edd. it is a premiss.

Aristotle adds one restriction to the scope of these equations. If A moves B over a given distance in a given time, it does not follow that A is strong enough to move twice the weight at all. If a gang of hauliers can move a ship a certain distance it does not follow that one haulier can move it a proportionately smaller distance in the same time or in any time.[107] Before saluting this acknowledgment of friction as a separate factor in motion we had better notice that Aristotle compares the failure of the haulier to move the ship with the failure of a falling grain to move the air;[108] that he at once generalizes the restriction to cover all kinds of change;[109] and that by the time he comes to write the eighth book of the *Physics* he seems to have forgotten the point completely.[110]

Briefly and too familiarly, the proportions Aristotle sets up are these. If A moves B over D in time T, then (1) A moves B/2 over 2D in T, (2) A moves B/2 over D in T/2, (3) A/2 moves B/2 over D in T; and, possibly as a fourth corollary but more probably as part of the premisses, (4) A moves B over D/2 in T/2. The conjunction of (1) and (2), and of (4) with the original premiss, shows that the speed of motion in the cases considered is taken to be uniform. So commentators naturally think of A as a force whose continued application is just sufficient to overcome the resistance due to gravity and friction and a medium, and to keep B moving at a steady speed. In such circumstances, they point out, propositions (3) and (4) – those concerned with the action of A on B or of the half of one on the half of the other – will yield results equivalent to those of Newtonian dynamics. The trouble then lies in the first two propositions, where the ratio of force to weight is doubled and the result in the later system will be not just a doubling of uniform velocity but acceleration up to some appropriate terminal velocity. And it would be quite perverse to play down the force of those two propositions, not merely because Aristotle gives them first place but because when he comes to apply these proportionalities in the eighth book of the *Physics* he makes substantial use of the first two[111] but it is still disputed whether he assumes or contradicts the third.[112]

Drabkin tried to find Aristotle a more secure bridge to later dynamics. He argued that in the condition envisaged by Aristotle, when the force applied is just sufficient to overcome the factors preventing motion, the force can be regarded as approximately proportional to the weight moved. But then Aristotle's account of *dunamis*, in terms either of weight and distance or (if we consider variations in time) of weight and distance and time, can be seen as prefiguring not the later idea of *force* but the concept of *work* or else of *power*; in the usual definition of those concepts we need only write 'displacement of the weight' for 'displacement of the force'.[113]

[107] 250a9-19.

[108] 250a19-25.

[109] 250b4-7.

[110] This is implied by *Phys.* VIII 10, 266a18, however the argument is construed; on the dispute see Ross, *Physics*, 722-3; Heath, *Mathematics in Aristotle*, 151-2.

[111] *Phys.* VIII 10, 266a26-28, 266b9-14, 17-19.

[112] See n.110 above.

[113] *NLM*, pp. 72-75.

This proposal has one evident virtue. It leaves Aristotle discussing the kind of case which is central to his dynamics, the carrying out of some finite task in a finite time. In his reply to Zeno he had given away too much: Zeno said that the arrow must be stationary at any moment of its flight, Aristotle answered that at a moment the arrow could be neither stationary nor in motion.[114] So for him there can be no talk of instantaneous velocity, or of velocity as a result of instantaneous application of a force.[115] The concept of work, once it is freed from this later idea of force, seems to answer well to his interests.

Yet after all the suggestion fails. Aristotle always supposes that, for an agent of a given sort or substance, the *dunamis* is multiplied in direct proportion to the size or quantity of the agent.[116] But to double the work done in a given time it is not of course necessary to double the agent in this way (say, a weight on a pulley). To suppose this would again be to overlook the difference between the conditions of uniform motion and of acceleration, and the result of passing from the first to the second.

In these cases of forced motion Aristotle does not claim that 'we see' so-and-so to be the case. Does he then give any argument for his statements of proportionality? Yes, frequently. It is that by accepting these propositions we preserve the rules of proportion.[117] So he is, in a modest way, applying mathematics here too. He starts from those rules of thumb for assessing the strength of a horse or of a work-gang that any hearer would accept, such as that a horse that can pull twice the load of another horse along the same road in the same time has twice the strength of the first; and he fills out the implications by the appeal to proportion. No doubt his neglect of acceleration comes from the nature of the cases he considers – cases, as Toulmin and Goodfield point out, in which the initial acceleration in getting the cart or ship moving will be negligibly small.[118] But I doubt whether they are right in suggesting that Aristotle saw all such movements as 'a balance between effort and resistance' or that 'whenever he theorized about a moving body he compared it for purposes of argument with a standard object being shifted at a steady rate against a uniform resistance'.[119] For in his accounts of forced motion, as we have seen, Aristotle seems not to calculate on resistance as a separate factor, whether as a property of a medium or in the form of continuous friction with the ground traversed. And this becomes doubly explicable when we consider the context and purpose of the arguments. Firstly, it would be not merely an irrelevance but an obstruction to the larger argument to provide a pioneer analysis of forced motion. He does not want to draw attention to more factors than would readily occur to a hearer assessing the *dunamis* of a horse; he hopes to have these agreed, and to use them for more important and surprising conclusions. And, secondly, the conclusions at which he aims concern the strength of a Prime Mover, able to keep the sky

[114] *Phys.* VI 3, 234a24-b9; VI 8-9, 259a23-b9.
[115] Cf. 'Zeno and the Mathematicians', above, Chapter 3.
[116] *Phys.* VII 5, 250a18-19; VIII 10, 266b7-14.
[117] *Phys.* VII 5, 250a3-4, cf. 8-9, 28; VIII 10, 266b10-12, 17-19; *Cael.* I 7, 275a9-10.
[118] Toulmin and Goodfield (n.56 above), 99-100, 101-2.
[119] Ibid., 99.

turning for all time; and this is patently not a case of pushing a body against uniform resistance.[120]

Both sides to our cold war have had to make concessions. The second party had to accept Aristotle's recognition of some higher mathematical abstractions as not incidental but integral to his physics. So far as we can tell, these were not innovations in mathematics but applications of an established discipline. On the other hand the party of the laws of motion faced the objection that they had pitched their search for mathematical abstraction on the wrong level. As a way of resolving a cold war, as with other ways, there may be no great hope in this. Let us turn briefly to our last question: what connection is there between the arguments we have been examining in Aristotle's physics and observation of the physical world?

The empirical data

Drabkin held that the success of Aristotle's dynamics was 'impeded not by insufficient observation and excessive speculation but by too close an adherence to the data of observation'.[121] 'The cause (of his failure) is rather an adherence to the phenomena of nature so close as to prevent the abstraction therefrom of the ideal case.'[122]

True, the equations of natural motion start with the claim that 'we see' something to be the case. One thing we are assured we see is that, other things being equal, a falling body moves faster in direct proportion to its weight.[123] In his accounts of forced motion, on the other hand, he builds expressly on conventional assessments of strength rather than on any inspection of the world. And this is quite in accord with his method in the central analyses of the *Physics*. The account of location, for instance, starts by setting out the 'accepted view' (what *dokeï*) about physical replacement;[124] it goes on to cite what some theorists 'say' and what Hesiod and most men 'believe', as well as making a more direct appeal to observation by pointing to the natural motions of bodies,[125] but it is on the first piece of evidence, the implications of our established ways of talking about physical replacement, that the analysis is built throughout.

I have argued elsewhere that this is not a departure from Aristotle's settled practice of arguing from the *phainomena*.[126] Common convictions and usage, and (less securely) the views of the wise, embody experience as securely as the accumulation of observed facts which underlies his natural history. In the

[120] In *Cael.* II 7 Aristotle considers the friction of the circling *aethêr* against the lower elements; but he thinks of it not as reducing motion but as generating heat, and he expressly locates this effect not in the moving body but in the stationary.

[121] *NLM*, 82.

[122] *NLM*, 69.

[123] *Phys.* IV 8, 216a13-16: this provoked celebrated experiments.

[124] *Phys.* IV 1, 208b1-8.

[125] 208b8-35.

[126] Cf. n.70 above.

first book of the *De Caelo* he remarks that his theory of *aethêr*, the fifth element, accords well with the *phainomena*; and the *phainomena* that he adduces are men's convictions that divinity lives in a high place, the consistency of such astronomical records as were available to him, and the etymology, or what Aristotle thinks to be the etymology, of the word '*aethêr*'.[127]

So much for a notorious cold war. If we cannot have détente, we must settle for confrontation.

[127] *Cael.* I 3, 270b4-5.

19

Aristotelian Pleasures

135 Aristotle's discussions of pleasure have figured largely in recent philosophical writing on the topic. Ryle, I think, showed English philosophers a way in; Kenny, Urmson, and many others have carried the explorations forward.[1] But there has been an air of piecemeal raiding about the enterprise rather than of connected exploration, for Aristotle seems to have no consistent account of pleasure to offer. I do not mean that the *Rhetoric* (1369b33-5, 1371a25-6, 33-4) and *Magna Moralia* (1205b7-8) repeat the Academic view of pleasure as a process of restoration which Aristotle rebuts in the *Eudemian* and *Nicomachean Ethics*. Both are in different ways *argumenta ad homines*, soon modified in the *Rhetoric* (1370a4-9) and directly rebutted in the *Magna Moralia*. I have in mind the more baffling inconsistency that seems to lie at the heart of the discussions of pleasure on which philosophers have chiefly drawn, the studies that now appear in the seventh and tenth books of the *Nicomachean Ethics*. This has exercised critics from the Greek commentators on. It led Miss Anscombe to say that the difficulty of the concept of pleasure, 'astonishingly reduced Aristotle to babble, since for good reasons he both wanted pleasure to be identical with and to be different from the activity that it is pleasure in'.[2] My first interest is to propose a different approach to this puzzle. My second is to discuss some arguments whose form will, I hope, be made clearer by such an approach. I shall end by confessing some residual puzzles, but their interest will be more historical than philosophical.

The mismatch of A and B

136 In a study of pleasure which is common to our texts of the/ *Eudemian* and *Nicomachean Ethics* Aristotle says that pleasures are *energeiai* (*EN* VII (= *EE* VI) 1153a9-15); in a second study which is found only in the *Nicomachean* he says that pleasures complete or perfect *energeiai*, but must not be identified with them (1174b14-1175b1, 1175b32-5). I shall follow Festugière[3] and distinguish the two studies, *EN* VII 11-14 and X 1-5, as '*A*' and '*B*' respectively. For '*energeia*' I shall use, pending later discussion, the

[1] A.J.P. Kenny, *Action, Emotion and Will* (London 1963) ch. 6; J.O. Urmson, 'Aristotle on Pleasure,' in *Aristotle*, ed. J.M.E. Moravcsik (New York 1967), 323-33.
[2] G.E.M. Anscombe, *Intention* (Oxford 1957), 76.
[3] A.J. Festugière, *Aristote: le plasir* (Paris 1946).

conventional translation 'activity'. What *A* says, and *B* appears to deny, is that pleasures are just the unhindered activities of our natural faculties. In both contexts the activities are such basic ingredients of a man's life as the exercises of his intelligence.[4] By identifying pleasures with such activities *A* can argue that the best life for man may simply be some pleasure or class of pleasures (1153b7-13). By distinguishing them *B* can leave it an open question whether we choose the life for the sake of the pleasure or *vice versa* (1175a18-21).

Traditionally the question has been whether the two accounts are too divergent to be compatible. I hope to show that they are too divergent to be incompatible. They are neither competing nor cooperating answers to one question, but answers to two quite different questions.

Since the ancient commentators the tendency has been to play the discrepancy down in the hope of finding Aristotle a unified thesis.[5] Commonly it is excused as the difference between an early draft and a finished version, *A* being the hastier and more polemical, *B* showing signs of refinement at leisure (e.g., Festugière, xxiv; Gauthier-Jolif, 783; Dirlmeier, 567, 580-1). Stewart dismissed it as 'of trifling and merely scholastic significance'. Hardie conflates *A* and *B* in speaking of *B* as propounding 'the view held by Aristotle, that it (sc. pleasure) is an/ activity (*energeia*) or the **137**
completion of an activity'. Sometimes the suggestion that *A* is rougher because more polemical is exaggerated into the claim that *A* is merely negative: Ross wrote that 'where there is contradiction, the preference must be given to Book X, for here Aristotle not only criticises the views of others but states his own position positively'.[6] But in both accounts a positive view is produced (Aristotle claims to be saying what pleasure is at 1154b33, 1174a13, and does so at 1152b33-1153a17, 1173a29-b20, 1174a13-1175a3). And in both it is reached by rebutting others. So another reason for assimilating them suggests itself: the positive account of pleasure in *A* and *B* must be essentially the same, since it is Aristotle's reply to the same mistaken view of pleasure. What he rejects in both contexts is the thesis that pleasure is a *genesis* or *kinêsis*, a process towards some state in which it terminates, as convalescence is a process to health.[7] On the strength of this Stewart proposed

[4] In *A* 1153a (retaining the *energeia* or *energeiai* of the MSS. with Festugière and Gauthier-Jolif against Bywater, who was probably mistaken to say that Aspasius did not have this reading (*in EN* 146.16-17, 20-21)). In *B* 1174b21.

[5] Gauthier-Jolif misrepresent the Greek commentators here (*Aristote: l'Ethique à Nicomaque* (Louvain 1970), 780). Pseudo-Alexander (*Apor.* 143.9-46.12) does not hold that *A* commits Aristotle to equating pleasure with enjoyed activities. If a good life consists in the latter, still if pleasure is *unhindered* activity the real source of happy living will be the virtue that ensures the unhinderedness. Nor does Aspasius (*in EN* 150.31-152.3) hold this view. He says that, if *A* is indeed by Aristotle, the argument is dialectical, *ad homines* (151.21, 26). So Dirlmeier (*Aristoteles: Nikomachische Ethik* (Berlin 1966), 567.

[6] J.A. Stewart, *Notes on the Nicomachean Ethics of Aristotle* (Oxford 1892), 221-2, n.1; W.F.R. Hardie, *Aristotle's Ethical Theory* (Oxford 1968), 304; W.D. Ross, *Aristotle* (London 1923), 228.

[7] The possible objection that the polemic in *A* concentrates on *genesis* (e.g. 1152b13,23) and that in *B* on *kinêsis* (1174a19-b9) would not show a substantial division between them. *Genesis* and *kinêsis* are coupled at 1152b28, 1173a29-30 (though the subsequent argument distinguishes them, 1173a31-b4, 1173b4-7), 1174b10 and 12-13, just as they are coupled in the specimen

a single Aristotelian 'formula', that pleasure 'is inseparable from *energeia*, enhances *energeia*, is *energeia*', and found the 'true significance' of this concoction in the fact that 'it asserts the opposite of "Pleasure is *genesis* or *anaplêrôsis*" '. ('*Anaplêrôsis*' or 'filling-up' is the less general but more vivid expression for a restorative process that Aristotle occasionally borrows from the opposition.)

This argument will not do. One reply is too obvious to spend time on. If a philosopher twice rebuts a given thesis and offers a substitute, that is not the least guarantee that he offers the same alternative on both occasions. The range of alternative options may be wide and his own view of it may be wider. But this reply does not find the root of the trouble. The root of it is the assumption that, when Aristotle argues that pleasure is not a *genesis* (coming into being) or *kinêsis* (change), he must have the same target in his sights on both occasions./

138 '*Hêdonê*', like its English counterpart 'pleasure', has at least two distinct though related uses. We can say 'Gaming is one of my pleasures' or, alternatively, 'Gaming gives me pleasure' or 'I get pleasure from (take pleasure in) gaming'. In the first use the pleasure is identified with the enjoyed activity, in the second the two are distinct and their relationship is problematic. Philosophers have sometimes concentrated on one of these uses to the near-exclusion of the other. Aristotle puts almost exclusive emphasis on the first in *A* and on the second in *B*. Thus what he takes himself to be rejecting in *A* is a thesis about what is *enjoyed* or *enjoyable* (in English, *a* pleasure): he wants to deny that what we enjoy is ever, in some last analysis, a process such as convalescing or relieving our hunger. But what he takes himself to be rejecting in *B* is a mistake about the character of *enjoying* or *taking pleasure*: he denies that the Greek equivalents of these verbs have the logic of process-verbs such as *building* something or *walking* somewhere. Neither rejection implies the other. Each determines the form of the positive thesis it introduces.

The distinction I have invoked is put by Kenny (*Action*, p.128) in this way: 'We get pleasure out of pleasures, and derive enjoyment from enjoyments'. But I doubt that the logic of his two plurals is the same. Given that I enjoy smoking and play-going, I can certainly say that among my pleasures is the pleasure of smoking and among my enjoyments the enjoyment of play-going. But the first 'of' seems identificatory ('the pleasure which consists in smoking', as in 'the honour of being your Mayor'), while the second marks a verb-object relation (as in 'the murder of Smith'). Pleasures are enjoyed activities (or feelings, etc.); enjoyments are enjoyings. Now the Greek plural '*hêdonai*' can be rendered either by 'pleasures' or by 'enjoyments'. *A* will normally require the first sense, *B* (e.g. 1176a22-9) the second.

---

argument about pleasure at *A.Pr.* 48b30-2. Building is an example of *genesis* in *A* (1152b13-14) and of *kinêsis* in *B* (1174a19-29). Lieberg (*Die Lehre von der Lust in den Ethiken des Aristoteles*, *Zetemata* 19 (Munich 1958), 104, n.1) thought the difference showed that after *A* Aristotle has reached some distinctions recorded in *Phys.* V 1, but he too thought the same form of thesis was under attack in both contexts.

The consistency of A

At the end of *A* (1154b32-3) Aristotle claims to have said what pleasure is. He evidently refers to his thesis (let us call it '*T*', for brevity) that pleasure is *anempodistos energeia tês kata phusin hexeôs* or, as Ross and others translate it, 'unimpeded activity of the natural state' (1153a14-15). *Hexis* or 'state' is
Aristotle's/ word for any settled condition or propensity of the agent that is **139**
exhibited in characteristic performances, and *energeia* or 'activity' is his word for the performances that exhibit it; or, more narrowly, when *energeia* is contrasted with *kinêsis* or *genesis* as it is here, it is his word for those performances which are not end-directed processes like convalescence but self-contained activities like the exercise of a healthy body. Aristotle wants to connect pleasure with the second, not the first. But what is the connexion? To sharpen the question, what does he mean here by 'the natural state'? Joachim described *A* as concerned with 'pleasure – the *feeling pleased*'. Is Aristotle speaking of some natural pleasure-faculty issuing, perhaps, in pleasure-feelings?

Emphatically he is not. He means that a pleasure is the unimpeded activity of *any* natural state. Any such exercise of our natural faculties or propensities *is* (and not: is accompanied by) pleasure. Let me try to clinch this as briefly as possible, before turning to some more interesting issues that arise. Consider first how the thesis *T* is put to work, then how it is reached.

(1) It is put to work in 1153b9-13. 'Given that there are unimpeded activities belonging to every state, it arguably follows that the activity either of all the states or of one of them – depending on which of these alternatives constitutes happiness – must, provided it is unimpeded, be the activity worthiest of choice. *And this is* (or, *is a*) *pleasure*. Consequently, even if most pleasures turned out to be unqualifiedly bad, the highest good would still be *some* pleasure'. One phrase deserves explanation. Aristotle is answering the thesis that the best life cannot be a pursuit of pleasure. He is presupposing an analysis of the good life which appears earlier in the *Nicomachean Ethics*: either happiness is made up of all the best activities or it is just one, the very best of these (1099a29-31), that which exhibits the 'best and completest excellence' (1098a16-18). This last option is what he means to leave open in speaking of 'the activity of all the states or of one of them'; he is looking forward to his thesis that happiness consists in the exercise of one superhuman faculty, pure intelligence (1177a12-1178a8). But on either alternative he takes one plain
conclusion to follow from *T*. It is that such activities, when they proceed/ **140**
unhindered,[8] are pleasures, not that they give rise to pleasure. Otherwise he

[8] Elsewhere Aristotle says something of hindrances to activity. (a) Misfortune may block our activities (1100b22-30) but so may too much good fortune (1153b17-25), too many friends (1170b26-9); note the asceticism of 1178b3-7. (b) The pleasure of one activity will interfere with another: people who enjoy fluteplaying cannot attend to arguments while a flute is being played (1175b1-22, cf. 1153a20-3; more on this later).

could not, as he does, envisage the good life as consisting in some pleasure or pleasures, or rebuff the opposition by allowing the good and rational man to aim at *some* pleasures even if not at all.

(2) There is the same use of 'pleasure' in the arguments leading to *T*. Aristotle lists three views about pleasure (1152b8-12) of which he wants to dismiss two. One of these is that no pleasure is good either intrinsically or even derivatively, the other is that even if all pleasures were good the greatest good could not be a pleasure. The two seem to him to share one principal argument: that pleasure is always a *genesis* or end-directed process and never the end-state of such a process (1152b22-3) – or, more specifically, that all pleasures are perceptible processes towards some natural or normal condition (1152b13-14). As Aristotle's reply shows, his opponents would have approved the obituarist who wrote 'Dining was among his pleasures; he valued the repleteness that resulted'. The pleasure, they held, was never 'in the same class' (1152b14) as its desirable outcome. Depending on the intransigence of the opponent this had been taken to show either that the pleasure had no value at all (cf. Plato *Philebus* 54c9-d12) or that it had the lesser value.

The point comes out sharply in the example Aristotle chooses to discuss, that of convalescence. We notice that we are getting better, and enjoy this (it is a *perceptible* process to a natural state); but what we want and value is ordinary health, which we scarcely notice but would not trade for any convalescence, however enjoyable. It is into this argument that Joachim introduced his identification of pleasure with 'feeling pleased'. But Aristotle is quite clear what the opposition intend: for them the pleasure is the convalescing. For him, as his reply will show, it is the activity of a healthy body. These are the only alternatives in the case that he considers./

141 At first, without directly challenging the assumption that pleasures consist in processes towards some desirable state, he tries a Platonic reply. Some such processes at least are not the pleasures they seem to be, namely those that involve discomfort for the sake of a cure – those that occur in the sick, for example. He is reminding his hearers of *Republic* 583b-586c, *Philebus* 51a. But then he turns to reject the assumption. He keeps another part of the opposition's case: in their view the valuable part of our lives is always some state or activity (1152b33), never the process leading to such a state or activity. Very well, even in convalescence there is a pleasure which is valuable by their standards, for the real pleasure is, as he will shortly put it (1153a14), 'an activity of the natural state'; not the trudge back to health but the exercise of actual health. But where is this healthy activity to be found in convalescence? 'The activity shown in the desires', he explains, 'is the activity of the state which still survives in us, our natural constitution' (or perhaps 'The activity is found in the desires of the state ...'; 1152b35-6, cf. 1154b18-20). He is claiming, I take it, that any actual pleasure associated with convalescence consists in the proper functioning of the healthy residue of the patient; without this the sick man would not want to get better.

That this is his point becomes clear in his summing-up (1153a7-12). Our pleasures are not to be contrasted as end-directed processes with their desirable ends. Pleasures are not such processes, they do not even all come

hand in hand with such processes (those which occur in convalescence do; theorising is one that does not). They are all activities constituting an end in themselves; in them we are not becoming so-and-so (healthy, say) but using the faculties we have. The only pleasures that have some further justification beyond themselves are those found in men who are being 'brought to the perfecting of their nature'; thus (as I gloss it) the functioning of the healthy parts in convalescence has a further point, that of promoting total health, but their comparable functioning in a wholly healthy man has no such further point. And Aristotle ends by rejecting the thesis that pleasure is a perceptible *genesis* and replacing it with *T*. The sense of 'pleasure' that was required to explain Aristotle's application of *T* is the sense needed to explain the steps by which it is introduced. In these contexts Aristotle's/ question 'What is **142**
pleasure?' means 'What is the character of a pleasure, what ingredients of a life are enjoyable in themselves?' The nature of enjoying does not come into question in *A*. If we are asked what is admirable about politics or detestable about beagling, we do not stop to ponder what admiring or detesting is before embracing the question.

Other evidence for the dominant use of 'pleasure' in *A* could be adduced. Is there evidence for a different use, in which the pleasure is a concomitant or consequence of some enjoyed activity? Not in 1153a6-7, where the 'pleasant things' contrasted with the 'pleasures' are not the enjoyed activities but their objects. But in 1153a20-3 there seems to be a sketch of the contrast we are after. Yet the point – that the enjoyment of an activity stimulates it and inhibits others – is made with nothing like the detail and perspicuousness of the comparable argument in *B*, 1175a29-b24. The conclusion remains that the central arguments of *A*, those which import and then apply *T*, are controlled by that first sense of 'pleasure'; and it is quite otherwise in *B*.

Corollaries

But the argument of *A* is too curious to put aside without more comment, particularly since *B* has had the lion's share of other discussions. How, to begin with, does Aristotle assure himself that he can identify the convalescent's pleasure with the activity of his healthy parts? His immediate argument (1152b36-1153a2) is that there are pleasures which do *not* involve wants and discomforts and which *are* the proper functioning of a natural faculty, such as the activities of theorising or rational contemplation. So he is looking for some common feature in all pleasures, some necessary and sufficient condition for anything to be enjoyable; and he uses something like a method of concomitant variations to isolate it. And his critics have long complained that this search for the unit is a delusion. Working at a crossword puzzle is surely an end-directed process, yet why should this not be more enjoyable than rationally contemplating the solution?

One more move is open to him. He has grasped, and never forgets, the essential point that pleasures are 'ends', that to enjoy *X*-ing is a reason for *X*-ing or for taking steps to bring/ *X*-ing about. True, this suggests that the **143**

X-ing I enjoy is always something I can choose to do (this seems to be Aristotle's view in *B*) or else can try to bring about (the healthy functioning in *A*). But I can enjoy receiving unexpected letters; in that case my enjoyment is a reason for others to send me letters. I can enjoy the knowledge that my horse has won; and if you think I shall enjoy that knowledge, that is a reason for imparting it to me, for making or letting me know. But I cannot make myself know that something is the case, as I can make myself go gardening or become a licensed plumber. And there are more teasing questions: can I claim without paradox to enjoy *believing* that my horse won? (Perhaps the oddity is that this could only be a reason for the ministrations of flatterers.) But these refinements do not touch Aristotle's clarity on the main issue, that a pleasure is or can be satisfying in itself. So if I find working at crossword puzzles more enjoyable than contemplating their solutions, that is surely because for me the puzzling has the form of a self-contained activity like juggling, not that of an end-directed operation like recovering one's stamina or building a house. At any moment that I say I am working at such a puzzle I can say I have worked at it (cf. *Meta.* 1048b18-35), and that use of the perfect would not be open to me if I described myself as solving the puzzle.

But there is a larger curiosity in Aristotle's argument. He seems to claim that we can misidentify the object of our enjoyment, and misidentify it systematically. When we say we enjoy convalescence we are always wrong about what we really enjoy. To find out what we are really enjoying we must resort to a curious induction – as though an enjoyment turned up and it had to be settled on some generalisation from other cases what it was an enjoyment of. But Aristotle cannot mean this absurdity. In *B* the complaint would be easily settled, for there Aristotle maintains, in Urmson's admirable summary ('Aristotle on pleasure', 324), that 'different activities are differently enjoyable. Just as perception and thought are different species of activity, so the pleasures of perception are different in species from the pleasures of thought. Every activity has its own "proper" (*oikeia*) pleasure; one could not chance to get the pleasure of, say, reading poetry from stamp collecting'. But that is *B*, not *A*. *A* is not concerned (save perhaps in
144 1153a20-3) with the relation between the/ enjoying and what is enjoyed. And *B* is not concerned with the misidentifying of the activity enjoyed.

Now in *A* Aristotle prefaces his own account of pleasure with the comment that the processes[9] which restore us to a natural state are only *incidentally, kata sumbebêkos*, pleasant (1152b34-5). Commonly he explains this expression by saying that an *A* is incidentally *B* when its being so is an exception (we should prefer to say, when under that description it is an exception): *A*s are not always or necessarily, or even usually, *B*s (cf. *Top.* I 5; *Meta.* V 30 and VI 2 with Kirwan's commentary (Oxford 1971)). But he cannot be concerned here to point out that convalescence is not always or usually a pleasure; his thesis is plainly much stronger than that. There is a more basic suggestion

[9] Understanding '*kinêseis kai geneseis*' at 1152b34 with Grant, Stewart, Ross, Dirlmeier, Gauthier. Rackham and Festugière understand '*hêdonai*'. Gauthier agrees with Ramsauer that this comes to the same thing, but the first reading is the more perspicuous.

that seems often to underlie his accounts of *to kata sumbebêkos*. Statements which hold good only 'incidentally' are formally misleading, suggesting a mistaken analysis or explanation of the fact they convey, and calling for rewriting or expansion into some unmisleading canonical form. This I suppose is the sense of Waitz's note (*Aristotelis Organon* I (Leipzig 1844), 443) that '*kata sumbebêkos* dicitur quod non nisi cum abusu quodam vocabuli dicitur', and it is the point of Aristotle's dictum that an *A* which is *B* is only incidentally so when it is not the *nature* of *A*s to be *B* or it is not *qua A* that this one is *B* (e.g. 1026b37-1027a8, 1025a28-9). 'A baker made this statue' is an example. Aristotle holds that the fact is better displayed by saying that what made the statue was a sculptor who happened to be (but for this purpose need not have been) a baker. Similarly with 'convalescence is a pleasure': the pleasure is the operation of the healthy parts which happens to occur in a process of convalescence but might have occurred apart from any such process.

Now this seems to give Aristotle a reply to the objection. The convalescent was wrong, we may say, not about the activity he was enjoying, but about the description under which it was enjoyable to him. For the functioning of the healthy residue does in this case happen to be also a process of convalescence. The baker who makes the statue *is* a baker; only it is not as a/ baker that he **145**
can be clarifyingly treated as responsible for the statue. And thus, it seems, the mistake that Aristotle claims to detect can be assimilated to one that has recently exercised philosophers, in which a subject, while enjoying *X*, rejects or overlooks the appropriate description of the *X* he is enjoying: the familiar schoolboy at the dormitory feast, who thinks he is enjoying eating cold bacon when he is really enjoying breaking the rules.

But this reply should give us qualms. It might indeed seem an anachronism. Aristotle does not speak unambiguously of identifying even a substance under different descriptions, let alone those intractable items, events. He does indeed speak of a thing as being 'one in number but two in *logos*', as the same mid-point of a line can be called both the end-point of one line and the beginning of another (*Phys.* 262a19-21, 263b12-14). But when he uses the same idiom to express the identity of a body with its matter (*GC* 320b14) we should cavil at the glib translation 'one thing under different descriptions'; the identity in question is too problematic. And it is worth recalling that Aristotle is prone to think of 'the sculptor is incidentally a baker' as importing two things which somehow combine into a unity (*Meta.* 1015b16-36, cf. 1017b33 and Kirwan's notes). Yet his discussion of the 'mixed' action at *EN* 1110a4-b17 is surely a treatment of one action under different descriptions: the jettisoning of the cargo which is *a priori* irrational, the jettisoning to save the ship which represents the rational choice. But those who distrust such aids in our context will prefer to say that Plato had after all argued that we can be mistaken about our real pleasures, and that Aristotle in *A* is still within that tradition. In *B* he is his own man, and there is no further hint that we may systematically misidentify what we enjoy.

The verb takes the stage

In *B*, as I have said, it is quite otherwise. Given any faculty of perception or intellect, Aristotle says, the exercise of that faculty will be best, and so most complete and pleasant, when the faculty is at its best and exercised on the finest kind of object. But the exercise of the faculty is not itself the pleasure; the pleasure comes to complete or perfect the activity (1174b14-23). Aristotle tells us something of what this means. The pleasure, he says, augments the
146 activity, in that people who engage in the/ activity with pleasure are more exact and discriminating (1175a30-b1); the stronger it is the more it prevents them from attending to other activities (1175b1-13), and the longer and better the activity goes on (1175b14-16). But its contribution to the completeness or perfection of the activity is not the same as that of the well-conditioned faculty or the fine object. It is more like the health the doctor produces than like such pre-existing contributing factors as the doctor (1174b23-6, taking '*kai ho iatros*' to follow and be governed by '*homoiôs*') or the health already in the patient (31-2). In brief it is an end in itself, something that gives the action a point different from that of exercising a good faculty on a good object. Enjoyment inevitably marks such exercises (1174b29-31) but it is still not, as we may put it, merely entailed by satisfying the conditions (1174a6-8). To say that Smith is using his excellent eyesight on some comely object is not to say, or say what entails, that he enjoys doing this, any more than to say that he is physically at his prime is to call him beautiful, though the beauty inevitably follows (1174b32-3). Yet the beauty and the enjoyment are not merely contingent benefits that might have been got otherwise. The beauty is that of a man in his prime, the pleasure can only be identified by reference to the activity it promotes.

Plainly Aristotle is refusing to identify the pleasure with the enjoyed activity. A little later he says so flatly. Unlike desires, pleasures are so bound up with the activities they complete that there is disagreement on whether the pleasure is simply identical with the activity. But it doesn't look as though the pleasure *is* just thinking or perceiving; *for that would be absurd* (1175b32-5).

There is the difference between *A* and *B*. How to explain it? Well, perhaps it occurred to Aristotle that the activities of the natural states which served as *A*'s paradigms of pleasure need not be enjoyable at all. Smith is exercising his wits on an argument; but his wits are blunt, he is tired, the argument is tangled. So *B* is spelling out the further conditions that are requisite for pleasure – sharp wits, impeccable object. But this does not explain the difference. For one thing, such conditions might be covered by *A*'s requirement that the activity proceed unhindered. For another, *B* does not conclude that when such conditions are satisfied the activity *is* a pleasure,
147 only that pleasure inevitably ensues. And for a third, *B* seems curiously/ unaware of the central claim of *A* that only self-contained activities and not end-directed processes are enjoyable. I shall take up the argument in

1173b9-15 later; meanwhile notice the kinds of activity that are promoted by their proper enjoyments in 1175a34-5. One is house-building, a paradigm of an end-directed process in both *A* and *B*. It is even odd that the senses, which provide a model of enjoyable activity in *B*, are so readily dismissed in *A*, in deference to convention, as neutral or a source of discomfort (1154b4-9).

Let us leave the attempt to build a bridge from *A* to *B* and consider a declaration of independence. I suggested that in asking what pleasure is, and concluding that it is not a process, *B* is engaged in a quite different sort of enquiry from *A*. It is concerned to say, not what is enjoyable, but what enjoying is. It is interested in the logic of the verb or verbs we translate by 'enjoying' and 'being pleased', and in the associated nouns just in so far as these go proxy for the verbs.

Notice first the quite different emphasis that *A* and *B* put on verbs connoting pleasure. Aristotle's standard noun for 'pleasure' is '*hêdonê*' (elsewhere, but not in *A* or *B*, he also uses '*apolausis*' and '*terpsis*'). The verbs he associates with it are *chairein, hêdesthai, areskein, terpein, agapân*. The difference is not just that in *B* the use of the verbs increases noticeably in proportion to that of the noun proper (from 8:47 in *A* to 23:83 in *B*). Nor is it only that the range of such verbs deployed in *B* is very much widened, though this deserves comment in view of Urmson's generalisation that 'the verb *hêdesthai* is far less common in the *EN* than *chairein*' (333). The fact is that in *A* only *chairein* occurs (8 times), whereas in *B* it is easily overtaken by *hêdesthai* (12 to *chairein* 7) as well as being joined by *terpein* (2), *agapân* (1) and *areskesthai* (1). This in itself is some evidence of the perfunctory treatment of the notion of enjoying in *A*, by contrast with the new sensitivity to it in *B*. But the most significant difference is that at various cardinal points in *B*, but never in *A*, the argument turns directly on an appeal to the behaviour of the verb. It will be worth reviewing the cases.

(1) 1173a15-22. Some hold that pleasure cannot be good, since pleasure is a matter of degree and goodness is not. But (objects Aristotle) if they base this conclusion on *being pleased*, the same difference of degree can be found in *being just* or *brave, acting/ justly* or *temperately* (the last expressions being single verbs **148**
in the Greek); so the supposed contrast with goodness is not there. Translators commonly render the pleasure-verb here in terms of 'feelings of pleasure', *Lustempfindung*, but Aristotle says nothing of feelings; he is recognising and finding parallels for one feature of the logic of pleasure-verbs, namely that we can say 'He is more pleased than I am', 'I enjoy it less than I used to'. Only the form of the argument matters for us, though there will be one implication to notice later.

Subsequently he turns to the more important business of collecting features of the logic of pleasure-verbs which show that pleasure is not a *kinêsis*, a process from some state to another.

(2) 1173a31-b4. Pleasure cannot be a process like walking (some distance) or growing (to some size), for these can be done quickly or slowly but one can't be pleased or enjoy something either quickly or slowly. One can of course *get* to be pleased as one can get angry quickly; but one can't be so. This mark of process-verbs, that they collect adverbs of relative speed, is of the first

importance for Aristotle, as Penner has pointed out (411-14). It is a corollary of his constant claim that any process must be such as to cover some distance in some time – the distance being either spatial, between two places, or an analogous stretch between different qualities, sizes, etc. This is why he subsequently says (1174b5) that 'the whither and whence make the form' of the process; the criteria of its identity must include the limits of the distance it covers. Now (to pursue the point) it is true that an enjoyment may have to be specified by some object of enjoyment – say the First Rasumovsky – which itself has a beginning and end and intermediate stages. The quartet may accordingly be played quickly or slowly. But if it is played quickly it does not follow that I enjoy it (or hear it) quickly. If it is left half-played then, in the sense of 'pleasure' appropriate to *A*, I have an unfinished pleasure; but, in the sense appropriate to *B*, I have not half-enjoyed something. (There is another sense, suggested by the argument under (1) above, in which I may only half-enjoy what I hear.)

149 (3) 1173b7-13. This passage may suggest that after all *B* does/ share *A*'s interpretation of the theory that pleasure is a *kinêsis*, for what Aristotle rejects here, as he does in 1153a2-4, is the claim that pleasure is 'a replenishment of nature'. But notice the radically different treatment of the thesis. In *A* he argued that not the process of replenishment but the resultant activity of the natural state was the pleasure, i.e. the proper functioning of the 'established nature'. This evidently allows the pleasure to be identified with the behaviour of the healthy body. But in *B* he argues that the enjoyment-verbs cannot have 'my body' as subject. It is the body that is replenished, so if '... is replenished' is treated as equivalent to or as a specification of '... is pleased', the subject-gap in the second should also be fillable by 'my body'; but we jib at this (*ou dokei de*). Rather, one (a person, *tis*) can be pleased when his body is being replenished. So once more, *A* asks what is enjoyed or enjoyable, and is accordingly ready to argue: a bodily function. But *B* asks what enjoying is, and by considering the logical requirements on subjects for enjoyment-verbs replies: not a bodily function.

(4) 1174b7-9. A process (Aristotle's examples have included building a temple, going for a walk) always takes time, but being pleased can be whole in an instant. Of course Aristotle does not mean that I can be pleased but pleased for no time; his point is rather that if I am enjoying doing something which takes time to complete, the construction appropriate to the subordinate verb does not transfer to the verb of enjoyment.

(5) 1174a14-b7. I shall not dwell on this text, possibly the most-discussed in *B*. Aristotle compares pleasure with seeing and contrasts it with processes such as temple-building, traversing a distance and other motions represented by verbal nouns. All these latter have stages and at any intermediate stage are still unfinished; one can't find a process complete of its kind at any arbitrary time in its progress. None of this holds good of enjoying or seeing (though, to be sure, it can hold good of what is enjoyed).

That Aristotle is concerned here still with the logic of enjoyment-verbs is, I think, clear. Conventionally he is represented as noticing that, if I say 'I am enjoying the First Rasumovsky', it would be bizarre to reply 'I am sorry you

have not yet/ enjoyed it', while the same form of reply to 'I am making myself 150
a winter coat' would be wholly in order. But he does not expressly import these familiar and debatable connexions between present- and perfect tense utterances into this passage (and indeed the verb '*hêdesthai*' had no known perfect tense). What he insists on is the unfinishedness of processes if we consider them stage by stage. They are complete, if at all, only in the whole time they take (1174a27-9 – but the 'if at all', '*eiper*', may mean only 'doubtless'). So it is natural to think that he is calling attention to the possibility that the building of a temple, unlike enjoyment, may be interrupted or remain unachieved. Now this could not be his point if some remarks of Vendler, which have been quoted as throwing light on Aristotle's analysis, give a correct account of the matter. Vendler wrote: 'If I say of a person that he is running a mile or of someone else that he is drawing a circle, then I do claim that the first one will keep drawing until he has drawn the circle. If they do not complete their activities, my statement will turn out to be false.'[10] But suppose you interrupt me when I am drawing a circle and the circle is never finished; it cannot follow that I was not drawing a circle. For if what I was drawing was not a circle but the circle-fragment left on my paper, you did not interrupt my drawing. If Aristotle's view were Vendler's, he could not accept the possibility of any process such as the building of a house or walking to London remaining finally incomplete. But there seems to be no ground for fathering this unsatisfactory view upon Aristotle.

(Indeed, I suspect that in *Metaphysics* VII 7-9 Aristotle runs into paradox concerning the role of 'a statue' in 'I am making a statue' partly because the truth of that statement does not require an actual statue to emerge. But that is another matter.)

You may indeed feel qualms at the suggestion that the world contains unfinished processes – as though there could be journeys from Oxford to London that ended at Reading. But that would mistake the point. If my journey to London remains incomplete I shall not be entitled subsequently to say that I *did go* or *have gone* to London on that occasion, only that I was going there; but that leaves the truth of my present claim 'I am going to London'
untouched. When Aristotle uses a present tense to/ describe a process he 151
standardly has in mind the imperfective sense represented by the continuous form in English; that is why he is unwilling to use that tense to say that something comes to have a certain character at some instant, and prefers to say that from the first instant it *has* come to have the character (*Phys.* 263b21-264a6). Nor, as his example of an object changing colour shows (ibid.), are such uses of the tense confined to contexts where the idea of intention need figure in the analysis.

So the point holds firm. There is no reason to deny that Aristotle is interested in the possibility of interrupting some process without falsifying the natural description of what is interrupted. And 'enjoying' can never stand for such a process.

[10] Z. Vendler, 'Verbs and Times', *Phil. Rev.* 66 (1957), 143-60.

Conclusions

There the case may rest. When Aristotle rejects the thesis that pleasure is a process in *A*, he is offering to tell us what our real pleasures are, what is really enjoyed or enjoyable. When he rejects a thesis in the same form of words in *B*, he is offering to tell us what the nature of enjoying is by reviewing the logical characteristics of pleasure-verbs. In *B* he moves naturally to the question what the enjoying contributes to the enjoyed activity, and apart from one peripheral hint there is no sign of that question in *A*.

No doubt the arguments of *B* suggest one explanation of the shift. What persuades him to decide there that it is 'absurd' to say the pleasure is the thinking or perceiving? He has noticed, we may guess, that many epithets of the thinking do not transfer to the pleasure, however much that pleasure may be the pleasure of that thinking. Circular or syllogistic thinking cannot without joking be called a circular or syllogistic pleasure. And the point comes out more sharply when processes are allowed to be enjoyable, as they are in *B*. If I enjoy building or dining quickly I do not quickly enjoy building or dining. So the question becomes: what can be said about enjoying *X*-ing that cannot be said about *X*-ing, and the converse? Verbs and their adverbs, and then their other logical features, take the centre of the enquiry; and for the philosophically suspect enterprise of *A* are substituted the admirable studies of *B*.

But the residual problem remains unresolved. It is not enough to say that
152 Aristotle shifts his interest, so that what he/ says in *A* is broadly compatible with what he says in *B*. The rub is that he uses the same expressions to identify the theories he rejects in *A* and *B*, and these are theories of quite different types. In both contexts he claims to be explaining *what pleasure is*. That remarkable and, I think, unremarked ambiguity I can only commend to your curiosity. But it is not clear that we need expect a philosophical explanation for it; and what had to be removed was a block to the philosophical assessment of Aristotle's arguments.

20

Philosophical Invective

Plutarch was shocked at a scandal about Pericles' private life which was 1
current in the great man's lifetime. 'For a historian,' he comments, 'there seems to be no easy way of tracking down the truth. Later generations find their knowledge of the facts blocked by the lapse of time, while the contemporary record of lives and deeds sullies and perverts the truth partly from envy and ill-will, partly from favour and flattery' (*Pericles* 13). Plutarch's pessimism arose from the fifth-century slander of a politician, but anyone who has tried to disentangle the evidence for the development of philosophical schools in the following centuries must feel the same dismay. Indeed I shall argue that concerning the fourth-century evidence we have not felt it often enough.

In centuries earlier than the fourth we are not likely to be misled by philosophical polemics. Heraclitus, to be sure, in a fragment whose authenticity need no longer be doubted, accuses Pythagoras of plagiarizing on a grand scale (22 B 129 Diels-Kranz); an accusation which may be illuminating at this early date, but which soon becomes a platitude of invective without ever losing its popularity. He also abuses Hesiod, Pythagoras, Xenophanes, and Hecataeus as polymaths who could not learn understanding (B 40); and Xenophanes himself makes a good joke at the expense, probably, of Pythagoras' doctrines of transmigration (21 B 7); but this is the worst of its kind. Zeno of Elea is often credited with publishing a polemic against Empedocles, but wrongly; the ascription rests partly on a mistranslation of the title *Exêgêsis tôn Empedokleous*,[1] partly on a failure to

[1] Suidas s.v. *Zênôn* = 29 A 2 DK *egrapsen ... exêgêsin tôn Empedokleous*. 'Of course Zeno did not write a commentary on Empedokles', says Burnet (*Early Greek Philosophy*[4] (London 1930), 312, n.1), referring to the argument of Diels (*Berl. Sitzgsber.* 1884, 359, n.2) that the title in the Suda can mean a polemic against Empedocles: on this some scholars build castles, notable Gaye in *Journal of Philology* 31 (1910), 114-15. But of the 'parallels' cited by Diels (*a*) Heraclides Ponticus' *exêgêseis Hêrakleitou* (Diogenes Laertius 5.88) need not and probably should not be construed as polemic (cf. *ho ton Hêrakleiton pasin exêgoumenos* (Antipanes apud Athen. 4.134b = Heraclides fr.10 Wehrli)); (*b*) the same writer's *pros ton Dêmokriton exêgêseis* (DL 5.88) is identified as polemic by the *pros* (cf. the *pros ton Dêmokriton* among Heraclides' *phusika* (DL 5.87): so Plutarch *pros Kôlôtên*, etc.); and (*c*) in Hipparchus' *Aratou kai Eudoxou phainomenôn exêgêseis* (Diels' prime 'parallel', but one which no subsequent writer has adopted) criticism is expressly coupled with the effort to show what is valuable and true in the texts expounded (I. i. 4); there is a good deal of straightforward historical explanation, and Hipparchus thinks it necessary to defend his critical interventions against Attalus who wrote an uncritical *exêgêsis* under the same rubric (I. i. 3-4 and I. iii. 2-4). None of these gives any ground for making the Suda title cover an Eleatic refutation of

2 notice that the/ *Exêgêsis* in question must be the work of another Zeno, Zeno of Citium, who wrote many such studies: for the Stoics, Empedocles was an ancestor almost as important as Heraclitus.[2]/

3 On the other hand, from the rise of Epicureanism at the end of the fourth century we are prepared for the worst. Indeed Epicurus sometimes figures in the textbooks as one who set the fashion for scurrility in the squabbles of philosophers. This is quite unfair: he was heir to a rich century of calumny whose measure the historians of philosophy are only starting to take. Yet we have had the clues in our hands. We know the scope and function of slander in the comedy, we are familiar with the idea of *diabolê* in rhetoric, both as a technical concept in the manuals of Anaximenes and Aristotle[3] and as a powerful weapon in the hands of Lysias and Demosthenes. But scholars have taken their examples from rhetoric and comedy without often asking how this knowledge bears on other fields of literature that show the influence of the first two; in particular, the field of the philosophical pamphleteers. And these literary influences are certainly important: they supplement Plutarch's diagnosis of slander as arising from envy and ill-will. Malice and sycophancy go only part of the way to explaining that fine field of abuse and adulation which surrounded the work of Plato and Aristotle and their contemporaries.

Let us start from a concrete case, a very important one for students of Aristotle. It is commonly supposed that we know a good deal about Aristotle's actions and motives in the year 347, the year in which Plato died and Speusippus succeeded to the headship of the Academy. Indeed those actions

---

Empedocles. Nor would Plato's account of Zeno (*Parm.* 128d-e) seem to leave him the time for writing an interpretation of Empedocles before adopting Eleaticism, and in any case Plato clearly implies that, at any rate at the dramatic date of the *Parmenides*, there was just one 'book' of Zeno's current (*Parm.* 127c-e, 128c-e). The other three titles credited to Zeno by the Suda would fit this one book well enough.

[2] I suggest that the title in n.1 above means what it says and that it has been transferred to Zeno of Elea from Zeno of Citium. That the later Zeno engaged in such historical studies is certain (cf. the anecdote in DL 7.2). It would be hard to believe that between Heraclides, whose four books of *exêgêseis Hêrakleitou* were 'one of the earliest full sources' for the Stoics (G. Kirk, *Heraclitus, the Cosmic Fragments* (Cambridge 1962), 11), and Cleanthes, who wrote a similar set of four books on the same subject (followed by Sphaerus with his five *diatribai* (DL 7.174, 178)), Zeno took no hand in expounding Heraclitus, to whom he owed or thought he owed important doctrines (Arius Didymus apud Diels *Dox.* 469. 27-470. 4; cf. Probus *in Verg.* 10.33ff. = *Dox.* 92b-93b, 'ex his [sc. quattuor elementis] omnia esse postea effigiata Stoici tradunt Zenon Citieus et Chrysippus Solaeus et Cleanthes Assius, qui principem habuerunt Empedoclem Agrigentinum') but still more in the converse importation of Heraclitean elements into the Stoic interpretation of Empedocles: the whole ekpyrotic cosmology that is fathered on Empedocles in Hippolytus (*Refutation of all Heresies* i.3 = 31 A 31 Diels-Kranz) and the evident connection between the *noêron pur*, with which Hippolytus identifies Empedocles' god, and the *phronimon pur* which the same source ascribes to Heraclitus (*RH* ix.10 = 22 B 64 DK). No doubt Empedocles' account of fire lent itself to this special treatment: Burnet is right to defend Aristotle's comment at *Meta.* 985a29-b2, *GC* 330b19-21 (op. cit., 231; contra H. Cherniss, *Aristotle's Criticism of Presocratic Philosophy* (Baltimore 1935), 56).

The transference of the title to the Eleatic Zeno may have been eased by the tendency of the Stoics to refer to their founder as 'the first Zeno' (Clement *Strom.* v. 9 = von Arnim *SVF*, i. 43). There was a later Stoic Zeno (DL 7.35).

[3] *Rhet.* 1415a24-34, 1416a4-1416b15; *Rhet. ad Alex.* 1436b36-1438a2, 1441b36-1442b27.

and motives have become a keystone in many explanations of Aristotle's philosophical development. Let me set the scene by listing some of the things on which the ancient authorities are sufficiently agreed and which it would be unreasonable to doubt.[4] We know that Plato died in Athens in the spring of 347, and that Aristotle left the city the same year.[5] We know that for twenty years before that time he had been a member of Plato's school in the Academy, ever since coming to Athens around the time of his seventeenth
birthday from his father's/ estate in Chalcidice.[6] We know that those twenty 4
years were the longest time he would ever spend in Athens. He was a man of nearly thirty-seven when Plato died, and when he came back from his travels some thirteen years later he was to have only twelve more years of writing and lecturing in the city before his exile and death.

We know too where Aristotle went when he left Athens in 347: he went to live with Hermias the ruler of Atarneus on the coast of the Troad, a patron who had established friendly relations with Aristotle's two main centres of interest, the Academy and the court of Macedon. After a few years in that region he was appointed tutor to young Alexander of Macedon, and he did not move back to Athens until Philip was dead and Alexander had inherited his army and his ambitions. All this is enough to show that the year 347 was a turning-point in Aristotle's life. For many critics it becomes the crux of his philosophical career. Werner Jaeger, as I need not remind you, argued in his book *Aristotle* that up to this date he had published nothing that was not piously Platonic, in a sense of that Humpty-Dumpty word drawn mainly from such middle-period dialogues as the *Phaedo* and *Republic*. Now, with Plato dead and the Academy far away and under uncongenial management, Aristotle could turn to criticizing Plato openly and constructing his own answers to the old problems.[7] And no doubt we might catch such professional and philosophical implications in his departure, if only we knew as much as we are held to know about the circumstances in which he left – that is to say, if we knew just when, and why, and with whom. So far as I can see, we do not know this at all. When we follow the evidence in any direction it peters out in a bog of libels and lampoons.

Jaeger, for example, knows that Aristotle left Athens *after* Plato's death,
when Speusippus had been appointed head of/ the school. And he can tell us 5
Aristotle's reason for going. Aristotle 'went to Asia Minor in the conviction that Speusippus had inherited merely the office and not the spirit' (*Aristotle*, tr. Robinson, 111). This picture of Aristotle as representing the old Academy in

[4] The evidence is collected and discussed in Düring, *Aristotle in the Ancient Biographical Tradition* (*AABT*), Studia Graeca et Latina Gothoburgensia 5 (1957).

[5] DL *Vita Arist.* 9; Dion. Hal. *Ep. ad Ammaeum* 5; Mubashir and Usaibia, cf. Düring, *AABT*, 199, 214.

[6] Düring, *AABT*, 254-5. We do not know that Eudoxus was deputizing for Plato in the Academy when Aristotle joined it: see n.24 below.

[7] Jaeger (*Aristotle*, trans. R. Robinson.[2] (Oxford 1948), ch. 5) is anxious to distinguish his own version of Aristotle's departure from this bleak picture by stressing Aristotle's continued admiration for Plato: 'When Aristotle had completed his destructive criticism of Plato's Idea, exact thinking and religious thinking went separate paths in him ... He reads Plato's works as poetry' (119 = tr. Robinson, 118).

exile takes its force from one further consideration. Aristotle was accompanied to Asia Minor by another celebrated and disappointed colleague – Xenocrates, who was himself to be elected as Speusippus' successor in the Academy eleven years later. The joint departure of Aristotle and Xenocrates amounted, so Jaeger tells us (op. cit.), to a 'secession'.

This is in some ways an attractive, and certainly an influential, picture of events. So it is unsettling to be assured, in another fine biography of Aristotle, that Aristotle left Athens *before* Plato's death[8] and so, very probably, before the appointment of his successor. In Ingemar Düring's view, it follows that Aristotle's reasons for going were not professional but political. Aristotle's family had long enjoyed close ties with the Macedonian court: his father had been one of the court doctors, and no doubt this connection was a major reason for Aristotle's later appointment as one of Alexander's tutors. But in Athens anti-Macedonian feelings were running high. In the previous year Philip had destroyed Olynthus. During that winter Aeschines, in his new role of war-leader, caught the ear of the Athenians.[9] So Aristotle, a foreigner with the wrong connections, found the city too hot for him. As for his failure to be appointed Plato's successor in the Academy, this carries no such professional or philosophical import as Jaeger read into it. For, even if there was a formal election after Plato's death (and this has been doubted by Jacoby),[10] Aristotle, by making himself a political refugee, had automatically removed his name from the short-list.

6 Here's a conflict, indeed. It is fair to add that Düring's/view of Aristotle's motives at this juncture suits his broader interpretation of Aristotle's development. To him, as to me, it seems that Jaeger has not made out his case for treating Aristotle as a careful adherent of Plato's theory of Ideas up to the time of Plato's death. When Jaeger tells us[11] that Aristotle's dialogue *Eudemus*, written soon after 354, maintains the theory of Ideas because one of the surviving fragments of that work refers to the 'sights yonder' (*ta ekei theamata*), the visions which the soul has in another world and forgets again when it is reborn on earth, it is enough to point out that the context in which this fragment is preserved shows beyond all question that the *theamata* are not the Ideas. Aristotle is using the paraphernalia of mythology, and the *theamata* are Styx and Lethe and all the traditional furniture of Hades.[12] There is no indication that he proposed to allegorize this material, and none that if he had done so his explanation would have introduced the Ideas. Nor can I find Jaeger's interpretation of the fragments which he assigns to Aristotle's

[8] Düring, *AABT*, 276, 388, 459.

[9] Aeschines, *In Ctes.* 58ff., *De Falsa Leg.* 12ff.

[10] *FGrH*, 328 F. 224 = Philodemus, *Ind. Ac. Herc.* 6. 28, p. 37 Mekler. The text says that Speusippus *diedexato tên diatribên* (cf. *diedexato d'auton*, DL 4.1) on account of his close family relationship, and goes on to describe a formal election (*psêphophorêsantes ... Xenokratên heilonto*) that took place on Speusippus' death. The author mentions that at this time Aristotle was still considered a member of the Academy, although his absence from the city apparently removed him from consideration. Cf. Düring, 259-60.

[11] *Aristotle*, 51.

[12] Cf. 'The Platonism of Aristotle', above, Chapter 11, n.4.

Protrepticus, a work which is generally supposed to date from just before the mid-century, more persuasive. But I have argued these broader issues elsewhere, and they do not concern us now. We are concerned only with the evidence for the events of 347.

There is one consideration that has often seemed to settle the matter, and Jaeger relies heavily on it. It is that when Aristotle left Athens he was accompanied by Xenocrates. Grote said roundly that this alone was enough to refute the suggestion that Aristotle left because of the political situation (*Aristotle*, 7), for Xenocrates was celebrated for his independence and probity in his dealings with Macedon (Diogenes Laertius (DL), 4.8-9). No scholar known to me disputes the assertion that Xenocrates went to Atarneus with Aristotle: it is a platitude of the textbooks, and solely on the strength of it Xenocrates appears as Aristotle's 'old and intimate friend'. Yet there is not a hint of this important fact in the extant lives of Aristotle and Xenocrates. It conflicts with the settled tradition that Xenocrates was a rival and not a
friend/ of Aristotle (DL 5.2-3, 10; 4.6), and with the equally firm tradition 7
that, whereas Hermias, his alleged host and patron, was closely connected with Macedon, Xenocrates' relations with Macedon were always cool and even insolent (DL 4.8-9, 11). So far as I know, no one even thought of portraying Xenocrates as a friend and colleague of Aristotle after Plato's death until it became fashionable in the last century BC to try to reconcile the Academy and the Lyceum (*Vita Marciana Aristotelis* 24). Aristotle himself dismisses Xenocrates' theories in the *Metaphysics* with a scathing reference that would be astonishing in an old friend (1083b1-3). And Diogenes Laertius, after saying that Xenocrates spent most of his time in the Academy (4.6), mentions various journeys he made out of Athens; needless to say, the excursion to Asia Minor is not one of them. So what is the evidence for the 'secession'?

Jaeger thinks that it was reported by a later commentator, Didymus, who survives in one papyrus, and that Didymus took it from Hermippus' life of Aristotle, written towards the end of the third century BC (*Aristotle*, 114-15). Yet Xenocrates' name does not appear in the papyrus: it has to be supplied to fill a gap.[13] And when Croenert looked at the gap he found that the name which originally filled it seemed to end not in *RATEN* but in *DOTON*.[14] (It might be argued that what Croenert very hesitantly identified as Δ̣Ọ̣ṬON is ACTON and that the missing name may be 'Theophraston'.[15]) Moreover, even if Xenocrates' name had appeared among those whom Didymus lists as Hermias' protégés in the Academy, this would not prove that Xenocrates left Athens after Plato's death; for there is some evidence that one or more of those named by Didymus had left for Asia Minor some years before that time.[16]

[13] Didymus, col. 5, 52 Diels-Schubart; cf. Jaeger, *Aristotle*, 114-15.

[14] 'Neue Lesungen des Didymuspapyrus', *Rheinisches Museum* 62 (1907), 380-9, cf. Düring, *AABT*, 273, 276.

[15] The letters in both names are equal in number.

[16] On Erastos and Coriscos see the debatable sixth Platonic letter; Erastos' name appears in the Didymus papyrus.

But those who imported Xenocrates' name into Didymus' text had other evidence in view. To be exact, they had one piece of evidence, embedded in a
8 passage of Strabo which is/ agreed on all hands to contain gross errors of fact and to derive, at any rate in part, from sources hostile to Aristotle. One of these sources has been readily identified: it is Theopompus the pupil of Isocrates, a writer whom later critics could pick out even in that golden age of the lampoon as *baskanos* ('slanderer') and *maledicentissimus* ('most slanderous').[17] As an earnest of his interest in philosophy you may like to recall his essay *Kata tês Platônos diatribês* ('Against the school of Plato') from which Athenaeus quotes in the course of that long and bitter polemic against Plato which takes up the end of his eleventh book. The comment he cites is that Plato's dialogues are not merely false and pointless but plagiarized, for the most part, from the works of Aristippus, Antisthenes, and Bryson (*Deipn.* 11.508c-d). With this warning in his mind let us look closer at the passage of Strabo. In his description of Assos he writes:

> Aristotle stayed here because of his connection with Hermias the tyrant. Hermias was a eunuch, and the servant of a banker. When he was in Athens he was the pupil of both Plato and Aristotle, and then on returning home he at first became a partner in the tyranny of his master, who had already launched an attack on the country round Atarneus and Assos, and subsequently succeeded him as tyrant. Thereupon he sent for Aristotle and Xenocrates and made himself their host; indeed he married his brother's daughter to Aristotle. But Memnon of Rhodes was then a general in the service of the Persians, and under the guise of friendship he invited Hermias to visit him, on the trumped-up pretexts of hospitality and business. He arrested Hermias and sent him up to the King, who had him hanged. The philosophers took to their heels and quit the region, which became Persian property. (Strabo 13.1.57, p.610)

It is hard to know where to start in assessing this farrago. Luckily much of the work has been done.[18] There is no doubt, for example, that the account of Hermias' death is far astray. Strabo or Strabo's source is wrong not only on the name of the Persian general but, far more revealingly, on the sequence of events. The consensus of our better evidence, deriving very probably from Philochoros, shows that Aristotle reached Macedon when Alexander was in
9 his fourteenth year,/ two years before Hermias was executed.[19] And the motive for this distortion of events is plain enough. It is to set the visitors from the Academy in a poor light, scuttling for their lives from the fate of their friend. Just the same bias can be seen throughout the passage. Hermias, we are told, having absorbed the teaching of Plato and Aristotle, goes home and forthwith takes shares in an aggressive tyranny; and to point up the connection, when the tyranny devolves on him alone he becomes host to not one but both of Speusippus' most celebrated rivals in the Academy. It is the

[17] Dion. Hal., *Ep. ad Cn. Pompeium* 6.8; Nepos, *Vita Alcibiadis* 117.

[18] Notably by Mulvany, 'Notes on the Legend of Aristotle', *CQ* 20 (1926), 155-67; Wormell, 'Hermias of Atarneus', *Yale Classical Studies* 5 (1935), 57-92; Düring, *AABT*, 276.

[19] Boeckh, *Kleine Schriften*, 6.196, cited by Düring, *AABT*, 252-6.

oldest and best-loved charge in all polemics against the Academy in Plato's time: the pupils of the Academy have a taste for tyranny, and ruthless tyranny at that. Athenaeus repeats the accusation and gives a long list of the followers of Plato and Xenocrates who took this road to perdition (*Deipn.* 11.508d-509b). No doubt there was some justification for the charge: the behaviour of Plato's friends and associates in Sicily had become a public scandal. But the Academy was not the only school with a taste for dynastic connections – it had a strongly entrenched rival in Theopompus' tutor, Isocrates. And the bitterness of the attack suggests a time when the Academy was not to be pitied but to be envied for its success in these manoeuvres. It sounds as though it may have started, not against the background of Plato's failure in Syracuse, but at a time when Isocrates' fingers were burnt: when his patrons the Evagorids had become friendly with the Persians and Aristotle took the opportunity of invading his field of patronage in Cyprus by addressing his *Protrepticus* to a Cypriot king.[20] However that may be, two strands must always be interwoven in such invectives. The tyrant must be blackwashed, and his connection with the Academy must be made as close as possible. No one doubts that Hermias is being blackwashed. Theopompus, to our certain knowledge,/ made him a eunuch, a slave, a barbarian, a **10**
money-lender, a miser, a ruthless despot;[21] and Strabo's report comes from this tradition. Indeed, no one who has written since Mulvany's paper in 1926 has doubted that Hermias is being traduced in a particular way, by being dressed up in the character of an earlier Hermotimus who came to Atarneus and was himself a eunuch and a slave.[22] For my part I doubt whether this recherché explanation is called for: we shall see later that the established categories of slander in the orators cover the case very accurately. Then Hermias' connection with the Academy must be made as close as may be. His period as a student at the Academy seems to be, if not an invention, at least an exaggeration: the sixth Platonic letter claims that Plato has never associated with Hermias (322e), and – more persuasively because it comes from a source with the opposite bias – there is no mention of Hermias in Athenaeus' list of tyrants who were pupils of Plato and Xenocrates (11.508d-509b). If the connection is exaggerated at this end of Hermias' career we may fairly be prepared for exaggeration at the other. Consider how tempting it would have been to link the eminently respectable Xenocrates with the blackguard Hermias by sending him too to Assos. Xenocrates had a consistently high reputation for moral probity, political independence, and courage:[23] picture him then first as the protégé of a jumped-up tyrant with

[20] Stobaeus cites Zeno of Citium for the anecdote which depends on Aristotle's addressing the *Protrepticus* to 'Themison, the king of the Cypriots' (4.32.21); but this is all we know of Themison, who seems to have left no coinage. His title suggests that he was king of Salamis, but there is no room for him in that succession; if he had a kingdom it was one of the smaller Cypriot cities, and it is natural to think of him as trying to overthrow the pro-Persian dominance of Salamis and being lost in the turmoil which brought the Evagorid Pnytagoras to power in that city.

[21] Quoted by Didymus, 5.21 = *FGrH*, II B 115 F 250.

[22] Mulvany, above n.18, cites Hdt. 8.104-6.

[23] Cf. *Kleine Pauly*, v. 1414; DL 4.6-11.

strong commitments to Macedon, then as running for his life from the fate of his patron. Just how tempting such a picture was is shown by Athenaeus' sly comment that Chairon of Pellene, a dictator who got rid of his leading citizens and made their wives marry their slaves, was a pupil not only of Plato but of Xenocrates too (11.509b). Tempting indeed then; but surely an invention. It is, is it not, flatly unreasonable to base a major interpretation of Aristotle's philosophical viewpoint at this time upon a single report, a report that is embedded in, and wholly explicable by, a context of calumny whose misrepresentations are known and whose motives are transparent?/

11 So much for the celebrated secession from the Academy. How far does its disappearance strengthen the case for saying that Aristotle's reasons for leaving Athens were after all not professional but political? The positive argument we were given for this thesis, you remember, was that Aristotle left the city before Plato's death, and it will be worth turning an equally curious eye on the evidence behind this claim. I am bound to warn you that it will prove to be a single report, conflicting with all the other evidence and embedded in a context – a context of the type you will now expect. But it will give us more material for such conclusions as may occur to us later.

In his work *On Philosophy* Aristocles, the teacher of Alexander of Aphrodisias, named and discussed the authors of the earliest invectives against Aristotle, *hoi prôtoi diabalontes Aristotelên* (apud Euseb. *Praep. Evang.* 15.13-15; Düring, ch.xv). Among them was Aristotle's contemporary Euboulides, and with him we move beyond the political malice of a Theopompus into the professional polemics of a fellow-philosopher. Euboulides was the best-known pupil of Eucleides of Megara, an important logician in his own right, and credited by the comedians with the *rhôpoperperêthra* (empty boastful talk) of a Demosthenes (Kock, C.A.F.iii.461, N.C. Adesp. 294). According to Aristocles, Euboulides ascribed some bad poems to Aristotle which were in fact forged; and then he accused Aristotle of three things. The second of them is the evidence that interests us. Aristotle, said Euboulides, had given offence to the court of Macedon; moreover he was not present at Plato's death (*teleutônti Platôni mê paragenesthai*); moreover he destroyed, or falsified (*diaphtheirai*), Plato's books. Now the salient feature of these charges is that they all have a distinguished service record behind them. The charge of giving offence to Macedon no doubt flew freely in Athens at some dates, but so far as philosophical polemic is concerned it had been levelled particularly against the Academy in the person of Plato: Speusippus was thought to have settled the matter by a blunt letter to Philip.[24] The third accusation is harder to pin down because of its ambiguity, but the words cannot mean, as some have supposed, that Aristotle criticized Plato's/
12 writings. It probably reduces to the standard charge of burning some or all of a philosopher's work. Aristotle himself blamed the disappearance of some of Empedocles' poems on the incendiarism of the poet's sister (DL 8.57), and for similar reasons the Athenians were accused of destroying all the copies they could find of Protagoras' book (DL 9.52); while Plato notoriously wanted to

[24] Athen., *Deipn.* 11.506e.

burn Democritus' work but – since the source of the story is Aristoxenus, whose adulation of the Pythagoreans is an exact measure of his dislike for Plato – the holocaust was courteously prevented by two Pythagoreans (DL 9.40 = Aristoxenus fr.131 Wehrli). Now this accusation too is plainly more at home if it is levelled at Plato and his contemporaries, rather than at his pupils. For it was the non-existence of Socrates' writings, not of Plato's, that had given a handle to slander. At the end of the century another philosophical pamphleteer, Menedemus of Eretria, knew another explanation of the deficiency: Plato's contemporary Aeschines had bought Socrates' writings from his widow, and passed them off as his own.[25] But the simpler accusation, that Socrates' writings had been suppressed by his followers, must have come readily to hand. And now the accusation that Aristotle was not present at his master's death falls into place. It too had seen service a generation earlier. In the very same form of words, Plato was accused of slandering Aristippus by saying that he had not been present at Socrates' death (DL 3.36); and it is obvious that the same charge, on Plato's own admission in the *Phaedo*, could be turned against himself. There is no reason to think that when an old and familiar complaint against the head of the Academy was transferred from him to his pupil either the author of the calumny or his audience would suppose that it still embodied sober fact. The fact in this case is attested by the same good sources on which we relied against Strabo. Philochorus records that Aristotle went to Assos after Plato's death; and the alternative story that he was in Macedon is no more than a confusion by Hermippus.[26]/

This suggestion, that a scandal which has been attached to one philosopher 13
can be transferred by a sinister inheritance to other members of his school, may seem hard to swallow. Strabo gave us a milder case of such contamination, when Xenocrates was involved in the *mésalliances* of Aristotle. In Euboulides, if I am right, we have much stronger examples of these legacies of slander. But it is only fair to recall two pertinent considerations. One is that later writers talk as though precisely the same technique had been used in another attack on Aristotle, the polemic in four books mounted against him by Isocrates' pupil Cephisodorus. While he was still a member of the Academy Aristotle had sought and fostered a professional rivalry with Isocrates. We cannot be sure when it began: some have thought that it was when Aristotle had been in Athens for only five or six years. According to a story reported by Cicero and Philodemus[27] Aristotle said, in a parody of Euripides, 'It is a shame to stay silent and let Isocrates talk', and thereupon

[25] DL 2.60; the slander is ascribed to the Epicurean Idomeneus by Athenaeus, *Deipn.* 13.611d-e.

[26] Philochorus as reported by Usaibia says that Aristotle joined Hermias after Plato's death (Düring, *AABT*, 214). Philodemus (ibid., 259) reports that Aristotle was in Macedon at the time: the report is traced to Philochorus by Düring but not Jacoby, and ascribed more probably to Hermippus by Merlan. Hermippus's probable confusion with a later episode is recognised by Düring (ibid., 58).

[27] Cicero, *De Orat.* 3.35, 141; Philodemus, *De Rhet.* col. 51.40 Sudhaus; Düring, *AABT*, 299, 311.

suddenly changed almost his whole style of teaching (mutavit repente totam formam prope disciplinae suae). In fact he began to teach rhetoric in rivalry to Isocrates. In his early dialogue *Grylos*, written after the death of Xenophon's son in 362, he seems to have debated whether rhetoric could be a matter of science and formal teaching at all: Friedrich Solmsen in his study of Aristotle's logic and rhetoric took the evidence to show that at this time Aristotle denied rhetoric the status of a *technê*,[28] but he did not allow for the fact that the *Grylos* was a dialogue in which, presumably, arguments were given on both sides.[29] At any rate Aristotle seems to have decided early in favour of rhetoric's claims to academic status, for he began to teach the
14 subject/ and to criticize Isocrates' methods and theories of education. In turn, and inevitably, he was attacked by Cephisodorus. Now the feature of Cephisodorus' reply which engaged the attention of later critics is that his attack on Aristotle as a philosopher was simply an attack on Plato. Numenius, for instance, in his lost work on the Dissension between Plato and the Academics, is said to have written:

> Cephisodorus saw his master Isocrates becoming the target of Aristotle's attacks, but he had no knowledge of Aristotle himself. He was led by the celebrity of Plato's views to suppose that Aristotle philosophized on the same lines as Plato: so while he was attacking Aristotle his shots were going home against Plato (*epolemei men Aristotelei, eballe de Platôna*). He began his criticism from the theory of Ideas and went on to other things; and even of these things he was ignorant and relied on a rough notion of what was commonly said on the subject. The fact is that Cephisodorus was not fighting the man he had a quarrel with; it was the man he did not want to quarrel with that he fought. (apud Euseb. *Praep. Evang.* 14.6)

Numenius can only explain the fact that Cephisodorus saddles Aristotle with Plato's theories, together with the old and tried objections to them, by supposing Cephisodorus wholly ignorant of Aristotle's actual views; and this is at least unlikely. Jaeger, holding more reasonably that Cephisodorus must have known something of the man he was attacking, argues ingeniously that Aristotle must have held the theories that came under fire in the polemic. Numenius, he says, knew only the writings which are preserved in the Corpus Aristotelicum. He did not know the dialogues and other early writings of Aristotle which reach us now in fragments if at all; but Cephisodorus knew these works and knew that in them Aristotle had written as a faithful exponent of the theory of Ideas.[30] Against this explanation stands the failure of many – perhaps, by now, most – critics to detect the Ideas in the fragments where Jaeger supposes them to lodge; and, more weightily, the consideration that some of the writings in which Aristotle attacks the theory of Ideas, such as the *Topics* and the earlier essay *Peri Ideôn*, must belong to Aristotle's apprentice years in the Academy. No serious critic of Aristotle in the ancient

[28] F. Solmsen, *Die Entwicklung der aristotelischen Logik und Rhetorik* (Berlin 1929), 196ff.

[29] Thus 'quaerendi gratia quaedam subtilitatis suae (not, as Ross, simplicitate sua!) argumenta excogitavit in *Grylo*' (Quint., *Inst.* 2.17.14 = Ross 2, Rose^2 58). That Aristotle did not appear as leader of the discussion is maintained by Jaeger, *Aristotle*^{2}, 29 nn.1, 2.

[30] Jaeger, *Aristotle*,^{2} Eng. tr. 37-8, omitted in second German edition.

world knows of him as an exponent of the theory which in his surviving work
he so powerfully rejects. So we come back/ to the simpler explanation. If 15
Cephisodorus belabours Aristotle with philosophical objections that have force only or originally against Plato, this is because he exploits a convention of some polemic. He is not required by the rules of the genre to ensure the historical accuracy of his complaints when he can beat the son with the stick that was cut for his father.

This mention of categories and conventions of slander points to a second, and clinching, consideration. It is that if we had been considering the orators and not the philosophers it would have seemed no more than a commonplace that there are stock forms of abuse in fourth-century invective, conventional slanders which can be employed with little or no care for the facts; and all the forms of slander with which we have so far been concerned take their familiar place among these standard types. When Housman filled the back of a notebook with abusive *obiter dicta* which were to be stored until some colleague or other called for the full treatment, he was working in a classical tradition which had been codified by Anaximenes and Aristotle and their forerunners; though of course it may be true of Housman, as Professor Nisbet says it is of the Romans, that 'invective came easily to him, even before it was fostered by study of the Greek classics' (*In Pisonem*, 193).

In *Ethos* (Leipzig 1910) Wilhelm Süss listed and documented the chief patterns of abuse favoured by the orators (247-54); and, as Professor Nisbet points out in his edition of the *In Pisonem*, they have not changed much by the first century BC. Briefly, the object of the attack is displayed where possible as a slave and the son of slaves; he is a barbarian; he follows a low trade; he is a common thief; he is sexually astray in some way or other; he hates those he should not hate and in particular he hates the people or city as a whole; his personal appearance is unsavoury or otherwise regrettable, for instance because of effeminate attire; he is a coward and at worst a *rhipsaspis*; he has wasted or lost his property. Needless to say, if the abuse cannot be brought home directly to the opponent it should be aimed at his parents in the reasonable expectation that something will rub off on him. If Aeschines' mother can be exhibited as the promoter of some shady mysteries Aeschines
can be taken to have followed the same/trade. This is a familiar piece of 16
licence in the orators, yet it is the precise analogue of the polemic which, with or without basis in facts, involves other members of a school in the misdemeanours of their leader. Like all the other charges it has a history in comedy: I do not pretend to know how much has been allowed to rub off on the Socrates of the *Clouds* from his supposed mentors in Athens. But in Euboulides and Cephisodorus we can see the principle working clearly enough. And the other material that we have considered shows the mark of many of these conventions of invective. According to Theopompus, for example, Hermias was a slave and a barbarian (*FGrH* 115 F 250 Jacoby); but the second charge is false, as Wormell proved long ago from the fact that the Eleans proclaimed the sacred truce to Hermias and from the language of the *hymnos* that Aristotle wrote to his dead patron (*Yale Classical Studies* 5 (1935), 73), so the first charge can be jettisoned with it. Hermias was, in particular,

the slave or servant of a banker, and again there is good evidence of the way in which a charge of serfdom can be thrown in as a bonne-bouche to the other abuse: in the *De Falsa Legatione*, as you will recall, Aeschines' father figures as a schoolmaster and his name is Atrometos (Dem. xix. 249, 281); when we meet him again in the *De Corona* (xviii. 129) he is the slave of a schoolmaster and his name is, of course, Tromes. Nor can we hope to rescue from the wreckage the information that Hermias was himself a banker: Pasion was only one of those who had popularized the notion of the self-made man as a banker risen from a banker's slave, and when no other (or no other discreditable) reason for a man's acquisition of great wealth suggests itself money-lending is a stock explanation. Socrates notoriously spent his days in *adoleschia* without ever coming to starvation, so Aristoxenus is ready with the explanation that he made his money from some canny loans and investments (DL 2.20 = fr.59 Wehrli). As for the description of Hermias as a eunuch, this seems to be a conflation of the claim that he was an Asiatic with the suggestion that he played a special role in his friendship with Aristotle: this is clear enough in the vicious epigram by Theocritus, and as later critics pointed out even Plato was not above repeating the gossip that Zeno enjoyed similar
17 relations/ with Parmenides (*Parm.* 127b). In fact it was a standard defamation of the relation between teacher and pupil: Satyrus (fr.12) describes the connection between Empedocles and Pausanias in the same terms.

There remains the conventional charge of being a thief. This too, you remember, was used against Socrates in the *Clouds*, but generally in philosophical invective it takes the more sophisticated form of a charge of plagiarism. We shall have examples of this on our hands shortly.

Once these parallels in contemporary rhetoric are stated, they are too obvious to press; but they lead to further explanations. For one thing they help to show why, so far as our record goes, none of the philosophers who were slandered in the ways we are examining took their detractors to court. By the fourth century, indeed, *kakêgoria* seems to be restricted in law to certain precise forms of defamation: the punishable *aporrhêta* (things one is forbidden to say) were such things as calling your opponent a murderer or a *rhipsaspis* (one who throws his shield away in battle). But Lysias makes his prosecutor in the *Kata Theomnestou* say that even over such slanders it would be ungentlemanly and pettifogging (*aneleutheron kai lian philodikon*) to go to law. 'If he had said that I killed *his* father, or any other of the established *aporrhêta*, I shouldn't have minded. But he said that I killed my own father, and that is going too far' (Lysias 10.2). Lysias is putting a good face on a bad business. Given the ordinary conduct of an Athenian trial it would be pointless to go to law over slander, for slander was a prescriptive feature of the trial itself. Aristotle's *Rhetoric* gives excellent advice on the delivering and evading of *diabolê* in court (*Rhet.* 3.15): among various methods it may be better to denounce your opponent's slander as irrelevant to the issue (1416a35-7), it may simply be better *antidiaballein ton diaballonta* ('to slander the slanderer in return', 14116a26-8). The last manoeuvre is one of which, among philosophers, Epicurus was the master though not the inventor. Later there grew up a sophistication on this procedure. One way of slandering a philosopher was to accuse him of slander. Plato's dialogues were ransacked for examples of malice against other philosophers.

But at once a new blood-relationship suggests itself for fourth-century polemic: a very obvious one. In drawing our rhetorical parallels we illustrated the ancestry of the methods/ from another kind of writing, the comedy; and 18
of course it is this genre in particular, with the special licence and immunity that belonged to it, that has most commonly been thought to throw light on philosophical invective. The alleged effect of Aristophanes' *Clouds* on the minds of Socrates' judges is largely responsible for the situation. And there is one historical consideration which makes it very tempting to see the philosophical pamphleteers of the fourth century as heirs to the comedians of the fifth. To be sure, we are no longer content with the scholiast's sharp distinction between Old and Middle Comedy.[31] Political lampooning on the stage did not go either out of fashion or beyond the law in 404. Any restrictive legislation introduced by the Thirty was cancelled by their fall, and the evidence for a running battle between the comedians and the politicians goes on until late in the century.[32] But against philosophers, as contrasted with politicians, the invective becomes weak and repetitive and generalized in the comedians in proportion as it becomes ruthless and uninhibited in the pamphlets of the sophists and philosophers themselves. How hard, and with what vanishing results, we have scoured the fragments of Middle Comedy for information on the philosophy of the time! How we have pored over the fragment of Epicrates in which he satirized the attempts of the Academy to classify a pumpkin,[33] hoping that the Sicilian doctor who is present may be Philistion on a lecture tour, until we remind ourselves of the settled tradition that doctors in comedy talk Doric – and apparently non-Spartan Doric at that.[34] How little the caricatures of the squalid, hungry Pythagoreans tell us, and how much less when we gather from Hermippus and Sosicrates that the tradition of Pythagorean squalor was a late fashion, perversely launched by a Pythagorizing Cynic Diodorus of Aspendos (Athen., *Deipn.* 4.163e-f). How hopefully we (or some of us) have interpreted Alexis' description of the Pythagoreans as living in starvation, dirt, *and* silence (Kock, 2.370, fr.197)/ as evidence for that famous vow of silence which prevented the Pythagoreans 19
from uttering the contents of Plato's *Timaeus* over a century before he published his notorious plagiarism, only to find Cratinus the Younger describing these same Pythagoreans as waylaying the innocent passer-by and practising on him every trick of rhetoric (Kock, 2.291, fr.7: the identification of the subject is supplied by DL 8.37). It is quite another matter when we turn to the pamphleteers. Athenaeus, that unrivalled scavenger in Greek comedy (he claimed to have read over eight hundred of them), says flatly that most

[31] Cf. schol. in Aristophanem, *Ach.* 67, *Aves* 1297.

[32] See K.J. Dover, *Greek Popular Morality* (Oxford 1974), 26-8, 30-3.

[33] Fr. 287 Kock.

[34] For Doric doctors in comedy, see Crates, fr. 41 Kock, Alexis fr. 142 Kock, Epicrates fr. 11 Kock, Menander, *Aspis* 374, 349ff.

philosophers are more slanderous than the comedians themselves (5.220a), and documents his case from the writings of Socrates' immediate followers. 'These men', he says, 'recognize no one as a good statesman or general or sophist or poet ... except Socrates. Time would come to an end before I could recite the solemn denunciations pronounced by philosophers.' But it must be remembered that Athenaeus is taking a hand in the invective himself. And in the earlier years of the fourth century pamphleteering was by no means confined either to solemnities or to Socrates' friends. Its affinity to comedy becomes clearer when we turn to an invective that was launched against Socrates and designed, so far as we can now tell, rather as a joke than as partisan polemic. I mean of course the *Accusation of Socrates* (*katêgoria Sôkratous*) written by Polycrates probably not more than twenty years, and certainly not less than five years, after Socrates' death.[35]

Polycrates was not himself a philosopher except in Isocrates' hospitable sense of the word (*Busiris* 1). He was a teacher of rhetoric. But his invective against Socrates, put into the mouth of Socrates' prosecutor Anytus, provoked brisk replies from those men whom Athenaeus describes as having nothing in common except their admiration of Socrates. The seriousness of the replies which have come down to us – Xenophon's *Apomnemoneumata* probably contains one of the earliest of them – has sometimes led scholars to regard Polycrates as a ruthless and committed opponent of the Socratics; and when Isocrates in his *Busiris* undertakes a brief reply to two of Polycrates' works,
20 the *Accusation of Socrates* and the *Encomium*/ *of Busiris*, it has been fancied, at least since the time of one Hellenistic argument attached to Isocrates' speech, that he was engaging – if only by innuendo – in a bitter polemic against Socrates' accuser. But Isocrates' own words are enough to dispel this myth. What he criticizes in Polycrates, superciliously but not in the least vindictively, are the technical railings. It is bad practice, he says, to write a defence of Busiris which includes the information that he was a cannibal; just as it is bad practice to attack Socrates on the score of his pupils and then to cite that outstanding man Alcibiades. The mood of the whole speech suggests that he is answering *jeux d'esprit*, and this agrees with what Demetrius says of Polycrates' *encomia*: 'Polycrates was playing, not serious. His general style is that of a *paignion*' (*Peri Hermeneias* 120). Remember that *paignion* can mean the performance of a comedy, and we seem to see the kind of literary licence that such writers expected to inherit.

This picture of the pamphleteers taking over from the comedians one of their stock subjects, together with the licence and the techniques of defamation appropriate to handling it, is attractive. But the example of Polycrates himself shows that it is at best only part of the larger picture. It takes no account of one of the salient features of fourth-century polemic: that the uninhibited invective is one side of a coin whose other face is uninhibited eulogy and adulation. An example of such eulogy is Isocrates' canonization of Evagoras I, a speech of which Jebb remarked that it is 'professedly an

[35] See E.R. Dodds, *Plato: Gorgias* (Oxford 1959), 28-9; A.H. Chroust, *Socrates, Man and Myth* (London 1957), ch.4.

encomium; but the praise which it awards does not, on the whole, appear to be exaggerated' (*Att. Or.* ii.113). When one recalls that after tracing Evagoras' family tree back to Zeus by way of Teucer Isocrates describes his seizure of power as the noblest instance of such manoeuvres and praises the war with Persia, which left him with no more than the possession of his own city, as the most successful of all wars including that against Troy, one feels that Jebb may have read the text in a variant MS tradition. Isocrates claims originality in this *genre* (8-11), and the sense and merits of the claim have been briskly debated.[36] It must at least be true/ that by this time the 21
Socratics were engaged on what Athenaeus regards as a comparable canonization of Socrates. Earlier there had been *encomia* of legendary celebrities, such as Gorgias' *Helen* and Polycrates' *Busiris*; and Isocrates himself shows that technically no division should be drawn between these essays and the praises of historical men by addressing the same criticisms both to Polycrates' praise of Busiris and to his polemic against Socrates and indeed by criticizing the faulty chronology of the first. In the manuals of rhetoric the techniques of the *encomium* and *loidoria* (abuse) are treated together,[37] and the doubling of these two forms of epideixis goes back at least to Isocrates' supposed teacher, Gorgias. Gorgias was celebrated as writing 'laudationes vituperationesque singularum rerum' ('praises and censures of extraordinary things'), and justifying this by the argument that the proper task of the orator was 'rem augere posse laudando, vituperandoque rursus affligere' ('to be able to build a thing up by praising it, and to strike it down again by censure', Aristotle apud Cic., *Brutus* 12.47). Whether Gorgias tried his hand at personal invective we do not know; but by the end of the Peloponnesian War Thrasymachus had made a name for his technical skill in both the use and the evasion of *diabolê* (Plato, *Phdr.* 267d), and Antiphon had published his *Loidoriai* of Alcibiades (Plut., *Alc.*3; Athen., *Deipn.* 12.525b).

Now it is one thing to practise the related techniques of calumny and adulation by way of an epideictic exercise; it is quite another thing to practise calumny on X as a corollary of your anxiety to eulogize Y. When not only the techniques but the subjects of praise and blame stand in this close connection we are beyond the field of technical display and into the morass of militant propaganda. It may be a short step, but Gorgias seems not to have taken it and I am willing to believe the same of Polycrates. No doubt Athenaeus is right in saying that some Socratics went this way and showed themselves inclined to canonize Socrates by defaming all competitors; it is a tendency that can be recognized in some of Plato's/ work, but not by any means in all of it, and 22
with Plato the deflating of Socrates' interlocutors is done with charm and humour. It is with Aristoxenus the pupil of Aristotle that we find the intimate propagandist coupling of praise and blame at its most ruthless and influential.

[36] Isocrates' claim was rejected by Wilamowitz in *Hermes* 35 (1900), 533 (reprinted in *Kleine Schriften* (Berlin 1962)). In support of Isocrates see: J. Sykutris, *Hermes* 62 (1927), 24-53, especially 43ff. (reprinted in F. Seck, ed., *Isokrates*, Wege der Forschung (Darmstadt 1976), 74-105, especially 94ff.); and K. Münscher, *Philologische Wochenschrift* 47 (1927), cols. 1063-70, 1098-103 (reprinted in Seck, 106-21).

[37] See Aristotle, *Rhet.* 1368a33ff.; *Rhet. ad Alex.* 35, 1440b; Cicero, *Partitiones Oratoriae* 70ff.

With him we may finish our excursion into the family tree of fourth-century philosophical polemic. The blood-relations fall into place. The licensed scurrility and the laughing-stocks of comedy, the rhetorical marriage of eulogy and defamation, join now with the precise and classifiable invective of forensic oratory to produce a genius of misrepresentation who is nevertheless in his own right a meticulous and exact scientist. His adulation of the Pythagoreans is known to be in exact proportion to his hostility towards Plato and Socrates. His reports of Plato and Socrates are received (despite an attempt to whitewash him which recurs every forty years or so) with general incredulity. His account of the Pythagoreans, and the connected account given by his friend and follower Dicaearchus, is still the basis of a great deal that the textbooks tell us about the first century and a half of Pythagorean doctrine.

In his *Rhetoric* Aristotle recommends a certain method of *diabolê*: abuse, he says, is all the more effective if it is mixed with a little praise (*Rhet.* 1416b4-8). Aristoxenus knew the device. Socrates, he reported in his life of that philosopher, was indeed uncommonly impressive in appearance and persuasive in speech – except, of course, when he was angry. When he was angry there was nothing he would not say or do (*hote de phlechtheiê hupo tou pathous toutou, deinên einai tên aschêmosunên. oudenos gar oute onomatos aposchesthai oute pragmatos* (fr.54a Wehrli)). Add to these pieces of information the further stock charges that he was seduced by his teacher Archelaus and that he made his money by loans and you have the character of Aristoxenus' writing when he leaves the
23 abstract field of/ harmonic theory. So it is not surprising to find him, in his life of Plato, reporting that practically the whole of the *Republic* had been pilfered from the writings of Protagoras (fr.67 Wehrli; and we can be virtually certain that it is on his authority that Plato is said to have bought certain Pythagorean writings in Sicily from which his own dialogues were duly supplied (fr.43)). This same polemical contrast between the Pythagoreans, on the one hand, and Plato and Socrates, on the other, recurs again and again in the reports that have reached us of Aristoxenus' lost books. It is Aristoxenus who is cited for the story that Plato was prevented from burning Democritus' works by two Pythagorean gentlemen. An anecdote which is elsewhere told about Plato's self-control (DL 3.38) is attached by Aristoxenus to his particular Pythagorean hero, Archytas (fr.30 Wehrli); and then it is duly repeated by the neo-Pythagorean Iamblichus as embodying a general rule of the Pythagorean order (ibid). The same language which is used at one point to describe Socrates' unpleasant impulses is used at another to describe the sort of behaviour that all Pythagoreans were forbidden by another rule of the order (frs.37, 54 Wehrli).

All this is plainly far more professional stuff than the reach-me-down methods of invective that we came upon in men who were probably slightly senior to Aristoxenus – Euboulides and Cephisodorus and Theopompus. But we must be all the warier of it; and in particular – though this hardly comes within the scope of a paper on calumny – we must be wary of the eulogistic face of the coin, the flattering inventions which are so much harder to identify than the slander when once they have been absorbed into the tradition.

Iamblichus makes a solemn rule of the Pythagorean order out of a floating anecdote about self-control which Aristoxenus attaches to the Pythagorean Archytas. There is one danger-signal to be watched: I mean the charges that later thinkers have plagiarized the ideas on which their reputation rests from Pythagorean scriptures. For in order to substantiate these claims the claimants have to involve the famous Pythagorean oath of secrecy which would allegedly prevent the order from publishing these valuable ideas earlier; and the oath (or at least, the rule) of secrecy is first clearly attested,
so far as/I can see, in a quotation from Aristoxenus' *Paideutikoi Nomoi* (fr.43 24
Wehrli = DL 8.15). Some scholars have professed to see a mention of it in a passage from Isocrates' *Busiris* (29), but I fail to follow them. What Isocrates seems to say is that the education of the Pythagoreans is known to be so good that they command more respect when they are silent than others who try to dazzle the company with rhetorical tricks. Much the same, on different grounds, was said of the Spartans; and, for that matter, according to Cratinus the comic poet the Pythagoreans were as ready as the next man to show their paces in rhetoric. Indeed, so far from being known to his contemporaries as a mystery-monger who divulged his principal doctrines only under oaths of secrecy, Pythagoras seems to have been denounced by Heraclitus as a pretentious polymath whose methods of research were well known; and it is said to be a theory of his about the reincarnation of the soul that is pilloried in the well-known joke of his contemporary Xenophanes. Nor can the mystery techniques that are satirized in the Phrontisterion of Aristophanes' *Clouds* be confidently connected with the Pythagoreans. No doubt there are Pythagorean elements in the picture – possibly the disciple's reference to Socrates as *autos* (though this would be a familiar enough usage in any event), more probably the final burning of the school which appeared seemingly in the second version of the play – but the old heresy propounded by Burnet that Socrates was a leading Pythagorean is surely refuted by Aristoxenus' treatment of him; and the suggestion that a philosophical school may impart *aporrhêta* to select pupils is for Plato in the *Theaetetus* (152c-e) a quite general joke that he plays on Protagoras and others, and may well have been the same for Aristophanes. Aristoxenus himself may have profited from it in his claim that almost the whole of Plato's *Republic* was plagiarized from some otherwise unknown writings of Protagoras.

Aristotle, to be sure, is said by Iamblichus to have recorded one of the Pythagoreans' 'greatest secrets' (*malista aporrhêta*) in his essay *On the Pythagorean Philosophy* (*Vita Pyth.* 6.30 = Arist. fr.187 R^2, 192 R^3), namely that the class *rational animal* is divided into 'god, man, and such as Pythagoras'.
Logikon zôion is a technicality of Aristotle's own day. Whether/ or not 25
Aristoxenus was his informant, the 'secret' was evidently too good to keep for long.

So the rule of silence which subsequently became an oath and which Aristoxenus finds it so profitable to claim for the Pythagoreans is sadly devoid of earlier and better support. No doubt – and this emerges as very probable from later sources – Pythagoras and his followers found it wiser to restrict some of their audiences to those competent in the matters to be discussed, and no doubt they had means of testing that competence. It would not be compatible with the early evidence we have to claim more than this. But to canvass Aristoxenus' treatment of Pythagoreanism as it deserves is a task which lies outside the scheme of this paper.

In sum, I am content if this brief review of the methods and family relationships of philosophical invective in the fourth century and later serves to put us on our guard against some evidence that wears an innocent face in the historians. I am more than content if the discussion of Aristotle's actions and motives rescues him from the libels on which some gimcrack interpretations have been built. But some uneasy thoughts remain. We have at many points identified the authors of scandal by relying on later sources. It is a characteristic of the scandal-maker to impute scandal to others. And where is our evidence then? The frustration may be reinforced by such thoughts as that, if Aristoxenus had been faced with the gross lack of evidence for any Pythagorean oath or rule of secrecy, he would surely have replied that it too was covered by the rule of secrecy. We walk on delicate and treacherous ground. With that thought I leave you.[38]

[38] Notes 9, 10, 28, 32, 34, 36, and 37 have been supplied by the editor, with warm thanks for assistance from Professor Albert Henrichs (Harvard University).

Index Locorum

References to pages in this book are in **bold** type

The editor wishes to thank Steven Hoekstra for preparing the indexes and to acknowledge the support of the National Endowment for the Humanities and of a Salamon Grant from Brown University.

General Index